Labour, Nature, Value

André Gorz Between Marxism and Degrowth

Emanuele Leonardi

Translated by Yari Lanci

VERSO

London • New York

This English-language edition first published by Verso 2026
First published *Lavoro Natura Valore. André Gorz tra marxismo e decrescita*
© Orthotes Editrice, Napoli-Salerno 2017
Translation © Yari Lanci 2026

The manufacturer's authorized representative in the EU for product safety (GPSR)
is LOGOS EUROPE, 9 rue Nicolas Poussin, 17000, La Rochelle, France
contact@logoseurope.eu

1 3 5 7 9 10 8 6 4 2

Verso
UK: 6 Meard Street, London W1F 0EG
US: 207 East 32nd Street, New York, NY 10016
versobooks.com

Verso is the imprint of New Left Books

ISBN-13: 978-1-80429-885-5
ISBN-13: 978-1-80429-887-9 (US EBK)
ISBN-13: 978-1-80429-886-2 (UK EBK)

British Library Cataloguing in Publication Data
A catalogue record for this book is available from the British Library

Library of Congress Cataloging-in-Publication Data
A catalog record for this book is available from the Library of Congress

Typeset in Minion by Biblichor Ltd, Scotland
Printed and bound by CPI Group (UK) Ltd, Croydon, CR0 4YY

To my father, *in memoriam*

Contents

Preface to the English-Language Edition

Lavoro Natura Valore: André Gorz tra marxismo e decrescita was originally published in November 2017. It was well received from the start – a dozen reviews, remarkable sales for Italian non-fiction standards and a few launching events throughout 2018 – but its 'lucky moment' was yet to come. In point of fact, Greta Thunberg's emergence as global icon of climate justice in 2019 dramatically boosted the interest for the book's key arguments. Finally, an academic reflection with militant ambitions had found its ideal audience: a powerful social movement whose political roots and scopes had to be reconstructed and debated, both internally and externally. Since the first Fridays for Future climate strike, which mobilized 1.6 billion people around the globe,[1] my work has received a kind of attention that would have been simply unimaginable a year prior: interviews on national radio broadcasting, public conferences, militant self-education workshops and so on.

Thunberg's direct and concise communicative style seemed to require historical contextualization and analytical assessment about actual contents, namely what the book aimed at providing. Take as an example the powerful words she uttered in Katowice (Poland), at COP 24: 'If solutions within the system are so impossible to find, maybe we should change the system itself. We have not come here to beg world leaders to care. You have ignored us in the past and you will ignore us again. We have run out of excuses, and we are running out of time. We have come here to let you

---

1   Mattias Wahlström, Piotr Kocyba, Michiel De Vydt and Joost de Moor (eds), 'Protest for a future: Composition, mobilisation and motives of the participants in #FridaysForFuture climate protests on 15 March 2019 in 13 European cities', *Cosmos: The Centre on Social Movement Studies*, 22 July 2019, cosmos.sns.it.

know that change is coming, whether you like it or not. The real power belongs to the people.'[2]

While the performative character of this speech is obvious, the same cannot be said of its political meaning and practical implications. Indeed, Thunberg's words constitute a remarkable shift in the history of the relationship between ecological issues and transnational governance. Quite abruptly, they put an end to the United Nations' Framework Convention on Climate Change as the *centripetal force for ecology-related imagination*, as the main attractor of climate-related policy efforts.[3] In the Italian context, the book proved instrumental in the collective effort to build an interpretive framework for the progressive disintegration of the UN-led governance process. To be sure, in 2017, such disintegration could be detected only as a trend (see chapters 6 and 7), whereas nowadays, after the implosion of COP 30 in Bèlem, it is nothing less than a stark reality.[4] However, the in-between years – roughly from the 2019 climate strikes to the 2021 mobilizations around COP 26 in Glasgow (Scotland) – represent key junctures to articulate two different but interrelated processes: the failure of ecological transition *from above*, and the elaboration of eco-social alternatives *from below*.[5]

As for the former aspect, the analysis focused on the twofold promise of this elite-driven green economy applied to global warming. In its

---

2   Greta Thunberg 'Speech at COP24', *Archives of Women's Political Communication (Iowa State University)*, 12 December 2018, awpc.cattcenter.iastate.edu.

3   Luigi Pelizzoni, Emanuele Leonardi and Viviana Asara (eds), *Handbook of Critical Environmental Politics* (London: Elgar, 2022); Luigi Pelizzoni, *Nature, Neoliberalism, and New Materialisms: Riding the Ungovernable* (Dublin: Bloomsbury, 2025).

4   The point was sadly exemplified by the following fact: as of March 2025, only 15 countries out of 194 (less than 8 per cent) had respected the Paris Agreement deadline to submit their NDCs (Nationally Determined Contributions) to cut carbon emissions (or at least to move towards net-zero scenarios), cf. Doug Specht, 'Only 15 countries have met the latest Paris agreement deadline. Is any nation serious about tackling climate change?', *Conversation*, 19 March 2025, theconversation.com.

5   Lorenzo Feltrin, Emanuele Leonardi, 'Working-class environmentalism and climate justice: Strategic converging for an ecological transition from below', *Relações Internacionais*, 2023 (Special Issue), 49–61.

assumption, the 'invisible hand' of the market would be capable of reducing greenhouse gas emissions and, simultaneously, of guaranteeing high profit rates. A quarter-century is undoubtedly a timespan long enough to evaluate the effectiveness of a public policy (and a business model), even more so in the case of the ecological crisis, as the urgency to take decisive action is in this regard fundamental. Therefore, the question is: have CO_2-equivalent emissions declined? The answer must be blunt: no, they have not.[6] Rivers of ink have been spilled to debate the reasons for such debacle, some of which had already been discussed in this book. However, what is more important is that a politically minded interpretation of the history of climate governance allowed Italian eco-activists to go beyond the usual rhetoric of unsuccessful COPs ('it's not enough, but it's a first step in the right direction'). In this sense, Harvard energy economist Rob Stavins provided a fitting, if misleading, metaphor when he stated that 'this is a marathon, not a sprint'.[7] Yet what climate justice movements eventually achieved was the ideological awareness that carbon trading is *not* an insufficient initial phase of a sensible road map, but rather an effective pillar of a highly dysfunctional ecological strategy. This is certainly a marathon, as Stavins suggests, but its final line is not climate stabilization – as per the UNFCCC alleged end goal – but 'climate

---

6   IEA, 'Global Energy Review 2025: CO2 Emissions', iea.org. Furthermore, it must be acknowledged that climatic translations of green economy – e.g. carbon trading – have unquestionably failed, even from an economic perspective. In chapter 6 of this book, I reported estimates from 2008–10 World Bank data, according to which 'the aggregate value of carbon markets could reach $2–3 trillion by 2020, and then $10 trillion by 2030' (p. 132). Recent data from financial consultancy 4IRE tell a different story: 'The 2023 carbon credit market valuation reached $414.8 billion, with a 2028 estimate reaching $1.6 trillion' (Helena Petrashuk, 'The Global Carbon Trading Market: Key Insights into Market Size and Trends', 5 January 2025, https://4irelabs.com/articles/carbon-trading-market-size-and-trends/). Given geopolitical uncertainty, it is very unlikely that the aggregate value of carbon markets will reach $1 trillion by 2030, making the comparison between hopeful expectations and actual performance quite striking.

7   Rob Stavins, *Harvard Gazette*, 'Separating Signal from Noise at COP 26', 17 November 2021, news.harvard.edu.

Darwinism', namely new techno-centred investments on adaptation coupled with indifference towards mitigation.[8]

In relation to the latter aspect, the book had (admittedly) less to offer. Its focus on negentropic work proved appealing for in-depth academic discussion, but rather out of sync with activists' needs.[9] Although a reference to the Just Transition is present, and the enabling role played by labour movements in politicizing the ecological crisis marks the core of chapter 4, what was missing in 2017 was a foundational reference to unions as (potential) climate actors. In other words, the link between labour and global warming was mostly explored in theoretical terms, from a categorial perspective, whereas the subjective dispositions of the working class *vis-à-vis* political ecology were relegated to past cycles of contention (in particular, the 1968–73 period) and basically disregarded insofar as contemporary cases were concerned. This situation would rapidly change, especially as a result of the research I conducted with Stefania Barca on the ex-ILVA steel plant in Taranto (Italy).[10] Since then,

---

8 To my knowledge, the term was coined by Italian journalist Ferdinando Cotugno in his podcast, 'Areale', for newspaper *Domani*, 8 April 2024, editoriale domani.it.

9 Giuseppe Allegri, Viviana Asara, Stefania Barca, Maura Benegiamo, Laura Centemeri, Alice Dal Gobbo, Andrea Ghelfi, Manlio Iofrida, Ottavio Marzocca, Luigi Pellizzoni and Salvo Torre, 'Simposio su *Lavoro Natura Valore: André Gorz tra marxismo e decrescita*, di Emanuele Leonardi', *Etica and Politica* XXI: 1, 2019, 134–230.

It is worth noting that, autonomously and compellingly, Enrique Leff developed a similar concept in his entry 'Negentropic production', in *Pluriverse. A Post-Development Dictionary*, ed. Ashish Kothari, Ariel Salleh, Arturo Escobar, Federico Demaria and Alberto Acosta (New Delhi: Tulika Books, 2019), 250–3.

However, my impression is that a rethinking of negentropic work may prove useful for a politico-ecological critique of artificial intelligence, in connection with key contributions such as: Vando Borghi, *The Ruins of Capitalism and Possibilism: Beyond Homo Faber* (London: Routledge, 2025); Antonio Casilli, *Waiting for Robots: The Hired Hands of Automation* (Chicago: Chicago University Press, 2025); Kate Crawford, *Atlas of AI: Power, Politics and the Planetary Costs of Artificial Intelligence* (Yale University Press, 2021); Nick Dyer-Witheford and Alessandra Mularoni, *Cybernetic Circulation Complex: Big Tech and Planetary Crisis* (London: Verso, 2025); Matteo Pasquinelli, *The Eye of the Master: A Social History of Artificial Intelligence* (London: Verso, 2023).

10 Stefania Barca, Emanuele Leonardi, 'Working-class Ecology and Union Politics: A Conceptual Topology', *Globalizations* 15: 4, 2018, 487–503.

I started to engage more substantially with *Environmental Labour Studies* and climate-related union politics.[11] I realized retrospectively that my analysis in *Labour, Nature, Value* fell short of explicitly showing how ecological transition *from above* – with its assumed elective affinity between environmental protection and economic growth – could only 'work' (in ideational terms) under the condition of relegating the labour movement, with its social function of contrasting inequality, to the margins. Or, even worse, by undermining its progressive stance by assigning it the role of retrograde actor resisting change in the name of protecting ecologically unsustainable jobs. After all, the subject of the green economy is financial 'self-entrepreneurship': daring, enlightened, smart. Its innovative charge springs from an indifference towards the shackles posed by intermediate bodies (unions in the first place) and the time-wasting panoply of institutional mediation (in particular democratic practices).

From this perspective, my encounter with the ex-GKN Factory Collective has been crucial. The unfolding of this industrial dispute in Campi Bisenzio (Florence) – from the stoppage of an offshoring project by means of occupying the factory to a re-industrialization plan based on sustainable public mobility, from a proposal for socially integrated ecological productions to three hugely successful editions of the Working-Class Literature Festival – is complex and tortuous, though by

---

11 Maura Benegiamo, Emanuele Leonardi, 'André Gorz's Labour-based Political Ecology and Its Legacy for the XXI Century', in *Palgrave Handbook of Environmental Labour Studies*, ed. Nora Rätzhel, Dimitris Stevis, and David Uzzel (Basingstoke: Palgrave, 2021), 721–41.

Such a stronger engagement with *Environmental Labour Studies* has been initially carried on at ECOSOC – *Oficina de Ecologia e Sociedade* (Centro de Estudos Sociais, University of Coimbra, ces.uc.pt/en/ces/ecosoc), especially in the framework of Horizon 2020 project JUST2CE (just2ce.eu). See Mario Pansera, Stefania Barca, Bibiana Martinez Alvarez, Emanuele Leonardi, Giacomo D'Alisa, Teresa Meira, Paul Guillibert, 'Towards a Just Circular Economy: Conceptualizing Environmental Labor and Gender Justice in Circularity Studies', *Sustainability: Science, Practice and Policy* 20: 1, 2024, 1–17; Viviana Asara, Marco Caligari, Emanuele Leonardi, 'Disrupting Carbon Lock-in from Below: Union Coalitions in Civitavecchia and the Making of a Just Transition in Italy's Energy Sector', *Transfer: European Review of Labour and Research* 27, 2026.

now fairly well known.[12] As I am here concerned about the labour movement as a climate actor, a brief recap would suffice. Up until 9 July 2021, GKN's blue-collar workers produced axle-shafts, mostly for luxury cars. However, on that day, Melrose Industries (the financial owner of the plant) sent out an email announcing the dismissal of more than four hundred workers. This dismissal was portrayed as the natural outcome of the 'ecological transition' in the automotive sector: 'Haven't you embraced Greta?!?', the mainstream narrative reproached radical unionists, 'Now accept the inevitable layoffs!' But they refused to do so and instead launched a permanent assembly within the factory, which is still operating today.

At first, these workers demanded only one thing: to get back their jobs. As weeks passed, however, they realized that the only way to keep production running was to advocate for a public and (territorially) integrated factory, which essentially meant profoundly changing production. In what direction? Well, here is probably their most significant intuition, as the answer was: *towards climate justice*. The Factory Collective explains this political wager as follows:

> All great cycles of historical mobilisation have coincided with a general vivacity in society, which feeds the workers' conflict, and vice versa. When we found ourselves jobless, on that 9th July, we reacted by bringing 40,000 people to the streets of Florence on 18th September. But a few days after we saw the mobilisation around the pre-COP in

---

12   Francesca Gabbriellini, Paola Imperatore, 'An Eco-Revolution for the Working Class? What We Can Learn from the Former GKN Factory in Italy', *Berliner Gazette*, 17 April 2023, berlinergazette.de; Paola Imperatore and Emanuele Leonardi, *L'era della giustizia climatica. Prospettive politiche per una transizione ecologica dal basso* (Naples: Orthotes, 2023); Leonard Mazzone, 'Dalla delocalizzazione al recupero cooperativistico della Gkn', *Meridiana* 109: 1, 2024, 49–72; Francesca Gabbriellini and Alberto Prunetti, '"We are not here to entertain you": Notes from the Italian Working-Class Literature Festival and from the GKN Florence Workers' Struggle', *Resistance: A Journal of Radical Environmental Humanities*, 11: 2–3, 2024, 232–46; Francesca Gabbriellini, Angelo Moro and Arianna Tassinari, 'A working-class road to radical industrial democracy. Workplace industrial relations and workers mobilization in the ex-GKN factory in Florence', *Studi organizzativi* 1, 2024, 79–104.

Milan [when Greta Thunberg gave her notorious 'blah blah blah' speech], with 50,000 people taking the streets for climate justice. And then we attended the Climate Camp, and we said to ourselves: these two movements need to add up and push the country toward a general and generalised strike.[13]

The process took some time to solidify, but eventually it produced long-lasting consequences. Fridays for Future (especially in Italy, but throughout Europe as well) is today one of the key partners in the co-op popular shareholding campaign (significantly dubbed GFF – GKN for Future – and still open). Furthermore, on 13 October 2024, Greta Thunberg herself showed up at the factory gates to give support and confirm the metamorphosis of climate activism, now deeply engaged in elaborating its foundational roots within the social question: 'Workers' rights and climate justice go hand in hand. A just and sustainable transition means putting power back in the hands of the workers, and that no one gets left behind.'[14]

A recent document put together by the Italian climate justice movements, shared by the Factory Collective through their social media, further confirms this eco-social convergence:[15]

We, the movements for climate and social justice, have a plan. A plan that we can explain in detail if necessary. Millions of jobs in Italy and tens of millions across Europe can be created with all the activities necessary to stop the climate catastrophe, to convert industry, agriculture and other productive activities, to move away from the fossil economy, and to create sustainable mobility. No, this is not yet another manifesto for green capitalism. This is a proposal for

---

13   Dario Salvetti (interview by Emanuele Leonardi and Domenico Perrotta), 'From overlapping to convergence: workers' struggle and climate justice at GKN', *Platforms, Populisms, Pandemics, Riots*, 7 November 2022, projectpppr.org.

14   Greta Thunberg, 'GKN: l'intervento di Greta Thunberg e i prossimi passi', *Fridays for Future Italia*, 2 November 2024, fridaysforfutureitalia.it.

15   Emanuele Leonardi and Alberto Manconi, 'Eco-social Convergence in Europe: Notes for a Renewed Internationalism in Times of War', *South Atlantic Quarterly* 124:4, 2025, 847–57.

grassroots activism, for change through participation and social awareness, for new power relations and priorities. Green capitalism is finally dropping its mask and giving way to war capitalism. Re-armament is the explicit negation of any climate transition goal . . . We also have a concrete example, perhaps not a model that can be repli-cated everywhere, but certainly a struggle that can be contagious: that of the ex-GKN workers.[16]

There is another point I find worthy of mention here. The articulation of Marxism and degrowth proposed in this book predates the incredible flourishing of such debate that followed the publication of Kohei Saito's more recent books on degrowth communism.[17] More importantly, how-ever, such articulation differs from Saito's, without necessarily being in opposition to it. A little historical detour may clarify this divergence. For a long time, the field of ecology has been seen as foreign, or even in plain opposition, to Marxism. Any discussion of nature, no matter how com-plex a role it played in Marx's texts, was often interpreted as a sign of the quasi-positivist, Promethean character of historical materialism. Such presumed 'Prometheanism' attributed to Marx constituted the spark that, starting from the 1960s, gave rise to the debate on eco-Marxism whose mapping, however, would take us much too far. If in the 1970s and 1980s only a few authors participated in the discussion – which, nonetheless, was already global in scope – the new millennium saw a steady expansion of contributions and, at times, the rise of caustic if not vicious polemical

---

16   Insorgiamo, *Facebook page*, insorgiamoconilavoratorigkn.

17   Kohei Saito, *Marx in the Anthropocene: Towards the Idea of Degrowth Com-munism* (Cambridge UP, 2023); and his *Slow Down: How Degrowth Communism Can Save the Earth* (London: Weidenfeld & Nicolson, 2024).

From a larger perspective, key contributions tho this debate are: Alyssa Battis-toni, *Free Gifts: Capitalism and the Politics of Nature* (Princeton: UP, 2025); Nic Beuret, *Or Something Worse: Why We Need to Disrupt the Climate Transition* (London: Verso, 2025); Wim Carton and Andreas Malm, *The Long Heat: Climate Politics When It's Too Late* (London: Verso, 2025); Lorenzo Feltrin, *In and Against the Ecological Crisis: Working-class Environmentalism between Workplace and Community* (London: Verso, 2026); Matt Huber, *Climate Change as Class War: Building Socialism on a Warming Planet* (London: Verso, 2022); Thea Riofrancos, *Extraction: The Frontiers of Green Capitalism* (New York: Norton, 2025).

debates. In recent years, such global conversations spread at incredible speed, so that, at the moment of writing this preface, the field of eco-Marxism is vast and steadily growing. Yet the main split remains the same. Some authors accept (at least partially) the criticism of Marx's alleged progressive triumphalism and focus on how to re-frame his methodological and political remarks around new socio-economic configurations; others choose the path of re-discovering Marx's supposedly *ante litteram* environmentalist insights.

Saito is, and already was in 2017, among the most prominent supporters of the second option. Quite differently, I followed (and still subscribe to) Gorz's argument according to which the encounter between Marx's corpus and ecological thought (degrowth being a sub-section of this) had emerged as a distinctively *political* problem from the very beginning. The event that set the stage for such an encounter to occur is the global cycle of struggles that emerged in the late 1960s and early 1970s, whose main character was the unprecedented centrality of what can be defined as the 'sphere of social reproduction' (de-colonial movements, feminist campaigns, health and safety grievances within factories, proto-environmentalist advocacy throughout society). Of course, this does not imply that the scope of eco-Marxism should be limited to contemporary mobilizations for environmental justice. Rather, it means that these function as a site of enunciation for inquiring about the ecological crisis as dependent on the labour-nature-value nexus. Contemporary struggles inspired by political ecology certainly reject an all-too-easy dismissal of Marx's relevance. Yet they simultaneously express the need to re-evaluate class theory along socio-ecological lines.

To clarify this statement, it may be useful to advance an analytical distinction between 'environmental degradation' and 'ecological crisis'. What distinguishes the former – a transhistorical phenomenon due to a dysfunctional configuration of the society-nature link – from the latter is the fact that only capitalism necessarily entails a modality of use of resources expressing a systemic tendency towards expansive accumulation. Environmental degradation belongs to pre-modern 'nature-idolatry'.[18]

---

18   Karl Marx, *Grundrisse: Foundations of the Critique of Political Economy*, trans. Martin Nicolaus (London: Penguin, 1993), 41.

By contrast, ecological crisis is a distinctively modern phenomenon. Therefore, the debate on eco-Marxism is a field of inquiry that focuses on the ecological crisis as an effect of capitalist development, starting from the politicization of such a crisis as articulated by the cycle of struggles between 1968 and 1973, in which labour movements met the central role of social reproduction.

Thus, from a Marxist perspective, degrowth emerges not so much as a *theoretical* issue – a matter of categories (bioeconomy, sustainability, physical limits, steady state, etc.) – but rather as a *historical discontinuity* (within the more general relationship with ecology) to be elaborated upon. Back in 2017, two questions were key for me. First, under which conditions could the leading role played by workers' organizations in politicizing ecology be so completely disregarded by degrowth scholars at the beginning of the twenty-first century? And second, under which conditions could an ecological critique of contemporary exploitation constitute a bridge between eco-Marxists and labour-sensitive degrowthers? This twofold *problématique* was dealt with by mobilizing the notion of the 'cycle of struggle' as a methodological filter.[19] Somewhat in keeping with the hegemonic sentiment of the alter-globalization movement, Latouche-inspired degrowth neglected the social question in its search for political legitimacy (hence its close ties with Solidarity Economy and critical consumption networks). By contrast, Catalan degrowth attuned itself with the anti-austerity cycle, putting class positionality back at the very core of revolutionary activity (hence its renewed interest for workers' instances of unrest, including the role of unions in pushing ecological transition *from below*).

Nevertheless, as anticipated, getting to degrowth via Marx's notebooks on natural science (as Saito did) or via rethinking Marx's critique of exploitation in ecological terms (as attempted in this book) does not necessarily entail dissent. Rather, Saito's passion for workers' co-ops manifestly echoes widespread degrowth support for democratizing work (including ex-GKN self-management proposals). Besides, I would

---

19   See Nick Dyer-Witheford, *Cyber-Marx: Cycles and Circuits of Struggle in High-Technology Capitalism* (Chicago: University of Illinois Press, 1999).

argue that a strategy of class struggle is more likely to achieve degrowth Communism than reformism based on the green economy or eco-fascism based on climate Darwinism.[20]

Parma, December 2025

20　Among the many degrowth authors who have recently manifested a class-sensitive political attitude, see Bengi Akbulut, 'Degrowth', *Rethinking Marxism* 33: 1, 2021, 98–110; Viviana Asara, 'Untangling the Radical Imaginaries of the Indignados' Movement: Commons, Autonomy and Ecologism', *Environmental Politics* 34: 1, 2025, 141–65; Stefania Barca, *Workers of the Earth: Labour, Ecology and Reproduction in the Age of Climate Change* (New York: Pluto, 2024); Ekaterina Chertkovskaya and Alexander Paulsson, 'Countering Corporate Violence: Degrowth, Ecosocialism and Organising Beyond the Destructive Forces of Capitalism', *Organization* 28: 3, 2021, 405–25; Corinna Dengler and Miriam Lang, 'Commoning Care: Feminist Degrowth Visions for a Socio-Ecological Transformation', *Feminist Economics* 28: 1, 2021, 1–28; Giacomo D'Alisa and Federico Demaria, 'Accumulation by Contamination: Worldwide Cost-Shifting Strategies of Capital in Waste Management', *World Development* 184, 2024, 1–15; Zac Edwards, 'Degrowth: What Is in It for the Labour Movement?', *Ecological Economics* 236, 2025, 1–10; Jason Hickel, *Less Is More: How Degrowth Will Save the world* (London: Windmill Books, 2021); Vilay Kolinjivadi and Aaron Vasintjan, *The Sustainability Class: How to Take Back Our Future from Lifestyle Environmentalists* (New York: New Press, 2023); Onofrio Romano, *Towards a Society of Degrowth* (London: Routledge, 2021); Bue Rübner-Hansen, *Batshit Jobs: Destroying Life to Make a Living* (forthcoming); Matthias Schmelzer, Aaron Vasintjan, Andrea Vetter, *The Future Is Degrowth: A Guide to a World Beyond Capitalism* (London: Verso, 2022).

Acknowledgements

If I were to thank each and every person who, directly or indirectly, contributed to this book with suggestions, criticisms, comments or anything else, the list would be very long – indeed too long. I hope I have managed to express my gratitude in person, through gestures and words: without the meetings, events, debates, discussions, seminars, conferences and convivial moments that have taken place over these ten years of work, nothing of this book would be what it actually is. I therefore thank my fellow travellers collectively.

To some people, however, I owe too much not to mention them explicitly: my deepest gratitude goes to Nick Dyer-Witheford, Stefania Barca, Luigi Pellizzoni and Ottavio Marzocca: their 'imprint' on this book is very recognisable, and I hope I have not distorted their teachings too much.

Thanks to Federico Chicchi and Stefano Lucarelli for their friendship and guidance.

Thanks to Federico Mazzini for turning his home into a library for the whole summer of 2017.

Thanks to Andrea Bui for a very long comradeship and for his invaluable contribution to greatly smoothing out the 'intellectualist' excesses of the book (some of which are still there, of course: responsibility for these and other limitations lies solely with me).

Thanks to the Orthotes Group (Diego and Laura, Luigi and Elisa, Riccardo and Stefania) because it was not easy to turn 23 June 2016 into a beautiful memory, but we did it.

Thanks to my mother, my sister and my grandmother.

Thank you to Sara and Margherita for reminding me every day that, despite the little problems that pop up here and there, I am a very lucky man.

Finally, I would like to take this opportunity to contribute in my own small way to keeping alive the memory of Heather Heyer, who was killed last August by a white supremacist while fighting new fascism in Charlottesville, Virginia, United States of America.

English Edition

My deepest gratitude goes to Yari Lanci for his careful translation.[21]

Special thanks to the community of *POE – Politics Ontologies Ecology*.

Many thanks to the participants of the 2019-born mailing list *Degrowth Communism*.

Thank you to all the people at CIDOSPEL research centre, especially Vando Borghi, and at the Department of Sociology and Business Law, University of Bologna: I could not have asked for better workplaces.

Grateful thoughts go to everybody at the Theory Centre (University of Western Ontario): your support is everywhere in this book.

Thanks to Marta and Adele: *piccole*!

Thank you to the ex-GKN Factory Collective and to Greta Thunberg: your political and moral stature is one of the few signs of hope for the dark times in which we live.

Finally, I would like to take this opportunity to contribute in my own small way to keeping alive the memory of Renée Nicole Good and Alex Pretti, who were killed last January by ICE while fighting new fascism in Minneapolis.

---

21   This was possible due to financial support from the European Union Horizon 2020 project JUST2CE GA: 101003491

Introduction

It has been shown that the indefinite growth of material goods would, on the one hand, encounter insurmountable limits in the exhaustibility of natural resources and, on the other hand, entail increasing environmental costs: air and water pollution, soil destruction, urban sprawl, congestion, and so on, which have already reached intolerable levels.

Claudio Napoleoni and
Carla Ravaioli, 'La politica degli orari di lavoro'

Until a few years ago, a book devoted to the relationship between the social sciences and the ecological crisis, as well as to the political implications of this relationship, would have required an introduction aimed at establishing the relevance of the question concerning the environment for both the general public and/or scientific debates. I think it is safe to say that this is no longer the case, as evidenced by the huge media coverage of the signing of the Paris Agreement at the end of the 21st Conference of the Parties to the United Nations Framework Convention on Climate Change in December 2015. Further proof, if needed, could be the significant economic-diplomatic investments linked to the recent G7 Environment Conference – held in Bologna in June 2017 – which marked an early moment of tense confrontation between the new American administration led by climate denier Donald Trump and the remaining governments of the most industrialized nations on the planet, who are seemingly quite committed to the fight against global warming.

I will briefly examine these two 'test-events', for they provide an opportunity to clarify the polemical focus of the arguments advanced in this book and to frame the research questions that guided it. Let us start with the Paris Agreement (henceforth PA), the international treaty that replaced the Kyoto Protocol (signed in 1997 and ratified in 2005 – henceforth KP) and which is going to serve as the foundation of global climate policy in the near future. Marica Di Pierri's insightful analysis describes the treaty as an undeniable diplomatic success (195 signatory countries), with ambitious goals (a maximum increase of 2 degrees Celsius by 2100, and an explicit desire to lower the bar to 1.5 degrees). However, it was crippled at the outset by insufficient commitments: the sum total of INDCs (Intended Nationally Determined Contributions) of individual states falls far short of even the minimum 2 degrees target. Moreover, Di Pierri's analysis shows how the treaty's toolkit was inadequate for the radical changes necessary to achieve these targets.[1]

I believe this inadequacy stems from reproposing the flexible mechanisms devised in Kyoto,[2] which assume that the market – treated as the exclusive organizing principle of production – must serve as the economic foundation of climate policy and thus the salvation of the planet. In other words, what is restated is the *marketization of the fight against global warming*, despite the proven inadequacy of this strategy.[3] On this point, US Secretary of State John Kerry, the chief negotiator at COP21, left no room for misunderstanding:

> What we're doing is sending the marketplace an extraordinary signal – that those 196 countries are really committed – and that helps the private sector to move capital into that, knowing there's a future that is committed to this sustainable path.[4]

---

1   Marica di Pierri, 'Scienza, Governance, Società', *EcoMagazine*, 10 February 2016, eco-magazine.info. Di Pierri also points at a number of serious shortcomings in the Paris Agreement's text, including: no reference to oil or fossil fuels, no reference to the need to reduce their extraction and eliminate subsidies and incentives; delayed entry into force (2020); delayed review of INDCs (2023).

2   A detailed analysis of these mechanisms will be proposed in chapter 6.

3   See for instance Joyeeta Gupta, *The History of Global Climate Governance* (Cambridge: Cambridge UP, 2014).

4   Jeff McMahon, 'John Kerry Calls for Climate Agreement With "Legally Binding Transparency System"', *Forbes*, 9 December 2015.

The insistence on this 'Paris Consensus' – i.e. the centrality of market logic in the climate arena, framing efficiency as both a cost-reducing measure and a means of ecological preservation – was recently reaffirmed by Italian Minister Gian Luca Galletti at the opening of the G7 Environment meeting in Bologna. I would add that this was not accidental, since it happened right before an audience of the Global Business Coalition led by Italian Confindustria:[5]

> We intend to reaffirm our commitment to promote further steps, on a voluntary basis, to improve efficiency and sustainability in the use of resources. We must decouple growth from consumption:[6] thus doing 'more with less'. Resource efficiency is one of the cornerstones of the transition from a linear economy to a circular economy, which is essential for sustainable development and for compliance with the Paris Agreement. If business and politics act together, we will achieve great results. Today, in some cases, companies are already ahead of governments: they realised early on that the circular economy is the future and are moving independently in that direction.[7]

Global elites have adopted the dictates of the so-called *green economy*, which posits that environmental limits should be perceived not as a constraint on development, but rather as an unprecedented business opportunity, a driver of sustainable growth and the foundation of a new cycle of accumulation. As will become clear, my aim is not only to invalidate the propositions underpinning this framework and how it is presented,

---

5   General Confederation of Italian Industry, Italy's largest and most influential employers' federation [translator's note].

6   It is quite likely that the minister meant 'resource consumption', i.e. the flows of matter and energy that traverse the economic system (also referred to as social metabolism or throughput). No criticism of consumerism, then, just a further endorsement of the 'green growth' advocated by ecological modernisation, i.e. the idea that so-called *decoupling* is indeed possible: increased capital accumulation (and accompanying GDP growth) with a simultaneous decrease in anthropic impacts on the biosphere.

7   Gian Luca Galletti, 'Ci sarà una "Bologna Road Map" per l'efficienza', *Environment Ministry*, 2017.

but also to trace its genealogy – that is, to examine its historical emergence – in order to critically analyse it and, ultimately, to overturn its political use. This leads to the two key research questions:

1. What historical transformations have shaped the conditions that lead most political decision-makers to view the green economy as a *reasonable* nexus between nature and value?[8]

2. Given that this approach has yielded little measurable success in over a decade of global implementation,[9] under what conditions is it possible to envision desirable and effective policy alternatives?

The remainder of this introduction is devoted to discussing and clarifying such research questions so that they can be adequately contextualized and developed in the following chapters of the book. In a nutshell, it could be said that, while the first question rests on a need to *understand* how ecology and the economy have historically intertwined, the second concerns the desire to *transform* the contemporary outcome of that very intertwining. This pattern has also guided my research, as it links an academic foundation informing the first question to a political foundation that gives substance to the second. However, it should be noted that this heuristic distinction ought not be taken to extremes. The specific political positioning in relation to the present – that is, the side we stand on when looking at reality – necessarily influences the questions we pose to the world around us. At the same time, it is good practice to cultivate curiosity and open-mindedness, allowing the answers the world presents to challenge and reshape the questions we ask. While it may be difficult, one must resist both the allure of detached impartiality – which conceals

---

8   Although it is undeniable that today this 'Paris Consensus' has found a strong critic in the person of Donald Trump, it should not be forgotten that the value-nature nexus referred to by the US president is precisely what, as I will discuss later, has 'produced' the ecological crisis as a distinctively political problem. In short, Trump criticizes the green economy for the wrong reasons, and a generalization of his environmental approach would be nothing short of disastrous.

9   Starting from the ratification of the KP in 2005.

the most repugnant ideology of all, *the post-ideological one* – and the belief that being on the 'right' side exempts us, as it were, from the intellectual labour of analysis, which is to say, from the type of conceptual work that ties the potential of an argument to the process that carves it into reality. Chapter 1 is devoted to a more in-depth examination of this methodological approach.

In order to correctly frame the first research question, it may be useful to further analyse an expression used previously: what exactly does the marketization of the fight against global warming (and, by extension, of the ecological crisis) mean? In response, I believe it may be useful to consider the current state of global carbon markets, exploring it through the lens of Hurricane Sandy (October 2012) and the particular coverage it received in US media.[10] The context is well known: Barack Obama was preparing to celebrate his second term of presidency after an electoral campaign in which neither he nor his Republican challenger, Mitt Romney, had felt the need to even mention climate change – a first since 1984 (Reagan vs Mondale). This indifference was compounded by the striking refusal of nearly all accounts to link Sandy – and, more generally, the increasing frequency of extreme weather events – to the anthropogenic CO_2-equivalent emissions in the atmosphere.

Against this backdrop, the first November issue of the influential business magazine *Bloomberg Businessweek* marked a significant exception. Indeed, its cover story, titled 'It's Global Warming, Stupid', highlights the dual character of the climate change debate. Journalist Paul Barrett first discusses a series of scientific findings suggesting a direct correlation between human activity and climate modifications. This represents the first register of such debate: it primarily concerns whether the root cause of climatic imbalances is human-induced or not. My reflection here does not engage with this issue. While climate science should not be regarded as the guardian of an eternal and indisputable truth, both scientific and experiential evidence supporting the anthropogenic nature

------

10   The hurricane, commonly referred to as Superstorm Sandy, caused over a hundred casualties across the Caribbean countries and the US East Coast. In the US alone, damages were estimated at $65 billion.

of climate change is now so abundant that controversies revolve more around its specific configurations than its actual existence.[11]

More interestingly from my perspective, Barrett's article also introduces the second register of the global warming debate, namely its possible solutions. Here, what I propose to call *carbon trading dogma* comes into full view, which is to say an extremely entrenched (yet empirically unproven) political belief according to which climate change, although a market failure, can only be viably solved through further marketization. The way Barrett articulates the shift from the first to the second register is quite telling:

> If all that [lists of scientific data] doesn't impress, forget the scientists ostensibly devoted to advancing knowledge and saving lives. Listen instead to corporate insurers committed to compiling statistics for profit.[12]

He then focuses on a report issued by financial insurance company Munich RE, which states that climate change is causing a rising number of natural catastrophes, especially in North America. His conclusion is peremptory: if brokers believe global warming is occurring, then there is no longer any point in questioning it.

This is a highly relevant passage, since it entails a curious reversal of modern rationality, ostensibly centred on the sharp distinction between facts (science) and values (politics and/or ethics). The financial colonization of climate change as a global political issue, in fact, relies on a paradoxical inversion of modern categories: 'you don't trust science? Fine. But you must surely believe in markets!'[13] In other words, in Barrett's

---

11   Naomi Oreskes and Erik M. Conway, *Merchants of Doubt* (London: Bloomsbury, 2010).

12   Paul M. Barrett, 'It's Global Warming, Stupid', *Bloomberg Businessweek*, 2 November 2012, bloomberg.com.

13   This dynamic complements rather than replaces the widespread perception that insurance analysts have more accurate information than is publicly known. This perception reveals that behind the political force of the market lies not only the ability to *produce truth*, but also profit as the driving force and criterion for evaluating scientific research considered reliable.

argument the market functions as a *site of veridiction*, to use Michel Foucault's formula as framed in his lectures on biopolitics from the late 1970s.[14] In this sense, the second register of the climate change debate postulates that an effective solution to climate issues exists only where there is an opportunity for profit. Any alternative is unthinkable. This is why I call this conceptualization the *carbon trading dogma*. On the one hand, it is defined by its nature as an exclusive belief (*aut-aut*), one that is not based on the rational analysis of the available empirical material. On the other hand, this dogma only emphasizes the salvific role of the price system, assuming that, even though climate change emerges as a market failure – which has historically failed to adequately account for the environment, essentially reducing it to a mere externality – it can nevertheless only be effectively addressed on the basis of further marketization. Put simply: 'give nature a price and the problem will disappear!' To put it more analytically: new, dedicated markets imply the production of new commodities, which in turn drive a new wave of primitive accumulation, sustainable at last (at least on paper). It is as if a patient were prescribed a treatment consisting of increased doses of the very pathogen recognized as the direct cause of the disease. The market, in fact, assumes a dual and ambiguous role in relation to climate change. It is both *executioner* (as the culprit of theoretical and practical neglect) and *redeemer* (as evidently able to include nature correctly in the price system).

As will become clear later, this is a dogmatic stance with an extreme social strength, indifferent to any practical refutation. Regardless of how one evaluates the concrete results of such a conceptual framework, it is worth highlighting from the outset the strikingly convoluted character of that formulation which, however, I believe is neither false nor irrational. Rather, this formulation presents itself as both *perfectly suited to the current regime of accumulation* and, at the same time, *manipulative in its treatment of the type of labour that produces value within this regime.* Almost everyone – the vast majority of people dispossessed of their

---

14   See Michel Foucault, *Security, Territory, Population: Lectures at the Collège de France 1977–78* and *The Birth of Biopolitics: Lectures at the Collège de France 1978–79*, ed. Michel Senellart, trans. Graham Burchell (Basingstoke: Palgrave Macmillan, 2009 and 2010).

territories, in the Global South as well as the Global North – loses out. A select few, mostly financial operators, profit from it. Meanwhile, no one seems particularly concerned with the question of what has happened to *labour* within the value-nature nexus that underpins the green economy. To borrow a fitting expression from Antonio Negri – yet applying it to a different context from the one in which it was originally conceived – the *carbon trading dogma* stands as a 'reasonable ideology' of the contemporary tendency of capitalist development.[15] This tendency reflects a context increasingly defined by the coexistence of expanding shares of cognitive labour and a growing centrality of financial markets in the framework of economic governance.

Now, before embarking on a detailed analysis of these aspects, it is necessary to emphasize their unprecedented character. At the turn of the 1970s – i.e. when the ecological crisis first emerged as a distinctively political issue – the idea that the deterioration of ecological conditions could be the driving force behind a new cycle of capitalist accumulation was simply unthinkable. Of course, some correctly warned of the potential for ecology to be weaponized against workers, just as there were visionary hypotheses about the adaptability of capital in its relationship to natural resources.[16] However, these were attempts to avoid underestimating

---

15   Negri elaborated this concept in 1970, in relation to Descartes's thought: 'It was a question for him, on the one hand, of confirming – from the metaphysical standpoint – the nascent power (*potentia*) of the bourgeoisie, the revolutionary potential of its action, the decision in favour of the autonomy of bourgeois reason: the "*I think*" is this determination . . . If the bourgeoisie presented itself as the hegemonic class, capable of constructing a new civilization, it was solely because it had recognised, as the foundation of such a civilization, a *new productive force* – that of labour . . . Descartes's philosophy can be read in this light: as *ideology* (ideology in the true sense, 'partisan' representation of reality, that is, affirmation of the class truth of the hegemonic bourgeoisie) and as *reasonable* ideology, rooted in the awareness of the actual relationships of forces and the progressive possibilities that could potentially open up to that new social body and to that truth.' Antonio Negri, *The Political Descartes*, trans. Alberto Toscano and Matteo Mandarini (London: Verso, 2007 [1970]), 322–3.

16   A. Dario Paccino, *L'imbroglio ecologico* (Turin: Einaudi, 1972); André Gorz (under the pseudonym of Michel Bosquet), *Critica al capitalismo di ogni giorno* (Milan: Jaca Book, 1978 [1972]).

capitalism's adaptive capacities, certainly not a prefiguration of the green economy. This was due not to analytical shortcomings or theoretical flaws, but to the simple reason that the conditions necessary for biophysical limits to be internalized in the valorization process had yet to materialize. At the time, the dominant conceptual framework saw nature acting as an 'edge' or 'limit' to value-producing activity, a 'margin' that is nonetheless infinite and free of cost. This conceptual framework sets very strict boundaries between the sphere of reproduction (comprising the environment and the unpaid labour extracted from domestic and slave labour), which guarantees the *conditions* of valorization, and the sphere of production mobilizing the *factors* of valorization (wage labour and capital).

This type of labour – embedded in what we might call the *energy-based* labour theory of value, which over time would take on an industrial-Fordist shape and flow into a quantitative institutional framework such as that of the wage-form – is undoubtedly responsible for ecological deterioration, which is to say, it presents itself as *entropic labour*.[17] From this perspective, it is appropriate to identify the capitalist organization of production as the direct cause of the ecological crisis, which differs from 'simple' environmental degradation – examples of which can be found in every age and society – precisely because of its dependence on the need for accumulation and growth that characterizes the cycles of capital. The entropic character of wage labour stems from the fact that, in this relationship between nature and value, the former acts as an unaccounted-for limit both at the beginning of the process (availability of raw materials) and at the end of the process (waste disposal). In short, in this model, nature is certainly internalized (appearing both as a 'free' component of the input and as an equally 'free' garbage bin for the wasteful output), but only in a way that defines the limits of productive abstract labour, limits that do not involve nature in the actual transformative activity.

The situation is quite different, however, when a scenario emerging from the energy crisis of the early 1970s is fundamentally marked by two elements: work that becomes increasingly cognitive and a more central

---

17   See Federico Chicchi, Emanuele Leonardi and Stefano Lucarelli, *Logiche dello sfruttamento* (Verona: ombre corte, 2016).

role of financial markets in economic governance. In this interweaving, work-knowledge transforms external and infinite nature into a primary factor of production and, therefore, overturns the 'classic' connection between value and nature. This sets a new wave of primitive accumulation in motion. As I will show in more detail later, the discrete units of 'nature-information' exchanged in carbon markets or in PES (Payments for Ecosystem Services) schemes have little to do with the extraction of raw materials or the disposal of waste. They are subjected to a very different process of commodification, and consequently present both different forms of exploitation – exerted on what Marx called the *general intellect* – and distinctive environment-friendly potentials (yet linked to the removal of socio-natural commons from a market-based governance).[18] Here, the relationship between labour and nature moves beyond a schematic dualism, where the former is active and the latter passive. Instead, there emerges a form of mastery that, by virtue of a new approach to data production in uncertain environments, embeds itself within a form of 'nature' that interacts with the economic system rather than merely providing the backdrop for its operations.[19] In the field of the so-called bio-economy – from bio-mimicry to synthetic biology, up to the frontier of bio-sensors – value extraction occurs as a process combining cognitive labour, technological innovation and the generative/evolutionary capacities of non-human natures.[20] The analysis of *this* kind of work – embedded in an *information-based* labour theory of value[21] – is the key to unveiling the manipulative structure of the green economy, taking its control away from the market, and thus revealing *negentropic* potential of the sphere of social reproduction, whose *direct productivity* has become more and more evident since the oil shocks in the 1970s.

---

18   Karl Marx, *Grundrisse: Foundations of the Critique of Political Economy*, trans. Martin Nicolaus (London: Penguin, 1993).

19   Luigi Pellizzoni, *Ontological Politics in a Disposable World: The New Mastery of Nature* (Farnham: Ashgate, 2015).

20   Elizabeth, R. Johnson, 'At the Limits of Species Being: Sensing the Anthropocene', *South Atlantic Quarterly* 116: 2, 2017, 275–92.

21   On this, see Matteo Pasquinelli, 'The Automation of the Anthropocene: On Carbosilicon Machines and Cyberfossil Capital', *South Atlantic Quarterly* 116: 2, 2017, 311–26.

Incidentally, it is worth noting that this new 'light' economy can be seen as a renewed opportunity for ambitious reformism, as a social compromise adapted to current coordinates of production. I would argue that the space for this option is very limited, but Aldo Bonomi, for example, takes a different view. He sees in these new conditions:

> The advent of a new generation of ICTs [Information and Communication Technologies], the centrality of economies reproducing life and territory, reinventing space and cities through ambiguous but also suggestive attributions such as smart, social and green. Underlying them is the qualitative and meaningful change in consumption, the high level of mass schooling, the acknowledgement of ecological and social sustainability as key criteria, the growing intolerance towards the dumping of common dimensions of living, dwelling and producing.[22]

To sum up this first part of the argument: Chapters 2 and 3 specify and critically discuss the labour-nature-value nexus that stemmed from primitive accumulation and was then synthesized by classical political economy; chapter 4 situates the crisis of this nexus, at least in the West, in the period between what Bruno Trentin called the 'second Red Biennium' (1968–9) and the first oil shock (1973);[23] chapter 5 examines the nexus between labour, nature and value that took shape between the mid-1980s and the early 2000s, while chapter 6 exemplifies this nexus through the Clean Development Mechanism, i.e. a particular aspect of the global CO_2 emissions markets. In sum, the aim is to analyse the transformations in the relationship between the theory of value – understood as a historical agent rather than a mere descriptive tool – and the natural environment. However, it is important to clarify from the outset that this transition implies not a complete substitution but rather the emergence of an

---

22   Aldo Bonomi, Federico Della Puppa and Roberto Masiero, *La società circolare: Fordismo, capitalismo molecolare, sharing economy* (Rome: DeriveApprodi, 2016), 35.

23   See Bruno Trentin and Guido Liguori, *Il secondo biennio rosso* (Rome: Editori Riuniti, 1999).

additional sphere within a valorization process that increasingly tends to differentiate its logics. If there is one overarching tendency, it is towards the *heterogeneity* of the forms of value production and extraction.[24] In other words, the green economy does not replace the fossil economy *tout court*; rather, it opens up a space of intra-capitalist conflict while also creating a new horizon for a post-capitalist articulation of the relationship between society and nature.

Finally, chapter 7 begins by addressing the political dimension of the labour-nature-value nexus or, more specifically, the invisibility of work in the arenas where environmental and climate policies are currently being discussed. It is true that, in recent years, a minoritarian (yet certainly not irrelevant) sector of the trade unions movement has started to engage with ecological issues, not only in terms of job blackmail, but also as a potential curb on unemployment.[25] However, it remains equally true that only rarely has the debate addressed how cognitive/digital work – a

---

24   Sandro Mezzadra and Brett Neilson, *Border as Method, or, The Multiplication of Labor* (Durham: Duke UP, 2013).

25   With 'job blackmail', I refer to what Marco Revelli, in describing the tragedy of the ILVA steelplant in Taranto, aptly condemned as a 'monstrous diktat' – the brutal ultimatum forced upon the city's working community: either die of hunger (due to lack of wages) or die of cancer (from an 'excess' of labour, from those specific forms of production of 'noxiousness' [*nocività*]). See Marco Revelli, 'Introduction', in Giuseppe de Marzo, *Anatomia di una rivoluzione: giustizia, ambiente e lavoro per invertire la rotta e battere la crisi* (Rome: Castelvecchi, 2010), 10. For an extensive analysis of 'job blackmail', see Stefania Barca, 'Labouring the Earth: Transnational Reflections on the Environmental History of Work', *Environmental History* 19: 1, 2014, 3–27; and Stefania Barca and Emanuele Leonardi, 'Working Class Communities and Ecology: Reframing Environmental Justice around the ILVA Steel Plant', in *Class, Inequality and Community Development*, ed. Mae Shaw and Marjorie Mayo (Brighton: Policy Press, 2017).

See, in particular, debates on 'Just Transition' and analyses of campaigns for the creation of climate jobs in the United Kingdom, South Africa and, more recently, Portugal: Stefania Barca, 'Greening the Jobs: Trade Unions, Climate Change and the Political Ecology of Labour', in *The International Handbook of Political Ecology*, ed. Raymond L. Bryant (London: Elgar, 2015); Dimitris Stevis and Romain Felli, 'Global Labour Unions and Just Transition to a Green Economy', *International Environmental Agreements* 15: 1, 2015, 29–43; Emanuele Leonardi, 'Finanza climatica e resistenze del lavoro: la critica del potere di definizione nella campagna sudafricana "One Million Climate Jobs"', *Sociologia del lavoro* 138, 2015, 240–54.

fundamental yet removed element of the green economy – gives rise to an unprecedented terrain of conflict in which it is possible to imagine a new relationship between society and nature. It is on this point that I intend to set up a dialogue between Marxism and degrowth, exploring how it should account for the transformations of the labour-nature-value nexus, starting with the fundamental contribution of André Gorz.

Here, it is important to make explicit the biographical (therefore largely accidental) reasons that prompted me to focus on this dialogue, which are, first and foremost, linked to my encounter with Gorz's essay *Sette tesi per cambiare la vita* ('Seven Theses to Change Life', Italian translation of the original French title *Écologie et liberté*). I fortuitously came across this essay among the shelves of a small but very rich library in the northern province of Varese, while browsing through the volumes as a way to delay my return to work. I remember reading it as one of the rare exciting moments of that time. The book addressed topics closely related to the research interests discussed previously, but it certainly did not limit itself to analytical-descriptive propositions. On the contrary, it forcefully attacked the contradictions of its time. I was deeply struck by its revolutionary charge and vitality, which was indirectly demonstrated by a dialogue I would have, shortly thereafter, with Maurizio Pallante.[26] Where I identified an essential contribution to the renewal of Marxism, he saw an explicit departure, a clean break with the tradition of historical materialism. I was initially astonished by the vast distance of our interpretations, but soon came to appreciate it as an enriching element inherent in the text. Since the version by the Italian publisher Feltrinelli had been out of print for decades, I thought that a new edition could reignite the debate on political ecology, which was not widely discussed in Italy.[27] I explored

---

26   In April 2011, I participated in a debate on degrowth organized by the Matteo Bagnaresi Foundation, with Maurizio Pallante, during which Gorz's essay was discussed at length. See Maurizio Pallante, *La felicità sostenibile* (Milan: Rizzoli, 2009).

27   However, there is no shortage of illustrious exceptions. The most significant figures in this regard include Laura Conti and Giovanni Berlinguer (as far as the PCI is concerned), Virginio Bettini, Giorgio Nebbia, Dario Paccino and Giovanna Ricoveri. An overview can be found in Stefania Barca, 'Lavoro, corpo e ambiente: Laura Conti e le origini dell'ecologia politica in Italia', *Ricerche Storiche*

this possibility in early 2011, while I was collaborating with the nascent publisher Orthotes on the translation of *The Indivisible Remainder*.[28] The publisher supported the initiative and took the first steps. However, as a result of a number of mostly minor mishaps, the project did not materialize. In retrospect, I believe the main reason for that torpor lay in the fact that, at the time, I could easily recognize the *theoretical* relevance of the book but did not perceive the *political* urgency of reintroducing it into debates in Italy about the social dimension of the global ecological crisis. At that moment, in fact, I felt there was a lack of both an expanded community of potential readers and, above all, a horizon of composition between different forms of activism, more or less linked to the question concerning the environment. In other words, what was missing – at least from my point of view – was a political space where different subjectivities could articulate themselves (also) through a new engagement with Gorz's analyses from his 'ecological phase'.[29]

The situation changed radically in September 2014, when I attended the Fourth International Degrowth Conference in Leipzig. Here too, chance played no small part. I had been involved with the Italian degrowth movement in its early years – between 2005 and 2007 – but I had distanced myself from it for two reasons: first, what I saw as an overemphasis on the issue of physical limits to growth (often at the expense of analysing the social limits to accumulation); second, a reluctance to incorporate a

---

3, 2011, 541–50; Michele Citoni and Catia Papa, 'Marxismo ed ecologia: prove di avvicinamento nella "stagione dei movimenti"', in *Karl Marx (in pillole)*, ed. Mario Boyer (Rome: Ediesse, 2010); Emanuele Leonardi, 'L'ecologia come frontiera mobile della questione operaia', *La società degli individui* 45: 1, 2013, 15–26; Luigi Pellizzoni (ed.), *Conflitti ambientali. Esperti, politica, istituzioni nelle controversie ecologiche* (Bologna: Il Mulino, 2011). For a broader discussion, see Stefania Barca, 'Labour and the ecological crisis: The eco-modernist dilemma in western Marxism(s) (1970s–2000s)', *Geoforum* 83, 2017, 91–100.

28   Slavoj Žižek, *The Indivisible Remainder: On Schelling and Related Matters* (London: Verso, 2007 [1996]).

29   I proposed an outline of the 'phases' of André Gorz's thought in my introduction 'L'ecologia politica di André Gorz', in André Gorz, *Ecologia e libertà* (Naples-Salerno: Orthotes, 2015 [1977]). A largely similar structure, though far more detailed and thorough, can be found in the brilliant biography written by Willy Gianinazzi, *André Gorz: A Life*, trans. Chris Turner (Calcutta: Seagull Books, 2022 [2016]).

class analysis of contemporary capitalism into the ecological critique. As a result, I had observed the first three international conferences (Paris 2008, Barcelona 2010, Venice 2012) from afar, and with a certain amount of scepticism. However, shortly before the deadline to submit a proposal for the fourth conference, a degrowther friend suggested to me that I submit one, for he sensed that there was a growing willingness within the movement to explore a possible ecological dimension of the critique of political economy. I was intrigued, then submitted the abstract – though with some hesitation – and remained undecided for a while as to whether to participate, even after my proposal had been accepted. In short, I did not have high expectations.

Instead, it provided an epiphany. Alongside a very significant academic and journalistic presence (over 500 people) was a vast array of civil society associations, political groups and grassroots movements (over 3,000 people). More than a conference, it was a festival of socio-ecological struggles, where different theoretical and political perspectives engaged with one another through concrete mobilizations, immediately raising the need for convergence among social movements that had previously been (almost) indifferent to one another. It was five days of conflict and discussion, an effervescence I had not experienced in several years. In other words, I had found the political space in which to embed *Écologie et liberté* in order to encourage the recognition between Marxism and degrowth and establish a possible horizon for their coalition. As will become clearer in the final chapter, much had changed since my scepticism in 2007. What changed was, of course, my own perspective, which had grown more open and curious. In addition, the composition of the degrowth movement itself had modified, particularly with the emergence of what I call *Catalan degrowth*,[30] that is, a group of scholars and activists far less reluctant to address the class dimension of the ecological crisis, often in dialogue with the revolutionary traditions of modernity – above all, anarchism and Marxism. I therefore returned to Italy, contacted the publisher to make

---

30   Cf. Giacomo d'Alisa, Federico Demaria and Giorgos Kallis, *Degrowth: A Vocabulary for a New Era* (London: Routledge, 2015); Marco Deriu (ed.), *La civiltà della decrescita* (Naples: Marotta e Cafiero, 2016); Giorgos Kallis, 'In Defense of Degrowth', *Open Commons*, 2017, indefenseofdegrowth.com.

sure that their interest in Gorz had not waned and, once reassured, I set to work. Within a few months, *Ecologia e Libertà* was back in circulation. While I was aware of the initiative's limitations, my impression was that the objective of the new Italian edition – reviving the thread of dialogue between certain Marxist streams interested in ecological issues and some areas of the degrowth movement – had been achieved.[31] Against this background, the aim of the final chapter is to intervene in that dialogical space with an autonomous formulation. It ties in with the epochal transformation of the labour-nature-value nexus analysed in the previous chapters of the book and highlights the need to rethink the *political* division of work that shaped the initial *rapprochement* between anti-determinist historical materialism (Marx/Gorz) and bioeconomy-inspired degrowth (Georgescu-Roegen). This division ultimately rested on the idea that the 1973 oil shock had unleashed a twofold crisis, both *social* (or of overproduction) and *environmental* (or of reproduction). In this context, the possibility of coalition was, so to speak, immediate: even though there remained significant differences regarding how to conceive of the root cause of the crisis (tendential fall in the rate of profit/workers' struggles vs violation of ecological limits), the critique of capitalism could proceed from converging positions – as it were, from *within* and from *outside* with respect to the capital relation.

The 'peculiar' defeat of the anti-authoritarian cycle of struggles (1960s and 1970s) showed the insufficiency of this solely 'additional' alliance between Marxism and degrowth, yet one could say that it did not certify its complete overcoming.[32] On the contrary, as we will see later, the ever-accelerating proliferation of extra-economic violence of contemporary capitalism – on the one hand, via accumulation by dispossession, as put forward by David Harvey;[33] on the other, via accumulation by contamination, as discussed by Giacomo D'Alisa and Federico Demaria – reasserts with even greater force the problem of the incompatibility between the

---

31   In particular, I am referring here to the debate hosted in the section 'Ecologia Politica' of the militant research collective *Effimera*, 2015–17, effimera.org.

32   Pier Paolo Poggio, 'Pensare il 68', *Sinistrainrete*, 14 March 2017, sinistrainrete .info.

33   David Harvey, *The New Imperialism* (Oxford: Oxford UP, 2003).

valorization process and healthy ecosystems.[34] Alongside all this, however, emerges a new dimension of the labour-nature-value nexus, in which the environment enters *directly* into valorization not merely as a *condition* of production but as a *factor* in its own right, as an expression of the *general intellect* and of the sphere of reproduction, that is, of work-as-information and care for the commons. Put differently, the political problem is how to produce conflict aimed at reducing pressure on the biosphere ('shrinking' entropic labour and social metabolism) *and* advancing the proliferation of care-based production of knowledge and society (multiplication of negentropic work). Fundamentally linked to the *general intellect*, negentropic work can only be realized within a techno-economic paradigm of a digital kind: only from this perspective can sustainability be politicized in such a way that non-commodified social knowledge may be placed at the service of environmental protection. This is not to say that information and communication technologies, in and of themselves, can 'solve' ecological issues. As things stand, their energy requirements are incompatible with a healthy planet. However, it remains possible to fight for a work-nature nexus that lies *beyond* the logic of value – namely, to construct relations of production that prioritize the development of negentropy over the imperatives of capitalist accumulation. Such relations will need to form the foundation on which to build a mode of production increasingly based on peer-to-peer networks linked to the care of commons and to environmental sustainability.

A final note regarding my approach to André Gorz's oeuvre. In this book, the reader will not find any systematic reconstruction of his socio-philosophical trajectory, for Willy Gianinazzi's biography and the book written by Françoise Gollain already provide a solid exegetical framework.[35] My aim is, rather, to use Gorz's work as a conceptual guide to reflect on some problems closely linked to current events. The 'Gorzian' passages in this book are always interwoven with suggestions from other

---

34 Giacomo D'Alisa and Federico Demaria, 'Alle frontiere del capitale', *Zapruder* 30, 2013, 38–51.

35 Gianinazzi, *André Gorz: A Life*, 2022; Françoise Gollain, *André Gorz, une philosophie de l'émancipation* (Paris: Éditions L'Harmattan, 2018).

political and cultural traditions, following a logic justified solely in the relationship between the issue at hand and the will to understand it fully, so that effective political mobilization becomes possible. Moreover, I would be pleased if I could assume Gorz's 'stance' – that of a *bridge-builder*. I have boundless admiration for his ability to promote dialogue and mutual recognition between disparate strands of anti-capitalism. It is also, perhaps above all, this *style of militancy* that needs to be rediscovered, ten years after his death (and that of Doreen, his lifelong companion).[36]

36   See *Omaggio a André Gorz nel decennale della morte*, special issue of *Etica e Politica* 19: 3, 2017, 81–167.

1

Political Ecology as Method: Analytical Premises and New Political Stakes of Social Transformation

The Divorce Between Wealth and Value

Marx says that revolutions are the locomotive of world history. But perpahs it is quite otherwise. Perhaps revolutions are an attempt by the passengers on this train – namely, the human race – to activate the emergency brake.

Walter Benjamin, Paralipomena to 'On the Concept of History'

It is quite likely that Benjamin – whose polemical object was the determinist belief in Progress, in other words in the idea that the quantitative accumulation of goods would spontaneously generate a classless society – was already correct at the time he formulated those words in 1940. However, there is no doubt that the ecological crisis, which erupted in the second half of the twentieth century, has only reinforced their validity. At a time when capitalist development is jeopardizing the very conditions that sustain human life on Earth, it is essential to recognize the inadequacy of any political strategy that does not contemplate a radical course reversal. Indeed, it is no longer sufficient to denounce capital's distributive irrationality, assuming that proletarian control of economic surplus would automatically resolve the environmental issue. What must be questioned are the fetish of accumulation, growth for growth's sake and the urge to expand social metabolism – or throughput, which is to say the amount of matter and energy flowing through the economic system. As early as 1977, André Gorz had already grasped the point with great clarity:

> Ecological concerns are fundamental; they cannot be compromised or postponed. Socialism is no better than capitalism if it makes use of the same tools. The total domination of nature inevitably entails a domination of people by the techniques of domination. If there were no other options, it would be preferable to have a non-nuclear capitalism than to have a nuclear socialism, for the former would weigh less heavily upon future generations.[1]

Rather than diverting the locomotive of universal history onto different tracks – while still aiming to increase its speed – it seems necessary to pull the revolutionary brake. This is not to deny the need for movement, but, rather, to reconsider first where one wants to go and then determine the most suitable means to get there. In the current situation, revolution as interruption is justified against the backdrop of what, drawing on the final phase of Gorz's research, we might call the *growing divorce between wealth and value*. In a 2005 interview, after predicting the great financial crisis that would erupt a couple of years later, Gorz states,

> Producing and producing more is not, then, a problem . . . The problem is the continually growing gap between the capacity to produce and the capacity to sell at a profit, between producible wealth and the commodity form, which is the form of value wealth must necessarily assume if it is to be able to be produced within the framework of the economic system currently in force.[2]

---

1   André Gorz, 'Ecology as Freedom', in *Ecology as Politics*, trans. Patsy Vidgerman and Jonathan Cloud (Boston, MA: South End Press, 1980 [1977]), 20. Since the mid-1950s, Gorz developed a fiercely critical analysis of so-called actually existing socialism. This, however, did not prevent him from placing his reflection within the context of the communist tradition, which is to say of a radical alternative to capitalist market economy.

2   'The secret of growth of the United States economy during the 1990s, years characterised by a quasi-stagnation of the European economy, resides in a policy that no other country can afford itself and which, sooner or later, will have fearsome

To better understand this distinction, and to fully grasp its ecological relevance, it is worth stepping back to examine the value-nature nexus that underpinned the modern conceptual framework – at least until the first oil shock in 1973 – and how the green economy and the carbon trading dogma emerged from its crisis. In particular, it seems apt to start from the element that these discursive formations, grounded in the transformation of the environmental constraint into a terrain for capital development, seek in every way to remove: labour. In this regard, an almost obligatory starting point is Marx's critique of the opening lines of the Gotha Programme, according to which 'labour is the source of all wealth':

> Labour is not the source of all wealth. Nature is just as much the source of use-values (and surely these are what make up material wealth!) as labour. Labour is itself only the manifestation of a force of nature, human labour power. This phrase can be found in any children's primer; it is correct in so far as it is assumed that labour is performed with the objects and instruments necessary to it. A socialist programme, however, cannot allow such bourgeois formulations to silence the conditions which give them the only meaning they possess. Man's labour only becomes a source of use-values, and hence also of wealth, if his relation to nature, the primary source of all instruments and objects of labour, is one of ownership from the start, and if he treats it

---

consequences . . . It is the growing indebtedness of "middle-class" households that was and remains the main engine of growth . . . However, this amazing state of affairs can last only so long as the Wall Street Stock Exchange continues to rise and the dollar doesn't fall in relation to other currencies. When Wall Street goes into long-term decline and the dollar begins to weaken, the fictional character of outstanding dollar balances will become evident and the world banking system will be in danger of collapsing like a house of cards. Capitalism is "teetering on the edge of the abyss".' André Gorz, 'Wealth Without Value, Value Without Wealth', in *Ecologica*, trans. Chris Turner (Calcutta: Seagull Books, 2010), 163–5. It is worth mentioning that the concluding phase of Gorz's research seems to be clearly influenced by the proponents of the 'critique of value', particularly Moishe Postone and Robert Kurz. On this, see Willy Gianinazzi, 'Quand André Gorz découvrit la critique de la valeur' (palim-psao.fr/2016/01/quand-andre-gorz-decouvrit-la-critique-de-la-valeur-par-willy-gianinazzi.html) [2016]; Gorz, 'Wealth Without Value, Value Without Wealth', 165–6.

as belonging to him. There is every good reason for the bourgeoisie to
ascribe supernatural creative power to labour, for when a man has no
property other than his labour power it is precisely labour's dependence
on nature that forces him, in all social and cultural conditions, to be
the slave of other men who have taken the objective conditions of
labour into their own possession. He needs their permission to work,
and hence their permission to live.[3]

The lucidity of Marx's analysis is simply extraordinary. Schematizing
somewhat – and even slightly stretching the letter of this passage to better
capture its spirit – we find here a tension between labour *in general*
(a transhistorical category that defines the mediating relationship between
society and nature)[4] and wage labour, which arises from the conditions
under which labour is performed in a specifically capitalist context. Such
a context is characterized by the separation of producers from the means
of production and the possibility – though in reality, the necessity – for
the former to sell their labour power to the owners of the latter.[5] As Marx

---

3   Karl Marx, 'Critique of the Gotha Programme', in *The First International
and After: Political Writings Vol. 3*, ed. David Fernbach (London: Verso, 2010), 341.

4   'Labour is, first of all, a process between man and nature, a process by which
man, through his own actions, mediates, regulates and controls the metabolism
between himself and nature. He confronts the materials of nature as a force of
nature. He sets in motion the natural forces which belong to his own body, his arms,
legs, head and hands, in order to appropriate the materials of nature in a form
adapted to his own needs.' Karl Marx, *Capital: A Critique of Political Economy, Vol. 1*,
trans. Ben Fowkes (London: Penguin, 1990), 283. For an ecological critique on
the concept of labour, a critique manifestly influenced by Gorz, see Françoise
Gollain, *Une critique du travail* (Paris: La Découverte, 2000).

5   A note added by Friedrich Engels to the fourth edition of *Das Kapital* further
clarifies this point: 'The English language has the advantage of possessing two
separate words for these two different aspects of labour. Labour which creates
use-values and is qualitatively determined is called "work" as opposed to "labour";
labour which creates value and is only measured quantitatively is called "labour", as
opposed to "work"'; Marx, *Capital Vol. 1*, 138.
    Distinguishing between 'activity' and 'labour', Romano Alquati formulated a
hypothesis that is different at the lexical level yet convergent at the political one.
Anna Curcio comments on this as follows: 'Labour is a specific activity within
human action (what Alquati defines as "labourised" action) that takes place within

himself notes, the freedom of exchange is as real as it is formal, since those who sell their labour power can only decide not to do so at the price of their own destitution.

To begin with, it is possible to distinguish between wealth and value as follows. Wealth is a concept that applies to all human epochs and is expressed through use values, contained in goods that satisfy historically defined needs and are, therefore, marked by inherent variability. The sources of wealth are, first, nature and, second, a particular expression of it: human labour power (or, in this context, labour in general).[6] Value, on the other hand, is a category peculiar to the capitalist mode of production and is embodied in exchange value – objectified in commodities produced not to satisfy needs but to be sold on the market. The source of value is abstract social labour, defined as follows: 'labour is not this or another labour, but labour pure and simple, abstract labour; absolutely indifferent to its particular *specificity* [*Bestimmtheit*], but capable of all specificities'.[7] It exists, on the one hand, as labour as result (dead labour embedded in the commodity form) and, on the other, as labour as activity (living labour, or labour in action, derived from labour power).[8]

In the following chapters, I will analyse in detail the categorial and historical relationship between value and nature. For now, what I would like to emphasize is that the conceptual distinction between wealth and

---

capital's processes of valorisation, bringing with it a whole burden of alienation and exploitation. Activity, by contrast, is at least potentially an autonomous expression of human action, escaping alienation by asserting independent control over the content and, above all, the times and timing of work, as well as autonomy in the knowledge and management of the labour process as a whole. In this sense, activity represents a moment of productive estrangement, where productivity is understood as capitalist valorisation and exploitation'; Anna Curcio, 'Lavoro, non lavoro, gratuità, *ATTAC Italia*, 27 October 2017, attac-italia.org.

6   We can find the same formulation in the first volume of *Capital* where Marx defines 'labour-power and land' as 'the two primary creators of wealth'; Marx, *Capital Vol. 1*, 752.

7   Marx, *Grundrisse*, 296.

8   Cf. Riccardo Bellofiore, 'Marx rivisitato: capitale, lavoro e sfruttamento', in *Il terzo libro del* Capitale *di Marx*, ed. Marco L. Guidi, special issue of *Trimestre* 1–2, 1996, 29–86.

value does not prevent us from formulating the hypothesis that, under certain conditions, the unfolding of the latter may lead to an increase in the former, at least partially. It is therefore possible to argue that, albeit with varying intensities over time and space, for at least two centuries the capitalist mode of production – i.e. the objective appearance of the (abstract-)labour theory of value – has increased the possibilities of satisfying needs through the use values contained in commodities, whose *raison d'être*, however, resides in their own exchange value. This relative overlap between the logic of value and the logic of wealth defines the so-called ameliorative element of capital, admired by Marx and undeniably reflected in a wide range of statistical indicators related to the growth in the supply of goods and services.[9] For example, humanity's per capita income has increased tenfold since 1820, while the total output has grown sixty times – with even higher peaks for the manufacturing sector – against a population that has risen from 1 to over 7 billion.[10] It should also be noted that per capita income tends not to account for the extraordinary advances in social welfare, particularly in the twentieth century, which include life expectancy, health, social security, access to consumption and availability of leisure time.[11]

Three clarifications before proceeding. First, the improvement in the general level of welfare is certainly not an inherent feature of capital; rather, it emerges as an outcome of subaltern struggles for a less unidirectional distribution of the value they themselves produce. Second,

---

9   'The bourgeoisie, during its rule of scarce one hundred years, has created more massive and more colossal productive forces than have all preceding generations together. Subjection of Nature's forces to man, machinery, application of chemistry to industry and agriculture, steam-navigation, railways, electric telegraphs, clearing of whole continents for cultivation, canalization of rivers, whole populations conjured out of the ground – what earlier century had even a presentiment that such productive forces slumbered in the lap of social labour?'; Karl Marx and Friedrich Engels, *The Communist Manifesto*, trans. Samuel Moore (London: Penguin, 2002 [1848]), 224–5.

10   See Robert W. Fogel, *The Escape from Hunger and Premature Death, 1700–2100: Europe, America and the Third World* (Cambridge: Cambridge UP, 2004).

11   Angus Maddison, *Contours of the World Economy 1–2030 AD: Essays in Macro-Economic History* (Oxford: Oxford UP, 2007).

acknowledging a so-called progressive side of capital in no way permits us to overlook the horrors of the world wars, the colonialist massacres perpetrated in the peripheries of the world-system – where the logic of wealth often proves irreducible to capitalist abstraction – and the violence intrinsic to the coerced labour of the proletariat at the centre of the world-system. Finally, the improvement in the living conditions of a significant segment of the world's population over the last two centuries cannot be taken as evidence that capitalism transcends the historicity of human events or constitutes an inescapable necessity, as Pierluigi Ciocca appears to suggest when he writes:

> Once we have ruled out what almost no one claims to really want – a radical upheaval – and once we have recognised that a different mode of production is not in sight, that it is not accepted by people, the question remains: wanting to avoid chaos and the extinction of life on the planet, can capitalism be saved?[12]

Where Ciocca derives his belief that people reject the prospect of radical upheaval, or that only capitalism can guarantee order and the persistence of life on the planet, is unknown. I merely note that the Marxian imperative to criticize the classical economists' purported naturalization of capitalism has lost none of its relevance.

André Gorz's Political Ecology

To sum up the reasoning carried out so far: growth and accumulation, which are unquestionably a problem today, were (at least until the 1970s) controversial phenomena and thus also endowed with positive elements. That is, for a long period, there was a partial yet significant overlap between value and wealth. The hypothesis I would like to put forward is that the energy crisis that erupted in 1973 – which had been incubating

---

12   Pierluigi Ciocca, 'L'economia di mercato capitalistica: un modo di produzione da salvare', in *Natura e capitalismo: un conflitto da evitare*, ed. Pierluigi Ciocca and Ignazio Musu (Rome: Luiss University Press, 2013), 38–9.

from a socio-political point of view since 1968 – disrupted this tendency towards convergence. To use a concept coined by Ivan Illich and deeply valued by Gorz, it can be said that the oil shock marked capitalism's crossing of the counterproductivity threshold.[13] As Illich explains, '[b]eyond a certain level of intensity of industrial production, externalities cannot be reduced but only shifted around', leading to the erosion of the material basis of welfare that this very production had previously helped to expand.[14] Developing this line of argument, Gorz emphasizes how the capitalist development in the 1960s and 1970s, though justifying its insatiable thirst for accumulation with the need to meet populations' primary needs, ultimately produced both new poverty (*relative scarcity*) and an irreversible deterioration of the biosphere (*absolute scarcity*).

It is against this backdrop that political ecology reveals its function as a methodological filter capable of accounting for the socio-environmental dimension underlying the divorce between wealth and value, as expressed by the severe crisis of 1973. In fact, Gorz's political ecology rests on two foundations. On the one hand, it offers an interpretation of the qualitative needs – namely, those that resist being subsumed within the quantitative framework of the wage form – expressed by the Western working class as a disruption from within the logic of value.[15] These are the so-called *struggles at the point of production* (in the Italian case, think of the 'Hot Autumn' of 1969). On the other hand, Gorz's perspective frames the environmental crisis as a product of the capitalist-industrial dynamic, though not entirely reducible to it. Indeed, the emergence of the ecological question represents an epochal and inescapable challenge, both for the analytical consistency of historical materialism and with a view to reconsidering an effective and desirable socialist strategy. In other words, it is about taking seriously the so-called struggles at the point of reproduction (consider, for instance, the struggles against the harmfulness of working environments – or 'noxiousness' [*nocività*] – and the feminist movement).

---

13   Ivan Illich, *Toward a History of Needs* (New York: Pantheon Books, 1978).

14   Ivan Illich, *Limits to Medicine – Medical Nemesis: The Expropriation of Health* (London: Marion Boyars, 2013 [1975]), 212.

15   See André Gorz, *Socialism and Revolution* (London: Allen Lane, 1975).

Herein lies, I believe, the fundamental core – first methodological and then strategic – of political ecology: the crisis of nature is not external to the economy, society, politics; if anything, it is their extreme face, their inescapable symptom, the injunction that cannot be avoided by dint of procrastination. Gorz is among the first to think of the environmental question in its *non-self-sufficiency*, in its impossibility to explain itself. Indeed, it unveils a crisis of Western productivism and industrial capitalism that has a precise historical origin and that brings about an unprecedented stake in social transformation.

As will be seen in more detail, the historical origin encompasses the constitution of the 'classical' nature-value nexus (Parts II and III), its crisis in the 1970s (Part IV), and its split development into the forms of the green economy and carbon trading dogma (Parts V and VI). However, as regards ecology as an element of political strategy (Part VII), it is worth presenting some elements here already. Firstly, it should be noted that, as Catherine Larrère suggests, ecology with Gorz becomes properly political.[16] Previously, the word referred either to a natural science – the study of the relations between living beings and their environment – or to a specialized field concerning the relations between human beings and their environment, particularly nature protection or risk prevention. Quite differently, Gorz made political ecology a global project for the transformation of society, capable not only of succeeding capitalism but also of redefining socialism, which is to say, freeing it from its productivist limitations. In short: *Gorz's political ecology is an anti-capitalism*, an active search for points of rupture within the logic of capital, a utopian effort to bring about what forces and ultimately breaks down the compatibilities of that techno-economic system.

Secondly, Gorz repeatedly emphasizes the exhaustion of the trade union strategy based on the centrality of the wage as an institutional dimension capable of accommodating the diverse conflicting demands of the working class. Indeed, the divorce between wealth and value implies the impossibility of both translating qualitative claims (health, environment, quality of life, culture and so on) into wages and satisfying them by

---

16   Catherine Larrére, 'André Gorz (1923–2007)', in *L'écologie politique d'André Gorz*, ed. Fondation de l'écologie politique, 2014, fondationecolo.org.

means of an increase in consumption. Willy Gianinazzi has very effectively shown how this shift from conflicts *over* wages to conflicts *beyond* wages – that is to say, this new relationship between struggles at the point of production and struggles at the point of reproduction – matured in Gorz through a close confrontation with the American counterculture and its broad conception of ecology, including, but not limited to, the working environment.[17]

Finally, I think it is important to emphasize the very close relationship between political ecology and the critique of the revolutionary subject (in the singular) made by the 1968 movements against the centripetal force exerted by the official labour movement – still imbued with the temporality of Progress – with respect to the heterogeneity of social conflicts. In this regard, I find Franco Piperno's words particularly effective:

> Before 1968, political life revolved around the ability to defer the clash between tradition and revolution, filling the interval produced by this deferral with the 'benefits of progress' – which, in turn, justified the deferral itself at the level of common sense. The 'here and now' heralded by 1968 abolishes this representation of the future; the revolution is realised, so to speak, in the very gesture of liquidating the time governed by progress . . . In the feminist and naturalist movements, there is a withdrawal of the mirage of modern morality. This was a mirage that concealed the misery into which passions were poured in modernity; a mirage that obscured the loss of meaning, the spectral character of industrial landscapes; a mirage that, in short, veiled the immoral universe of modern morality.[18]

In this context, Gorz's approach is particularly interesting: starting from an analysis of the transformation of the working class in the 1960s, he identifies the rejection of capitalism's monopoly of knowledge applied to production as the most promising terrain of conflict for a communist

---

17   See Willy Gianinazzi, *André Gorz: A Life*, trans. Chris Turner (Calcutta: Seagull Books, 2022 [2016]), in particular Part Three (Chs 10, 11 and 12), 151–209.
18   Franco Piperno, *'68: l'anno che ritorna* (Milan: Rizzoli, 2008), 142–8.

strategy. The struggle for emancipation, therefore, begins *within* labour, aiming at self-determining the labour process from below, and then extends *beyond* labour with the goal of establishing a convivial society free of productivism. 'There can be no communism without communist culture':[19] by this, Gorz means that workers' autonomy, in relation to knowledge (and technology), implies a radical rupture with the capitalist imperative of endless accumulation and growth. However, this rupture redefines the centrality of the working class itself. In Gorz's view, 'communist culture' is not synonymous with 'working-class culture'. The latter is necessarily bound to a specific location in the productive structure, whereas the former encompasses the multiplicity of forms of social and communal autonomy in the definition of what matters the most – namely, the qualitative composition of production: what, how, when, where, how much to produce.

Political ecology thus incorporates the fundamental element of 1968 and its aftermath; in other words, it absorbs and reflects the conflictual emergence of differences. The relationship between conflict and difference is crucial, making it worth examining more closely. In a recent speech, Simona de Simoni rightly stressed – speaking about feminism, though the same could be applied to ecological movements – the need to 'articulate differences in such a way that they give rise to conflict; differences do not count for less than conflict, and conflict without differences points to a road that is no longer viable'.[20] Within our reconstruction of Gorz's reading of the 1968–73 conjuncture, one could argue that factory struggles originate in workers asserting their identity and fighting for self-determination *within* (waged-productive) labour. At a later stage, this oppositional drive expands to incorporate broader social differences (particularly those inhabiting the sphere of reproduction) specifically to lay the foundations for a 'communist culture' on a non-capitalist base, which means *beyond* (waged-productive) labour. Ultimately, political ecology highlights the stakes of class struggle when conflicts over workers' control of the production process open up the space to imagine

---

19   André Gorz, *Critique de la division du travail* (Paris: Seuil, 1973), 19.

20   Simona De Simoni, 'Femminismo, differenza e conflitto', *InfoAut*, 14 May 2017, infoaut.org.

and practise communism beyond the wage form and its ability to translate social demands in quantitative and developmental terms.

It is on this terrain – where differences are articulated through conflict – that Gorz meets Félix Guattari and his proposal to conceive of *ecosophy* as the horizon of struggle capable of connecting the three ecologies (environmental, social, mental):

> Our survival on this planet is not only threatened by environmental damage but by a degeneration in the fabric of social solidarity and in the modes of psychical life, which must literally be reinvented. The refoundation of politics will have to pass through the aesthetic and analytical dimensions implied in the three ecologies – the environment, the socius and the psyche. We cannot conceive of solutions to the poisoning of the atmosphere and to global warming due to the greenhouse effect, or to the problem of population control, without a mutation of mentality, without promoting a new art of living in society . . . We cannot conceive of a collective recomposition of the socius, correlative to a resingularisation of subjectivity, without a new way of conceiving political and economic democracies that respect cultural differences – without multiple molecular revolutions.[21]

Further Considerations: The Concept of Nature, the Theoretical Status of the Theory of Value, and Class Composition

This chapter sheds light on a kernel of the analytical approach developed in this book, namely the effort to rethink (with Gorz's aid and through his work) both the ecological crisis against the backdrop of the transformations of labour and the conflictual subjectivities in relation to shifts and

---

21   Félix Guattari, *Chaosmosis*, trans. Paul Bains and Julian Pefanis (Indianapolis: Indiana UP, 1995 [1992]), 20–1. The close proximity of Gorz's analyses to those of Guattari is confirmed both biographically (cf. Gianinazzi, 'Quand André Gorz découvrit la critique de la valeur') and developed in original ways by Tiziana Villani, *Ecologia politica: nuove cartografie dei territori e potenza di vita* (Rome: Manifestolibri, 2013); and Ubaldo Fadini, *Divenire corpo: soggetti, ecologie, micropolitiche* (Verona: ombre corte, 2015).

mutations of the value-nature nexus. Before proceeding with the actual research, however, I believe it is useful to clarify three aspects that could lead to misunderstandings. First, when I refer to the concept of nature, I do so, as it were, from a governmental perspective – concerned with how environmental issues interact with power dynamics – rather than in an ontological sense, which would seek to define what nature ultimately is and what consequences follow from such a definition. My choice does not stem from underestimating the ontological dimension of Nature but from the fact that engaging with it with the depth, complexity and rigour it requires would take me far beyond the scope of this book – that is, the investigation of the transformation of the labour-nature-value nexus and, on this basis, the reactivation of a dialogue between certain strands of Marxism and degrowth. I will therefore limit myself to a minimal but necessary analytical step: following Manlio Iofrida in his interpretation of the later Maurice Merleau-Ponty, I adopt an understanding of Nature that grants it a degree of autonomy from human productivity. This simply means ruling out the possibility that the labour-nature-value nexus *entirely* encompasses Nature's space of unfolding, in other words, the idea that the biosphere can be reduced to capital in a framework that is stable, durable and conflict-free. As Iofrida puts it,

> The essential point of Merleau-Ponty's position is that the world of culture arises from a natural foundation that is never fully absorbed into culture, or 'culturalised': as it renews itself, every culture can once again draw upon this stratum of precultural experience. Now, we cannot help but think that, for Merleau-Ponty, this stratum corresponds to our bodily experience: it is through the body and its immediate, 'horizontal' apprehension of the world that we are able to continually renew our cultural constructs.[22]

The second aspect concerns the theoretical status of value, a particularly ambiguous term since it directly pertains to at least two fields of

---

22   Manlio Iofrida, 'È ancora attuale oggi il concetto di natura di Merleau-Ponty?', in *Emergenza ecologica, alienazione, lavoro*, ed. Manlio Iofrida (Modena: Mucchi, 2016), 77.

knowledge: economics and ethics.[23] The reader must be made aware from the start that I will deal only with the first meaning. In this book, I treat value as a fundamental category for the analysis and critique of the capitalist mode of production, an institutionalized social system founded on the need to extract and accumulate surplus value.[24] I justify this choice by drawing on two recent philosophical positions. The first concerns 'value pluralism',[25] which either assumes the economic determination of value as a neutral background against which the various ethical options confront each other, or treats it as just one instance of value among (formally identical) others. The second emerges instead at the crossroads between a certain strand of feminism and the set of reflections on postmodernity, identifying the hierarchizing dualisms of modernity (human, male, white, heterosexual, etc. vs Nature, woman, black, homosexual, etc.) as discursive formations that perpetuate power asymmetries between 'evaluators' and 'evaluated'.[26]

To clarify my decision to approach value theoretically from an institutional and economic-political perspective, it is useful to cite Jason Moore, a Marxist geographer best known for extending world-systems analysis to incorporate an in-depth reflection on environmental issues.[27] This led him to propose the notion of *world-ecology*, the idea that capitalism does not *have* an ecological regime, but *is* itself an ecological regime in the way it embodies a specific manner of organizing nature. Moving beyond any

---

23   Rahel Jaeggi, *Forme di vita e capitalismo*, trans. and ed. Marco Solinas (Turin: Rosenberg & Sellier, 2016).

24   I believe it is important to emphasize that the approach I am about to present is neither the only one nor the dominant one within the field of economics. Far more widespread is the approach centred on the monetary valuation of the environment, which will be subject to critique in Part V. See Francesco La Camera, *Misurare il valore dell'ambiente* (Milan: Edizione Ambiente, 2009).

25   Isaiah Berlin, 'Two Concepts of Liberty', in *Liberty*, ed. Henry Hardy (Oxford: Oxford UP, 2002 [1958]), 166–217.

26   Val Plumwood, *Feminism and the Mastery of Nature* (London: Routledge, 1993).

27   Jason W. Moore, *Ecologia-mondo e crisi del capitalismo. La fine della natura a buon mercato*, ed. Gennaro Avallone (Verona: ombre corte, 2015). In English, see his *Capitalism in the Web of Life: Ecology and the Accumulation of Capital* (London: Verso, 2015).

residual Cartesian dualisms, Moore's concept of world-ecology refers to an original entanglement of social dynamics and natural elements comprising the capitalist mode of production, shaping its historical trajectory and in its tendency to become a world market. From this perspective, the abstractions necessary for the emergence of the theory of value as a structuring principle of reality – particularly the division of 'society/labour' as the exclusive realm of human production and 'nature' as a reservoir of humans and non-humans devoted to reproduction – are not merely illusory, deceitful or purely immaterial constructs. Rather, they channel a profoundly violent way of organizing nature. In addition to obscuring the entwinement of humans and non-humans in historical development, these abstractions affect and shape social reality itself to the extent of making it functional to the perpetuation of the logic of value. According to Moore,

> Capitalism's governing conceit is that it may do with Nature as it pleases, that Nature is external and may be coded, quantified, and rationalized to serve economic growth, social development, or some other higher good. This is capitalism as a project. The reality – the historical process – is radically different. While the manifold projects of capital, empire, and science are busy making Nature with a capital 'N' – external, controllable, reducible – the web of life is busy shuffling about the biological and geological conditions of capitalism's process. The 'web of life' is nature as a whole: nature with an emphatically lowercase n. This is nature as us, as inside us, as around us. It is nature as a flow of flows. Put simply, humans make environments and environments make humans – and human organization.[28]

Capitalism as a project corresponds to the aim of value (as a theory) which, while unfolding, posits the conditions for its historical validity, that is, it produces (capitalism as a process) a world conceived of as inherently commensurable through exchange-value. The theory of value is thus not merely one hypothesis that economic science develops among many. Rather, it is a political design that in its unfolding constitutes the

---

28   Moore, *Capitalism in the Web of Life*, 14.

necessary conditions for its own reproduction. Within this framework, nature is positioned as external, reproduction as subordinate, deviance as stigma. Consider the example of coal, which is particularly significant from the standpoint of the value-nature nexus. Moore accurately reconstructs how the social relations emerging during the long sixteenth century transformed coal from a simple rock to a fossil fuel, alongside the body of biological, physical and geological knowledge necessary to make the very concept of 'fuel' thinkable and usable. It follows that coal-based productive development would have been inconceivable outside the value relations established in early modernity: 'Coal changed the world once the relations of class and capital activated its potential.'[29]

Let us now return to the philosophical positions mentioned earlier. With respect to the liberal-pluralist position, it is crucial to highlight here the non-neutrality of value as a capitalist world-praxis, which functions more like the rules of the game than a legitimate course of action among others. In contrast to the postmodernist position, it is important to emphasize the constitutive proximity between value and power. Indeed, while it is true that without evaluators there would be no evaluation, it is equally undeniable that a system of economic criteria shaped by the historical force of capital holds a vastly disproportionate effectiveness and efficacy compared to alternative parameters voluntarily elaborated by diverse social groups. Alternative valuation systems, being as they are phenomena of the utmost importance, should thus be examined in relation to the theory of value as an agent of historical transformation and the struggles of alterities shaped as subaltern and marginalized. This leads us, unlike Moore, to focus not only on the imperatives of capitalist valorization but also on the resistances to it.

And so we arrive at the third and final consideration. It seems to me that the power asymmetries associated with modern dualisms are not independent of class dynamics – specifically, the practices determining who produces value (through labour) and who appropriates it. Non-independence means that, while class does not directly determine

---

29   Jason W. Moore, 'The Capitalocene Part II: Accumulation by Appropriation and the Centrality of Unpaid Work/Energy', *Journal of Peasant Studies* 45: 2, 2018, 246.

'binary' subalternity, neither is it indifferent to it. Rather, one could say that the emergence of dualisms as forms of social organization has a class dimension. Besides, the concept of class is not a monolithic category but, rather, denotes the historical variation of the collective subject that produces surplus value yet is dispossessed of it.[30] In this book, I aim to focus on this variability in a way that sheds light on its ecological dimension, with a view to showing the historical articulations of the labour-nature-value nexus.[31] To this end, I will draw on a key concept of Italian *operaismo*,[32] class composition, which integrates two interrelated dimensions.[33] On the one hand, there is a *technical* composition, referring to the working class as labour power organized by the capitalist division of labour or, in other words, determinate – that is, determined by the relationship between tasks, technological level and hierarchy within production (labour power as commodity *within* capital). On the other hand, in constitutive relation to it, there is a *political* composition, which pertains to the sphere of values, experiences and dispositions of living labour – its ways of being and its propensity for struggle (working class as a subjectivity *against* the capital relation). Mario Tronti captures this ambivalence with great precision:

---

30   Erik Olin Wright, *Understanding Class* (London: Verso, 2015).

31   In this sense, the book's methodological structure harks back to Carolyn Merchant's concept of 'ecological revolution'. These revolutions point to epochal transformations in the relationship between human beings and the non-human natural world, driven by shifts, frictions and contradictions between modes of production and ecology, as well as between modes of production and modes of reproduction. See Carolyn Merchant, *Ecological Revolutions: Nature, Gender and Science in New England* (University of North Carolina Press, 1989). For a discussion of Merchant's contribution to environmental history, see Marco Armiero and Stefania Barca, *La storia dell'ambiente: un'introduzione* (Rome: Carocci, 2004).

32   [Translator's note] In keeping with other recent English translations of this term, henceforth I will follow Clara Pope's decision to use the Italian word 'operaismo' in order to distinguish Italian operaismo from other workerisms with the anglicization 'operaist' as its adjective. See Clara Pope note in Gigi Roggero, *Italian Operaismo: Genealogy, History, Method*, trans. Clara Pope (Cambridge, MA: The MIT Press, 2023), 187n1.

33   Steve Wright, *Storming Heaven: Class Composition and Struggle in Italian Autonomist Marxism* (London: Pluto, 2002).

So, yes, when we are talking about the working class within the system of capital, the same productive force really can be counted twice: one time as a force that produces capital and another time as a force that refuses to produce it; one time within capital, another time against capital.[34]

The chief advantage of the category of class composition, and perhaps of *operaismo* as a whole, is methodological.[35] Indeed, it allows us to focus on the dynamic process through which social subjects are constituted, particularly those from whom surplus value is unduly extracted. These subjects are not pre-existing entities but are shaped through their own 'making', through the tension between their position within the circuits of value and their potential capacity to constantly challenging this positioning. To speak of class composition, then, is to adopt a methodological view that recognizes conflict as an intrinsic and irreducible dimension of social existence. In Tronti's words:

> We too saw capitalist development first and the workers second. This is a mistake. Now we have to turn the problem on its head, change orientation, and start again from first principles, which means focusing on the struggle of the working class. At the level of socially developed capital, capitalist development is subordinate to working-class struggles; not only does it come after them, but it must make the political mechanism of capitalist production respond to them.[36]

From this perspective, one of the core objectives of this study is to analyse the ecological dimension corresponding to the different forms of class composition in the transition from the so-called classical to the new, contemporary value-nature nexus. Specifically, the hypothesis is that

---

34   Mario Tronti, *Workers and Capital*, trans. David Broder (London: Verso, 2019), 173.

35   Cf. Michele Filippini and Federico Tomasello, 'Il pensiero come arnese: note sul metodo operaista degli anni Sessanta', in *Dal pensiero critico: filosofie e concetti per il tempo presente*, ed. Alessandro Simoncini (Udine: Mimesis, 2015).

36   Tronti, *Workers and Capital*, 65.

(wage) labour, as embodied in the subjective figure of industrial mass worker, has a tendentially *entropic* character, while cognitive labour, both expressed *and* obscured through devices such as the green economy and carbon trading dogma, carries a potentially *negentropic* element.

2

Nature in Classical Political Economy and in Its Critique: Primitive Accumulation, Valorization and Abstract Social Nature

> *One could conquer the globe only if one could see it. Here the early forms of external nature, abstract space, and abstract time enabled capitalists and empires to construct global webs of exploitation and appropriation, calculation and credit, property and profit, on an unprecedented scale.*

> Jason W. Moore, 'The Rise of Cheap Nature'

The history of the labour-nature-value nexus begins with the emergence of capitalism. This is so because the latter category of the trinomial must be understood as the peculiar modality of social abstraction representing the *differentia specifica* between the capitalist mode of production and previous economic systems. Our discussion therefore must be set in motion with three preliminary questions: how is the relationship between labour and nature established in the forms that precede the capitalist mode of production (in relation to the latter)?[1] Also: how does the

---

1   The assumption of a point of view that is situated *in the present* is a key element within Marx's complex methodology: 'Human anatomy contains a key to the anatomy of the ape. The intimations of higher development among the subordinate animal species, however, can be understood only after the higher development is already known. The bourgeois economy thus supplies the key to the ancient, etc. But not at all in the manner of those economists who smudge over all historical differences and see bourgeois relations in all forms of society. One can understand tribute, tithe, etc., if one is acquainted with ground rent. But one must not identify them . . . Although it is true, therefore, that the categories of bourgeois economics

transition occur from societies based on that relationship to societies founded on the abstraction of value? And, lastly: how is the labour-nature-value nexus posited in capitalism?

Marx: Nature as Capital

As to the first question, Marx shows in the *Grundrisse* that, in pre-capitalist societies, '[t]he aim of work is not the *creation of* value', but, rather, the sustenance or simple reproduction of the 'total community'.[2] In this context, Marx continues, individuals working the soil relate to it 'naively . . . as the *property of the community*', which is to say, as their 'natural workshop'.[3] It follows that

> [t]he individual relates simply to the objective conditions of labour as being his; [relates] to them as the inorganic nature of his subjectivity, in which the latter realizes itself; the chief objective condition of labour does not itself appear as a product of labour, but is already there as nature.[4]

Therefore, nature and labour are two sides of the same coin, namely, production aimed at preserving the members of the community. Within the worker cohabit, on the one hand, productive activity as 'organic body' (*der organische Leib*) and, on the other, 'inorganic nature' (*die unorganische Natur*) as the objective condition of production.[5] Put differently, producers relate to the means of production as owners.

In relation to this framework, the emergence of the capitalist mode of production establishes itself in terms of a *radical historical rupture*. This is what Marx emphasizes in the XXVI chapter of the first volume of *Capital*:

---

possess a truth for all other forms of society, this is to be taken only with a grain of salt.' Karl Marx, *Grundrisse: Foundations of the Critique of Political Economy*, trans. Martin Nicolaus (London: Penguin, 1993), 105–6.

2   Ibid., 472.
3   Ibid., 471.
4   Ibid., 485.
5   Ibid., 488.

The capital-relation presupposes a complete separation between the workers and the ownership of the conditions for the realization of their labour. As soon as capitalist production stands on its own feet, it not only maintains this separation, but reproduces it on a constantly extending scale . . . So-called primitive accumulation, therefore, is nothing else than the historical process of divorcing the producer from the means of production. It appears as 'primitive' because it forms the pre-history of capital, and of the mode of production corresponding to capital.[6]

This process of separation of the producers from the land deeply revolutionizes the relation between labour and nature. Whereas in pre-capitalist forms of production nature is conceived of as a transcendent force, as an external normative entity, nature's function in capitalism is mediated from the beginning by the social production of surplus value:

Thus capital creates the bourgeois society, and the universal appropriation of nature as well as of the social bond itself by the members of society. Hence the great civilizing influence of capital; its production of a stage of society in comparison to which all earlier ones appear as mere local developments of humanity and as nature-idolatry. For the first time, nature becomes purely an object for humankind, purely a matter of utility; ceases to be recognized as a power for itself; and the theoretical discovery of its autonomous laws appears merely as a ruse so as to subjugate it under human needs, whether as an object of consumption or as a means of production.[7]

Here it should be noted that the type of nature capital refers to is immediately *internal* to its mechanisms of production and reproduction. Nature, far from presenting itself as transcendent or external to the interaction between productive forces and capitalist relations of production, appears *as* capital and as its specific mode of existence. In this regard, two

6 Karl Marx, *Capital: A Critique of Political Economy*, Vol. 1, trans. Ben Fowkes (London: Penguin, 1990), 874–5.
7 Marx, *Grundrisse*, 409–10.

things should be considered. First, it is necessary to highlight once again the partially progressive character of the logic of value, its localized super-imposition onto the logic of wealth, which is to say, 'the great civilizing influence of capital'. I believe it is worth clarifying this point further: Marx is convinced that, with regard to the ends of production, wealth (which aims at the satisfaction of needs through use values) is to be pre-ferred to value (which instead strives for profit through the sale of commodities exchanged on the market). At the same time, Marx also holds that 'the bourgeois society and the universal appropriation' – those results obtained only through the logic of value – open up a novel horizon of development for humankind, yet a horizon that calls for the over-coming of that very logic and towards a broader unfolding of the logic of wealth. The following passage is exemplary:

> [T]he old view, in which the human being appears as the aim of pro-duction, regardless of his limited national, religious, political character, seems to be very lofty when contrasted to the modern world, where production appears as the aim of mankind and wealth as the aim of production. In fact, however, when the limited bourgeois form is stripped away, what is wealth other than the universality of individual needs, capacities, pleasures, productive forces etc., created through universal exchange? The full development of human mastery over the forces of nature, those of so-called nature as well as of humanity's own nature? The absolute working-out of his creative potentialities, with no presupposition other than the previous historic development, which makes this totality of development, i.e. the development of all human powers as such the end in itself, not as measured on a predetermined yardstick? Where he does not reproduce himself in one specificity, but produces his totality?[8]

The second consideration concerns nature's role within an understanding of value as a self-propelling agent that aims at its own expansion by means of the exploitation of its source, that is to say, abstract social labour as the imposition of the wage-form on labouring activity (a shift from labour *in*

---

8   Ibid., 487–8.

general to *wage* labour). With its compulsive search for limits to overcome, capital posits nature as a primordial 'foothold', as the relatively stable surface on which multiple circuits of valorization unfold. Immanent and manipulable, nature's function is to provide an *internal limit to the valorization process*, i.e. a set of *reproductive conditions* – the environment and unpaid work (human, such as slave and domestic work, and animal) – which, once established, allow *productive factors* (wage labour and capital) to be activated and generate surplus value.

Nature and Political Economy

What can be found in Marx's analysis of classical political economy is the emergence of this specific modality of the nexus between labour-nature-value, where the first term causes the propulsion of the third, while the second functions as the 'edge' or inner limit of their encounter in the shape of accumulation. It is well known that Marx intended his theoretical production as a *critique* of political economy, a critique of the capitalist science of capital. Marx's object of dispute with the elaborations of Quesnay, Smith and Ricardo concerned their attempt at 'naturalizing' capitalism, at describing its origins as pacific or idyllic in character, as if capitalism's beginnings had been a case of a smooth transition rather than plunder and theft. Indeed, Marx showed both the violence of primitive accumulation – 'written in the annals of mankind in letters of blood and fire'[9] – and the violence of exchange value as the abstraction whose 'hidden background [is] *the appropriation of alien labour without exchange*, [the] complete separation of labour and property'.[10]

However, classical political economy is the unescapable point of departure leading Marx to his most crucial 'discovery', that of *surplus value*. The first condition that ensures such a discovery is constituted by the physiocratic intuition according to which, in contrast to the mercantilists' propositions, the source of wealth's surplus lies in production and not within exchange. From this standpoint, the concept of 'net product'

---

9   Marx, *Capital, Vol. 1*, 875.
10 Marx, *Grundrisse*, 509.

constitutes an embryonic form of surplus value, though a limited form since the physiocrats, lacking a theory of value, could only focus on the *physical* element of production. It is for this reason that agriculture was considered as the sole actually productive sector and that surplus assumed the form of nature's free gift, particularly as regards the fertility of the soil. Marx deeply admired the physiocrats, yet he reproached them for not grasping the subordination of use value to exchange value under capital-ism. Nature's gifts, indeed, produce the former in multiple shapes without contributing to the formation of the latter.[11] Quesnay and fellow physio-crats, in other words, did not grasp the passage from labour in general to wage labour, as well as the qualitative shift this entails in terms of abstrac-tion. As Marx puts it:

> The land is not yet capital; it is still a particular mode of existence of capital whose value is supposed to lie in its natural particularity. But land is a universal natural element, whereas the mercantile system considered that wealth existed only in precious metals. The object of wealth, its matter, has therefore attained the greatest degree of univer-sality possible within the limits of nature – in so far as it is directly objective wealth even as nature . . . Labour is therefore not yet grasped in its universal and abstract form, but is still tied to a particular element of nature as its matter and is for that reason recognized only in a par-ticular mode of existence determined by nature.[12]

Adam Smith surely represents a significative theoretical development, but he makes a specular mistake. In order to emphasize that human labour is the source of value, Smith goes as far as to argue that in manufactures 'nature does nothing, man does all'.[13] One should note in passing that, from this viewpoint – and exclusively from this – Smith's position seems

---

11   See Paul Burkett, *Marxism and Ecological Economics: Toward a Red and Green Political Economy* (Leiden: Brill, 2006).

12   Karl Marx, 'Economic and Philosophical Manuscripts', in *Early Writing of Karl Marx* (Harmondsworth: Penguin, 1992), 343–4.

13   Adam Smith, *An Inquiry into the Nature and Causes of the Wealth of Nations*, ed. R. H. Campbell, A. S. Skinner and W. B. Todd (Indianapolis: Liberty Classics, 1981 [1776]), 364.

to anticipate the neoclassical model of growth that Robert Solow elaborated in 1956, one in which the land is erased from its productive function on the basis of the implicit assumption that nature's *inputs* could be substituted with equivalent *inputs* of labour or capital.[14] Going back to the debates in classical political economy, let us focus on the reply given to Smith by Ricardo, who provides an extraordinarily interesting point for the articulation of the labour-nature-value nexus.

> Does nature nothing for man in manufactures? Are the powers of wind and water, which move our machinery, and assist navigation, nothing? The pressure of the atmosphere and the elasticity of steam, which enable us to work the most stupendous engines – are they not the gifts of nature? To say nothing of the effects of the matter of heat in softening and melting metals, of the decomposition of the atmosphere in the process of dyeing and fermentation. There is not a manufacture which can be mentioned, in which nature does not give her assistance to man, and give it too, generously and gratuitously.[15]

This is thus the outline that we draw from classical political economy: the circuit of value posits nature as the *condition* of the economic process aimed at the production of surplus value – a condition that is unlimited and free of charge both upstream (raw materials) and downstream (waste disposal) – while at the same positing labour (as organized by capital) as a *factor* of that very process. Marx adds two essential elements to such an outline. Firstly, he introduces the distinction between *objects of labour* – whose paradigm is the land as an 'original larder' and 'original tool house' – and *raw materials*, which are constituted as the initial elements of valorization through the filter of previous labour.[16] In this sense, what

---

14   Robert M. Solow, 'A Contribution to the Theory of Economic Growth', *The Quarterly Journal of Economics* 70: 1, 1956, 65–94. For a critical discussion, see also Erik Gómez-Baggethun et al., 'The History of Ecosystem Services in Economic Theory and Practice: From Early Notions to Markets and Payment Schemes', *Ecological Economics* 69: 6, 2010, 1209–18.

15   David Ricardo in Karl Marx, *Theories of Surplus Value*, in *Collected Works* (London: Lawrence & Wishart, 1975–2005), Vol. 30, 369.

16   Marx, *Capital, Vol. 1*, 284–5.

is unlimited is not so much the availability of raw materials but, rather, the possibility to produce them by means of the simple application of labour to the free gifts of nature. In contrast to the objects of labour, indeed, raw materials generate a rent and are thus not assumed to be unlimited and free of cost, even though from the perspective of valorization they must constantly be kept at a low cost.[17]

Secondly, Marx exercises his critical acuity with the usual efficacy in order to counterbalance capital's 'progressive character'. In the capitalist mode of production, the increase in levels of social well-being is secured at the cost of worker exploitation and environmental degradation. The following passage best illustrates such an ambivalence:

In modern agriculture, as in urban industry, the increase in the productivity and the mobility of labour is purchased at the cost of laying waste and debilitating labour-power itself. Moreover, all progress in capitalist agriculture is a progress in the art, not only of robbing the worker, but of robbing the soil; all progress in increasing the fertility of the soil for a given time is a progress towards ruining the more long-lasting sources of that fertility . . . Capitalist production, therefore, only develops the techniques and the degree of combination of the social process of production by simultaneously undermining the original sources of all wealth – the soil and the worker.[18]

Bringing to a close the argument delineated so far, we could for instance use the *input/output* model that Wassily Leontief formulated in the years between 1945 and 1955 as a perfect reflection of this type of relation between labour, nature and value.[19] Such a model consists in thinking general production starting from the combination of a set of components that originate from a natural environment (populations, objects of labour/raw materials, energy sources), and which constitute a final product (indeed,

---

17   Ibid.; cf. Jason W. Moore, *Capitalism in the Web of Life: Ecology and the Accumulation of Capital* (London: Verso, 2015).

18   Marx, *Capital, Vol. 1*, 638.

19   Cf. Luigi Pasinetti, *Lezioni di teoria della produzione* (Bologna: Il Mulino, 1984), Ch. 4.

an *output*) through the transformation obtained by means of a technical system (fixed capital and wage labour). Assembling different economic sectors within such a structured matrix allows one to infer economy's 'golden ratio', namely, the imperative to maximize the value of the final product (*output*) while minimizing the cost of the initial components (*input*). Although further critical considerations could be made, here I wish to show how nature in this model functions as a limit that is unaccounted for, both at the beginning of the process (objects of labour for production) and at its end (disposal of production's waste). Conversely, during the process, capital encounters labour to bring valorization into being. In short, nature in this model is certainly internalized: it exists (though invisibly) both as *input*'s free component ('tap') and as the equally free recipient of *output*'s waste ('sink').[20] Yet nature is internalized only to define the limits of the productive process, those limits that do not include it in actually transformative activity. Nature is, in this sense, a condition, but not a factor, of valorization.[21]

Moore: Abstract Social Nature

Keeping firmly in mind this articulation of the labour-nature-value nexus, an articulation that may be defined as 'classic', we can now shift the discussion to the work of Jason Moore, because two different perspectives in his analysis are particularly useful. Firstly, the fundamental concept of *abstract social nature* allows us to better understand the specific terms through which 'nature' is internalized in the valorization process as an enabling yet invisible limit – that is, the necessary

---

20   Since 1971, nature's internalized form is also visible. Leontief added to his model a table that included environmental elements as well. This table provided the basis to build an economic accounting system that comprised both monetary and physical units. See Gianni Cannata, ed., *Saggi di economia dell'ambiente* (Milan: Giuffrè, 1974).

21   Piero Bevilacqua has aptly noted that such a scheme invalidates from the outset the possibility that an intrinsic value, one that is incommensurable to the price system, could be assigned to nature. See Piero Bevilacqua, *Demetra e Clio* (Rome: Donzelli, 1994).

condition for the encounter between capital and wage labour, without being a factor directly involved in the act of creating value. Moore identifies in the epochal transition from land to labour – as the primary source of productivity, a shift that took place during the long sixteenth century – the *conditio sine qua non* for nature's internalization into value. In this context, as Gennaro Avallone has rightly observed, the relationship between the environment and capital is anything but immediate: 'in capitalism, nature is abstract social nature'.[22] What does this mean? It means that, for valorization to occur, the vital activities of which nature is expression must be transformed in ways that would *conform* them to the logic of value. The framework that emerges could be schematically summarized as follows: abstract social labour – which is to say, wage labour organized by capital and measured in discrete units of labour time – is undoubtedly the only source of value, a source located in the sphere of production. However, for valorization's mechanisms – which Moore locates in the area of commodification or *accumulation by capitalization* – to be set in motion, it is necessary that a large amount of unpaid (and thus unwaged) work be made available to capital. Moore calls this movement *accumulation by appropriation*: it defines the sphere of abstract social nature in which the elements traditionally relegated to the sphere of reproduction (domestic work, slave work, 'free gifts') converge. In addition, abstract social nature includes those practices that reshape nature to make it 'visible' or 'quantifiable', therefore 'appropriable' or that can be 'internalized' as a condition of value – this also implies a linear/homogenous conception of time and a flat and geometric idea of space. As Moore puts it,

> Capitalist technics seek to mobilize and to appropriate the (unpaid) 'forces of nature' so as to make the (paid) 'forces of labor' productive in their modern form (the production of surplus value). This is the significance of the production of nature; nature is not a pre-formed object for capital. Rather, historical natures are those webs of relations

---

22   Gennaro Avallone, Introduction to Jason W. Moore, *Ecologia-mondo e crisi del capitalismo. La fine della natura a buon mercato*, ed. Gennaro Avallone (Verona: ombre corte, 2015), 10.

that capital reshapes – through the double internality of the oikeios – so as to advance the contributions of biospheric 'work' for capital accumulation.[23]

The second useful element in Moore's argument lies in his passionate critique of Cartesian dualism and its derivates (*res cogitans* vs *res extensa*, mind vs body, Man vs Nature, etc.). Moore's concept of world-ecology refers to an original mixture of social dynamics and natural elements that make up the capitalist mode of production in its historical development, in its tendency to become a world market. As already recalled, capitalism does not *have* an ecological regime but *is* itself an ecological regime. Exploitation and value creation take place not *on* nature but *through* it – that is to say, *within* the socio-natural relationships that stem from the variable articulation of capital, power and the environment. Salvo Torre has maintained that this is a matter not of integrating the environmental element in the theory of value but, rather, of 'reformulating it in socio-ecological terms, considering the system's ecological core, and also incorporating a theory of conflict within such a perspective'.[24] At the same time, one should always keep in mind that, as previously mentioned, the theory of value is not a set of descriptive lucubrations but a 'gravitational field exerting durable influence over the long-run and large-scale patterns of the capitalist world-ecology'.[25]

This point is fundamental, since most of the 'environmentalist' critique of the labour-nature-value nexus (as found in classical political economy) goes only as far as highlighting its lack of 'realism' and ascribing to it a 'metaphysical' dimension, the incapacity to 'discover the real source of economic value, which is the value that life displays for every individual organism'.[26] From this perspective, nature as an element that is invisible and unaccounted for, its being the necessary yet not determining

---

23   Jason W. Moore, *Capitalism in the Web of Life: Ecology and the Accumulation of Capital* (London: Verso, 2015), 106.

24   Salvo Torre, 'Per una nuova teoria socio-ecologica del valore', *Effimera*, 10 July 2017, effimera.org.

25   Moore, *Capitalism in the Web of Life*, 188.

26   Federico Falcitelli and Silvano Falocco (eds), *Contabilità ambientale: L'ambiente nei conti, i conti per l'ambiente* (Bologna: Il Mulino, 2008), 27.

condition for value creation, is a scientific error, a false perception, a die-hard prejudice that however could be eventually remedied with a solid analytic reference, since 'no other conception could be the furthest from reality'.[27] According to Mercedes Bresso, for example, it would be sufficient to develop a new paradigm based on concepts that are alien to standard economics (limit, complexity, uncertainty), patiently and scientifically showing that things are not as Ricardo says, or as Solow would want them, but are as asserted in physics and ecology: the planet is as finite as its free gifts, nature is the only producing entity while the economy is limited to transforming low-entropy resources into high-entropy waste.[28]

At times, the unfolding of such an argument leads to very particular assertions, such as those framing the fundamental presupposition of an institutionalized order as 'the coherence which an economic system maintains with the physical limits dictated by thermodynamics and the maintenance of an ecosystem's vitality'.[29] I wonder how one could overlook that the economic system in which we live has been holding as its fundamental presupposition, for at least two and a half centuries, precisely the *lack* of coherence with the physical limits of the planet. As Pierluigi Ciocca has noted, the capitalist mode of production 'based on fixed capital, competition, innovation, and profit *coincides* with the incessant urge to produce ever more commodities'.[30] Of course, this does not mean that capitalism is *destined* to break biospheric balances – even though the empirical evidence we have today quite obviously suggests precisely that. Rather, it means that the 'classic' nexus between labour-nature-value as a structure of social power that is constitutively entropic – certainly not as a mere analytic operation, no matter how 'wrong' – is at the origins of the ecological crisis, an ecological crisis becoming politically perceivable in the early 1970s but that had been incubating since the long sixteenth century.

⅘

---

27 Ibid., 29.

28 Mercedes Bresso, *Economia Ecologica* (Turin: La Nuova Italia, 2003).

29 Falcitelli and Falocco, *Contabilità ambientale*, 33.

30 Pierluigi Ciocca, 'L'economia di mercato capitalistica: un modo di produzione da salvare', in *Natura e capitalismo: un conflitto da evitare*, ed. Pierluigi Ciocca and Ignazio Musu (Rome: Luiss UP, 2013), 38.

The following chapters will be dedicated to clarifying the passage just mentioned, with particular reference to the historical development of an entropic economy and the 1968–73 period, marked as it was by global political unrest and a worldwide energy crisis. Nevertheless, it was important to specify the particular way in which I will use political ecology as a method, namely, by refusing to separate the interpretative dimension from a critique of power.

3

An Entropic Device: The Rise of the Labour-Nature-Value Nexus from Fossil Capitalism to the Fordist Pact

Nothing has corrupted the German working class so much as the notion that it was moving with the current . . . From there it was but a step to the illusion that the factory work which was supposed to tend toward technological progress constituted a political achievement . . . The Gotha Program already bears traces of this confusion . . . The new conception of labor amounts to the exploitation of nature, which with naïve complacency is contrasted with the exploitation of the proletariat. Compared with this positivistic conception, Fourier's fantasies, which have so often been ridiculed, prove to be surprisingly sound. According to Fourier, as a result of efficient co-operative labor, four moons would illuminate the earthly night, the ice would recede from the poles, sea water would no longer taste salty, and beasts of prey would do man's bidding. All this illustrates a kind of labor which, far from exploiting nature, is capable of delivering her of the creations which lie dormant in her womb as potentials. Nature, which, as Dietzgen puts it, 'exists gratis', is a complement to the corrupted conception of labor.[1]

Walter Benjamin, 'Theses on the Philosophy of History'

---

1   In relation to the concluding reference to Dietzgen, Michael Löwy clarifies that 'Benjamin opposes the "progressive" ideology of a certain "scientific" socialism – represented here by the German social positivist Joseph Dietzgen, long forgotten today, but immensely popular in German Social Democracy at the turn of the century.' Michael Löwy, *Fire Alarm: Reading Walter Benjamin's 'On the Concept of History'*, trans. Chris Turner (London: Verso, 2005), 75.

In a remarkable passage in the *Grundrisse*, Marx discusses what he believes to be one of capital's essential characters, namely, its inherent and self-referential *cannibalism*, its uncontainable compulsion to violate the bounds that it had itself previously established: 'Every boundary [*Grenze*] is and has to be a barrier [*Schranke*] for it.' From this, it follows that '[t]he quantitative boundary of the surplus value appears to it as a mere natural barrier, as a necessity which it constantly tries to violate and beyond which it constantly seeks to go'.[2] This formulation is particularly interesting in that it allows us to suggest a methodological distinction between what is posited as formally constant in capitalism's becoming (the compulsion to overcome self-imposed limits) and what appears instead as historically contingent in its development (the specific configuration of the 'natural barrier'). In other words, for as much as it is true that limits must be always laid down, it is equally true that their concrete qualities vary according to coordinates that are both spatial and temporal.

In order to mobilize value's invariant logics and the historical changes in the forms of valorization, one needs to assume that capital never confronts nature *per se*, nature in its generic indeterminacy. Rather, capital confronts what Marx and Engels called *historical nature*. Indeed, society and nature, production and reproduction are not separate entities relating to each other *a posteriori* but are instead the mutable historical result of a univocity in the making. Put differently, as Gennaro Avallone has argued, 'nature does not pose the material world in an immutable way; the material world is a historical product'.[3] Marx and Engels had already articulated this point in the chapter on Feuerbach from *The German Ideology*:

> The cherry-tree, like almost all fruit-trees, was, as is well known, only a few centuries ago transplanted by commerce into our zone, and

---

2   Karl Marx, *Grundrisse: Foundations of the Critique of Political Economy*, trans. Martin Nicolaus (London: Penguin Books, 1993), 334–5.

3   Gennaro Avallone, 'Introduction' to Jason W. Moore, *Ecologia-mondo e crisi del capitalismo. La fine della natura a buon mercato*, ed. Gennaro Avallone (Verona: ombre corte, 2015), 10.

therefore only by this action of a definite society in a definite age has it become 'sensuous certainty' for Feuerbach.[4]

In the previous chapter of the book, we looked into the logical form of the 'classic' labour-nature-value nexus and highlighted its main characters. Now we need to add a historical element that could help us reveal its entropic dimension. My hypothesis is indeed that this nexus is the main cause of an ecological crisis that, though already present in an embryonic form since the long sixteenth century, assumed a fully political form starting from the Second World War only to erupt at the turn of the 1970s.[5] The environmental issue is therefore going to be read as a crucial – yet not the only – element within a broader *ecological critique of political economy* capable of accounting for the social forces that determined the emergence of the 'classic' nexus of labour-nature-value.

Resisting Value Theory: Struggles Against and Within Valorization

In Part I, we saw how the theory of value appears both as the capitalist *project* to ensure the functioning of its productive dynamics and as the historical *process* to transform reality on the basis of that model. Let us try to apply this distinction to the 'classic' labour-nature-value nexus so as to formulate a few hypotheses concerning the modalities of its development. In such a project, that nexus becomes central in the sphere of production (active entities: wage labour and capital) to the detriment of the sphere of

---

4   Karl Marx and Frederick Engels, *The German Ideology*, in *Collected Works* (London: Lawrence & Wishart, 1975–2005), Vol. 5, 39.

5   Daniel Worster suggests defining this period as the 'age of ecology', characterized by the reversal of the promises of emancipation inherent in humanity's attempt to 'dominate nature'. In his words: 'The age of ecology opened on the New Mexican desert, near the town of Alamogordo, on July 16, 1945, with a dazzling fireball of light and a swelling mushroom cloud of radioactive gases . . . [The] dream of extending man's empire over nature . . . had suddenly taken a macabre, even suicidal, turn.' Donald Worster, *Nature's Economy: A History of Ecological Ideas* (New York: Cambridge University Press, 1994 [1977]), 342–3.

social reproduction (passive entities: unwaged human work and environmental free activity). For the process of valorization to occur 'correctly' – that is, in order to result in the accumulation of capital – wage workers must be industrious yet docile, and the subjects of reproduction must be reduced to invisible and silent objects. Historically, in the attempts at putting into practice these requirements, the theory of value as a process encountered endless forms of resistance: domestic work, slave work, factory labourers.[6] This resistance had a twofold aim: safeguarding the portion of autonomy guaranteed to the natural community and prospecting an expansion of the logic of wealth that could be independent of the logic of value. These forms of resistance thus had the wage-form as their problematic horizon, which is to say, the device that at once internalizes workers as productive factors and reduces the subjects of reproduction to the rank of conditions for valorization. In Gorz's words, wage labour is mainly 'a means of dominating the workers. They are divested of their means of labour, dispossessed of the purpose and product of their work and deprived of the opportunity to determine its nature, length, and tempo . . . Commodity labour engenders the pure consumer of commodities.'[7]

In this sense, the first front of anti-capitalist struggle concerns the *refusal of the wage-form* as the 'subalternity proof' of the workers in relation to the qualitative composition of production and, correlatively, as the confirmation of demotion to the endless and gratuitous backdrop of social reproduction. Gorz contends that the phase in which this first front prevailed constituted 'the heroic age of trade-unionism, of workers' cooperatives and mutual-aid societies, workers' education associations and class unity and belonging'.[8] As he continues,

At that stage, workers' struggles were mainly conducted in the name of the right to a living, demanding a sufficient wage to cover the needs

6   For more on this triad, see, respectively: Silvia Federici, *Caliban and the Witch: Women, the Body and Primitive Accumulation* (London: Penguin, 2021 [2004]); Peter Linebaugh and Marcus Rediker, *The Many-Headed Hydra: The Hidden History of the Revolutionary Atlantic* (London: Verso, 2002); E. P. Thompson, *The Making of the English Working Class* (London: Penguin, 2013 [1963]).

7   André Gorz, 'Wealth Without Value, Value Without Wealth', in *Ecologica*, trans. Chris Turner (Calcutta: Seagull Books, 2010), 151–2.

8   Ibid., 153.

of workers and their families. This norm of sufficiency was so influential that craftworkers stopped work when they'd earned enough to live in a manner to which they were accustomed, and workers paid by their output could be forced to work 10 or 12 hours a day only by reducing their hourly wages.[9]

Although the theory of value as a process practically enforced the wage-form as a social norm, the solidity of this form has always been challenged by the conflicts linked to it. Alongside it, however, a second front of struggle progressively emerged in a context where the wage-form represented not so much what is at stake but rather an institutional framework. This is indeed the *wage-institution*, that is, the normative terrain where sellers and buyers of labour power meet and clash in order to negotiate its price. For such an organizational space to appear, it is necessary that the commodity-form shaped society to itself. Put differently, it is imperative that the theory of value – though in the not-eternal and reversible status of its own hegemony – progressively fashioned reality to correspond to its project.

Now we need to ask: *what is the wage?* What is the salary agreement within this perspective characterized by the commodity-form? From the capitalist's point of view, the wage is the price of labour power calculated in units of time; from the point of view of the workers, it is the value of labour power as a potential, as capacity to produce.[10] Labour power is indeed a very special commodity, one that creates more value than the value crystallized in the amount of money that pays it. What follows is that an excess portion of value emerges, namely, *surplus value*. Therefore, the allocation of the discrepancy between the price of labour power (time) and the value of labour power (potential capacity) represents the second front of class struggle in capitalism: when the rate of exploitation is high (periods of low conflict), surplus value predominantly flows into profit; when the rate of exploitation is low (periods of high conflict), a part of surplus value is directly and indirectly channelled towards wages.

---

9   Ibid. See also Ariel Salleh, ed., *Eco-Sufficiency and Global Justice: Women Write Political Ecology* (London: Pluto Press, 2010); Nancy Fraser, 'Behind Marx's Hidden Abode', *New Left Review* 86, 2014, 55–72.

10   Riccardo Bellofiore, 'La questione del salario', *Reblab*, 28 May 2015, https:// ilcomunista23.blogspot.com/2016/08/la-questione-del-salario-riccardo.html.

Gorz expresses a very severe judgement of this second front of conflict, which according to him emerges in the US with the New Deal and in Europe with the so-called thirty glorious years (1945–73). As he puts it,

> Labour treated as a commodity – employment – renders labour structurally homogenous with capital. Just as the determining goal of capital isn't the product the enterprise puts on the market but the profit which the sale of that commodity enables it to achieve, so the determining goal of the wage-earner is not what he produces but the wage that his productive activity brings him. Labour and capital are fundamentally complicit in their antagonism, inasmuch as 'earning money' is their determining goal. In the eyes of capital, the nature of production is of less importance than its profitability; in the eyes of the worker, it is of less importance than the jobs it creates and the wages it distributes . . . This is why the labour movement and trade unionism are anti-capitalist only insofar as they question not just wage levels and working conditions, but the purposes of production and the commodity form of the labour that effects it.[11]

The 'Classic' Labour-Nature-Value Nexus as Entropic Device

I believe Gorz's remarks here excessively emphasize the separation between the two fronts of class struggle in such a way as to render it too clear-cut and unequivocal, almost as though the two fronts were mutually exclusive.[12] At the same time, finding a profound tension between the struggle *against* and *within* valorization represents a very significant moment because, through various Gorz passages, we could also articulate

---

11   Gorz, 'Wealth Without Value, Value Without Wealth', 150–1.

12   We saw earlier how the analysis of *operaismo* leads to regard as true the emergence of a conflict which is simultaneously *within* and *against* capitalist development. With respect to the 'classic' nexus between labour-nature-value, the interpretation that Italian *operaismo* proposes seems to be more convincing than that of Gorz (as we will see in the following chapter of the book). Nevertheless, Gorz's criticism undoubtedly hits the mark when levelled at the social-democratic tendency of the official workers' movement.

the components of this tension in terms of political ecology. Conflicts against the wage-form, indeed, aim at the combined abolition of the exploitation of human labour and of society's domination of nature. For instance, Walter Benjamin sets wage labour in opposition to a utopian model of liberated activity – work as play – that could bring to the light a labour-nature nexus separated from value: 'Such work inspired by play aims not at the propagation of values, but at the amelioration of nature.'[13] In a similar vein, Kristin Ross, in her masterpiece on the imaginary of the 1871 Paris Commune, shows how, in the reflections advanced by the anarcho-communists Élisée Reclus and Pyotr Kropotkin, the elimination of the wage-form was the necessary condition to put an end to unsustainable industrialization, and to bring forth a new work-nature nexus mediated by art and finalized at the production of 'communal luxury' based on the logic of wealth: 'For solidarity with nature to exist, rather than purely mercantile interests, a transformation of values must occur that is itself predicated on a complete transformation of the social order: the abolition of private property and of the state.'[14]

The situation is different with regard to conflicts within valorization. Since they take on the wage-form as their institutional frame, these conflicts move, from the outset, within the 'classic' labour-nature-value nexus and thus never challenge its status as an *entropic device* oriented to economic growth.[15] It was Nicholas Georgescu-Roegen who, in the 1960s, introduced the theme of entropy in economic thought.[16] He maintained that any process producing material commodities decreases the future availability of energy and thus the possibility to produce additional

---

13　Walter Benjamin cited in Löwy, *Fire Alarm*, 76. What is meant by 'amelioration of nature' is a complex issue to which only a broad democratic movement can provide a definitive answer. I will outline some thoughts on this subject in chapter 7.

14　Kristin Ross, *Communal Luxury: The Political Imaginary of the Paris Commune* (London: Verso, 2015), 216–17.

15　In the context of classic thermodynamics, entropy is a state function of a thermodynamic system that quantifies a system's unavailability to generate work. It is introduced with the second principle of thermodynamics, according to which the state of entropy of the entire universe, as an isolated system, will increase over time.

16　See Nicholas Georgescu-Roegen, *Bioeconomia. Verso un'altra economia ecologicamente e socialmente sostenibile*, ed. M. Bonaiuti, trans. G. Ricoveri and E. Messori (Turin: Bollati Boringhieri, 2003).

material commodities. Moreover, in the economic process, matter will degrade as well, which is to say that matter's possibilities to be used again diminish tendentially. Once dispersed in the atmosphere, the raw materials that were previously concentrated in subsoil deposits can only be reintegrated into the economic cycles to a limited extent and at the cost of a high expenditure of energy.

The result is what sociologist Allan Schnaiberg defined as the 'treadmill of production'.[17] This is a socio-environmental relation that develops across three main trajectories: society's economic expansion implies an increase in 'withdrawals' from nature (raw materials) and 'discharges' in the environment (waste); the incremental 'usage' of the environment leads to ecological imbalance; when this imbalance reaches specific thresholds, it seriously restricts the economy to expand further, even though such an expansion is a necessary prerequisite in the capitalist mode of production.[18] In this sense, therefore, one could say that the 'classic' labour-nature-value nexus is the entropic device lying at the centre of what Andreas Malm called 'fossil capital', namely, 'an economy of self-sustaining growth predicated on the growing consumption of fossil fuels, and therefore generating a sustained growth in emissions of carbon dioxide'.[19] Such is the definition shaping the argument according to which a model of capitalist development based on fossil fuels could not do anything but increasingly endanger the atmospheric conditions that make it possible to have life on earth. For instance, since this model considers the environment as inexhaustible and free of cost, on the one hand it loses its reference in relation to any norm about what is sufficient and, on the other, it has the tendency to overuse resources aimed at accumulation. This means that the mechanism of production cuts off every fundamental link it has with a set of historically given needs and with a variety of use values necessary to its correct functioning: what matters is the endless expansion of exchange value. It is for this reason that it seems correct to indicate that the direct

17   Allan Schnaiberg, *The Environment: From Surplus to Scarcity* (Oxford: Oxford UP, 1980).

18   Allan Schnaiberg, 'Social Syntheses of the Societal-Environmental Dialectic: The Role of Distributional Impacts', *Social Science Quarterly* 56: 1, 1975, 5–20.

19   Andreas Malm, *Fossil Capital: The Rise of Steam Power and the Roots of Global Warming* (London: Verso, 2016), 11.

causes of the ecological crisis are to be found in the logic of value and the resulting imposition of the wage character onto labour.

It should also be highlighted here that accepting the wage-institution as the frame of struggle within valorization always implies that a possible 'agreement' between sellers and buyers of labour power can be reached *only* when based on the marginalization of the subjects of social reproduction. In other words, to return to Ariel Salleh's suggestive formula, the meta-industrial labour of these subjects is both ignored by not being paid and denied as a negentropic eco-factor, meaning that it is thus irreducible to the extractive-industrial dimension.[20] Moreover, such a discrimination of the reproductive sphere is historically reflected in two types of *unequal exchange*. (Neo)colonial in nature, the first type is socio-economic, involves a disequilibrium between the terms of exchange (i.e. the sum of imports financed by exports) between the periphery and the centre of the world-system, and is measured in quantities of labour-time.[21] The second type is ecological and, for the countries at the periphery, entails exporting goods with high ecological use value and importing damaged/spoiled products or even harmful products (such as toxic waste).[22]

Both of these types strengthen the sphere of valorization in the central countries of the world-system and, therefore, also indirectly benefit the

---

20   Negentropy is the opposite of entropy. By showing entropy's relative validity with respect to closed systems, negentropy affirms itself as a process of reintegration of order. These two phenomena do not exist in pure forms but rather stem from an original interaction. For instance, as concerns the metabolism of living organisms, on the one hand is catabolism (the organism's consumption and destruction of organic molecules) and on the other is anabolism (the reconstruction of these molecules powered by different forms of energy). Regarding the formula, see Ariel Salleh, 'From Metabolic Rift to "Metabolic Value": Reflections on Environmental Sociology and the Alternative Globalization Movement', *Organization and Environment* 23: 2, 2010, 205–19.

21   Cf. Andre Gunder Frank, *Latin America: Underdevelopment or Revolution* (New York: Monthly Review Press, 2009 [1969]).

22   The anthropologist Alf Hornborg suggests the following example: in 1850, by exchanging 1,000 lbs of textiles produced in Manchester for 1,000 lbs of raw cotton coming from American plantations, the British Empire would earn 46 per cent in terms of incorporated labour (unequal socio-economic exchange) and 6,000 per cent in terms of incorporated hectares (unequal ecological exchange). See Alf Hornborg, *Global Ecology and Unequal Exchange: Fetishism in a Zero-Sum World* (London: Routledge, 2011).

working class in the Global North. Besides, it is no accident that 'union-isation was, or least became, a directly capitalist exigency or need' with Roosevelt's New Deal.[23] In relation to this passage, too, Gorz's analysis is apt:

> From 1920 onwards in the United States and after 1948 in Western Europe, basic needs offered capitalism too tight a market to absorb the volume of commodities it was capable of producing. Only if the production of superfluities increased more and more markedly at the expense of necessities could the economy continue to grow, the accumulated capital be valorised and profits reinvested . . . Capitalism needed to produce a new type of consumer and a new type of individual: it needed individuals who wanted to free themselves, by their consumption and purchases, from the shared norm; to distinguish themselves from others and 'stand out from the crowd'.[24]

Gorz's argument, once again, appears to be excessively partial because he loses sight of the liberating dimension of escaping the shared norm and the possibility of emancipation from original circles (social, geographic or cultural). At the same time, he grasps with precision the key elements that supported Keynes's theoretical edifice (implicit in the New Deal), namely the incorporation of the working masses into consumption dynamics, and the access – guaranteed by a broad range of social rights – that these same masses would gain to various mechanisms of social protection. During the 'thirty glorious years' the wage-form as a terrain of recognition between the subjects of class struggle within valorization crystallized in the so-called *Fordist pact* in the sphere of production.[25] Here, the buyers of labour-power attained (a relative) social peace and kept every right on

---

23   Luciano Ferrari Bravo, 'The New Deal and the New Order of Capitalist Institutions', trans. Evan Calder Williams, *Viewpoint Magazine*, 2 October 2014 [1972], viewpointmag.com.

24   Gorz, 'Wealth Without Value, Value Without Wealth', 153–4.

25   We are, of course, referring here to the US and Western Europe. Indeed, it should not be overlooked that the Soviet 'threat' was one of the necessary conditions to establish the Fordist pact. One would indeed suspect that, had it not been for the risk of Bolshevik 'contagion', the Western ruling classes would have never felt the need to integrate the working class in capital's plans.

the qualitative composition of production, whereas the sellers of labour-power witnessed the confirmation of their own legitimacy as the productive class and obtained social integration by means of mass consumption (directly, through their salaries) and the welfare state (indirectly, through social security).[26]

In this context, it is necessary to shed light on two fundamental conditions that held the Fordist pact together. The first was *sustained economic growth*, understood in quantitative terms. Following the principle that 'growing the pie' would allow all the commensals to eat more, Keynesian policies increased as much as they could the volume of production, in point of fact releasing it from social needs and, instead, sustaining a multiplication of these that was not always autonomous (artificially induced needs) coupled with an accelerated substitutability (planned obsolescence). The second condition concerns the status of the reproductive sphere within the 'agreement among producers'. Even though the sphere of reproduction was evidently involved in the mechanisms of social protection provided by the welfare state, it would enter these mechanisms in *conditions of subalternity*. Indeed, the welfare state, in its 'classic' form, had established a specific relationship with the productive system. While the latter functioned as a central element (direct creation and primary distribution of wealth), the former operated as a peripherical institution (redistributive action aimed at individual and collective protection in case economic projects failed). If we couple this form of subalternity to the assumption that nature is unlimited and free of cost, we can then understand why the Fordist pact may be thought of as an *entropic device*. By considering the subjects of reproduction as secondary to those of production, and by assuming that nature as a resource is inexhaustible, the goal of quantitative growth at all costs becomes the unquestionable premise of any economic policy. The social inclusion of the working class in the Global North – a process of enormous historical significance – comes at

---

26 In particular, I refer to the concept of 'social property' as it determines the possibility for 'non-owners' (understood as a collective subject) to increase their share of value by virtue of its partial transformation in public assets. See Robert Castel, *From Manual Workers to Wage Labourers: The Transformation of the Social Question* (New York: Routledge, 2003 [1995]).

a high cost: the relinquishment of autonomy in defining its own needs and the allocation to the reproductive sphere of negative socio-environmental externalities.

It should be noted that such a pact was never implemented in its pure form. It did, however, function as the ideal rule of the Fordist accumulation regime and, as such, it deeply affected class relations for nearly half a century (in the Global North at least). This regulative ideal supported the advent of what the sociologist Robert Castel defined as the 'wage-earning society', that is, the integration of wage labour in the ambit of the circulation of value. On the one hand, the limits of capitalist accumulation opened up markets to a new class of consumers; on the other, the subordination of wage labour to production ended up being, as it were, 'normalized' with the acquisition of social rights.[27] The wage-earning society, in turn, took advantage of the *virtuous circle* of the cumulative process inherent in the specifically Fordist capitalist development, whose fundamental elements are: increase in productivity in the industrial sector, driven by technological innovations; reduction of the product's cost per unit following market expansion; direct proportionality in the relation between rise in production, increase in employment, and consumption growth; redistribution of substantial shares of the value produced in the form of better social services.

Such a 'virtuosity', however, had significant social and ecological costs. It was indeed a highly dissipative expansion cycle. The steady growth in the Fordist period was characterized by energy greed and exponential increase of ecological footprint.[28] As Christophe Bonneuil and Jean-Baptiste Fressoz have indicated, while in the first half of the twentieth century an annual global rate of 2.1 per cent of corresponded to a 1.7 per cent increase in the consumption of fossil fuels, during the 'thirty glorious years' a yearly growth rate of 4.2 per cent corresponded to an annual increase in fossil fuel consumption of 4.5 per cent. This reduction in efficiency also applies to mineral raw materials: while between 1950 and 1970

---

27 See Federico Chicchi, *Lavoro e capitale simbolico* (Milan: Franco Angeli, 2003).

28 The ecological footprint is an indicator that evaluates the human consumption of natural resources relative to the Earth-system's capacity to regenerate them.

global GDP grows by 2.6 times, the consumption of minerals and mining products triples, and that of construction materials almost triples as well. The global ecological footprint thus jumps from 63 per cent of Earth's bio-(re)productive capacity in 1961 to over 100 per cent by the end of the 1970s.[29] In other words, we have since then exceeded the planet's capacity to produce the resources added in production processes and to absorb their waste.[30]

Before analysing the way in which capitalism confronted the impossibility of facing the ecological crisis, something needs to be clarified. Even though the subjects of production are the active entities of the 'classic' labour-nature-value nexus as an entropic device, it would be inaccurate to distribute the responsibility for the environmental degradation equally between capitalists and wage labourers. Once again Gorz's reflections seem accurate:

> The workers and their organisations – that is to say, commodity labour – share the responsibility for this pillage and destruction only to the extent that they defend employment at all costs in the existing context and, to that end, fight everything that reduces economic growth and the financial profitability of investment in the immediate term.[31]

We can infer from this not solely the obvious observation that those holding the power to decide on the qualitative composition of production should be regarded as being more to blame than those who were subjected to those decisions, but also a less intuitive consideration. What causes the ecological crisis is not wealth in a general sense, or a broad social well-being understood abstractly, and not even a less unilateral distribution of the fruits of production. Analysing the increase in pollution rates in the United States between 1946 and 1976 (from 200 per cent to 2,000 per cent),

---

29   Christophe Bonneuil and Jean-Baptiste Fressoz, *L'Événement Anthropocène* (Paris: Seuil, 2013).

30   In 2017, Earth Overshoot Day, which is the date when global production reaches 100 per cent of the Earth bio-(re)productive capacity, was marked on 2 August.

31   Gorz, 'Wealth Without Value, Value Without Wealth', 157.

Barry Commoner shows that the per capita quantity of goods accounts for only 1 per cent to 5 per cent; the population increase accounts for 12 per cent and 20 per cent, with the remainder attributed to the types of products and technology.[32] Put differently, as Michele Nobile has rightly remarked, 'it is the profit-driven commercial demand that makes necessary the adoption of polluting technologies, both process- and product-related'.[33] We could add a further note: the ambivalent position of the working class relative to the 'classic' labour-nature-value nexus – the working class gains in material wealth as active factor of production, though it is subjected to an increasingly intense exploitation[34] – can be (also) explained with a historical dynamic that shows the partial overlap between the logic of value and the logic of wealth. As it will be shown hereafter, the political and energy crises between 1968 and 1973 would deeply question this very overlap, paving the way for new developments of the interaction between work, environmental impacts and processes of valorization.

---

32   Barry Commoner, *The Politics of Energy* (New York: Alfred A. Knopf, 1979).

33   Michele Nobile, *Merce-natura ed ecosocialismo* (Bolsena: Massari Editore, 1993), 237.

34   This formulation, though seemingly paradoxical, is actually a recurring element of the development of the working class from the very outset: '[I]t is perfectly possible to maintain two propositions which, on a casual view, appear to be contradictory. Over the period 1790–1840 there was a slight improvement in average material standards. Over the same period there was intensified exploitation, greater insecurity, and increasing human misery.' Thompson, *The Making of the English Working Class*, 231.

4

The Twofold Crisis of the 'Classic' Labour-Nature-Value Nexus: Social Struggles and Physical Limits to Growth at the Root of the First Oil Shock (1968–73)

By the end of the 1960s, a period begins in which the central issue of class conflict in large-scale industry tends to be the capitalist organisation of labour and the hierarchical structure that sustains and reinforces it . . . What must be highlighted here is that the emergence, alongside these wage-related demands [concerning salaries and pay equity], of other demands for power and freedom (both individual and union-related) reflects an inseparable connection between these two aspects of class action within large-scale industry . . . This second set of demands includes . . . the right to collective investigation and knowledge regarding the hygiene and safety conditions in the workplace, as well as the 'physical and mental' health of workers, and the right to education (the '150 hours' programme) . . . Taken as a whole, this second set of demands is characterised by the rejection of union agreements with employers or the subordination of new autonomous forms of worker organisation to employer control.

Bruno Trentin, 'Economia e politica nelle lotte operaie
dell'ultimo decennio'

The aim of this chapter is to analyse the crisis of the 'classic' labour-nature-value nexus previously described as a project and as a process. That crisis emerges out of the irruption of May '68 in France (political rupture of the temporality of Progress) and spans to the ensuing energy crisis (socio-environmental rupture in the abundance [and low cost] of fossil fuels, most notably oil). In the previous chapters, I deployed the method of political ecology, as it were, retrospectively – i.e. applying it to an epoch when the collateral effects of capitalist development had yet to manifest in all their destructiveness.[1] Now, I will instead try to grasp political ecology in its 'making', in its emergence within the Marxist tradition as a transformative element and, ultimately, including the environmental crisis as a significant dimension within it. As always, Gorz will be my guide. Even though, in his analysis, the social aspect prevailed over the ecological one, this does not mean at all that Gorz considered the latter as irrelevant. Simply, his conviction is that the best way to face the inescapable issue of the physical limits to growth is not to deify Nature, immediately making it a normative concept, but to develop a theory of the relation between the capitalist mode of production and the surrounding environment. As Gorz writes,

> Nature is not untouchable. The 'promethean' project of 'mastering' or 'domesticating' nature is not necessarily incompatible with a concern for the environment. All culture (in the double sense of this word) encroaches upon nature and modifies the biosphere. The fundamental issue raised by ecology is simply that of knowing:
>
> - whether the exchanges, which human activity imposes upon or extorts from nature, preserve or carefully manage the stock of nonrenewable resources; and
> - whether the destructive effects of production do not exceed the productive ones by depleting renewable resources more quickly than they can regenerate themselves.[2]

In this sense, ecology and Marxism can distinctly divide up tasks between themselves. Whereas Marxism studies and advances a critique of the *internal limits* of productive activity, ecology deals with registering its

---

1   J. R. McNeill and Peter Engelke, *The Great Acceleration: An Environmental History of the Anthropocene since 1945* (Cambridge, MA: Harvard UP, 2016).

2   André Gorz, 'Ecology and Freedom', in *Ecology as Politics*, trans. Patsy Vidgerman and Jonathan Cloud (Boston, MA: South End Press, 1980 [1971]), 21.

external limits and reporting whether such limits are crossed. Therefore, ecology is not *in itself* a subversive science since, in order to become so, it needs political intervention. Here, then, is explained the possible complementarity of ecology and Marxism, but with two warnings. First, within Gorz's theoretical system, such an outline only functions on the condition that Marxism is not understood in its 'vulgar' version, and that any prophetic element is purged from it. Indeed, starting from the 1950s, Gorz showed a great deal of scepticism in relation to any philosophy of history, and particularly with regard to the historicist tendencies of dialectical materialism.[3]

Besides, and we are shifting here to the second warning, the participation of the 'official' labour movement (major unions and communist parties) in the productivist paradigm can be directly ascribed to an understanding that sees the succession of different modes of production (feudal, capitalist, communist) as automatic, linear and progressive. Gorz would always insist on the idea that socialism, in order to live up to its emancipatory ambition, must necessarily break the hegemony of capital over economic policies and the means of production. Supporting growth as a remedy for all ills, such policies not only reveal their own deceptive nature (since the social gap has continued to widen), but also nail political imagination to the seemingly neutral ground of *quantity*.

A further aspect I will tackle concerns the (absolutely not obvious) way in which the ecological crisis makes its entrance into the political arena, creating for the first time in Italy what, following Rodolfo Lewanski, could be termed as 'demand for environmental quality'.[4] A rather widespread interpretation holds that the material self-evidence of physical limits would appear in all its unmovable character once specific critical thresholds are surpassed – thresholds that would be scientifically identifiable and that would simply need to be respected: ultimately, a matter of political will.[5] The path taken in this chapter diverges significantly from such

---

3   André Gorz, *La morale de l'histoire* (Paris: Seuil, 1959).

4   Rodolfo Lewanski, *Governare l'ambiente* (Bologna: Il Mulino, 1997).

5   Donella H. Meadows et al., *The Limits to Growth: A Report for* The Club of Rome's *Project on the Predicament of Mankind* (New York: Universe Books, 1972).

a picture. This is so not because the profound relevance of the physical limits to growth is denied, but rather because their political emergence maintained an extremely close relationship with two phenomena. On the one hand, with an extraordinary cycle of workers' struggles that challenged and, in some cases, rejected abstract social labour. On the other hand, with the disruptive irruption of social reproduction as a terrain of mass contestation, namely: the feminist and anti-colonial interruption of the invisibility to which these subjectivities had been relegated (explosion of abstract social nature). With particular reference to the Italian context, the environmental issue is thus addressed as a crucial (but not the only) element within a wider ecological critique of political economy that is capable of accounting for the social forces that determined the crisis of the 'classic' nexus between labour-nature-value, both *from within* and *from outside* the logic of value.

Gorz's Theory of the Twofold Crisis (1968–73)

According to Giorgio Nebbia, '1973 was the last year of ecology's spring'.[6] The trouble started with the cholera epidemics that hit Bari and Naples in August and continued in Chile in September with the overthrow of Salvador Allende's socialist government, which managed to remove mineral resources (particularly copper) from the control of large American companies. Pinochet's military dictatorship would promptly provide a 'remedy' to this. The countries at the periphery of the world-system, Nebbia maintains, 'understood that they could have managed the internal natural resources independently only by means of a direct confrontation, on their own territories, with the industrialised countries'.[7] The year ended with the first oil shock, and the second would follow in 1979, just after the Iranian Revolution, which was triggered by the unilateral decision of the producing and exporting countries, united in the Organization of the Petroleum Exporting Countries (OPEC), to suddenly

---

6	Giorgio Nebbia, *La contestazione ecologica: Storia, cronache e narrazioni* (Naples: La Scuola di Pitagora, 2015), 102.

7	Ibid., 103.

quadruple the price of crude oil, from about 3 dollars per barrel to 12.[8] The abrupt price increase and the US boycott set off a wave of speculation that fixed the free-market price well above the list price. In Augusto Graziani's words, 'throughout 1980 the price of crude oil on the Antwerp stock exchange reached and at times exceeded the price of 40 dollars per barrel'.[9]

Fixing the price so high could be interpreted in two ways. On the one hand, such a choice tended to be read as a 'crisis of raw materials', in other words, a relatively haphazard reaction to the 'discovery' of the physical limits to growth, which just the previous year had been high-lighted in the report of the Club of Rome.[10] On the other hand, it could appear to be an attempt to take advantage of a severe capitalist crisis in order to both dismantle the so-called workers' inflexibility (*rigidità operaia*), which is to say the power labour movements had gained, and to disintegrate the strength of the new revolutionary subjectivities that had emerged since 1968.[11]

These two interpretive lines, in general, have never crossed and remained indifferent to each other in the majority of cases. From this perspective, Gorz's contribution is truly remarkable in that he developed a coherent theory of the capitalist crisis exploded in 1973. On the one

---

8   Founded in 1960, the OPEC sits at the centre of the process that, at the turn of the 1970s, marked the transfer of control of oil resources from large international private companies to the producing countries. The price of crude would almost triple in 1970, reaching the hitherto almost unthinkable price of 32 dollars per barrel.

9   Augusto Graziani, *Lo sviluppo dell'economia italiana: dalla ricostruzione alla moneta europea* (Turin: Bollati Boringhieri, 1998), 112.

10   Nebbia, *La contestazione ecologica*, 104.

11   In point of fact, there is a third (and crucial) interpretation, which would however extend the unfolding of our argument beyond its specific focus. It is important to frame the decision made by the majority of the Arab countries in the OPEC within a geopolitical strategy aimed at putting the Palestinian question at the centre of the international agenda after the defeat of Egypt and Syria in the Yom Kippur War against Israel. Indeed, it is quite possible that, had the US withdrawn their support for Israel, the rise in the price of crude oil would have been immediately revoked. See Timothy Mitchell, *Carbon Democracy: Political Power in the Age of Oil* (London: Verso, 2011), Ch. 7 in particular.

hand, starting by essentially accepting the indication that Marx gave about the tendency of the rate of profit to fall – that is, the impossibility in the long term to replace the valorizing function of workers' living labour with dead labour crystallized in machinery – there emerges a situation of *overproduction*, which capital meets with countervailing factors, including the planned obsolescence of commodities and the creation of induced and pre-packaged needs. On the other hand, Gorz locates a *crisis of reproduction* in the rising costs that capital has to bear in order to regenerate the environment, until then used as an inexhaustible resource and as a free landfill, so that it could pollute it again (with the unavoidable result of a hike in prices).[12] Let's read a passage of particular importance:

> This forward flight [planned obsolescence and artificially induced needs], which was in any event bound to culminate in economic crisis, came to a stop with the so-called oil crisis. The latter did not cause the economic recession; it merely revealed and aggravated the recessionary tendencies which had been brewing for several years. Above all, the oil crisis revealed the fact that capitalist development had created absolute scarcities: in trying to overcome the economic obstacles to growth, capitalist development had given rise to physical obstacles.[13]

The argument is examined in depth while lucidly indicating the socio-environmental causes of the twofold crisis:

––––––––––––

12   Already in 1973, James O'Connor described the capitalist attempt to socialize the costs of reproduction of a healthy – from the standpoint of the productive processes – environment by means of the intervention of 'government money' within the project of 'total environmental planning'. As he argued, 'industries such as paper, chemicals, primary metals, and other large-scale polluters cannot afford to treat and dispose of their waste properly without financial help in one form or another'. James O'Connor, *The Fiscal Crisis of the State* (London: Transaction Publishers, 2002 [1973]), 176–7. With a few exceptions noted by Gorz and O'Connor (e.g. steel in Pittsburgh and chemicals in the Ruhr region), it is worth noting how the *directly* capitalist use of the welfare state – for instance, public intervention once the logic of value and the logic of wealth begin to separate – in no way undermines the key dynamics discussed in this chapter of the book, that is, the exhaustion of the 'classic' labour-nature-value nexus.

13   Gorz, 'Ecology and Freedom', 24.

The crisis did not begin in October 1973 with the Yom Kippur War. Nor is it due to the decision by oil-producing countries to quadruple the nominal price of oil. Its cause is not to be sought in the forecasting errors of technocrats, and it will not be overcome through better management of the current economy and apparatus of production. The present crisis began towards the end of the 1960s. It is a systemic crisis, that is, a simultaneous crisis of the economy, society, and capitalist civilisation. Its fundamental cause lies in the exhaustion of the factors deemed conducive to growth which, in 1945, had allowed the increasing mass of accumulated capital to produce profits that were likewise increasing . . . The physical and ecological limits to growth were not the primary cause of the crisis. Yet they accelerated and exacerbated it from an economic standpoint, further highlighting the absurdity of a system in which the growth of production went hand in hand with increasing inequality and suffering.[14]

Now, we need to ask: what caused the depletion of the factors of economic growth, in other words the maintenance of the wage-institution as the entropic device based on the exploitation of paid labour and the 'free' appropriation of the sphere of social reproduction? According to Gorz, the fundamental element in this process is the year 1968 understood as a cultural earthquake that shattered at once the progressive temporality of modernity and its political representation. For the Marxist left, such a representation was based on the exclusive individuation of the subject of transformation – the working class (*class in itself*) – and on the division of tasks between the party (*class for itself*) and unions (tactical transmission belt, a mere connector). Gorz's 1968 stages the multiplication of political practices through *conflict* and *difference*:[15] within the overall

---

14 André Gorz, *Ecologia e politica* (Bologna: Cappelli, 1978), 15–16. Ricciotti Antinolfi shares with Gorz a similar analysis of the crisis, particularly in reference to events that occurred in Italy, though with no particular focus on environmental aspects. See Ricciotti Antinolfi, *La crisi economica italiana 1969–1973* (Bari: De Donato, 1974).

15 Gorz expresses this passage with particular clarity in the Introduction to the Italian edition of *Écologie et politique*, written in May 1978 and significantly titled 'Politics is no longer in the political'. As he claims: 'No longer represented by

struggle against the capitalist order, social actors could finally recognize their irreducibility and mingle according to their own needs. The profound roots of political ecology are to be found here:

> Consciously or (more often) unconsciously, ecologists ultimately lend scientific rigour to all those who, in an apparently irrational way, perceive the current order as a barbaric disorder and reject it, refusing the existing forms of production, consumption, labour, and technology. They also insist that it is possible to live better while producing and consuming less, provided that production, consumption, and life itself are thought of differently and reimagined. In a sense, the protagonists of May 1968 were saying nothing different.[16]

These *molecular revolutions*, to use Guattari's terms, certainly concern the working class both as the active subject of protest (living labour yearning for autonomy from the capitalist organization of production) and as a polemical object (abstract social labour aimed at the production of value).[17] It is not by chance that Gorz identified the central core of the

---

political parties, the field of aspirations for radical change is now occupied by an abundance of movements, associations, and organisations with specific and partial objectives. These movements have a clear advantage over traditional parties. Since they do not defend a comprehensive vision of society or adhere to a predetermined political strategy, they need not concern themselves with the interests their campaigns might undermine or the difficulties their success might pose for governance. These movements, autonomous precisely because of the limits of their objectives, are the only spaces where latent aspirations can find expression and give shape to a new conception of social relations when the opportunity arises. However, they are careful not to define this conception as "political" as it rejects the logic of government-oriented parties that claim politics as their exclusive possession and domain. In this case, the refusal of politics does not connote apoliticism but rather the refusal to subordinate freedom of expression, of contestation, and of imagination to the needs and logic of power.' Gorz, *Ecologia e politica*, 8–9.

16 André Gorz (as Michel Bosquet), *Critica al capitalismo di ogni giorno* (Milan: Jaca Book, 1978 [1972]), 178. See also André Gorz, *Letter to D: A Love Story*, trans. Julie Rose (Cambridge: Polity, 2009); and Willy Gianinazzi, *André Gorz: A Life* (Calcutta: Seagull Books, 2022 [2016]).

17 On this, see Félix Guattari, *Molecular Revolution*, trans. Rosemary Sheed (Harmondsworth: Penguin, 1984 [1977]). In the Preface to the Italian edition of the

uprising in the complex relationship between workers and students: 'It was as though the workers had decided that they were as good as the students in taking powers wherever they were and to make the places of work into places of living. To me, the real revolution of 1968 was that.'[18]

As a result, even the role of the union is modified, as exemplified by a text Gorz wrote in 1971 and addressed to the metalworkers' union of West Germany (IG Metall). In this text, Gorz argues that, once the 'increase in the costs of production' – following the expensive necessity to safeguarding (*ex ante*) or reclaiming (*ex post*) the environment – is identified as the main factor of the crisis, the union must renew itself and engage in a project of civilization centred more on 'extra-economic "qualitative" goals' than on wage disputes.[19] This is the theme of 'qualitative needs' that

---

book, Guattari highlights that 'the alliance between the new liberation movements, which day after day increasingly transform our political context, and the struggles of the working class is necessary and inevitable. However, we should not lose sight of the fact that the struggles of desire, those against the dominant conformism, and the defence of minorities against the oppressive consensus of the majority have as their target the working class *as well*, especially its apparatuses which are particularly saturated with the modes of thought, ways of organisation, ways of life of capitalist power and its substitutes in the "socialist" states', in *La rivoluzione molecolare*, trans. Bruno Bellotto, Anna Rocchi Pullberg and Alfredo Saisano (Turin: Einaudi), xi.

18 Gorz interviewed in Conrad Lodziak and Jeremy Tatman, *André Gorz: A Critical Introduction* (London: Pluto Press, 1997), 125. It is worth noting that Gorz's interpretation does not differ much from that of *operaismo* as found in the article 'Maggio '68 in Francia' written by Sergio Bologna and Giairo Daghini for *Quaderni Piacentini* (VII, 35, July 1968). This is how the authors provide a comment on this text forty years after its publication and in its Italian context: 'Here, our "operaismo" comes back into play, our theoretical and political expertise returns to the forefront with respect to existential experience. Writing a reportage? Just traces on water. The alternative was to try to build a paradigm, May '68 in France as an exemplification of political theory, a theory of class dynamics, and as such to the movement as a reflection with a precise political intent: the point was to shift its focus from the anti-authoritarian and Third-Worldist student phase to a worker phase. Thinking about how things subsequently unfolded, we succeeded. The sequence is still shocking: struggles at Pirelli in the autumn, strikes at Fiat in the summer of 1969, Hot Autumn, Workers' Statute of May 1970.' Sergio Bologna and Giairo Daghini, *Maggio '68 in Francia* (Rome: DeriveApprodi, 2008 [1968]), 8.

19 André Gorz, 'Labor and the "Quality of Life"', in *Ecology as Politics*, 133.

are rooted in the following paradox. The capitalist mode of production, although it exploits labour and impoverishes the sphere of social reproduction, entails in the long run a certain material well-being for important sectors of the population, thereby liberating them from the inescapable obligation to fight on a daily basis for their survival. New qualitative aspirations grow in importance specifically at that moment. And yet capitalism prevents their full realization while its power gradually becomes more capillary. The division of labour imprisons workers for their entire life in tight meshes of functions and tasks, in such a way as to inhibit their individual and collective development.[20]

Class unions are thus invoked to directly organize the opposition to capital not only (and not primarily) to challenge unequal distribution, but rather to provide a fundamentally alternative vision of the aims of production. Already in 1966 Gorz maintained that:

> This is why it is impossible to divorce the labor struggle for better wages and working conditions from the broader political and economic struggle embracing, for example, education, city planning, social services, regional development, and so on – all problems to which no lasting solution can be found except in terms of an anti-capitalist policy.[21]

The Environmental Causes of the Twofold Crisis: The Physical Limits to Growth

After tracing the historical framework (1968–73) in which Gorz offered his interpretation of the twofold crisis (of overproduction and reproduction), we now need to take a closer look at the factors that caused it, starting from abstract social nature's 'refusal' to remain in a state of supposedly infinite abundance and total ('free') availability. Let us begin with

---

20   See André Gorz, *Stratégie ouvrière et néo-capitalisme* (Paris: Seuil, 1964).

21   André Gorz, *Socialism and Revolution*, trans. Norman Denny (London: Allen Lane, 1975 [1967]), 93.

the physical limits to growth as discussed by the Club of Rome in the 1972 report *The Limits to Growth*, a report widely commented upon in public discourse (newspapers, magazines, etc.). A very succinct summary of the report highlights two conclusions:

a) if the current rates of global population growth, of industrialization and corresponding pollution, of food production and generally of the use of natural resources persisted, the critical bio-physical thresholds to economic development on planet Earth will be reached in conjunction with a breaking point that is not yet determinable with precision, but which can be placed in the course of the twenty-first century. As for the form of such a breaking point, the most plausible scenario is a sudden and unmanageable decline of the population and its productive capacity;

b) there is the possibility of revising the growth rate downward in such a way that it would not undermine either ecological or economic stability, thus preserving the prospects for development even in the long term. This scenario, however, requires meticulous planning so that individual needs are satisfied and everyone may receive the same possibilities to realize their human potential.

It is not known precisely what those *needs* are and how those *possibilities* might specifically emerge. As Gorz maintained already in 1972, 'the American researchers from MIT are very careful not to politicise the debate'.[22] Despite this, the report had a global impact; it arrived as a profound shock and as such generated violent reactions. The most common trait among these reactions was a sort of uncanny bewilderment, the consequence of coming to terms with something that, after all, was known yet actively shunned. A substantial part of the public opinion welcomed the scenarios presented by Donella Meadows and her colleagues with a bizarre mixture of palingenetic enthusiasm and fear of

---

22   Gorz (Bosquet), *Critica al capitalismo di ogni giorno*, 175.

imminent catastrophe. For instance, the fourth president of the European Commission, Sicco Mansholt, drew a manifesto based on the report that gathered numerous adherents.[23]

Moreover, others replied with disjointed retorts ranging from irritable to disdainful. According to Giorgio Nebbia, part of the establishment reacted by deeming the attack on growth unreasonable and accusing the writers of the text of class betrayal or even collusion with the communist enemy. A few economists reasserted that the market, as always, would have dealt with the problem of scarcity and that the physical limits to growth did not represent a significant novelty in this regard. The Catholic world read the report as an indirect invitation to birth control and thus took distance from its recommendations. Lastly, the reaction of a few orthodox Marxists was 'cruder'. The latter group maintained that, on the one hand, the report struck at the legitimate proletarian aspirations to consumer well-being while, on the other hand, it muddied the waters by ignoring that the problems of limits could retain a certain validity in the capitalist West but would have never emerged in the socialist regimes, led by the Soviet Union, which, at this point, were supposedly free from the imperative to accumulate.[24]

A small minority made an effort to read the Club of Rome's text *politically* with a view to shaping it into a weapon of struggle in the hands of ecological movements and the labour vanguards. Gorz was the main representative of this line of thought. In an article written in 1972, significantly titled 'For a Good Use of Mansholt', we read the following:

An official document has rarely provided so much ammunition to the socialist and revolutionary movement. Mansholt, with all his ambiguities, cunning, and caution, ultimately suggests this: the preservation of civilised life on Earth, even humanity's very survival, is incompatible with the capitalist mode of production and requires its transcendence . . .

---

23   Johan van Merriënboer, 'Sicco Mansholt and "Limits to Growth"', in *Europe in a Globalising World: Global Challenges and European Responses in the 'Long' 1970s*, ed. Claudia Hiepel (Baden-Baden: Nomos, 2014).
24   Giorgio Nebbia, *Le merci e i valori* (Milan: Jaca Book, 2002), 73.

Did he [Georges Marchais][25] fail to grasp the advantage that communists could draw from these documents? Or did he conclude that the masses in France were not yet ready to receive such revolutionary truths? That there were, in fact, more votes to be gained by banking on their scepticism, their attachment to the habits and myths of 'consumer society'? Either way, a great opportunity was lost.[26]

Within such a framework, it is worth emphasizing that *all* social sectors felt that it was inconceivable to keep the capitalist mechanism in the same form it had retained up to that point. The elites reacted in a dual way to the revelations of the Club of Rome. First, frightened by an ecologically uncertain future yet unable to slow down the rhythms of growth since the Cold War was in full swing, they invested resources in order to adapt their companies to environmental risks. Indeed, as Romain Felli has lucidly illustrated, within discussions on climate change the issue of adaptation dates back to the mid-1970s and thus precedes by more than a decade the register of mitigation.[27] Second, the elites arranged an extraordinarily aggressive class politics – what we today call neoliberalism[28] – aimed at unfolding on a global scale a degree of social polarization that was unknown since the First World War.[29] The Fordist pact began to creak.

---

25   General Secretary of the French Communist Party from 1972 to 1994.

26   Gorz (Bosquet), *Critica al capitalismo di ogni giorno*, 162–3. The emphasis on the politicization of Mansholt's manifesto, alongside its necessary *class* dimension, is reiterated even more clearly in an article published a few months later: 'With few exceptions, ecologists and ecological movements remain silent on the issue of *means*. Theirs is a subversive sensibility and a revolutionary aspiration without class as a foundation, a *moral* revolt that, more often than not, rejects capitalist civilisation as a whole without explicitly addressing the *class nature* of the emergence of such a civilisation.' Gorz (Bosquet), *Critica al capitalismo di ogni giorno*, 180.

27   Romain Felli, *The Great Adaptation: Climate, Capitalism and Catastrophe* (London: Verso, 2021 [2016]).

28   Pierre Dardot and Christian Laval, *The New Way of the World: On Neoliberal Society* (London: Verso, 2013 [2009]).

29   'Not long after *The Limits to Growth* report was issued, the norms of public provision, which had ensured a degree of social equity in the Fordist compact, fell under attack. Tax reform, fiscal austerity, deregulation and privatization, structural adjustment, crumbling of secure work, and the general shredding of social welfare dramatically eroded most of the postwar gains for workers, and pushed them

The movements, for their part, acknowledged the crucial significance of *The Limits to Growth* and sharply emphasized the stakes involved: 'democracy of the associated producers or planetary regimenting; *socialism* or *eco-fascism*'.[30] In short, the idea that capitalism could integrate the limits of the biosphere within valorization, and thus shape these limits into drivers of development (rather than restrictions), was not on the agenda.[31] This idea would have emerged later, starting from 1987 with the concept of 'sustainable development' and more markedly during the 1990s with the 'green economy'.

Apart from the reactions to it, the report provides the key for an interpretation that allows us to establish a direct connection between the American 'peak oil' – which could be dated in 1970 since the United States has never again extracted as much as in that year[32] – to the dramatic effects of the 1973 crisis. From an economic point of view, the following

---

underwater. The only compensation on offer was a lottery ticket in the speculative housing market – sparking a highly unsustainable round of land development which ended in the worst global recession since the 1930s. In retrospect, it is fair to conclude that the message of *The Limits to Growth* was not ignored. It did get through to its elite audiences, and they responded by squirreling away whatever resources they could carry off from the commonwealth.' Andrew Ross, 'Vita e lavoro nell'epoca del cambiamento climatico', in *Lavoro in frantumi*, ed. Federico Chicchi and Emanuele Leonardi (Verona: ombre corte, 2011), 31.

30   Gorz, *Ecologia e politica*, 15–16. Two years earlier, Gorz had been even more radical as he titled an article 'Communism or eco-fascism?', see Gorz (Bosquet), *Critica al capitalismo di ogni giorno*, 223–40.

31   An exception to this is a truly prophetic, albeit isolated, passage Gorz wrote in 1972: 'At a later stage . . . the most powerful groups will have secured a monopoly over the production and sale of purified air, potable water, recycled minerals, and preserved environment. This, in turn, will enable a new cycle of accumulation, one rooted in the capitalisation of nature itself, in capital's subsumption of the *totality of factors and conditions that sustain life on Earth*. The circle will thus be complete; the law of profit will have infiltrated the last remaining pockets of nature; even air will have become a commodity. The totalitarianism of capital will be fully perfected and realised, along with the monopolisation of the economy.' Gorz (Bosquet), *Critica al capitalismo di ogni giorno*, 183.

32   See Richard H. K. Vietor, *Energy Policy in America Since 1945: A Study of Business–Government Relations* (New York: Cambridge UP, 1984); and James Howard Kunstler, *The Long Emergency: Surviving the End of Oil, Climate Change, and other Converging Catastrophes of the 21st Century* (New York: Grove, 2005).

period would be marked by both a substantial contraction of consumption and stagflation (i.e. a general increase in prices in the absence of growth).[33]

In this sense, the crisis could be seen as a kind of *nemesis of finitude*, considering that Morris Adelman, an expert on world oil markets for MIT, still in 1972 extensively criticized the Nixon administration precisely for taking on the natural scarcity argument, one about the shortage of physical resources:

> Minerals are inexhaustible and will never be depleted . . . A stream of investment creates additions to proved reserves from a very large in-ground inventory. The reserves are constantly being renewed as they are extracted. How much was in the ground at the start and how much will be left at the end are unknown and irrelevant.[34]

Two years later, Robert Solow toned down that analysis by showing with great precision the subtle difference between the 'classic' labour-nature-value nexus and its subsequent version: 'it is very easy to substitute other factors for natural resources, then there is in principle no "problem". The world can, in effect, get along without natural resources, so exhaustion is just an event, not a catastrophe.'[35] In this passage, we can spot the idea that biophysical scarcity could be substituted entirely with equivalent units of capital and/or wage labour and, as such, it encapsulates the market's self-regulating capacity in its purest form. From this perspective, the oil shock would perfectly demonstrate the law of supply and demand:

---

33   I need to reveal in advance some of the long-term effects that will be analysed in more detail in the next chapter of the book: processes of tertiarization, industrial delocalization from the Global North, informatization and cognitivization of labour (Information and Communication Technologies are indeed born in the 1970s), financializaton of the economy. Therefore, one could argue that the oil shock supported the emerging neoliberal rationality; see Matthew T. Huber, *Lifeblood: Oil, Freedom, and the Forces of Capital* (Minneapolis: University of Minnesota Press, 2013).

34   Morris Adelman in Mitchell, *Carbon Democracy*, 188.

35   Robert M. Solow, 'The Economics of Resources or the Resources of Economics', *The American Economic Review* 62: 2, 1974, 11.

a good becomes scarce, its price increases, research and technology provide cheaper alternatives, alternatives spread and progressively render the scarce good obsolete, thereby lowering its price.[36]

The Social Causes of the Twofold Crisis: Feminist Revolution and Liberation of Work / Liberation from Labour

In effect, once the energy crisis gets reduced to its environmental dimension, it becomes difficult to escape its technocratic interpretation. Such an interpretation comprises two opposite yet specular forms: one picturing an insurmountable scarcity to 'manage' or 'govern' (according to unspecified criteria) and another depicting an irrelevant scarcity to be replaced. Actually, as Gorz noted, physical limits are not at the origin of the crisis, even though they made it worse. The crisis should thus be read starting from its social causes. And, indeed, as shown by Matthias Schmelzer, the revolutionary turbulence of 1968 was the crucial factor that pushed technocratic organizations such as the OECD – within which the Club of Rome saw its birth – to rethink and reassess the paradigm of economic growth.[37]

Before exploring this important topic further, I need to add a caveat: to maintain that environmental causes are 'secondary' to social ones does not in the least entail considering them as merely conjunctural, accessory or superficial. Being the first moment in which the ecological crisis acquired global political visibility, the oil shock is an epoch-making event that marks a profound discontinuity in the overall historical experience of humanity. As Salvo Torre has argued,

The turning point in the interpretation of human history arrived only with the understanding of the limits of development, the moment when

---

36   Cf. Robert M. Solow, 'Is the End of the World at Hand', *Challenge* 2, 1973, 39–50.

37   OECD: Organisation for Economic Co-operation and Development, established in 1948. See Matthias Schmelzer, '"Born in the corridors of the OECD": the forgotten origins of the Club of Rome, transnational networks, and the 1970s in global history', *Journal of Global History* 12, 2017, 26–48.

the complex of planetary resources and the biosphere began representing a tangible boundary that human history could not overstep.[38]

Put differently, as we will see, the 1973 crisis cannot be *exclusively* reduced to its bio-physical roots. In order to become an ecological crisis – that is, the evidence of the breakdown of the nexus between labour-nature-value – the environmental degradation represented by the oil shock had to be understood in its multidimensional character. The main forces that made this passage possible were the feminist revolution and the workers-centred tension between liberation *of* work and liberation *from* labour.

In the previous chapter, we saw how the 'classic' labour-nature-value nexus required the demotion of social reproduction to the role of *condition* of production. 'Operaist' feminism in the 1970s also criticized the *naturalization* of the woman within the domestic-private sphere, that is to say, the operation that made women disappear within a space unworthy of theoretical or conceptual status.[39] The effect of such dual capture is that some subjects (women) and some activities (those attributed to women and enfolded within the sphere of reproduction) end up being subordinated and ruled as a 'natural force of social labour', according to Leopoldina Fortunati's incisive formulation.[40] The wage-institution, therefore, not only acts within the sphere of production but also operates as a device for the disciplining and governing of reproduction. Contrary to what Marx thought, Fortunati shows how the wage-institution both certified the division of the working day in necessary labour and surplus labour, *and* transformed women's working day into 'non-labour'. As she

---

38 Salvo Torre, *Dominio, natura, democrazia: Comunità umane e comunità ecologiche* (Milan: Mimesis, 2013), 75.

39 Carolyn Merchant traced the origins of this process within the Scientific Revolution linked to the name of Francis Bacon, which marks the triumph of male violence over nature-woman. See Carolyn Merchant, *The Death of Nature: Women, Ecology, and the Scientific Revolution* (San Francisco, CA: Harper & Row, 1980). See also Gea Piccardi, *Produzione e riproduzione: una critica femminista alla teoria del valore*, MA thesis (Università di Roma Tre, 2015).

40 Leopoldina Fortunati, *The Arcana of Reproduction: Housewives, Prostitutes, Workers and Capital*, trans. Arlen Austin and Sara Colantuono (London: Verso, 2025 [1981]), 16.

put it, 'it is not true that all labour appears as paid labour. Only the labour provided in the production process appears as paid labour. The labour provided in the reproduction process [which Ariel Salleh calls "meta-industrial labour"] appears as non-labour, or, more specifically, it is positioned as non-labour; it is represented as a personal service and functions as indirectly waged labour.'[41]

Now, the 1970s feminist revolution specifically concerns the refusal of such a twofold subordination (naturalization and becoming-invisible). From this standpoint, I believe that the ecological dimension of this refusal should be strongly emphasized. By rupturing the forced separation between production and reproduction, feminism cuts off the assumptions of infinity and gratuity from the conditions of value.[42] It shatters abstract social nature altogether. In this regard, the International Wages for Housework campaign emerging at the beginning of the 1970s is particularly instructive. As early as 1975, Silvia Federici very convincingly highlighted the 'revolutionary implications' of the campaign:

> *It is the demand by which our nature ends and our struggle begins because just to want wages for housework means to refuse this work as the expression of our nature,* and therefore to refuse precisely the female role that capital has invented for us . . . In this sense, it is absurd to compare the struggle of women for wages for housework to the struggle of male workers in the factory for more wages. In struggling for more wages, the waged worker challenges his social role but remains within it. When we struggle for wages for housework we struggle unambiguously and directly against our social role. In the same way, there is a qualitative difference between the struggles of the waged worker and the struggles of the slave for a wage against that slavery. It should be clear, however, that when we struggle for a wage we do not struggle to enter capitalist relations, because we have never been out of

---

41   See Ariel Salleh, 'From Metabolic Rift to "Metabolic Value": Reflections on Environmental Sociology and the Alternative Globalization Movement', *Organization and Environment* 23: 2, 2010, 205–19. Fortunati, *The Arcana of Reproduction*, 38.

42   See for instance Maria Mies and Vandana Shiva, *Ecofeminism* (London: Zed Books, 2014 [1993]).

them. We struggle to break capital's plan for women, which is an essential moment of that division of labor and social power within the working class through which capital has been able to maintain its hegemony.[43]

In *Farewell to the Working Class* (1980), Gorz commented very critically upon the feminist campaign for family allowances, identifying its basis in the willingness to participate in the 'benefits' that the wage-institution reserved only to male waged workers. Federici's revolutionary implications, however, show without fear of contradiction the extent to which Gorz's concerns were unfounded. The idea expressed there was not to achieve integration, but to *blow up* the system. Since housework can coexist with the logic of value only by being made invisible, made unlimited and 'free', 'accounting' for it as a factor of value would have had highly destabilizing consequences. A complete compensation in wages for domestic work would have meant the end of value. This is exactly why 'operaist' feminism claimed it. By contrast with the wage-institution, whose function is to naturalize exploitation within production, the demand for paid housework is a 'lever of power' aimed at de-naturalizing the practices of appropriation within social reproduction.[44]

In this sense, the feminist revolution is at the core of the crisis of the 'classic' labour-nature-value nexus. It represents the irruption of the reproductive sphere into production, thus placing itself on the same level as the workers' struggles, which, starting from within wage labour, would extend their reach up to question the logic of value *tout court*. We should not forget, for instance, that the oil shock was also (or above all) an international attack led by the United States against the high level of workers'

---

43 Silvia Federici, 'Wages against Housework', in *Revolution at Point Zero: Housework, Reproduction, and Feminist Struggle* (Oakland, CA: PM Press, 2012 [1975]), 18–19, emphasis in original. See also Mariarosa Dalla Costa, 'Women and the Subversion of the Community', in *The Power of Women and the Subversion of the Community* (Bristol: Falling Wall Press, 1972), 21–56. See also, in the same volume, Selma James, 'A Woman's Place', 57–79.

44 See Louise Toupin, *Wages for Housework: A History of an International Feminist Movement, 1972–77*, trans. Käthe Roth (London: Pluto Press, 2018 [2014]), 62ff.

power and against the (relative) cultural hegemony the labour movement had achieved through social struggles over a period of five years of intense battles.[45] Sergio Bologna wrote on this matter in 1974 for *Quaderni Piacentini*:

> The 'energy crisis' has been an instrument that allowed selective oper-ations: to worsen the attack on the mass vanguards of the car factories and to 'integrate' the process of forming an Arab proletariat to the historical stage of the petrochemical sector, undermining its growth rates from the outset . . . Furthermore, the changes in demand required a restructuring that will have long-term effects and leave a lasting mark on what too many still insist on considering a crisis merely linked to the present conjuncture.[46]

In the next chapter, I will put forward a few reflections on this 'restructur-ing', for it has important consequences as regards the transformation of the nexus between labour, nature and value. For now, however, it is nec-essary to pay some attention to the way in which a high level of workers' power could emerge in the years between 1968 and 1973. From the per-spective of the labour-nature-value nexus, the crucial point is that the ecological issue in Italy became a truly political issue *through* workers' struggles, not *despite* them.[47] Struggles against 'noxiousness' [*nocività*]

---

45   Midnight Notes Collective, 'The Post-Energy Crisis US Working Class Composition', in *Midnight Oil: Work, Energy, War 1973–1992* (New York: Autono-media, 1992), 59–66.

46   Sergio Bologna, 'Petrolio e mercato Mondiale: cronistoria di una crisi', in *Banche e crisi: dal petrolio al container* (Milan: DeriveApprodi, 2013), 103–17.

47   This is exactly the opposite of what Franco La Cecla argued in his essay (co-written with Charlene Spretnak), *Green Politics: The Global Promise* (London: Paladin Grafton Books, 1984). Describing this essay a few years later, La Cecla claimed the following: 'I argued that the background from which our homegrown environmentalism emerged had in some way remained outside the crises and the turmoil of the Italian Left of the 1960s. In particular, I was referring to the antimil-itarist movements inspired by nonviolence and the movement of conscientious objection. Around that world – and around religious components, nonviolent anar-chism, and inspirations somewhat unorthodox in relation to the Italian Catholic sphere, such as Quakers, Gandhian groups, those linked to Lanza del Vasto – a need

emerge at the turn of the 1970s and begin to fiercely criticize the so-called *monetization of risk*, that is, the idea that a salary increase could 'compensate' for exposure to very dangerous pollutants.[48] What breaks this mechanism and posits the environmental crisis as an issue that cannot be evaded is the strength of organized workers,[49] and definitely not a 'new' sensitivity of the urbanized middle classes as suggested by the sociological theories of ecological modernization and post-materialism, or by the economic theory of the environmental Kuznets curve.[50] The idea underlying these approaches is that a particularly polluting first phase of industrial development, based on quantitative growth, was to be followed by a more 'environment-friendly' phase, triggered by the greater prosperity of social actors that, freed from the necessity of providing for basic needs, could at

---

arose for a much more grassroots and general way of doing politics. I identified Capitini as one of the key inspirations for this, alongside the influence of the "alternative way of life" coming from Anglo-Saxon countries, which cultivated this new focus.' Franco La Cecla, 'Le tre ecologie più una: la pornoecologia', in Félix Guattari, *Le tre ecologie* (Casale Monferrato: Sonda, 1991 [1989]), 57.

48   This idea is quite widespread even within unions: 'The entire approach of the official workers' organizations, at least until 1966, shows acceptance of the organization of labour under capital as a natural and inevitable fact. Indeed, while the spontaneous forms of self-defence against risk highlight, even to a superficial analysis, the refusal to succumb to the labour conditions imposed by capital, the demands of the organizations, which aim at the monetization of risk, do not question the causes of such a risk. Addressing these causes would have immediately challenged that organization of labour. Technical progress [according to the words of Vittorio Foa], is 'the cruel fate that I must pay for, in one way or another'. Therefore, the possibility of eliminating the causes of risk is not questioned, only ensuring compensation for those who have to endure them in any case.' Sebastiano Bagnara and Francesco Carnevale, 'La costruzione di una linea di intervento sull'ambiente e la nocività', *Classe – Quaderni sulla condizione e sulla lotta operaia* 7, 1973, 112–13.

49   There are at least two fundamental militant magazines and two persons that must be mentioned in relation to the struggle for health in Italy: on the one hand, *Sapere* and *Medicina Democratica*; on the other hand, Giulio Maccacaro and Luigi Mara. Reflections and contributions on these magazines and these militants can be found in *Altronovecento*, available at altronovecento.fondazionemicheletti.eu.

50   An outline of this approach can be found in Giorgio Osti and Luigi Pellizzoni, *Sociologia dell'ambiente*, (Bologna: Il Mulino, 2003); and Ignazio Musu, *Introduzione all'economia dell'ambiente* (Bologna: Il Mulino, 2003).

last commit themselves to ecological themes by setting off a mechanism of 'clean' growth.[51] This is a colossal blunder, which nonetheless endures in sociological common sense and at times also in union rhetoric.[52]

It is thus important to reiterate that the ecological perspective is the result of the struggles *against* 'the gospel of eco-efficiency': environmental justice in the Global South,[53] working-class environmentalism and feminism in the Global North.[54] As Stefania Barca has aptly remarked: 'The workplace had to be understood as a particular type of ecosystem, and the working class was the subject that knew it best.'[55] Qualitative needs, therefore, are not the step following basic needs on a hierarchy that is secretly predetermined. Rather, they are the contingent outcome of the conflictual passage from the quantitative demands wholly tied to the working conditions – wages and level of employment – to broader and more general subject matters: environment, culture (think about the 150 hours), care for the territory, control of investments.[56] In sum, ecology is primarily a class issue. In this regard, I believe that the line of reasoning already proposed in 1976 by Alfredo Milanaccio and Luca Ricolfi is particularly sound:

---

51   See for instance Wilfred Beckerman, *Economic Development and the Environment: Conflict or Complementarity?* (Washington, DC: The World Bank, 1992).

52   For a lucid critical overview on this, see Oscar Krüger and Mladen Domazet, 'Climate Change: Introducing the European Egalitarian Environmentalist', *Social Ecology* 25: 1–2, 2016, 167–89. See also, Laura Pennacchi, *Tra crisi e 'grande trasformazione': Libro Bianco per il Piano del Lavoro 2013* (Rome: Ediesse, 2013).

53   Joan Martínez-Alier, *The Environmentalism of the Poor: A Study of Ecological Conflicts and Valuation* (Cheltenham: Edward Elgar, 2002).

54   See Stefania Barca, 'Labour and the ecological crisis: The eco-modernist dilemma in western Marxism(s) (1970s–2000s)', *Geoforum* 83, 2017, 91–100.

55   Stefania Barca, 'Pane e veleno: Storie di ambientalismo operaio in Italia', *Zapruder* 24, 2011, 103.

56   The Italian experiment of 150 hours refers to the workers' right to receive time off work for educational purposes. In Italy, this right had been included in several collective agreements since 1973. Most of these agreements were to be found in industry (metalworking, textiles and clothing, glassworks, tanneries, publishing, wood and cork, ceramics, etc.), while some in services or agriculture. On this, see Filippo Maria De Sanctis, 'A Victory by Italian Workers: The "150 Hours"', in *Learning and Working*, ed. Zaghloul Morsy (Paris: UNESCO, 1979), 309–23. The experiment also had a huge impact on women, see Leslie Caldwell, 'Courses for Women: The Example of the 150 Hours in Italy', *Feminist Review* 1, 1983, 71–83.

When what is at stake is exclusively or fundamentally the level of the rate of exploitation, the problem is not 'what' to ask for, or 'how' to obtain it, nor even 'evaluating' the results of the struggles. In these conditions, control is ensured, 'automatically' one might say, by the measurability and the defined, given nature of what is at stake. The decisive variable, power relations, comes into play to determine the outcome of the clash but not its content, which is given. In relation to this framework, 1968 represents a true turning point. The refusal to delegate and active participation do not come out of nowhere, but arise at the very moment when a new universe of needs and demands begins to emerge from the factory, different from the traditional ones and essentially new because it broadens the scope of the experience of workers. What is truly new in the struggles in those years is that they do not involve only the levels of exploitation in the factory but immediately raise, within the fight against the level of exploitation, the issue of the social legitimacy of the organising model of the entire society.[57]

Similarly to how Trentin put it in the epigraph used at the beginning of this chapter, wage demands and requests for 'power and freedom' are tied in an indivisible connection that forms the basis of the exponential growth of the workers' power between 1968 and 1973. Oppositional class subjectivation was the necessary (yet not sufficient) condition for the unfolding of a truly disruptive cycle of struggles.

However, as concerns qualitative struggles, we need to shed light on the tension between the perspectives of liberation *of* work (supported by Trentin himself, at that time the general secretary of the Italian Federation of Metalworkers [FIOM/FLM],[58] and the radical Left) and the ambition of liberation *from* labour (embraced by operaist organizations [Potere Operaio at first, then Autonomia Operaia]).[59] Both options, as we said, place their analyses beyond the mere level of wages and thus shape themselves as

---

57   Alfredo Milanaccio and Luca Ricolfi, *Lotte operaie e ambiente di lavoro: Mirafiori 1968–1974* (Turin: Einaudi, 1976), 23.

58   For an outline of Bruno Trentin's trajectory in union politics, see Simone Fana, 'Da sfruttati a produttori: sindacato e politica in Bruno Trentin', *404: file not found*, 16 December 2016.

59   Cf. Nicola Pizzolato, 'A New Revolutionary Practice: *Operaisti* and the "Refusal of Work" in 1970's Italy', *Estudos Históricos* 30: 61, 2017, 449–64.

forms of *critique of the logic of value*. In other words, therefore, they execute what Karl Heinz Roth defined as the 'opening up of the wage struggles'.[60] Nonetheless, they have different horizons that are not easy to reconcile.[61] The first option, for instance, assumes that it is possible to 'redeem' wage labour in the name of work understood in the generic sense of human activity in which individuals externalize their own authentic personality through cooperation. It is a matter of dis-alienating wage labour by virtue of workers controlling the productive process so that the irreducible singularity of every worker can eventually develop. In this sense, the request for wage egalitarianism (i.e. salary rises identical for all, detached from productivity gains) represents, according to Trentin, a 'desperate defence of existing conditions' on the one hand and a 'radical negation of personhood, of its diverse possibilities of self-realization, of its diverse conditions of cultural autonomy and appropriation of knowledges' on the other.[62]

By contrast, the second option advocates for the *refusal of labour* as an activity imposed by capital,[63] which is also deemed useless in an era when information technologies make their entrance on the scene of production. The expression 'refusal of labour' is not only aimed at establishing a radical critique of waged work (labour as toil, labour as employment, expropriated labour), but is also (and especially) deployed to express the determination to take control of the power to influence the qualitative

---

60   Karl-Heinz Roth, 'External and internal militants: Workers' autonomy in Porto Marghera seen from West Germany 1971–1974', *libcom.org*, 2012 [2009], libcom.org.

61   See for instance Egidio Pasetto and Giuseppe Pupillo, 'Il gruppo "Potere Operaio" nelle lotte di Porto Marghera (primavera '66 – primavera '70)', *Classe – Quaderni sulla condizione e sulla lotta operai* 3, 1970, 95–119.

62   Bruno Trentin and Guido Liguori, *Il secondo biennio rosso (1968–1969)* (Rome: Editori Riuniti, 1999), 65–6.

63   In this regard, Maria Turchetto maintains the following: 'I have the impression that too often the history of the modern idea of labour is conflated with the history of the organised workers' movement which, while it has certainly interiorised this idea, in part at least, it is not its architect . . . I would rather . . . trace the genesis of labour, evidently belonging to modernity, to the processes of formation of national states that inaugurate the emergence of techniques of "biopower".' Maria Turchetto, 'Lavoro senza fine', *Zapruder* 3, 2004, 8–26.

composition of production in the era of increasing automation: 'the principle of refusal of labour, controlled and directed by the "generalized social intelligence", could bring about a use of technology and the machine which is capable of freeing human beings from the slavery of waged work'.[64] Hence, it is a matter not of claiming the right to idleness, following Paul Lafargue, but rather of abolishing value altogether and reaffirming the logic of wealth by means of claims such as reduction of working hours, slowing down productive rhythms, refusal of exposure to noxiousness (including environmental risks) and claims for the right to health, for wage egalitarianism.[65]

Incidentally, it is interesting to note how Gorz himself oscillated between these two options. Up to 1973, his critique of the division of labour depended on factory struggles – in particular the alliance between the figure of the mass worker and the technician – which could revert the aims of production through workers' control of the productive process and a subsequent expansion in the form of self-management.[66] Starting from 1977, Gorz's attention shifts from the factory to society as a whole and goes as far as theorizing, in 1980, the birth of a 'non-class of non-workers' or of a 'post-industrial neo-proletariat' for whom 'it is no longer a question of freeing themselves *within* labour . . . The point now is to free oneself *from* labour by rejecting its nature, content, necessity and modalities.'[67]

---

64   Nanni Balestrini and Primo Moroni, *The Golden Horde: Revolutionary Italy 1960–1977*, trans. Richard Braude (Calcutta: Seagull Books, 2021 [1997]).

65   Lafargue was widely misunderstood. As pointed out by Bernard Marszalek, author of the introduction to the English version of Lafargue's *Le Droit à la paresse*, what is to be understood as 'other' than labour is not idleness or indolence, but rather 'autonomous and creative collective activity – ludic activity – that develops our unique humanity and grounds our practice of reversing perspective [of reality and society]'. Bernard Marszalek, 'Introduction' to Paul Lafargue, *The Right to be Lazy* (Oakland, CA: AK Press, 2011), 19.

66   See André Gorz, 'Le despotisme d'usine et ses lendemains', in *Critique de la division du travail* (Paris: Seuil, 1973).

67   André Gorz, *Farewell to the Working Class*, trans. Michael Sonescher (London: Pluto Press, 1987 [1980]), 67 (translation modified). In order to provide a partial corrective to the manifold misunderstandings that accompanied the publication of this book, it should be emphasized that, although Gorz stated that 'the

Let us return to Italy. From 1969 onwards, the development of the dispute over the noxiousness of working environments at the petrochemical plant in Porto Marghera (Venice) constitutes a paradigmatic example of the friction between liberation *of* work and liberation *from* labour.[68]

___

class itself has entered into crisis', his following analysis does not at all accept those crude simplifications arguing for the extinction of social classes. On the contrary, here Gorz is engaged in a critical cartography of the subjective figures emerging alongside the mass worker during struggles – in Italy, Toni Negri would talk about 'social worker' and Sergio Bologna would term it 'disseminated worker'. The following passage, which I would argue can be criticized for its excessive optimism (a character that we will find again later), should nonetheless provide enough of a reason to support the hypothesis of a persistence of class analysis in Gorz's reflection: 'In contradistinction to the working class, this non-class [of non-workers] has not been engendered by capitalism and marked with the insignia of capitalist relations of production. It is the result of the crisis of capitalism and the dissolution of the social relations of capitalist production – a process stemming from the growth of new production technology. The negativity which, according to Marx, was to be embodied in the working class has by no means disappeared. It has been displaced and has acquired a more radical form in a new social area. As it has shifted, it has acquired a new form and content which directly negate the ideology, the material base, the social relations and the juridical organisation (or State form) of capitalism. It has the added advantage over Marx's working class of being immediately conscious of itself; its existence is at once indissolubly subjective and objective, collective and individual.' Ibid., 68.

However, we cannot infer from this that *operaismo*'s and Gorz's perspectives on the refusal of labour coincide. In the words of Franco 'Bifo' Berardi: 'Gorz's position is very different from the operaist hypothesis of the refusal of labour. Indeed, refusal of labour indicates the workers' stubborn deconstruction of the capitalist castle which aims at rearranging and redefying the boundaries that separate labour and the firm, breaking down and recombining the collective body of work. It does not mean the realization of a work-free paradise. The hypothesis of Italian *operaismo* and André Gorz's utopian post-work hypothesis are two different perspectives. However, they should not be considered as in opposition.' Franco 'Bifo' Berardi, 'La congiura degli estranei', *Carmilla*, 27 October 2007, carmillaonline.com.

68   In this series of events, we can find further proof of the fact that the origins of politicization of the ecological crisis in Italy are to be found in workers' struggles. According to the architect and city planner Alberto Magnaghi, for instance, the bulletin of the Autonomous Assembly of Porto Marghera, *Lavoro Zero*, can be considered the first ecologist magazine in Italy. See *Futuro Anteriore*, ed. Guido Borio, Francesca Pozzi and Gigi Roggero (Rome: DeriveApprodi, 2002); and Guido Borio, Francesca Pozzi and Gigi Roggero, *Gli operaisti* (Rome: DeriveApprodi,

Whereas the workers' mobilization in the previous year was mainly connected to wage egalitarianism, 1969 marks at once the emergence of factory councils and the transition from the critique of the division of labour to the issue of the types of goods to be produced and, more generally, to social reproduction. This is a turning point. Indeed, in 1966, the 'price' of the poisons generated by the petrochemical sector had regularly been at the centre of union negotiations. In the spring of 1967, CGIL did not sign the hazard pay agreement that had been signed by CISL and UIL.[69] What can be thus observed is 'the first attempt to find solutions other than the plain and simple "monetization" of risk, so starkly at odds with the demand for full dignity of the workers'.[70] For the union, then, it is a matter of fighting against noxious conditions through contractual means. As Trentin put it:

> The issue of physical and mental health, against any form of compensation in wages or 'monetisation' of its degradation, to the point of evolving in many factories into the practice of genuine self-protection, both individual and collective, drawing impulses from the interaction between organised workers and the field of medical science and setting a new course for research in occupational medicine . . . All these events would remain inexplicable were they not linked to a true transformation of the contractual cultures and the practices of demand in the Italian trade union movement.[71]

The 1969 contract, in effect, contains the idea of a maximum acceptable concentration (MAC) of hazardous substances. However, 'the MAC=0

2005). *Lavoro Zero* was distributed for the first time in 1973. It would later become a magazine and from 1977 would be complemented by a weekly insert called 'Controlavoro – Foglio del Comitato proletario territoriale' (Counterlabour – a Paper of the Proletarian Committee of the Territory).

69   CIGL: Confederazione Generale Italiana del Lavoro (Italian General Confederation of Labour); CISL: Confederazione Italiana Sindacati Lavoratori (Italian Confederation of Workers' Union); UIL: Unione Italiana del Lavoro (Italian Labour Union).

70   Gilda Zazzara, *Il Petrolchimico* (Padu: Il Poligrafo, 2009), 45.

71   Bruno Trentin, *La città del lavoro: Sinistra e crisi del fordismo* (Milan: Feltrinelli, 1997), 27–8.

position – no harm, ever, in the factory – bogs down in complex technical-scientific discussions and must soon be corrected in "socially acceptable MAC"'.[72] The United Federation of Chemical Workers in Italy (FULC, comprising CGIL, CISL and UIL) accepts the plan for managing hazardous substances by means of innovation and maintenance. Therefore, it proposes the remediation of old plants and the adoption of new, low-impact technologies.

By contrast, Potere Operaio uses the condemnation of noxiousness as a leverage to advance a radical critique of the system of wage labour which 'consumes human life piece by piece. It is upon the impossibility to be indemnified, more visible in the case of noxiousness, that one of the toughest cores of the political thought of that time is built.'[73] Indeed, in the words of Augusto Finzi (militant in Potere Operaio), 'what is noxious [*nocivo*] is having to go to work every morning, noxious is following the rhythms, the modalities of production, noxious is working a shift, noxious is going home with a wage that forces you day after day to go back to the factory'.[74] In this case, the objective is the refusal of the labouring condition understood as the kernel of the overall capitalist system. Such a refusal, in turn, paves the way to attempts at modulating the application of science to production in opposition to the logic of value:

> Workers are not against machinery, but against those who use the machines to make workers toil. To those who say that working is necessary, we answer that the quantity of accumulated science (see for instance the expeditions on the Moon) is such that it could instantly reduce labour to a mere accessory to human life, rather than conceiving of it as 'the very reason for human existence'.[75]

It is worth highlighting here that this conception perfectly aligns with the roots of 1970s ecological thought that, according to Gorz, is to be found

---

72   Zazzara, *Il Petrolchimico*, 51.

73   Devi Sacchetto, 'Esperienze di classe', in *Quando il potere è operaio*, ed. Devi Sacchetto and Gianni Sbrogiò (Rome: Manifestolibri, 2009), 221.

74   Augusto Finzi in Zazzara, *Il Petrolchimico*, 46.

75   Porto Marghera Workers' Committee, 'Il rifiuto del lavoro', in Sacchetto and Sbrogiò (ed.), *Quando il potere è operaio*, 162.

in the rupture between *more* and *better* (in the language deployed so far: the growing divorce between the logic of value and the logic of wealth).[76] In other words: the productive potential has expanded to such a point that an increase in socially necessary labour time no longer corresponds to an increase in material well-being. Hence, it is necessary to reduce working hours, confine the wage-institution to minimum requirements and increase the time available for autonomous activities. Thus, the refusal of labour is nothing but a pedagogical procedure that entails learning to live without having to sell one's own labour power (or buying that of others).[77] Here we enter Gorz's paradigmatic utopia: the civilization of liberated time.

For the moment, I want to signal that, even though the fault line between liberation *of* work and liberation *from* labour is far from being merely ideological, the inability to find inclusive forms of struggles underpins the epochal defeat of the workers' movement starting from the second half of the 1970s, a defeat in which we are still deeply immersed (especially in Italy). As Nanni Balestrini and Primo Moroni put it:

And thus the effect of restructuring has been, for the most part, exploitation, dependence and a ruinous political division between employed and unemployed. This has only been the case because, over the course of the 1970s, the revolutionary movement failed to bring its programme of workers' leadership of the internal process of productive transformation to its apex. Union mediation and extremism confronted each other over this point without finding a final outcome, which would have been the generalized reduction of working hours, i.e. the redistribution of socially necessary labour time; in other words, workers' power over the conditions of post-industrial transition, over the conditions of de-industrialization and the transformation of the entire world of production.[78]

---

76   See Gorz, 'Ecology and Freedom', *passim*.
77   Cf. Stevphen Shukaitis, 'Learning Not to Labor', *Rethinking Marxism* 26: 2, 193–205.
78   Balestrini and Moroni, *The Golden Horde*, 443.

I will return to this passage in the last chapter of this book because I believe that reopening a discussion concerning the saturation of the field of possibilities that, thanks to social and ecological struggles, emerged between 1968 and 1973 is a necessary step in order to establish a dialogue not only between Marxism and degrowth, but also more generally between social and environmental justice.

5

Nature as a Direct Element of Valorization: Cognitive Labour and Financialization in the Green Economy

I believe it is an epochal necessity for capitalism to abandon old products and invent new ones . . . Only the environmental issue can nowadays provide a strong push on products. Capital needs environmentalism in order to reach the frontier of a new industrial revolution.

Sergio Bologna, 'Emarginazione e ambientalismo'

At the end of the previous chapter of the book, we saw that the 'Long 1968' ended with an undeniable failure. Indeed, the aim of replacing the logic of value with a plural logic of wealth was not achieved. Rather than shaping a form of workers' power over the qualitative composition of production – within a framework that had profoundly changed, as we will see – there emerged capital's tremendously violent reaction: fragmentation of labour, dismantling of the welfare state and accelerated financialization (starting from the US unilaterally abandoning the gold standard in 1971). However, it must be noted that the defeat of that cycle of struggles was peculiar and also entailed a significant change in the structure of capitalist valorization, which increasingly became detached from labour-time as its unit of measurement. What developed was a situation where increasing exploitation and diffused class violence coexisted (and still coexists) with an unprecedented potential for emancipation. As Gorz observed, the wage-earning society entered a crisis, 'but we are exiting backwards from it and walking (still backwards) into a civilization of free time, incapable of visualizing and desiring that civilization, and thus incapable of *civilizing* the free time which is coming our way'.[1]

The aim of this chapter of the book is the analysis of this constitutive ambivalence from the point of view of the transformations of the labour-nature-value nexus. The main theme is that, with the language and rhetoric of the 'green economy', the ecological crisis starts being thought of *also* as a field of capitalist development, thus no longer *only* as a moment of blockage, as pure cost or as an unwanted yet necessary collateral effect. The causes of this shift must be found in phenomena such as the increased relevance of cognitive labour ('cognitivization') and the financialization of the economy, which are based on the becoming-productive of the sphere of social reproduction. Such phenomena, in turn, derive from the modifications in class composition during the 1970s and 1980s. The first section of this chapter will analyse these aspects.

The second section, on the other hand, will deal with the entirely new transition originating from these processes. It is true that nature has never been external to the capital relation, yet the theory of value posited nature as the 'limit' or 'enabling boundary' of value itself. In such a context, knowledge served as a connector between the productive needs that oriented value (abstract social labour) and the reproductive sphere to which

---

1   André Gorz, *Capitalism, Socialism, Ecology*, trans. Chris Turner (London: Verso, 1994 [1991]), 45. In this regard, see Lapo Berti's lucid analysis: 'The world imagined by Marx and then by Keynes, a world where most of the work intended to the reproduction of men and society is done by machines, and where men see the time they have to dedicate to their labour drastically reduced, is getting dangerously nearer. Dangerously because, on the contrary, we perceive as extremely distant – we cannot visualise them – institutions able to govern a world where the necessary labour time is severely reduced, and potentially nullified, but where paradoxically humanity's ability to secure means of subsistence and all that offered by an immense production apparatus is attached exactly to that necessary labour. And this paradox generates another one, even more terrible, that is, the time thus liberated does not bear any freedom, but only an increase in needs. The more scientific and technological development instilled in the regime of these machines frees human lifetime from the burden of labour, the poorer humanity will get.' Lapo Berti, *Accelerated Fantasies: An Emergency Exit for the Left?*, trans. Ettore Lancellotti, Letizia Rustichelli and Paolo Davoli (Rizosfera, 2017), 50 (translation modified).

it ended up being applied (abstract social nature). What we see here is thus a dualist logic in which society (understood as an active entity) operates on the environment (understood as a passive entity). The transformations of capitalism following the crisis of Fordism radically modify this structure. They generate a space of valorization within which work-knowledge (or labour-information) is not applied *onto* nature as a limit but, rather, shapes it as a direct element of the value logic.[2] Alongside the 'classic' labour-nature-value nexus, we are dealing here with the rise of a 'new' nexus based on the exploitation of different types of labour that are not necessarily remunerated with a wage – cognitive and/or reproductive labour, work drawn into financial whirlpools. The key expression of this novel labour-nature-value nexus is the *green economy*. The type of exploitation it performs is no less violent than that which occurs within the wage relationship. Moreover, the productive potential of labour expressed in the green economy is manipulated to the point of concealment, just as it happened with wage labour originally – indeed, it was Marx who 'discovered' surplus value and, with it, both the *potentia* of labour power and the discrepancy between its value and its price. The green economy, therefore, incorporates at once the potential of social labour, now finally aware of the entropic dimension of the wage-institution, and its capitalist manipulation, which is to say, its forced reduction to the logic of value, characterized by the imperatives of accumulation and growth. In other words: the becoming-productive of social reproduction reveals the *negentropic potential of work* at the very heart of valorization processes, not only within the sphere of reproduction, as Ariel Salleh suggests with the concept of 'metabolic value', but also within production itself. However, the capitalist need to accumulate infinitely and grow irreparably wastes such a potential. The negentropic capacity of work, in fact, could be fully expressed only by virtue of a simultaneous double movement: replacing the logic of wealth to the logic of value and reducing social metabolism, two conditions that are incompatible with the capitalist mode of production. The seventh and final chapter will examine in more details this political indication that strives to reconcile a certain strand of Marxism with a certain form of degrowth.

---

2   A concrete example of this shaping process, related to the markets for CO_2-equivalent emission trading, will be presented in the next chapter of the book.

Ecology and Class Composition

The main subjective figure underpinning the factory-based struggles described in the previous chapter is undoubtedly the 'mass worker' (*operaio massa*), which is the generic worker positioned on the assembly line, devoid of specialized skills, assigned to perform repetitive tasks within a productive process that is increasingly parcelled out and automated. Workers of this type were capable of expressing in their struggles an element of inflexibility that, on the one hand, provided the foundations for welfare gains but, on the other hand, marked workers' (partial) participation in Fordism as an entropic device (yet without direct responsibilities). As mentioned before, the attempt to thoroughly overturn the logic of value failed. However, it remains true that it was the social opposition of the mass worker (in its connection with a more general anti-authoritarian uprising) that lent political visibility to the ecological dimension, laying the groundwork for its transition from being a collateral effect of development mechanisms to a significant element of the post-industrial form of the capitalist mode of production. Put differently, here I want to reframe in an environmentalist sense the central theoretical core of Italian *operaismo*, which is that the driving force behind capitalist development is to be found in the innovative character of working-class conflict, in the generative dimension of its antagonism. Of course, this does not erase the defeat, but it shows how social struggles profoundly modified the historical conditions of the labour-nature-value nexus, which should thus be approached from the perspective of class composition. It is certainly not by chance that the first in Italy who explored in depth the relationship between class composition and ecology were the operaist thinkers contributing to the journal *Primo Maggio*.[3] As early as 1977, Sergio Bologna speculated that an important shift was occurring within the processes of mutation in class composition. Influenced by feminism and environmentalism, the multifarious needs for self-management started moving from the new

----

3   See Cesare Bermani (ed.), *La rivista 'Primo Maggio'* (Rome: DeriveApprodi, 2010).

metropolitan subjectivities towards the factory through the emergence of a new social figure, namely the 'disseminated worker', a figure that is subsequent but not antithetical to the mass worker.[4] Within this framework, Bologna lamented the dearth of importance that the 1977 movement seemed to attach to environmental degradation.

Unfortunately, there are many Marxist comrades who consider the hypothesis of biological destruction as millenarian and smile at any mention that reminds them of 'ecology'. Seveso[5] and many other cases reminded us that the era of biological destruction, of irreversible processes, has already begun and our children are born and grow up in this era. What is underway is a process representing something more horrifying than fascism. The political system, represented by local authorities, has been totally complicit with the productive structures that have set this process in motion.[6]

---

4   Antonio Negri, by contrast, would use the term 'social worker' (*operaio sociale*), which emphasizes even more its irreconcilability with the mass worker. In his words: 'Instead of increasing profit, restructuring consolidates the crisis in the presence of a further massification of abstract labor, socially diffused living labor, which is predisposed to struggle . . . An overwhelming hypothesis then begins to take shape: *the category of the "working class" goes into crisis, but as the proletariat it continues to produce all the effects that are proper to it on the social terrain as a whole* . . . The proletarian once made himself into the worker, but now the process is inverted: the worker makes himself into the tertiary worker, the socialized worker, the proletarian worker . . . We have seen the mass worker (the first massive concretization of the capitalist abstraction of labor) produce the crisis. Now we see restructuring, far from overcoming the crisis, unfolding and lengthening its shadow over the whole of society'; Antonio Negri, *Books for Burning: Between Civil War and Democracy in 1970s Italy*, trans. Arianna Bove, Ed Emery, Timothy S. Murphy and Francesca Novello (London: Verso, 2005 [1997]), 125–6. See also Steve Wright, *Storming Heaven: Class Composition and Struggle in Italian Autonomist Marxism* (London: Pluto, 2002), ch. 7 in particular, 152–75; and Daniele Ilardi, 'La classe tra primo e secondo operaismo: operaio massa e operaio sociale a confronto', *Effimera*, 18 July 2017, effimera.org.

5   For a thorough analysis of the incident at the ICMESA chemical plant in Seveso in 1976, see Laura Centemeri, *Ritorno a Seveso: Il danno ambientale, il suo riconoscimento, la sua riparazione* (Milan: Mondadori, 2006).

6   Sergio Bologna, 'La tribù delle talpe', *Primo Maggio* 8, 1977, 8.

Primo Maggio's reflections on environmentalism continued into the 1980s, ultimately leading, in 1987, to the first critical formulation of the elective affinity – representing the cornerstone of the green economy – between economic management of the ecological crisis and capitalist valorization.[7] More specifically, Sergio Bologna suggested not to limit the analysis of environmentalism to its relationship with revolutionary subjectivities but, rather, to expand the analytical focus to critically and pragmatically include the possible proximity between capital's needs and the protection of the biosphere. Starting from the premise that the financial element of surplus value production had become particularly tied to the military-industrial complex, Bologna noted that civilian production suffers from a crisis of competitive obsolescence that could only be alleviated by a decisive injection of product innovation (and not just process innovation, as happened in the past). This leads to what was mentioned in the epigraph of this chapter, namely the (capitalistic) necessity to appropriate environmentalism, and environmental issues, to trigger a new industrial revolution.[8]

It is important to note here how Bologna approaches this kind of 'revolution from above' with great caution, as he interprets it in its inherent ambivalence. If it were to be accompanied by the utopian dimension that emerges from the new working condition (diffused, territorial, multi-level), then such a revolution could lead to the creation of new products and the establishment of a new way of working, which would mark the end of Fordist workers' 'indifference' towards the use values they themselves produce. However, if the revolution failed to strongly emphasize the necessity of this inclusion of workers in the decision-making centre of production, then 'it will be an aborted revolution or merely an incentive to social cooperation and productivity *tout court*'.[9]

Apart from the obvious observation that the second aspect of this ambivalence has ultimately weighed far more heavily than the first in the

---

7   Cf. Sergio Bologna, 'Operaismo e i "nuovi movimenti" in Germania', *Primo Maggio* 19–20, 1983–4, 41–9; and Jussi Raumolin, 'L'uomo e la distruzione delle risorse naturali: la *Raubwirtschaft* all'inizio del secolo', *Primo Maggio* 26, 1986–7, 25–33.

8   See Bologna, 'Emarginazione e ambientalismo', *Primo Maggio* 27–8, 1987–8, 38.

9   Ibid., 42.

three decades that have passed since the publication of the article just discussed, another trait should be highlighted as well. The importance of this thesis lies primarily in its ability to structure the labour-nature-value nexus outside of the opposing frameworks that would conceive of ecology and capitalism either as essentially irreconcilable or as purely super-imposable. In this regard, as early as the end of the 1980s – though the recommendation remains as relevant as ever – Riccardo Bellofiore warned against

> reproposing a red-green version of the theory of collapse. Rather, the real problem is to identify new forms of conflict to both drive and navigate the processes of capitalist change in which one could continue the struggle against exploitation. It is also essential to abandon the illusion that the destruction of the environment today, like the market anarchy of the past, reveals alleged insurmountable contradictions within capitalism.[10]

These considerations open up the possibility to address, beyond any determinism, the topic of a new potential articulation of the labour-nature-value nexus. Such an articulation should thus be thought (and acted upon) by considering the underlying tendencies and dynamics of capitalist development, while also not losing sight of the terrain of poten-tial emancipation it unfolds. That this potential is currently mystified by the rhetoric of the green economy should not overshadow the fact that the contemporary condition of (disseminated) workers finds in it the oppor-tunity to influence the qualitative composition of production *beyond* the logic of value. In short, diffused workers still inhabiting productive terri-tories, which are marked by processes of 'multiplication of labour', must find the opportunity to have their voices heard on *what, how* and *where to produce*, based not on apocalyptic threats but on the inalienable right to build a desirable future (also from an environmental point of view).[11]

---

10   Riccardo Bellofiore, 'Il rosso, il rosa e il verde: Considerazioni inattuali su centralità operaia e nuovi movimenti', *Quaderni del CRIC* 3, 1988, 21.

11   Sandro Mezzadra and Brett Neilson have proposed a remarkable investiga-tion into contemporary living labour from which emerges a multiplied image of

This means that, within the growing divorce between the logic of value and the logic of wealth, there is space for both the intensification of deregulated exploitation and the development – to be politically constructed and consolidated – of new forms of liberation *of* work and *from* labour. Therefore, there are no required outcomes, but only scenarios whose actual realization will be the result of class struggle in the twenty-first century, a struggle of which the ecological crisis is an essential part.

Cognitive Capitalism and the Becoming-Productive of Social Reproduction

Let us take a step back and pose the following questions: under what conditions can the ecological crisis become the focus of a new industrial revolution marked by sustainability? How can an obstacle to valorization morph into a mechanism for capitalist development? I believe the answer to these questions lies in the *peculiar defeat* of the so-called Long 1968, which is to say, in those processes of restructuring and innovation that have their roots in the post-1973 capitalist offensive but that start to be fully realized only midway through the 1980s. Until then, indeed, no one could have imagined a 'developmental' exit – in terms of accumulation – from the environmental problem. In particular, I will refer to two phenomena to which Gorz paid great attention in the final phase of his theoretical work: cognitive capitalism and the growing weight of financial markets in the overall economy – without leaving behind their intertwined relationship, which Mauro Turrini, referring to the biotechnological sphere, aptly

---

global working practices. First, labour intensifies and tends to progressively colonize people's time of life. Second, it diversifies and follows the expansion of the needs that characterized so-called globalization. And, finally, labour becomes increasingly heterogeneous from the standpoint of the legal and social regimes of its organization. This tripartite fragmentation is 'reshaping labouring lives and conditions across the diverse spaces and scales of capital's global operations, but it produces very different concrete assemblages of employment and unemployment, misery, subsistence and exploitation, flight, refusal, and struggles'. Sandro Mezzadra and Brett Neilson, *Border as Method, or, The Multiplication of Labor* (Durham and London: Duke UP, 2013), 92.

defines as the 'financialisation of scientific discovery'.[12] In point of fact, it is from the unfolding of these processes that the crisis of the 'classic' labour-nature-value nexus – based on the subordination of the reproductive sphere to the productive sphere, as we said – witnesses the emergence of a new mode of articulation among these three terms, characterized precisely by the overcoming of that historical-categorial foundation.

It should be noted from the outset that nature as a direct element of valorization *does not* replace nature as a condition for value production. Rather, it complements it and, in doing so, constitutes an appendix or a supplement that is at times well integrated and other times generating friction. The specific modality of their relationship thus takes the semblance of what Luigi Pellizzoni suggests calling 'nested problematisation'.[13] Within the 'classic' labour-nature-value nexus, a problem arises historically, whose solution (in theory) is a constrained rearticulation of that very nexus, which thus takes on a dual form that is not always easy to harmonize.

Let us now turn to cognitive capitalism, an issue that both Gorz and Italian *operaismo* have revisited (while updating it) from a famous and prophetic passage in Marx's *Grundrisse*, known as the 'Fragment on Machines'. Given its crucial importance, it is worth quoting extensive excerpts from it.

The exchange of living labour for objectified labour – i.e. the positing of social labour in the form of the contradiction of capital and wage labour – is the ultimate development of the value-relation and of production resting on value. Its presupposition is – and remains – the mass of direct labour time, the quantity of labour employed, as the determinant factor in the production of wealth. But to the degree that large industry develops, the creation of real wealth comes to depend less on labour time and on the amount of labour employed than on the power of the agencies set in motion during labour time, whose 'powerful effectiveness' is itself in turn out of all proportion to the direct labour

---

12   Mauro Turrini, 'Introduction', in *Biocapitale: Vita e corpi nell'era del controllo biologico*, ed. Mauro Turrini (Verona: ombre corte, 2016), 16.

13   Luigi Pellizzoni, *Ontological Politics in a Disposable World: The New Mastery of Nature* (Farnham: Ashgate, 2015), 7.

time spent on their production, but depends rather on the general state of science and on the progress of technology, or the application of this science to production . . . In this transformation, it is neither the direct human labour he himself performs, nor the time during which he works, but rather the appropriation of his own general productive power, his understanding of nature and his mastery over it by virtue of his presence as a social body – it is, in a word, the development of the social individual which appears as the great foundation-stone of production and of wealth. The theft of alien labour time, on which the present wealth is based, appears a miserable foundation in face of this new one, created by large-scale industry itself . . . Nature builds no machines, no locomotives, railways, electric telegraphs, self-acting mules etc. These are products of human industry; natural material transformed into organs of the human will over nature, or of human participation in nature. They are organs of the human brain, created by the human hand; the power of knowledge, objectified. The development of fixed capital indicates to what degree general social knowledge has become a direct force of production, and to what degree, hence, the conditions of the process of social life itself have come under the control of the general intellect and been transformed in accordance with it. To what degree the powers of social production have been produced, not only in the form of knowledge, but also as immediate organs of social practice, of the real life process.[14]

Two brief considerations on this extraordinary passage: first, following Adelino Zanini, it is important to highlight that, by disentangling the 'powerful effectiveness' of the general intellect from labour-time, what emerges is the potential autonomy of general social knowledge, which implies the priority of knowledge as a productive force over value.[15] Second, drawing on an insight from Paolo Virno, it seems relevant to note that, in the crisis of Fordism, the general intellect ceases to be identified

---

14   Karl Marx, *Grundrisse: Foundations of the Critique of Political Economy*, trans. Martin Nicolaus (London: Penguin, 1993), 705–6.

15   See Adelino Zanini, *Filosofia economica: Fondamenti economici e categorie politiche* (Turin: Bollati Boringhieri, 2005).

with the development of fixed capital and instead becomes a fundamental character of living labour.[16] It is against this backdrop that Carlo Vercellone formulates the hypotheses of cognitive capitalism and of a new configuration of the division of labour whose essential character is represented by 'the hegemony of *savoirs* in a process of diffused intellectuality and the driving role of the production of knowledge by means of knowledge'.[17] Such a novel configuration is made possible by a dual process: on the one hand, by the rise of a mass intellectuality linked to the extraordinary increase in levels of education and the democratization of teaching; on the other hand, by the decentralization of the mechanisms for the circulation of knowledge that was made possible by a series of innovations – from personal computers to the World Wide Web – in the field of Information and Communication Technologies. As recently suggested by researchers involved in the European project D-CENT (Decentralised Citizen ENgagement Technologies), this dual process 'since the 1980s has played a role comparable to that of the steam engine during the first Industrial Revolution'.[18]

There are two elements in the hypothesis of cognitive capitalism that are of particular interest for our purposes. The first concerns the 'crisis' of the *law of value-labour time*, the mode of valorization we analysed in the previous chapters. According to Vercellone, this mechanism of

---

16   Cf. Paolo Virno, *A Grammar of the Multitude: For an Analysis of Contemporary Forms of Life*, trans. Isabella Bertoletti, James Cascaito and Andrea Casson (Los Angeles, CA: Semiotext(e), 2004).

17   Carlo Vercellone, 'Elementi per una lettura marxiana dell'ipotesi del capitalismo cognitivo', in *Capitalismo cognitivo: Conoscenza e finanza nell'epoca postfordista*, ed. Carlo Vercellone (Rome: Manifestolibri, 2006), 40. Specifically, there are three historical roots of cognitive capitalism: 'the opposition to the scientific organisation of labour'; 'the expansion of the collective services and insurances of welfare'; 'The constitution of a diffuse intellectuality developing from the "democratisation of education" and a rise in the general level of training', see Carlo Vercellone and Alfonso Giuliani, 'An introduction to cognitive capitalism: A Marxist approach', in *Cognitive Capitalism, Welfare and Labour: The Commonfare Hypothesis*, ed. Andrea Fumagalli, Alfonso Giuliani, Stefano Lucarelli and Carlo Vercellone (Abingdon, Oxon: Routledge, 2019), 23.

18   D-CENT, 'Managing the Commons in the Knowledge Economy', 2015, dcentproject.eu.

valorization, which is essentially based on labour-time as the measure of value produced socially, only represents a determinate historical variant of the more general *law of surplus value*, which remains valid since it decrees that surplus labour is to be considered as the basis of the formation of profit and rent, without anticipating the specific modalities through which this surplus labour actually generates profit and rent. As Vercellone puts it,

> The origin and historical significance of the law of value-labour time are directly tied to the configuration of the capital-labour relationship that emerges in the wake of the Industrial Revolution and to the logic of real subsumption of labour under capital. From this perspective, the law of value-labour time appears as the concrete expression of the drive to discipline and to abstraction the very content of labour, where the clock, and later the stopwatch, became the ultimate instruments for quantifying the economic value generated by labour, prescribing its operational modalities, and increasing its productivity.[19]

By contrast, in the new reality produced by the hegemony of the cognitive dimension of capitalism, the circuits of valorization rather concern themselves with capturing the general intellect or intercepting the positive externalities that are produced by what Yann Moulier-Boutang defines, following Gabriel Tarde, as the 'invention power' inherent in social cooperation.[20] In the current conditions, to cite Vercellone one last time, 'labour measured by the time spent in and validated by the business enterprise is often no more than a fraction of the actual social time of labour. *Here we enter into the realm of the beyond-measure [fuori misura].*'[21]

This approach does not negate but rather *expands* the hypothesis that labour is the source of value. Indeed, alongside wage labour, there emerge new forms of social activity that appear to be productive even though they

---

19   Carlo Vercellone, 'Lavoro, distribuzione del reddito e valore nel capitalismo cognitivo: Una prospettiva storica e teorica', *Sociologia del lavoro* 115, 2009, 36.

20   Yann Moulier-Boutang, *Cognitive Capitalism*, trans. Ed Emery (Cambridge: Polity, 2011 [2007]).

21   Vercellone, 'Lavoro, distribuzione del reddito e valore nel capitalismo cognitivo', 38.

cannot be measured with labour-time. In other words, the crisis of the wage-earning society has led to a *broadening of the base of accumulation* that, in turn, has resulted in a *metamorphosis of the concept of labour as understood within capitalism.*[22] This sort of reshuffling is predominantly related to a fundamental issue: the *valorization of the sphere of social reproduction*, both in its elements traditionally tied to wages (though not perfectly equivalent to them) – such as consumption and savings – and in its dynamics that were once considered 'unproductive' (relational/ affective/communicative spheres, education, natural environment).

From this point of view, we need again to highlight the foundational role of the feminist critique of political economy. Questioning the subordination of the reproductive moment to the productive one is, indeed, the necessary condition for analysing the post-wage scenarios we are facing. One should therefore speak of the *feminization of work* not so much to indicate 'the quantitative increase of the female labour force at the global level' but rather, and above all, to define 'the *quality* of contemporary work . . . the paradigmatic character of the role that women play in the global economy'.[23] Contemporary work progressively adopts *care* as a reference model and tends to display typically 'feminine' traits – affective, relational, oriented towards sharing and so on. Put differently, the separation between the *accounted* productive sphere and the *invisibilized* reproductive sphere has completely collapsed. Today, 'subjectivity and relationships, passion and affect, traditional characteristics of the private and reproductive sphere of human existence have become fundamental resources in the world of commodity production'.[24] This shift, whose novel character is fairly evident, is neatly grasped by Melinda Cooper and Catherine Waldby: 'these debates [on reproductive labour in the 1970s] were eventually disabled by their attachment to an industrial model of labor and valorization and their inability to conceptualise forms of productive activity that did not involve expenditures of metric time or produce

---

22   See Federico Chicchi, Emanuele Leonardi and Stefano Lucarelli, *Logiche dello sfruttamento* (Verona: ombre corte, 2016).

23   Cristiana Morini, *Per amore o per forza: Femminilizzazione del lavoro e biopolitiche del corpo* (Verona: ombre corte, 2006), 49.

24   Alisa del Re, 'Produzione/Riproduzione', in *Lessico Marxiano* (Rome: Manifestolibri, 2008), 149.

tangible commodities'.[25] A paradoxical consequence of this centrality of reproduction is that, in the era of an identifiable crisis of wage labour, actual working time expands disproportionately and ends up overlapping with the time of life, making these two temporalities almost indistinguishable.[26]

This is the backdrop against which another question Gorz posed in his 2003 book titled *The Immaterial* comes into play: can cognitive capitalism fully appropriate a type of economy predominantly based on knowledge? If so, under what conditions? Now, that such an appropriation was indeed possible became clear as early as the appearance of the *dot-com* speculative bubble in the late 1990s, and it remained clear even after it burst in 2001, so much so that Gorz wrote,

> To treat knowledge as capital and as a means of production is, ultimately, to reduce the whole of human activity – all cognitive, aesthetic, relational and bodily capacities, etc. – to instrumental activities of production, that is to say to capitalist productivism and its indifference to contents. The paradigm of production for production's sake and accumulation for accumulation's sake is simply extended from the field of commodities and capital to that of innovation and of knowledge-productive-of-productive-knowledge, regarded as an end in itself with no concern for the orientation and sense of that accumulation. It is from this angle that cognitive capitalism is an extension of capitalism while at the same time perverting the specificity of the social relations of knowledge.[27]

I would say that the general framework here is described correctly. However, Gorz's analysis assumed that the knowledge economy, as based on a type of good that is not subject to scarcity and thus is abundant and free, inherently carried an oppositional element in relation to processes of commodification and, therefore, undermined the long-term stability

---

25   Melinda Cooper and Catherine Weldby, *Clinical Labor: Tissue Donors and Research Subjects in the Global Bioeconomy* (Durham and London: Duke UP, 2014), 105.

26   Andrea Fumagalli, *Bioeconomia e capitalismo cognitivo: Verso un nuovo paradigma di accumulazione* (Rome: Carocci, 2007).

27   André Gorz, *The Immaterial: Knowledge, Value and Capital*, trans. Chris Turner (Calcutta: Seagull, 2010 [2003]), 95.

of cognitive capitalism.[28] In other words, '[s]o-called cognitive capitalism *is* itself the crisis of capitalism'.[29] Now, I believe that this hypothesis was excessively optimistic even when it was formulated. Perhaps what played a role were the good health of alter-globalization social movements and of free software circles. At any rate, Gorz's hypothesis cannot in any way be offered in the current phase. This is due not only to the increasingly widespread diffusion of degrading forms of digital Taylorism but also (and most importantly) to the emergence of so-called *platform capitalism* – based on Information and Communication Technologies (ICTs) – which embodies a mode of organizing exploitation based on the expropriation of an immense amount of data produced by the interconnected collectivity carried out by a few monopolistic companies (Amazon, Apple, Google, Facebook, Microsoft).[30] In this regard, it is worth remembering that the 'big data' fuelling these companies hold value that is proportional to the vastness of the databases. Individually, user profiles are worth little to nothing.[31] According to some analysts, the information produced by the digital activities of millions of people (mostly outside their working hours) is to capitalism what oil was to late nineteenth-century capitalism – specifically, the capitalism of the Second Industrial Revolution.[32] Moreover, the production of information appears as not remunerated. While it generates value, it is neither acknowledged nor accounted for. Morini concludes the following:

> The extraction of value from reproductive processes enabled by online interactions allows the system to remain firmly intact and to ignore

---

28   André Gorz, 'Economia della conoscenza, sfruttamento dei saperi', *Etica e Politica* 19: 3, 2019 [2007], 115–26.

29   Gorz, *The Immaterial*, 55.

30   On Taylorism, see Carlo Formenti, *La variante populista. Lotta di classe nel neoliberismo* (Rome: Derive Approdi, 2016).

31   Cf. Emiliana Armano, Annalisa Murgia and Maurizio Teli (eds), Platform Capitalism *e confini del lavoro negli spazi digitali* (Milan: Mimesis, 2017); Benedetto Vecchi, *Il capitalismo delle piattaforme* (Rome: Manifestolibri, 2017); and Nick Srnicek, *Platform Capitalism* (Cambridge: Polity, 2017).

32   See 'Fuel of the Future: the Data Economy', *The Economist* 423: 9039, 6 May 2017, economist.com; and Ben Tarnoff, 'Silicon Valley siphons our data like oil', *Guardian*, 23 August 2017, theguardian.com.

issues related to the crisis of wage measurement or the decline in consumption driven by mass precarity and impoverishment. The application of technologies to the reproductive process allows the most immediate and direct form of socialisation of labour ever seen, along with the resulting profits without the need for too many mediations, especially those related to wages.[33]

Incidentally, the error in Gorz's hypothesis regarding the inherent irreducibility of the knowledge economy to cognitive capitalism should not, in my opinion, lead us to throwing the baby out with the bathwater. The tensions between those two categories remain, but the outcome of their interaction depends on the political development of class struggle, not on the intrinsic characteristics of one or the other. Put differently, the widespread and multiplied working potential that is being valorized in a myriad of ways today certainly has the possibility to politically challenge the commodification of knowledge in its various forms. Indeed, the growing divide between the logic of value and the logic of wealth makes it increasingly unlikely that the Fordist pact will be revived in new forms, thus the appeal of quantitative growth is constantly reduced and, conversely, the likelihood of direct confrontation increases. However, such a challenge cannot take place but through direct conflict.

Let us return to the issue of platform capitalism. My hypothesis is that the general intellect, i.e. a form of productive work that is not necessarily waged, lies at the foundation of the data that serve as the raw materials for digital accumulation. This profoundly modifies the 'classic' nature-labour-value nexus, as it is precisely through the general intellect that nature moves from the sphere of reproduction to that of production, thereby becoming a direct element of valorization. This is a crucial shift because it shows that labour in a generic sense is not exiting the circuit of valorization. Rather, what is being reduced, though by no means exhausted, is the relevance of waged labour. The type of nature valorized

---

33   Cristina Morini, 'Divenire donna del lavoro e maschilizzazione dell'esclusione: Gratuità, crisi del modello salariale e della divisione sessuale del lavoro', in *Salari Rubati: Economia politica e conflitto ai tempi del lavoro gratuito*, ed. Francesca Coin (Verona: ombre corte, 2017), 67.

within cognitive capitalism is essentially information, a blend of environment and collective knowledge. It is not the tree, the ocean or the soil themselves but their potential to absorb carbon dioxide in keeping with the needs of financial markets; not the seed but the genetic sequence that makes it resistant to a particular pesticide produced by the biotech industry. Therefore, there is a leap of abstraction in the contemporary labour-nature-value nexus, which, however, does not negate but rather supplements the 'classic' one. As Daniel Bensaïd aptly highlighted, 'The incommensurability between market values and ecological values ["wealth", in the terms developed in this book] marks one of the historical limits of the capitalist mode of production.'[34]

In the next chapter of the book, this point will be illustrated in more detail through the example of 'carbon commodities', namely the commodities produced by 'carbon markets'. We can, however, already highlight its conditions of possibility. In order to establish a significant connection between a weather event – no matter how extreme – and global warming, a large-scale mobilization of the general intellect in its various forms (i.e. the different knowledge factories: universities, think tanks, counterarguments advanced by social movements, etc.) is invariably required.

This new relationship between knowledge, ecology and exploitation – a direct outcome of the 'new' labour-nature-value nexus – can be briefly illustrated referring to what Melinda Cooper calls 'bioeconomy'. The term defines the capitalist attempt to extract surplus value directly from living organisms and relies entirely on the scientific 'de-standardization' of these organisms that is aimed at their 'manipulation'.[35] The entrance of the logic of profit into biotechnological practices (both medical and agricultural) is clearly evident in the gradual disappearance, starting from 1980s, of the distinction between *discovery* and *invention* in the context of patentability of biological material. Until then, 'discovering' meant bringing to light objects that existed in nature but were previously

---

34   Daniel Bensaïd, *The Dispossessed: Karl Marx's Debates on Wood Theft and the Right of the Poor*, trans. Robert Nichols (Minneapolis, MN: University of Minnesota Press, 2021 [2007]), 56.

35   Melinda Cooper, *Life as Surplus: Biotechnology and Capitalism in the Neoliberal Era* (Seattle, WA: University of Washington Press), 31ff.

unknown, while 'inventing' referred to the creation of something that had not existed before. A patent could be granted only to objects belonging to the latter category. In that year, however, the Supreme Court of the United States – in the well-known case of *Diamond v. Chakrabarty* – authorized the extension of intellectual property rights to genetically modified forms of life (which were thus neither completely natural nor entirely artificial).[36] The boundary between nature-as-discovered and artifice-as-invented became blurred, as demonstrated by the case of Roundup Ready soybeans – designed by Monsanto, the world leader in the Genetically Modified Organisms (GMOs) sector. As Cooper points out, commenting on Monsanto's decision to shift its core business from agricultural chemistry to biotechnology,

> The commercial calculus was straightforward – instead of profits from mass-produced chemical fertilizers and herbicides, the agricultural business would displace its claims to invention onto the actual generation of the plant, transforming biological production into a means for creating surplus value. Moreover, it was predicted that biotechnology would expand the geological spaces open to commercial agriculture, making it possible to create plants that would survive on arid land or flourish in the degraded environments created by industrialized agriculture. Indeed, according to some prognoses, life itself would soon be put to work to remediate all kinds of industrial waste – from chemical pollutants to nuclear fallout (so-called bioremediation).[37]

Monsanto's economic success, which began commercializing Roundup Ready soybeans in 1996, clearly demonstrates that, in the context of the 'new' labour-nature-value nexus, exploitation occurs not *on* nature-reproduction but *through* it, *by virtue of* its becoming productive. The general intellect permeating biotechnological practices brings the environment into the very core of the valorization process. Specifically, it does so by blurring the boundaries between artificial and natural, between production and reproduction, and between abstract social labour and

---

36   Sheila Jasanoff, *Designs on Nature: Science and Democracy in Europe and the United States* (Princeton: Princeton UP, 2005).

37   Cooper, *Life as Surplus*, 23.

abstract social nature. Such indistinctness is well illustrated by the ambiguous notion of 'substantial equivalence'. In order to be quickly distributed on the market, GMOs must be deemed suitable by the relevant institutions, such as the Food and Drug Administration (FDA) in the United States or the Food and Agriculture Organization (FAO) at the UN. This means that the genetically modified products must have metabolic and protein profiles that are compatible with the range of variation displayed by the biochemical profiles of natural seeds. In such cases, the former are declared 'substantially equivalent' to the latter. This procedure, already problematic in itself, becomes paradoxical when one starts considering the issue of intellectual property rights. Indeed, given the legal impossibility of patenting a living organism in its natural form, biotech companies like Monsanto have developed a complex discursive apparatus that, by bending the deployment of the general intellect to their advantage, allows them to claim the criterion of substantial equivalence with the FDA while simultaneously asserting precisely the opposite, the criterion of sufficient difference, with the United States Patent and Trademark Office (USPTO).

The identical and the different coexist in this type of nature shaped in the image and likeness of capital. In this context, it becomes clear that it is not the environment as such that produces value, but, rather, the blend of nature and labour/knowledge (exploited general intellect) that allows these commodities to swing between the registers of the artificial and that of the natural, depending on the convenience of those who control the balance of power relations. Hence, we can now see the difference between the abstract social nature that Moore speaks of and this type of nature that is 'mixed' with labour/knowledge. The first is appropriated by capital, while the second is exploited. As Sandro Chignola has put it, 'nature is re-semanticised in linguistic-communicative terms, which is to say, as a sequence of information. Like a grammar. And it is on this materiality . . . that a significant transformation in the regimes of capital accumulation is simultaneously grafted.'[38] To conclude: using Marxian terminology in a technical sense, one could say that the *exploitation of nature* is a very recent phenomenon.

---

38   Sandro Chignola, 'Vita, lavoro, linguaggio: Biopolitica e biocapitalismo', *Euronomade*, 20 October 2015, euronomade.info.

Financialization of the Economy and Ecological Crisis

To better understand the specific modalities of this type of exploitation, we must first focus on the process of financialization and, subsequently, on its elective affinity with the so-called market-based management of the ecological crisis – meaning, as it will be soon shown, the green economy. Therefore, what should we understand by financialization? I believe that the most effective definition remains the one proposed by Stefano Lucarelli:

> First of all, financialization can be defined as the diversion of domestic economy savings to stock market shares. Ever since the 1980s, the American economy has been characterized by the process of financial market liberalization and the consequent explosion of new financial tools: thus the passage from a Keynesianism built on a pact between producers in an environment of a monetary system that binds currency and financial manoeuvres – already weakened by president Nixon's declaration of the inconvertibility of the dollar to gold in 1971 – to a financial Keynesianism based on private deficit spending, in which the largest financial market deregulations are accompanied by the diminution of social incomes distributed by the welfare state.[39]

This refers to a series of practices through which businesses, institutions and citizens end up being drawn into the vortex of financial transactions. This results in a situation where virtually *everything* depends on unstable markets traversed by volatile currencies – from food to services, from education to income. It is objectively difficult to think of productive activities that are not somehow caught up in financial flows: from the diffusion of pension funds to microcredit that embeds people in poverty,[40] from the

---

39   Stefano Lucarelli, 'Financialization as Biopower', in *Crisis in the Global Economy: Financial Markets, Social Struggles, and New Political Scenarios*, ed. Andrea Fumagalli and Sandro Mezzadra, trans. Jason Francis McGimsey (Los Angeles, CA: Semiotext(e), 2010), 125.

40   Marco Fama, *Il governo della povertà ai tempi della (micro)finanza* (Verona: ombre corte, 2017).

growth-driving role of mortgages in the real estate sector to the blatant power wielded by rating agencies over national governments, and the increasing reliance on private debt to bridge the gap between falling wages and steady cost of living. Also, it should be pointed out that the instability of these markets is not at all an unintended side effect, but, rather, a tool of political governance and social control by virtue of which finance gradually and in progressively deeper ways influences the circuits of value.[41] It is no coincidence that finance links the creation of petro-dollars during the oil shocks and their subsequent use in the debt economy – which emerged during the 1980s and was supported by the infamous Structural Adjustment Programmes imposed by the International Monetary Fund on many countries in the Global South – to the processes of globalization, and finally to the great crisis of 2007–8 in which we are still dramatically immersed.[42]

Ultimately, the attempt is to extract value from incorporating every aspect of social life into the financial sphere. As Christian Marazzi has observed,

> The thesis that is being put forth here is that financialization is not an unproductive/parasitic deviation of growing quotas of surplus-value and collective saving, but rather the form of capital accumulation symmetrical with new processes of value production . . . Apart from the role of finance in the sphere of consumption, what happened in these last 30 years is a veritable metamorphosis of production processes of this very surplus-value. There has been a transformation of valorization processes that witnesses the extraction of value no longer circumscribed in the places dedicated to the production of goods and services, but, so to speak, extending beyond factory gates, in the sense that it

---

41   See Stefano Lucarelli and Emanuele Leonardi, 'Financial Governmentality: Wealth-Effect as a Practice of Social Control', in *The Global Financial Crisis and Educational Restructuring*, ed. Michael Adrian Peters, João M. Paraskeva and Tina Besley (New York: Peter Lang, 2015), 91–120.

42   See Midnight Notes Collective, 'Oil, Guns and Money', in *Midnight Oil: Work, Energy, War 1973–1992* (New York: Autonomedia, 1992), 3–22; and George Caffentzis, *In Letters of Blood and Fire: Work, Machines, and the Crisis of Capitalism* (Oakland, CA: PM Press, 2013).

enters directly into the sphere of the circulation of capital, that is, in the sphere of exchanges of goods and services. It is a question of extending the processes of extracting value from the sphere of reproduction and distribution – a phenomenon, let it be noted, for a long time well known to women.[43]

What does such a finance-dominated regime of accumulation have to do with the 'new' labour-nature-value nexus that emerged alongside the 'classic' one with the crisis of Fordism? Let us recall two key points of the analysis. First, financial markets exert direct control over contemporary capitalist production. Second, what made the attempt to integrate ecological objectives and creation of profit 'thinkable' was the economic background shaped by the struggles of the 1960s and 1970s. The connection between these two elements entails that, in today's scenario, the management of the environment as a direct element of valorization – rather than as an obstacle to it – is largely ensured by finance. For instance, the creation of the Dow Jones Sustainability Indices (DJSI) in 1999, and most importantly their success, reveal how large multinational corporations are seeking to reinvent ecological challenges by transforming them into sources of competitiveness.[44] This pervasive marketization of the environment by means of financial instruments represents the real face of the shift – as a raising level of abstraction – from considering *nature as a limit* to seeing it *as a driver* of value.

---

43   Christian Marazzi, 'The Violence of Financial Capitalism', in Fumagalli and Mezzadra, *Crisis in the Global Economy*, 36–7. It is worth noting here that the late Gorz agrees entirely with this analysis, as expressed in the following article: 'Penser l'exode de la societé du travail et de la marchandise', *Mouvements* 50, 2007, 95–106.

44   The DJSI provide a system of global measurement of corporate sustainability based on the so-called triple bottom line, which evaluates economic performance along three axes, namely monetary, social and environmental. The performance of these indices are often deployed to confirm the so-called Porter hypothesis, which suggests that economic competitiveness and environmental protection are not mutually exclusive, but rather complementary. In particular, the indices appear to indicate a positive correlation between the adoption of good environmental management practices (Corporate Environmental Governance) and the market value of the companies that adhere to them. See also, John Grant, *The Green Marketing Manifesto* (Chichester: John Wiley & Sons, 2007).

From the viewpoint of financial handling of the ecological crisis, I would like to focus on a 2008 article published by Paul Mills, Senior Economist of the International Monetary Fund, titled 'The Greening of Markets'. Referring specifically to the fight against climate change, Mills lucidly outlines the role that, in his view, financial markets can play. Firstly, they support various *mitigation* strategies (i.e. the reduction of greenhouse gases to a given level of economic activity), both by optimizing the trading of emission permits and by allocating investments towards 'clean' technological innovations, those that are focused on increasing energy efficiency rather than labour productivity. Secondly, financial markets enable the reduction of *adaptation* costs – the costs associated with reacting to the adverse effects of global warming – at once through incentives for shifting investments towards new, zero-impact (or, at least, low-impact) sectors of production and strategies for the reduction of financial risk linked to weather-related hedge funds. The mitigation aspect is crucial in demonstrating how the management of climate change is increasingly being translated into the grammar of value, while the adaptation aspect is particularly interesting in that it comprises a set of hybrid instruments (both financial *and* ecological), such as weather-derivatives and catastrophe bonds (CAT bonds).

Weather derivatives aim to price and make tradable both the scientific uncertainties and the social fears related to global warming. Catastrophe bonds, on the other hand, are a form of insurance that, at least theoretically, should pre-emptively reduce the risks of natural disasters and thus protect vulnerable sectors such as agricultural areas or coastal properties. In his article, Mills extensively discusses both limitations and potentialities of these financial instruments. He notably does not hide the constant political support they require to function properly. However, in the overall economy of our discussion, it is sufficient to highlight the conclusions of his argument:

It seems likely that financial markets will play an integral role in climate change mitigation and adaptation in the future. Securities markets will reward those companies that successfully develop or adopt cleaner technologies. Cap-and-trade [the establishment of an emissions cap alongside the simultaneous possibility of purchasing pollution quotas] seems to be becoming the mitigation policy of choice in high income countries, in which case the global market in permits for GHG emissions is likely to become the largest global commodity market. Although weather derivatives and CAT bonds do not offer a complete panacea—as yet, only hedges against weather and catastrophe risks are available out to five years—recent rapid innovation and deepening in these markets prompt optimism that they will continue to innovate and further help adaptation to climate change.[45]

Of course, none of this has materialized in the decade since Mills's prediction. Yet his projections perfectly capture the deep connection between finance and ecology, their elective affinity (of a neoliberal nature). Finance has become the chief governance mechanism through which ecological challenges are transformed into opportunities aimed at the creation of surplus value. What demonstrates this is the experience of the world's largest climate market, the European Union Emissions Trading System. Between 2005 and 2012, when trading was limited to the compliance market – i.e. defined by the cap on emission permits – the results were nothing short of disastrous, both economically and ecologically. Though only from an economic perspective, things improved once very special commodities such as emission permits were allowed to be traded on secondary markets – those including riskier financial instruments (particularly derivatives).[46] As Sarah Bracking wrote: '*The game itself* [climate politics] *is financialised.*'[47]

---

45   Paul Mills, 'The Greening of Markets', *Finance and Development* 45: 1, 36.

46   To my knowledge, the best critical definition of what a derivative is has been provided by Brian Holmes: 'The idea was that all risks, including collective ones, should be made into saleable products, formatted for the market by private actors in search of a profit. Yet although it is saleable, the derivative cannot be understood as an ordinary commodity of the industrial era. Marx described the commodity as that product of human labour whose exchange value, seemingly animated with a life of its own, acts to render invisible the social relations that produced it. Derivatives, however, have nothing directly to do with production; instead they are conceived to manage the environmental risks that weigh on the future of speculative activity. In this sense they are *meta-commodities* that govern the unfolding of the contemporary economic model.' Brian Holmes, 'Is It Written in the Stars? Global Finance, Precarious Destinies', *ephemera* 10: 3/4, 230.

47   Sarah Bracking, 'The Anti-Politics of Climate Finance: The Creation and Performativity of the Green Climate Fund', *Antipode* 47: 1, 2015, 296. See also by the

Green Economy: Exploitation and Manipulation of Cognitive Labour in Biomimicry

The most evident consequence of the converging impact among cognitive shift, becoming-productive of social reproduction and processes of financialization on the 'classic' labour-nature-value nexus is the emergence of the *green economy* during the 1990s. The green economy is defined by its ability to internalize the ecological constraints not as a limit to development, but as a novel opportunity for valorization and a cornerstone of a new accumulation cycle. To simplify, one could say that the green economy represents a radicalization of the principle of *sustainable development*, which held that effective governance could be achieved by politically balancing economic growth, environmental protection and the will to ensure a liveable planet for future generations. In other words, what sustainable development (as formulated in the well-known Brundtland report of 1987)[48] sees as a negotiation scenario in which the intended outcome is the result of self-imposed limitations that are distributed among the involved actors, the green economy transforms into a positive-sum game. This entails a situation where the pursuit of self-interest by various actors naturally leads to the achievement of different goals. Business, environment and future humans: it looks like everyone wins with the green economy!

But what exactly *is* the green economy? In short, two things: a theory of environmental economics based on the crucial function of *eco-efficiency* and a theory of capitalist *eco-development* founded on the combination of nature and labour/knowledge. Essentially, the green economy assumes that the pressure of economic activity on nature depends on three factors: i) scale growth (*how much* is produced); ii) the qualitative composition of productive structures (*what* is produced); iii) technological development

---

same author, 'Performativity in the Green Economy: how far does climate finance create a fictive economy?', *Third World Quarterly* 36: 12, 2015, 2337–57. Some of these aspects will be analysed further in the next chapter of the book.

48   See Brundtland Commission, *Our Common Future* (Oxford: Oxford UP, 1987).

(*how* production is organized). As for the first factor, the constraints of the 'classic' labour-nature-value nexus are unavoidable. Indeed, if the scale of productive activity increases, the pressure of the economy on the environment inevitably increases as well. However, the other two factors, which together are defined as the *aggregate coefficient of environmental impact per unit of Gross Domestic Product* – could potentially counterbalance (or even overcompensate) the negative effects of the first. Put differently, if this coefficient decreases at a rate faster than GDP growth, then the environmental pressure of economic growth can progressively diminish.[49]

The tools developed to achieve the goal of reducing the aggregate coefficient of environmental impact are essentially two: i) appropriate environmental policies that would restructure both demand and supply in a 'green' direction; ii) suitable innovation policies that would discourage high-impact technologies and support those that enhance energy efficiency. In this regard, we can observe a shift from eco-efficiency – which essentially only patches up the 'social organisation of waste'[50] – to eco-development. For the green economy to function effectively, in point of fact, energy savings must represent and serve as a springboard for a *radical transformation of the productive structure*. In the words of Ignazio Musu, 'environmental innovations requiring specific support policies are not so much the "incremental" ones, which merely improve existing technologies by increasing their efficiency, but rather the "radical" innovation that alter the technological regime'.[51] Enzo Rullani explained with great clarity under what conditions such radical innovation becomes conceivable:

> Today's industrial economy has transformed into a network economy and knowledge economy. This is an economy that generates economic value by promoting the flexibility of networked organisations, individual creativity, and collective intelligence, and concentrating them

---

49   See Ignazio Musu, 'Crescita economica: una sfida alla sostenibilità', in *Natura e capitalismo: un conflitto da evitare*, ed. Pierluigi Ciocca and Ignazio Musu (Rome: Luiss UP, 2013), 59–93.

50   Piero Bevilacqua, *Il grande saccheggio: L'età del capitalismo distruttivo* (Rome-Bari: Laterza, 2011), 34.

51   Musu, 'Crescita economica', 78.

around a few key ideas shared by many people and companies, which assign (monetizable) value to certain meanings and experiences ... Today [compared to Fordism], producing value requires something else. And more. This is so not only to minimise dissipation to the bare minimum, but also to create meanings, experiences, and qualities that, in terms of value, compensate for the negative value produced by the dissipation that is technically necessary. Besides, innovations that make the use of knowledge more efficient, flexible, and creative no longer rely on playing the (dissipative) card of wasting environmental resources, once considered abundant and cheap. Rather, they move in the opposite direction: they tend to 'enlist' the environment as a resource to be valorised and translated into positive meanings, recognised by markets and thus shared and exchanged among the various interested producers and consumers.[52]

In order to grasp the specific operation of the green economy – namely, the transformation of the ecological crisis from an obstacle to a driver of value – it is necessary to address the presence of a *negentropic potential* in contemporary production, which, in Rullani's terms, is the element enabling the process for 'overcompensating' the technically necessary dissipation. 'Enlisting' the environment in the valorization process means precisely this. Alongside this potential, however, we can also find the concealment of its source, which is to say, cognitive and/or reproductive labour that is drawn into financial vortexes. It is because of this that in the introduction I referred to Negri's term of 'reasonable ideology' to define the green economy: it is both *adequate* to the current regime of accumulation and, at the same time, *manipulative* with respect to the type of labour that produces value within such a regime. It is only in this coexistence of adequacy and manipulation that we can understand why the green economy is doomed to fail. On the one hand, it exploits a type of labour that cannot be reduced to the logic of value and the wage-form, but, on the other hand, it maintains the accumulation of capital and quantitative economic growth as unquestionable objectives. In other

---

52   Enzo Rullani, *Modernità sostenibile: idee, filiere e servizi per uscire dalla crisi* (Venice: Marsilio, 2010), 135.

words, the green economy is caught up in an irreconcilable tension. To succeed, it would have to renounce to grow and accumulate (since reproduction, now turned productive, can no longer be conceived as subordinate, infinite and free). Yet, given that accumulation and growth are the green economy's very reasons for existing, it cannot afford to do so. Every good practice that is linked to eco-efficiency, therefore, transforms into an investment in eco-development that has to be measured in quantitative terms. Sooner or later – more often sooner than later, as we will see in the next chapter of the book – the short-circuit between environmental preservation (i.e. a form of wealth) and profit (the essence of valorization) inexorably comes to light.

The negentropic work that the green economy simultaneously mobilizes and represses is incompatible with the Fordist scheme, no matter how revised. Being rooted in reproduction during the epoch in which reproduction itself had become central, negentropic work reveals the growing divorce between the logic of value and the logic of wealth. 'Liberating' it thus requires at once the abandonment of the capitalist imperative of accumulation and growth, and the recognition of a shrinking of social metabolism as a key goal – whose level has long been hypertrophic and incompatible with a good life for all the inhabitants of planet Earth.

In the final chapter, I will enquire in more depth into the theme just mentioned. Before that, however, I would like to provide an example of how the manipulation of cognitive labour in the green economy reconfigures the idea of nature and its relationship with political economy, in a way that is far from neutral. Specifically, I will focus on the concept of biomimicry, which has been discussed since the 1990s in circles linked to the green economy. Initially, this concept tended to express a strong opposition to the dissipative growth models that were typical of industrial-Fordist capitalism and to the pro-fossil lobbies that resisted a more or less sustainable revision of its operating mechanisms. In more recent years, however, the widespread adoption of the green economy as both a business model and a policy framework – epitomized by the approval of the Clean Energy and Security Act by the first Obama administration in 2009 – seemed to have considerably diluted the critical potential of biomimicry. With Donald Trump's election to the White House and his strategy to revive the fossil industry, the fortunes of this notion are certainly at risk of receding, at least in the United States. However, what remains is a considerable economic relevance built over more than two decades of implementation. According to Biomimicry 3.8, the most important consultancy in the field, 'it is estimated that by 2030, bio-inspired [*sic*] goods and services will generate $1.6 trillion in global GDP. Drawing from the powerful intelligence of evolutionary processes – which have been ongoing for 3.8 billion years – we have collaborated with more than 250 companies to provide them with competitive advantages through biomimicry.'[53]

Apart from the trends in its reception, what is important to show here is the silent paradox upon which the concept of biomimicry rests. In itself, abstracted from its material context, it appears rather linear and almost self-explanatory: given the unsustainable levels of pollution and con-sumption of non-renewable resources, the industrial system is, first, destined to economic unsustainability (a soaring increase in the prices of raw materials) and then, inescapably, to collapse. This happens because the system, in its artificiality, does not heed the feedback from environ-mental factors. According to Janine Benyus – an important voice within the array of reflections on biomimicry – it is less a matter of negligence than of *oblivion*. The industrial system has indeed forgotten the nine explanatory keys that illuminate the 'laws, strategies, and principles of nature':

Nature runs on sunlight / Nature uses only the energy it needs / Nature fits form to function / Nature recycles everything / Nature rewards cooperation / Nature banks on diversity / Nature demands local expertise / Nature curbs excesses from within / Nature taps the power of limits.[54]

This forgetfulness could be resolved by conceiving of productive systems as living systems, in such a way that the former would 'imitate' the latter and thereby free themselves (as much as possible) from the very concept

---

53   See 'What is biomimicry!', 2016, biomimicry.net.

54   Janine M. Benyus, *Biomimicry: Innovation Inspired by Nature* (New York: HarperCollins, 1997), 7.

of 'waste', which, as is well known, does not exist in nature.[55] Therefore, it is necessary to change perspective and base it on a model that 'is not reliant on linear processes that are indifferent to waste; rather, on circular processes ("cradle to cradle"), which reuse waste by getting inspiration from the most effective and efficient biological system we have ever encountered: nature'.[56] A precise articulation of the link between green economy and biomimicry is advanced by Paolo Ricotti, heterodox economist who has dedicated the last years of his research to this issue:

> In the green economy there is full awareness of operating with high strategic and competitive value. Also in nature there is strategy, intelligence, capability of action in any observed case in point. Also in nature there is competition and, in fact, the fittest and the genetically strongest survives. Or the one who adopts the best procreation strategy . . . The green economy and the social model which it shapes are fully sustainable insofar as their general processes are engrained in a closed-cycle, 'systemic' vision. Such a vision is similar to the natural one, whose basic logics are determined by chemical-physical-biological elements.[57]

As is easily noticeable – beyond a caricatured Darwinism – the arguments put forward are not lacking in a certain reasonableness and simplicity that seem to render them somewhat indisputable: 'nature knows best', so all one needs to do is to imitate procedures and processes to 'return to it', reintegrating the realm of anthropogenic production within the broader

---

55   This is the first principle of the so-called circular economy, an economy designed to regenerate autonomously through the connection of different industrial sectors: the waste from some production could serve as raw materials for others. See Ken Webster, *The Circular Economy: A Wealth of Flows* (Geneva: Ellen MacArthur Foundation Publishing, 2015). For a critical perspective, see Mario Pansera, 'The Origins and Purpose of Eco-innovation', *Global Environment* 4: 7–8, 2011, 128–55.

56   Davide Reina and Silvia Vianello, *GreenWebEconomics: la nuova frontiera* (Milan: EGEA, 2011), 50. See also Aldo Bonomi, Federico Della Puppa and Roberto Masiero, *La società circolare: fordismo, capitalismo molecolare, sharing economy* (Rome: DeriveApprodi, 2016).

57   Paolo Ricotti, *Sostenibilità e Green Economy. Quarto settore* (Milan: Franco Angeli, 2010), 103–4 and 171.

realm of the living. Yet this is not exactly the state of things. Under what conditions, in fact, can it be claimed that natural cycles work 'better' than anthropic-industrial ones? Only under the assumption that we can compare their performances. In other words, it is necessary to transform nature from the material base for the reproduction of living systems into a provider of biological or ecosystem services.[58] Therefore, in order to support biomimicry as a political programme, it is first necessary to have 'economized' the environment, forcibly imprinting the logic of value on it (together with the associated imperatives: to accumulate capital, to grow quantitatively). This is a perfect example of the creation of *neoliberal environments*: one enters into the paradox of proposing a 'return to nature' that is nothing else than another dive into the economistic liquid in which one was already floating.

To demonstrate this, we should consider that, according to the advocates of biomimicry programmes, the main way to act like living systems is to measure and enforce their monetary value. 'Putting a price on nature' was one of the slogans of the *Grenelle de l'environnement*, the ambitious general assembly of the environment-capitalism alliance initiated in 2007 by then French President Nicolas Sarkozy.[59] One of the most interesting points was that, by considering raw materials (freshwater, air,

---

58   In their influential volume titled *Natural Capitalism*, Paul Hawken, Amory Lovins and Hunter Lovins frame the issue of monetarily measuring nature as provider of biological services in the following terms: 'Valuing natural capital is a difficult and imprecise exercise at best. Nonetheless, several recent assessments have estimated that biological services flowing directly into society from the stock of natural capital are worth at least US$36 trillion annually. That figure is close to the annual gross world product of approximately US$39 trillion – a striking measure of the value of natural capital for the economy. If natural capital stocks were given a monetary value, assuming the assets yielded "interest" of US$36 trillion annually, the world's natural capital would be valued at somewhere between US$400 and US$500 trillion – tens of thousands of dollars for every person on the planet. That is undoubtedly a conservative figure given the fact that anything we can't live without and can't replace at any price could be said to have an infinite value.' Paul Hawken, Amory B. Lovins and L. Hunter Lovins, *Natural Capitalism: The Next Industrial Revolution* (New York: Back Bay Books, 1999), 5.

59   See Joseph E. Stiglitz, Amartya Sen and Jean-Paul Fitoussi, *Mismeasuring Our Lives: Why GDP Doesn't Add Up* (London: The New Press, 2010).

virgin forests, minerals, etc.) as 'free commodities', what follows are 'distortions in the marketplace'.[60] Here, we encounter once again the core of the manipulation of cognitive-reproductive work. By transforming the environment from a condition to a direct element of production, it becomes a crucial factor of the process of value creation, thereby opening up fresh opportunities for profit. It is as if capital finally recognized nature as (no longer) being 'unlimited and free of charge' only to shape it in its own image, transforming it into the archetype of a profit-oriented enterprise. Only in this way does it become possible (or even 'natural') to imagine 3.8 billion years of evolution as the immense archive of a corporate research and development department, from which useful information can be extracted for the profitability of capital. This is a perfect example of what Jessica Dempsey calls 'enterprising nature'.[61] In a similar vein, Jesse Goldstein and Elizabeth Johnson show how biomimicry sets in motion a twofold process of enclosure. On the one hand, nature is reduced to intellectual property (an artificial production of scarcity as a strategy for capitalist accumulation); on the other hand, nature ceases to be conceived as a passive entity (raw material or waste receptacle) only to be transformed into an active subject pursuing the logic of value.[62]

In conclusion, I need to hark back to the problem that I will develop in the following chapters, namely the profound ambivalence characterizing the green economy and biomimicry. The crucial question is the following: does their elective affinity with the logic of value render them ecologically and socially useless (if not harmful), or does it merely signal the economic-political background on which struggles for a just transition to sustainability – those struggles connected to the logic of wealth – can be fought? Given that only by connecting theoretical research and conflictual practices can the ambivalence comprised in this question be resolved, for the moment I will limit myself to highlighting the emergence of a new field

60   Hawken, Lovins and Hunter Lovins, *Natural Capitalism*, 15.

61   Jessica Dempsey, *Enterprising Nature: Economics, Markets and Finance in Global Biodiversity Politics* (Oxford: Wiley, 2016), 10.

62   See Jesse Goldstein and Elizabeth Johnson, 'Biomimicry: New Natures, New Enclosures', *Theory, Culture and Society* 32: 1, 2015, 61–81.

of analysis. If the critique of classical political economy aimed at demystifying the bourgeois attempt to *naturalize capitalism*, today's ecological critique of value must also be able to dismantle the financial attempt to *capitalize nature.*

6

For a Critique of Carbon Markets: Historical and Economic Notes on the Peculiar Commodification of the Climate

Offsets are not like products that you can touch or feel. I might sell you an offset for planting a tree, but how do you know that I have not also sold that offset to someone else?

James Kohm, associate director of enforcement at the US Federal Trade Commission's Bureau of Consumer Protection

If we zoom into a category and question the relations stabilising its inside we are confronted with ontological politics. It is a politics about what kind of carbon is constructed and, eventually, emitted into social and economic reality.

Ingmar Lippert, 'Carbon classified? Unpacking Heterogeneous Relations Inscribed into Corporate Carbon Emissions'

The aim of this chapter of the book is to show how global carbon markets constitute an example of the 'new' labour-nature-value nexus that emerged from the becoming-productive of social reproduction (cognitivization of labour and financialization of the economy). In particular, I argue that, within carbon markets, nature acts as a direct element of value creation and not merely as an internal limit (as was the case with the 'classical' labour-nature-value nexus). I also draw attention to the fact that this production of value, contrary to the promises of the carbon trading dogma, is not in the least accompanied by an improvement in environmental quality. Rather, 'green' valorization further undermines planetary health. Indeed, as Carlo Vercellone puts it, 'far from emancipating itself from the productivist logic of industrial capitalism, cognitive capitalism subsumes it, reproduces it, and extends it, leading to a dramatic rupture of those balances that are necessary for the reproduction of the ecosystem'.[1] This means that the negentropic potential of contemporary work – the true original element engendered by the green economy – is defused and obscured by the profit imperative and ultimately deprived of its emancipatory force. In the final chapter of the book I will advance the hypothesis that this 'incapacitation' of reproductive work unmistakeably illuminates its constitutive irreducibility to the logic of value. However, this does not mean that it cannot be commodified, or that its mere presence prevents capitalist dynamics from functioning. The data in this chapter show the exact opposite. Perhaps less ambitiously, I would argue that for contemporary work to become a lynchpin in the strategy of ecological conversion of society, the logic of value must necessarily be replaced by the logic of wealth.[2] It is on this basis, which entails placing conflict at its core, that a convergence between a certain version of Marxism and a certain strand of degrowth can come into being.

Before embarking on our analysis, it is necessary to reiterate that the 'new' labour-nature-value nexus does not replace the 'classical' one but, rather, emerges beside it. To put it schematically, one could thus characterize the current relationship between capitalist accumulation and the environment as in the following. To the extent that the 'classical' nexus continues to perform the function of a *condition of value*, the pressure on the biosphere can assume two forms: accumulation by dispossession, as described by David Harvey,[3] and accumulation by contamination as discussed by Giacomo D'Alisa and Federico Demaria. While the former

---

1 Carlo Vercellone, 'André Gorz: reddito social garantito ed ecologia politica', *Etica e politica* 19: 3, 2017, 150.

2 The need for such a replacement does not in any way imply that the logic of wealth is a preconceived strategy simply awaiting implementation. Rather, it presents itself as a field of tensions that is inherently open to multiple interpretations of what precisely the centrality of use-value politically means.

3 David Harvey, *The New Imperialism* (Oxford: Oxford UP, 2003).

responds to the need to ensure, by means of extra-economic violence, the separation of workers from the means of production in order to subjugate areas hitherto outside the capital's reach (such as the privatization of commons or of land grabbing), the latter refers to

> the socialisation of environmental costs through which the capitalist system contaminates the means of subsistence (and existence) of human beings. Indeed, the expanded social metabolism of industrial capitalist economies generates significant consequences on the environment, on people's health, often eradicating subsistence economies which, by contrast, are characterised by a less environmentally destructive metabolism.[4]

Alongside these two forms, which have continued to proliferate in recent years, emerges the novelty constituted by that sphere of the labour-nature-value nexus inscribing the environment into valorization as a *direct element of production* (hence, no longer merely a condition), as an expression of the general intellect, i.e. labour-information. This chapter is dedicated precisely to a particular instance – constitutively linked to climate change – of nature as a direct element of valorization.

Carbon Trading *in actu*: The Kyoto Protocol (1997)

In order to contextualize the analysis of global CO_2 emissions markets, we need to revisit a concept already outlined in the Introduction, that of *carbon trading dogma*. This is defined by the exclusive emphasis placed on the 'saviour role' of the price system, ultimately assuming that, even though climate change configures itself as a market failure – which, in the past, was not capable of adequately accounting for the environmental element, essentially relegating it to 'invisible' negative externalities – it can be effectively addressed only on the basis of further marketization.

---

4 Giacomo D'Alisa and Federico Demaria, 'Alle frontiere del capitale', *Zapruder* 30, 2013, 42–3.

Rather than a rational solution, the application of market logics to global warming thus proves to be an element of a wider regime of truth that renders any alternative, be it political or economic, literally 'unthinkable'. This leads to the emerging idea that 'putting a price on nature' means doing it justice. In other words, the carbon trading dogma prescribes that the creation of new markets exclusively dedicated to 'pricing' climate change determinants will at once unleash a new wave of primitive accumulation and an unprecedented spread of sustainable practices (at least on a formal level). Reformulating a recent proposal by Larry Lohmann,[5] this 'market-as-truth-producer' gives rise to the following dogmatic equation:

climate stability = CO_2 emissions reduction = carbon trading = sustainable economic growth

This shift entirely depends on the emergence of the 'new' labour-nature-value nexus. Framing climate change as a primarily political issue helps clarify this point. As Paul Edwards has suggested, the very visibility of global warming rests on complex and controversial *knowledge infrastructures*, which provide not granitic certainties but rather a sort of informational matrix, in other words, a mixture of nature and general intellect:

Instead of thinking about knowledge as pure facts, theories, and ideas – mental things carried around in people's heads, or written down in textbooks – an infrastructure perspective views knowledge as an enduring, widely shared sociotechnical system. Here is a definition: knowledge infrastructures comprise robust networks of people, artifacts, and institutions that generate, share, and maintain specific knowledge about the human and natural worlds.[6]

---

5   Larry Lohmann, 'The Endless Algebra of Carbon Markets', in *Durban's Climate Gamble: Trading Carbon, Betting the Earth*, ed. Patrick Bond (Braamfontein: University of South Africa Press, 2011).

6   Paul N. Edwards, *A Vast Machine: Computer Models, Climate Data, and the Politics of Global Warming* (Cambridge: MIT Press, 2010), 17.

As mentioned in the previous chapter of the book, no one experiences an atmospheric-planetary event without the support of climate science. Indeed, establishing a link between a weather-related event (no matter how extreme) and climate change is only possible on the premise that the machinery of social knowledge, in its various forms, is effectively set in motion. The same applies to the construction of complex markets for exchanging emission of what could be termed 'pollution rights'.

Against this theoretical background, it may be useful to begin our brief historical excursus by quoting some figures the World Bank provided.[7] In terms of total market value, carbon trading – including both markets with legislative compliance (i.e. linked to maximum emission thresholds set by states) and voluntary ones – amounted to about $10 billion in 2005, then tripling the following year to around $30 billion. The increase in transaction volumes slowed slightly in 2010, only to resume in 2011, despite the severe global economic crisis, reaching the more than remark- able figure of $176 billion. In general terms, despite the frequent collapses of both allowance and credit prices, the market trend has grown at first exponentially and then semi-steadily. Robert Fletcher, analysing three different estimates made by the World Bank, hypothesizes that the aggre- gate value of carbon markets could reach $2–3 trillion by 2020, and then $10 trillion by 2030.[8]

These are clearly significant figures, which is particularly surprising given the young age of these markets. Even though the direct proportion- ality between carbon dioxide levels in the atmosphere and the Earth's surface temperature had been known since the late nineteenth century, the collective realization of the damaging potential of global warming can be dated to nearly a hundred years later. As seen in the previous chapters, the ecological crisis erupts within the 'classical' labour-nature-value nexus but only becomes politically manageable, from the perspective of

------

7   See World Bank, 'State and Trends of Carbon Pricing' (Washington, DC: The World Bank, 2008); and 'State and Trends in the Carbon Markets' (Washington, DC: The World Bank, 2011–12).

8   Robert Fletcher, 'When Environmental Issues Collide: Climate Change and the Shifting Political Ecology of Hydroelectric Power', *Peace and Conflict Review* 5: 1, 2010, 14–30.

capital, with the emergence of the 'new' nexus, which is to say, with the possibility of conceiving its inclusion within the logic of value.

The Intergovernmental Panel on Climate Change (IPCC) was founded in 1988, and in 2007 was awarded no less than the Nobel Peace Prize (together with Al Gore, author of the well-known documentary *An Inconvenient Truth*). Published in 1990, the IPCC's first report produced an intensification of the public debate on climate change and led to the crucial UN Conference on Environment and Development – otherwise known as the Earth Summit – held in Rio de Janeiro in 1992. One of the most significant outcomes of that conference was the international environmental treaty known as the United Nations Framework Convention on Climate Change (UNFCCC), whose primary objective is to stabilize the concentration of climate-changing gases in the atmosphere at a level that can avert harmful consequences. Fundamental to the treaty was its acknowledgement of the principle of common but differentiated responsibilities between 'developed' and 'developing' countries in relation to global warming.[9] Since 1995 (the year following the ratification of the UNFCCC), signatory countries (originally 189, now 196) have met annually at Conferences of the Parties (COPs) to discuss and improve global climate policies.

Held in Kyoto in 1997, COP 3 was particularly important. Here, member countries signed a protocol to the UNFCCC, known as the Kyoto Protocol (KP). Ratified in 2005, the KP is the first legally binding agreement on global warming. It mandates that the thirty-seven countries in Annex I (the so-called developed nations) commit to reducing emissions of six greenhouse gases (an average of 5.2 per cent over the 2008–12 period, with 1990 as baseline year). Though the KP proposes to achieve a global reduction in emissions through a diversified series of instruments (international cooperation, technology transfer, safeguarding the natural carbon sinks), there is no doubt that the fundamental innovation it envisions is carbon trading, i.e. the idea that the allocation and exchange of carbon commodities through market mechanisms represent the most efficient solutions to the climate crisis. In this regard, the KP establishes

9   Due to the impressive development of China – and more generally of the BRICS countries – this principle has been extensively revised by the Paris Agreement in 2015.

three flexibility mechanisms: Emissions Trading (a cap-and-trade system in which public authorities set maximum emitting thresholds and companies trade pollution allowances and credits); the Clean Development Mechanism (which entails the indirect inclusion of Annex II countries in global carbon markets); Joint Implementation (which regulates the trading of credits between Annex I countries).[10] A detailed analysis of the three flexible mechanisms would take us far beyond the purposes of this book. Yet it is sufficient here to point out the fundamental principle of economic theory structuring them, which runs as follows. Trading carbon allowances and credits (i.e. pollution rights) on dedicated markets would simultaneously: reduce the aggregate cost of achieving abatement targets set by the KP; promote sustainable development in non-industrialized countries; and create a positive atmosphere for the growth of green business. In short, what is illustrated here with particular eloquence is the transformation of the question concerning the environment from an obstacle to capital accumulation into an opportunity for the extraction of value.

Plenty has been written about the innumerable flaws of the KP. For instance, an influential and detailed literature review on climate policy has not recorded any reference to actual positive effects of the Protocol on reducing greenhouse gas emissions.[11] In terms of emissions containment,

---

10   In Kyoto, the main alternative to carbon trading (the market-based 'solution') was the carbon tax (the fiscal 'solution'), i.e. the idea of taxing emissions in order to discourage them. It may be worth remembering that the European Union advocated the idea of an emissions tax but had to capitulate in the face of opposition from the US delegation – led by Al Gore and fully committed to the market-led approach – and then found itself in the curious situation of being the only entity to experiment with a cap-and-trade market (George W. Bush's first administration, in fact, did not ratify the KP and did not engage in emissions trading). Ironically, a very similar dynamic occurred in relation to the Paris Agreement: the absence of legal constraints, on the one hand, and the persistence of a market-centred logic, on the other, were undoubtedly victories for Barack Obama's second administration, which hoped in this way to bypass ratification by Congress and galvanize green business. However, with the victory of Donald Trump in the 2016 elections, the US left the Paris Agreement.

11   See Joyeeta Gupta, *The History of Global Climate Governance* (Cambridge: Cambridge UP, 2014).

the rare 'positive' performances are in fact due to the devastating economic crisis that broke out in 2007 and certainly not to the effectiveness of flexible mechanisms. Even the World Bank argued in its report that the KP had produced substantially insignificant outcomes.[12] By contrast, in the period between the signing of the Protocol and its ratification (1997–2005), CO_2-equivalent emissions grew in aggregate by 24 per cent, and then continued to increase in the implementation periods (2005–8, 2008–12 and 2012–present). It should also be noted that the cap-and-trade markets – the most significant of which is the European Union Emissions Trading System (EU ETS) – displayed a certain (economic) resilience only due to the so-called grandfathering, namely the free allocation (not through public auctions, as initially anticipated) of emission allowances by public authorities.[13] Even more serious, and indeed often denounced and sanctioned, is the frequent recourse to fraud and corruption in the context of the Clean Development Mechanism.[14]

Productive Failure of Carbon Markets and Climate Rent

Here we face a curious (if only apparent) paradox. From an environmental point of view – the one giving rise to carbon trading – it can safely be said that carbon markets are useless when they are not harmful. Quite trivially, they either do not achieve their own targets, or even make such achievement impossible. At the same time, from an economic point of view, such markets represent a gold mine for financial operators, as the figures given previously indicate. Thus, it is only fair to ask: do carbon markets work or not? The answer cannot but be multi-layered. Firstly, as Larry Lohmann noted, Michel Foucault's arguments in relation to the French penitentiary system during the Classical Age also applies to these

12   World Bank, 'World Development Report: Development and Climate Change' (Washington, DC: The World Bank, 2010).

13   Carl Knight, 'What is grandfathering?', *Environmental Politics* 22: 3, 2013, 410–27.

14   Larry Lohmann, 'Carbon Trading – A Critical Conversation on Climate Change, Privatisation and Power', *Development Dialogue* 28 (Uppsala: Dag Hammarskjöld Foundation, 2006).

markets – that is, they have constantly been presented as their own remedy. In other words, failure should be considered as a constitutive element of their very deployment.[15] Secondly, there seems to emerge an obvious short-circuit between the (supposed) *ecological goal* and the (actual) *economic means* of carbon markets. For although no environmental improvement has been achieved through carbon trading, a significant amount of value has been created and usually transferred to the shareholders of fossil-intensive enterprises. This is where we can appreciate how deeply entrenched the carbon trading dogma is socially. While its ecological irrelevance has been proven countless times on a practical-empirical level, the assumption of a harmonious compatibility between climate stability and economic growth continues to guide the actions of both legislators and market actors.

Let us clarify the mechanism through which labour-information extracts financial value from global warming while contributing next to nothing to its mitigation. Here, I believe the best definition is *climate rent*, but this needs to be immediately qualified. In classical political economy, rent designates income from land (just as wages come from labour and profit from capital). In this 'classical' context, what distinguishes rent is that it derives from the ineliminable *scarcity* of land as a condition of production, which means that such income is justified solely by the 'luck' of being born a landowner (thus not by skill and effort, as is the case with wages and profit). It is precisely because of this parasitic nature of rent that John Maynard Keynes hoped for the *euthanasia of the rentier*. Things change profoundly with the advent of cognitive capitalism, within which, according to Carlo Vercellone,

> it is the traditional frontiers between ground rent and corporate profit that are increasingly losing their relevance. This blurring of the boundaries between rent and profit finds one of its manifestations in the way

---

15   See Larry Lohmann, 'Financialization, Commodification and Carbon: The Contradiction of Neoliberal Climate Policy', in *Socialist Register 2012: The Crisis and the Left*, ed. Leo Panitch, Greg Albo and Vivek Chibber (New York: Monthly Review Press, 2012); and Michel Foucault, *Discipline and Punish: The Birth of the Prison*, trans. Alan Sheridan (London: Penguin, 1991 [1975]).

the power of finance reshapes the criteria of corporate governance around the exclusive objective of value-creation for shareholders . . . The competitiveness of companies depends less and less on internal economies and increasingly on external ones, that is, on their capacity to capture the productive surpluses generated by the cognitive resources of a given territory . . . Capital appropriates, free of charge, the benefits of society's collective knowledge, as if these were a 'gift of nature'.[16]

It is worth exploring further this passage, given its centrality both in this, so to speak, 'analytical' part of my research and in its more 'political' dimension, which will be addressed in the next chapter. Let us thus follow Christian Marazzi's reasoning:

It could be said that the forms of life innervating the social body [the becoming productive of reproduction, in the terminology of this book] are equivalent to land in Ricardo's theory of rent. Only that, unlike Ricardo's rent, today's rent is assimilable to profit precisely in virtue of financialization processes themselves. Financialization, with its specific logic—particularly the autonomisation of the production of money via money through directly productive processes—is the other face of the externalization of value production typical of biocapitalism. Financialization not only contributes to the production of the effective demand necessary for the realization of the product of surplus-value (i.e., it does not only create the mass of rent and consumption without which the growth of the GDP would be modest and stagnant) but also fundamentally determines continuous innovations and continuous productive leaps in biocapitalism, imposing on all companies—quoted or not—and on the whole of society its hyper-productive logics centred around the primacy of shareholder value.[17]

---

16   Carlo Vercellone, 'Lavoro, distribuzione del reddito e valore nel capitalismo cognitivo: una prospettiva storica e teorica', *Sociologia del lavoro* 115, 2009, 49–50.

17   Christian Marazzi, *The Violence of Financial Capitalism*, trans. Kristina Lebedeva and Jason Francis McGimsey (Los Angeles, CA: Semiotext(e), 2011), 63–4.

It is for these reasons that climate rent (and, more broadly, ecological rent) stands out as the clearest expression of the 'new' labour-nature-value nexus. Indeed, it designates an income that produces value (thus is not parasitic) precisely because it is based on the exploitation of that labour-information that forcibly inscribes nature in the register of (financial) capital – which is to say, it makes it *conform to the imperative of profit*.[18]

Let us now return to carbon markets. One might ask, at this point, why they expose themselves to that peculiar form of *productive failure* described here (environmental irrelevance and economic profitability). A first interpretative hypothesis is to consider the marketization of global warming as a primarily ideological operation. For instance, according to Patrick Bond, the ultimate goal of capital's green rhetoric – based on the unprovable affinity between environmental preservation and economic growth – would be at once to favour the oil industry while deceptively ensnaring social opposition. In short, carbon trading would be little more than a smokescreen aimed at concealing the impossible compatibility – on both logical and historical grounds – between a healthy environment and the capitalist mode of production.[19] It seems undeniable to me that this argument has solid foundations. However, I believe that the plastic-adaptive qualities that capitalism displayed throughout its centuries-long history are equally undeniable. Indeed, following Michel

---

18   See Alberto Pierobon, 'La cosiddetta "finanziarizzazione" dell'ambiente', in *Nuovo manuale di diritto e gestione dell'ambiente*, ed. Alberto Pierobon (Sant'-Arcangelo di Romagna: Maggioli Editore, 2012). Besides, it should be noted that this analysis of climate rent is not universally accepted. For instance, in a compelling article, Romain Felli does not address the thesis of the becoming-rent of profit and therefore conducts an 'orthodox' analysis of carbon commodities, concluding that they are not actual commodities – i.e. they do not incorporate abstract labour – and should therefore be considered as forms of economically parasitic but politically useful rent for maintaining imperialist power relations on a global scale; see Romain Felli, 'On Climate Rent', *Historical Materialism* 22: 3, 2014, 251–80. More generally, an important attempt to bring a critical perspective on contemporary forms of rent, within the field of political ecology, can be found in Diego Andreucci, Melissa García-Lamarca, Jonah Wedekind and Erik Swyngedouw, '"Value Grabbing": A Political Ecology of Rent', *Capitalism Nature Socialism* 28: 3, 2017, 28–47.

19   Patrick Bond, *Politics of Climate Justice: Paralysis Above, Movement Below* (Durban: Kwazulu-Natal UP, 2012).

Callon, it cannot be ruled out in advance that markets are adaptive entities, in that they present themselves not as impenetrable monoliths but rather as social experiments open to improvement.[20] Moreover, it is not clear where a full and unreserved rejection of the link between climate change and the market would lead. Beyond a problematic nostalgia for a non-existent Golden Age that resurfaces from time to time, the greater risk, in my view, is to lose sight of negentropic work, the emergence of its ecological potential (brought about by social struggles) and its neutralization by the logic of value.

So we are back to square one. After these considerations, how is the productive failure of carbon markets justified? I believe that a preliminary element for an adequate answer to this question is to be found in the peculiarly abstract nature of the commodities produced and traded within these markets. As Tamra Gilbertson and Oscar Reyes wrote: 'These [carbon trading's] failings are not caused by teething problems, but are symptomatic of the extreme difficulties of assessing the value of "carbon", which is a commodity which bears little relation to any real-world object.'[21] Similarly, Philippe Descheneau and Matthew Paterson have argued the following:

> While new products such as the iPad are clearly hyped enormously, the hype has some relationship to the (purported) use-value of the object. By contrast, the products in the carbon market have no use-value. The tonne of carbon refers to a tangible unit of measure, but demands for the right to emit it arise purely out of government regulatory activity. The tonne of carbon has thus to be abstracted to something more tangible for market actors, i.e. financial or monetary products. Thus, what is being sold is not the tonne per se but rather the financial or discursive representations of it.[22]

---

20   Michel Callon, 'Civilizing markets: Carbon trading between *in vitro* and *in vivo* experiments', *Accounting, Organizations and Society* 34: 3–4, 2009, 535–48.

21   Oscar Reyes and Tamra Gilbertson, 'Submission to Environmental Audit Committee Inquiry on the role of carbon markets in preventing dangerous climate change', *Carbon Trade Watch*, 2 March 2009, carbontradewatch.org.

22   Philippe Descheneau and Matthew Paterson, 'Between Desire and Routine: Assembling Environment and Finance in Carbon Markets', *Antipode* 43: 3, 2011, 667–8.

These considerations are very important because they show how the relationship Marx established between use value and exchange value requires further investigation, if one wishes to apply it to carbon-commodities. To simplify, Marx can be said to hold that, in a capitalist system, the relationship between use value (the practical utility of an object understood as the quality of the needs it satisfies – that is, a 'natural distinction') and exchange value (the monetary unit of measurement of a commodity understood as the quantity of socially necessary labour-time it contains, namely an 'economic equivalence') takes the form of mutual indifference.[23] Capital does not concern itself with the specific qualities of individual commodities. For the conditions of capitalist circulation to emerge, commodities must be exchangeable on the basis of money as a general equivalent, i.e. as a functional abstraction enabling commensurability between otherwise incomparable commodities. It becomes clear, then, that this interface between use value and exchange value proves unusable when analysing the peculiar commodification of climate. What natural need, after all, is satisfied by 'the financial or discursive representation' of a tonne of carbon-equivalent? Obviously, none. Are we therefore to conclude, with Descheneau and Paterson, that such commodities lack use value altogether? I do not think so, not least because this would imply the absence of any intentionality in the circuits of valorization, effectively diagnosing the economic system as a whole with an irredeemable obsessive-compulsive disorder.

A possible alternative is to call into question the 'new' labour-nature-value nexus, namely to conceive of the use value of commodities as *information* (a mixture of nature and general intellect). As such, this kind of use value would transcend the relationship of indifference between natural distinction and economic equivalence while maintaining a foundational link with it. Indeed, we may ask: what makes climate information 'useful'? Answering this question requires establishing a deep connection between the production of climate information and the carbon trading dogma advocating for a perfect overlap between atmospheric-environmental balance and the logic of value. Against this backdrop, the use value of carbon

---

23   Karl Marx, *Grundrisse: Foundations of the Critique of Political Economy*, trans. Martin Nicolaus (London: Penguin, 1993), 141.

commodities is nothing other than the unquestionable assumption that carbon markets make the transition to a low-emission society more efficient and desirable than any other political strategy. If this is true, then the informational use value of carbon commodities can only exist in so far as it conforms to the carbon trading dogma. Thus, economic equivalence splits and produces a kind of self-indifference of exchange value. We could define such a self-referential twist as a *second-order abstraction*, to differentiate it from the first-order abstraction that marks the transition from use value as a natural distinction to exchange value as economic equivalence. From this follows that the process of 'climate valorization' unfolds in the stratification of 'carbon' as a commodity. For value to be created, diverse sources of social knowledge must be valorized in such a way that the resulting permanent uncertainty enables carbon markets to maintain their exclusive hegemony over other approaches to managing global warming. All this, it is worth repeating, takes place even in the face of the clearest empirical evidence against the effectiveness of these markets.

How to Produce a Certified Emissions Reduction: In the Lab of Carbon Commodities

To better understand the second-order abstraction that is typical of carbon commodities, I will now turn to the production process of Certified Emissions Reductions (CERs), the credit units or offsets that are traded within the Clean Development Mechanism (CDM). Let us take a step back. In the context of KP's flexible mechanisms, whose market-based nature remains intact in the framework of the Paris Agreement, the CDM was structured around two conceptual axes: the positive connotation of economic flexibility and the cost-efficiency of transitioning to a low-carbon economy. Put simply, the only agent deemed capable of effectively tackling global warming is the 'free' market.

Around these two axes gravitate three crucial assumptions, which we might describe as intermediate instruments of the carbon trading dogma: a) reducing emissions at source, where they are actually produced, is inefficient; b) emissions reductions are measured on a plane of perfect commensurability (it does not matter where and when reductions occur:

a tonne of CO_2-equivalent is independent of its space-time coordinates); c) in order for the efforts to de-carbonize the economy to succeed, countries in the Global South must be included in the transitional process. With the possible exception of the third assumption, whose geopolitical nature is self-evident, the truth-value of this framework entirely rests on the unconditional adherence to the aforementioned dogmatic equation. In fact, there is no empirical evidence for market superiority in terms of economic efficiency, nor for the inefficiency of reductions at source, let alone for full commensurability between different forms of emissions.

Therefore, what gives substance to the categorical apparatus of the CDM is the impossibility of conceiving of global warming outside its market-centred dimension. The rhetoric of economic competition functions as a pre-analytical lens through which the ecological question is framed. Beyond its translation into the homogeneous grammar of money, environmental depletion simply does not exist for CDM actors – or, if it does, it is not that important (certainly less so than financial returns on 'investments'). Climate justice movements have widely criticized this centrality of the *lex mercatoria*. First, it has been noted that the low price of CERs has indeed drawn financial interest towards CDM projects, but at the cost of depriving those same projects of their *raison d'être* – namely, incentivizing not speculative investments but policy-driven transitions towards low-carbon productive systems.[24] Second, the recurring and fraudulent practice of 'double counting' was denounced, as CDM participants frequently recorded the expected emissions reduction in two accounting registers (those of the proposing and the host country). The high frequency of this fraudulent practice suggests it should not be treated as an exceptional occurrence. Rather, it should be thought of as a widespread and conscious *modus operandi*, intimately tied to the complexity of project design mechanisms that inherently lend themselves to corruption and fraud.[25] Finally, attention has been drawn to the persistence of colonialist dynamics and

---

24   Mike Childs, 'Privatising the atmosphere: A solution or dangerous con?', *ephemera* 12: 1–2, 2012, 12–18.

25   Larry Lohmann, 'Regulation as Corruption in the Carbon Offset Markets', in *Carbon Trading in Africa: A Critical Review*, ed. Trusha Reddy (Pretoria: Institute for Security Studies, 2011), 139–60.

unbalanced power relations between Global North and Global South. Having exhausted its share of 'pollutable' atmosphere, the North now appears to be colonizing the South's 'climate reserve', thereby also preventing it from experimenting with alternative development trajectories.[26]

In general, these evaluative remarks are more than justified and would certainly suffice to support a full rejection of the CDM as a tool for managing the climate crisis. However, from a theoretical point of view, it is even more instructive to critically examine one of the four prerequisites for the eligibility of CDM projects: *additionality*.[27] In brief, additionality is defined as the difference between the counterfactual estimate of a course of action related to carbon markets (the approval of a given CDM project) and an equally counterfactual scenario based on the hypothetical continuity of past industrialization patterns ('business as usual' [BAU]). Additionality thus measures the 'emissions savings' between two irreconcilable futures: the BAU scenario, marked by global warming as a market failure, and the CDM one, shaped by the carbon trading dogma, which is to say the belief that a new market will redeem the failure of the previous one.

Although apparently simple and straightforward, when subjected to closer analysis the notion of additionality reveals several problematic elements, both technical and conceptual. First of all, it is worth emphasizing how the intricate, highly complex structure of design protocols (in particular, the Project Design Document) produces two major effects. On the one hand, it excludes subjects lacking the necessary skills to navigate through the labyrinths of 'climate bureaucracy', in other words, almost all local communities, which are also supposed to be the actors 'to be developed'. On the other hand, those subjects who do possess such skills tend to move beyond the confines of consultancy work and take on a leading role as investors in carbon markets. Consider, for instance, the

---

26   Heidi Bachram, 'Climate fraud and carbon colonialism: the new trade in greenhouse gases', *Capitalism Nature Socialism* 15: 4, 2004, 1–16.

27   Further requirements, which are nevertheless only formally valid, include: a) compatibility between the project and the host country's sustainable development strategy; b) priority of the environmental dimension over the economic dimension; and c) supplementary of the project with respect to existing environmental policies.

EcoSecurities affair. This company developed a large number of CDM projects, many of which were approved (more than 300 as of 2009). The issue is that the same company is also the most important buyer of CERs, since its primary source of profit lies not in the approval of projects but in the exchange of credits at the financial level. It is therefore not surprising that the risk of a conflict of interest is extremely high.

Nevertheless, I believe that the main problematic issue of the CDM and CERs lies in the conceptual distinction between *financial* additionality and *environmental* additionality. The former expression makes us question whether a given project would have been implemented even without the gain of CERs. In principle – i.e. according to the predicament of the KP (left unchanged by the Paris Agreement) – for a project to be approved, the gain of carbon credits must be the decisive financial factor. In short, the presence of these credits should serve as an incentive for investors to finance a project that, in and of itself, would be perceived as ecologically sustainable but economically unattractive. However, this perspective cannot be reconciled with the logic of (speculative) value, which prescribes financing initiatives with the highest possible profit margin. A new short circuit is thus produced between (supposed) *ecological goal* and (actual) *economic means*. The financial actors of the CDM find themselves in the paradoxical situation of having, on the one hand, to persuade investors of the profitable character of a given project regardless of CERs and, on the other, to convince the members of the CDM Executive Board that without CERs that same project would be financially pointless. As already noted, the carbon trading dogma works by apparent paradoxes that constantly run the risk of becoming ossified.

We encounter similarly serious difficulties when inquiring into the notion of environmental additionality. This expression allows us to thematize the technocratic *sequestration of the future* enacted by the CDM. Indeed, as mentioned before, determining the extent of environmental additionality requires, first, a counterfactual future projection that crystallizes past development strategies – that is to say, BAU – making them unchangeable for the purposes of calculating additionality; second, it requires an equally counterfactual future projection of emissions abatement, should a given CDM project become operational. In other words, as defined according to CDM criteria, additionality is both a *calculating* device (centred on arbitrary quantification procedures) and a *promissory* device ('carbon markets must be trusted for they will undoubtedly open up a better future'). This device functions primarily by means of a *de-politicization of public decision-making*. In order to shape a plane of commensurability between the radiant future based on the production of CERs and the catastrophic future announced by the continuation of BAU, one must first accept a radical presupposition, namely, that only CDM represents an alternative to the nefarious projection of past models of industrialization into the future. In the terminology proposed in this book: only negentropic work subordinated to the logic of value can come after the entropic labour experienced in the context of Fordism.

The corollary of this theorem is no less surprising: the projection of past patterns must be one and *only* one, and it must be calculated on the basis of an otherwise unchangeable present. Put differently, the dark future drawn today by climate change can only be avoided through the proliferation of CERs. It is this new articulation between historical determinism (the past prescribes the future . . .) and market freedom (. . . unless the future itself conforms to economic competitiveness) that signals the presence of the fideistic element of carbon trading dogma at the very root of CERs. Once more, the market is the only agent whose agency is not given as already inscribed in the laws of historical becoming. Yet again: second-order abstractions are the means of production that activate the use value of carbon-commodities. Indeed, it is clear that if placed outside the assumption that only carbon markets can avoid climate disaster, CERs would be revealed for what they actually are: empty stylistic exercises within the logic of value in the era of its increasing divorce from the logic of wealth – in this case, from safeguarding the health and habitability of the planet.

As a final note to this chapter, I would like to briefly linger over how the self-indifference of exchange value mentioned previously warrants the very advanced state of the divorce between the logic of value and the logic of wealth. From a climatic (and, more generally, ecological) standpoint, the more the former logic deepens, the more the latter is eclipsed. It seems appropriate here to indicate that, so long as labour-information is forced to conform to the carbon trading dogma, there will be no escape from the short-circuit between (supposed) environmental goals and (actual) economic means. The result is that the political space for a pact between a reproductive sphere that has become productive and financial capital does not appear to be in sight, even remotely. I will elaborate on this hypothesis in the next chapter. For now, I would simply like to point out that the lack of a mediating space between capital and labour *does not* imply that labour-information is devoid of a potentially positive negentropic dimension in an ecological perspective. It only means that this potential cannot be conveyed in a fully capitalist context. Put differently: for work to play its part in the fight against global warming, it must increasingly free itself from the logic of value – now marked by self-indifference – and instead bind itself to the logic of wealth, to the sustainable production of use values capable of satisfying those needs that societies will democratically decide to define as *fundamental*.

Between Marxism and Degrowth: Shrinking Social Metabolism and Liberating Negentropic Work

> In the future, much more than the simple defence of nature will be required; we will have to launch an initiative if we are to repair the Amazonian 'lung', for example, or bring vegetation back to the Sahara. The creation of new living species – animal and vegetable – looms inevitably on the horizon, and the adoption of an ecosophical ethics adapted to this terrifying and fascinating situation is equally as urgent as the invention of a politics focussed on the destiny of humanity. New stories of the permanent recreation of the world replace the narrative of biblical genesis.
>
> Félix Guattari, *The Three Ecologies*

The purpose of this concluding chapter is to offer some reflections on the political perspectives emerging from the transformation of the labour-nature-value nexus previously outlined. The central hypothesis is that establishing a dialogical space between certain strands of Marxism and certain approaches to degrowth could reopen the Pandora's box of potentials that surfaced between 1968 and 1973 but ultimately remained unfulfilled. This blockage resulted from a set of complex factors, at least three of which warrant a mention: the extremely violent response by capital; the constrained manoeuvring space imposed by the Cold War; and the inability of social movements to unify the various demands presented by disparate political identities into a cohesive strategy.

This final issue, in particular, requires us to move beyond Gorz's analyses from the 1980s – valuable as they may be – which suggest that the overall effect of territorial struggles would almost automatically entail the reduction of the sphere of heteronomy (state and markets) and the expansion of the sphere of autonomy (time freed for multiple activities that find their *raison d'être* in themselves).[1] Even in 1992, when Gorz advocates for reinstating a 'norm of sufficiency' (abolished by industrial development) to protect both the living environment and the 'lived world' from the predation of economic reason, the question of how to politically organize the forces of change is not even considered.[2] It is worth noting that this issue is not confined to André Gorz; rather, it poses a challenge to the broader field of heterodox Marxism that takes the ecological crisis seriously. A telling example is Guattari's aforementioned essay *The Three Ecologies*. Here, Guattari's reference to the need to address the environmental, social and mental aspects of the crisis in unison is, unfortunately, not accompanied by a discussion of the *actual ways* in which that convergence might be practically achieved.

Instead, the issue of political organization runs like a red thread through this chapter, the basic thesis of which can be summarized as follows. By approaching Marxism and degrowth through the co-presence of the 'classical' labour-nature-value nexus (entropic labour exploited alongside accumulation by dispossession and accumulation by contamination) and the 'new' labour-nature-value nexus (negentropic work exploited in the green economy), it becomes possible to politically articulate two different instances into a singular demand: *shrinking social metabolism* (less entropic labour, in quantitative terms) and *liberating negentropic work* (the multiplication of reproductive activities that have become productive, in qualitative terms). The aim is to develop a logic of wealth capable of translating the dynamism of the logic of value onto a qualitatively different plane (where it is necessary not to 'grow' but to 'prosper'; not so much by 'competing' as by 'cooperating', etc.). At the same time, what emerges as key is repairing the damage produced by Fordism as an

---

1 See André Gorz, *Farewell to the Working Class: An Essay on Post-Industrial Socialism*, trans. Michael Sonenscher (London: Pluto, 1987 [1980]); André Gorz, *Paths to Paradise: On the Liberation from Work*, trans. Malcolm Imrie (London: Pluto, 1985 [1983]).

2 André Gorz, 'Political Ecology: Between Expertocracy and Self-Limitation', in *Ecologica*, trans. Chris Turner (Calcutta: Seagull, 2010 [1992]). In keeping with this interpretation, see Stefania Barca, 'Labour and the ecological crisis: The eco-modernist dilemma in western Marxism(s) (1970s–2000s)', *Geoforum* 83, 2017, 91–100.

entropic device through a care-based practice aimed at maintaining what is common (natural environments, social relations, affect, knowledge and so on). In other words, while Marxism emphasizes a twofold critique of value, degrowth provides a criterion for selecting among different regimes of political action: some productive practices must be reduced in quantitative terms, while others require a process of qualitative diffusion. The focus of the economy shifts from the wage-institution to the dimension of collective caring for relationships and the environment.

I think it should be emphasized from the outset that this strategy of reducing one type of labour (wage-industrial) and liberating another type of work (cognitive-relational/reproductive) is driven primarily by its *desirability*. Social metabolism is to be streamlined not because an impending catastrophe imposes it but because the full enjoyment and widespread realization of negentropic work requires, on the one hand, a process of de-commodification and, on the other, an intervention to secure the environment as the material basis for the reproduction of social life and economic activity, an economic activity freed from the profit-imperative.

In order to unfold this argumentative line, I will first discuss the relationship between Marxism and (proto)degrowth in the 1970s, followed by the contemporary form of the Marxism-degrowth relationship – with particular reference to both *operaismo* and what I propose to call the *Catalan* degrowth.

୫

Before turning to these analyses – which, to be fully transparent, represent working hypotheses more than fully formed research outcomes – I would like to highlight a new element of the contemporary political scenario that, in my view, makes them particularly urgent: the unprecedented centrality assumed by socio-ecological conflicts (often, though not exclusively, at the territorial level). This is not merely a question of quantity, even though this aspect is certainly relevant.[3] Rather, I am referring here to a qualitative leap that Salvo Torre describes as in the following:

---

3   Socio-ecological conflicts are numerous (if often overlooked) and spread across the globe. As for Italy, see the 'Atlas of environmental conflicts', atlanteitaliano.cdca.it; for a global overview, see the Global Atlas of Environmental Justice, ejatlas.org; also of great interest is the recent ACKnowlEJ, acknowlej.org.

For several years now, planetary social movements have shown that they can represent a major political novelty and possess the capacity to act decisively in major contexts of transformation . . . Movements for environmental justice and ecological conflicts worldwide are the expression of a new political space and of a new issue for sovereignty because they now operate on a different level. The environmental justice debate makes this shift clear, as its historical trajectory has paralleled the expansion of the neoliberal model. Since the 1980s, as instances of environmental conflict have multiplied, alongside various forms of opposition to interventions that destroy the biosphere, awareness of a distinctive novelty in the functioning of the economic system has grown.[4]

This novelty is in direct connection with the becoming productive of reproduction and, therefore, with the emergence of the 'new' labour-nature-value nexus (alongside, not substituting, the 'classical' one). The point is thus to conceive of contemporary socio-ecological struggles as a broad and diversified horizon of political composition, potentially providing consistency and univocity to disconnected oppositional frontlines. Yet with one caveat, that to 'compose' in this context does not mean to place side by side or 'pile up' the various conflicting instances, conceiving them as watertight, homogeneous compartments. To 'compose' means to foreground a *relational processuality*, namely the practice of organizing convergences. It is a matter of showing how elements not directly attributable to the wage relation – i.e. ultimately based on the separation of producers from the means of production – are also included in the *definition of class*. The key role of reproduction by means of struggles, expressed but co-opted in the 'peculiar' defeat of the Long 1968, has reshuffled *technical* class composition. Class can no longer claim to be indifferent to gender dynamics, environmental issues, segmentations along the 'colour line' and so on. All these elements concur to define the logics of contemporary exploitation and, therefore, the strategies for resisting it. Consequently, *political* class composition is also traversed by the centrality of the reproductive moment.

----

4   Salvo Torre, *Contro la frammentazione: Movimenti sociali e spazio della politica* (Verona: ombre corte, 2017), 7 and 82.

For this reason, socio-ecological struggles are inherently transversal. Their chances of success largely depend on their ability to maintain a precise and recognizable strategic horizon without falling into ossifying their identity. Guattari understood this perfectly in 1989, as he warned about a precise risk. In the absence of an overarching 'ecosophy' capable of connecting the three ecologies – environmental, social, mental – two mutually reinforcing processes would take place. First, the *infantilization of public opinion* (what Bernard Stiegler would later define as the generalized proletarianization of knowledge) and, second, the *neutralization of democracy* (the outcome of the technocratic passion of neoliberalism, aptly analysed by Pierre Dardot and Christian Laval).[5] To address this dual threat, Guattari pointed to the growing divorce between the logic of value and the logic of wealth:

> The notion of collective interest ought to be expanded to include companies that, in the short term, don't profit anyone, but in the long term are the conduits of a processual enrichment for the whole of humanity . . . It is up to the new ecological components to polarize them and to affirm their importance within the political and social relations of force.[6]

It is hardly a coincidence that the arguments proposed by Guattari are often referenced in relation to the most significant and enduring socio-ecological conflict in Italian history: the No TAV movement. In the Susa Valley, the 'territory' appears to have played a strongly compositional role. Infantilization was met with a formidable process of bottom-up knowledge production and dissemination, and the neutralization of democracy was countered through mass popular participation and the creation of new institutions – the garrisons.[7] All of this occurred in

---

5   Bernard Stiegler, *The Re-enchantment of the World: The Value of Spirit against Industrial Populism*, trans. Trevor Arthur (London: Bloomsbury, 2014 [2006]); Pierre Dardot and Christian Laval, *Never-Ending Nightmare: The Neoliberal Assault on Democracy*, trans. Gregory Elliott (London: Verso, 2019 [2016]).

6   Félix Guattari, *The Three Ecologies*, trans. Ian Pindar and Paul Sutton (London: The Athlone Press, 2000 [1989]), 65–6.

7   Emanuele Leonardi, 'Foucault in the Susa Valley: The No TAV Movement and Struggles for Subjectification', *Capitalism Nature Socialism* 24: 2, 2013, 27–40.

strong continuity with the tradition of the workers' movement. To para-
phrase novelist Wu Ming 1, the No TAV struggle is class struggle in the
open field.[8]

Therefore, I believe it is worth sharing Andrea Ghelfi's reflections on
the ecological potential of a *politics of matter*:

> An ecological perspective . . . could highlight not only the relevance of
> the numerous material and environmental conflicts unfolding globally,
> but also the political character of the many alternative ways of existing
> evident within indigenous, peasant, and ecological movements. This
> perspective could also complement the critique of political economy
> with a political critique of capitalism's development and the disasters it
> has produced. What I have in mind is an ecological critique of capitalist
> progress and the underlying drive for extraction and accumulation –
> on behalf of the many material worlds that still exist (and now require
> to be defended), or that do not yet exist (and must be built).[9]

હ

Before embarking on the comparison between Marxism and degrowth, it
is important to delimit this potentially boundless field of inquiry.[10]

---

8   Wu Ming 1, *Un viaggio che non promettiamo breve: Venticinque anni di
lotta* No Tav (Turin: Einaudi, 2016).

9   Andrea Ghelfi, 'Ecologie del comune', *Effimera*, 25 May 2017, effimera.org;
written by the same author, see also *Worlding Politics: Justice, Commons and Tech-
noscience*, doctoral thesis, University of Leicester, 2016. On the relevance of the
other-than-human for an (ecological) politics of the common, see Miriam Tola,
'Species, Nature, and the Politics of the Common: From Virno to Simondon', *South
Atlantic Quarterly* 116: 2, 2017, 237–55; and Miriam Tola, 'Dentro e contro l'Antro-
pocene: sfide per il post-operaismo', *Effimera*, 29 June 2017, effimera.org.

10   It must be said that I am not the first to engage with this topic. Limiting
ourselves to works published in Italian, see Marino Badiale and Massimo Bontempelli, *Marx e la decrescita* (Trieste: Abiblio, 2010); Claudio Lucchini, *Il bene come
processo possibile concreto: Natura umana e ontologia sociale* (Milan-Udine:
Mimesis, 2010), see in particular Part III ('Estraneazione e democratizzazione
nel capitalismo assoluto: alcune riflessioni'), 245–339; Anselm Jappe and Serge
Latouche, *Uscire dall'economia. Un dialogo fra decrescita e critica del valore: Letture
della crisi e percorsi di liberazione* (Milan-Udine: Mimesis, 2014); Giovanni Mazzetti, *Critica della Decrescita* (Milan: Punto Rosso, 2014). For works published in

Regarding Marxism, here I will not deal with analyses that have sought to highlight the fallacy of the so-called productivist prejudice within Marx's *oeuvre*. I refer in particular to John Bellamy Foster, Paul Burkett and Kohei Saito,[11] whose main goal is to show how the contradiction between capitalist accumulation and environmental health was clearly theorized by Marx, particularly in relation to the so-called metabolic rift – i.e. the rupture of the closed energy circularity between town and country since the second half of the eighteenth century. To be clear: these are studies of the utmost importance. They successfully restore the wide range of Marx's curiosity and convincingly show his awareness of the negative impact of capitalist dynamics on their own bio-physical substratum. Yet I believe these authors do tend to depict a proto-ecological Marx, fully aware of the catastrophic consequences of a technological development divorced from social needs and entirely oriented towards profit. This conclusion seems to be far-fetched. The ecological crisis as a specifically political problem, that is, one that confronts the globality and depth of environmental change within the transformation of the labour-nature-value nexus, and as a vector of subjectivation (which is claimed by certain actors to the point of defining their social identity) emerged in the late 1960s and 1970s. Although extraordinarily innovative, Marx's thought belongs to a different epistemological horizon (that of the nineteenth century), and it is within those confines that his – very relevant, to be sure – contribution to an ecological critique of the capitalist mode of production must be assessed.

Things get quite different if one shifts attention from Marx's writings to his method, and even more to Marxism as a political and intellectual movement constitutively linked to that method. In this context, it becomes

---

French, see the excellent analysis by Françoise Gollain, *Pour une pensée de l'écosocialisme* (Neuvy-en-Champagne: Le Passager Clandestin, 2014). The main difference between my approach and those listed here lies in the fact that my attempt depends entirely on the hypothesis that a radical transformation of the labour-nature-value nexus has taken place.

11   John Bellamy Foster, *Marx's Ecology: Materialism and Nature* (New York: Monthly Review Press, 2000). Paul Burkett, *Marx and Nature: A Red and Green Perspective* (New York: St Martin's Press, 1999). Kohei Saito, *Karl Marx's Eco-socialism: Capital, Nature, and the Unfinished Critique of Political Economy* (New York: Monthly Review Press, 2017).

possible to activate a very rich historical archive in an original way by projecting new issues onto it, such as those raised by the biospheric deterioration. The question, therefore, is: given that Marx was never indifferent to the environmental conditions of capitalist development, how did Marxism respond to the emergence of the ecological crisis as a fundamentally political issue? The significance of the 1968–73 period is demonstrated by a crucial book written by Alfred Schmidt titled *The Concept of Nature in Marx*.[12] Originally published in 1962, the ecological crisis is entirely absent from it as the approach is exclusively epistemological. The reason for this absence is explained by the author in the Preface to the French edition of the book, written in 1993 with the title of 'For an Ecological Materialism'. At the end of the 1950s (when Schmidt was conducting his research) concepts such as 'ecological consciousness', 'limits to growth', 'alternative civilization' or 'ecological crisis', which today dominate both everyday debates and scientific discussions, were still virtually unknown.[13] In 1971, in a Post-scriptum to the second German edition of his book, Schmidt could still acknowledge only in passing the risk of the 'destruction of the natural foundations of social life'.[14] By 1993, however, the collapse of the Soviet Union and the worsening of environmental degradation had compelled him to supplement his text with an 'ecological critique of the destructive aspect of modern industrial development'.[15] With this critique,

[t]he dialectical and historical materialism expands into an 'ecological materialism'. The latter understands that the dialectic of productive forces and relations of production is itself enveloped in and driven by an elementary dialectic of the earth and man, the a-historical condition of all history. Here the idea [already present in Engels's Dialectics of

---

12   Alfred Schmidt, *The Concept of Nature in Marx*, trans. Ben Fowkes (London: Verso, 2014 [1962]).

13   Alfred Schmidt, 'Préface de l'auteur à l'édition française – "Pour un matérialisme écologique"', in *Le concept de nature chez Marx* (Paris: Presses Universitaires de France, 1994), 1. I would like to thank Riccardo Bellofiore for pointing out the importance of this preface, and Hervé Baron for kindly making it available to me.

14   Alfred Schmidt, 'Préface à la seconde édition allemand' [Post-scriptum 1971], in *Le concept de nature chez Marx*, 23.

15   Alfred Schmidt, 'Pour un matérialisme écologique', 2.

Nature] that the world is a material unity is confirmed. We would have already gained much if humanity, by renouncing unlimited growth, could arrange itself so as to live the future in better harmony with the system of nature.[16]

Cases such as that of Schmidt are by no means exceptional. On the contrary, I would be tempted to call it paradigmatic. Indeed, between the 1970s and 1980s, the dominant reaction to ecologism from the official left was one of disregard, if not outright rejection. Hence, even considering Marx's indications to the contrary,[17] it is not inaccurate to identify a rather profound productivist/industrialist tendency in 'orthodox' Marxism. Not all Marxists, however, reacted in this way. As we have seen previously, Gorz was the most far-sighted, and in 1977 he theorized the emergence, together with the crisis of overproduction, of a crisis of reproduction due to the capitalist need to invest in recycling procedures to restore the natural conditions of production:

The need for such recycling has a precise economic significance: it means that from now on it has become necessary to reproduce that which was previously abundant and free. Air and water, in particular, have become means of production like any others: industries must now assign a portion of their investments to antipollution equipment in order to restore to the air and water some of their original properties. The consequence of this requirement is a further increase in the organic composition of capital (i.e., in the share of capital per amount of commodities produced). But there is no corresponding increase in the amount of merchandise produced; the air and water recycled or depolluted by the chemical industry cannot be resold. The falling rate of profit is thus aggravated; the productivity of capital encounters physical limits. And those limits created by pollution are not the only ones.[18]

---

16   Ibid., 17–18.

17   Besides, in the first two chapters of this book, I have tried to highlight some of these indications.

18   André Gorz, *Ecology as Politics*, trans. Patsy Vidgerman and Jonathan Cloud (Boston, MA: South End Press, 1980 [1977]), 25.

Essentially fallen into oblivion for a decade, Gorz's insight was taken up by James O'Connor in the late 1980s, by which time the great revolutionary thrust of the Long 1968 had receded, giving way to the neo-liberal counteroffensive. Recalling the Marxian focus on both 'external physical' (environment) and 'personal' (labour-power) conditions of production, O'Connor develops a theory of the ecological crisis as the cause of the disproportionate rise in the cost of reproducing productive conditions, which opens up the possibility for the 'underproduction of capital'.[19] As he puts it, 'It is conceivable that total revenues allocated to protecting or restoring production conditions may amount to one-half or more of the total social product – all unproductive expenses from the standpoint of self-expanding capital.'[20] The analysis continues by showing both the politicized nature of the conditions of production – thus also the central role of public mediation by the state – and the centrality of new social movements.

From my perspective, the Gorz–O'Connor trajectory is significant because it highlights how, within the 'classical' labour-nature-value nexus, class struggle and ecological conflicts converge through, as it were, an *additional modality*.[21] On one hand, since the post-oil shock capitalist crises (1973 and 1979) assume an environmental form, Marxism can comfortably settle into ecology; on the other, since the ecological crisis is a side effect of capitalist development, environmentalism finds a natural place in Marxist analysis. Here, ecology is not an element of class composition. If anything, it acts as the vector of a process of political subjectivation that may align with the interests of the working class. What we are dealing with, then, are two distinct entities that can come together with a view to a common goal: the overcoming of the capitalist mode of production. Moreover, the field of convergence is represented by breakdown theory or *theory of collapse* – which is to say, the idea that capitalism is destined to implode – elaborated in one case on the socio-economic level (the

---

19   James, O'Connor, *L'ecomarxismo*, trans. G. Ricoveri (Rome: Datanews, 2000), 13.

20   James O'Connor, 'Capitalism, Nature, Socialism: A Theoretical Introduction', *Capitalism Nature Socialism* 1: 1, 1988, 26.

21   Yet not only Gorz–O'Connor. Particularly important is also Carla Ravaioli, *La crescita fredda: Occasione storica per la sinistra* (Rome: Datanews, 1995).

unmanageability of market anarchy), in the other on the ecological level (metabolic hypertrophy being doomed to catastrophe).

It is worth noting that this union of distinct but compatible entities can function either by emphasizing their social side (where relations of production are central) or by emphasizing their environmental side (where the destructive capacity of productive forces takes precedence). There is no doubt that Gorz and O'Connor – and, generally speaking, every Marxist – chose the first option. Equally certain is that one of the fundamental precursors of degrowth, Nicholas Georgescu-Roegen, instead favoured the second, insisting since 1970 on the entropic limits to which the economic system is subject. As Mauro Bonaiuti, who has dedicated important studies to the Romanian economist, argues: 'Since economic processes are based on finite stocks of fossil energy (coal, oil, gas, etc.), it follows that the fundamental objective of the economic process – the unlimited growth of production, consumption and incomes – is at odds with the fundamental laws of thermodynamics.'[22]

I will return to degrowth and its 'roots' shortly. For the moment, however, I would like to focus on Riccardo Bellofiore's review of O'Connor's essays (in their Italian translation), which appeared in the journal *Marx 101* in 1990. According to Bellofiore, the American sociologist's 'additive' perspective fails, despite his good intentions, in that it is both 'internally contradictory and simplistically consolatory'.[23] The basic idea is that 'much more courage' is needed to operate both a profound self-critique of the productivist root of the labour movement, and a critique of the new social movements (including feminism and environmentalism) that 'separate labour and needs, production and reproduction'. In Bellofiore's view, the starting point is the centrality of both labour-power as a socio-natural element of the conditions of production, and its antagonism – which is not a given, but a *potential*:

---

22   See Mario Bonaiuti (ed.), *Nicholas Georgescu-Roegen: La sfida dell'entropia* (Milan: Jaca Book, 2017), 21; and Nicholas Georgescu-Roegen, *Bioeconomia*, ed. Mauro Bonaiuti, trans. Giovanni Ferrara degli Uberti, Pier Luigi Cecioni, Leo Maletti, Giovanna Ricoveri, Milly Messori and Mauro Bonaiuti (Turin: Bollati Boringhieri, 2003).

23   Riccardo Bellofiore, 'Recensione a James O'Connor – *Ecomarxismo*', *Marx 101* 1, 1990, 178.

Labour power may indeed be antagonistic, but it is also, as a rule, a subordinate part of capital. The entire social mechanism drives it to such outcome: to break this rule . . . entails a crisis. Workers live if their opposite, capital, lives. Workers are bound to it for wages, for employment, for the thousand threads of an industrialist culture. This is a culture that ended up devastating Marxism itself, soon causing the Marxian centrality of wage labour's struggles to be exchanged for its opposite, i.e. for an exaltation of the centrality of production as expressed in the political demands of workers' representatives.[24]

It is only when the antagonism of labour-power has materialized into action (and, I would add, following Ubaldo Fadini, has produced new institutions) that it will be possible, as Bellofiore hopes, 'to go beyond the centrality of labour' and for workers to politically take on 'the feminine [*sic*] value of "care"' and 'respect for nature as "other"'.[25] A final consideration in this regard: beyond the obviously debatable outcomes, the aim of my research is precisely to show how the practices of feminist care and ecological otherness must be thought of *within* class composition, against the backdrop of the 'new' labour-nature-value nexus.

୫

Let us now turn to degrowth. It seems appropriate to begin the argument from the definition offered by its most prominent exponent, Serge Latouche:

The failure of the goal of happiness for all promised by the growth society forces one to question the content of the promise itself. Material over-consumption leaves an ever-larger part of the population in penury and does not even ensure true well-being for others. The redefinition of happiness as 'frugal abundance in a solidary society' – this is the rupture proposed by the Degrowth project. This is a rupture that entails breaking free from the vicious circle of endlessly creating needs and products, along with the growing frustration that this process generates, while simultaneously countering the selfishness produced

---

24   Ibid., 179–80.
25   See Ubaldo Fadini, *Il tempo delle istitutzioni* (Verona: ombre corte, 2016). Ibid.

by an individualism reduced to standardised massification by virtue of conviviality.[26]

In Latouche's intentions, it would take a 'semantic bomb' (or 'missile word') to critically address the notion of sustainable development, which is to say, the idea that economic growth, environmental health and intergenerational justice can coexist:

> To rail against the imposture of that successful slogan we needed a strong word, and all in all 'Degrowth' – which sounds blasphemous because we live in the religion of growth – was a rather successful provocation, because immediately people began saying: 'These people are crazy. How can you support degrowth?' Yet, at the same time while facing the provocation, some quite curious people wondered: 'What on Earth do these nutters want? What's behind this?'[27]

Over the years, however, degrowth evolved from an effective provocation to a social movement, and, ultimately, also became an academic research agenda.[28] The history of degrowth can be approached in various ways. According to Latouche, the symbolic starting point dates back to 2002, specifically to an article he wrote for the ecological French magazine *Silence*.[29] However, in this book, I prefer the periodization proposed by

---

26   Serge Latouche, *Per un'abbondanza frugale: Malintesi e controversie sulla decrescita*, trans. Fabrizio Grillenzoni (Turin: Bollati Boringhieri, 2012 [2011]), 13.

27   Serge Latouche, *L'economia è una menzogna*, trans. Fabrizio Grillenzoni (Turin: Bollati Boringhieri, 2014), 55–6.

28   See Federico Demaria et al., 'What Is Degrowth? From an Activist Slogan to a Social Movement', *Environmental Values* 22, 2013, 191–215. See also Martin Weiss and Claudio Cattaneo, 'Degrowth – Taking Stock and Reviewing an Emerging Academic Paradigm', *Ecological Economics* 137, 2017, 220–30.

29   See Serge Latouche, 'À bas le développement durable! Vive la décroissance conviviale', *Silence* 208, 2002. However, Latouche clarified that 'the idea was in the air. There was a background, and the word arrived at the right moment.' He also immediately made explicit the strong continuity with 1970s political ecology: '[the choice of the term degrowth in 2002] was a good move, because if the message is fundamentally the one that Castoriadis, Illich, and Gorz had been preaching in the desert for thirty years, that slogan began to gain traction from the moment we found it'. Serge Latouche, *L'economia è una menzogna*, 56.

Timothée Duverger, which broadens rather than denying Latouche's perspective and offers significant advantage of fitting more closely with the historical framework I deployed to advance my argument. According to Duverger, degrowth is an anti-systemic movement that emerged in the 1970s as a direct outcome of the seismic event of May 1968.[30] It recognizes two fundamental themes, the propensity to 'revolt' and the orientation towards 'quality of life'.[31] Accepting these prerogatives, which are admittedly rather generic, five currents appear, distinct from a heuristic point of view, yet actually intertwined: bio-economics (Nicholas Georgescu-Roegen); critique of technology (Jacques Ellul); culturalist critique of development (Ivan Illich); political ecology (André Gorz); and Third-Worldism (François Partant). In passing, it should be noted that, with the very notable exception of Gorz (and to some extent Illich), none of the other currents explicitly confronts the 'classical' labour-nature-value nexus, which was itself entering into a crisis during those years. Instead, there is a tendency to emphasize (or at least to assume) a certain objectivity, a 'givenness' of environmental limits, relegating the political problem to defining the best method for 'respecting' them.

However, Barbara Muraca, who shares with Duverger the hypothesis that degrowth emerged under the sign of anti-capitalism, notes that in the public debate this radicality is often overshadowed by three distinct discursive formations: the critique of GDP as a measuring tool; the rhetoric of sustainability; and the anthropological critique of the concept of growth.[32] I mention these important works to emphasize that, just as with Marxism, there is no degrowth monolith composed of linear and universally accepted arguments. On the contrary, degrowth is a horizon of

---

30   It should be noted that the term 'degrowth' was not in circulation at that time. It was coined by André Gorz, who used it in a neutral sense during a 1972 debate in *Le Nouvel Observateur* on the Club of Rome's report. Later, in 1979, Jacques Grinevald titled a collection of Georgescu-Roegen's writings *La décroissance* with the Romanian economist's approval. From that point on, until 2002, the term fell into disuse.

31   Timothée Duverger, *La décroissance: une idée pour demain. Une alternative au capitalisme – Synthèse des mouvements* (Paris: Sang de la Terre, 2011), 73.

32   Barbara Muraca, 'Décroissance: A Project for a Radical Transformation of Society', *Environmental Values* 22, 2013, 147–69.

thought and political practice within which quite divergent positions coexist. Among other things, Duverger's book proposes to date the decline of early degrowth precisely to the period following the 1973 oil shock, which allows me to draw the following conclusion. Before the crisis of the 'classical' labour-nature-value nexus, partly due to the socio-ecological struggles of 1968–73, anti-capitalist forces were practising a sort of 'division of political work'. Critical Marxism concerned itself with attacking the *internal limits* of the nexus (through liberation *of* work and liberation *from* labour), while the centrality of reproduction (feminism and [proto]degrowth) sought to unhinge the *external limits* of the nexus.

Such a 'division of political work' showed an extraordinary radicality but could not avoid the 'peculiar' defeat I described earlier. Thus, revisiting today the relationship between Marxism and degrowth means adopting this 'peculiar' defeat as a starting point and following Riccardo Bellofiore's invitation for greater courage in criticizing, on the one hand, the productivism of the labour movement and, on the other, those subjects of social reproduction who refuse to acknowledge their own involvement in valorization – in other words, their own entanglement with the 'new' labour-nature-value nexus. Put differently, it is necessary to examine the relationship between labour and ecology *within* class composition in a context in which it is *first* politically desirable – and only *then* dramatically necessary – to reduce (quantitatively) the share of entropic labour and to expand (qualitatively) the share of negentropic work in social production.

℘

Before tackling this issue, it is necessary to propose an interpretive hypothesis on what Duverger calls the 'degrowth *renaissance*', as it emerged in the twenty-first century associated with the name of Serge Latouche, in France, and with two distinct movements in Italy, the Association for Degrowth and the Movement for Happy Degrowth, led by Maurizio Pallante.[33] Broadly speaking, the political project of this phase

---

33 Timothée Duverger, *La décroissance*, 75. See Mauro Bonaiuti (ed.), *Obiettivo decrescita* (Bologna: EMI, 2005). See Maurizio Pallante, *La decrescita felice* (Rome: Edizioni Decrescita Felice, 2005); Maurizio Pallante, *Felicità sostenibili* (Milan: Rizzoli, 2007).

can be summarized through the articulation of the 'revolutionary' horizon of the 8 Rs (Re-evaluate, Reconceptualize, Restructure, Relocate, Redistribute, Reduce, Reuse, Recycle) alongside a 'reformist' electoral programme presented to all candidates in the 2007 French presidential elections. This programme comprises ten points:

1. Re-establish a sustainable ecological footprint
2. Reduce transport through appropriate eco-taxes
3. Re-localize activities
4. Re-establish peasant agriculture
5. Redistribute profits from increased productivity to reduce working time and create jobs
6. Relaunch the 'production' of relational goods
7. Reduce energy waste
8. Substantially reduce advertising space
9. Redirect scientific and technical research
10. Re-appropriate money[34]

Beyond a certain vagueness of the proposals – for instance, what exactly does 're-appropriating money' mean? – it is important for the purposes of this book to place this 'second-stage' degrowth into historical context. It is undoubtedly an essential component of the global movement for an alternative globalization,[35] which first emerged between Seattle 1999 and Genoa 2001, then ascended to the role of a 'second world power' – as famously described by the *New York Times* following the demonstrations against the war in Iraq on 15 February 2003 – before gradually dissipating around the mid-2000s. To simplify somewhat, this movement represented the first significant refutation of Francis Fukuyama's thesis concerning the supposed 'end of history' that was meant to follow the collapse of

---

34 See Serge Latouche, *Breve trattato sulla decrescita serena* (Turin: Bollati Boringhieri, 2008 [2007]).

35 Among the many possible references on this theme, see Luciana Castellina (ed.), *Il cammino dei movimenti. Da Seattle a Porto Alegre 2003 ai cento milioni in piazza per la pace* (Naples: Intra Moenia, 2003).

the USSR.[36] This point is crucial, as I have the impression that the spectre of actually existing socialism played a key role in the theoretical elaboration of this degrowth. In short, in order to easily dismiss the historical burden represented by the failure of the bureaucratized regimes of the Eastern bloc, the entire body of Marx's work – but also Marxism overall and other radical traditions of the labour movement – was effectively reduced to what Latouche, still in 2010, calls the 'productivist paradox':

> The Marxist critique of capitalism and modernity is compromised by a terrible ambiguity – what we might call the productivist paradox. While the capitalist economy is criticised and denounced, the growth of the forces it unleashes is always characterised by the Marxist tradition as 'productive' – even though these forces are, at least to an equal extent, if not more so, destructive . . . From the viewpoint of production/employment/consumption, this growth is credited with nearly all benefits. Yet, when viewed through the lens of capital accumulation, it is held accountable and responsible for a litany of afflictions: the proletarianisation of workers, their exploitation and impoverishment, as well as imperialism, wars, crises (including, of course, ecological ones).[37]

The underlying syllogism thus appears as follows: productivism/Progress constitute the root of the ecological crisis; liberalism and Marxism share a positive orientation to productivism/Progress; hence, effectively addressing the ecological crisis requires the simultaneous rejection of both liberalism and Marxism. In between the lines, two highly problematic equations seem to emerge. Marx's work is equated with orthodox Marxism (or considered as such in a derogatory sense), while the international communist movement is conflated with the Communist Party of the Soviet Union.

---

36   Francis Fukuyama, *The End of History and the Last Man* (Harmondsworth: Penguin, 1992).

37   Serge Latouche, 'Prefazione all'edizione italiana', in *L'invenzione dell'economia* (Turin: Bollati Boringhieri, 2010), xii–xiii.

Clearly, there is no space here for the 'courageous' self-criticism called for by Bellofiore, nor for an analysis of the transformations of the labour-nature-value nexus. Rather, everything must be discarded, for, in Marx, 'the economy is criticised as ideology, never as symbolic practice'.[38] I have no intention of assessing this approach morally, despite my disagreement with it, as it is entirely legitimate for a political-cultural movement to decide to sever a significant root of its intellectual heritage in order to reach a broader audience. Undoubtedly, in the early 2000s, a strategy aimed at building consensus around words like 'communism', 'Marx' and 'Soviet Union' would have met limited success. It is no coincidence that *La décroissance*, a bi-monthly publication launched in 2004 and dedicated entirely to anti-productivism, sold over 25,000 copies per issue on newsstands. Furthermore, the rejection of this heritage also enabled the recovery of certain themes from utopian socialism, a development not to be overlooked.[39]

What I wish to stress is that the decision to reduce Marx to the 'productivist paradox' has, in effect, prevented the possibility of a meaningful and fruitful dialogue between Marxism and Latouchean degrowth. Indeed, the most promising attempts at bridge-building have either dismissed any potential of common ground altogether (Mazzetti) or reverted to the 'additive' logic previously outlined and criticized (Badiale and Bontempelli). However, the landscape changed significantly following the 2007–8 economic crisis, which restored Marx's analysis to the forefront of anti-capitalist discourse within social movements. At the same time, a new generation of degrowth activists emerged, determined to reconnect the red

---

38   Ibid., xiv.

39   '"Socialist" modernisation [in the Global South] wiped the slate clean of the past with even more violence and fervour than capitalist modernisation, thus paving the way for the task of ultra-liberal globalisation that followed the failure of the socialist experiments. The extraordinary diversity of the paths and voices within early socialism (hastily dismissed as romantic or utopian) was annihilated by the monolithic thinking of historical, dialectical, and scientific materialism. Since then, plurality has merely been tolerated, allowed only as a temporary, tactical concession, pending the inevitable return to the one true socialism. The project of degrowth is, precisely, that other voices may once again be heard.' Serge Latouche, *Per un abbondanza frugale*, 84–5.

thread of workers' movement traditions (particularly Marxism and anarchism) with the urgent need for a concrete strategy of ecological transition.

℘

I propose defining this new generation as the *Catalan* degrowth, given its strong connection to the unique context of a city like Barcelona. As a symbolic milestone for this transition, I choose 2014, the year of the Fourth International Conference held in Leipzig (and briefly mentioned in the Introduction). Initially, Catalan degrowth (which would soon gain global traction) was associated with the name of Joan Martínez-Alier, author of seminal books, including *Environmentalism of the Poor*.[40] However, in recent years, it has been increasingly identified with the work of Giacomo D'Alisa, Federico Demaria and Giorgos Kallis, the three editors of *Degrowth: A Vocabulary for a New Era*.[41]

The reflections of these authors draw from studies on social metabolism – specifically, the relationship between the quantity of matter and energy flowing through the production system and the institutions that regulate its functioning – carried out by a number of ecological economists since the late 1980s. Yet they transpose their findings onto an explicitly political level. For instance, while still in 2010 the

---

40   Barbara Muraca and Matthias Schmelzer recently showed how the Southern European debate on degrowth has expanded to include Anglophone and German-speaking streams; see their 'Sustainable Degrowth: Historical Roots of the Search for Alternatives to Growth in Three Regions', in *History of the Future of Economic Growth: Historical Roots of Current Debates on Sustainable Degrowth*, ed. Iris Borowy and Matthias Schmelzer (London: Routledge, 2017). Joan Martínez-Alier, *The Environmentalism of the Poor: A Study of Ecological Conflicts and Valuation* (Cheltenham: Edward Elgar, 2002).

41   Giacomo d'Alisa, Federico Demaria, Giorgos Kallis (eds), *Degrowth: A Vocabulary for a New Era* (London: Routledge, 2015). In Italian, elements of this analytical framework can be found in Marco Deriu (ed.), *Verso una civiltà della decrescita* (Naples: Marotta e Cafiero, 2016). However, we should highlight here that the distance between the *second* degrowth and the *Catalan* one does not in any way imply a rupture. I think it is more accurate to speak of an emphasis placed on different elements. Moreover, there are authors who would be genuinely difficult to categorize. One such figure is Marco Deriu himself, whose 'Introduction' to the volume just mentioned is a piece that significantly opens up to dialogue with other movements and political traditions.

proposed definition of degrowth referred to an 'equitable downscaling of production and consumption', it has since become commonplace to speak of an alternative social ecology.[42] The emphasis has shifted from *less* to *different*, broadening the scope without discarding the original premise:

> Degrowth signifies a society with a smaller metabolism, but more importantly, a society with a metabolism which has a different structure and serves new functions. Degrowth does not call for doing less of the same ... In a degrowth society everything will be different: different activities, different forms and uses of energy, different relations, different gender roles, different allocations of time between paid and non-paid work, different relations with the non-human world.[43]

Two consequences follow from this new definition. The first is a renewed interest in the conflictual traditions of the labour movement. In the *Vocabulary*, one finds frequent references not only to Marx but also to Marxist scholars such as Silvia Federici, Massimo De Angelis and David Harvey. This opens up a new path of dialogue between degrowth and Marxism.[44] The second consequence is a certain terminological elasticity. Today, some parts of the degrowth mosaic refer to concepts such as

---

42   François Schneider, Giorgos Kallis and Joan Martínez-Alier, 'Crisis or opportunity? Economic degrowth for social equity and ecological sustainability', *Journal of Cleaner Production* 18: 6, 2010, 511–18.

43   D'Alisa, Demaria and Kallis, *Degrowth*, 4.

44   I think we can assume positive retrospective feedback concerning Latouche's own positions, as reflected in a 2013 article: 'Growth is but the "vulgar" name for the phenomenon that Marx analysed as endless accumulation of capital, the source of all the failures and injustices of capitalism. Profit is the end of capital accumulation just as capital accumulation is the end of profit. To speak of good growth or capital accumulation, of good development, is therefore tantamount to saying that there is good capitalism (green or sustainable, perhaps) and good exploitation. In order to emerge from a crisis that is inextricably ecological and social, we need to get out of the logic of the infinite accumulation of capital and the subordination of all essential decisions to the logic of profit'; Serge Latouche, 'Decrescita con Marx', *ComuneInfo*, 5 October 2013, comune-info.net.

the German *Postwachstum* or the English *post-growth*.[45] Within this framework, the reorganization of society proposed by the Catalan degrowth theorists revolves around three axes: *limits, care, dépense* (Bataille's concept of expenditure).[46]

Regarding the first aspect, Kallis writes:

Degrowth proposals generally incorporate collective limits, such as caps on carbon emissions or 100% reserve requirements for banks. These are understood as 'self-limitations', collective decisions to refrain from pursuing all that could be pursued.[47] Moreover, only social systems of limited size and complexity can be governed directly rather than by technocratic elites acting on behalf of the populace. Fossil fuels and nuclear power are dangerous not only because they pollute, but also because an energy-intensive society based on increasingly sophisticated technological systems managed by bureaucrats and technocrats will grow less democratic and egalitarian over time. Many degrowth advocates, therefore, oppose even

---

45   See Matthias Schmelzer and Alexis J. Passadakis, *Postwachstum* (Hamburg: Verlag, 2011). Cf. Christian Garmann Johnsen et al., *Organizing for the Post-Growth Economy* (London: Mayfly, 2017).

46   It is worth noting that, ironically, none of the three editors of the *Vocabulary* was born in Catalonia.

47   In this regard, I feel it is important to point at an unresolved issue in political ecology overall, namely the existing tension between the semantic fields it brings into communication: *interdependence* (i.e. the specific dynamic of ecology) and *autonomy* (i.e. the goal of political action [in this case]). It is a very complex philosophical problem, which in the context of this book I will merely summon by referring to a research path that I think would be worth pursuing so as to overcome the impasse. I am referring to the hypothesis proposed by Gilbert Simondon according to which 'autonomy pre-exists independence'. Broadening the meaning of this proposal, one could read the question of (environmental) self-restraint as the outcome of specific conflicts for political autonomy that correspond to, and retroact on, a given (historical) configuration of ecological interdependence. Gilbert Simondon, *L'individuation à la lumière des notions de forme et d'information* (Grenoble: Million, 2005, 195). See also the reflections on the possibility of an 'ecological philosophy' that rejects neither science nor technics in Gilbert Simondon, *Sulla tecnica* (Naples-Salerno: Orthotes, 2017).

'green' megastructures like high-speed trains or industrial-scale wind farms.[48]

With respect to the centrality of care:

Care can become the hallmark of an economy based on reproduction, rather than expansion. Reproduction refers to the activities that sustain the life cycle, typically within the family. But more generally, it encompasses all processes of sustenance and restoration. In the present economy, care work remains gendered, undervalued, and pushed into the shadow of the formal economy. Degrowth calls for the equal distribution of care work and the re-centring of society around it. A caring economy is labour-intensive precisely because human labor is what gives care its value. It thus has the potential to offset rising unemployment today while fostering a more humane society.[49]

Finally, in relation to *dépense*:

Dépense refers to the unproductive expenditure of the social surplus. How civilizations allocate their surplus, the expenditures they make above and beyond what is necessary to meet basic human needs, gives them their collective character. The Egyptians devoted their surplus to pyramids, the Tibetans to an idle class of monks, and the Europeans of the Middle Ages to churches. In today's capitalist civilization, as the surplus is accumulated and invested to produce more growth, dépense is displaced to privatized acts of exuberant consumption. Since limiting excessive consumption alone would fuel even more saving and investment, degrowth envisions radically reducing the surplus and deploying it for a festive society in which citizens devise new, non-harmful ways to dispense it, ways that help build community and collective meaning.[50]

---

48   Giorgos Kallis, 'The Degrowth Alternative', *Great Transition Initiative: Toward a Transformative Vision and Praxis*, February 2015, greattransition.org.
49   Ibid.
50   Ibid. This issue has entered the degrowth debate following the work of Onofrio Romano. In addition to his entry 'Dépense' in the Vocabulary, see 'Bisogna

I am interested in emphasizing three aspects of these excerpts. First, economic limits are not *objectively given* but *politically posited* by collective action, which is to say that they are the always potentially reversible outcome of the class struggle. Second, conflicts within the sphere of reproduction are interpreted as fundamental and, with respect to my aims, only the last step remains to be taken (namely assuming the productive nature of reproduction in contemporary capitalism). Third, the reversal of the point of view is clear-cut: the problem is not scarcity but surplus, and this reinforces the critique of the logic of value implicit in so-called consumerism and frames the desirability of commoning as an expression of the logic of wealth – that is, entirely within a *qualitative* framework.

It is on this basis that I propose a new terrain for discussion between degrowth and Marxism or, more specifically, a certain strand of Marxism, as we will see shortly. It should be noted, however, that even at the level of concrete political proposals, Catalan degrowth marks an improvement over previous iterations, not least because these proposals arise in constant reference to the struggles of social movements against the brutal effects of the crisis. Indeed, the Research and Degrowth collective (based in Barcelona) has drawn up a decalogue of *non-reformist reforms* – borrowing André Gorz's expression – to address both the immediate objective of the crisis and the long-term objective of transcending capitalism:

1. Debt audit (aimed at the restructuring and partial abolition of debt)
2. Reduction of working hours (thirty-two hours per week and incentives for job-sharing)[51]
3. Basic income with income and wealth caps
4. Eco-taxes

---

distruggere la società', in *Governare l'ambiente? La crisi ecologica tra saperi, poteri e conflitti*, ed. Ottavio Marzocca (Milan-Udine: Mimesis, 2010).

51   In this regard, it is worth highlighting the excellent feminist interpretation of degrowth-oriented work-sharing put forward by Corinna Dengler and Birte Strunk, 'The Monetized Economy Versus Care and the Environment: Degrowth Perspectives on Reconciling an Antagonism', *Feminist Economics* 24: 3, 2018, 160–83.

5. Immediate end of public subsidies to highly polluting activities
6. Incentives to alternative production (non-profit, cooperative system, short supply chains, etc.)
7. Ecological retrofitting of buildings
8. Substantial reduction of advertising space
9. Introduction of limits to environmental pollution
10. Abolition of GDP as an indicator of economic progress[52]

℘

As mentioned earlier, my attempt to juxtapose Marxism and degrowth on the basis of the co-presence of the two, distinct labour-nature-value nexuses (the 'classical' and the 'new') actually refers to a certain form of degrowth (the Catalan one) and to a certain strand of Marxism. As it will not be difficult to infer, given the analysis conducted in the previous chapters, the theoretical current I am interested in discussing here is Italian *operaismo* and, more specifically, the contemporary efforts to update its theoretical toolbox.

Let us quickly recall the main features of the operaist experience. From a historical perspective, the development of *operaismo* is closely linked to the revolutionary cycle of the 1960s and 1970s in Italy (and beyond).[53] At least the journals *Quaderni Rossi*, *Classe Operaia* and *Rosso*, as well as political formations such as 'Potere Operaio' and 'Autonomia Operaia', must be mentioned. From a methodological perspective, the theory unfolds through four key steps, aptly described by Michele Filippini and Federico Tomasello. These are the partiality of the point of view, the constitutive unity of thought and struggle, the ambivalence of workers'

---

52 Giorgos Kallis, *In Defense of Degrowth: Opinions and Minifestos*, ed. Aaron Vansintjan (Open Commons, 2017). In particular, see Part IV, 104–39.

53 In Germany, *operaismo* disseminated rapidly through the journal *Autonomie* and the work of Karl Heinz Roth; in France, it spread through journals such as *Matériaux pour l'intervention*, *Camarades* and the work of Yann Moulier Boutang; in the United States, through the journal *Zerowork* and the analyses of Harry Cleaver. See Sandro Mezzadra, 'Italy, Operaism and Postoperaism', in *International Encyclopaedia of Revolution and Protest*, ed. Immanuel Ness (Oxford: Blackwell, 2009), 1841–5.

conditions (labour-power/abstract labour *within* capital, working class/ living labour *against* capital) and the centrality of class composition.[54] Finally, from a political perspective, I believe that two key innovations accompany *operaismo*. First, the refusal of labour (specifically, of the wage-form as such) and, second, the so-called 'Copernican revolution' according to which class conflict *precedes* the organization of capital (thus establishing both a *causal* and an *incremental* link between workers' struggles and capitalist development).

With regard to the latter, it must be stressed that the rupture of the logic of value must necessarily occur where this logic is most powerful and dynamic. In this sense, capitalist backwardness is also a limiting factor for workers' struggles. Roughly, the argument appeared as follows. Since the driver of development lies in working-class struggles, the attack must be carried to the highest point of capitalist development because only from there will it be possible to redirect the aims of co-operation without depowering it, without dispersing its political force. The need for the bifurcation between the logic of value and the logic of wealth is therefore not at the root but, to stick to the tree metaphor, at the level of the fruit.[55] I quote here two passages from an important interview Sandro Mezzadra gave in 2001 to Guido Borio, Francesca Pozzi and Gigi Roggero, in which the main strength and the key limit of *operaismo* are simultaneously discussed.[56] As for the former:

> The strength I continue to see lies in the attempt to read social realities through categories charged with strong subjective tension. In a nutshell, what seems to me the most valuable aspect of the operaist legacy is that it keeps open a reflection on the capitalist mode of production

---

54 Cf. Michele Filippini and Federico Tomasello, 'Il pensiero come arnese: note sul metodo operaista degli anni Sessanta', in *Dal pensiero critico: filosofie e concetti per il tempo presente*, ed. Alessandro Simoncini (Milan-Udine: Mimesis, 2015), 313–31.

55 Sara Baranzoni and Paolo Vignola, 'Biforcare alla radice: Su alcuni disagi dell'accelerazione', *Effimera*, 25 August 2016, effimera.org.

56 See Guido Borio, Francesca Pozzi and Gigi Roggero, *Futuro Anteriore* (Rome: DeriveApprodi, 2002) and, by the same authors, *Gli operaisti* (Rome: DeriveApprodi, 2005).

that has at its centre the element of scission – subjectivity as an engine (among other engines, I might add) of the process of development.

With respect to the latter:

If I have to talk about the limits of operaismo, well, it is at once easier and more difficult. More difficult because even the very definition of operaismo is debatable. It can be understood in a very broad sense, holding together different historical moments and subjective elaborations. Personally, when it comes to the operaist experience and theoretical heritage that still circulates in our country – particularly within social movements circles – I think the greatest limitation lies in a tendency to indulge at times in a sort of foundational organicism, whereby this subject I spoke of earlier is no longer the subjective drive but is a preformatted subject, already entirely disposed towards communism, etc. The second limitation – and this perhaps applies more broadly to operaismo as a whole – is a kind of implicit progressivism. As I said, this limit is likely applicable for operaismo as a whole, even if there are many distinctions to be made. By implicit progressivism, I obviously mean the constant reference to the highest point of development as the point at which the potential for rupture is also the highest, according to the famous lesson of Tronti's 'Lenin in England'. These two limits have obviously gone hand in hand, and still do, so that the search for the highest point of development immediately becomes a search for the preformatted subject around which class recomposition (even if described in other terms) can be determined. In my view, all of this, especially in the current conditions, frequently tends to take on somewhat mystical overtones.[57]

☙

I will now try to specify what is at stake in this discussion between *operaismo* and Catalan degrowth. I will do so by drawing on a recent analysis by Franco 'Bifo' Berardi, who argues that social movements would do well to get rid of two fetishes that have become increasingly cumbersome over the years, *wage labour* and *economic growth*. As he argues, '[m]aybe the

---

57   Sandro Mezzadra, 'Intervista', *Futuro Anteriore*, 3 April 2001, autistici.org.

emancipation from contemporary depression coincides with the prospect of disentangling social desire from the model of growth and wage labour'.[58] I fully agree with this view and intend to show, on the one hand, how these two fetishes have a profound affinity and, on the other, how liberating ourselves from both is today nothing less than a strategic necessity. In this framework, contemporary reflections on *operaismo* can find in Catalan degrowth the resources needed to move beyond the implicit progressivism Mezzadra mentioned. For its part, this degrowth can find in the analysis of the 'new' labour-nature-value nexus the *subjective tension* through which to ground its transitional project. As Stefania Barca has rightly pointed out, social change needs real subjects, and good arguments are not enough to reach them. In this sense, the analysis of the concrete work through which both value and wealth are created remains fundamental.[59] By investigating the relationship between workers' position within the labour process (technical composition) and concrete interests/orientations to the multiplication of wealth (political composition), Catalan degrowth might identify the workers on whom to rely.

Now we need to go back to reflect on the relationship between wages and growth. In this regard, I need to quickly hark back to the thesis discussed in chapter 3. The wage as an institution is at the heart of the Fordist pact – obedience in exchange for security – that is, of the entropic device whose prerequisites are quantitative economic growth and the subordination of the subjects of reproduction (guaranteed by a form of welfare state conceived as a peripheral and redistributive entity). In short, the pact holds if the economic 'pie' grows for the subjects of production at the expense of those who are external to the productive sphere.

With respect to this framing, two clarifications must be added. The first concerns the concept of growth (and its relation with the notions of capital accumulation and expanding social metabolism). The second concerns the historicity of the analytical context. On the first point, the most promising approach is, in my view, that of Schumpeter.[60] We can

---

58   Franco 'Bifo' Berardi, 'Il rifiuto del lavoro ai tempi della precarietà', in *Salari rubati*, ed. Francesca Coin (Verona: ombre corte, 2016), 129.

59   Stefania Barca, 'The labor(s) of degrowth', *Entitle blog*, 31 January 2017, entitleblogdotorg3.wordpress.com.

60   Adelino Zanini, *J.A. Schumpeter: Teoria dello sviluppo e capitalismo* (Milan: Mondadori, 2000).

think of accumulation as consisting of two moments, a qualitative one (development marked by creative destruction from which emerges a tech-no-economic paradigm that opens a cycle of accumulation)[61] and a quantitative one (growth that progressively 'saturates' the cycle while awaiting for an innovation capable of setting the mechanism in motion again on a different, and higher, level).[62] Two movements, then: one 'verti-cal', opening up a new space for the self-valorizing movement of capital; the other 'horizontal', gradually colonizing and eventually 'exhausting' that space. From this perspective, growth cannot claim any predominance – logical, historical or political – over the accumulation of capital. On the contrary, it can quite easily be detached from it.

It is in this context that the vast majority of Marxists have argued, and continue to argue, for the possibility of and also the social desirability of a *different kind of growth* decoupled from capitalist imperatives. I refer here to the positions of authors I hold in high regard, who variously posi-tioned themselves in relation to *operaismo*: rejection, critical interlocution or adhesion. I start with Bruno Trentin:

> I always emphasise the need to start from a transformation of labour in order to achieve a qualitatively different development, one that is more compatible with the environment. In order to interrupt the disastrous circuit of growth without quality, which multiplies ecological degradation, it is necessary to reconcile the person who works and who seeks greater spaces of freedom within labour with environmental issues, with health issues, concerning both the human species and the planet. If they continue to remain separate, if not at times opposed, they are both doomed to defeat.[63]

---

61 Carlota Perez, *Technological Revolutions and Financial Capital: The Dynamics of Bubbles and the Golden Ages* (Cheltenham: Edward Elgar, 2002).

62 However, we should specify that, for Schumpeter, growth (in proportional terms) without development is merely a logical-analytical device. The real dynamic lies in development, which is nonetheless always underpinned by expectations of rising profits.

63 Carla Ravaioli and Bruno Trentin, *Processo alla crescita* (Rome: Editori Riuniti, 2000), 118–19.

I continue with Riccardo Bellofiore and Emiliano Brancaccio. When prompted by Carla Ravaioli to express an opinion on economic growth as a direct cause of the ecological crisis, they write,

> The ideal choice we have before us is not so much zero growth, but rather negative growth; or, alternatively . . . a different quality of development, which should certainly have very little to do with the military and consumerist Keynesianism of the golden age of capital, and which would be compatible with the growth of some sectors and the decline of others . . . The first path seems to us to be difficult to follow both on a global and on a national scale, and incompatible with democracy. It is therefore a matter of taking the second path, that of a possible quality-based development going hand in hand with a different internal and international distribution of income and wealth.[64]

I conclude with Alex Foti:

> Today we need a simultaneous revision of both social and ecological regulation of capitalism . . . Growth must be restarted, so that it can jump above the profit rate, and reduce capital-labour disparity. However, this 'red' (social) objective is posed to clash with the 'green' (environmental) objective, since additional growth would lead to even greater carbon emissions, pushing the planet further towards environmental chaos . . . Yet, economic growth only has meaning if measured in monetary terms, not in physical terms. Thus, in principle, a social regulation of capital can be envisaged where there is growth in monetary terms (thus overcoming the economic crisis), but not in entropic terms (thus forestalling climate catastrophe). This would be a stage of the economy where immaterial growth becomes the norm, along with the maximization of collective knowledge and social well-being, rather than corporate profit or private wealth. An economy where people mostly exchange immaterial services, rather than material goods.[65]

---

64 Riccardo Bellofiore and Emiliano Brancaccio, 'L'economia della natura', in *Lettera aperta agli economisti: Crescita e crisi ecologica*, ed. Carla Ravaioli (Rome: Manifestolibri, 2001), 60–1.

65 Alex Foti, *General Theory of the Precariat: Great Recession, Revolution, Reaction* (Amsterdam: Institute of Network Cultures, 2017), 40 and 148. Foti

The common thread running through these three visions seems to be the idea that the problem of productivism constitutively pertains to only the capitalist mode of production and that, therefore, what lies beyond value is a kind of wealth that may grow infinitely. From an (post)operaist perspective, such an endlessness is grounded on the general intellect and, more broadly, on the becoming productive of reproduction, thus unbound by the principle of scarcity. I must admit that this is a conceptual move with its own compelling force, one I do not feel comfortable in fully abandoning. Yet this does not negate the fact that a positive relationship between an expansion in social metabolism and an increase in the compound growth rate is empirically observable. Even if one conceives of intangible wealth as the creation of cognitive labour freed from the yoke of exploitation, we should nonetheless avoid overlooking the (very high) energy requirements of the digital economy. The accelerationist dream of planned full automation could all too easily turn into an (socio)ecological nightmare.[66] Moreover, it should be highlighted that we are starting not from scratch but rather from a planet already deeply scarred by ecological crisis. To cite but one recent example, *The Lancet*'s Commission on Pollution and Health reported that, in 2015, air pollution contributed to 9 million deaths, one sixth of the total.[67]

Therefore, I find Kallis's observation persuasive: he argues that, historically, throughput and growth indices show a positive correlation, and, while it is theoretically possible to imagine a decoupling between

---

mentions the issue of degrowth particularly with reference to Latouche's strand. Unfortunately, he confuses it with negative growth or recession, thereby making any fruitful conversation impossible.

66   Nick Srnicek and Alex Williams, *Inventing the Future: Postcapitalism and a World Without Work* (London: Verso, 2015). Andreas Roos, Vasilis Kostakis and Christos Giotitsas, 'The Materiality of the Immaterial: ICTs and the Digital Commons', *tripleC* 14: 1 2016, 48–50. On the (desirable) dialogue between accelerationism and degrowth, Aaron Vasintjan has put forward a compelling analysis, suggesting that the sharpness of the former regarding transformations in technological regimes should be paired with the analysis of social metabolism advanced by the latter. See Aaron Vasintjan, 'Accelerationism . . . and Degrowth? The Left's Strange Bedfellows', *Institute for Social Ecology*, 28 September 2016, social -ecology.org.

67   See '*The Lancet* Commission on pollution and health', *Lancet*, 20 October 2017, thelancet.com.

GDP growth and material and energy consumption, we should approach this prospect with considerable caution, for at least four reasons. First, if the objective remains to maximize growth over the long term, then decoupling can only be relative and temporary. Second, we must not forget that practical feasibility does not necessarily follow from logical possibility. Third, energy gigantism (like industrial gigantism) does not lend itself to democratic control and tends to require technocratic management. Fourth, if energy demands were to continue growing at recent rates over an extended period, then even a complete transition from fossil fuels to renewables might prove undesirable, as vast areas of land would need to be dedicated to energy productions (renewables are preferable if the substitution of sources is accompanied by a reduction in overall demand).[68]

&

There is a further issue that seems to me fundamental, a highly effective provocation by Kallis, Demaria and D'Alisa. Assuming we have exited the logic of value, what need is there, indeed, to talk about 'growth'? Sure, we need *more* reproductive activities and *less* pollution, *more* communal sharing and *fewer* privatizations. Yet affective relations 'intensify', they do not 'grow'; arts and pleasures 'flourish', they do not 'grow'. And so on. 'Of course some sectors, such as education, medical care, or renewable energy, will need to flourish in the future, while others, such as dirty industries or the financial sector shrink . . . The desired change is qualitative, like in the flourishing of the arts. It is not quantitative, like in the growth of industrial output.'[69] It should also be emphasized that, as we saw in the previous chapter, the commodification of the reproductive sphere poses a serious problem. In order for it to create value, labour-information mixed with nature must certainly be commodified, but often its ecological utility gets lost in the process. When reproductive goods multiply without growing (i.e. they produce wealth and not value), they are not included in the GDP calculation and are therefore capitalistically invisible. In short, the point is that, once we abandon the exclusively quantitative terrain of

---

68   Giorgos Kallis, 'Socialism Without Growth', *Capitalism Nature Socialism* 30: 2, 2019, 189–206.

69   D'Alisa, Demaria and Kallis, *Degrowth*, 5.

the growth-wage nexus, why exactly do we the need to maintain a system of measurement based on it?

With this question, I come to the second clarification on the concept of growth, which shifts the focus of the argument from economic theory to historical contextualization. GDP as an instrument for measuring national performance was introduced in 1934 in the United States – in almost perfect alignment, and certainly not by coincidence, with Roosevelt's New Deal. It was adopted by the international community at the Bretton Woods Conference in 1944 and underwent a transformation into a political panacea for all ills around the mid-1950s.[70] However, its connection with the Fordist pact is not only chronological. What matters most is the socio-institutional aspect, which Matthias Schmelzer masterfully captures with the concept of 'growth paradigm':

> I use the term 'growth paradigm' to describe a specific ensemble of societal, political, and academic discourses, theories, and statistical standards that jointly assert and justify the view that economic growth as conventionally defined is desirable, imperative, and essentially limitless. These assumed (1) that GDP, with all its inscribed reductions, assumptions, and exclusions, adequately measures economic activity; (2) that growth was a panacea for a multitude of (often changing) socio-economic challenges; (3) that growth was practically the same as or a necessary means to achieve some of the most essential societal goals such as progress, well-being, or national power; and (4) that growth was essentially unlimited, provided the correct governmental and inter-governmental policies were pursued.[71]

The effects of the growth paradigm were of the utmost relevance, since the paradigm

---

70   Diane Coyle, *GDP: A Brief but Affectionate History* (Oxford: Princeton UP, 2014).

71   Matthias Schmelzer, 'The Growth Paradigm: History, Hegemony, and the Contested Making of Economic Growthmanship', *Ecological Economics* 118, 2015, 264.

promised to turn difficult political conflicts over distribution into technical, non-political management questions of how to collectively increase GDP. By thus transforming class and other social antagonisms into apparent win-win situations, it provided what could be called an 'imaginary resolution of real contradictions' and played a key role in producing the stable postwar consensus around embedded liberalism . . . It helped integrate labor and the political Left, rendered rearmament feasible without a decline in living standards, it helped stabilize the Bretton Woods system, and in the context of global inequalities it offered the (post)colonial countries in the global South a possible route out of poverty towards what came to be defined as 'progress'.[72]

Schmelzer's analysis seems to corroborate the reasoning in the earlier chapters. As long as the logic of value and the logic of wealth partially overlap, the paradigm of growth – within the institutional framework of the wage-form – remains ambivalent, as it increases social welfare while impoverishing workers and the subjects of reproduction, particularly the environment. In this sense, therefore, the growth-wage nexus is at the heart of the Fordist pact as an entropic device. However, it is crucial to emphasize that the appeal of the growth paradigm is both the outcome of past class struggles and a deferral of future ones. By striving to expand the 'pie', so that all beneficiaries of the pact can get more of it, what remains untouched is relative income distribution. This is incompatible with increasing the share of wages relative to the share of profits. As Henry C. Wallich (who later became a Federal Reserve Governor) put it with admirable clarity in 1972: 'Growth is a substitute for equality of income. As long as there is growth there is hope, and that makes large income differentials tolerable.'[73] It is important to note that, within this framing, degrowth is by no means synonymous with recession but with equality of

---

72 Ibid., 266.

73 Henry C. Wallich in Matthias Schmelzer, *The Hegemony of Growth: The OECD and the Making of the Economic Growth Paradigm* (Cambridge: Cambridge UP, 140).

income.[74] This means that degrowth advocates liberation 'from the prescriptive expectations of the capitalist model' that 'can usher in a time of lived wealth as opposed to accumulated value'.[75]

However, the socio-ecological struggles of 1968–73 challenged this model and marked the emergence of a 'new' labour-nature-value nexus alongside the 'classical' one – in the historical context of the 'peculiar' defeat of the Long 1968. As we are reminded every day by news reports and political talk shows, this shift does not mark the end of growth as an objective but certainly entails a significant transformation of the growth paradigm. By placing reproduction at the centre of valorization – with some even openly describing the common as a mode of production – contemporary capitalism brings negentropic work to the forefront.[76] The

---

74   James Hickel, 'Why less is more. There's only one way to avoid climate catastrophe: "de-growing" our economy', *IPS*, 2 October 2017, ibs-journal.eu.

75   'Bifo' Berardi, 'Il rifiuto del lavoro ai tempi della precarietà', 128. Bifo offers these considerations in what appears to be a polemic with 'some theorists who propose degrowth as a political project to be realised' (127, presumably referring to Latouche), and concludes: 'It is not therefore a question of promoting degrowth: it is a question of semiotising it [growth] within categories other than those of capital, it is a question of distinguishing the process of enrichment of the useful sphere from the process of capital valorisation' (128). I hope that the argument developed so far shows not only the compatibility, but also the direct convergence between the proposals of Catalan degrowth and Bifo's reflections. After all, in the same article, there are statements such as the following, which many degrowther would most likely endorse: 'This completely unreasonable situation [the increase in working hours alongside the intensification of productivity caused by technological innovations] is the price that society must pay for its inability to emancipate itself from the economic growth model. The concept of growth, according to which the mass of value produced must expand consistently every year to avoid crises and economic catastrophes, is articulated in a series of economic, social, and financial devices that no longer serve any function in the current era' (123–4).

76   See Carlo Vercellone et al., *Il comune come modo di produzione* (Verona: ombre corte, 2017); Andrea Fumagalli, *Economia politica del comune* (Rome: DeriveApprodi, 2017). Other terms referring to the same phenomenon are 'digital mode of production' or P2P (peer-to-peer) as a mode of production. On this, see Aldo Bonomi, Federico Della Puppa and Roberto Masiero, *La società circolare: Fordismo, capitalismo molecolare, sharing economy* (Rome: DeriveApprodi, 2016); and Michel Bauwens and Vasilis Kostakis, *Peer-to-Peer: A Manifesto for a Commons Transition* (P2P Foundation, 2017).

idea that GDP growth and increased social metabolism can be decoupled registers this novelty, and it certainly does so correctly. What must be emphasized, however, is that this potential enters into strong tension with the growth paradigm in that the negentropic kernel of labour-information can multiply according to the logic of wealth, but it cannot grow according to the logic of value. In other words, such a potential 'flourishes' in commoning and 'degrades' in private appropriation. It is certainly possible to commodify negentropic work, forcibly returning it to the logic of value, but in doing so its socio-ecological potential wanes rather than increases.

The example of the so-called fiscal crisis of the state, or the hypertrophy of the welfare state from the early 1970s onwards, may be illustrative.[77] Giovanni Mazzetti shows that such a crisis could (and should) have been addressed by accepting 'the specific narrowness of production mediated by money' (in the terminology deployed in this book: the logic of value). This would entail recognizing that the expansive relationship between public expenditure and multiplier, which had functioned up to that point, 'could no longer ensure further development without being violated'.[78] According to Mazzetti, it would have been correct to 'transgress the principle of equivalence implicit in the value relationship'. This means that, in order to survive and prosper, the Keynesian welfare state would have had to transform itself and at least partially accommodate the logic of wealth. In other words, it would have had to overcome the exclusivity of the wage-growth nexus. Remaining on a hypothetical level, in a situation in which

---

77   James O'Connor, *The Fiscal Crisis of the State* (London: Transaction Publishers, 2009 [1973]).

78   '[From a Keynesian point of view] public spending, by replacing the shortfall in private expenditure, would have enabled the direct utilisation of a significant portion of existing resources. But above all, it would have generated income which, transforming into additional expenditure (demand), would have indirectly supported employment in the private sector, thereby leading to a recovery in investment. The sum of the income produced directly and that produced indirectly would thus be significantly greater than the initial public expenditure (multiplier effect)'. Giovanni Mazzetti, 'Imparare dalla crisi: e se ci spingessimo al di là del Welfare?', in *Una crisi mai vista: Suggerimenti per una sinistra cieca*, ed. Massimo Loche and Valentino Parlato (Rome: Manifestolibri, 2001), 80–1. The multiplier effect is the clearest expression of the partial overlap between the logic of value and the logic of wealth. Ibid., 90.

the state had financed welfare measures in the absence of subsequent fiscal compensation (due to the exhaustion of the virtuous circle public expenditure-multiplier-public expenditure), Mazzetti asks rhetorically whether

> wage labour set in motion by public deficit spending would have been useless and unproductive or, if appropriately directed through planning it would instead have been able to produce precisely what society needed, without making it subject to the condition that it creates an equivalent value.[79]

It seems to me that Mazzetti indicates with great clarity both the becoming productive of reproduction – that is, the increasing redundancy of the wage as a necessary measure – and the growing divorce between the logic of value and the logic of wealth. Paradoxically, what in the passage just quoted Mazzetti calls 'wage labour' (mobilized by public deficit spending) would actually embody a reproductive (and negentropic) activity remunerated through a basic income that liberates this activity from being 'subject to the condition that it creates an equivalent value' (i.e. measurable with the parameters of the wage-institution).[80] In other words, the welfare state 'fails' because of its 'success'. The specific production of society that takes place during the post–World War II Fordist era, and which culminates in the socio-ecological struggles discussed here, ultimately erodes its own foundations, revealing the political artificiality of maintaining the logic of value. So long as this logic partially overlapped with the logic of wealth, investing in the production of society (also) entailed a return in terms of valorization. But, since these two logics started diverging, investment in social welfare no longer implies a surplus of value – which is to say, the multiplier effect of public expenditure declines. Today, valorization acts more as a brake on than as a driver of the production of wealth.

A final consideration in this regard. The depletion of the propulsive thrust (in capitalist terms) of the wage-growth nexus does not mean that

---

79   Ibid., 81.

80   See Emanuele Leonardi and Giacomo Pisani, 'Il reddito di base contro la nuova logica dello sfruttamento', *Etica e Politica* 19: 1, 2017, 19–31.

the subjects of reproduction, now rendered productive, are revolutionary *per se*. The first limitation of *operaismo* recalled by Mezzadra would re-emerge here in the form of a social cooperation already autonomous and ready to reap the fruits of the general intellect. The reality, however, is quite different. Processes of commodification continue – one only has to look around to realize this – and may potentially continue for a long time yet. Left to its own devices, it may well be that 'capitalism's centuries are numbered'.[81] Hence, Gorz's optimism regarding cognitive capitalism as a crisis of capitalism *tout court* should at least be relativized.[82] The point, however, is that in the context of the divorce between the logic of value and the logic of wealth, room for manoeuvre in the search for a new social pact, which some call a Green New Deal, seems to be shrinking.[83] The slogan of *Occupy!* ('We are the 99 per cent') precisely registers the capitalist difficulty of finding a functional equivalent of the now-dismantled wage-institution. Christian Marazzi aptly notes this obstacle:

> Monetary authorities can create all the money they want, but if this created money is not integrated into the sphere of commodity circulation in the form of monetary incomes (I insist: incomes), its creation does not serve in any way to transform the surplus value of commodities into money . . . The question to be asked is about where all this liquidity [the European Central Bank's quantitative easing] goes. And the answer is quite simple: on the financial markets, where the investors' incomes are monetarily realised . . . The problem is that this wealth realised on the financial markets, quite contrary to the claims of neoclassical theory (according to the trickle-down principle) does not drip downwards, towards the so-called real economy, but remains within the one per cent of the very rich, thus contributing to exacerbate existing inequalities and the polarisation between rich and

---

81   Giorgio Ruffolo, *Il capitalismo ha i secoli contati* (Turin: Einaudi, 2008).

82   However, it seems that Paul Mason's book, though interesting, remains caught in the same misunderstanding, see Paul Mason, *Postcapitalism: A Guide to Our Future* (London: Penguin, 2015).

83   Antonio Cianciullo and Gianni Silvestrini, *La corsa della green economy: Come la rivoluzione verde sta cambiando il mondo* (Milan: Edizioni Ambiente, 2010).

poor that has been a clear feature of the evolution of our societies in recent years.[84]

In his generous attempt to outline a high-level reformism for current times, Alex Foti seems nonetheless to overlook the fact that, in a finance-led growth model, the redistribution of income through the welfare state is complicated because the 'flourishing' of society is no longer matched by the creation of surplus value, at least not in the direct form typical of Fordism. Quite the contrary, in order for the production of surplus value to grow continuously, society must indeed restrict what Guattari calls 'existential territories' – think of the rhetorics of human capital and self-entrepreneurship, which require people to think of themselves as enterprises in order to access income. Of course, it cannot be ruled out that new spaces for a Green New Deal may emerge in the future. Nevertheless, the current impasse must be acknowledged and its difficulties addressed. For instance, Foti sees in carbon markets a first, if imperfect, form of ecological regulation for a new social compromise, a sort of necessary evil ('a carbon tax would be better, but at least they are a first step . . .'). Yet he simply avoids taking into account carbon trading's short circuit between environmental ends and economic means, which I examined in the previous chapter. Put differently, the negentropic potential of labour-information would require a post-capitalist context to be actualized, a scenario capable of both ensuring universal access to the fruits of the general intellect (unconditional basic income and universal basic services) and providing a roadmap to the re-localization of manufacturing activities (as proposed by the Italian *Società dei Territorialisti*).[85]

∽

We can now return to Bellofiore and Brancaccio's reflections to begin discussing the central thesis of this chapter. To Ravaioli, who pressed them on the need to reduce the rate of growth, the two economists replied with an *aut-aut*: either a reduction in the level of production or a

---

84　Christian Marazzi, *Che cos'è il plusvalore?* (Bellinzona: Casagrande, 2016), 44–5.

85　On the key concept of local self-sustainable development, see Alberto Magnaghi, *Il progetto locale* (Turin: Bollati Boringhieri, 2010).

radical change in its structure. Now, the analysis carried out so far aims to avoid this either/or. I believe that a political programme capable of bringing Catalan degrowth and *operaismo* into dialogue must strive for a *reduction in entropic labour* (which refers to the logic of value) and, simultaneously, for an *expansion of negentropic work* (which revolves around the logic of wealth). The either/or is avoided because the process of diminution and that of extension *do not* occur on the same level. The former requires a weakening of the 'classic' labour-nature-value nexus, while the latter rests on liberating the ecological potential contained in the 'new' labour-nature-value nexus. Nevertheless, they form a unified strategy. They are two sides of the same coin: class struggle in the twenty-first century. I find it difficult to disagree with Kallis when he argues that

> [a] sustainable socialism would only be one that plans with popular support for declining material and energy use, which in most likelihood entails decreasing, not increasing, industrial output. This serves as a reminder of the monumental transformation of desires, and the preparatory pedagogical work (yes, also at the level of values and imaginaries) that would have to take place if an eco-socialism were ever to become real. Refuting this stark bio-physical challenge postpones the work that needs to be done.[86]

Therefore, it is good that value decreases. However, the same cannot be said of wealth. Wealth can expand or 'flourish' precisely because of the becoming productive of reproduction. Yet it is clearly impossible to ignore the previous (and radical) redistribution of wealth from the 1 per cent to the 99 per cent. This redistributive process, similar in scale but opposite in direction to the class polarization that has occurred since the late 1970s, stands as the essential condition for the socio-environmental sustainability of a reduction in entropic work together with an increase of negentropic work.

A useful way to visualize this two-sided strategy is offered by the 'Doughnut Economy' proposed by economist Kate Raworth (overleaf):

---

86 Kallis, 'Socialism without Growth', 196.

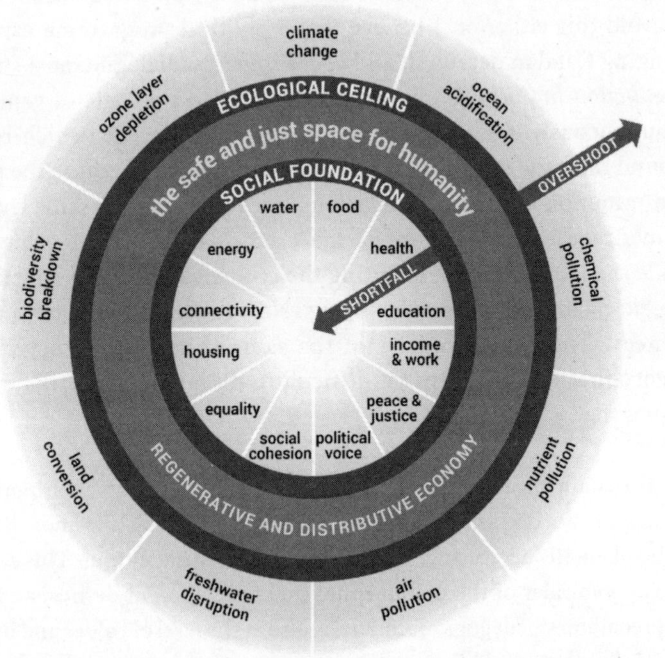

The latest iteration of the Doughnut

What exactly is the Doughnut? Put simply, it is a radically new compass for guiding humanity this century. And it points towards a future that can provide for every person's needs while safeguarding the living world on which we all depend. Below the Doughnut's social foundation lie shortfalls in human well-being, faced by those who lack life's essentials such as food, education and housing. Beyond the ecological ceiling lies an overshoot of pressure on Earth's life-giving systems, such as through climate change, ocean acidification and chemical pollution. But between these two sets of boundaries lies a sweet spot – shaped unmistakably like a doughnut – that is both an ecologically safe and socially just space for humanity.[87]

---

87   Kate Raworth, *Doughnut Economics: Seven Ways to Think Like a Twenty-First-Century Economist* (London: Business Books, 2017), 44–5.

Raworth's merits are several. First, she shed light on the inseparability of the economic and ecological moments. Second, she returned a strong idea of socio-environmental justice to the centre of economic discourse. Finally, she made immediately intelligible the simultaneous need for reduction (of the environmental ceiling) and expansion (of the social foundation). What is missing from the perspective outlined here is the centrality of conflict within both modes of the labour-nature-value nexus. The Doughnut risks remaining, at best, a good intention without the imposition of a radical redistribution of wealth and a deep transformation in the qualitative aspects of production. If capitalism genuinely had the fate of 'all humanity' at heart, there would be no reason to debate these problems.

This is why I would argue that it may be useful to place reproductive dynamics at the core of the analysis of class composition in order to constantly connect the inner and outer boundaries membranes of the Doughnut. Indeed, in doing so, we can appreciate the convergence of ecological struggles against alienation and practices of refusal of (wage/entropic) labour within the *liberation of negentropic work*. With regard to the first typology, Stefania Barca's reflection is fundamental:

> For the working class to become the political subject of a new system of ecological relations, a new consciousness must be shaped: an ecological class consciousness, grounded in a renewed, plural process of subjectivation, capable of transforming the working class into the main historical subject for a green revolution aimed at emancipation, rather than at new forms of oppression (as would be the case in a 'green capitalism'). In order to become the subject of this coming ecological revolution, trade unions must undergo a profound transformation, placing ecology at the centre of their political visions and strategies . . . But it is not only the labour movement that needs to be transformed. Besides, work cannot be transformed in a social vacuum. A far-reaching process of emancipation and cultural shift is needed, one that is capable of creating the space to form new solidarities and alliances, in order to reclaim the forgotten subject of work outside domination and exploitation.[88]

---

88   Stefania Barca, 'Lavoro e cambiamento climatico: verso una coscienza di classe ecologica', *Effimera*, 18 February 2016, effimera.org. By the same author, see

As Barca points out, this is exactly what is happening at Ri-Maflow, a former automotive factory that was reclaimed after its production was relocated to Poland.[89] It is an experience of 'conflictual self-management' that has chosen an alternative path to 'industrialist productivism' and now aims for the goal of zero waste through the reuse and recovery of electrical and electronic equipment (EEE) and wooden pallets, working 'in three phases, in order of priority: prevention, reuse and recycling'. The core idea is that of the 'open factory', an economic activity that guarantees both a decent income for workers and direct involvement of the local community in the definition of production choices.[90] In addition, in the Ri-Maflow warehouses is 'Fuorimercato' (*Outside-the-Market*), an experience that seeks to create a space for local food exchange, also due to its proximity to the Parco Agricolo Sud Milano (*South Milan Agricultural Park*), as an alternative to large-scale retail trade. A worker from Ri-Maflow puts forward the following considerations:

> Recovered factories can serve as a pragmatic solution to the destruction of both productive forces and the environment. They preserve jobs and control over these within local territories. We can't wait any longer, a transition is necessary. It is imperative to change the modalities and paradigms that govern the production of goods and their consumption. We must decide whether we want to find a solution to the two crises of our time [economic and environmental] or whether we want to continue focusing on palliatives that will only make them worse in the long run.[91]

---

her 'Labor in the Age of Climate Change', *Jacobin*, 18 March 2016, jacobin.com; and the already cited 'The labor(s) of degrowth'.

89   Barca, 'The labor(s) of degrowth'. As concerns Ri-Maflow, and generally on the phenomenon of reclaimed factories, see Francesca Gabbriellini, *Le fabbriche recuperate Scop.Ti e Ri-Maflow: Dalla delocalizzazione all'autogestione*, MA thesis (Università di Pisa, 2017).

90   Luca Federici, 'Ri-Maflow, una fabbrica recuperata', in *Riconversione: un'utopia concreta*, ed. Marica Di Pierri, Silvano Falocco and Laura Greco (Rome: Ediesse, 2015), 168.

91   Ibid., 169.

I would just add that the issue of ecological conversion is not limited to the factory perimeter.[92] On the one hand, it implies a process of reconciliation between existential dimensions and working practices (which Lucia Bertell calls 'eco-autonomous work').[93] On the other hand, it involves a radical rethinking of the structure of property, moving towards the new centrality of 'collective uses' as investigated by Nicola Capone.[94]

∽

The necessity – and, at the same time, the desirability – of a re-localization of labour (particularly the entropic labour that needs to decrease) and of the decision-making power over the qualitative composition of production suggest we return to and expand the line of thought concerning what Mezzadra called the 'implicit progressivism' (which we may re-label as 'implicit productivism') of *operaismo*. However, let us start from a fact. It is precisely on the basis of this 'productivism', which is typical of the political strategy of struggling 'within and against' the capital relation, that something like a 'beyond' the logic of value has become socially perceptible (once again, the reference here is the cycle of conflicts against 'noxiousness'). Historicizing the argument is crucial here. In my hypothesis, the second half of the 1970s marks the crossing of a *threshold of counter-productivity*, as Illich would describe it. It is at that specific point that the logic of value and that of wealth begin to diverge, and it is at that specific moment that the strategy of struggling 'within and against' begins to lose its exclusivity.

That being said, it seems that contemporary reflections about *operaismo* are united in the observation that, between the refusal of labour (active element) and the fragmentation of work (passive element), the increasingly extreme multiplication of practices of valorization makes it impossible to identify the highest point of development today. Against the backdrop of becoming productive of reproduction, the tendency is towards heterogeneity.[95] If the linear immediacy of the connection

---

92   See Guido Viale, *Conversione ecologica* (Rimini: NdA Press, 2011).

93   Lucia Bertell, *Lavoro eco-autonomo* (Milan: Elèuthera, 2016).

94   See Nicola Capone, 'Del diritto d'uso civico e collettivo dei beni destinati al godimento dei diritti fondamentali', *Politica del diritto* XLVII: 4, 2016, 597–636.

95   Sandro Mezzadra and Brett Neilson, *Border as Method, Or, The Multiplication of Labor* (Durham and London: Duke UP, 2013).

between workers' struggles and capitalist development is lost, and with it the relatively straightforward identification of the revolutionary subject responsible for the bifurcation, for the rupture, the logic of 'within and against' starts revealing its problematic side. Without going so far as to support Carlo Formenti's (quite unclear) position according to which 'if you are within you are not against' – from which it can be inferred that workers should position themselves 'outside and against' – it may not be unhelpful to question, on the one hand, the different ways of being 'within' and, on the other, the transformative potentials of the 'outside'.[96] It is contemporary valorization that suggests we interpret 'within' and 'outside' in their non-exclusivity (and, above all, subordinate to 'against').

It seems to me that the path to an ecologically desirable anti-capitalism should pass both through a coalition between the heterogeneous segments that participate in the production of value (from manufacturing labourers and industrial farmers to knowledge workers) and an alliance between the multifarious expressions of the 'outside' (indigenous cosmovisions, subsistence farming communities, workers in the 'informal' economy).[97] In other words, I believe we should consider more carefully the question of the relationship between those who perceive what lies *beyond* value based on what was once the highest point of capitalist development and those who see the *other* than value from a position of (relative, temporary, reversible) externality. The stakes are high: it is truly necessary that the rights of Pachamama and resistance to wage theft be on the same revolutionary boat. Moreover, it is on this non-progressive level that we can better understand the central role of the South, which finds expression in socio-ecological struggles (at least since the alter-globalization cycle),[98] and that we see at all levels: the driving force of the African, Asian and Latin American indigenous-peasant

---

96   Carlo Formenti, *La variante populista* (Rome: DeriveApprodi, 2016), 177.

97   It should also be emphasized here that referring to *Buen Vivir*, *Sumak Kawsay* or *Ubuntu* does not mean grounding the analysis in a sort of 'naturalistic outside' – in the mould of reproduction within the 'classic' labour-nature-value nexus – but, rather, recovering traditions that have experienced the economy in forms other than those of capitalism (*within* conflicts, *with* political curiosity and *without* unjustifiable feelings of superiority).

98   Cf. Valentino Parlato and Giovanna Ricoveri, 'Ascoltiamo i segnali spediti dal Sud', in Ravaioli, *Lettera aperta agli economisti*, 79–82.

movements on a global level, of the Indignados on a continental level, of the Neapolitan municipal experimentations on a national level.

To be clear: this is not a question of indulging in improbable pre-modern mythologies. The fact is that the disarticulation of the 'Fordist' relationship between 'within' and 'against' makes it necessary to reject the idea that the 'outside' (along with the 'low' and 'intermediate' points of development) could be thought of as *residual*. This, in turn, opens up the political problem of the composition of subjectivities that are exposed in different ways to the violence of capitalist exploitation, a problem that is best addressed by recognizing the leadership of the South.

To reiterate: once it has become productive, reproduction acts as the backdrop to this anti-productivist reading of the logic of 'within and against'. It follows that the dual strategy of re-localizing manufacturing activities and ensuring global access to the general intellect refers to the virtuous coexistence of an equally dual temporality. On the one hand, the reversibility of deteriorating historical processes – such as the uncontrolled diffusion of the megacity, increased environmental degradation and the worsening of democracy – allows for a selective recovery of certain aspects of past experiences (including peasant civilizations and those linked to indigenous worldviews). On the other hand, the opening towards a future horizon allows us to socially experiment with new forms of production and new knowledge (including those related to rurality and the relationship between humans and non-humans).

Ultimately, it is a question of rethinking work, perhaps returning to question the physiocratic concept of the *sterile class*, as suggested by Christian Marazzi – that is, 'a class that is productive insofar as it is transformative and not because it is the origin of an addition of value, namely that surplus which is then alienated, sucked up by the market, by the exchange with other goods. It is thus fundamental to reclaim unproductivity *even* within transformative action . . . Why not think of ourselves as those who transform without adding value?'[99]

℘

---

99 Marazzi, *Che cos'è il plusvalore?*, 20–1.

Therefore, we need to imagine a kind of working activity that is capable of: a) transforming matter; b) without adding value; c) while being essential to the production of wealth. Differently put, the question becomes: can we politically construct, today, an ecological dimension of the refusal of wage labour? I pose the question with Anna Curcio in mind, who argues that we need to look at *new forms of refusal* without confining them to

> those of the past, as it is all too obvious to stress that every collective practice is linked to a historically determinate phase. Instead, we must dig within new behaviours to see what real or potential forms of refusal are occurring or may occur, what their specific ambivalences are, and what are the possible paths to transform them into processes of organisation and subversion.[100]

I want to start with a suggestion by Paolo Cacciari, founding member of the Association for Degrowth:

> The right question then is: 'how can we restore meaning within work?' How can we make work a life experience and a meaningful social relationship, capable of bringing real benefits for oneself and for others? Discussing work therefore means, first of all, discussing what its purpose and its aim should be. And it is equivalent to debating what type of economy, technology and society we want. Indeed, it is difficult to think that there can be good work in a bad economy and good economy in a classist, despotic, violent society.[101]

Therefore, to speak of the 'centrality of work' in the era of the becoming productive of reproduction means, first, to focus attention on what, how, how much, where and for whom the production is intended – that is, on the goals of the activity that creates wealth. Second, as Cacciari tells us,

---

100   Anna Curcio, 'Lavoro, non lavoro, gratuità', *ATTAC Italia*, 27 October 2017, attac-italia.org.

101   Paolo Cacciari, 'Quale lavoro per quale società', *Comune-info*, 21 September 2017, comune-info.net. For a precise and considered overview of the practices that restore meaning to work, see Cacciari's *101 piccole rivoluzioni* (Milan: Altreconomia, 2016).

it means bringing to the forefront the technologies through which we intend to achieve those objectives. The subject is vast and I certainly do not intend to exhaust it with only a few notes.[102] I limit myself to putting forward an interpretative hypothesis and to proposing a tendency. Following Bifo, I think it is reasonable to argue that the refusal of labour in the 1960s and 1970s indicated 'a propulsive dynamic that drives technical innovation, that stimulates collective intelligence and that makes possible a progressive reduction of how social time depends on the domination of money, wages and capital'.[103] Yet this possibility has not materialized. On the contrary, far from destroying the wage cage, digital technology has brought with it new forms to exploit subjectivity. However, this does not mean that the microelectronic revolution should (or even simply could) be completely rejected. Rather, it signals a specific area of conflict in the broader context of the 'peculiar' defeat of the Long 1968.

And this is where the tendency I would like to shed light on originates. Investing politically in the logic of wealth at the expense of the logic of value means approaching the technological tool from the point of view of the dual strategy we have outlined (reduction of entropic labour and expansion of negentropic work). It is here, in the simultaneous disarticulation of the wage-institution and the growth paradigm, that I believe one of the new forms of refusal of labour is situated.

An excellent example of this perspective is the 'Design Global, Manufacture Local' (DGML) model (Figure 2).[104]

In a nutshell, the DGML model points to a confluence between knowledge-based commons and productive technologies (ranging from 3D printers to old screwdrivers). The basic idea is that the design of products

---

102   In the field of degrowth, and aimed at analysing the diminishing returns of advanced capitalist societies, it is worth noting the important critical work of Mauro Bonaiuti, *La grande transizione: dal declino alla società della decrescita* (Turin: Bollati Boringhieri, 2013). For a sophisticated but ultimately specious critique of the supposed technophobia of degrowth advocates, see Luca Simonetti, *Contro la decrescita: perché rallentare non è la soluzione* (Milan: Longanesi, 2014).

103   Berardi, 'Il rifiuto del lavoro ai tempi della precarietà', 122–3.

104   See Vasilis Kostakis, 'Are there alternative trajectories of technological development? A political ecology perspective', *Entitle blog*, 6 October 2017, entitle-blogdotorg3.wordpress.com.

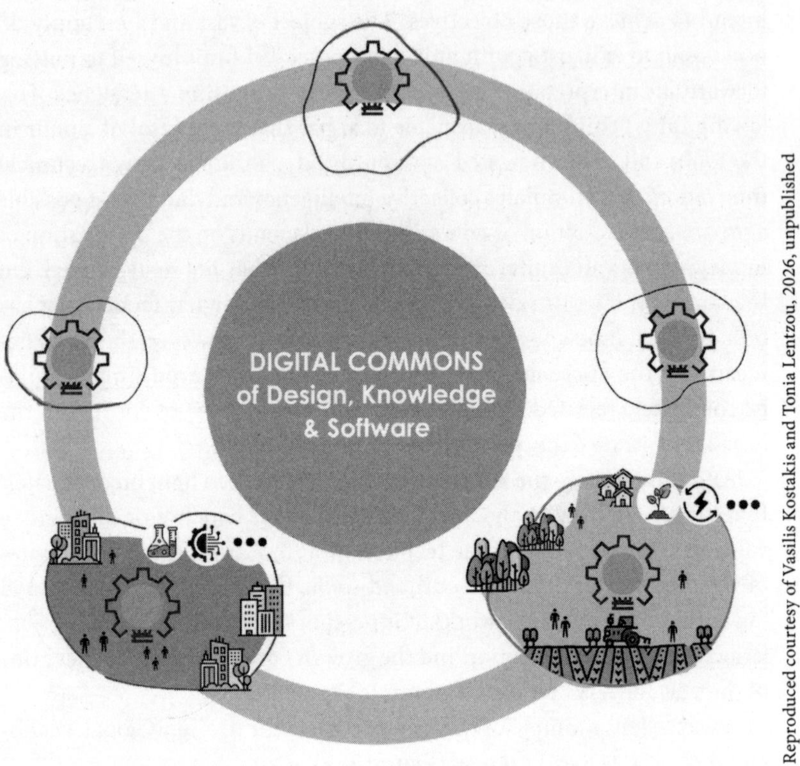

Latest iteration of the DGML image

is developed as a digital common, while the actual manufacturing process takes place locally, using shared infrastructures and paying attention to the biophysical conditions of each territory. According to research conducted by Vasili Kostakis et al., three interconnected practices make the DGML model particularly interesting from the standpoint of political ecology and (for our purposes) in relation to the dual strategy of reducing entropic labour and increasing negentropic work. These practices concern the incentives to integrate environmental sustainability into the design process, the possibility of on-demand production (with a consequent reduction in waste), and the shared use of both digital and physical infrastructures.

Furthermore, DGML technologies tend to be low-cost, are compatible with small-scale operations and are adaptable to local needs. Like other initiatives oriented towards the commons, the DGML model also advocates technological sovereignty by encouraging the autonomy of users' communities and promotes universal access to collective knowledge.[105]

It still remains necessary to more precisely calculate the reduction in environmental impact where such experiences are already in place, and to produce reliable estimates of the potential energy savings from a broader adoption of peer-to-peer models.[106] Nonetheless, the virtuous interplay indicated by this model is already evident: against the backdrop of a socio-ecological conflict, it brings together autonomous decision-making, the reduction of negative externalities and the diffusion of sharing practices as an alternative to individual competition.

Despite all its limitations, the DGML seems to me a promising first step towards a strategy of reducing throughput, accompanied by the expansion of the general intellect according to the logic of care. It is along this same trajectory that Matteo Pasquinelli seems to move when, borrowing a classic concept from *operaismo*, he states that 'a new political composition of energy and information must be thought against the technical composition that bifurcated them since the industrial age'.[107] This passage would also allow for the construction of connections between struggles centred on energy (such as those for climate justice) and those centred on information (from hacktivism to the digital precariat).[108]

---

105   Cf. Vasilis Kostakis, 'The convergence of digital commons with local manufacturing from a degrowth perspective: Two illustrative cases', *Journal of Cleaner Production* 197: 2, 2018, 1684–93.

106   See also Vasilis Kostakis, Andreas Roos and Michel Bauwens, 'Towards a political ecology of the digital economy: Socio-environmental implications of two competing value models', *Environmental Innovation and Societal Transitions* 18, 2016, 82–100; and Céline Piques and Xavier Rizos, *Peer-to-Peer and the Commons: A Matter, Energy and Thermodynamic Perspective* (P2P Foundations, 2017). Cf. Chris Giotitsas, Alex Paxaitis and Vasilis Kostakis, 'A peer-to-peer approach to energy production', *Technology in Society* 42, 2015, 28–38.

107   Matteo Pasquinelli, 'The Automaton of the Anthropocene: On Carbosilicon Machines and Cyberfossil Capital', *The South Atlantic Quarterly* 116: 2, 2017, 322.

108   Nick Dyer-Whiteford, *Cyber-Proletariat: Global Labour in the Digital Vortex* (New York: Pluto Press, 2017).

Of course, there is always the possibility, at least in theory, that these developments could be made compatible with a new social pact, a Green New Deal. Even in a scenario marked by a growing divorce between the logic of value and the logic of wealth, there are those who continue to promote 'high-level' reformist proposals. This is the case of Aldo Bonomi, Federico Della Puppa and Roberto Masiero, who have recently introduced the concept of a 'circular society'. From the perspective of the relationship between energy and information, the central element is the idea of a smart grid diffused throughout the territory:

> The fundamental principle is to develop all forms of alternative and renewable energy and, above all, to ensure that all the economic and social benefits remain in the areas of production. For instance, this is possible by promoting territorial energy plans entrusted to public and private entities on the basis of regional agreements and by simultaneously activating start-up processes, hence new entrepreneurship.[109]

More than its practical feasibility, however, the real issue is the social desirability of this scenario. In the 'relational economy' Della Puppa and Masiero dream of, 'the individual is at the centre, with their needs, demands, necessities and aspirations', together with the 'enterprise as an active subject'. The role of politics is even more explicit, particularly that of local administrators, as they are expected to 'invite private investors to play and prepare the support for the gaming table; but they should not decide the game'.[110] This is not exactly the centrality of the socio-ecological struggles that I have placed as the heart of the reflection developed in this chapter.

Nevertheless, a 'circular society' is certainly not the worst-case scenario. It remains entirely possible that the reformist hypothesis will fail, leaving us to helplessly witness the commodification of the general intellect, with its potential for emancipation subjugated and inequalities deepened. Hence, let me repeat: there is no reason to be particularly optimistic. There is no 'automatic' mechanism that would carry us beyond

---

109   Bonomi, Della Puppa and Masiero, *La società circolare*, 151.
110   Ibid., 164–5.

capitalism. However, it is possible to transform a line of flight, one mistaken for an already existing process, into a political objective of contemporary socio-ecological struggles. In this light – conceiving of anti-capitalism as a task and not as a given – one could fully agree with the final reflection by André Gorz, the thinker who made it possible for me to initiate this new dialogue between Catalan degrowth and *operaismo*, and to whom I can only express my deepest gratitude:

It is the fact that relations of domination are inherent in the industrial mode of production – which remains structurally a capitalism even when industry is 'collectivised' – that explains the persistence of nostalgic utopias that link degrowth, de-industrialisation and a return to largely autarkic village, communal and/or family economies, in which production is essentially craft production. However, the possibility of a quite different simultaneous exit from industrialism and capitalism is currently emerging. Capitalism itself is working involuntarily towards its own extinction by developing the tools for a kind of hi-tech craft production that makes it possible to manufacture almost any three-dimensional objects with a much higher level of productivity than industry and with a minimal consumption of natural resources . . . ['Digital fabricators', or 'fabbers'] would enable groups that are excluded or doomed to inactivity or underemployment by the 'development' of capitalism to come together in communal workshops to produce everything they and their communities need . . . An economy beyond 'employment', money and commodities, based on the pooling of the products of an activity originally conceived as shared – a zero-cost economy – begins to seem possible.[111]

---

111   André Gorz, 'Global Crisis', in *Ecologica*, trans. Chris Turner (Calcutta: Seagull Books, 2010), 128–30.

Conclusion

If the hope that new technologies and the new economy could revive the cycle of accumulation once reflected in the self-referential goals of neoclassical economics, perhaps today it is time to go back to the origins of the crisis that began in the 1970s and rethink the role of work in a society that can finally provide for its own needs, and rethink the role of knowledge no longer as an object of utility whose value is defined by the immediate needs of the market, but as an end in itself.

Francesca Coin, 'La fine della conoscenza?'

To recall some of the fundamental analytical points in this book through a provocative comparison, one could say that, just as at the beginning of the twentieth century, Progress was always right, even when it was wrong, so at the beginning of the twenty-first century socio-ecological struggles are always right, even when some of their assessments might prove imprecise.

It is well known that, about a century ago Filippo Tommaso Marinetti, Italian Futurist poet, pronounced these words: 'Have faith in Progress, which is always right, even when it is wrong, for it is movement, life, struggle, and hope.'[1] What he meant was that, whatever form such Progress may take, its costs would pale in comparison to its benefits. Moreover, this was an idea common to all futurisms. As Vladimir Mayakovsky wrote, 'after electricity, I could no longer be interested in nature: so imperfect'.[2]

---

1   Filippo Tommaso Marinetti, *Critical Writings*, trans. Doug Thompson, ed. Günter Berghaus (New York: Farrar, Strauss and Girous, 2006), 251.

2   Vladimir Mayakovsky in Fausto Borrelli, *Poesia della tecnica: Majakovskij, due chiacchiere con la Tour Eiffel e il Ponte di Brooklyn*, in *Energia Ambiente e Innovazione* 1, 2006, 71.

Which, if read in the light of Lenin's revolutionary equation (communism = soviet + electrification), means: humanity's dominion over nature by means of technology (over productive forces) represents a positive achievement regardless of the social project to which that dominion is directed (the social relations of production). At the beginning of the twentieth century – and up until the crisis of Fordism – I believe that this conceptual framing was essentially reasonable.[3]

However, this is simply no longer the case today. The apparent autonomy of the productive forces and the telluric seduction of Progress were, in fact, grounded in a real (though partial) overlap between the logic of value and the logic of wealth. Now that their growing separation presents itself as self-evident, the terms of the problem have changed. Political intervention in the realm of productive forces has become an essential element of the social relations of production. The conflict arises no longer at the level of mere use of technology but directly at the level of the goals to which technological development must be directed. This is why, even if in the future a wonderfully well-meaning engineer were to assure us that constructing a high-speed railway (*Treno ad Alta Velocità*, TAV) between Lyon and Turin would not harm the health of the people of the Susa Valley or damage the Alpine ecosystem,[4] the reasons for the popular struggle would still stand. This is because the model of development embodied in that high-speed train has nothing to do with the concept of well-being shaped through a struggle that has lasted more than a quarter of a century. In short, whatever form *this* Progress may take, its benefits pale in comparison to its costs. Unlike a century ago, the quantitative terrain is no longer the one on which costs and benefits are compared. Increasingly, we are faced with socialized costs and privatized benefits. It is in this discrepancy that quality breaks the logic of value and ushers in the sphere of the beyond-measure (*fuori misura*). But this does not mean that comparability vanishes. Rather, comparability no longer pre-exists

---

3   In this regard, I would like to highlight the impressive (visual) reflection by Davide Ferrario, namely the documentary *La zuppa del demonio: quando l'industria e gli operai facevano sognare l'Italia* (Rossofuoco / Rai Cinema, 2014).

4   This is a hypothesis that, as things stand at present, is absolutely nonsense: mine is an attempt at proof by absurdity.

the things being compared; it must, instead, be produced as the outcome of a prior negotiation between social actors. The logic of wealth is the realm not of cultural relativism but of political mediation between fundamentally incommensurable instances.

As Francesca Coin suggests in the epigraph of this Conclusion, it is time to 'go back to the origins of the crisis that began in the 1970s and rethink the role of work in a society that can finally provide for its own needs'. In other words, contemporary socio-ecological struggles express a class composition that is shaped not by the neutrality of the productive forces but by their immediate incorporation into the social relations of production and the struggles that traverse them. What kind of producers do we want to be? What kind of society do we want to live in? What kind of relations do we seek with the otherness within us, and with the alterity that surrounds us? These are not distant, imaginary questions to be deferred until after the Winter Palace has been stormed. They are strategic questions for the present.

If there is a red thread running from beginning to end through this book, it is the conviction that the political stakes of the present reconfigure our interpretation of the past in such a way that their urgency can be fully expressed. The key point structuring my reflections here is the need to conceive of the ecological crisis as constitutively linked to the transformations of labour and to capitalist development. I thus examined the emergence and consolidation of the 'classical' labour-nature-value nexus, aiming to highlight both its internal tensions – namely, the simultaneous impoverishment of workers in production and of all subjectivities in reproduction – and its so-called progressive side, that is, the broad (if uneven) rise in the level of living standards. I then analysed the crisis of the 'classical' nexus and the emergence from within it of a 'new' nexus between labour-nature-value. I also clarified that this relationship should be understood in terms not of substitution but rather of complementarity. In this light, the central hypothesis is that the growing divorce between the logic of value and the logic of wealth – as the outcome of the socio-environmental struggles of 1968–73 – produced a widening split between *entropic* wage labour and (potentially) *negentropic* cognitive-reproductive work. It is within this shift from a partial overlap between value and wealth to their increasingly pronounced decoupling that capital's progressivism embarks on its downward trajectory, a trend further exacerbated by the major crisis we have been living through over the past decade.

Entropic labour and (potentially) negentropic work today coexist in ways that can range from mutual consolidation to open friction. Among the former are phenomena such as the incorporation of climate rent into the budgets of oil companies – or, more broadly, of enterprises with strong links to fossil capital – or the equivocal attitude of various governments, including Italy's, which pay lip service to the Paris Agreement but, when faced with the necessity to act concretely, fatally succumb to the allure of the drill. Instances of the latter include the fierce battles over the distribution of subsidies and incentives – where the fossil industry does everything in its power to obstruct (especially fiscal) support for 'decarbonization' strategies. Also, they include the repugnant mobilization of the (strictly white) working class by Donald Trump in his nationalist offensive against the global green economy, which he portrays as the domain of financiers and liberals.

Given the centrality of labour issues in my argument, I believe that this point deserves brief elaboration. On 28 March 2017, as he prepared to sign the Executive Order promoting energy independence and economic growth, Trump, surrounded by visibly pleased representatives of the white working class, declared,

That is what this is all about: bringing back our jobs, bringing back our dreams – and making America wealthy again . . . Finally, I want to acknowledge the truly amazing people behind me on this stage: our incredible coal miners. (Applause) We love our coal miners. Great people. Over the past two years, I've spent time with the miners all over America. They told me about the struggles they've endured. I actually, in one case, I went to a group of miners in West Virginia and I said, how about this: Why don't we get together, we'll go to another place, and you'll get another job; you won't mine anymore. Do you like that idea? They said, no, we don't like that idea – we love to mine, that's what we want to do. I said, if that's what you want to do, that's what you're going to do. And I was very impressed. They love the job. That's what their job is. I fully understand that. I grew up in a real estate family, and until this recent little excursion into the world of politics, I could never understand anybody who would not want to be in the world of real estate. (Laughter) Believe me. So, I understand it. And we're with you, 100 percent, and that's what you're going to do. Okay? (Applause)[5]

This is a dramatic situation that allows for no shortcuts. Indeed, it would simply be absurd to accuse these miners of selfishness – as if defending their immediate class interests were somehow shameful – or even of environmentalist ignorance. The job blackmail (in its various forms: either wage or health, either wage or social stigma and so on) is not a matter of shortcuts. It is a real tragedy, rooted as it is in the 'peculiar' defeat of social movements in the Long 1968. However, it is also an impasse that must be addressed. In the face of a president testing miners' willingness to change jobs, while an opportunistic refusal may well be understandable, the social desirability and ecological necessity for a less extractivist economic model should no longer be in question. A key political objective of trade union strategy should be to ensure that workers' identity and pride, certainly an indispensable requirement of class struggle, no longer coalesces primarily around entropic labour. It is in this sense that the ecological class consciousness theorized by Stefania Barca is indeed a fundamental issue.

The practical imagination of a society marked by the dual strategy of shrinking entropic labour and liberating negentropic work is already, in point of fact, an internal dimension of contemporary class composition. The task is to learn, by means of conflict, how to articulate this more effectively. And it is along this path that a confrontation between Catalan degrowth and *operaismo* acquires its distinctly political sense. This entails the construction of a shared horizon of struggle capable of bringing together different subjects (trade unions, civil society organizations, anti-austerity movements and so on) around a basic programme whose cornerstones might include: reduction of working hours; joint introduction of a minimum wage, unconditional basic income and universal basic services; shrinking of social metabolism; and autonomy of

---

5   'Remarks by President Trump at Signing of Executive Order to Create Energy Independence', *trumpwhitehouse*, 28 March 2017, trumpwhitehouse.archives.gov.

territorial struggles.[6] Each of these elements directly shapes class composition. And each one, in turn, traces an ever-deeper divide between the logic of wealth that inspires them and the logic of value that limits their potential.

To conclude, I hope to have shown at least two things. First, that the effort to liberate the negentropic dimension of contemporary work represents an important terrain of class struggle in the twenty-first century. And second, that engaging with this struggle may well benefit from opening a channel of dialogue between degrowth and Marxism. I would therefore like to end with another excerpt from Carla Ravaioli's interview with Claudio Napoleoni, the same interview from which the epigraph to this book's Introduction was drawn:

RAVAIOLI: At this point, class conflict should be reborn in a form that is quite different from the traditional one . . .

NAPOLEONI: Yes, because the terrain of the struggle changes. Now, it lies in the implementation of the second industrial revolution [meaning the microelectronic revolution that began in the 1970s].

RAVAIOLI: So, you agree with me that the Left should by all means encourage and promote the widespread adoption of microelectronic technologies, rather than opposing them and, at the same time, launch a major battle for the radical and generalised reduction of working hours?

NAPOLEONI: Certainly, these are the two essential fronts. First and foremost, we must ensure that the innovation process takes place.

---

6   In this regard, it is worth mentioning the extraordinary political work of the German degrowth movement, which in the 2017 project *Degrowth in Bewegung(en)* set up a highly participative and wide-ranging ground for discussion between various campaigns and movements, including: 15M, Buen Vivir, Care Revolution, Climate Justice, Food Sovereignty, Free Software, Refugees' Movements, Basic Income and Trade Unions; see Corinna Burkhart, Matthias Schmelzer and Nina Treu (eds), *Degrowth in Movement(s): Exploring Pathways for Transformation* (London: zer0 Books, 2020).

The replacement of human labour by the 'intelligent machine' is a goal to be pursued as something good in itself, and should be taken up by the Left as a programme priority above all other actions. Yes, I agree that the second terrain of struggle, which follows politically and immediately from the first, is the commitment to reduce working hours. For trade unions, in particular, this means shifting the focus from the traditional objective of workers' movements: no longer using the increase in productivity from technical progress solely to increase wages, but instead to reduce the amount of work performed per unit of time . . . The very economic mechanism on which the market is based, namely competitiveness, would lose relevance. And competitiveness is an aggressive, violent mechanism in which the life of each depends on the death of others. The entire social process it enables presupposes the existence of winners and losers. I repeat: reducing working hours, also as a precondition for women to enter the world of wage labour in far greater numbers and with a far more qualified presence than in the past, would amount, as it were, to the sanction of a social transformation in which the element of femininity emerges as a characteristic feature of a new society.

RAVAIOLI: Besides, a policy aimed at reducing the share of labour provided would also mark a trend reversal with respect to recent history, a history shaped by productivist myths, by a belief in technology as a cure for all ills, by the blind faith in the acquisitive economy, in quantitative growth as the guarantor of Progress, and in the fetish of GDP as the sole and supreme measure of well-being. These myths, which have also taken hold on the Left, now are not only being exposed as increasingly hollow, but are also leading us to environmental catastrophe.[7]

---

7   Claudio Napoleoni and Carla Ravaioli, 'La politica degli orari di lavoro', in *Tempo da vendere, tempo da usare: lavoro produttivo e lavoro riproduttivo nella società microelettronica*, ed. Carla Ravaioli (Milan: Franco Angeli, 1988), 158–61.

Index

Etliche Sekunden lang reagierte ich nicht. Er versuchte, mich zu ködern. Ich senkte die Stimme und sprach ganz ruhig. „Das geht zu weit. Ich sage Ihnen was. Ich möchte, dass Sie gehen. Sie können herzlich gerne meinen Anwalt kontaktieren." Ich zog eine Show ab und tippte auf meinem Device herum, so als riefe ich Informationen auf, um sie ihnen zu schicken. Ich hatte keinen Anwalt. Ich glaubte nicht, dass sie meinen Bluff durchschauen würden.

„Wir entschuldigen uns, Colonel Butler", sagte Mallory. „Sie haben recht. Das ging zu weit. Sergeant Burke hat es nicht so gemeint. Sagen Sie ihm, dass es Ihnen leidtut, Burke."

„Tut mir leid", sagte Burke. Es tat ihm nicht leid.

„Nicht der Rede wert", sagte ich. Ich vergab ihm nicht.

„Sind Sie sich sicher, dass Sie uns nichts sagen können, das uns vielleicht helfen könnte?", fragte Mallory.

„Ich nehme an, dass es kein natürlicher Tod war?", fragte ich.

Mallory dachte darüber nach, wieder wog sie ab, was sie mir mitteilen sollte. „Nein. Es war nicht natürlich."

„Er sollte gestern um drei Uhr nachmittags zu einem Treffen erscheinen. Im Gerard's, wie gesagt. An der Ecke Vine Street und Latten."

Burke schaltete sich ein. „Ich glaube, ich kenne den Laden. Viel falsches Holz?" Er verhielt sich zwanglos, aber er war vermutlich schon dort gewesen. Sie wussten, dass wir uns zwei Tage zuvor zum Mittagessen getroffen hatten, also hatten sie den Laden mit ziemlicher Sicherheit überprüft.

„Ja, das ist er", sagte ich. „Wir haben uns auch vorgestern dort zum Mittagessen getroffen."

„Worum ging es bei Ihrem Treffen?", fragte Mallory.

„Eine gemeinsame Freundin hat uns miteinander bekannt gemacht. Eine andere Soldatin. Sie weiß, dass ich nicht viele Freunde in der Stadt habe, also dachte sie, das wäre vielleicht gut für mich." Ich hatte nicht das Bedürfnis, die ganze Wahrheit zu erzählen, besonders nicht, solange ich nicht wusste, ob sie mich für einen Zeugen oder einen Verdächtigen hielten.

Sie tippte etwas in ihr Device. „Und Sie haben sich so gut verstanden, dass Sie beschlossen, sich gestern Nachmittag wiederzusehen?"

Ich lächelte sie mit einem falschen Lächeln an. „Ich habe es Ihnen schon gesagt. Ich habe keine Ahnung, worum es ging. Er hat mich kurz nach zwei angerufen und gebeten, zu kommen. Ich hatte nichts zu tun, also sagte ich: ‚Wieso nicht?'" Ich dachte mir, dass sie die Anrufliste hatten und den Anruf sehen würden, also ergab es Sinn, das zu erzählen. Angestellt bei Omicron hatte er vermutlich eine Leitung mit High-End-Verschlüsselung, so wie ich, aber bei einem Mord – angenommen, dass es einer war – konnte die Polizei die Anrufe vielleicht doch nachverfolgen. „Als er nicht auftauchte, rief ich ein paar Mal in seinem Büro an, aber es ging sofort der Anrufbeantworter dran."

„Haben Sie das gemeldet?", fragte sie.

„Was gemeldet? Dass ein Typ nicht zu einem Meeting aufgetaucht ist?"

Burke sah aus, als wolle er mich etwas fragen, aber Mallory machte eine beinahe unsichtbare Handbewegung, um ihn davon abzuhalten. Sie wandte sich mir zu und lächelte. „Colonel Butler, es tut mir leid, Ihnen so früh am Tag eine solche Nachricht überbracht zu haben. Wenn Ihnen irgendetwas einfällt, das uns vielleicht hilft, rufen Sie mich an. Sie finden meine Nummer in Ihrem Sicherheitssystem – seit dem Scan vorhin."

„Sicher." Ich folgte ihnen zur Tür, Burke blickte sich noch immer in der Wohnung um, als könne er irgendwo ein blutiges Messer erspähen.

Mallory drehte sich zu mir um, nachdem sie draußen war, sprach beinahe über ihre Schulter mit mir. „Ach, und Colonel Butler? Bitte verlassen Sie den Planeten nicht."

„Sagen Sie mir, dass Sie was Gutes für mich haben", sagte ich, als Plazz meinen Anruf entgegennahm. Ich hatte vielleicht eine halbe Stunde gewartet, nachdem die Polizei weg war, und gehofft, in besserer seelischer Verfassung zu sein. Es hatte nicht geklappt.

„Schön, von Ihnen zu hören, Carl. Es geht mir großartig, wie geht es Ihnen?"

„Nun, ich wurde gerade von der Polizei befragt, und ich nehme an, es geht um den Mord an einer Führungskraft auf mittlerer Ebene von Omicron, also–"

„Heilige Scheiße."

„Ja. Auf meiner Seite stehen die Dinge also ziemlich still, und ich weiß nicht, wo ich als Nächstes hinsoll. Also hoffe ich, dass Sie etwas für mich haben."

„Wer ist tot?"

„Ich will nicht drüber reden", sagte ich. „Was haben Sie über den Einbruch rausgefunden?"

„Vergessen Sie's. Sie können nicht einfach ein *,Es gibt da diesen Toten'* fallen lassen und dann sagen, dass Sie nicht drüber reden wollen", sagte sie.

„Ja, das ist fair." Ich erzählte ihr von Gylika und dem Besuch der Polizei.

„Danke, Carl."

„Wofür?"

„Dafür, dass Sie wirklich Ihre Informationen mit mir teilen."

Ich schüttelte den Kopf und grinste unwillkürlich. „Sie sind ein Arsch."

„Arschlöcher kriegen Sachen geregelt."

„Das ist wahr", sagte ich. „Also, erzählen Sie mir von dem Einbruch."

„Ihre offizielle Antwort auf meine Nachfrage ist Ahnungslosigkeit."

Ich grunzte. „Na toll."

„Das ist nicht sonderlich überraschend. Es ist nichts öffentlich und sie wollen nicht, dass es an die Öffentlichkeit gelangt. Denken Sie drüber nach, wie die Aktienteilhaber reagieren würden, wenn sie rausfinden würden, dass es eine Sicherheitslücke gibt, die vielleicht jemand ausgenutzt hat."

Ich seufzte. „Verstehe. Aber das hilft uns nicht gerade."

„Es gibt abgesehen von den offiziellen Kanälen andere Wege, an Informationen zu gelangen. Das wissen Sie."

„Also haben Sie was." Ich konnte es in ihrer Stimme hören.

„Ich habe *vielleicht* etwas. Ich kann mit ziemlicher Sicherheit sagen, dass es eine Lücke gegeben hat, und dass ein paar Leute bei Omicron deswegen ziemlich aufgeregt sind. Nicht im positiven Sinne."

„Das ist etwas", sagte ich.

„Ist es, aber ich finde nicht heraus, was passiert ist."

„Shit. Wie sieht es mit dem Wie aus?", fragte ich.

„Keine Chance. Von der Quelle, die ich jetzt habe, erfahre ich das nicht. Und ich glaube nicht, dass jemand, der Bescheid weiß, mit mir reden wird. Es ist ein ziemlich kleiner Kreis, nach dem, was ich so höre."

„Ich verstehe. Und ich glaube, dass der Kreis heute um eine Person kleiner geworden ist. Das ist eine sichere Leitung, richtig?" Ich hätte vorher daran denken sollen. Beim Militär hatte ich das nie fragen müssen.

„Absolut. Sie glauben, Ihr Typ wusste Bescheid?", fragte sie.

„Gibt es eine andere Erklärung? Als er mich anrief, klang es, als hätte er mir etwas mitzuteilen. Jetzt ist er tot."

„Lassen Sie mich diesen Tod untersuchen", sagte sie. „Omicron kann dichtmachen und mich ausschließen, aber die Polizei kann das nicht. Da gibt es zu viele Lecks. Ich lasse Sie wissen, was ich finde."

„Danke", sagte ich.

„Sehen Sie, wie das funktioniert? Sie teilen Informationen mit mir und ich besorge Ihnen Antworten. Es ist beinahe so, als würden wir zusammenarbeiten."

„Ja, ja. Wir sprechen uns später."

Kapitel sieben

Ich wollte Dernier aus dem Weg gehen, als ich zur Arbeit ging. Ich würde ihm von Gylika erzählen müssen, er würde weitere Informationen verlangen und in meiner psychischen Verfassung wollte ich mich damit nicht auseinandersetzen. Er würde es herausfinden, aber ich wollte warten. Trotz meines Verlangens, es mit niemandem zu teilen, glaubte ich nicht, dass ich damit durchkäme, Javier außen vor zu halten, also ging ich in sein Büro, nachdem ich meinen ersten Kaffee getrunken hatte. Ich hatte noch eine zweite Agenda. Ich würde ihm von Gylika erzählen, aber ich wollte ihn auch nach seiner ursprünglichen Quelle beim Militär fragen. Seine Sekretärin bot mir einen weiteren Kaffee an, dann führte sie mich in sein Büro.

Javier sprach, ohne von seinem Bildschirm aufzusehen. „Carl. Sie gehen dem Anwalt, den ich Ihnen zugewiesen habe, aus dem Weg.“

„Was? Nein. Ich war lediglich beschäftigt.“ *Aber es ist gut zu wissen, dass er Ihnen Bericht erstattet.*

„Sie sind ein schlechter Lügner, Carl.“

Das bin ich, wenn ich will, dass man mich dabei ertappt. „Okay. Ich hatte nichts, also bin ich ihm aus dem Weg gegangen.“

„Aber jetzt haben Sie etwas.“

Ich atmete hörbar aus. „Nein.“

„Aber …“ Er klappte seinen Bildschirm zu und sah mich an.

Ich zuckte mit den Schultern. „Ich dachte, ich hätte etwas. Dann gab es einen Toten.“

Er zögerte einen Moment. Er hatte es noch nicht gewusst. Gut. „Oh, Shit. Was meinen Sie damit?“

Ich nahm mir einen Moment Zeit, ihn über Gylikas Tod, die Ereignisse des vergangenen Tages und alles andere, was sonst vorgefallen war, auf den neusten Stand zu bringen. Ich erwähnte weder Plazz noch Ganos. Er brauchte meine Quellen nicht zu kennen, nur die Informationen und warum ich nicht weiterkam.

„Tja … Scheiße. Was machen wir jetzt? Wir müssen uns aus dieser Sache verabschieden, richtig?“ Er stand auf und begann, auf und ab zu gehen. „Die Polizei hat sich eingeschaltet. Das könnte schlecht für uns aussehen.“

„Ich glaube nicht“, sagte ich. „Ich bin es nicht gewesen. Die Optik mag nicht toll sein, aber am Ende habe ich mich mit dem Mann nur zum Mittagessen getroffen. Er hat mir nichts erzählt und eine gemeinsame Freundin hat das Treffen vereinbart. Wir waren nur zwei Ex-Militärs, die Zeit miteinander verbracht haben.“

„Aber die Leute werden es nicht so sehen“, sagte Javier.

„Ich kann es fallen lassen, wenn Sie wollen“, sagte ich. „Aber Sie haben mir diesen Auftrag erteilt, weil Sie sich Sorgen wegen der Sicherheitslücke gemacht haben. Für mich wird die Sache dadurch nicht weniger beunruhigend, sondern noch besorgniserregender. Was, wenn sich die Leute, die für den Einbruch bei Omicron verantwortlich sind, auch um Gylika gekümmert haben?" Damit überraschte ich mich selbst. Ich hatte nicht vorgehabt, darauf zu drängen, den Auftrag weiterzuführen, aber als ich es sagte, fühlte es sich augenblicklich richtig an. Gylika war vielleicht wegen etwas gestorben, das ich in Gang gesetzt hatte, und ich wollte Antworten haben.

„Halten Sie das für wahrscheinlich?", fragte er. „Egal … darum geht es nicht. Der Punkt ist, dass es jetzt eine Polizeiangelegenheit ist. Es geht uns nichts mehr an."

„Doch, das tut es. VPC ist vielleicht in Gefahr. Es ist unsere Pflicht, zu handeln, um die Firma so gut es geht zu schützen."

Er hielt inne und dachte nach. Dann nickte er und sagte: „Ich schätze schon. Okay, bleiben Sie dran. Aber Sie müssen wohlüberlegt vorgehen. Was haben Sie vor?"

„Ich könnte versuchen, noch eine Kontaktperson bei Omicron zu finden, aber ehe die Polizei nicht herausgefunden hat, was Gylika zugestoßen ist, wäre das ziemlich verantwortungslos."

„Richtig", sagte er. „Das ist definitiv der falsche Weg."

„Ich habe noch einen anderen", sagte ich und legte meinen Köder aus.

„Welchen?"

„Wer war Ihre ursprüngliche Quelle beim Militär? Wenn ich das wüsste, hätte ich gute Chancen, mich mit ihm … oder ihr … in Verbindung und dort neu anzusetzen." Ich versuchte, meinen Atem nicht anzuhalten. Javier hatte meinen einzigen Anhaltspunkt, und ich ertappte mich dabei, sehr am Ausgang der Sache interessiert zu sein.

Er atmete tief durch die Nase ein, dann ging er auf die andere Seite des Raumes und starrte aus dem Fenster. Ich folgte ihm, kam ihm aber nicht zu nahe.

„Ich bin mir nicht sicher, ob ich das tun kann", sagte er, nachdem er mindestens eine Minute geschwiegen hatte. Entweder hatte er ernsthaft darüber nachgedacht oder so getan. Ich vermutete, dass es Ersteres gewesen war. Wenn ich eine Möglichkeit gehabt hätte, ihn unter Druck zu setzen, glaube ich, dass er mir die Information gegeben hätte. Stattdessen hielt ich mich zurück. Er schien abzuwägen, ob er überhaupt weitermachen wollte, und ich wollte nicht, dass er mir sagte, ich solle die Sache ganz fallenlassen.

Ich ließ die Stille solange wie möglich andauern. „Ich werde einen anderen Weg finden."

Er dachte noch etwas länger nach. „Ja. Sie haben recht. Wir müssen etwas tun. Finden Sie einen anderen Ansatzpunkt." Er starrte mich mit diesem Alphamännchen-Blick an, den manche Führungskräfte bekommen, als würde er mich herausfordern, ihm zu widersprechen.

„Das kann ich tun." Ich hatte noch Karten, die ich hätte spielen können. Ich sagte nicht, dass jemand gestorben war, und dass es uns in größere Gefahr brachte, wenn er Informationen zurückhielt. Er wusste das, und musste Gründe dafür haben, mir seine Kontaktperson nicht zu nennen. Er musste sich als Chef um mehr Dinge einen Kopf machen als ich. Alles, was die Firma traf, traf auch ihn. Ich würde einen anderen Weg finden. Das tat ich immer.

„Sir, wo gehen wir hin?"

„Man nennt es Mittagessen, Ganos. Menschen essen.“ Ich suchte einen Weg durch die Menge, die den Bürgersteig zu dieser geschäftigsten Zeit des Tages bevölkerte, Ganos im Schlepptau.

„Richtig. Sir, Sie gehen nicht auswärts zum Mittagessen.“

„Sicher tue ich das.“

„Lassen Sie mich das umformulieren. *Ich* gehe nicht auswärts zum Mittagessen.“

„Exakt. Das ändern wir.“

„Wir sind draußen. Ich arbeite in der IT. Ich bin nicht fürs Mittagessen angezogen.“ Sie trug violette Yogapants und einen grauen Hoodie. Sie hatte nicht ganz unrecht.

„Wir gehen irgendwohin, wo es zwanglos ist.“

„Da ich davon ausgehe, dass Sie etwas von mir wollen, zahlen Sie. Gehen wir irgendwohin, wo es gute Fritten gibt.“

„Verstanden.“ Ich sah mich um, um sicherzustellen, dass uns niemand folgte. Ich hatte angefangen, zu glauben, dass meine Paranoia etwas Gutes sein könnte. Natürlich war das an und für sich paranoid, aber Vorsicht ist die Mutter der Porzellankiste.

Ich ging an zwei Läden vorbei, ehe ich mich schließlich für einen entschied, der ein Stück die Straße hinunter lag. Ich hatte es Ganos nicht erzählt, aber ich wollte nicht, dass irgendjemand aus der Firma – besonders Dernier – uns gemeinsam essen sah, was bedeutete, dass wir uns weiter vom Firmengebäude entfernen mussten.

„Wir hätten in eins der anderen Restaurants gehen können, die näher waren“, sagte sie, sobald wir uns setzten. „Moment mal … Oh, heilige Schei– … Sie schämen sich, mit den kleinen Leuten aus der Firma gesehen zu werden, nicht wahr?“

„Waren Sie schon mal hier?“

„War ich nicht.“ Sie lachte. „Ich werde einen Milchshake bestellen.“

„Bestellen Sie, was Sie wollen.“

„Sir … was ist los? Sie verhalten sich echt seltsam. Es geht um die Sache, die ich untersucht habe, richtig?“

„Ja.“ *Natürlich hatte sie es sich zusammengereimt.* „Es war eine harte Woche. Schauen Sie, ich werde Sie bitten, etwas zu tun. Sie können nein sagen.“ Das war natürlich Bullshit. Ich wusste, dass Sie nicht ablehnen würde. Ich hasste mich dafür, dass ich so ein Arschloch war. Okay, das stimmt nicht, aber ich tat so, als ob, damit ich mich nicht so mies fühlte.

Wir verstummten, als die Kellnerin kam und unsere Bestellung aufnahm. Ganos hielt Wort und bestellte die ungesundesten Sachen auf der Karte. Ich bestellte einen Geflügelsalat. Ich machte Smalltalk, bis das Essen kam, und beobachtete die Tür, um zu sehen, wer das Lokal betrat. Niemand schien misstrauisch zu sein. Sobald ich so entspannt war wie möglich, kam ich zum Punkt.

„Ich will, dass Sie sich in Javier Sanchez’ Computer hacken.“

Ich hatte gewartet, bis Ganos den Mund voller Milchshake hatte, ehe ich es sagte. Wie gesagt: Arschloch. Ich musste ihr zugutehalten, dass sie ihn nicht ausspuckte.

„Ich lehne mich mal aus dem Fenster und sage, dass das keine gute Idee ist.“

„Sie können es also nicht?“, fragte ich.

„Ich bitte Sie", sagte sie. „Mit wem reden Sie hier? Ich *kann* es. Die Frage ist, ob ich es tun *sollte.* Mr. Sanchez weiß nicht, wer ich bin. Ich würde es bevorzugen, wenn das so bliebe."

Ich hatte genau genommen nach demselben Grundsatz gelebt, bis er mir diese Sache zugewiesen hatte. Ich konnte das nachvollziehen.

Aber ich drängte sie dennoch.

„Was, wenn ich sage, dass er es genehmigt hat?"

„Er hat genehmigt, dass man seinen eigenen Account hackt?" Sie verdrehte die Augen nicht, aber ich glaube, nur aus Respekt.

„Ich arbeite im Bereich Sicherheit", sagte ich. „Es ist mein Job, nach Schwächen zu suchen, besonders nach der Sache bei Omicron, von der ich Ihnen erzählt habe. Er will Lösungen. Er hat mir die Erlaubnis gegeben, ungewöhnliche Wege zu finden, um mir das potenzielle Problem anzusehen."

Sie hielt meinen Blick ein paar Sekunden lang. Sie kaufte es mir nicht ab. Kluge Frau. Und doch war da ein Funke, es ratterte in ihr. Ich hatte sie.

„Angenommen – und ich meine *angenommen* –, ich täte es ... wonach würde ich suchen?"

„Nichts Heikles. Wir brauchen lediglich etwas, um zu beweisen, dass wir drin waren. Sagen wir ... seine Adressliste."

„Seine Adressliste. Mehr nicht?"

„Ja. Das wäre ein eindeutiger Beweis, dass er gefährdet ist."

Sie nahm sich einen Moment Zeit, um darüber nachzudenken, und aß währenddessen Pommes. „Wo ist der Haken?"

„Der Haken ist, dass es besser wäre, wenn er uns nicht erwischt.“

Sie lachte. „Sir, was führen Sie im Schilde?“

Ich begegnete ihrem Blick. „Es ist besser, wenn Sie das nicht wissen. Können Sie es machen, ohne erwischt zu werden?“

„Falls ich es tue, ist es ausgeschlossen, dass man mich erwischt.“ Sie nippte an ihrem Milchshake, um mehr Zeit zum Nachdenken zu haben. „Okay. Bin dabei. Geben Sie mir einen Tag.“

„Wirklich?“

„Sicher, wieso nicht? Außerdem macht es mir Spaß, die Leute von der Sicherheit zu verarschen. Das wird lustig.“

„Danke, Ganos.“

„Ich schätze, ich soll niemandem in meiner Abteilung erzählen, was ich tue. Immerhin haben Sie sich große Mühe gegeben, dass uns niemand gemeinsam beim Mittagessen sieht“, sagte sie.

Ich verschluckte mich beinahe an meinem Wasser. Ich dachte, ich hätte mich schlau angestellt, aber ich hatte sie nicht eine Minute zur Närrin gehalten. „Das wäre am besten, ja.“

Es stellte sich als gute Vorsichtsmaßnahme heraus, dass ich Ganos vor mir zur Arbeit zurückgeschickt hatte, denn in der Lobby stieß ich mit Dernier zusammen. Seine Absätze klackerten auf dem polierten Boden, als wären selbst sie überspannt. „Ich habe von der neusten Entwicklung erfahren“, sagte er.

„Welcher Entwicklung?“, fragte ich.

„Warren Gylika“, sagte er.

„Oh, das. Ja.“

„Sie fragten, welche Entwicklung. Gibt es noch andere?", fragte er.

„Nein, eigentlich nicht."

„Würden Sie mir davon erzählen, wenn dem so wäre?"

Ich dachte darüber nach, wie ich antworten sollte. Er kannte die Antwort bereits, also erschien es mir sinnlos, es zu leugnen. „Vermutlich nicht."

„Ich weiß nicht, was ich getan habe, das Sie gegen mich eingenommen hat. Wieso erlauben Sie mir nicht, Ihnen zu helfen?"

Ich hatte keine gute Antwort darauf. Kurz nachdem ich ihm erzählt hatte, dass ich eine Spur habe, war der Mann tot. Ich gab Dernier nicht die Schuld – zumindest nicht der vernünftige Teil in mir –, aber ich konnte es auch nicht ausblenden. Das konnte ich ihm nicht sagen, also dachte ich mir eine Ausrede aus. „Es ist nichts Persönliches. Ich habe lediglich das Gefühl, dass Sie Ihrem Boss über alles, was ich ihnen erzähle, Bericht erstatten."

„Selbstverständlich erstatte ich meinem Boss Bericht. Warum sollte ich auch nicht? Wir sind die Rechtsabteilung. Es ist unser Job, die Firma aus Schwierigkeiten herauszuhalten."

„Ich glaube, Sie und ich sehen die Dinge in dieser Hinsicht unterschiedlich. Denn das halte ich für *meinen* Job."

Er blieb stehen, was mich dazu zwang, ihn entweder zurückzulassen oder ebenfalls stehen zu bleiben. Ich erwog Ersteres, überlegte es mir aber anders. „Das wird ein Problem sein", sagte er. „Ich will das nicht tun, aber ich werde es Mr. Sanchez zutragen. Ich werde nicht riskieren, gefeuert zu werden, nur weil Sie keine Lust haben, zu kooperieren."

Ertappt. Sein Gesichtsausdruck und seine Stimmlage sagten mir, dass er nicht bluffte, und ich konnte es mir nicht leisten, dass er noch mal zu Javier ging. Nach unserem letzten Meeting wusste ich, dass der CEO mich von dem Projekt abziehen würde, wenn die Rechtsabteilung auch nur einen winzigen Einwand erhob. „Also gut. Gehen wir."

„Wohin?", fragte er.

„An die Arbeit."

Ein paar Minuten später saßen wir in meinem Büro und sahen uns über meinen eleganten, aber nicht zu ausgefallenen Firmenschreibtisch hinweg an.

„Wie sehen Sie Ihre Rolle in dieser Sache?", fragte ich.

„Zuerst einmal darin, das Unternehmen vor Haftbarkeit zu schützen."

„Da wir gerade davon reden: Ich brauche vielleicht einen Anwalt. Die Polizei hat mich zu Gylikas Tod befragt."

„So ein Anwalt bin ich nicht. Und Sie wechseln das Thema", sagte er.

„Sie haben gefragt, was mir helfen würde. Ich könnte vermutlich juristischen Rat gebrauchen, obwohl ich nichts mit seinem Tod zu tun hatte."

„Sorry."

Ich seufzte. Also gut, dann würde ich eben einen anderen Kurs einschlagen. „Wie kann ich Ihnen dabei helfen, Ihren Job zu machen?"

„Ich muss wissen, was der Plan ist. Was werden Sie als Nächstes tun? Wo geht die Reise hin?"

„Ich sagte Ihnen doch schon, dass ich das für gewöhnlich erst weiß, wenn ich dort bin.“

„Damit kann ich nicht arbeiten. Ich muss meinem Boss irgendetwas geben. Können wir nicht wenigstens eine Liste potenzieller Vorgehensweisen aufsetzen?“, fragte er.

Ich war kurz davor, ihn anzublaffen, hielt mich aber zurück. Ich war zu defensiv, und das würde zur Folge haben, dass er sich mehr in die Sache reinhängte, anstatt sich zurückzuhalten. Gleichzeitig konnte ich ihm nicht von meinem tatsächlichen Plan erzählen, denn der beinhaltete den Hack des Accounts unseres CEOs, und ich musste annehmen, dass die Rechtsabteilung das missbilligen würde. Also dachte ich mir stattdessen irgendwelchen Bullshit aus. „Schauen Sie, ich stelle mir Dinge aus anderen Blickwinkeln vor als andere Leute. Das ist nicht besser oder schlechter, es ist lediglich meine Vorgehensweise. Manchmal, wenn mein Boss mich überanalysiert, sieht er ob all der Teile nicht das Gesamtbild. Ich habe es vielleicht selbst noch nicht zusammengesetzt.“

Er schien empfänglich dafür zu sein, also fuhr ich fort. „Sie und ich wollen unterschiedliche Dinge. Wir wollen beide das Beste für die Firma, aber Sie wollen ihren Boss briefen und ich will Kontrolle über die Informationen, sodass ich keine Fragen von oben bekomme, ehe ich Antworten habe. Ich will niemanden nervös machen. Diesen fundamentalen Unterschied müssen wir überwinden.“

„Wieso geht nicht beides? Was ist falsch an ein paar Fragen, wenn Sie das Richtige tun?“, fragte er.

Über diese Naivität musste ich beinahe lachen. Wie war der Typ mit dieser Einstellung Firmenanwalt geworden? „Weil ich, wenn ich Antworten vom Chef zu beantworten versuche, damit beschäftigt bin, Sachen zu verfolgen, die mir vielleicht nicht helfen, echte Antworten zu finden. Ich behalte Dinge gerne unter Kontrolle, bis ich etwas Wissenswertes zu berichten habe, dann präsentiere ich ein zusammenhängendes Bild."

Er dachte einen Moment darüber nach, ohne den Blick abzuwenden. „Okay. Ich verstehe. Vielleicht können wir uns ein System ausdenken, bei dem Sie mir mitteilen, was Sie herausfinden, aber mich wissen lassen, was ich weitergeben kann und was ich für mich behalten soll. Aber Sie müssen mit mir zusammenarbeiten. Sie müssen mir irgendetwas geben, mit dem ich die Bestie füttern kann."

Das klang so vernünftig, dass ich mich fragte, ob ich nicht von Anfang an weniger Arschloch hätte sein sollen. Das konnte ich nie ausschließen. „Damit kann ich arbeiten."

„Was den juristischen Rat betrifft, würde ich empfehlen, dass Sie nicht noch mal mit der Polizei sprechen, ohne dass ein Anwalt zugegen ist. Das gilt eigentlich für jede Situation."

„Danke. Ich schätze, dann werde ich mir jemanden suchen müssen."

„Ich kann Ihnen ein paar gute Leute empfehlen", sagte er.

Der weiße Raum stank antiseptisch und das mechanische Piepen von einem Dutzend Maschinen waren der Soundtrack dazu. Ich bewegte meine Arme, aber sie waren an das schmale Bett gebunden, eines von acht identischen im Raum. Ich war allein, hatte aber das unangenehme Gefühl, dass sich mir bald jemand anschließen würde. Ich riss meine rechte Hand vor und zurück, bis ich schließlich meine Fesseln löste. Ich befreite meinen anderen Arm und schwang meine nackten Füße auf die kalten Kacheln. Ich blickte zur Tür und erwartete, dass jeden Moment jemand hereinkäme, dann eilte ich zu einem Schaltpult hinüber.

Es passte nicht zum Rest der Szenerie. Das hier war eine medizinische Einrichtung, aber die Bedienelemente sahen aus wie etwas, das auf ein Schiff gehörte. Ein Zielcomputer. Ich schob den Gedanken beiseite und ließ meine Finger wie schon viele Male zuvor über die Tasten fliegen. Muskelgedächtnis. Ich musste die Basis zerstören. Wir hatten genug Feuerkraft im Orbit.

Ich hielt inne.

Ich war auf der Basis. Dem Planeten. Wenn ich den Feuerbefehl ausführte, unterschriebe ich mein eigenes Todesurteil. Die Szenerie verschwamm und veränderte sich, während ich das Problem zu lösen versuchte. Ich suchte in meinem Gehirn nach Antworten, aber je intensiver ich suchte, desto mehr schlüpften sie mir durch die Finger. Ich gab die Koordinaten ein und authentifizierte den Befehl. Auf dem Bildschirm erschien ein Timer und zählte herunter. Das passte nicht. Kein System beim Militär hatte einen solchen Timer. Er sah eher aus wie etwas aus einem schlecht geschriebenen Holo-Video.

Piep, piep, piep …

Ich setzte mich im Bett auf und rang nach Luft. Die Kleider, in denen ich eingeschlafen war, waren klatschnass vor Schweiß. Ich brauchte einen Moment, um

mich zu orientieren, da aufgrund der Verdunkelungs-
vorhänge kein Licht ins Zimmer drang. Ich holte mehrmals tief Luft und versuchte, meinen galoppierenden
Herzschlag zu beruhigen. Ich sank zurück ins Kissen
und schloss die Augen. Ich musste mich ausruhen, fand
aber den Rest der Nacht keinen Schlaf.

Kapitel acht

Da ich nicht schlafen konnte, tat ich das, was ich in dieser Situation immer tue. Ich ging ins Fitnessstudio. Während ich trainierte, merkte ich mir alle Dinge, die mir in den Sinn kamen. Sobald ich eine physische Liste erstellt hatte, wurde es einfacher, damit klarzukommen; weniger überwältigend. Als ich geduscht hatte und einen Kaffee trank, hatte ich eine Art Plan, und das entspannte mich stets. Das Kommando zu übernehmen und vorwärts zu marschieren, war immer besser, als stillzusitzen und darauf zu warten, dass andere tätig wurden. Wenn andere handelten, musste ich reagieren, was mich augenblicklich ins Hintertreffen brachte.

Ich konnte nicht kontrollieren, wann Ganos sich mit den Informationen aus Javiers Account bei mir melden würde, also kümmerte ich mich um andere Aufgaben. Da sich die Untersuchung verzögerte, konzentrierte ich mich auf mein übriges Leben. Ich musste mich um meine Paranoia kümmern, darum, dass ich glaubte, jemand würde mich verfolgen. Ich konnte das nicht ausschließen, und ich kannte mich gut genug, um zu wissen, dass ich nicht aufhören würde, darüber nachzudenken, solange ich keinen empirischen Beweis dafür fand, dass ich mit meinem Verdacht falschlag. Ich würde weiter darüber nachdenken und das würde dazu führen, dass ich wieder in der Praxis der Psychiaterin säße und darüber spräche, was ich zu sehen geglaubt hatte. Ich verbrachte genug Zeit mit ihr, auch ohne ein neues Thema hinzuzufügen.

Ich machte ein paar Einkäufe. Der Wind blies schneidend, und dass an diesem frühen Morgen am Wochenende so wenige Menschen unterwegs waren, machte es zwar schwieriger, in der Menge unterzugehen, bedeutete aber auch, dass ich weniger Blicken ausweichen musste. Ich stieg dreimal um, um auf die Westseite der Stadt zu fahren. Die Straßen wurden immer schmaler, die Schilder an den Geschäften weniger kunstvoll. Bei Nacht würde ich diesen Teil der Stadt nicht betreten, und selbst tagsüber machte er mich etwas nervöser, als ich es sonst war. Ich lief etwa drei Blocks von der Haltestelle und fand den Laden, den ich suchte. Auf dem digitalen Schild waren einige Pixel ausgefallen, sodass man es kaum lesen konnte, und die dicke Plexiglasscheibe verhinderte, dass man ins Ladeninnere gucken konnte, aber ich war schon mal hier gewesen und wusste, dass ich an der richtigen Adresse war.

Eine dünne, hellhäutige Frau stand hinter dem Tresen, sie war allein. Sie trug ihr schwarzes Haar auf der einen Seite lang, auf der anderen hatte sie es abrasiert, und sie hatte auf der einen Seite ihrer Unterlippe drei Nieten. Sie musterte mich mit einem Blick, der sagte, dass ich nicht hierhergehörte, obwohl sie ihren Kopf leicht neigte und mich auf diese Weise grüßte. „Was kann ich für Sie tun?"

„Ich suche nach Überwachungsausrüstung."

„Sie sind nicht von der Westside. Sie sind nur dafür den ganzen Weg hergekommen? Suchen Sie nach etwas, womit Sie aus der Entfernung Bilder machen können?"

„Ich suche nach etwas, das man nicht überall bekommt", sagte sie.

Jetzt betrachtete sie mich eindringlicher. „Was brauchen Sie?"

„Eine programmierbare Drohne", sagte ich.

„Es ist illegal, in der Stadt eine Drohne zu fliegen."

„Ich habe ein Haus draußen auf dem Land." Ich lächelte.

Sie schnaubte. „Klar. Also dieses ... Haus auf dem Land. Ich nehme an, Sie wollen etwas, das man nicht so leicht sieht?"

„Richtig", sagte ich. „Sie wissen schon ... damit sie die Tiere nicht vertreibt."

„Ich habe genau, was Sie suchen. Tiere werden gar nicht wissen, dass sie da ist. Fliegt bis zu fünfzig Meter hoch und ist leise genug, dass man sie aus fünf Metern Entfernung nicht hört."

„Videoübertragung?", fragte ich.

„Nein", sagte sie. „Nur zum Download. Nur so kriegt man sie so klein, wie Sie sie haben wollen. Außerdem reduziert das die elektronische Signatur." Sie hielt inne. „Für den Fall, dass die Tiere Elektronik aufspüren können."

Ich kicherte. „Ja. Kluge Tiere. Wie funktioniert sie?"

„Passive Sensoren. Sie setzen den Sensor auf das ... Tier an, das Sie betrachten wollen, und die Kamera der Drohne bleibt drauf. Nach einer voreingestellten Zeit kehrt sie zur vorprogrammierten Basis zurück."

„Wie groß ist sie?", fragte sie.

Sie zeigte mir etwas, das etwa halb so groß war wie eine Walnuss.

„Klingt so, als wäre es genau das, was ich suche."

„Sie ist nicht billig", sagte sie. „Und nur Bargeld."

„Ich habe Bargeld."

„Hoffentlich haben Sie viel davon."

Den Rest des Morgens verbrachte ich damit, mich durch die Nachrichten auf meinem Terminal zu scrollen. Ich suchte nach allem, was ich zu Gylikas Tod finden konnte.

So etwas konnte nicht lange geheim bleiben, selbst wenn die Polizei das wollte. Der Mann hatte vermutlich Familie – Menschen, die ihn liebten. Jemand musste darüber reden, denn selbst in einer Stadt mit 15 Millionen Einwohnern schaffte es ein Mord in die Nachrichten.

Nur, dass dem nicht so war.

Nicht direkt. Der Standardartikel, den alle Quellen brachten, ließ verlauten, dass er im Parkhaus unter dem Hauptquartier von Omicron „tot aufgefunden" worden war, nirgendwo aber wurden Mord oder die Todesursache erwähnt. Niemand veröffentlichte Bilder, abgesehen von einem Foto in der Todesanzeige, das von der Familie stammte. Omicron hatte ein offizielles Statement veröffentlicht, in dem die Firma den Verlust betrauerte und der Familie Beileid bekundete. Die Familie selbst hatte nichts geäußert; zumindest nichts, das Reporter aufgeschnappt hatten. Ich fragte mich kurz, wie viel die Familie wusste, aber ich konnte sie nicht kontaktieren, um sie das zu fragen. Das wäre unglaublich geschmacklos, ganz zu schweigen davon, dass die Polizei mich noch mehr verdächtigen würde als ohnehin schon.

Also tat ich das Nächstbeste. Ich ignorierte den juristischen Rat, den Dernier mir tags zuvor gegeben hatte und rief Lieutenant Mallory an. Ich wollte herausfinden, was sie wusste, aber sie würde es mir nicht umsonst mitteilen, also entschied ich, ein kleines Spiel zu spielen und so zu tun, als hätte ich ihr etwas zu sagen, um zu schauen, was ich von ihr erfahren konnte.

„Ich hoffe, es ist okay, dass ich Sie am Wochenende anrufe", sagte ich, nachdem ich mich vorgestellt hatte.

„Das ist kein Problem. Ich arbeite sowieso. Haben Sie was für mich?"

„Ich habe mich gefragt, wie der Status des Falles ist", sagte ich. „Haben Sie herausgefunden, was passiert ist?"

„Wieso interessiert Sie das so?", fragte sie.

Die Frage hatte ich erwartet. „Ich darf den Planeten nicht verlassen, bis Sie mich aus dem Kreis der Verdächtigen ausschließen. Ich habe Pläne."

„Was für Pläne?", fragte sie.

„Ich will mich mit einem alten Geschäftskollegen treffen, wegen einer Arbeitsangelegenheit."

Sie grunzte. „Der Fall ist noch nicht abgeschlossen."

„Keine Spuren?"

„Schauen Sie", sagte sie. „Ich bin eine viel beschäftigte Frau. Haben Sie was für mich oder nicht?"

„Vielleicht", sagte ich.

„Mr. Butler, ich empfehle Ihnen dringend, mich nicht zu verarschen. Ihnen wird das Ergebnis nicht gefallen. Jetzt sagen Sie mir, was Sie haben, oder ich lege auf."

„Ich würde gerne zu Ihnen kommen, um mit Ihnen zu reden", sagte ich.

„Dann kommen Sie."

„Da ist der Haken. Ich glaube, jemand folgt mir. Ich will nicht rausgehen." Eine Halbwahrheit, aber wahr genug.

„Ich schicke Ihnen einen Wagen. Fünfzehn Minuten." Sie legte auf.

Das Hover-Auto erschien wie versprochen pünktlich, weiß mit dem goldenen Symbol der Polizei an den Seiten und auf dem Dach, und es setzte mich ein paar Minuten später am Revier ab. Eine große Frau empfing mich am Vordereingang und führte mich nach hinten in einen fensterlosen Raum mit einer einzelnen Tür. Ein Verhörzimmer. Ich saß auf einem einfachen Stuhl mit harter Rückenlehne und wartete, bis Mallory ein paar Minuten später eintrat und die Tür schloss.

Ich zeigte in den kahlen Raum. „Ist das wirklich nötig?"

„Ich nahm an, dass wir ungestört sein wollten. Ich habe kein Büro, nur einen Schreibtisch im Großraumbüro."

„Wo ist ihr böser Bulle? Burke."

„Er ist nicht da. Lassen Sie den Scheiß, Butler. Was haben Sie?"

„Abgesehen davon, dass jemand mir folgt?"

Sie begegnete meinem Blick, ohne zu blinzeln, sagte aber nichts.

„Es fiel mir das erste Mal an dem Tag auf, als ich mich mit Gylika treffen wollte. Dem Tag, an dem er starb."

Sie zögerte einige Sekunde. „Wieso haben Sie uns das nicht erzählt, als wir in Ihrer Wohnung waren?"

„Ich konnte nicht klar denken. Vielleicht stand ich ein bisschen unter Schock, als ich herausfand, dass der Mann, mit dem ich mich treffen wollte, tot war.“

Sie kommentierte das nicht, aber ihr Gesichtsausdruck sagte: „Bullshit“.

Sie war echt gut und ich musste vorsichtig sein. „Die Person, die Ihnen gefolgt ist. Wie hat sie ausgesehen?“

„Beige Jacke“, sagte ich. „Ich bin mir nicht sicher, ob es ein Mann oder eine Frau war.“

„Also haben Sie die Person nicht genau gesehen?“

„Nein.“

„Woher wissen Sie, dass sie Ihnen gefolgt ist?“

„Instinkt“, sagte ich.

„Instinkt“, wiederholte sie mit einer Spur von Sarkasmus.

„Ich habe gelernt, darauf zu vertrauen.“

„Mr. Butler, Sie wissen, dass ich damit nichts anfangen kann.“

„Ich bin mir sicher genug, dass ich darüber nachgedacht habe, meinen alten Ansprechpartner im Militärsicherheitsdienst zu kontaktieren“, sagte ich. „Vor ein paar Jahren wurde mir ein Team an die Seite gestellt. Es hat damals ein paar Morddrohungen gegeben.“

„Wieso haben Sie ihn nicht angerufen?“

„Ich dachte, ich gebe erst Ihnen eine Chance“, sagte ich.

Sie hielt inne und sah mich nachdenklich an. „Morddrohungen. Gab es in jüngster Zeit so was?“

„Ich habe keine erhalten“, antwortete ich. „Sie müssten sich mit dem Sicherheitsdienst in Verbindung setzen, um zu schauen, ob sie welche erhalten haben, von denen ich nichts weiß.“

„Das ist nicht wirklich hilfreich", sagte sie, tippte aber eine kurze Notiz in ihr Device.

„Ich bin hier", sagte ich. „Ich versuche, zu helfen." Sie hatte mich in der Defensive, was mich davon abhielt, Informationen aus ihr rauszuholen.

„Sie sind hier, das muss ich Ihnen lassen." Sie starrte mich einige Sekunden lang eindringlich an. „Wieso sind Sie hier?"

„Weil nirgendwo in den Nachrichten steht, was dem Mann zugestoßen ist. Ich kannte ihn, wenn auch nur kurz, und ich will es wissen."

„Mr. Butler, wissen Sie, wie viele Leute in dieser Stadt Verbrechen gestehen, die sie nicht begangen haben?"

„Ich habe keine Ahnung."

„Mehr als nur ein paar. Wenn wir also publik machen, wie ein Tod zustande gekommen ist, haben wir plötzlich ein halbes Dutzend falsche Spuren. Das können wir nicht gebrauchen. Normalerweise können wir es nicht kontrollieren. Dieses Mal hatte die Sicherheitsabteilung von Omicron die Sache bereits eingedämmt, als wir eintrafen, und das Unternehmen sowie die Familie waren einverstanden, Stillschweigen zu bewahren. Militärfamilie, Sie verstehen. Gute Menschen."

Endlich hatte ich eine Möglichkeit. Mallory hatte bereits bestätigt, dass Omicron die Situation eingedämmt hatte. Zeit, zu kriegen, weswegen ich hergekommen war. „Also, wie *ist* es passiert?"

Sie sah mich an wie eine Lehrerin, die einen besonders schwierigen Schüler anschaut. „Wirklich?"

„Sind Sie sich sicher, dass er ermordet wurde?"

„Offiziell? Wir wissen nichts mit Sicherheit."

„Aber ...", bot ich an und hoffte auf einen Trostpreis.

„Wir sind uns sicher, ja.“

„Also ist er im Omicron-Gebäude gestorben. Ziehen Sie in Erwägung, dass jemand aus dem Unternehmen ihn erledigt hat?“

„Erledigt hat?“, fragte sie. „Ist das hier ein schlechtes Detektiv-Holo-Video?“

„Sie wissen, was ich meine.“

„Wir haben alles erwogen. Wenn Sie mir nichts anderes anzubieten haben, ich habe Verbrechen aufzuklären.“

„Sicher. Ich finde selbst hinaus.“

„Sollen wir Sie nach Hause fahren?“, fragte sie.

„Nicht nötig.“

„Die Person, die Ihnen gefolgt ist ...“

„Das ist echt“, sagte ich. „Ich habe vielleicht übertrieben, was das Ausmaß meiner Angst angeht.“

Sie sah mich ausdruckslos an. „Sie nehmen ein Auto.“

Kapitel neun

Ich verbrachte den Rest des Wochenendes damit, mit meiner Drohne herumzuspielen und sie in die Umgebung zu schicken. Ich fand nichts, aber damit zu spielen machte mir eine Menge Spaß, und ich lernte, sie dazu zu kriegen, dass sie tat, was ich wollte, ohne in irgendwelche Gebäude zu krachen. Meistens.

Am nächsten Morgen kam Dernier etwa fünfzehn Minuten, nachdem ich eingetroffen war, in mein Büro. Ich wusste das zu schätzen, weil es mir erlaubte, mir einen Kaffee zu holen, ehe ich wieder in die Sackgassen meiner Ermittlung abtauchen musste. „Ich habe etwas gefunden, das Sie vielleicht sehen wollen."

Ich schaltete meinen Bildschirm aus, sodass er mich nicht ablenkte und ich Dernier meine volle Aufmerksamkeit schenken konnte. „Was haben Sie?"

„Ich bin mir nicht sicher, ob es etwas ist, aber Sie haben erwähnt, dass Sie manchmal nicht wissen, wo ihre Spuren herkommen, und Sie deswegen viele Informationen bevorzugen. Ich hätte es beinahe auf unsere Seite geladen, aber ich bin mir nicht sicher, wie weit Sie damit gekommen sind–"

„Dernier", sagte ich und ließ meine Stimme so freundlich wie möglich klingen, als ich ihn unterbrach, „sagen Sie mir, was Sie haben."

„Ich habe am Wochenende über Mr. Gylika nachgedacht und über das, was ihm zugestoßen ist. Und ich habe angefangen, darüber nachzudenken, wie wir überhaupt auf seinen Namen gestoßen sind."

Es interessierte mich, dass er über Gylika nachgedacht hatte, weil ich mich unterbewusst immer noch fragte, ob er bei dessen Tod versehentlich seine Hand im Spiel gehabt hatte, aber ich schob diesen Gedanken beiseite. Ich musste ihm vertrauen. Täuschung brachte ihm nichts ein … und ich hatte keinen besseren Anhaltspunkt. „Was ist damit?"

„Er stammte aus dem Artikel, den Sie mir geschickt haben. Über das Phoenix Project", sagte er. „Ich habe diesbezüglich nachgeforscht. Es ist alles streng geheim, was Verlautbarungen des Unternehmens und die Nachrichten betrifft, selbst Wirtschaftszeitungen. Aber ich bin drangeblieben und über einen seltsamen Hinweis gestolpert. Ich habe einen unveröffentlichten Forschungsbericht von einem jungen Arzt aus einer medizinischen Hochschule auf Ferra 3 gefunden."

„Wie haben Sie ihn gefunden?", fragte ich.

„Rohe Gewalt. Wortsuche über das gesamte Netz, dann ein KI-Programm, das mir dabei half, die Einträge zu durchsuchen, bis ich jene gefunden hatte, die zu genügend meiner Kriterien passten, um sie manuell zu durchsuchen."

„Das müssen eine Menge Treffer gewesen sein."

„Nachdem die KI fertig war? Zweitausendzweihundertsiebenundvierzig." Er sagte es nebensächlich, aber es sollte mich beeindrucken. Und das tat es. Es war eindeutig ein besserer Beitrag zu dieser Sache, als eine Drohne herumfliegen zu lassen.

„Das ist viel Lesestoff."

„Ich habe bei etwa siebenhundert aufgehört, als ich etwas Vielversprechendes gefunden hatte."

Ich lehnte mich vor, mein kälter werdender Kaffee war vergessen. „Okay. Jetzt haben Sie wirklich meine Aufmerksamkeit."

„Das Paper erörterte Fortschritte im Bereich der Medizintechnologie und erwähnte nebenbei das Phoenix Project als eines der wenigen, das Potenzial habe. Viel war es nicht."

„Was war sein Fachgebiet? Von dem Typen, der das Paper geschrieben hat."

„Ortho-Robotik", sagte er.

Es war gut, dass ich gerade keinen Kaffee trank, sonst hätte ich ihn ausgespuckt. Es konnte nicht sein. Aber der Zufall war bedrohlich wie ein Asteroid, der auf eine Raumstation zurast. Ich konnte ihm nicht ausweichen.

„Was?", fragte er. „Was ist los? Sie sind gerade ganz blass geworden."

Ich war immer noch erschüttert und suchte nach einer Antwort. „Ich habe im Krieg einen Fuß verloren. Ich habe eine Menge unangenehme Zeit in Ortho-Robotik-Abteilungen verbracht."

„Oh, das tut mir leid." Sein Gesicht spiegelte ehrliche Besorgnis. „Ich wusste nicht–"

„Sie konnten es nicht wissen. Und es sind wichtige Informationen, für die Sie hart gearbeitet haben. Wenn wir sie mit anderen zusammenfügen, könnte es etwas bedeuten." Ich war wirklich zufrieden, sodass ich ihm gegenüber etwas offener war. Aber mein gerade gefasster Plan, ihm zu vertrauen, beinhaltete nicht, ihm von meiner Geschichte mit der Ortho-Robotik auf Cappa zu erzählen. Ich konnte ihm immer noch später von meinem wirklichen Verdacht erzählen, wenn sich die Sache zu etwas Ernstem entwickelte.

Natürlich log ich mir selbst in die Tasche. Kaum dass ich es gehört hatte, glaubte ich, dass es etwas Ernstes war.

„Okay, aber ich wollte wirklich nicht–“

„Denken Sie sich nichts dabei“, sagte ich. „Es war vor langer Zeit und ich habe es so gut wie überwunden.“

Er glaubte mir nicht, nickte aber und zog sich zurück. Leute tun das, wenn Soldaten von alten Dämonen aus dem Krieg erzählen. „Ich komme morgen noch mal auf Sie zu, falls keiner von uns vorher etwas anderes findet.“

„Klingt gut“, sagte ich. Ich leerte meinen Kaffee in den Mülleimer, dann stand ich auf, um mir frischen zu holen. Ich musste etwas tun. Irgendetwas.

Ich konnte mich nicht konzentrieren, also rief ich Dr. Baqri an, um zu schauen, ob sie mich in ihrem Terminplan unterbringen konnte, und sie sagte, ich solle vorbeikommen.

„Sie klangen verzweifelt, als Sie anriefen“, sagte sie, nachdem ich mich gesetzt hatte.

„Danke, dass Sie mich empfangen.“ Ich saß auf meinem gewöhnlichen Platz und starrte auf den teuren Teppich, der den falschen Steinfußboden bedeckte.

„Woran denken Sie?“

„Zufälle“, sagte ich.

„Sie haben mir schon mal gesagt, dass Sie nicht an Zufälle glauben.“

„Tue ich nicht. Aber das ist es ja gerade.“ Ich dachte einen Moment darüber nach und sie gab mir Zeit. „An welchem Punkt wird das zu Paranoia? Wenn ich denke, dass jedes kleine Teil mit anderen Teilen verbunden ist ... was, wenn ich zu viel über Dinge nachdenke?"

„Sie sind schon immer ein zuversichtlicher Mensch gewesen, richtig?"

Ich zuckte mit den Schultern. „Sicher."

„Was also ist jetzt anders?"

„Ich schätze, die Welt hat sich verändert."

Sie sah mich mit dem Blick einer Ärztin an. „Hat sich die Welt verändert oder ihr Blick darauf?"

„Seit ich Zivilist bin?"

„Genau, seitdem. Aber auch in anderen Zusammenhängen."

„Ah", sagte ich. „Seit ich getan habe, was ich getan habe. Sie wollen also sagen, dass ich, seit ich bedaure, was ich auf Cappa getan habe, in Zweifel ziehe, wie ich über andere Dinge denke."

Sie lächelte. „Das habe ich nicht gesagt."

Ich mochte sie. Manchmal wollte ich einfach, dass sie mir die Antworten gab, denn sie hatte sie. Aber es funktionierte anders, und so ungern ich zu ihr in die Praxis gehen wollte, am Ende ging es mir nach einer Sitzung immer besser als vorher. „Wie überwinde ich das? Die Selbstzweifel?"

„Nun, vielleicht müssen Sie das als neuen Normalzustand akzeptieren. Zweifel ist nichts Schlechtes."

„Aber so bin ich nicht."

„Vielleicht doch. Vielleicht ist es auch etwas, an dem Sie arbeiten könnten."

Ich nickte. Was sie sagte, ergab für mich Sinn. Ich musste an mich glauben. Wenn ich etwas sah, musste ich darauf vertrauen, egal, wie ich mich dabei fühlte.

Ich kehrte in mein Büro zurück und verbrachte dort die Mittagspause. Trotz des beruhigenden Einflusses von Dr. Baqri, konnte ich nicht stillsitzen. Jetzt, da ich fast ein ganzes Jahr lang untätig in diesem Büro gesessen hatte, erschien es mir unmöglich. Es wäre klug gewesen, die ganze Sache aufzugeben; die Ermittlung oder sogar den Job. Ich hätte mir irgendeine Entschuldigung einfallen lassen und verschwinden können. Javier würde eiligst den Stecker ziehen, wenn ich ihn darum bat.

Aber ich wollte nicht.

Irgendein Teil von mir – ein großer Teil – wollte der Sache auf den Grund gehen. Ich wollte all die Zufälle nehmen und sie nach meinem Willen gewaltsam zu einer Antwort formen. Es gab mir irgendwie das Gefühl, mehr am Leben zu sein. Es gab mir zum ersten Mal, seit ich Cappa verlassen hatte, das Gefühl, wieder relevant zu sein – und für mein eigenes Schicksal verantwortlich.

Ich bewegte mich bezüglich Dernier und den Jungs aus der Rechtsabteilung immer noch auf einem schmalen Grat. Nach meinen anfänglichen Vorbehalten hatte ich begonnen, den Mann zu mögen, aber ich musste ihn dennoch ein bisschen im Dunkeln lassen. Sobald er dachte, dass ich mich in eine Richtung bewegte, die irgendwie Aufmerksamkeit auf die Firma lenken könnte, würde er es melden. Keine wie auch immer geartete Verbindung zwischen uns würde das ändern.

In der Zwischenzeit machte ich mich auf den Weg in die IT und fand Ganos. Zehn Minuten später waren wir draußen und entfernten uns vom Gebäude.

„Die Mittagszeit ist vorbei", sagte sie.

„Noch mal Fritten zu essen würde ich nicht ertragen.“

„Es wird seltsam aussehen, dass wir zusammen weggehen.“

„Nee, die Leute werden lediglich denken, dass Sie eine Affäre haben“, scherzte ich.

„Igitt.“

Ich griff mir an die Brust. „Autsch.“

„Verstehen Sie mich nicht falsch, Sir. Für Sie wäre es ein guter Deal. Jüngere Frau, brillant, all das. Aber ich wäre das Mädchen, das mit dem alten Kerl schläft.“

Ich lachte und während ich das tat, wurde mir bewusst, wie sehr ich es brauchte. „Wir können zurückgehen. Ich wollte nicht im Gebäude reden. Zu viele VPC-Augen. Haben Sie es?“

„Sir. Was glauben Sie denn, wen Sie hier vor sich haben? Natürlich habe ich es.“ Sie fischte ein paar Seiten aus ihrer Tasche und faltete sie mehrmals. „Der Kerl hat eine Menge Kontakte. Ich habe sie nirgendwo elektronisch hinkopiert, denn das hätte–“

„Sie müssen es nicht erklären“, sagte ich. „Ich nehme an, es ist Computermagie.“

„Richtig. Magie. Magie, bei deren Wirken ich nicht erwischt werden will.“ Sie reichte mir das gefaltete Papierquadrat, ich nahm es und steckte es ohne es mir anzusehen in meine Jackentasche.

„Danke, Ganos. Das ist eine große Hilfe.“ Ich hielt inne. „Hey, falls irgendjemand das herausfindet und Sie fragt–“

„Es wird niemand herausfinden“, sagte sie. „Es sei denn, Sie erzählen jemandem davon.“

„Aber alles, was Sie tun, kann nachverfolgt werden, richtig?“

„Theoretisch? Sicher. In diesem Fall ... habe ich es so tief vergraben, dass Sie es nur finden würden, wenn sie wüssten, wonach *genau* sie suchen – wenn sie gewusst hätten, dass ich etwas tue, während ich es tue, und was genau ich vorhatte. Wenn das jemand wüsste, würde er es finden. Also ja. Es ist eine Chance von eins zu einer Million."

„Immerhin."

„Es ist okay – ich würde deshalb nicht mal gefeuert werden, Sir. Es sind eigentlich keine sensiblen Informationen. Verdammt, selbst wenn ich gefeuert werden würde, würde ich es als Prank verkaufen und behaupten, dass ich den Chef verarschen wollte. Ich hätte innerhalb von sechs Stunden einen neuen Job."

„Großartig", sagte ich. Sie hätte innerhalb von sechs Stunden einen neuen Job. Ich musste mich fragen, ob dasselbe auch für mich galt, wenn Javier herausfand, was ich getan hatte. Er wollte seine Kontaktperson geheim halten, und jetzt hatte ich das womöglich sabotiert. Ja, er würde mich definitiv feuern.

Ich widerstand dem Verlangen, mir Ganos' Papiere während der Fahrt mit den Öffentlichen anzuschauen. Ich wusste nicht, was ich darin zu finden erwartete, oder ob das, was ich finden würde, mir etwas brächte. Vielleicht fände ich seinen Kontakt beim Militär und könnte nichts damit anfangen. Vielleicht gab es keinen. Ich hielt den Kopf oben, mehr als sonst. Die Leute blickten mich an, während sie so taten, als täten sie es nicht, und mindestens eine Person flüsterte das Wort „Geißel", obwohl sie es nicht laut genug sagte, dass ich erkennen konnte, ob sie es voller Abscheu aussprach oder lediglich ihren Begleiter auf mich aufmerksam machte. Ein gut gebauter Mann mit schwarzen Haaren und goldener Haut starrte mich länger als die meisten an, länger als höflich war. Normalerweise war ich nicht auf Streit aus, aber aus irgendeinem Grund machte es mich wütend, also starrte ich zurück. Er hielt meinen Blick ein paar Sekunden, ohne ihm wirklich zu begegnen, aber dann wandte er den Blick ab, als hätte er mich nie gesehen.

Ich erstarrte.

Als er wegsah, veränderte sich die Form seiner Augen, und für den Bruchteil einer Sekunde glaubte ich, dass es cappanische Ovale waren. Ich begann zu schwitzen, kalt und klamm, und senkte den Blick zu Boden, auf meine Füße. Der Bus hielt mit einem Ruck an, eine Haltestelle vor meiner, aber ich stand auf und stolperte zur Tür. Wäre ich im Bus geblieben, hätte ich dort Wurzeln geschlagen, fürchte ich. Ich musste weg von hier. Ich ging schnell und sah mich erst um, als ich mich zwanzig Meter von der Tür entfernt hatte. Der Bus rumpelte weiter und die Leute, die ausgestiegen waren, verstreuten sich, aber der dunkelhaarige Mann war nicht darunter.

Ich holte mehrmals tief Luft und versuchte, mich zu konzentrieren. Ich steckte meine Hand in die Tasche, berührte die Papiere und versicherte mich ihrer Anwesenheit. Abgesehen von einer optischen Täuschung, verursacht durch das sich bewegende Fahrzeug, hatte ich nichts abgesehen. Ich hatte eine Mission, ein Ziel, und durfte nicht wieder von einer Panikattacke übermannt werden. Ich schaltete meinen Kopf aus, lief den verbliebenen halben Kilometer zu meiner Wohnung, ließ den ganzen Weg meine Hand in der Tasche und hielt die Liste wie einen Talisman fest.

Ich schaltete mein Sicherheitssystem aus und warf einen Blick auf die Flasche auf dem Beistelltisch, entschied mich aber dagegen. Ich faltete die Seiten auf und zerriss sie dabei fast vor Hast. Drei Seiten handgeschriebene Namen in grüner Tinte starrten mich an. Ganos' Buchstaben waren klobig und zweckmäßig, aber leicht zu lesen. Ich erkannte die meisten Namen auf Seite eins, weil ich mit ihnen zusammenarbeitete. Ich war beinahe unten auf Seite zwei angekommen, als mich ein Name ansprang.

Serata.

Shit.

Kapitel zehn

General Serata war etwa zur gleichen Zeit aus dem Militär ausgeschieden wie ich, aus denselben Gründen, allerdings war seine Pensionierung viel ruhiger verlaufen. Es hatte etwas damit zu tun, dass ich zu der Zeit die Schlagzeilen bestimmt hatte. Niemand meldete sich zu Wort und sagte, warum er zurückgetreten war, und soweit ich wusste, fragte niemand öffentlich nach. Ich hatte immer angenommen, dass es politische Gründe hatte. Es gab Gerüchte, dass er freiwillig zurückgetreten war, damit die Behörden mich im Gegenzug nicht strafrechtlich verfolgten. Er selbst hatte das nie bestätigt, aber ich schloss es nicht aus.

Er war weich gefallen. Das tun die meisten Generäle. Er hatte jetzt einen Teilzeitjob als Motivationsredner und arbeitete außerdem als Berater für hochrangige Militärmanöver. Er bekam einen Haufen Geld dafür, ein paar Tage im Monat zu arbeiten. Ich konnte das nachvollziehen, da auch VPC mich gut bezahlte. Nicht so gut wie Serata, aber ich konnte nicht klagen. Obwohl er wie ich auf Talca lebte, besuchten wir einander nie. Sein spärliches Arbeitspensum erlaubte es ihm, außerhalb der Stadt zu leben, also wohnten wir nicht nahe genug beieinander, sodass wir es einfach hatten.

Wir kommunizierten alle paar Monate, und wir redeten auch immer davon, dass wir uns treffen sollten, schafften es aber nie.

Ich gab ihm keine Schuld. Nicht dafür zumindest.

Ich hatte viel Zeit gehabt, darüber nachzudenken – wie die Sache auf Cappa geendet hatte. Viele dieser Gedanken endeten damit, dass ich schweißnass wach lag oder mein Abendessen in den Mülleimer erbrach. Aber es hatte auch klare Momente gegeben, in denen ich objektiver darüber hatte sinnieren können. Wenn ich nicht darüber nachdachte, was ich getan hatte, sondern wie es dazu gekommen war.

Die Antwort war klar: Er hatte mich reingelegt.

Ich hatte es schon vermutet, als ich noch auf Cappa gewesen war, aber als ich nach Hause kam, versuchte ich, eine andere Erklärung zu finden. Eine, die mir erlaubte, ihn immer noch als meinen Mentor zu betrachten, aber die existierte am Ende nicht. Serata hatte jemanden gebraucht, der einen Job erledigte, den er selbst nicht machen konnte, und ich war der Richtige gewesen. Ich glaube nicht, dass er gezielt nach einem Sündenbock gesucht hatte. Vielleicht bin ich, was das betrifft, naiv. Aber Serata ist ein kluger Mann, und er wird gewusst haben, welche der möglichen Ausgänge am wahrscheinlichsten waren. Vielleicht hatte auch jemand über ihm einen Sündenbock gebraucht und er hatte herhalten müssen.

Und doch, obwohl ich wusste, dass er mich benutzt hatte, warf ich ihm das nicht vor. Er hatte einen Job zu tun und er hatte ihn erledigt. Ich hatte einen Job zu tun und hatte ihn ebenfalls erledigt. Ich hatte selbst am Ende die Wahl, und ich habe sie getroffen. Er hat den Knopf nicht gedrückt. Ich hatte einen Arsch voll Cappaner getötet und als Bonus meine Ehe zerstört und mich zu einem Aussätzigen gemacht. Und so darüber nachzudenken – wie das Ganze mich beeinträchtigt hatte – führte lediglich dazu, dass ich mich nur noch mieser fühlte: Wie konnte ich es wagen, im Vergleich zu all den Leben, die ich beendet hatte, über mein kleines Leben nachzudenken? Aber ich hatte bereits auf diese Weise über die Cappaner nachgedacht, und wie es sie beeinflusst hatte, und das endete für mich stets an einem noch dunkleren Ort. Ich musste das um meiner geistigen Gesundheit willen lassen.

Wir machten den Job. Ich hasste ihn und wünschte, ich wäre nie in die Lage geraten, ihn zu machen. Wenn ich in der Zeit zurückreisen könnte, hätte ich Serata an jenem Tag in seinem Büro Nein gesagt. Schließlich hatte er mir keinen Befehl erteilt. Er hatte mich gebeten. Vielleicht hätte er jemand anderen gefunden. Hätte er das getan, wäre die Person vielleicht klüger gewesen und hätte eine andere Lösung gefunden. Eine, die nicht zum Verlust so vieler Leben geführt hätte. Vielleicht wäre diese andere mythische Person blind gewesen und hätte die Verschwörung nicht aufgedeckt, es hätte viel weniger tote Cappaner gegeben und ein immer noch fortlaufendes Projekt, bei dem genetische Experimente gemacht werden.

Ich tanzte so sehr um all die Was-wäre-wenn-Fragen herum, dass mir schwindelig wurde.

Aber ich konnte nicht in der Zeit zurück. Ich hatte Ja gesagt und war rausgeflogen nach Cappa, ich hatte getan, was ich getan hatte, und das war's. Serata hatte mich geschickt und er hatte es mit voller Absicht getan. Aber wie gesagt, ihm gab ich keine Schuld.

Ich gab mir selbst die Schuld.

Und jetzt musste ich mit ihm reden, und das bedeutete, dass ich einen Weg finden musste, um eine Brücke zu schlagen. Ich konnte ihn nicht einfach anrufen und fragen, wieso er in Javiers Kontaktliste auftauchte. Das würde mir nicht das bringen, was ich brauchte. Ich musste ihn persönlich treffen. Ich musste ihm gegenüberstehen und schauen, wie er reagierte. Vor drei Jahren hätte ich das nicht gesagt. Ich hätte ihn über den Kommunikator gefragt und ihm seine Antwort geglaubt. Jetzt nicht mehr. Ich gab ihm keine Schuld, aber das hieß nicht, dass ich ihm vertraute. Ich glaube, dass ich deswegen verbittert bin, mehr als andere, wenn es um Serata geht. Mir fehlte unsere Beziehung. Ich brauchte jemanden, dem ich vertrauen konnte, und das hätte er sein sollen.

Ich verfasste eine Nachricht auf meinem Device – an seine Privatnummer, nicht sein Büro.

Sir, ich bin morgen geschäftlich in Ihrer Nähe. Würde mich freuen, wenn wir uns treffen könnten, sofern Sie Zeit haben. Ich bin flexibel. Lassen Sie von sich hören.

Ich wartete einen Moment und las sie ein paarmal durch. Es hätte mehr drinstehen können, ein Grund, aber das würde nur zur Folge haben, dass er sich Fragen stellte. Das hier war genug. Ich drückte auf Senden.

Etwa zehn Minuten später bekam ich eine Antwort.

Carl, schön von Ihnen zu hören, Kumpel. Wieso kommen Sie nicht zum Abendessen? Sagen wir, gegen 18.30 Uhr.

Perfekt.

Ich näherte mich der Tür von Seratas Haus, das an einem Ort stand, der als Stadtrand durchging. Ein sehr reicher Teil des Stadtrands, mit großen Häusern, gepflegten Gärten und Sicherheitstoren. Ich blieb unvermittelt stehen, als Serata die Tür öffnete. Er war schon immer ein körperlich imposanter Mann gewesen, und ich weiß nicht, wieso ich etwas anderes erwartet hatte. Ich hatte mich gedanklich darauf vorbereitet, ihn wiederzusehen, aber jetzt, da er vor mir stand, war ich irgendwie verschlossen.

„Carl. Sie sehen scheiße aus, Kumpel."

Ich lachte. Ich wusste nicht, was ich von ihm erwartet hatte, aber das war es nicht gewesen. Plötzlich war alles gut. „Ich schlafe in letzter Zeit nicht gut. Sie sehen so aus, als würde es Ihnen gut gehen."

„Ich versuche, fit zu leiben. Ist aber hart. Alt zu werden ist scheiße." Er hielt inne, nicht lange genug, dass es peinlich wurde. „Kommen Sie rein", sagte er. „Lizzie macht gerade das Abendessen fertig. Wir haben noch ein paar Minuten."

Ich reichte ihm eine Flasche Whisky. „Ich habe Ihnen etwas mitgebracht."

Er nahm sie und bewunderte das Etikett. „Der gute Stoff."

„Nie mit leeren Händen dastehen. Das hat meine Mom immer gesagt."

„Kluge Frau." Er führte mich in ein Arbeitszimmer, das aussah, als gehörte es in ein Holo-Video: dunkles Holz und ein dichter brauner Teppich. Er öffnete eine

Vitrine und nahm zwei Gläser heraus. Er goss zwei Finger breit in jedes Glas, gab einen kleinen Spritzer Wasser dazu und reichte mir eins. „Wie geht es Ihnen, Carl?"

„Es geht mir gut", antwortete ich.

Er schüttelte den Kopf. „Nein. Wirklich. Wie geht es Ihnen?"

Ich nahm einen Schluck von meinem Schnaps und genoss die Wärme in meiner Kehle. „Etwa gleich. Manche Tage sind okay, manche nicht so."

Er nickte. „Treffen Sie sich mit jemandem?"

„Sie meinen eine Frau? Nein, seit Sharon weg ist, war mir nicht wirklich danach."

„Ich meine professionell", sagte er.

„Ah. Eine Seelenklempnerin. Ja, ich gehe ein paarmal im Monat hin. Bringt nicht viel. Ist ja nicht so, als gäbe es eine Selbsthilfegruppe für Leute, die das Leben von Millionen zerstört haben."

„Es hilft trotzdem, drüber zu reden."

„Sie haben vermutlich recht", sagte ich. „Vertrauen Sie denen? Ich meine, wenn ich anfange, über Sachen zu reden und das rauskommt, werden die Leute anfangen, über das zu sprechen, was ich erzähle."

Er nahm einen Schluck Whisky, dann schwenkte er den Rest in seinem Glas herum. „Ich glaube, Sie können ihr vertrauen, wenn Sie die Richtige gefunden haben. Sie müssen vorsichtig sein. Sehen Sie sich um, wenn Sie müssen. Ich mache mir Sorgen um Sie, Kumpel."

Ich nickte leicht und starrte meinen Drink an, ehe ich einen Schluck nahm und den Geschmack auskostete. Wir tranken einen Moment lang schweigend. Er meinte, was er sagte; das bezweifelte ich nicht. Nicht nur, dass er sich Sorgen um mich machte.

Kumpel.

Ich verspürte Druck hinter meinen Augen, Kopfschmerzen davon, dass ich bestimmte Sachen nicht aussprach. Ich nahm einen weiteren Schluck, um sie vertreiben. Manchmal half das.

„Was ist mit Ihnen, Sir? Wie geht es Ihnen?"

„Ich komme klar. Ich hatte einen Job zu erledigen, und ich habe ihn erledigt. Die Leute können es anschließend hinterfragen, aber ich habe die beste Entscheidung getroffen, die ich angesichts der Informationen, die ich zu dem Zeitpunkt hatte, treffen konnte."

„Ich war derjenige, der es getan hat, Sir. Wirklich. Ich weiß, dass Sie mich geschickt haben, aber ich habe die Ziele programmiert."

„Was ich getan habe, ist größer. Sie ... Ihre Rolle ist nur ein kleiner Teil davon. Und es tut mir leid. Was ich Ihnen angetan habe, tut mir leid. Aber was ich getan habe ... Ich habe mich dem Willen der zivilen Führung widersetzt, und obwohl ich immer noch glaube, das Richtige getan zu haben, war das nicht in Ordnung. Ich dachte, ich hätte eine bessere Lösung, und die habe ich umgesetzt. Ich *hatte* eine bessere Lösung. Aber das ist wirklich nicht der Punkt."

Ich trank aus. Diese Diskussion hatte ich nicht erwartet – eigentlich beinahe eine Beichte –, aber irgendwie brachte es die Dinge in Ordnung. Nicht für den Rest der Galaxis, aber zumindest zwischen Serata und mir.

„Wollen Sie sich setzen?", fragte Serata.

„Sicher." Ich setzte mich auf einen schweren ledergepolsterten Stuhl. Überall sonst hätte ich es für Kunstleder gehalten, aber bei Serata bezweifelte ich das.

Er ging zur Anrichte und schenkte mir etwas mehr Schnaps ein, goss auch sich etwas in sein eigenes halb ausgetrunkenes Glas und setzte sich dann ebenfalls hin. „Also, was ist los? Es sei denn, Sie erwarten, dass ich glaube, Sie wären aus heiterem Himmel aufgetaucht."

Ich lachte. „Was? Kann ein Kerl nicht in der Stadt sein und zum Abendessen vorbeischauen?"

Er lächelte und seine Augenfalten wurden sichtbar. „Könnte er. Aber Sie nicht."

Er war nicht verärgert. Eher neugierig. „Ja, Sir, Sie haben mich erwischt. Es gibt da eine Sache bei der Arbeit. Die ist etwas seltsam. Ich dachte, Sie wüssten vielleicht etwas."

Er lehnte sich in seinem Stuhl zurück. „Schießen Sie los."

„Ich wurde gebeten, eine potenzielle Sicherheitslücke zu untersuchen."

„Klingt normal", sagte er.

„Wäre es, aber die vermutete Lücke war bei Omicron."

Er legte seine Stirn in Falten und er dachte ein paar Sekunden darüber nach. „Hm."

Ich beobachtete ihn genau, während ich so tat, als würde ich meinen Drink mustern. Ich konnte an seiner Reaktion bisher nichts ablesen. „Was es seltsamer macht, ist, dass ich diese Art Arbeit eigentlich nicht mache. Wenn ich ehrlich bin, arbeite ich überhaupt ziemlich wenig."

„Also haben die das Ihnen zugewiesen, weil Sie verfügbar waren?" Er klang nicht so, als würde er das glauben.

„Unwahrscheinlich. Besonders, da der Auftrag von ganz oben kam.“

„Von Javier?“

„Ja.“

„Wir sind nicht befreundet, aber ich habe ihn ein paarmal getroffen. Als ich in Ruhestand ging, haben wir darüber geredet, ob ich bei ihm anfangen soll. Sind Sie sich sicher, dass es von ihm kam?“

„Er hat mich in sein Büro bestellt, was nie zuvor passiert ist, und hat mir den Auftrag persönlich erteilt.“

„Hm.“ Serata nippte an seinem Drink. Ich verstand das nicht als Ablenkung, eher so, als bräuchte er einen Moment zum Nachdenken. „Ich nehme an, dass Sie das untersucht haben.“

„Habe ich. Ich habe eine Kontaktperson bei Omicron gefunden und mich mit ihm getroffen. Ein Kerl namens Gylika.“

„Warren Gylika?“

„Ja, Sir.“

„Ich kenne ihn nur vom Hörensagen, aber ich habe gehört, dass er ein guter Mann ist.“

„War. Er ist tot.“

Serata hob gerade sein Glas zum Mund und hielt auf halbem Wege in der Bewegung inne. „Shit. Das wusste ich nicht.“

Er sagte die Wahrheit. Darauf hätte ich eine Menge Geld gesetzt. „Er hat mich nach unserem Treffen angerufen, weil er sich noch mal mit mir treffen wollte. Hat mir gesagt, dass er mir etwas mitteilen wolle. Er hat es nicht geschafft.“

Serata holte tief Luft. „Verdammt. Glauben Sie, dass es etwas mit dem zu tun hatte, was er Ihnen sagen wollte?“

„Die Polizei sagt, es war Mord. Gibt es eine andere Erklärung?“, fragte ich.

„Es ist eindeutig verdächtig.“ Er dachte etwas länger nach. „Und wie führt Sie das hierher, um mit mir zu reden?“

Jetzt kamen wir zum Kern der Sache. Wenn er sich entschied zu lügen, hätten wir diesen Punkt erreicht. „Kaum dass jemand gestorben war und die Polizei anfing, mir Fragen zu stellen, begann ich, die Sache etwas ernster zu nehmen. Ich ging wieder zu Javier und fragte ihn nach seiner Quelle. Ich wollte wissen, woher er von der Sicherheitslücke bei Omicron wusste, wenn in den Nachrichten nichts gestanden hatte. Es war überhaupt nichts an die Öffentlichkeit gedrungen.“

„Und Sie dachten, ich hätte ihm davon erzählt?“

„Ich habe ihn gefragt, und er sagte mir, dass seine Quelle vom Militär stamme, aber mehr wollte er mir nicht sagen. Ich wusste, dass er Sie kennt, weil er sie auf einem Foto in meinem Büro erkannt hat, also dachte ich, ich versuche es mal und schaue, ob ich Glück habe.“ Ich glaubte nicht, dass ich offenbaren sollte, dass ich Javiers Computer hatte hacken lassen. Ich wusste immer noch nicht, welche Verbindung er zu Javier hatte.

„Nein. Ich war es nicht.“

„Wussten Sie von der Sicherheitslücke?“ Ich versuchte, die Frage nebensächlich zu stellen. Wir waren nicht länger beim Militär und ich musste mich ihm nicht mehr unterordnen, aber ich wollte ihm auch nicht ans Bein pissen. Er konnte mir immer noch den Arsch versohlen.

„Gerüchte", sagte er. „Mehr als Gerüchte. Starke Gerüchte. Als wäre etwas passiert, aber niemand sagte, was. Ich habe nicht dran geglaubt … nein, das stimmt nicht. Es ist nicht so, als hätte ich die Gerüchte nicht geglaubt … Ich habe nie wirklich drüber nachgedacht, bis Sie es eben angesprochen haben."

„Erschien es Ihnen nicht wichtig?"

„Nein. Niemand hat eine große Sache daraus gemacht, wissen Sie? Und wenn etwas Großes an die Öffentlichkeit gelangt wäre, *hätte* jemand eine große Sache daraus gemacht. Wenn kein Alarm ertönt, brennt es auch nicht."

Ich setzte das Glas an die Lippen und musterte ihn über den Rand hinweg. Ich glaubte ihm. Er konnte gut lügen, wenn er es für nötig hielt, aber das spürte ich jetzt nicht. Er wusste wirklich nichts davon. „Irgendeine Ahnung, wen Javier noch kennen könnte, der diese Information haben könnte?"

Er dachte darüber nach. „Kann ich nicht mit Sicherheit sagen, aber nach dem, was ich über Javier weiß, würde ich sagen, dass es unwahrscheinlich ist, dass er irgendetwas Unüberlegtes tut. Er erscheint mir nicht wie jemand, der übereilte Entscheidungen trifft."

„Sehe ich auch so", sagte ich.

„Ich habe Gefühl, dass er etwas mit relativ großer Sicherheit gewusst haben muss, wenn er Sie zu sich gerufen und Ihnen diesen Auftrag erteilt hat. Ich glaube nicht, dass ein Gerücht ausgereicht hätte."

„So wie er es sagte, kam es nicht rüber wie etwas, bei dem ich herausfinden sollte, *ob* es passiert war. Er wollte wissen, *was* passiert war."

„In diesem Fall weiß ich nichts Hilfreiches. Ich bin nicht mehr so gut vernetzt wie früher. Ich könnte mich umhören, ein paar Gefallen einfordern."

„Danke, Sir. Das wäre großartig." Für ein paar flüchtige Sekunden kam mir in den Sinn, dass Gylika kurz vor seinem Tod etwas Ähnliches gesagt hatte, aber das hatte ich Serata bereits erzählt, also kannte er das Risiko. Er konnte auf sich aufpassen.

„Was werden Sie tun?", fragte er.

Ich zuckte mit den Schultern. „Dranbleiben."

„Carl, den Gesichtsausdruck kenne ich. Was haben Sie vor?"

„Nichts, Sir. Es ist ... Ich frage mich, ob es einen Grund gibt, warum Javier *mich* auf diese Sache angesetzt hat. Etwas Konkretes, das mit mir zu tun hat."

„So als hätten Sie damit zu tun?"

Ich schüttelte den Kopf. „Ich weiß es nicht. Es klingt lächerlich, wenn ich es laut ausspreche."

„Tja." Er hielt inne. „Manche Dinge klingen lächerlich und sind es nicht. Manchmal guckt man sich eine Sache an und alles deutet in eine Richtung, und doch hat man das Gefühl, dass etwas anderes zutrifft. Wissen Sie, was ich meine?"

Und manchmal nutzen Leute mit Macht einen aus. Ich nickte. „Weiß ich."

„Wir trainieren die Leute darauf, ihre Gefühle außen vor zu halten. Wir sagen ihnen, dass sie sich die Fakten anschauen und die Gefühle raushalten sollen. Aber wir wissen beide, dass das Bullshit ist. Man kann das nicht tun und gleichzeitig etwas taugen. Deswegen lassen wir die Entscheidungen von Menschen treffen, nicht von Computern."

„Sie sagen also, dass ich dranbleiben soll", sagte ich.

„Ich weiß es nicht. Versuchen Sie es mit einem anderen Ansatz. Wenn Javier Sie aus gutem Grund damit beauftragt hat, was könnte dieser Grund dann sein? Finden Sie das heraus und Sie finden die Verbindung, wenn es eine gibt."

Lizzie rief uns zum Essen und wir beendeten das Gespräch, sprachen über angenehmere Dinge, erinnerten uns an alte Freunde und brachten uns auf den neusten Stand, was alte Bekannte betraf und was diese jetzt taten. Ich hatte diese Unterhaltung nötig. Mir war nicht klar, wie sehr, bis ich dasaß, lachte und feststellte, dass ich mich zum ersten Mal seit Jahren wohlfühlte. Nach dem Essen blieb ich nicht lange. Ich wollte nicht wieder ins Arbeitszimmer und über tiefgründige Dinge reden. Ich wollte, dass die guten Zeiten für eine Weile an erster Stelle standen.

„Danke für die Einladung, Sir", sagte ich, als ich an der Tür stand. Serata hatte ein ehrliches Lächeln im Gesicht. Ich denke, auch ihm war unser Gespräch wichtig gewesen.

„Ich bin froh, dass Sie gekommen sind, Carl. Es ist schön, Sie zu sehen."

„Ich fand es auch schön, Sie zu sehen, Sir." Ich meinte es ernst. Ich hätte ihn eher besuchen sollen. Nicht wegen der Sache mit Omicron, sondern wegen allem anderen. Nichts von dem, was er oder ich getan hatte, hatte sich verändert, aber die gemeinsame Erfahrung

verteilte irgendwie das Gewicht und ließ es nicht ganz
so schwer erscheinen.

Und auch das hatte ich gebraucht.

Kapitel elf

Das Gespräch mit General Serata hatte meinem Wohlbefinden wirklich gutgetan, mir aber nicht bei meiner Mission geholfen. Dennoch erinnerte ich mich immer wieder an seine Worte. Er hatte Javier überlegt genannt, hatte gesagt, dass er nichts täte, ohne es vorher durchdacht zu haben. Das führte mich dazu, zu überlegen, wie es dazu gekommen war, dass ich überhaupt bei VPC gelandet war. Javier hatte mich meiner Verbindungen wegen angestellt. Vielleicht könnte ich einen Weg finden, das zu nutzen, obwohl ich mich nicht wieder direkt in die Causa Omicron stürzen wollte, ohne zu wissen, was dort auf mich warten mochte. Falls Omicron mich mit Gylika in Verbindung gebracht hatte, könnten sie beobachten, ob irgendjemand anders mit mir reden würde.

Mir fielen zwei andere mögliche Orte ein, an denen ich nach Informationen suchen könnte: MEDCOM und SPACECOM. Eine Menge MEDCOM-Leute waren vor zwei Jahren verschwunden, nachdem Elliot sich erschossen hatte und das ganze Schlamassel ans Licht gekommen war. Sicher hatte MEDCOM nicht alle eliminiert, die Bescheid gewusst hatten, aber genug Leute, sodass alle anderen sich von allem fernhielten, was auch nur im Ansatz mit dem Projekt zu tun hatte. Aber eine Akte könnte immer noch existieren. Wenn eine

Person die durchsickern ließe, könnte der Kopf von Omicron den Rest besorgen.

Unglücklicherweise hatte ich keine Möglichkeit, bei MEDCOM nachzufragen, also konzentrierte ich mich stattdessen auf die andere Möglichkeit. Eine, die mich sowieso seit einiger Zeit heimgesucht hatte.

Einige der Subjekte hatten es von Cappa heruntergeschafft.

Einiges davon mag Paranoia gewesen sein – meine Einbildung – aber ich konnte die Möglichkeit nicht ausschließen, dass tatsächlich Cappaner-Mensch-Hybride hier waren. Falls Leute, die die Behandlung bekommen hatten, überlebt hatten und geflohen waren, bräuchten sie medizinische Versorgung. Da Elliot tot war, mussten sie, um weiterbehandelt zu werden, jemanden ausfindig machen, der sich mit der Technologie auskannte und eine entsprechende Ausstattung besaß. Ich hatte gesehen, was mit Leuten wie Colonel Karikov auf Cappa passiert war, wenn sie nicht behandelt wurden. Wenn die potenziellen Geflüchteten jemanden fanden, der sie behandelte, gehörte für die entsprechende Ärztin nicht viel dazu, jemanden in Amt und Würden zu kontaktieren, ob sie nun von dem Programm wusste oder nicht. Sobald das passierte, war eine Verbindung zu Omicron einfach.

Ich hatte bei meinem Angriff alle interstellaren Waffen der Cappaner vernichtet, also mussten sie sich davor vom Planeten entfernt haben. Ich war auf der Raumstation in einen Hinterhalt gelockt worden, ich konnte also nicht ausschließen, dass sie nicht sowieso schon vom Planeten runter gewesen waren. Sie hätten sich auch während der Evakuierung unter die Menschen mischen können, ehe ich den Angriffsbefehl gab. Viele Cappaner – Millionen – hatten überlebt. Sie hatten jetzt keine Möglichkeit mehr, vom Planeten herunterzukommen. Sogar Bergbaubetriebe hatten ihre Arbeit eingestellt. Menschen kamen nicht mehr nach Cappa; Cappaner verließen den Planeten nicht mehr. Dafür sorgte das Embargo der Regierung. Wenn sie nicht gegangen waren, ehe ich auf den Planeten gekommen war – und ich glaubte nicht, dass sie das getan hatten – ließ das nur ein kurzes Zeitfenster, in dem sie hätten fliehen können. Ich wusste, wo ich nach diesem Zeitfenster suchen musste, aber ich brauchte Hilfe. Ich schickte Serata eine Nachricht.

Sir, ich brauche Zugang zu einigen alten Akten von SPACECOM. Wen kennen wir dort, der vielleicht helfen könnte?

Seine Antwort erfolgte fast augenblicklich.

Stirling ist Direktor für Aus- und Weiterbildung. Soll ich ihn anrufen?

Ich lachte.

Nein, Sir. Danke für den Hinweis. Ab hier übernehme ich.

Ich hatte Sterling seit Cappa nicht mehr gesehen und mir war nicht bewusst gewesen, dass er in meiner Nähe lebte. Ich wusste, dass er zum Brigadegeneral befördert, aber nicht, wo er stationiert worden war. Wir waren nicht in Kontakt geblieben. Direktor für Aus- und Weiterbildung bei Space Command klingt nach einem eindrucksvollen Job, ist es aber nicht. Die Beförderung hatte vermutlich mehr damit zu tun, dass er so getan hatte, als hätte es auf Cappa keine Probleme gegeben, weniger damit, dass er sie wirklich verdient hatte. Meinem und Seratas „Ruhestand" sehr ähnlich. Er war in einem Sackgassenjob gelandet, wo er für ein paar Dinge verantwortlich war, die keine große Rolle spielten und hauptsächlich von selbst funktionierten. Er würde den Rest seiner Dienstzeit im Verborgenen ableisten. Ich wusste, wie das war, weil ich vor ein paar Jahren auf demselben Abstellgleis gelandet war. Der Unterschied war, dass ich es akzeptiert hatte. Stirling würde es von innen heraus auffressen. Er hatte nicht den Charakter, um mit so etwas fertigzuwerden.

Ich freute mich darauf, ihn zu sehen.

Am Tor zur Basis zeigte ich meinen Ausweis, der mich als Ruheständler auswies, und sie ließen mich ohne Nachfrage ein. Eine Audienz bei dem Mann zu bekommen, den ich sehen wollte, war eine etwas größere Herausforderung. Man kann einen Brigadegeneral nicht einfach besuchen gehen, besonders nicht, wenn er einen nicht sehen will – und er wollte mich mit ziemlicher Sicherheit nicht sehen. Ich hätte Serata bitten können, ein Treffen zu vereinbaren, aber wo blieb da der Spaß? Ich ging unangekündigt zu seinem Büro.

Der Lageplan der Basis führte mich zu einem hässlichen, einstöckigen Gebäude, das vierzig Jahre alt sein musste. Die Steine, die den Gehweg säumten, waren sauber gestrichen, und der Bau schien brauchbar zu sein, aber er war nicht entworfen worden, um Besucher zu beeindrucken. Die Tür hatte ein Touchpad und ich war nicht autorisiert, also wartete ich darauf, dass jemand anderes eintrat, dann folgte ich der Frau, der dieses Los zufiel. Ich hatte mir eine Geschichte zurechtgelegt, für den Fall, dass sie mich fragte, aber sie würdigte mich keines Blickes. Ich vermute, dass Sicherheit keine große Priorität war, was vielleicht einen Hinweis darauf gab, wie wichtig das war, was in diesem Gebäude vor sich ging.

Ich fand mich in einem spärlich beleuchteten Flur wieder, und berief mich auf meine übliche Methode: Ich tat so, als gehörte ich hierher. Ich kam an einem Major vorbei und stellte keinen Augenkontakt her.

Ich brauchte ein besseres Ziel. Ich ging um die Ecke und sah einen jungen Soldaten, der mit einem Mopp aus einer Abstellkammer kam. „Entschuldigung, ich habe eine Verabredung mit General Stirling. Wo geht es zu seinem Büro?"

Der Soldat zeigte nach rechts. „Hier runter und dann nach links, Sir."

„Danke."

Ich betrat Stirlings Vorzimmer, als jemand anderes herauskam, sodass ich nicht klingeln musste. Ich ging direkt auf seine Sekretärin zu, eine Zivilistin, die etwa in meinem Alter war, mit kurzem blondem Haar, durch das sich etwas Grau zog. „Carl Butler. Hier um Brigadegeneral Stirling zu sehen."

Sie blickte mich einige Sekunden lang an und taxierte mich. Ich wusste augenblicklich, dass ich sie mit meinem Bullshit nicht zur Närrin halten würde. Leute blieben nicht lange Sekretärinnen von Generälen, ohne gut in ihrem Job zu sein. „Mr. Butler, ich sehe Sie nicht in der Terminliste."

„Er wird mich sehen wollen."

„Er ist in einem Meeting. Ich weiß nicht, wann er fertig ist." Sie hatte ihren Blick auf mich geheftet, ohne zu blinzeln.

„Sagen Sie ihm meinen Namen. Wir kennen uns lange."

Sie starrte mich noch einige Sekunden länger an und seufzte. „In Ordnung. Aber er macht keine Akquise. Was auch immer Sie verkaufen, Sie verschwenden Ihre Zeit."

Das brachte mich beinahe zum Lachen. Sie hielt mich für einen Vertreter. Natürlich. Vermutlich kamen vielen von denen her, und es wären alles Typen wie ich. Offiziere im Ruhestand. „Ich verkaufe nichts. Wir haben zusammen auf Cappa gedient."

Ihre Augen weiteten sich. Ich kannte diesen Blick, weil mich eben dieser Blick jeden Tag traf. Dieser Moment der Erkenntnis, wenn jemand die Verbindung herstellt und mich erkennt. „Butler. Sie sind *dieser* Butler?"

„Bin ich."

„Der General ist wirklich in einem Meeting", sagte sie. „Das habe ich mir nicht ausgedacht."

„Ich dachte nicht, dass Sie sich das ausgedacht hätten", sagte ich. „Ich kann warten."

„Setzen Sie sich dort drüben auf das Sofa. Ich lasse ihn in der nächsten Pause wissen, dass Sie hier sind. Möchten Sie einen Kaffee?"

„Gut Sie zu sehen, Carl", log Stirling, immer noch so durchsichtig wie Glas.

„Dito, Aaron." Ich log ebenfalls. Aber ich wollte etwas von ihm, also log ich selbstverständlich.

Er saß hinter einem großen, modernen Schreibtisch mit Polymerplatte, der ordentlich und so glattpoliert war, dass er glänzte. „Ich bin mir sicher, dass Sie nicht nur vorbeigeschaut haben, um mich auf den neusten Stand zu bringen."

Ich kicherte. „Nein. Ich brauche Hilfe."

Er zögerte eine Sekunde zu lang. „Sicher. Was immer Sie brauchen, natürlich." Er meinte das ernst, aber hauptsächlich sagte er es, weil er keine andere Wahl hatte. Er schuldete mir was, und wir beide wussten es. Ich hatte für Cappa den Kopf hingehalten und öffentlich nie erwähnt, wie sehr er die Dinge vermasselt hatte, und wie das zu dem, was ich hatte tun müssen, beigetragen hatte. Er hatte sich sicherlich nicht so viel zuschulden kommen lassen wie ich, aber ich hätte es ihm schwer machen können, tat es aber nicht.

Was nicht bedeutete, dass er zu schätzen wusste, dass ich auftauchte, um die Schulden einzutreiben.

Es kümmerte mich nicht.

„Ich muss wissen, ob irgendwelche Schiffe Cappa verlassen haben. Irgendwelche unerlaubten Schiffe. Könnten Minenarbeiter oder als solche verkleidet gewesen sein. Es wäre kurz vor dem Ende gewesen. Innerhalb von ein paar Tagen."

Er dachte einen Moment lang nach. „Wir hatten die Blockade."

Ich änderte meine Haltung in dem abgenutzten Polsterstuhl, der seinem Schreibtisch gegenüberstand. „Richtig. Ist irgendetwas durchgekommen?"

„Wie ich sagte: Nein. Aber wir hatten nicht genug Schiffe für die Evakuierung. Also ... weiß ich es nicht. Ich schätze, ausschließen kann ich es nicht.“

„Irgendeine Möglichkeit, um es sicher herauszufinden?“ Ich kannte die Antwort bereits, wollte aber, dass er selbst darauf kam.

„Ist es wichtig?“

„Ich habe Grund zur Annahme, dass ein paar Cappaner es vom Planeten runtergeschafft haben. Oder Leute, die mit ihnen zusammengearbeitet haben. Oder beides. Sie scheinen sich für mich zu interessieren und ich will wirklich nicht, dass all dieser Kram noch mal hochkommt.“ Ich ließ unausgesprochen, dass auch *er* das nicht wollte. Ich nahm an, ihm genug von der Wahrheit gesagt zu haben, um ihn zum Handeln zu bewegen.

Er dachte darüber nach. „Wir können auf die Aufzeichnungen des Hauptquartiers zugreifen. Wir lagern dort alles, und wenn sie es nicht sofort haben, können wir es abrufen.“

„Gibt es eine Möglichkeit, wie ich mir das ansehen kann? Ich schätze, ich brauche etwa die Aufzeichnungen von zwei Tagen.“

„Haben Sie immer noch eine Freigabe?“, fragte er.

„Ja. Ich brauche sie für meinen Job, also bezahlt das Unternehmen, damit sie aktuell bleibt.“

„Ich mache einen Anruf.“

„Das können Sie? Beim Hauptquartier anrufen?“, fragte ich. Wenn er das konnte, würde es die Sache einfacher machen als ich gedacht hatte. Ich hatte erwartet, zwei Besuche zu benötigen, um zu kriegen, was ich brauchte, aber mit dieser Hilfe konnte ich es vielleicht in einem bekommen.

Er schnaubte. „Ich mag in einer Sackgasse stecken, aber ich bin immer noch General. Niemand wird lange fackeln wegen einer solch unbedeutenden Sache. Sie werden aber eine Coverstory brauchen, es sei denn, Sie wollen verraten, aus welchem Grund Sie die Daten haben wollen."

Er hatte nicht ganz Unrecht. „Sicher. Sagen wir, ich schreibe meine Memoiren und ich will ein paar Sachen verifizieren, bezüglich der letzten Tage vor dem Angriff. Es wird natürlich anonym bleiben, und ich werde nichts verwenden, was der Geheimhaltung unterliegt. Sie tun lediglich einem alten Kameraden einen Gefallen."

„Das sollte funktionieren." Er nahm seinen Telefonhörer in die Hand und bekam sofort jemanden an die Leitung. Er hatte es in weniger als einer Minute organisiert.

„Danke, Aaron", sagte ich.

„Nicht der Rede wert."

Ich lief den zehn Minuten langen Weg zum Operations-Hauptquartier und war froh, dass er das Treffen am selben Tag vereinbar hatte. Ich musste schnell handeln, denn sobald Stirling Zeit zum Nachdenken hatte, würde er jemandem davon erzählen, und je nachdem, wem er davon erzählte, verlöre ich vielleicht meinen Zugang zu den Informationen. Wenn die Geheimdienstleute herausfanden, was ich vermutete, war es wahrscheinlich, dass sie mich für eine Einsatznachbesprechung einbestellen würden. Das würde ich lieber vermeiden.

Ich betrat dasselbe moderne Wunder von einem Gebäude, in dem ich Serata vor drei Jahren aufgesucht hatte. Ein weiblicher, dunkelhäutiger Major, die ihr schwarzes Haar in einem strengen Dutt trug, empfing mich an der Tür zum Hauptquartier und ging mit mir nach unten, in die entgegengesetzte Richtung meines letzten Treffens mit Serata. Sie führte mich zwei Stockwerke hinunter und durch ein Labyrinth aus Korridoren, ehe sie ihre Handfläche auf ein Bedienfeld legte und so eine Tür öffnete, die in einen Raum mit niedriger Decke führte, der keine Trennwände hatte. Etwa vierzig Arbeitsplätze säumten die Ränder des großen Raumes, an etwa der Hälfte saßen Leute.

„Wow", sagte ich. „Eindrucksvolle Einrichtung."

„Es gibt fünf Räume wie diesen, Sir", sagte der Major. „Wir überwachen jede entfernte SPACECOM-Station. Nicht in Echtzeit, natürlich. Zeitverzögerung durch die Sprünge."

„Richtig", sagte ich. Ich wusste, dass SPACECOM Vieles im Auge behielt, aber ich hatte nie darüber nachgedacht, was für einen Aufwand das erforderte.

Sie führte mich zu einem großen, weiblichen Sergeant mit breiten Schultern, die neben zwei unbenutzten Terminals stand und uns beobachtete. „Sir, das ist Sergeant Kobiaski. Sie ist eine meiner besten Technikerinnen. Wenn sie Ihnen nicht helfen kann, kann es niemand."

Ich streckte Kobiaski meine Hand hin. „Schön, Sie kennenzulernen."

„Freut mich auch, Sir." Sie senkte für den Bruchteil einer Sekunde verlegen den Blick. „Es ist mir eine Ehre, Sir, wenn ich das sagen darf."

„Danke. Die Ehre ist ganz meinerseits. Ich weiß es wirklich zu schätzen, was Sie hier tun." Niemand hatte ihr eine Wahl gelassen, aber es schadete nie, Soldatinnen und Soldaten zu danken, auch wenn sie lediglich ihren Job machten.

„Ich lasse Sie dann allein, Sir, wenn das in Ordnung ist?", fragte der Major.

„Sicher. Wenn es akzeptabel für Sie ist, kann der gute Sergeant hier mich hinausbegleiten, wenn wir fertig sind. Dann müssen Sie hier nicht herumhängen."

„Wenn Sie sich sicher sind, dass das okay ist, Sir." Der Major hatte bereits begonnen, sich zu entfernen. Das Letzte, was sie brauchte, war, eine Stunde eines geschäftigen Tages zu verschwenden, weil sie für einen Colonel im Ruhestand die Babysitterin mimen musste. Das passte mir ebenfalls. Ich machte mir keine Illusionen. Ich war nicht unsichtbar. Wenn ich heute etwas Interessantes fand, würde es fast augenblicklich die Befehlskette raufwandern. Aber mit dem Sergeant hatte ich eine bessere Chance, die Verbreitung der Information zu kontrollieren, als mit dem Major.

„Vollkommen okay. Danke. Sergeant K, wollen wir loslegen?"

„Ja, Sir. Sie können hier sitzen. Ich brauche ein paar Informationen von Ihnen. Daten, Orte. Alles, was Sie mir geben können, um die Suchparameter einzuschränken."

Ich hatte die Daten griffbereit, eingebrannt in meinem Gehirn. Ich gab sie ihr und sie beugte sich über ihr Terminal und begann, so schnell auf die Tasten zu tippen, dass ich ihr nicht folgen konnte.

„Es wird ein paar Sekunden dauern, bis es da ist, Sir. Wir holen Daten von einem entfernten Server."

„Sicher", sagte ich. „Wie schwer ist das?"

„Gar nicht schwer. Es ist eine ungewöhnliche Anfrage, aber nicht beispiellos. Ich habe schon Sachen aufgerufen, die weiter zurückliegen.“

„Wie weit gehen unsere Aufzeichnungen zurück?“, fragte ich. Interesse an ihrer Arbeit zu zeigen, war ein kluger Schachzug, aber ich ertappte mich dabei, ehrliches Interesse zu haben.

„Ewig, glaube ich, Sir. Ich habe nie nachgesehen, aber ich habe auch noch nie nach etwas gesucht, das dann nicht da war.“

Es lief mir kalt den Rücken runter, bei der Erinnerung an andere Daten aus der Vergangenheit, die hatten da sein sollen, es aber nicht gewesen waren. „Ich weiß Ihre Mühe zu schätzen.“

„Los geht’s, Sir.“ Ein computerisiertes Bild des Profils eines Planeten, von dem ich annahm, dass es Cappa war, erschien auf dem Bildschirm, umgeben von blauen Punkten, die freundliche Schiffe symbolisierten. Zwei grüne Schiffe waren ebenfalls zu sehen. Grün stand für neutral, wie Söldner oder Schiffe von Bergbauunternehmen. „Wir haben die Daten für sechzig Stunden. Wie wollen Sie sich die ansehen?“

„Lassen Sie mich Ihnen sagen, wonach ich suche, und dann überlasse ich es Ihnen, wie wir es finden. Sie sind die Expertin.“ Sie nickte, also fuhr ich fort.

„Ich suche nach allen Schiffen, die es vielleicht durch die Blockade geschafft haben. Alle, die den Planeten verlassen haben, ohne durchsucht worden zu sein.“

Sie dachte einen Augenblick darüber nach. „Sollte nicht allzu schwer sein, wenn man bedenkt, wo die blauen Schiffe fliegen. Das ist ein ziemlich hoher Orbit.

Die Schiffe, nach denen Sie suchen, müssen vom Planeten aus starten?"

„Ja."

„Sagen wir also zehn Minuten vom Start bis zum Erreichen der Blockade. Wir können uns sechs Datenpunkte pro Stunde ansehen und uns entgeht nichts. Machen wir sieben, damit wir auf der sicheren Seite sind. Das sind nur etwas über vierhundert Bilder, die wir checken müssen. Wo wir eine grüne Spur sehen, setzen wir einen Marker, dann gucken wir es uns noch mal an und schauen, ob sie von Blau abgefangen wurde."

Ich atmete durch geschürzte Lippen aus. „Das sind ganz schön viele Daten."

„Ich schätze, wir können das in etwa drei Stunden durcharbeiten."

Ich sah auf die Uhr. „Drei Stunden geht über das Schichtende hinaus."

„Ich werde bezahlt, um 24/7 Soldatin zu sein, Sir. Ich bin dabei, wenn Sie dabei sind."

Ich lächelte. „Sie sind eine gute Soldatin, Kobiaski. Sie helfen mir wirklich weiter."

Ihr Gesicht erhellte sich. „Fangen wir an, Sir." Sie drückte auf ein paar Tasten und der Bildschirm sprang in der Zeit vorwärts. Sie ließ den Mauszeiger über das eine grüne Symbol schnellen, das zu sehen war, und markierte es, dann sprang sie weiter zum nächsten Bildschirm.

Zweieinhalb Stunden später fühlte ich mich, als hätte jemand meine Augen mit Schleifpapier bearbeitet. Wir waren vierhundertzwanzig Raster durchgegangen und hatten neunzehn Schiffe markiert, die den Planeten verlassen hatten. Gott segne die Techniker, die jeden Tag auf diese Weise Bildschirme anstarrten. Nach einer kurzen Kaffeepause setzten wir uns wieder und verfolgten die Spur jedes einzelnen Schiffs, das Cappa verlassen hatte. Kobiaski ließ das Display mit vierfacher Geschwindigkeit laufen, aber da das All so riesig war, konnten wir sie mühelos verfolgen. Eins nach dem anderen kroch über den Bildschirm, und eins nach dem anderen traf auf ein blaues Schiff.

Als das neunzehnte Schiff auf ein freundliches traf, seufzte ich. „Tja, das war's dann."

Kobiaski antwortete nicht. Sie starrte auf den Monitor und ließ die Spur des letzten Schiffs rückwärtslaufen. Sie zoomte raus und wieder rein. Sie grunzte. Ich unterbrach sie nicht. Wenn eine Technikerin tief in ihrer Maschine versinkt, lässt man sie machen. „Was verdammt noch mal ist das?", fragte sie beinahe im Flüsterton.

„Was haben sie gefunden?" Ich spähte auf den Bildschirm und versuchte zu ergründen, was sie gesehen hatte.

„Sehen Sie das?", fragte sie.

Ich sah nichts, abgesehen von blauen Schiffen, die grüne abfingen. „Wo?"

„Hier drüben." Sie bewegte den Mauszeiger auf die rechte Seite des Planeten, weit entfernt von dem grünen Schiff, und deutete auf eine leere Stelle des Bildschirms.

„Tut mir leid, ich sehe nicht–"

„Warten Sie, Sir ... dort." Sie pausierte das Display.

Ich war mir nicht sicher, ob ich es gesehen hatte, aber für den Bruchteil einer Sekunde sah es so aus, als würde ein grüner Punkt aufleuchten und dann wieder verschwinden. „Ich glaube, ich habe es gesehen. Was war das?“

Sie schüttelte den Kopf. „Keine Ahnung, Sir. Aber da stimmt was nicht.“

„Können wir reinzoomen?“

Sie hantierte an ihrer Tastatur herum. „Nicht wirklich, Sir. Das Display ist auf dieser Seite des Planeten nicht so genau.“

„Das ergibt Sinn“, sagte ich. „Die andere Hemisphäre von Cappa ist nicht bevölkert. Die besteht nur aus Ozean und öden Kontinenten.“

Sie verzog das Gesicht ein wenig. „Das sollte keine Rolle spielen, Sir. Wir bekommen unseren Feed von Satelliten, die den Planeten umkreisen …“ Ihre Stimme verstummte, dann drückte sie wieder ein paar Knöpfe und etliche goldene Symbole erschienen im Orbit. „Heilige Scheiße.“

„Was?“, fragte ich.

„Entschuldigung, Sir.“ Sie errötete leicht.

„Keine Entschuldigung erforderlich. ‚Heilige Scheiße‘ ist okay. Was ist passiert?“

„Die Satelliten. Wir benutzen ein Netzwerk aus geosynchronen und kreisförmigen Umlaufbahnen.“

„Okay“, sagte ich.

„In exakt diesem Moment, sind die beiden Satelliten auf den kreisförmigen Umlaufbahnen, die den vom Planeten abgehenden Weltraumverkehr aufzeichnen sollten, auf dieser Seite des Planeten.“

„Das erscheint mir ziemlich unüberlegt“, sagte ich.

„Eigentlich nicht, Sir. Wir befinden uns nicht in einem Krieg im All, und sämtlicher Verkehr vom Planeten wird für freundlich gehalten. Ein Satellit braucht rund neunzehn Minuten, um den Planeten einmal zu umkreisen. Wir reden von einem vielleicht zehn oder fünfzehn Minuten langen Zeitfenster. Es sollte keine Rolle spielen."

Die Haare auf meinem Arm stellten sich auf. „Es sollte keine Rolle spielen, es sei denn, jemand kannte das Zeitfenster und hat sich von der gegenüberliegenden Seite des Planeten davongestohlen."

Sie nickte. „Das kann man nicht ausschließen, Sir."

„Das ist unmöglich, oder nicht? Dort drüben gibt es keine Möglichkeit, ein Schiff zu starten."

Sie dachte darüber nach. „Ich weiß nicht, Sir. Wie offen sind Sie für Verschwörungstheorien?"

„In diesem Fall? Verdammt offen."

„Unsere Systeme kümmern sich nur um Aufzeichnungen in großer Höhe. Ich nehme an, dass bodengestützte Systeme die untere Atmosphäre überwachen."

„Das ist richtig", sagte ich und erinnerte mich an meine Zeit auf Cappa. „Die Cappaner hatten ihre eigene Luftsicherung innerhalb der Atmosphäre."

„Wenn Sie also von der Rückseite den Planeten verlassen wollten, müssten Sie nur tief genug fliegen, um unsere bodengestützten Systeme zu umgehen, und kämen so ungesehen auf die gegenüberliegende Seite."

„Und all unsere bodengestützte Ausrüstung wurde zu der Zeit vom Planeten gebracht."

„Was es noch einfacher macht", sagte sie.

„Irgendeine Möglichkeit, das zu überprüfen?"

Sie sah mich einen Moment lang an. „Die Satelliten arbeiten auf Basis voreingestellter Muster. Die können wir uns ansehen.“

„Wenn wir uns also jeden Zeitpunkt ansehen, zu dem sie teilweise verdeckt sind ...“

„Ist einen Versuch wert, Sir. Ich spule um die Zeitspanne eines Satellitenorbits um den Planeten zurück. Das sind ... achtundachtzig Minuten und siebenundzwanzig Sekunden.“

„Denken Sie an etwas Puffer“, sagte ich. Sie wusste das, aber ich konnte mir nicht helfen.

„Ja, Sir. Ich füge auf jeder Seite vier Minuten hinzu.“ Sie tippte auf ihrer Tastatur herum, lehnte sich zurück und beobachtete den Bildschirm.

Ich vergaß beinahe zu atmen, während ich die kleinen Farbpunkte anstarrte. Nach ein paar Minuten hörten sie auf, sich zu bewegen. „Ist etwas passiert? Ich habe nichts gesehen.“

„Ich auch nicht.“

„Spulen Sie nochmal zurück“, sagte ich. „Nehmen Sie einen anderen Orbit.“

Sie tat es. Wir schauten es uns an. Nichts.

„Gibt es irgendeine andere Erklärung für das, was wir auf der ersten Aufzeichnung gesehen haben?“, fragte ich. „Ist es möglich, dass es kein Schiff ist?“

„Ja ... ja, Sir. Es könnte sein ... ich weiß nicht. Es könnte eine Störung sein.“

„Aber Sie glauben nicht dran“, sagte ich, nachdem ich ihren Tonfall gehört hatte.

„Nein, Sir.“

„Sie sind der Profi. Spulen Sie noch einen Orbit zurück und wir schauen nach.“

Sie gab die Daten ein und ließ die Aufzeichnung laufen. „Dort!"

Sie hielt das Programm an und scrollte zurück. „Sehen Sie es, Sir? Es ist das Gleiche wie eben."

„Ich sehe es", sagte ich. „Schauen wir, wie viele wir finden."

Als wir fertig waren, war es eine Stunde vor Mitternacht. Wir hatten vier Zeitpunkte gefunden, zu denen Schiffe den Planeten verlassen hatten, alle zeitlich so geplant, dass sie nicht entdeckt wurden. Beinahe. Sie hatten nicht mit einem brillanten Sergeant mit einem Computer gerechnet. Wir konnten nicht herausfinden, was für ein Schiffstyp oder wie groß sie waren, und wir konnten uns nicht sicher sein, dass wir sie alle gefunden hatten. Das System war nicht genau genug. Für mehr Genauigkeit brauchte ich Daten von der cappanischen Flugsicherung, und irgendetwas sagte mir, dass sie mir die nicht anbieten würden, selbst wenn ich sie kontaktieren könnte.

Trotz meiner Müdigkeit arbeitete mein Verstand daran, zu verstehen, welche Konsequenzen unser Fund hatte. Basierend auf meinen Erfahrungen auf Cappa hatte ich keinen Zweifel daran, dass sie Zugang zu Satelliteninformationen hatten und die Fähigkeit, diese zu manipulieren. Als ich dort gewesen war, hatte ich angenommen, dass das auf Karikovs Leute zurückging, aber angesichts der Dinge, die ich seitdem gesehen hatte, konnte ich nicht ausschließen, dass die Cappaner selbst das System gehackt hatten. Ich wollte allerdings keine Vermutungen anstellen, denn das würde mein Blickfeld einschränken. Vielleicht würde mir etwas entgehen. Aber *irgendjemand* hatte die Satelliteninformationen gehabt und sie absichtlich genutzt, um Schiffe vom Planeten herunterzubekommen. Auf diesen Schiffen konnten Cappaner gewesen sein oder Truppen der Special Forces. Verdammt, es hätten Schmugglerschiffe sein können, bis unters Dach voll mit Silber. Keine Vermutungen.

Allerdings war ich der festen Überzeugung, dass wenigstens ein *paar* Menschen aus Elliots Experimenten entkommen waren, immerhin hatte ich einen von ihnen im Bus gesehen.

Zumindest glaubte ich das.

Kobiaski führte mich zum Hauptausgang des Gebäudes, ich trat in die Nacht hinaus und wünschte mir augenblicklich, eine dickere Jacke mitgenommen zu haben. Ich dankte ihr zum fünften Mal. Ich hätte sie für eine Auszeichnung vorgeschlagen, aber das hätte bedeutet, einem hohen Tier zu erzählen, was sie gefunden hatte. Sie würden es irgendwann herausfinden – ich hatte sie nicht gebeten, es geheim zu halten, weil ich sie nicht in diese Lage versetzen wollte. Aber ich hatte einen Vorsprung, und selbst wenn sie es herausfänden, würden sie nicht sofort begreifen, was es bedeutete. Kobiaski hatte das Unmögliche zuwege gebracht und ich schuldete ihr was. Ich schrieb sie auf meine lange, gedankliche Liste großartiger Menschen, die Dinge getan hatten, für die sie nie Anerkennung bekommen würden.

Kapitel zwölf

Am nächsten Tag hatte ich frei, aber ich konnte nicht untätig in meiner Wohnung herumsitzen, ich wäre durchgedreht. Die Informationen über die Cappaner hatte mich überwältigt und ich hatte niemandem, mit dem ich darüber sprechen konnte. Ich vertraute Dr. Baqri, aber selbst das hatte seine Grenzen. Ich entschied, etwas anderes zu tun, wenn ich schon nichts mit meinem Wissen anfangen konnte. Ich wusste immer noch nicht, was bei Omicron vor sich ging, die Polizei verdächtigte mich in einem Mordfall und ich glaubte immer noch, dass mich jemand beobachtete. Handeln war besser als Untätigkeit, also improvisierte ich. Ich programmierte meine Drohne auf die Funkfrequenz eines Senders und startete sie von Dach meines Hauses aus. Ich steckte mir den Sender in die Tasche und ging nach draußen. Wenn mir jemand folgte, müsste die Drohne ihn theoretisch mit der Kamera aufzeichnen.

Ich hatte nicht viel zu verlieren. Das war ein Vorteil davon, in der Welt der Zivilisten tätig zu werden, nicht in der des Militärs. Bei der Army hätte ich eine Menge Leute, die mir halfen und meine Befehle befolgten. Das hatte sein Gutes und Schlechtes. Es lastet der unglaubliche Druck auf einem Anführer, seine Sache richtig zu machen. Mach einen Fehler und Leute, die dir vertrauen, bezahlen mit dem Leben. Manchmal starben sogar Leute, selbst wenn man keinen Fehler gemacht hatte. Ich hatte in meiner Karriere Entscheidungen getroffen, die ich immer noch in Gedanken durchspielte, wieder und wieder, und ich fand nichts, was ich heute anders gemacht hätte. Aber manchmal landete man eben doch in der Scheiße.

Wenn ich in der Welt der Zivilisten einen Fehler machte, betraf der nur mich. Damit konnte ich leben. Nicht für die Leben anderer Leute verantwortlich zu sein, machte es leichter, etwas auszuprobieren, von dem ich nicht wusste, ob es funktionieren würde oder nicht.

Ich hatte kein Ziel, aber das half meinem Vorhaben. Es war ein kalter Tag, aber nicht zu kalt, also konnte ich herumlaufen und schauen, was passierte. Ich lief mit schnellen Schritten los, so als hätte ich es eilig, zu einer wichtigen Verabredung zu kommen. Ich kämpfte gegen das Verlangen, nach oben zu schauen. Ich würde die Drohne ohnehin nicht sehen können. Ich versuchte, mich natürlich zu verhalten. Falls mir *wirklich* jemand folgte, wollte ich nichts tun, das die Person misstrauisch werden ließ. Ich konnte mir aber auch nichts vormachen. Ich erwartete, jemanden vorzufinden.

In meiner Vorstellung würde es nicht lange dauern, bis aus der einen theoretischen Person, die mir folgte, eine Gruppe wurde. Es erschien mir logisch, dass ein größeres Ziel verfolgt wurde, wenn mich jemand beschattete, und dieses Ziel deutete auf eine größere Organisation hin. Ich versuchte, nicht darüber zu grübeln, wer diese Organisation sein könnte, obwohl ich tief drinnen ein Kribbeln verspürte. Ein positiver Nebeneffekt des Spazierengehens war, dass es mir dabei half, den Kopf freizukriegen, und es mir Zeit gab, meine Gedanken zu ordnen.

Am wahrscheinlichsten war, dass Omicron mich beschattete. Sie waren das Opfer einer Sicherheitslücke gewesen, also wären sie auf der Hut vor allem, was ungewöhnlich war. Gylika war tot, und sie wussten ziemlich sicher, dass wir uns getroffen hatten. Das ließ mich an das erste Mal zurückdenken, dass mir cappanische Augen aufgefallen waren, und ich fragte mich, ob das vor oder nach meinem Treffen mit Gylika gewesen war. Das führte mich weiter in den Kaninchenbau und ich stellte fest, dass die Verbindung, die Dernier zwischen dem Phoenix Project und Ortho-Robotik gefunden hatte, immer noch an mir nagte. Eine Menge Zufälle deuteten auf Omicron hin.

Aber ich zwang mich dazu, andere Möglichkeiten in Betracht zu ziehen. Es könnte eine Klatschzeitung sein oder sogar eine seriöse Nachrichtenquelle. Vielleicht folgten sie mir in der Hoffnung, dass ich sie zu einer Story führte – nicht über Omicron, aber über irgendetwas. Ich *war* schließlich die Geißel, und ein schlechter Ruf sorgte für Klickzahlen. Ein Foto von mir, wie ich etwas Zwielichtiges tat, würde es ihnen erlauben, meinen Namen wieder durchs Netz zu zerren. Das schien mir aber nicht wahrscheinlich. Wohin ich auch ging, kannten mich die Leute, und wenn ich irgendetwas Derartiges getan hätte, wäre es bereits herausgekommen. Davon abgesehen mussten sie mir nicht folgen. Es gab überall Augen und Kameras. Es könnte sogar Plazz sein. So sehr ich ihr auch vertraute, machte ich mir keine Illusionen darüber, wie weit sie für eine wichtige Story gehen würde.

Es könnte jemand aus der Rechtsabteilung von VPC sein, der mir folgte, um mich aus Schwierigkeiten herauszuhalten. Scheiße, es könnten sogar Sharons Anwälte sein, die versuchten, noch mehr Geld aus mir herauszuholen.

Aber am Ende glaubte ich nichts davon. Egal mit wieviel Logik ich die Situation betrachtete, ich kam immer wieder auf die Cappaner zurück. Ich hatte diese Augen gesehen. Vielleicht. Vielleicht ließ mich auch die neue Information, dass sie den Planeten verlassen hatten, an Gespenster glauben. Es ist nicht schwer, seine Beobachtungen den eigenen Annahmen anzupassen, wenn man nicht diszipliniert mit seinen Gedanken umgeht. Früher hatte ich damit kein Problem. Ich war stets ein strukturierter Denker gewesen, in der Lage, alles zu ordnen und Gefühle außen vor zu halten. In letzter Zeit war ich mir da nicht mehr so sicher.

Ich drehte eine etwa fünf Kilometer lange Runde, blieb ein paarmal stehen, um mir interessiert etwas anzusehen, und kaufte mir in einem örtlichen Laden, dessen Besitzer ich mochte, ein Wasser. Dann ging ich in meine Wohnung zurück. Ich löste die Funktion aus, die die Drohne zu ihrer Basis zurückbrachte. Ich holte sie vom Dach, nahm die Basis mit, und schloss sie an mein Terminal an, um das Video herunterzuladen. Ehe ich es mir ansah, brachte ich die Drohne zurück aufs Dach zurück und programmierte sie mit der Standardeinstellung, die ich entwickelt hatte, um mein Wohnhaus zu überwachen. Falls mir jemand auf meinem Spaziergang gefolgt war, war die Person irgendwohin gegangen, als ich nach Hause zurückkehrte. Vielleicht hatte die Drohne sie aufgenommen.

Ich hatte viel für die Drohne gezahlt, und die Angestellte hatte nicht gelogen, was die Qualität betraf. Ich konnte Gesichter erkennen, Straßenschilder und so ziemlich alles andere, was ich wollte. Wenn ich reinzoomte, konnte ich beinahe lesen, was Leute auf dem Bildschirm ihres Devices hatten. Ich hatte die Überwachung bewusst auf Weitwinkel eingestellt, da die Drohne mich als Zentrum hatte, ich aber jemanden finden musste, der ein ganzes Stück hinter mir sein würde. Alle fünf Minuten machte ich ein Standbild und schickte es auf meinen großen Bildschirm. Ich stellte acht Fotos nebeneinander, um zu schauen, ob dieselbe Person mehr als einmal auftauchte.

Ziemlich schnell fand ich eine Person, die im ersten und letzten Foto auftauchte, aber als ich sie näher untersuchte, stellte ich fest, dass sie sich nicht bewegt hatte. Ich war lediglich zweimal an ihr vorbeigelaufen, an derselben Stelle, einmal, als ich aufgebrochen, und einmal, als ich zurückgekommen war. Das schloss nicht aus, dass sie vielleicht meine Wohnung observierte, aber sie war mir zumindest nicht gefolgt.

Ich verglich andere Fotos. Ich brauchte dreißig Minuten, bis ich sie fand. Eine dunkelhäutige Frau in einem beigefarbenen Pullover mit hohem Kragen tauchte auf Bild zwei und Bild sieben hinter mir auf. Ich brauchte nicht lang, bis ich sie auch in zwei anderen Einstellungen gefunden hatte. Ich erfasste ihr Gesicht aus jedem Winkel, der mir zur Verfügung stand, dann sah ich mir das gesamte Video noch einmal an, mit dem Fokus auf ihr. Als ich einmal wusste, wonach ich suchen musste, war es einfach, ihr zu folgen. Sie entfernte sich ein paar Minuten, ehe ich in meine Wohnung zurückkam, und tauchte auch nicht wieder auf, als wüsste sie, wohin ich gehen würde, und wäre gelangweilt. Oder sie hatte jemand anderes, der meine Wohnung observierte, und brauchte sich nicht selbst zu nähern. Wieso war sie mir auf meinem kleinen Spaziergang gefolgt, hatte aber nichts unternommen? Sie hatte nichts herausgefunden, weil es nicht herauszufinden gab. Abgesehen von meinen regelmäßen Wegen, ging ich selten irgendwohin. Ich fragte mich, wie lange sie mir schon folgten. Und wieso? Mir nur zu folgen ergab keinen Sinn. Es sei denn, ich war nicht die Zielperson. Vielleicht wollten sie, dass ich sie irgendwo hinführte, aber wenn das der Fall war, war mir nicht klar, was das Ziel sein sollte.

Ich nahm jedes der Fotos und fütterte mein System damit, um zu schauen, ob sie zu bekannten Bildern passten. Ein Scan des Netzes brachte nichts hervor, aber ich hatte nur Zugang zu öffentlichen Daten und selbst eine kompetente Amateurin konnte die eigenen Spuren mit wenig Aufwand daraus entfernten. Leute taten das pausenlos als Routinemaßnahme, um ihre Privatsphäre zu schützen. Um tiefer zu graben, bräuchte ich Zugang zu einem besseren System. So etwas, wie es die Polizei oder das Militär hatten. Das schloss ich aus. Ich glaubte nicht, dass ich weit käme, wenn ich mit irgendwelchen Bildern eine Polizeistation betrat. Ich schloss es allerdings für die Zukunft nicht aus. Wenn sie den Mord aufklärten und mich nicht länger als Verdächtigen führten, waren sie vielleicht in versöhnlicherer Stimmung. Andererseits fragten sich mich dann vielleicht, woher ich die Bilder hatte, und ich wollte nicht zugeben, dass ich eine illegale Drohne besaß, die ich in der Stadt über mir fliegen ließ, um zu überwachen, wer mir vielleicht folgte.

Ich ging erneut aufs Dach, um die Drohne zu holen, mir das Überwachungsmaterial anzusehen und zu schauen, ob ich jemanden in der Nähe meiner Wohnung entdeckte. Ich war einen Treppenabschnitt hochgegangen, als mich das Geräusch von Schritten ein paar Stockwerke unter mir zögern ließ. Ich konzentrierte mich und glaubte, drei Personen ausmachen zu können, die eindeutig nach oben kamen. Mein Herz begann zu klopfen. Abgesehen von mir nahm niemand in unserem Gebäude die Treppe. Die Leute fuhren mit dem Fahrstuhl. Und sie waren definitiv nicht zu dritt unterwegs. Ich schoss die Stufen hinunter und eilte zu meiner Wohnung. Ich schaffte es durch meinen Sicherheitscheck, als die Schritte das Stockwerk unter mir erreichten. Ich rannte hinein, warf die Tür zu und eilte zum Schreibtisch, um meine Pistole zu holen.

Wie ich so dastand, mit meiner Waffe in der Hand, kam ich mir dämlich vor. Ich konnte nicht durch die Tür schießen, sie konnten nicht rein, und es war verdammt noch mal ausgeschlossen, dass ich rausgehen würde. Dennoch legte ich sie nicht weg. Ich stand da und strengte mich an, etwas durch die dicke Sicherheitstür zu hören. Als es klingelte, bekam ich beinahe einen Herzinfarkt. Nach einem Augenblick beruhigte ich mich genug, um mich an mein Kamerasystem zu erinnern, und aktivierte es.

Die Frau aus dem Drohnenüberwachungsvideo starrte mich vom Bildschirm aus an, und obwohl ich sie sehen konnte, sie mich aber nicht, zuckte ich etwas zusammen. Sie hatte Leute bei sich, aber ich konnte sie nicht genau sehen. Ich kam nicht über die Pupillen der Frau hinweg. Ovale.

Ich erstarrte, meine Hand auf halbem Weg zum Knopf, der die Gegensprechanlage aktivierte. Ich wollte mit ihr reden, sie fragen, wieso sie hier waren, wieso sie mir gefolgt waren. Aber ich konnte mich nicht bewegen.

Es klingelte wieder, und dann noch einmal. Ich weiß nicht, wie oft. Ich weiß nicht, wie lang ich dastand. Schließlich gingen sie weg.

Trotz meines kompletten Zusammenbruchs hatte der Besuch des Cappaner-Mensch-Hybrids zwei Vorteile: Erstens wusste ich jetzt, dass ich es mir nicht eingebildet hatte. Sie waren real. Zweitens hatte ich zusätzlich zu den Fotos der Drohne ein gutes Foto von meinem Sicherheitssystem. Die beiden Leute, die die Frau dabeigehabt hatte, hatten sich so hingestellt, dass mein System sie nicht aufnehmen konnte – das würde ich beheben müssen – aber von ihr hatte ich ein deutliches Bild.

Ich versteckte mich am folgenden Tag in meiner Wohnung, weil ich fürchtete, dass sie draußen auf mich warten würden, aber am Tag danach musste ich zur Arbeit gehen, also scannte ich den Flur mit meinem Sicherheitssystem, ging aufs Dach und startete meine Drohne, um rasch die Umgebung zu scannen. Ich fand keine Spur von der Frau und entdeckte niemand anderen, der meine Wohnung observierte, also machte ich mich eilig auf den Weg. Dennoch sah ich mich ununterbrochen um, während ich ging, und ich scannte den Bus, während ich einstieg. Dieselben Augen sahen mich an, die mich jeden Tag ansahen – einige voller Ehrfurcht, andere voller Hass. Keine Ovale. Als ich bei VPC eintraf, ging ich nach unten in die IT, und traf Ganos, die sich mit einer Runde aus Sweatshirts tragenden Programmierern unterhielt. Als ich mich näherte, zerstreuten sie sich wie Mäuse, wenn man in der Küche das Licht einschaltet.

„Entschuldigen Sie, dass ich Ihre Gruppe auflöse."

Ganos lachte. „Sie sind nicht daran gewöhnt, dass hier zufällig Anzugträger auftauchen. Ernsthaft, das passiert nie."

Ich reichte ihr das Bild meiner Besucherin. „Wie schwer ist es, ein Bild zu prüfen und jemanden zu identifizieren? Ich habe es mit der öffentlichen Standardsuche probiert und nichts gefunden. Ich habe Grund zur Annahme, dass diese Person sich zu verbergen versucht."

Sie blickte sich um, dann senkte sie die Stimme. „Ist das geheim?"

„Nein, das ist offiziell. Von der Firma genehmigt. Sie hat etwas mit der Ermittlung zu tun, die ich durchführe. Nichts Illegales, aber ich würde mich freuen, wenn wir eine bessere Informationsquelle anzapfen könnten als die, die mir zur Verfügung steht." Es war keine komplette Lüge. Die Frau *könnte* mit meinem Fall zu tun haben. Ich fühlte mich berechtigt, Firmengelder dafür einzusetzen.

„Alles klar, Sir. Ich sorge dafür, dass alles legal bleibt."

„Danke", sagte ich.

Sie grinste. „Soweit Sie wissen.“

Ich lachte schnaubend, was sie ebenfalls zum Lachen brachte. „Ich vertraue Ihrer Einschätzung.“

„Vermutlich nicht Ihre beste Entscheidung, aber ich weiß es zu schätzen. Ich melde mich morgen bei Ihnen. Ich will von zu Hause daran arbeiten.“

Kapitel dreizehn

Ganos hielt Wort und wartete am nächsten Morgen in meinem Büro auf mich, mit den Füßen auf meinem Schreibtisch.

„Muss nice sein, Führungskraft zu sein und zu kommen und zu gehen, wann Sie wollen", sagte sie.

Ich lachte. „Ist nicht schlecht, das kann ich Ihnen sagen."

Sie schwang ihre Füße vom Tisch. „Ich habe das Bild gecheckt, das Sie mir gegeben haben. Sie werden es nicht glauben, Sir."

„Ich weiß nicht. Ich würde eine Menge glauben."

„Also diese Frau, sie existiert nicht, okay? Nirgendwo, wo eine normale Person sonst existieren sollte. Keine Accounts bei sozialen Netzwerken, keine Bilder im offenen Netz, nirgendwo. Nicht *zu* ungewöhnlich, aber eindeutig jemand, der sich die Mühe gemacht hat, im Verborgenen zu bleiben."

„Wie also haben Sie etwas gefunden?"

„Stellen Sie keine Fragen, auf die Sie keine Antworten haben wollen, Sir."

„Verstanden."

„Auf einem entwickelten Planeten wie Talca ist es so ziemlich unmöglich, aus dem All zu kommen, ohne durch eine Sicherheitskontrolle zu gehen. Also habe ich vermutet, dass sie nicht hier geboren wurde und aufgewachsen ist, und habe bei der Einreisebehörde einen Treffer gelandet."

„Sie haben Zugang zur Einreisebehörde?"

„Erinnern Sie sich dran, dass wir sagten, Sie würden diese Art Fragen nicht stellen? Jedenfalls ist sie vor etwa neun Monaten nach Talca gekommen." Ganos hielt mir ein Blatt Papier hin, auf dem ein schlechtes Foto der Einwanderungsbehörde zu sehen war, dazu der Name Jane Cantella und eine Adresse auf dem Planeten, die vermutlich nicht echt war.

„Großartige Arbeit", sagte ich, während meine Gedanken bereits rasten. Wenn es stimmte, dass sie vor neun Monaten auf den Planeten gekommen war: Was war der dafür Grund gewesen? Und wieso war sie mir erst vor Kurzem aufgefallen? Alle möglichen Antworten konnten zutreffen und ich musste sie durchgehen.

„Da ist noch mehr", sagte Ganos. „Ich dachte mir, dass sie von irgendwoher gekommen sein musste, wenn sie auf den Planeten gekommen war. Also folgte ich einer Eingebung. Etwas an dem Bild erinnerte mich ans Militär, und niemand führt besser Buch als die Army."

„Also haben Sie eine militärische Datenbank gehackt."

„Sir ... bitte. Das wäre illegal. So oder so, sie ist Ex-Militär. Hat als Infanteristin angefangen, später dann ist sie zu einer–"

„Spezialeinheit", unterbrach ich sie.

„Stimmt, Sir. Woher wissen Sie das?"

„Erinnern Sie sich dran, dass wir keine Fragen stellen wollten? Vertrauen Sie mir, Sie wollen das nicht wissen."

„Verstanden, Sir. Sie war bei einer Spezialeinheit, also konnte ich nicht viel von ihrer Akte ausgraben. Die halten sie gut unter Verschluss, und es gibt Orte im Netz, bei denen nicht mal ich dumm genug bin, um dort herumzuschnüffeln. Eine Sache habe ich allerdings gefunden. Den Grund, warum sie den Dienst verlassen hat."

Ich hatte eine Vermutung, entschied mich aber, sie für mich zu behalten. „Was war der Grund?"

„MIA, Sir. Missing in Action. Wie kommt das? Wenn man MIA ist, ist das wie der Code des Militärs dafür, dass man tot ist, aber niemand deine Leiche finden kann, um das zu beweisen."

„So ziemlich", sagte ich.

„In was für eine Scheiße sind Sie verwickelt, Sir?"

„Dieselbe Sorte, in die ich immer verwickelt zu sein scheine." Ich schüttelte den Kopf. „Ehrlich, ich weiß es wirklich nicht. Es wird immer seltsamer."

„Ich weiß, dass es etwas mit Omicron zu tun hat. Ich will dabei sein", sagte sie.

„Wie meinen Sie das?"

„Verschaffen Sie mir Zugang zu ihrem System, Sir. Lassen Sie mich herumstochern."

„Ich wüsste nicht, wie ich das anstellen sollte."

„Finden Sie einen Weg."

„Die Tage, als Sie nur meine Untergebene waren, fehlen mir."

„Nein, tun sie nicht."

Nein, taten sie nicht.

Als ich nach der Arbeit in meiner Wohnung herumsaß, versuchte ich, *nicht* darüber nachzudenken. Aber ich hätte genauso gut versuchen können, mir Flügel wachsen zu lassen und zu fliegen. Ich trank ein wenig und wurde wütender, also trank ich noch mehr. Irgendwo in diesem Prozess hatte ich genug davon, mich zu verstecken. Ich würde den Cappaner-Mensch-Hybriden, die mich beschattet hatten, nachstellen. Zumindest wäre das *etwas*. Klugerweise entschied ich zu warten, bis ich wieder nüchtern war. Das Tageslicht würde mir vielleicht zeigen, wie lächerlich meine nächtliche Idee gewesen war.

Wenn überhaupt, wachte ich noch wütender auf. Das passierte nie. Ich hatte tatsächlich geschlafen, obwohl ich absonderlich geträumt hatte und immer wieder durch verschiedene Umgebungen gejagt worden war, was mich immer wieder kurz hatte hochschrecken lassen. Aber alles in allem fühlte ich mich dennoch erholt. Ich sprang schnell unter die Dusche, schaute nach dem Wetter und überflog die Nachrichten, dann schnappte ich mir meine Pistole und steckte sie in die übergroße Tasche meiner Jacke. Das Gewicht war ungemütlich, aber es würde gehen müssen. Ich erwog eine kurze Suche mit der Drohne, aber das hätte mich vielleicht verunsichert. Die Sonne hatte begonnen, den Himmel zu erhellen, und die Straßen waren noch nicht voll, wenn also jemand dort draußen war, würde ich ihn oder sie wahrscheinlich sehen. Davon abgesehen wollte ich eine Konfrontation, und wenn ich jemanden fand, der meine Wohnung observierte, bekäme ich sie.

Ich erreichte das Erdgeschoss und die kleine, leere Lobby meines Gebäudes, wo der Geruch irgendeines Reinigungsmittels in meiner Nase stach. Ich schaute durchs Fenster hinaus und als ich niemanden sah, drückte ich auf den Knopf, um die Tür zu öffnen. Ich wandte mich nach links und war fünfzehn oder zwanzig Meter weit gekommen, als ich spürte, dass mich jemand beobachtete. Eine Frau stand auf der anderen Straßenseite, halb verborgen von einem Schatten, was vermutlich der Grund dafür war, weshalb ich sie von der Tür aus nicht gesehen hatte. Ich drehte mich um, ging über die Straße auf sie zu und beschleunigte meine Schritte, aber ohne zu rennen.

Ich hatte beinahe ihre Straßenseite erreicht, als sie plötzlich weglief.

Ohne nachzudenken rannte ich ihr hinterher, meine Pistole schlug schmerzhaft gegen meinen Hüftknochen. Sie rief etwas, das ich nicht verstehen konnte, entweder sprach sie in ein Kommunikationsdevice oder rief jemandem in der Nähe etwas zu. Das war nicht gut. Wenn sie Verstärkung hatte, wurden meine Chancen dadurch deutlich schlechter.

Sie vergrößerte ihren Vorsprung und bog in eine Seitenstraße ein. Wenn sie wirklich ein Cappaner-Mensch-Hybrid war, hatte ich keine großen Chancen sie einzuholen, aber ich verfolgte sie trotzdem weiter. Ich rannte schnell um die Kurve und verlor beinahe das Gleichgewicht, dann sah ich, dass sie fast schon an der nächsten Ecke war. Ich verlangsamte meine Geschwindigkeit zu einem schnellen Joggen, um meinen Atem zu schonen, folgte ihr aber weiter. Vielleicht machte sie einen Fehler und ich hatte Glück. Ich bog noch zwei Mal ab und verlor sie jedes Mal nur gerade so nicht aus den Augen. Wir arbeiteten uns durch schmale Seitenstraßen und Gassen hindurch. Ich kam an ein oder zwei Zaungästen vorbei, aber sie blickten kaum in meine Richtung, sondern waren konzentriert auf irgendein Ziel, das sie an diesem frühen Morgen ansteuerten.

Etwa dreißig Meter von der nächsten Straßenecke entfernt trat die Frau, die vor meiner Wohnungstür gestanden hatte, vor mir auf die Straße. Ich stolperte beinahe beim Versuch, stehen zu bleiben. Während ich mein Gleichgewicht wiederherstellte, schloss sich ihr ein Mann mit goldener Haut an, der eine dunkle, leichte Jacke trug.

„Colonel Butler", sagte die Frau. „Wir wollen Ihnen nichts Böses. Wir wollen lediglich mit Ihnen reden."

Tja, Scheiße. Das war eine ziemliche Kehrtwende. Sie hatten keine Waffen in den Händen, allerdings hatte ich das auch nicht. Ich widerstand dem Verlangen, nach meiner Pistole zu tasten. Kein Grund, ihnen zusätzliche Informationen zu geben. „Wieso sind Sie dann weggelaufen?"

„Sie haben mich verfolgt", sagte sie.

„Sie wissen, wovon ich rede. Sie waren draußen vor meiner Wohnung. Wieso haben Sie mich beschattet?"

Sie hob ihre Hand etwas, was vielleicht als beschwichtigende Geste gemeint war. „Wie gesagt, wir wollen uns mit Ihnen unterhalten."

Ich fühlte mich nicht beschwichtigt. Ich ließ zwanglos meine Hand in die Tasche mit der Pistole gleiten. „Das kaufe ich Ihnen nicht ab. Sie hätten mich jederzeit ansprechen können. Haben Sie aber nicht."

„Wir sind zu Ihrer Wohnung gegangen, aber Sie sind nicht an die Tür gekommen." Sie machte einen Schritt auf mich zu, obwohl wir immer noch fünfzehn Meter voneinander entfernt waren. „Jetzt sind wir hier."

„Jetzt, da ich Sie erwischt habe." Ich zog die Pistole aus meiner Tasche. Ich hob sie nicht, um auf sie zu zielen, aber ich zielte auch nicht anderswo hin. Falls die Waffe sie nervös machte, ließen sie sich das nicht anmerken.

Die Frau machte zwei weitere Schritte auf mich zu, langsam, die Hände halb erhoben, ihren Partner ließ sie zurück. „Hören Sie uns an und wir lassen Sie in Ruhe. Wir brauchen Ihre Hilfe."

„Wer sind Sie?"

„Ich bin–"

Ein Schuss ertönte und unterbrach sie. Projektil, keine Pulswaffe. Der Knall hallte von den Häuserwänden wider und ich brauchte eine Sekunde, bis mir bewusst wurde, dass der Schuss von hinter mir gekommen war. Während ich mich umdrehte, um den Schützen zu finden, feuerten auch die Hybride, die jetzt hinter mir waren. Ohne nachzudenken suchte ich Deckung, mein Körper reagierte instinktiv. Ich suchte nach den Leuten, die das Feuer eröffnet hatten, aber von meiner tiefen Position aus, an eine Hauswand gepresst, konnte ich sie nicht ausmachen. Dem Winkel des Feuers nach zu urteilen schlussfolgerte ich, dass sie von einer erhöhten Position aus schossen, vermutlich aus einem Fenster oder von einer Feuertreppe aus. Das verschaffte ihnen in dieser schmalen Gasse einen ernsthaften Vorteil. Nach einer weiteren Sekunde machte ich zwei verschiedene Quellen aus, eine auf jeder Straßenseite. Instinktiv erkannte ich die Waffen an ihrem Geräusch. Pistolen, keine Gewehre. Dem Himmel sei Dank für die kleinen Wunder.

Ich stieß mich vom Boden hoch und schaute, ob ich einen Schuss abgeben könnte. Etwas traf mich hart am

Bein und warf mich wieder zu Boden, ich krachte auf die Knie und zerschrammte sie mir durch die Hose hindurch. Meine Pistole fiel mir polternd aus der Hand und ich kroch hinterher, bis eine Kugel in die Straße vor mir einschlug und Funken aufwarf. Ich warf meinen Kopf erst nach links, dann nach rechts, wo ich einen Blick auf die Hybridfrau erhaschte, die sich unmenschlich schnell bewegte und um die Ecke verschwand.

Ich versuchte, wieder aufzustehen und fiel hin. Mein Bein brannte und schmerzte gleichzeitig, direkt oberhalb des Knies. Ich befühlte die Stelle und meine Hand wurde klebrig und nass.

Shit.

Ich wusste nicht, wer mich angeschossen hatte und ob es absichtlich geschehen war, aber es spielte keine Rolle. Aus beiden Richtungen wurde weiterhin geschossen, während ich mich zusammenkauerte und zu zittern begann. Meine einstigen Verfolger erwiderten das Feuer auf den- oder diejenigen, die uns eine Falle gestellt hatten, aber die Angreifer feuerten doppelt so viel. Nach ein paar Sekunden ließen die Schüsse nach, wie die letzten Maiskörner in einer Tüte Mikrowellen-Popcorn. Ich suchte die oberen Stockwerke nach dem Überfallteam ab, aber meine Sicht wurde unscharf. Ich vermutete, dass sie uns immer noch beobachteten, auch wenn sie das Feuer eingestellt hatten. Ich wusste nicht, ob das gut oder schlecht war. Sie hatten auf die Cappaner-Mensch-Hybride gefeuert, aber das musste sie nicht zu Freunden von mir machen. Mit meinem Bein waren sie eindeutig nicht befreundet.

Das pochte jetzt und ich presste meine Hand auf die Wunde, um die Blutung zu verlangsamen. Es floss trotzdem durch meine Finger hindurch. Arterielles Blut. Die Schützen waren egal. Ich würde hier auf der Straße verbluten.

Ich fingerte an meinem Hemd herum und versuchte, es auszuziehen, weil ich einen Druckverband brauchte. Meine Finger kamen mit den Knöpfen nicht zurecht, meine Hände funktionierten nicht richtig. Ich versuchte es noch mal, irgendwie spürte ich, dass es um Leben und Tod ging, obwohl mein Verstand zunehmend vernebelt war. Eine Sirene ertönte in der Entfernung, kam näher, obwohl sie beinahe so klang, als wäre sie unter Wasser. Irgendetwas surrte in der Luft über mir. Polizeidrohne, dachte ich, obwohl ich nicht wusste, wieso diese Erkenntnis ihren Weg in mein Bewusstsein fand, wenn mein übriges Urteilsvermögen schon den Dienst eingestellt hatte.

Es spielte keine Rolle.

Ich wurde ohnmächtig.

Kapitel vierzehn

Ich war hellwach, versuchte, mich aufzusetzen, und blinzelte ob des hellen Lichts. Mir wurde schwindlig und mein Kopf fiel wieder auf das weiße Kissen zurück. Ein Krankenhausbett. Ich hatte kein Gefühl in meinem rechten Bein. Mein Blickfeld war eingeschränkt und an den Rändern war es dunkel. Mir drehte sich der Magen um. Ich streckte eine Hand aus und fürchtete, das Bein würde nicht da sein. Ich atmete auf, als meine Hand meinen Oberschenkel erfühlte, auch wenn ich meine Berührung dort nicht spüren konnte.

„Sie sind wach", sagte ein Krankenpfleger. Ich wusste nicht, ob er gerade eintrat oder bereits im Zimmer gewesen war. „Gut. Die Bluttransfusion hat funktioniert."

„Ich spüre mein–"

„Sie haben eine Nervenblockade im Bein, deswegen können Sie es nicht spüren."

Mein Blick wurde rasch schärfer und meine Gedanken klar, was vermutlich bedeutete, dass sie mich nicht allzu sehr unter Drogen gesetzt hatten. Ich betrachtete das als gutes Zeichen und als Hinweis darauf, dass die Beinwunde die einzige Verletzung war. Angesichts der Nervenblockade brauchte ich keine Schmerzmittel, zumindest so lange nicht, bis sie nachließ. „Kommt das wieder in Ordnung?"

„Wird wieder so gut wie neu", sagte der Pfleger. „Die Kugel hat Ihre Arterie getroffen, aber wir haben Ihnen eine neue verpasst. Die Ärztin sagt, sie erholen sich in ein oder zwei Tagen, sobald sie die fortgeschrittenen Wachstumszellen einpflanzt, was bald passieren sollte.“

„Großartig.“ Ich ließ mich ein bisschen ins Kissen sinken.

„Da sind ein paar Leute, die mit Ihnen reden wollen.“

Mein Herz pochte gegen meinen Brustkorb. Ich blickte mich im Zimmer um und suchte nach meiner Waffe, die ich nicht fand. Sie waren mir ins Krankenhaus gefolgt. Natürlich waren sie das. „Ich muss hier raus.“

Der Pfleger sah mich an, das Gesicht vor Verwirrung verzogen. Ehe er etwas sagen konnte, traten zwei Personen ein. Mallory und Burke. Die Polizei.

„Colonel Butler. So sehen wir uns wieder, und wieder ist es unter ungewöhnlichen Umständen“, sagte Mallory. Burke bedeutete dem Pfleger, das Zimmer zu verlassen, und der Mann tat es. Er musste sich kleinmachen, um sich an ihnen vorbeizuschieben.

„Ich habe nichts getan“, sagte ich.

„Sie wurden angeschossen. Sind beinahe gestorben“, sagte Mallory.

„Das ist kein Verbrechen.“

„Ich habe nicht gesagt, dass es das wäre.“ Sie zog einen Rollhocker heran und setzte sich, sodass unsere Augen auf derselben Höhe waren. „Ich muss aber sagen, dass Sie in letzter Zeit in seltsame Situationen geraten.“

„Mittagessen ist keine seltsame Situation.“

„Ist es, wenn der Typ, der sich am nächsten Tag mit Ihnen treffen will, als Leiche endet.“

Sie versuchte absichtlich, mich zu reizen. Im Stillen dankte ich der Abwesenheit von Drogen in meinem Kreislauf. Ich musste mich konzentrieren, herausfinden, wieviel sie wussten. Es wäre unklug zu lügen und dabei erwischt zu werden, aber ich wollte auch nichts preisgeben, das ich nicht preisgeben musste.

„Wir haben Ihre illegale Waffe gefunden", sagte Burke.

„Das ist nicht meine", sagte ich.

„Ihre Fingerabdrücke sind drauf."

„Die können gefälscht sein."

„Wir haben Sie auf Video, und da haben Sie die Waffe in der Hand", sagte Burke.

Video. Richtig. Da war eine Drohne gewesen, zusätzlich zur Videoüberwachung, die sowieso die Straße sicherte. „Leute fälschen pausenlos Videos."

„Lassen wir die Pistole mal für einen Moment aus dem Spiel", sagte Mallory. „Das ist ein geringfügiger Verstoß. Nichts, an dem wir im Moment interessiert sind. Sagen Sie uns, was passiert ist, und wir schauen, was wir tun können."

Sicher. Erst erwähnte Burke, dass sie meine Pistole gefunden hatten, dann ließ Mallory das außer Acht, um guten Willen zu zeigen, in der Hoffnung, dass ich dankbar wäre und ihr etwas erzählen würde. „Eine Frau hat mein Haus observiert. Ich bin rausgegangen, um sie zur Rede zu stellen, sie rannte weg, ich habe sie verfolgt." Soviel hatten sie auf den Bändern gesehen, also schadete es nicht, wenn ich das erzählte.

„Und dann haben Sie auf sie geschossen?", fragte Mallory.

„Netter Versuch“, sagte ich. Falls sie meine Waffe untersucht hatten – und das hatten sie definitiv –, wussten sie, dass sie nicht abgefeuert worden war. Ich hatte nicht einen Schuss abgegeben. „Ich habe auf niemanden geschossen.“

„Wer ist es dann gewesen?“, fragte sie.

„Sie sind die mit dem Überwachungsmaterial“, sagte ich. „Haben die Drohnen irgendetwas aufgenommen?“

„Ich muss schon sagen, Sie sind ziemlich ruhig für einen Mann, der angeschossen wurde.“

„Was soll ich sagen? Ist nicht das erste Mal.“ Mir fiel auf, dass sie meine Frage nicht beantwortet hatte. Nicht dass ich das erwartet hätte. Ich hatte ihre Fragen auch nicht beantwortet.

„Also, was ist passiert?“, fragte sie.

Ich beschloss, etwas zu mauern. „Wenn ich mir etwas ansehen könnte, würde das vielleicht meinem Gedächtnis auf die Sprünge helfen. Video oder so was.“

Sie dachte darüber nach. „Wir haben Videoaufnahmen von Leuten, die vom Tatort fliehen, aber nichts, das besonders nützlich wäre. Schlechte Winkel und nicht genug Licht. Wir überprüfen andere Überwachungskameras in der Gegend, aber wir sind nicht optimistisch. Es scheint, als hätten sie gewusst, wo die Kameras sind.“ Mallory überraschte mich mit ihrer Ehrlichkeit – oder zumindest ihrer teilweisen Ehrlichkeit.

„Interessant“, sagte ich, mehr weil ich das Gefühl hatte, dass sie mich etwas sagen hören wollte, weniger weil ich wirklich daran glaubte. Ich hatte noch ein paar Karten, die ich spielen konnte. Ich konnte von den Cappaner-Mensch-Hybriden erzählen oder davon, dass Ganos von einer von ihnen ein scharfes Bild hatte. Ich wollte definitiv nicht ihren Namen nennen, aber ich könnte mir etwas einfallen lassen, wie ich an die Informationen gekommen war, wenn es mir mit der Polizei half. Aber ich wusste nicht, was es mir bringen sollte, meine Druckmittel aus der Hand zu geben. Ich wollte nur Informationen preisgeben, wenn ich glaubte, dass ich im Gegenzug etwas dafür bekam, und bis jetzt hatte Mallory mir nichts von Wert angeboten.

„Sie sind dran", sagte sie, als würde sie an meinem Schweigen meine Absichten erkennen. „Da wir so in Austauschlaune sind, wieso erzählen Sie uns jetzt nicht was?"

„Ich habe die Frau verfolgt, als sie weglief, wie gesagt. Sie war schneller als ich, aber ich bin drangeblieben. Ich kam um eine Ecke und da war sie, mit einem Partner. Ich blieb stehen und ehe wir viel anderes tun konnten, begann die Schießerei."

„Haben Sie zuerst geschossen?", fragte sie.

„Sie wissen, dass ich das nicht getan habe", sagte ich. Sie wiederholte dieselbe Frage und versuchte, mich aufs Glatteis zu führen. Obwohl es eine Standardtechnik war, ging es mir auf Sack.

„Woher sollten wir das wissen?"

Netter Versuch. Sie wollte, dass ich zugab, meine Pistole nicht abgefeuert zu haben, sodass sie mir die Pistole eindeutig zuordnen konnten. „Sie haben Videoaufzeichnungen."

„Es ist nicht klar, wer wann gefeuert hat", sagte sie.

„Wie ich es Ihnen bereits sagte, habe ich keine Waffe abgefeuert."

Sie legte die Stirn in Falten. Vielleicht war sie meinetwegen frustriert. Ich hatte diesen Effekt auf Leute. „Sie machen es sich schwerer als es sein muss. Ich will ganz offen sein. Entweder Sie fangen an zu reden oder wir lassen Sie in ein Arrestzimmer verlegen, bis es Ihnen gut genug geht für den Knast."

Ich dachte einen Moment lang darüber nach, um herauszufinden, wie wenig ich ihnen sagen und gleichzeitig in Freiheit bleiben konnte. Ich hätte einen Anwalt verlangen können, wie es Dernier vorgeschlagen hatte, aber ich erhielt immer noch die Hoffnung aufrecht, dass sie mir Informationen geben würden, wenn ich mitspielte. Das war wichtiger als nicht in Haft zu kommen, zumindest für den Moment. Davon abgesehen glaubte ich, dass sie blufft. Sie würde einen verletzten Veteran nicht verhaften.

„Da waren zwei Gruppen. Die Frau, die ich verfolgt hatte, und ihr Partner waren auf der Straße, vor mir. Anfangs hatten sie keine Waffen, und ich habe nicht gesehen, wie sie welche gezogen haben, aber ich glaube, ich habe sie feuern gehört. Ich kann das nicht beschwören, da ich sie zu diesem Zeitpunkt aus den Augen verloren hatte. Eine andere Gruppe – die habe ich nicht gesehen – hat angefangen zu schießen. Ich weiß nicht, ob sie auf mich geschossen haben oder auf die anderen beiden, weil sie hinter mir waren, als sie das Feuer eröffnet haben, aber ich bin mir sicher, dass sie von einer erhöhten Position aus gefeuert haben. Es klang nach Pistolen und da sie aus vielleicht fünfunddreißig Metern Entfernung schossen, erklärt das vielleicht, wieso der erste Schuss vorbeiging. Es ging schnell. Eben redete die Frau noch, dann explodierte alles – mein Bein eingeschlossen. Sie sehen, dass ich verwundet bin, oder nicht? Ich kann nicht glauben, dass Sie keine Spuren

haben." Sie hatte versucht, mich anzustacheln, also re-
vanchierte ich mich.

„Abgesehen von der Leiche haben wir nichts", sagte
Mallory.

Ich ließ mir nichts anmerken. Meine Stichelei gegen
sie hatte ins Schwarze getroffen, und jetzt wollte sie
mich verunsichern, also war meine Reaktion selbstverständlich, ihr das nicht zu erlauben. Sie weckte allerdings meine Neugier. „Sie haben eine Leiche gefunden?"

„Das scheint bei Ihnen öfter zu passieren", sagte
Burke.

Ich würdigte ihn keines Blicks und sah weiterhin
Mallory an. Burke hatte mich bei unserem ersten Treffen kalt erwischt, aber diesmal war ich vorbereitet. „Ich
kann die beiden Leute beschreiben, die ich gesehen
habe, falls das hilft, die Leiche zu identifizieren."

„Wir glauben, es war jemand von der zweiten
Gruppe", sagte Mallory. „Es scheint, als wäre die Person
irgendwo heruntergefallen, was zu Ihrer Information
passen würde, dass sie von einer erhöhten Position aus
gefeuert haben. Die beiden Leute, die sie zur Rede gestellt haben, sind geflohen, obwohl eine von ihnen vielleicht verwundet wurde."

„Sie haben sie auf einem Video gesehen?", fragte ich.
„Ja."

„Ist Ihnen irgendetwas Merkwürdiges an Ihnen aufgefallen? Wie sie sich bewegt haben?"

Mallory hielt inne, warf ihrem Partner einen raschen
Blick zu, dann sah sie wieder mich an. „Kann sein, dass
es Unregelmäßigkeiten gegeben hat."

Ich kicherte. „Unregelmäßigkeiten. So kann man es natürlich auch ausdrücken."

„Haben Sie was gesehen?", fragte sie.

„Kann sein, dass mir einige Unregelmäßigkeiten aufgefallen sind", sagte ich.

Burke unterbrach, ehe seine Partnerin fortfahren konnte. „Klar. Sie sind mitten in einer Schießerei und Ihnen *fallen einige Unregelmäßigkeiten auf.* Bullshit."

„Verzeihung?" Ich drehte mich langsam um, um ihn anzusehen; zum Teil, um eine Show abzuziehen und zum Teil, weil es schwierig ist, sich mit einem betäubten Bein zu bewegen. Ich hatte einen nichtssagenden Ausdruck im Gesicht.

„Überall fliegen Kugeln herum, Sie suchen Deckung und erwarten, dass wir Ihnen abkaufen, Sie hätten andere Leute beobachtet und drauf geachtet, wie sie sich bewegen? Wieso lügen Sie uns an?"

„Was verfickt noch mal ist Ihr Problem, Burke?"

Er machte ein paar Schritte auf mich zu, die Hände zu Fäusten geballt.

Ich wich nicht zurück. „Na, los. Verpassen Sir mir eine. Schlagen Sie den Kerl, der bereits im Krankenhausbett liegt."

Mallory stellte sich zwischen uns, ehe die Dinge noch weiter eskalierten. „Okay, jetzt beruhigen Sie sich mal. Sie beide."

„Ich liege nur hier", sagte ich, mit einem passiv-aggressiven Tonfall, der Burke sauer machen sollte. Ein Teil von mir wollte, dass er mich schlug. Es wäre unangenehm, aber dann hätte ich ein Druckmittel. Mallory aber war okay, also richtete ich das Wort an sie. „Schauen Sie, ich bin nicht Ihr typischer Zeuge, okay?

Wenn Kugeln fliegen, erstarren die meisten Leute. Das passiert andauernd, ich weiß das, ich habe es mitangesehen. Aber wenn man das ein paarmal mitgemacht hat, verlangsamen sich die Dinge. Der Körper reagiert und das Gehirn stellt den Dienst nicht vollständig ein. Also ja. Ich habe gesehen, wie die beiden sich zurückgezogen haben, und sie haben sich sehr, sehr schnell bewegt.“

„Möchten Sie uns sagen, was Sie davon halten?“, fragte Mallory.

„Wovon?“

„Den beiden. Wie sie sich bewegt haben? Fällt Ihnen dazu was ein?“

„Kommt drauf an“, sagte ich. „Sprechen Sie mich von allen Anklagepunkten frei, einschließlich dem, was sie über Gylika zu haben vorgeben, sodass ich den Planeten verlassen darf, wenn ich will? Ich bekomme allmählich das Gefühl, dass es hier nicht sehr sicher ist.“

„Das hier ist keine Verhandlung“, sagte sie.

Ich lächelte. „Natürlich ist es das.“

„Wir könnten einfach gehen“, sagte Burke. „Die Schießerei war in den Nachrichten, und Sie sind eine Berühmtheit, also wissen die Leute mittlerweile, dass Sie hier sind. Vielleicht lassen wir keine Leute zu Ihrem Schutz hier.“

„Ihre Partnerin wird mich nicht hierlassen, um ermordet zu werden, Arschloch. Davon abgesehen habe ich innerhalb von dreißig Minuten Militärsicherheit hier.“ Ich bluffte. Zumindest teilweise. Wenn ich Gefallen einforderte und sagte, dass ich in Gefahr war, schickten sie *vielleicht* jemanden.

„Können Sie beide verdammt noch mal aufhören damit?" Mallory blickte erst Burke und dann mich wütend an. „Diese Sache ist kompliziert genug, auch ohne, dass Sie beide alles anpissen, um Ihr Revier zu markieren."

Ich tat so, als sei ich eingeschüchtert, weil es das war, das sie sehen wollte. Es war mir aber egal. Wenn sie mich nicht freisprachen davon, etwas mit Gylikas Tod zu tun zu haben, schuldete ich ihnen nichts. Ihnen noch mehr Informationen zu geben, würde nicht helfen. Wenn ich ihnen erzählte, dass Kreuzungen aus Cappanern und Menschen durch die Stadt liefen, würden sie sich bestenfalls eine Notiz machen. Wahrscheinlicher war, dass sie mich in die Geschlossene sperren würden. „Alles, was ich Ihnen sagen kann, ist, dass sie sich ungewöhnlich schnell bewegt haben. Einer von ihnen konnte außergewöhnlich hoch springen."

„Mehr haben Sie nicht?"

„Das ist alles, solange ich den Planeten nicht verlassen darf, ja."

„Mr. Butler, Sie machen es sich selbst schwer", sagte sie.

„Vielleicht", stimmte ich zu. „Das würde definitiv zu meinem Charakter passen."

Sie lächelte beinahe, schüttelte aber den Kopf. „Ich fürchte, Sie sind zu sehr in diese Sache verwickelt, um Sie jetzt freizulassen, besonders angesichts dieser neuen Situation und der ausstehenden Anklage wegen Waffenbesitzes. Betrachten Sie sich bis auf Weiteres als an dieses Zimmer gebunden. Wir lassen ein Personenschutzteam hier."

„Ich kann das Militär einschalten“, sagte ich.

„Tun Sie, was Sie wollen“, sagte sie, „aber Sie dürfen nicht gehen.“

„Hat die Leiche, die Sie gefunden haben, Ihnen irgendwelche Erkenntnisse vermittelt?“, fragte ich. Sie hatte keinen Grund, mir das zu beantworten, ich hatte durch die Frage aber auch nichts zu verlieren.

„Nicht viel. Ex-Militär, glauben wir, basierend auf der Körperkunst.“

„Die könnte ich mir angucken. Schauen, ob ich etwas erkenne.“

„Nein, danke. Sie haben genug geholfen.“ Sie stieß sich von dem Hocker hoch, trat ihn unter den Tisch und ging zur Tür. „Rufen Sie uns an, wenn Sie sich an irgendetwas erinnern, das uns tatsächlich hilft. Ach ja, und wir behalten Ihre Pistole.“

Shit. Nachdem sie gegangen waren, spielte ich das Gespräch in meinem Kopf noch mal durch. Ich hätte mich besser anstellen können. Vielleicht hätte ich über die Cappaner-Mensch-Kreuzungen auspacken sollen. Cappaner-Mensch-Kreuzungen verloren ohne Behandlung den Verstand. Die beiden, die ich zur Rede gestellt hatte, hatten nicht irrational gewirkt, aber das hatte Mallot anfangs auch nicht. Karikov allerdings schon. Sie konnten gefährlich werden, nicht nur mir, sondern auch anderen.

Doch nichts über die Cappaner-Mensch-Kreuzungen erklärte die anderen Schützen. Ex-Militär, hatte Mallory gesagt. Das half nicht gerade. Man konnte in dieser Stadt keinen Fahrstuhl betreten, ohne dass ein ehemaliger Soldat mit darin war. Die Gegend zog sie an. Zog *uns* an. Ehemalige Soldaten dienten nicht nur im industriell-militärischen Bereich, sondern als Polizeikräfte, private Sicherheitsleute und in so ziemlich jedem anderen Job, bei dem man Waffen tragen musste. Anscheinend dienten einige als außergerichtliche Mordkommandos.

Sie hatten mich nicht töten wollen, und wenn doch, hatten sie den Job gründlich versaut. Ich wusste immer noch nicht, welche Seite mich angeschossen hatte, und ich wusste nicht, ob es absichtlich passiert war. Es war eine schmale Gasse gewesen, und Kugeln wurden manchmal zu Querschlägern. Als ich die Szene noch mal in meinem Kopf durchspielte, erinnerte ich mich daran, dass ich mich nach links weggeduckt hatte und meine rechte Seite zu den Hybriden und meine linke zu den anderen gezeigt hatte. Aber danach hatte ich mich umgedreht. Die Kugel hatte mein rechtes Bein getroffen, das in Richtung der Nicht-Hybriden gezeigt hatte, aber das war nicht genug, um sicher zu sein. Es war möglich, dass das Überfallteam absichtlich vorbeigeschossen hatte, aber mir fiel kein plausibler Grund dafür ein.

Das Einzige, das ich mit absoluter Sicherheit sagen konnte, war, dass ich vollkommen gescheitert war bei meinem Versuch, mich vom Verdacht des Mordes an Gylika freizusprechen, und dafür konnte ich niemandem außer mir selbst die Schuld geben. Wenn überhaupt hatte ich es schlimmer gemacht. Mallory wusste, dass ich nichts damit zu tun hatte, aber sie konnte die Sache nicht auf sich beruhen lassen, weil sie sonst kein Druckmittel gegen mich gehabt hätte. Und jetzt hatte sie Vorwurf des Waffenbesitzes. Sie würde daran festhalten, um mich dazu zu kriegen, ihr zu sagen, was ich über andere Dinge wusste. Sie vermutete wahrscheinlich, dass ich ihr etwas verheimlichte, was gerechtfertigt war, denn genau das tat ich. Ich konnte ihr etwas verraten, aber ich kannte Leute von ihrer Sorte. Wenn ich ihr jetzt etwas erzählte, würde sie ihren Griff um mich nicht lockern, weil sie mich dazu kriegen wollte, noch mehr preiszugeben. Es half ihr nicht, mich gehen zu lassen, also würde sie es nicht tun, egal was ich ihr erzählte.

Ich musste mir etwas einfallen lassen, um das zu ändern und sie mir zur Verbündeten zu machen.

Kapitel fünfzehn

Eines der schlimmsten Dinge an einem Krankenhausaufenthalt ist, dass jeder weiß, wo man zu finden ist. Manchmal fühlen Leute sich verpflichtet, vorbeizukommen, obwohl sie es eigentlich nicht wollen. Dank der Medikamente, die man mir gegeben hatte, nachdem die Blockade abgeklungen war, hatte ich ziemlich gut geschlafen, und am nächsten Morgen fand ich mich in einer peinlichen Unterhaltung mit Javier Sanchez wieder. Er trug einen maßgeschneiderten grauen Anzug und stand in der Türöffnung, als würde er sich in Gefahr begeben, wenn er den Raum betrat. Ich war kurz davor, ihm zu sagen, dass Kugeln im Bein nicht ansteckend waren.

„Hat die Polizei Ihnen irgendwelche Informationen darüber gegeben, wieso das passiert ist?", fragte er.

„Sie waren nicht sehr entgegenkommend. Ich glaube, Sie haben mich verhaftet."

„Was? Moment … wie kommt es, dass Sie das nicht sicher wissen?"

„Sie haben mir gesagt, dass ich das Zimmer nicht verlassen darf", sagte ich. „Sie haben Leute draußen. Aber niemand hat ausdrücklich gesagt, dass ich verhaftet bin."

„Gibt es eine bestimmte Anklage?"

„Ich hatte eine Pistole."

Javier legte für eine halb Sekunde die Stirn in Falten, dann setzte er wieder einen neutralen Gesichtsausdruck auf. „Wieso hatten Sie eine Waffe?“

Ich zuckte mit den Schultern. „Alte Soldatenangewohnheit. Und in den letzten Jahren wollten mir eine Menge Leute ans Leder. Ich habe mich dadurch sicherer gefühlt.“

„Ich setze die Rechtsabteilung drauf an.“ Sein Gesichtsausdruck sagte mir, dass er noch mehr Fragen hatte, aber er behielt sie für sich.

„Das weiß ich zu schätzen, aber es ist keine große Sache. Ich bin mir sicher, dass sich das von selbst regeln wird.“ Ich war mir dessen *ganz und gar nicht sicher*, aber ich wollte nicht, dass VPCs Rechtsabteilung in der Sache herumstocherte – und in dem, was wirklich passiert war. Ich würde die Schwierigkeiten mit der Polizei vermutlich aus der Welt schaffen können. VPC allerdings würde mich vermutlich feuern, wenn sie die ganze Wahrheit herausfanden. Sie mussten das Unternehmen schützen und ich machte mir keine Illusionen darüber, was passieren würde, wenn ich zu einer Belastung wurde. Als hätte ich diese Grenze nicht schon überschritten.

„Was werden Sie also tun?“, fragte er.

„Ich wollte das Zimmer eh nicht verlassen.“ Ich musste ihn und das Gespräch in eine andere Richtung bewegen. „Es ist ein Polizeiteam hier, aber ich glaube, es ist zu meinem Schutz hier, nicht um mich einzusperren.“

„Glauben Sie, dass Sie noch in Gefahr sind?“

„Ich bin mir nicht sicher, ob ich *überhaupt* je in Gefahr war. Vielleicht war ich einfach nur zur falschen Zeit am falschen Ort."

Er dachte einen Moment lang darüber nach, aber ich fürchte, er glaubte mir nicht. Er war nicht dumm. „Sie glauben … Sie glauben doch nicht, dass es etwas mit Ihrer Arbeit zu tun hat, oder?", fragte er.

Ich lachte beinahe, konnte es mir aber verkneifen. Es gibt nichts Besseres, als den Arsch des Unternehmens zu retten, um das Beste aus dem Chef rauszuholen. Damit konnte ich arbeiten. „Ich wüsste nicht, wie. Sie?"

„Nein, nein. Natürlich nicht. Wenn Sie irgendetwas brauchen, während Sie hier drin sind, müssen Sie nur was sagen. Bei VPC kümmern wir uns um unsere Leute."

„Das weiß ich zu schätzen", sagte ich. „Ich sollte nur ein paar Tage hier sein. Es war eine ziemlich saubere Wunde." Eine peinliche Stille trat ein, die ich schon nach wenigen Sekunden nicht mehr aushielt. „Sie sehen aus, als hätten Sie noch was auf dem Herzen, Chef."

„Es ist … nein, vergessen Sie's. Alles ist gut."

„Javier. Es geht mir gut. Ich bin schon mal angeschossen worden. Ich werde es überleben. Was gibt es?"

„Ich glaube …" Er hielt inne. „Vielleicht sollten wir noch mal überdenken, was Sie für die Firma tun."

„Sie meinen, mich in eine andere Abteilung versetzen?"

„Nein, nichts dergleichen", sagte er. „Es ist vielleicht an der Zeit, diese spezielle Mission abzubrechen, das ist alles."

„Sie glauben also *doch*, dass es eine Verbindung gibt.“ Ich konnte ihm für den Gedanken keinen Vorwurf machen, immerhin dachte ich dasselbe.

„Ich bin mir nicht sicher. Sie haben offensichtlich eine Menge durchgemacht. Wie auch immer, wir müssen jetzt keine Entscheidung treffen. Kommen Sie in mein Büro, wenn Sie wieder arbeiten können, dann reden wir drüber.“

„Mache ich“, sagte ich.

Javier war schon seit einer Weile wieder gegangen, als eine Krankenpflegerin zur Tür hereinschlich und sich umsah, als wollte sie sehen, ob sie jemandem auffiel. Ihre blauen Haare unterschieden sich im Farbton nur wenig von der OP-Kleidung, die sie trug, waren aber etwas heller. „Ganos, wieso sind Sie angezogen wie eine Krankenpflegerin?“, fragte ich.

„Dieser Laden wird beobachtet“, sagte sie. „Ich dachte mir, es wäre am besten, wenn niemand mitbekommt, dass ich Sie besuche.“ Ich gab mein Bestes, um nicht zu reagieren, was schwierig war, weil sie sich so amüsant verrückt anhörte. „Die Polizei beobachtet uns.“

„Von der wissen wir.“ Ich machte sie nicht darauf aufmerksam, dass ihre blauen Haare nicht gerade unauffällig waren und jeder, der uns beobachtete, uns bereits zusammen gesehen hatte. Sie steckte eine Hand in den Stoffbeutel, den sie mitgebracht hatte, und zog ein Tablet heraus. „Ich habe Ihnen etwas mitgebracht, um sich die Zeit zu vertreiben.“

„Danke. Aber sie haben mir mein eigenes Device wiedergegeben.“

„Benutzen Sie das nicht. Sie wissen nicht, was die Leute damit angestellt haben, während Sie nicht bei Bewusstsein waren. Sie könnten es überwachen. Wenn Sie es mir geben, mache ich einen Scan. In der Zwischenzeit habe ich auf das hier alle möglichen Sachen zur Unterhaltung geladen. Außerdem ist es nicht registriert. Sie können Sachen suchen, zumindest für eine Weile, und niemand wird wissen, dass Sie es sind.“

„Ganos ... was glauben Sie, geht hier vor?“

Sie blickte sich um, als wollte sie sichergehen, dass niemand in der Nähe war, dann kam sie näher an mein Bett heran und senkte die Stimme. „Was soll ich glauben? Es hängt alles zusammen, richtig? Wir stellen fest, dass eine ehemalige Angehörige einer Spezialeinheit Sie beschattet, und am Tag darauf werden Sie angeschossen. Kommt mir nicht wie ein Zufall vor.“

„Es könnte willkürlich sein“, sagte ich.

Der Sarkasmus in ihrem Gesichtsausdruck war so eindrucksvoll, dass ich mich fragte, ob sie das vor dem Spiegel geübt hatte.

„Es *könnte* so gewesen sein“, wiederholte ich.

„Aber das war es nicht, oder? Ist sie es gewesen? Die Spezialeinheits-Lady?“

„Sie war da“, gab ich zu.

„Sie hat das getan?“ Sie zeigte auf mein Bein.

„Ich weiß es wirklich nicht. Kugeln flogen und ich ging zu Boden.“

„Ich werde sie aufspüren“, sagte Ganos.

„Wie?“

„Ich habe ein Foto von ihr. Es gibt etwa eine Million Kameras in dieser Stadt, und sie sind alle mit Computern verbunden. Ich werde sie finden.“

Ein Teil von mir wollte sie umarmen, aber der klügere Teil wollte ihr eine kleben. Ich hatte keinen Zweifel daran, dass sie es tun würde. Sie sah die Gefahr nicht, so sehr war sie in die imaginäre, undurchdringliche Rüstung der Jugend gehüllt. Aber ich wollte nicht, dass sie sich um meinetwillen in so eine Situation brachte. Diese Leute hatten Waffen. Und ich hatte keine. Selbst wenn ich eine hätte, würde es nicht viel bringen, solange ich an dieses Krankenzimmer gebunden war. Davon abgesehen konnten wir, wenn Ganos sie aufspürte, nicht viel mehr tun, als diese Information an die Polizei weiterzugeben, was zu peinlichen Fragen darüber führen würde, wie wir diese Information in die Finger bekommen hatten. Das schadete unserem Verhältnis zu den Behörden vermutlich mehr als es nützte. „Versprechen Sie mir, dass Sie das nicht tun", sagte ich.

„Wieso nicht, Sir? Sie muss bezahlen."

„Wir sind nicht in der Position, irgendjemanden zahlen zu lassen", sagte ich. Ich war mir nicht sicher, dass sie bezahlen *musste*, aber das war keine Unterhaltung, die ich führen wollte, während man mich belauschen konnte. „Es gibt gefährliche Leute da draußen, und bis ich weiß, was sie im Schilde führen, ist es besser, sich für eine Weile zurückzulehnen."

„Und was *können* wir tun?", fragte Ganos.

Ich dachte darüber nach. Obwohl ich Ganos nicht weiter involvieren wollte, hatte ich keine anderen Helfer. Ich rechtfertigte es vor mir selbst damit, dass ich mir sagte, ihr eine Beschäftigung geben zu müssen, weil sie sonst auf eigene Faust etwas unternehmen würde. Diese Sache ging mittlerweile weit über die Sicherheits-

lücke bei Omicron hinaus. Ich war persönlich verstrickt, und Ganos zu sagen, dass sie sich raushalten
sollte, würde sie verletzen. Wir hatten zusammen gedient. Das bedeutete etwas: uns beiden, nicht nur mir.
„Erinnern Sie sich daran, dass Sie sagten, ich solle Sie
ins Netzwerk von Omicron reinbringen?"

„Ja. Wir stellen wir das an?"

„Langsam", sagte ich. „Im Moment ist es nur ein Gedanke. Ich muss darüber nachdenken. Und hier können wir nicht drüber reden."

Sie nickte, ihr gesamter Körper wippte beinahe mit.
„Wenn Sie eine Idee haben, lassen Sie es mich wissen.
Ich bin dabei."

„Werde ich. Aber Ganos ... versprechen Sie mir, dass
Sie vorsichtig sind, bis Sie von mir hören."

Sie schnaubte. „Natürlich, Sir. Mit wem reden Sie
denn hier?"

Genau darum machte ich mir Sorgen.

Niemand sonst kam mich besuchen. Halb erwartete
ich, dass Dernier vorbeischauen würde, was mich ge-
zwungen hätte, mir noch mehr auszudenken, um ihn
von der Existenz der Hybride abzulenken.

Plazz besuchte mich nicht, rief aber an. „Sie sind überall in den Nachrichten. Es ist erstaunlich, wie viel Mühe
Sie sich machen, um mir aus dem Weg zu gehen."

Ich mochte sie. Kein Bullshit bezüglich meiner Gesundheit oder „Oh, es war so schrecklich!". Direkt zur
Sache. „Ja. Können Sie was tun, um die Medien zurück-
zupfeifen? Das sind Ihre Leute."

Sie lachte. „Sicher. Ich sage allen, dass sie aufhören
sollen, darüber zu berichten, wenn wir alle zu unserem
Medien-Agenda-Meeting zusammenkommen."

„Sie meinen, so läuft es nicht? Was, wenn ich jemanden dazu kriege, ein Kätzchen wie einen Roboter anzuziehen?"

„Keine Sorge. Geben Sie der Sache noch einen Tag und sie wird vorüberziehen. Das hält sich nicht langfristig. Sie sind eine berühmte Person, die in eine Schießerei geraten ist, das ist alles."

„Das ist gut. Ich würde mich nur sehr ungern aus dem Krankenhaus schleichen."

„Selbstverständlich könnte es länger gehen, wenn Sie mir sagen würden, worum es wirklich geht." Sie ließ ihre Stimme leicht klingen, scherzte, aber der Hauch einer ernst gemeinten Frage blieb.

„Wie Sie schon sagten. Nur ein halbberühmter Typ, der zufällig in eine Schießerei geraten ist."

„Sie wissen, dass ich Ihnen nicht glaube, Carl."

„Das verletzt mich. Ich dachte, wir hätten ein Vertrauensding am Laufen."

„Ha! Ich weiß nicht, was in dieser Situation passiert ist, aber ich kenne Sie. Wenn Sie damit zu tun haben, ist es alles andere als zufällig."

Ich versuchte zu entscheiden, ob ich mich geschmeichelt oder beleidigt fühlen sollte. „Zwingen Sie mich nicht, Sie anzulügen. Ich habe gerade nicht die Energie, mir etwas auszudenken."

„Verstehe", sagte sie. „Ich musste es versuchen."

„Logisch."

„Wissen Sie, woran ich gemerkt habe, dass Sie lügen?", fragte sie.

„Woran?"

„Weil Sie mich das letzte Mal, als wir sprachen, baten, Informationen über den Fall Gylika zu suchen, und mich dann nicht zurückgerufen haben. Das bedeutet, dass Sie mir vermutlich etwas verheimlichen."

Hm. Darüber hatte ich nicht nachgedacht. Sie hatte recht damit, dass ich es vermieden hatte, sie anzurufen, auch wenn Gylika eine etwas niedrigere Priorität geworden war. „Wissen Sie, das habe ich ganz vergessen."

„Sie haben einen Mord vergessen."

„Eine Kugel ins Bein zu kriegen, kann so was verursachen", sagte ich.

„Verständlich. Hey, wenn Sie sich entscheiden *sollten*, drüber zu reden, rufen Sie mich zuerst an, okay?"

„Selbstverständlich."

Schüsse schlugen über meinem Kopf in die Wand ein und ließen Betonbruchstücke auf meine Blende regnen. Mein Display zeigte an, dass ein Soldat am Boden war, ein anderer war schwer verwundet. Der Vogel, der uns evakuieren sollte, war vier Minuten entfernt, aber wir hatten keine vier Minuten. Wir hatten nicht mal eine.

„Raketen", schrie ich, obwohl mein Transmitter auch ein Flüstern wahrgenommen hätte. Meine Ohren klingelten wegen all der Explosionen und ich hatte es schwer, meine Stimme unter Kontrolle zu kriegen.

„Raketen, Roger." Mindestens fünf verschiedene Stimmen bestätigten meinen Befehl. Gut. All unsere verbliebenen Raketen einzusetzen würde dazu führen, dass wir jämmerlich wenig Feuerkraft übrighatten, aber sie nicht einzusetzen, würde bedeuten, dass uns die Luft ausging. Einfache Entscheidung. Aber wir mussten dafür sorgen, dass sie saßen, was bedeutete, dass jemand Ziele markieren musste. Das war ich.

„Bereithalten für Ziele." Diesmal sprach ich mit leiserer Stimme. Ich holte zweimal tief Luft, dann sprang ich auf die Füße und schob meinen Kopf über die Wand, die mir Deckung gab. Die Zielmatrix in meinem Helm suchte nach den Feinden. Ich brauchte drei Sekunden, um sicherzustellen, dass ich verlässliche Daten hatte. Ich hatte vermutlich zwei Sekunden, bis sie mich sahen und anfingen, auf mein Gesicht zu schießen.

Ich zählte im Stillen. Zwischen zwei und drei übertrug ich die Ziele. Den Bruchteil einer Sekunde später splitterte meine Blende–

Ich bekam keine Luft. Ich erwachte, rang nach Luft und klammerte mich an die Bezüge. Ein mechanischer Ton brachte mich in die Wirklichkeit zurück. Ich warf einen Blick auf die Quelle – mein Pulsmessgerät. Einhundertzweiundsechzig. Medizinische Geräte erschufen einen schwachen Schimmer im Zimmer, verstärkt durch etwas Licht, das durch die Tür hereinfiel, die einen Spalt offenstand. Das erlaubte mir schnell, mir zusammenzureimen, wo ich war, was mich etwas beruhigte.

Was meine Träume betrifft, war das im Vergleich nicht schlimm gewesen. Eine echte Erinnerung. Ein Gefecht gegen eine Gruppe von Aufrührern, vor einer langen Zeit. Eins meiner ersten. Meine Blende hatte mir das Leben gerettet, und ich war mit einer leichten Fraktur des Genicks davongekommen, verursacht von der kinetischen Energie, die meinen Kopf zurückgeworfen hatte. Es hatte mich an einen Ort katapultiert, der dem, an dem ich jetzt war, ziemlich ähnlich war. Ich würde gerne glauben, dass mein jüngeres Selbst nicht dasselbe Grauen verspürt hatte, nicht dieselbe Sorge vor dem, was vor der Tür wartete. Vielleicht war ich damals zu jung gewesen, um es besser zu wissen.

Ich wollte Ganos nicht in den wie auch immer gearteten Schlamassel reinziehen, in den ich geraten war, aber je länger ich darüber nachdachte, desto mehr vermutete ich eine Verbindung zwischen den Cappaner-Mensch-Kreuzungen und der Sicherheitslücke bei Omicron. Das Phoenix Project, was immer es war, war ein zu großer Zufall; ich konnte das nicht auf sich beruhen lassen. Und wenn ich zurück an die Arbeit ging und mit Javier sprach, würde er mich vermutlich von dem Fall abziehen und ich würde die Verbindung für immer verlieren. Omicron konnte ich ignorieren – das war geschäftlich.

Die Hybride ... die machten es persönlich.

Ich verbrachte den Tag damit, den riesigen Haufen Daten durchzugehen, den Dernier in unserem gemeinsamen Ordner abgelegt hatte, und versuchte, einen anderen Weg zu finden. Nach weniger als zwei Stunden wollte ich mit meinem Gesicht den Bildschirm einschlagen. Mir fiel immer wieder auf, dass ich etliche Seiten gelesen hatte, ohne mich an irgendetwas zu erinnern, also scrollte ich zurück. Mein Kopf war voll und wenn etwas in Derniers Unterlagen war, bin ich mir nicht sicher, ob ich es gefunden hätte. Die Antworten, die sich mir immer irgendwie erschlossen, wenn ich etwas Stumpfsinniges tat, kamen nicht. Ich markierte die gelesenen Akten. Hoffentlich bekam Dernier so wenigstens das Gefühl, dass ich seine Arbeit wertschätzte. Vielleicht hielt ihn mir das für eine Weile vom Hals.

Ich kam immer wieder auf das zurück, was Ganos darüber gesagt hatte, sich bei Omicron einzuschleusen, dann verdrängte ich es aus meinen Gedanken. Ich brauchte jemanden, an dem ich meine Ideen ausprobieren konnte, aber ich hatte niemanden, dem ich genug vertrauen konnte. Eindeutig nicht Dernier. Ich dachte über Serata nach, aber sobald ich ihn hinzuzog, verlöre ich die Kontrolle über die Ermittlung. Er würde sich vielleicht verpflichtet fühlen, jemanden beim Militär zu informieren, und das würde jede Spur, die ich zu Omicron haben mochte, im Keim ersticken, ehe ich verstand, welche Verbindung es gab.

Ich glaube, es hätte geholfen, wenn ich jemandem von meinen Ideen hätte erzählen können, wenn mir jemand dabei geholfen hätte, mir einen Reim daraus zu machen. Ich glaube, wenn ich diese Möglichkeit gehabt hätte, wären die Dinge anders gekommen. Aber zwei Jahre, in denen ich mich absichtlich isoliert und Menschen und besonders enge Beziehungen gemieden hatte ... dafür zahlte ich jetzt den Preis. Menschen nah zu kommen, brachte sie in meine Welt, und niemand musste so leben.

Ich rief Ganos an.

Kapitel sechzehn

Die Idee war einfach: Ganos ins Netzwerk von Omicron reinkriegen. Der Idee fehlte Finesse, aber meine andere Wahl war, wieder den Cappaner-Mensch-Hybriden nachzujagen. Soweit ich das beurteilen konnte, waren sie verschwunden, und wenn nicht, galt immer noch, dass ich das letzte Mal, als ich sie zur Rede gestellt hatte, angeschossen worden war. Ich zog es vor, diesen Ausgang zu vermeiden, und was immer meinem Plan für Omicron auch fehlte, das Unternehmenshauptquartier würde nicht auf Schusswaffen zurückzugreifen.

Um die Dinge in Gang zu setzen, rief ich Omicrons Direktor der Personalabteilung an – einen Mann namens Turkov – und ließ ihn wissen, dass ich über einen Stellenwechsel nachdachte. Er schluckte den Köder und vereinbarte ein Meeting, für das ich sein Büro nahelegte, indem ich andeutete, dass ich mit der Sache hinter dem Busch halten musste, und oh, ob er nebenbei vielleicht verhindern könnte, dass ich während meines Besuchs von irgendwelchen Kameras aufgenommen wurde, weil ich nicht wollte, dass mein Arbeitgeber davon erfuhr. Der Plan hatte Lücken, aber ich hatte keine besseren Ideen.

Ich holte Ganos und machte mich mit ihr auf den Weg zum Hauptquartier von Omicron. Wir nahmen drei verschiedene Privatautos, um sicherzugehen, dass uns niemand folgte. Die Hybride machten mir am meisten

Sorgen, aber ich konnte auch nicht ausschließen, dass uns jemand von VPC folgte. Ganos hatte ihre blauen Haare gegen ein nüchternes Braun getauscht und trug einen grauen Hosenanzug, der sie aussehen ließ wie jede mittlere Angestellte bei einer von Tausend verschiedenen Firmen. Sie mitzubringen brachte sie in Gefahr, aber ich konnte niemand anderem vertrauen, und sie war sehr hartnäckig gewesen.

„Schicke Haarfarbe", sagte ich.

„Freut mich, dass sie Ihnen gefällt, denn Sie zahlen fürs Färben."

Ich lachte. „Wenn Sie meinen."

Die Lobby von Omicron erinnerte mich an jede andere, vielleicht mit etwas mehr poliertem Kunststein, falls das möglich war. Sie roch sogar gleich, nach aufbereiteter Luft und irgendeiner Chemikalie, die ich irgendwo zwischen ätzend und parfümiert einordnete. Die flachen Absätze von Ganos' Schuhen klackerten auf dem Boden und wenn ich sie ansah, fiel es mir schwer, keine Miene zu verziehen. Ich bezweifelte, dass selbst Parker sie erkennen würde.

Ich ging auf den Empfang zu, Ganos folgte einen Schritt hinter mir. Ich suchte erst Augenkontakt mit dem Gentleman hinter dem Tresen, als ich direkt vor ihm stand.

„Kann ich Ihnen helfen, Sir?", fragte er mit höflichem, geschäftsmäßigem Tonfall.

„Ich habe ein Meeting mit Mr. Turkov", sagte ich.

Der Mann richtete sich auf, als er den Namen hörte. Beiläufig den Namen des VP der Personalabteilung zu erwähnen, hatte diesen Effekt. „Ja, Sir. Sie finden ihn im 17. Stock. Fahrstühle sind gleich dort drüben."

Ich sah ihm direkt in die Augen und setzte ein künstliches, geschäftsmäßiges Lächeln auf. „Danke", sagte ich und sah auf sein Namensschild, „Aaron." Ich wollte, dass seine Aufmerksamkeit auf mir lag, nicht auf Ganos. Je weniger Leute sie identifizieren konnten, desto sicherer wäre sie, wenn die Sache in die Hose ging.

„Ist mir ein Vergnügen, Sir", sagte er, aber ich hatte mich bereits abgewandt und ging zu den Fahrstühlen.

Als ich im 17. Stock aus dem Fahrstuhl stieg, spielte ich weiter meine Rolle als Businesstyp, der ein bisschen zu viel von sich hält. Es machte mich beinahe unsichtbar. Ich fand Turkov ohne Probleme, da er das größte Büro auf dem Stockwerk hatte und alle ihn kannten. Sein ausgefallenes Vorzimmer war mit einem Sekretär ausgestattet und einem großen Mann, der aufsprang, kaum dass wir eintraten. Er hatte allein in dem Zimmer gesessen, das voll von hochwertigem Businessteppich und dunklem Kunstholz war. Seinem Schreibtisch stand ein zweiter gegenüber, der war aber gegenwärtig ungenutzt.

„Kann ich Ihnen helfen?", fragte er.

„Ich bin hier, um Mr. Turkov zu sehen", sagte ich so ausdruckslos ich konnte, und versuchte, gelangweilt zu wirken. Ich blickte nicht zu Ganos zurück, von der ich annahm, dass sie ein Stück hinter mir stand.

Ehe der Sekretär antworten konnte, kam ein übergewichtiger Mann in einem Anzug, der ihm eine halbe Nummer zu klein war, aus dem Büro und füllte den Türrahmen aus. „Colonel Butler. Ich bin Yergei Turkov. Kommen Sie rein."

„Danke, dass Sie mich so kurzfristig empfangen", sagte ich, sobald wir das Büro betreten hatten. Ganos folgte mir und wich der Tür aus, als Turkov sie ihr vor der Nase zumachen wollte. „Ich weiß, dass Sie ein beschäftigter Mann sind.“

„Nicht der Rede wert“, sagte er. „Kann ich Ihnen etwas anbieten? Wasser, Kaffee? Whisky?“

„Danke, nein.“ Ich wusste zu schätzen, dass der Mann seine Hausaufgaben gemacht hatte.

„Also, was kann ich für Sie tun?“ Sein fragender Blick ruhte auf Ganos.

„Entschuldigen Sie“, sagte ich. „Das ist meine Assistentin, Ms. Gabbert."

„Ihre … Assistentin“, sagte Turkov.

Ich wandte den Blick ab, um seinem nicht zu begegnen, und versuchte Scham auszustrahlen. Ich warf Ganos einen Blick zu. Sie stand da, als würden wir nicht über sie sprechen. Ich seufzte. „Ms. Gabbert ist nicht wirklich meine Assistentin.“

Turkov setzte sich auf seinen Kunstlederstuhl und lehnte sich zurück, die Hände hinter dem Kopf. Er sagte nichts, aber sein Gesichtsausdruck verlangte eine Erklärung.

Ich warf Ganos erneut einen Blick zu, diesmal länger als nötig, dann sah ich wieder Turkov an. Ich versuchte, nervös zu wirken. „Ms. Gabbert gehört zum Sicherheitsdienst von VPC.“ Ich sah ihn bedeutungsschwanger an und versuchte zu vermitteln, dass sie mehr war als nur mein Bodyguard.

„Sie brauchen Personenschutz?“, fragte Turkov, wie auf Stichwort.

„Das Unternehmen findet, dass ich wichtig bin. Sie wollen nicht, dass ich … sie wollen nicht, dass mir irgendetwas zustößt.“ Ich sah Ganos jetzt eindringlicher an, als forderte ich sie auf, etwas zu sagen. Sie stand unerbittlich da, wie wir es geprobt hatten.

Turkov lächelte das Lächeln eines Mannes, der sich für clever hielt. „Ich dachte mir schon, dass das der Fall ist."

Ich lächelte zurück. Die zweite Lüge erwarteten Leute nie. Sie erwarteten, dass man einmal log, aber wenn sie einen erwischten, glaubten sie ausnahmslos die nächste Sache, die man ihnen erzählte. Turkov enttäuschte mich nicht. „Ich würde gerne mit Ihnen über eine … Gelegenheit sprechen." Ich warf Ganos einen schnellen Blick zu, dann sah ich wieder Turkov an. Ich wollte ihn glauben machen, dass ich allein mit ihm sprechen müsste, das aber nicht vor Ganos sagen konnte.

„Wieso führe ich Sie nicht herum?" Turkov stand auf und kam hinter seinen Schreibtisch hervor.

Ich hielt inne. „Ja. Das wäre großartig." Ich sah Ganos an. „Ich bin davon überzeugt, ganz und gar in Sicherheit zu sein, Ms. Gabbert."

Ganos blickte erst Turkov und dann mich nervös an.

„Sir … ich sollte wirklich bei–"

„Er wird schon klarkommen, Ms. Gabbert", sagte Turkov.

„Ich komme klar, Ms. Gabbert", sagte ich. „Ich werde Mr. Sanchez nicht erklären müssen, dass ich irgendwelche Probleme mit Ihrer Arbeit hatte." Ganos blickte zwischen uns hin und her, dann blickte sie zu Boden. „Ich warte hier."

Turkov schleppte seinen massigen Körper zur Tür und führte mich rasch hinaus. „Wir sind für ein paar

Minuten nicht im Büro", sagte er zu seinem Sekretär, als wir an ihm vorbeigingen.

„Danke für Ihr Verständnis." Ich wollte Ganos ansehen, tat es aber nicht. Ich hoffte, dass ihr Teil des Plans funktionierte. Wichtiger noch war meine Hoffnung, dass sie nicht erwischt werden würde.

Er lächelte. „Selbstverständlich. Wollten Sie sich wirklich das Unternehmen ansehen?"

„Nicht wirklich, nein", gab ich zu. „Ich wollte meinem Firmenaufpasser entkommen, sodass ich frei sprechen kann, ohne dass meinem Boss davon berichtet wird. Das ist lästig."

„Darauf wette ich. Also, was kann ich für Sie tun?"

„Ich denke über meine Möglichkeiten nach. Ich weiß, dass Sie Interesse hatten, als ich anfangs nach einer Stelle suchte, und ich denke, es könnte Zeit für eine Veränderung sein, wenn ich die richtige Position fände. Die Dinge bei VPC ... sagen wir einfach, dass ich anderswo glücklicher sein könnte."

Sein Gesicht erhellte sich. Ich hatte ihn. „Nach was für einer Position suchen Sie?"

Ich zuckte mit den Schultern und tat unvermittelt so, als wäre ich nicht interessiert. Ich musste das Spiel so spielen, wie er es erwartete, damit es sich echt anfühlte. „Ich bin für viele Dinge offen."

Er unterdrückte ein Kichern. „Natürlich. Irgendein bestimmter Job, für den Sie sich qualifiziert fühlen?"

„Einen, der nicht bedeutet, dass mir jemand vom Unternehmen folgt, sobald ich das Gebäude verlasse?"

Diesmal lachte er. „Das können wir arrangieren, da bin ich mir sicher. Ich kann nicht genau sagen, was wir aufs Namensschild an Ihrer Tür schreiben würden, aber das spielt nicht wirklich eine Rolle, oder?"

„Ich bin flexibel, solange es derselbe Rang ist wie jetzt. Oder höher."

Er nickte. „Ich schaue mich um. Rede mit ein paar Leuten. Briefe den Boss. Aber ich glaube nicht, dass das ein Problem sein sollte."

„Kein Problem ist gut", sagte ich.

„Kommen Sie", bot er an. „Ich zeige Ihnen den Laden ein wenig. Dann wird Ihre ... Assistentin ... nicht misstrauisch."

„Danke für Ihre Diskretion", sagte ich.

Ganos und ich verließen Omicron ohne zu reden und fuhren zu ihrer Wohnung, unterwegs wechselten wir einmal den Wagen. Ich wollte woanders hin, aber sie hatte das Equipment, das sie brauchte, und ich nicht. Ganos' Wohnung überraschte mich, weil sie so zweckmäßig und sauber war. Da sie sich für gewöhnlich ohne große Sorgfalt kleidete, glaube ich, übertrug ich das auch auf ihre Wohnverhältnisse. Ihre Wohnung konnte es größentechnisch mit meiner aufnehmen, aber wegen der spärlichen Möblierung wirkte sie größer. Sie hatte einen gemütlichen Stuhl und drei Hocker an der Bar, die die effiziente Küche umgab. Der gekachelte Boden funkelte und Staub schien nicht zu existieren. Die gesamte Wand des Wohnbereichs zog meinen Blick auf sich. Sie hatte drei Tische längs nebeneinandergestellt, die alle unter High-Tech-Maschinen begraben waren. Fünf Monitore auf dem Tisch in der Mitte formten einen Halbkreis, davor stand ein Kapitänsstuhl, der aussah, als wäre er das teuerste Möbelstück im Zimmer. Lichter tanzten durch die Türme aus Prozessoren und weiß Gott was noch für Technologien.

Alles stand ordentlich an seinem Platz, abgesehen von einem kleinen, zwei Kilogramm schweren, pelzigen Schrecken, der über den Boden hüpfte und mich anbellte, als wäre er nicht bloß so groß wie einer meiner Schuhe.

„Netter Hund", sagte ich.

„Francisco! Mach Sitz! Er ist okay." Die pelzige Ratte wich einen halben Meter zurück und hörte auf zu bellen, behielt mich aber im Blick. „Kümmern Sie sich nicht um Cisco. Er bellt nur."

„Das muss er auch. Was soll er sonst tun? Über meinen Knöchel herfallen?"

„Er leistet mir Gesellschaft", sagte sie.

„Natürlich. Also, Omicron ... was haben Sie herausgefunden?"

„Nichts", sagte sie. „Nun, ich habe gelernt, dass man nicht eingeloggt bleiben sollte, wenn man sein Büro verlässt. Aber das wussten wir ja schon. Nicht, dass es eine Rolle gespielt hätte. Ich hätte sein Terminal auch so geknackt."

„Also haben Sie es reingeschafft?"

„Selbstverständlich habe ich es reingeschafft, Sir. Aber ich habe keine Informationen. Ich hatte keine Zeit, und wenn ich Zeit gehabt hätte, hätte jemand gesehen, wie Turkovs Terminal Sachen abruft, die er nicht abrufen sollte, und das hätte die Alarmglocken läuten lassen. Das ist nichts, was wir machen wollen, während wir in ihrem Gebäude sind."

„Verstanden“, sagte ich. „Aber wenn Sie nichts herausgefunden haben, was hatte es dann für einen Sinn, dass ich Ihnen Zugang zu seinem Büro verschaffe?“

„Ich habe mir eine Tür gebaut.“

„Eine Tür?“

„Richtig. Ein winziges Loch, um ehrlich zu sein. Eins, das ich von außen nutzen kann.“

„Werden sie das nicht sehen?“

„Werden sie. Abhängig davon, wie gut ihr Sicherheitsdienst ist, finden sie es in den nächsten zwölf Stunden, spätestens in drei Tagen. Sie werden sich fragen, wie es da hingekommen ist, und abhängig von Ihrem Protokoll, werden sie es entweder untersuchen oder als Routine behandeln. Die Quoten stehen auf Routine.“

„Aber Sie haben gesagt, dass sie es sehen würden, wenn Sie Informationen an Turkovs Terminal sendeten.“

„Würden sie, wenn ich es von dort aus tun würde. Aber da ich jetzt alle Zeit habe, die ich brauche, werde ich subtiler vorgehen. Also fällt es ihnen vielleicht nicht auf. Und wenn doch, werde ich auf meinem Weg rein durch tausend verschiedene Proxys geleitet.“

„Also ist es nicht nachzuverfolgen?“

Sie ging zu ihrem System hinüber und legte ein paar Schalter um. „Alles ist nachzuverfolgen. Aber ja, so ziemlich.“

„Das ist eine ganz nette Einrichtung“, sagte ich.

„Ich mag meine Arbeit“, antwortete sie. „Also landet hier mein gesamtes Geld, abgesehen von dem, was ich brauche, um Cisco zu verwöhnen. Sie können es sich genauso gut gemütlich machen. Das braucht einen Moment, um hochzufahren.“

Ich nahm mir den bequemen Stuhl und Ganos setzte sich hinter ihre computerisierte Schöpfung. Ventilatoren summten und noch mehr Lichter tanzten, und sie verschwand an einen anderen Ort, als wäre ich gar nicht da. Cisco entschied offenbar, dass ich seinen Anforderungen genügte, und legte sich zwischen meine Füße. Ich zog mein Device hervor, scrollte durch die Nachrichten und prüfte, ob die Polizei irgendetwas Neues über den Mord an Gylika hatte. Hatten sie nicht, aber ein Artikel führte zum nächsten und ich vergrub mich in einigen anderen Storys, bis Ganos mich unterbrach.

„Sir, was ist Project Phoenix?"

„Phoenix. Shit. Etwas im medizinischen Feld, an dem Omicron arbeitet. Ich weiß nicht genau, was es ist, aber es ist wichtig. Was haben Sie gefunden?"

„Ich glaube, das war die Sicherheitslücke. Oder anders, Phoenix hat die Sicherheitslücke nicht verursacht. Die Sicherheitslücke war *bei* Phoenix."

„Das ergibt keinen Sinn", sagte ich. „Gylika ... er war meine Kontaktperson bei Omicron. Er hat an Phoenix gearbeitet, zumindest in irgendeiner Funktion. Aber ich habe mich mit ihm getroffen, nachdem es zu der Sicherheitslücke gekommen war, und er hat nichts davon gewusst."

„Es gibt hier ein paar E-Mails. Medizinische Forschung ... bla, bla, bla ... geschätzter Ertrag. Heilige Scheiße, das sind viele Nullen."

„Steht da irgendetwas über Ortho-Robotik?", fragte ich.

„Ja, Sir. Wussten Sie das? Es sieht aus, als hätte es irgendetwas mit DNA-Splicing zu tun."

Ich erstarrte. Ich weiß nicht, wie lange ich schweigend dasaß. Ich hatte das schon mal gehört, aber dieses Mal drang es wirklich in mein Bewusstsein. Ich konnte es nicht länger leugnen.

„Sir, Sie sind ganz blass geworden. Was ist los?"

Ich holte langsam und tief Luft, um mich zu beruhigen. „Können Sie sagen, wer eingebrochen ist? Wer hat die Unterlagen gestohlen?"

„Lassen Sie mich nachsehen ..." Ihre Finger flogen über die Tasten. „Wow. Es ist nicht medizinisch. Es ist militärisch. Mehr oder weniger. Hat etwas damit zu tun, DNA zu manipulieren. Irgendwie soll es Leuten ermöglicht werden, Kybernetik besser zu tolerieren. Ich verstehe es nicht, aber ich glaube, sie versuchen, mechanische Soldaten zu erschaffen. Oder teilweise mechanisch. Ich kann es nicht sagen – hier sind nicht genug Informationen."

„Ganos ... ich will, dass Sie das dichtmachen und von dort verschwinden." Ich hatte genug gehört. Ich wollte wissen, wer eingebrochen war, aber diese Information war explosiv. Ich hatte einen Verdacht gehabt, aber das bestätigte ihn. Ich musste Ganos um ihrer selbst willen davon abziehen.

„Warten Sie, Sir. Ich versuche, herauszufinden, wer eingebrochen ist." Sie vergrub ihr Gesicht wieder hinter den Monitoren.

„Machen Sie dicht", sagte ich.

„Ich bin gerade rein. Lassen Sie mich etwas von dem Zeug auf meinen lokalen Speicher runterladen."

Ich stand auf und in meiner besten „Ich bin Colonel"-Stimme sagte ich: „Machen Sie alles dicht und versiegeln Sie es. Verbergen Sie so gut Sie können, dass Sie dort gewesen sind. Ergreifen Sie alle Vorsichtsmaßnahmen. Tun Sie alles, was Sie können."

Sie blickte mich über einen ihrer Monitore hinweg an. „Sir, Sie machen mir Angst. Was ist los?"

„Tun Sie einfach, was ich sage", sagte ich. „Ich verspreche Ihnen, ich werde alles erklären. Aber Sie müssen da jetzt sofort raus."

Meine Gedanken rasten, während die Tasten ihrer Tastatur klapperten. Sie hatten das Projekt nie eingestellt. Sie hatten es an einen anderen Ort verfrachtet, ihm einen anderen Namen gegeben und es von einem militärischen Projekt zu einem Unternehmen gemacht. Und jetzt gab es Cappaner-Mensch-Kreuzungen, vermutlich instabil, die mich durch die Stadt jagten und auf Rache aus waren. Ich stand auf und ging im Zimmer auf und ab. Cisco huschte an eine Stelle zwischen Ganos und mir und begann zu knurren. Selbst der Hund konnte meine Angst spüren.

Ich konnte nicht klar denken, aber eine Sache war sicher: Ich konnte Ganos nicht weiter involvieren. Das würde mich in eine Zwickmühle bringen, wenn ich weitere Informationen einholen wollte, da sie bisher meine einzige zuverlässige Quelle und die einzige Person war, der ich vertraute. Aber ich hatte sie genug in Gefahr gebracht, und ich hatte den Hinweis, den ich brauchte. Ich hatte ein dummes Spiel gespielt, bei dem mir der Einsatz nicht bewusst gewesen war, und jetzt, da er vollkommen klar geworden war, musste ich feststellen, dass ich drei Züge zurücklag.

„Haben Sie Urlaubstage angespart?", fragte ich. „Es wäre vielleicht gut, wenn Sie für ein paar Tage die Stadt verlassen."

Sie hielt mitten im Tippen inne. „Sir, was verfickt noch mal geht hier vor?“

„Eine große Sache, Ganos. Es hängt mit dem zusammen, was ich auf Cappa getan habe, als ich den Planeten in die Luft gejagt habe.“

Sie hörte auf zu tippen, ihre Hände hingen über dem Keyboard. „Sir … erzählen Sie mir alles.“

„Erledigen Sie das zuerst, dann erzähle ich es.“

Sie tat es, und ich auch. Ich erzählte ihr alles. Was mit Elliot auf Cappa passiert und alles, was seitdem geschehen war. Als ich fertig war, erwartete ich, dass sie etwas sagte. Mich anbrüllte, weil ich sie da hineingezogen hatte. *Irgendetwas.*

Stattdessen nickte sie ein paar Mal langsam. „Wow. Das ist eine große Sache.“

„Das denke ich auch. Sind Sie sich sicher, dass Sie Ihren Zugang zum System gut verborgen haben?“

„Ja, Sir. Ich habe das Loch so gut gestopft, wie ich kann. Es bräuchte die besten Techies der Galaxis, um den Scheiß aufzuspüren. Ich mache mir keine Sorgen.“

Ich wünschte, ich hätte ihre Zuversicht.

Kapitel siebzehn

Die Personalabteilung sagte mir, dass ich mir nach meinem Krankenhausaufenthalt ein paar Tage freinehmen solle, aber ich konnte nicht in meiner Wohnung herumhängen und mir über das, was Ganos gefunden hatte, den Kopf zerbrechen. Kurz nach dem Mittagessen verließ ich die Wohnung und nahm eine alternative Route zur Arbeit, sah mich auf dem gesamten Weg immer wieder um und hielt Ausschau nach meinen cappanischen Hybrid-Freunden. Mein gerade gerichtetes Bein brauchte das Training eh. Sirenen spielten eine Symphonie, die sich auf die normalen Hintergrundgeräusche der Stadt setzte, aber ich kam ihnen nie nah genug, um zu sehen, was die Rettungsmannschaften zu tun hatten.

Ich hatte kaum mein Büro erreicht, als Ganos hereinhüpfte. Sie zitterte praktisch vor Aufregung. „Sir! Sie sind hier."

Ich legte die Stirn in Falten. „Ich dachte, wir hätten besprochen, dass Sie sich ein paar Tage freinehmen."

„Technisch gesehen haben *Sie* das gesagt. Aber genug der Semantik. Sie werden nicht glauben, was passiert ist."

„Leute sagen das immer wieder", sagte ich. „Sagen Sie mir nicht, dass Sie noch mal an den Ort gegangen sind, von dem ich Ihnen sagte, dass Sie nicht dort hingehen sollen."

„Bin ich nicht. Aber ich habe das Bild von der Frau genommen, das wir hatten, und habe ein bisschen herumgestöbert, nach bekannten Partnern gesucht, anderen Bildern, so was."

„Und Sie haben was gefunden?" So sehr ich wollte, dass sie nichts mehr mit dieser Sache zu tun hatte, so wenig konnte ich auf diese Art Informationen verzichten. Davon abgesehen würde es nichts ändern, wenn sie mir davon erzählte, jetzt, da sie die Arbeit bereits getan hatte.

„Ja. Nein. Mehr oder weniger." Sie wedelte mit den Händen, während sie sprach.

„Langsam, Ganos. Fangen Sie von vorne an."

Sie holte tief Luft. „Okay. Ich habe nach Dingen gesucht, in einem Haufen verschiedener Datenbanken. Auf eine tiefgehende Art, aber nichts super Technisches oder etwas besonders Gefährliches. Dann, ganz plötzlich, schloss jemand die Tür, wo immer ich mir Zugang verschaffte."

Ich ließ sie meine Verwirrung in meinem Gesicht sehen. „Helfen Sie mir."

„Die Orte, an denen ich suchte ... die haben nicht gerade öffentlichen Zugang, okay?"

„Sicher. Bis hierhin komme ich mit."

„Jedes Mal, wenn ich eintrat, hat mich jemand rausgeworfen. Nicht einmal. Jedes. Mal. Egal, wohin ich ging. Beim ersten Mal dachte ich, es sei Zufall. So was passiert. Beim zweiten Mal habe ich mich gewundert. Beim fünften Mal?"

„Also waren die Leute, die die Datenbanken betreiben, Ihnen auf der Spur?", fragte ich.

Sie schüttelte den Kopf. „Ausgeschlossen. *Alle* von ihnen? Sie gehören nicht zum selben System. Jede Aktion war unabhängig von den anderen."

„Ich verstehe das nicht. Wie ist es dann passiert?"

„Darüber habe ich lange nachgedacht", sagte sie. „Jemand anderes muss dieselben Datenbanken gehackt und mich rausgeworfen haben."

„Das ist möglich?"

„Sollte es nicht sein. Um das zu tun ... müsste man jedes einzelne System da draußen überwachen. Und jetzt kommt das Beste. Es passiert niemandem sonst in der Hacker-Gemeinde. Davon hätte ich gehört. Sie haben ausdrücklich *mich* ins Visier genommen."

Mir lief es kalt den Rücken runter. Ich dachte an meine eigene Situation und wie sie mir gefolgt waren. „Ich weiß nicht viel über Computer, aber Sie haben gesagt, dass jemand dafür alles überwachen müsste. Was, wenn sie stattdessen Sie überwacht haben?"

Sie nickte. „Zu dem Schluss bin ich auch gekommen. Ich habe alles durchsucht, was ich habe. Ich habe einen Tag gebraucht, aber ich habe es gefunden. Gerade so. Den Hauch einer Spur in meinem System. Sie haben mich gehackt und es dann so gut verborgen, dass ich es beinahe nicht finden konnte. Irgendwie peinlich, um ehrlich zu sein."

„Wie haben die das angestellt?"

Sie zuckte mit den Schultern. „Ich arbeite noch daran, das herauszufinden. Aber es hat mir Angst gemacht, das sage ich Ihnen."

„Mir auch." Sie schien darauf fokussiert zu sein, wie sie es technisch angestellt hatten. Ich machte mir Sorgen darum, woher sie wussten, dass man sie überhaupt überwachen musste. Ich wusste einen Scheiß über Computer, aber es musste Omicron sein. Ich wollte es nicht laut sagen. „Welchen Schaden haben sie angerichtet?"

„Das ist es ja gerade. Keinen. Wer auch immer das getan hat, hätte Alarm in den Systemen auslösen können, während ich drin war, und ich wäre vielleicht erwischt worden. Aber das haben sie nicht getan. Sie haben mich rausgeworfen und die Tür abgeschlossen. Das war's. Die Administratoren wussten nicht mal, dass es passiert ist."

„Das ist–"

„Colonel Butler?" Ein Kollege, den ich erkannte, aber nicht zuordnen konnte, steckte seinen Kopf zur Tür herein und unterbrach mich.

„Ja?"

„Sir, Sie müssen mit mir kommen."

„Geben Sie mir einen Moment", sagte ich.

Er blieb in der Tür stehen. „Es tut mir leid, Sir. Es muss jetzt sofort sein."

Ich blickte ihn wütend an, bekam aber keine echte Wut zustande. Mir schwirrte immer noch der Kopf von dem, was Ganos mir gerade berichtet hatte. „Ich sagte–"

Er unterbrach mich. „Sir, die Polizei ist in der Lobby, und sie bestehen darauf, Sie augenblicklich zu sehen."

Ich verkniff mir die Antwort, die ich gerade geben wollte, und sah Ganos an, als ich zur Tür ging. „Verlassen Sie die Stadt. Besser noch den Planeten. Verstanden?"

„Ja, Sir", sagte sie. Ich glaubte ihr nicht, aber darauf konnte ich mich im Moment nicht konzentrieren.

Als wir um die Ecke kamen und die Lobby betraten, überraschte es mich nicht, dass Mallory und Burke auf mich warteten, obwohl sie in dieser Umgebung fehl am Platz wirkten: Zwei Cops in billigen Anzügen umgeben von der Opulenz von VPCs Lobby.

„Was gibt es?", fragte ich.

„Colonel Butler, Sie müssen uns begleiten", sagte Mallory, während ihr Partner hinter ihr lauerte.

Meine Gedanken rasten. Da ich gerade mit Ganos gesprochen hatte, fragte ich mich, ob sie ihre semilegalen Computeraktivitäten irgendwie mit mir in Verbindung hatten bringen können. Aber das war nicht möglich. Allenfalls war es höchst unwahrscheinlich, dass nur mich hatten sprechen wollen. Die Rechtsabteilung hatte mir versichert, dass es mir freistand, das Krankenhaus zu verlassen, also konnte es das nicht sein. „Wollen Sie mir sagen, worum es geht?"

„Eigentlich nicht, nein", sagte Mallory.

„Was, wenn ich sage, dass ich nicht mitkomme?"

„Sie kommen mit. Wir können das auf die leichte oder die harte Tour machen." Mallory klopfte auf die Handschellen an ihrem Gürtel.

„Bitte sagen Sie ‚die harte Tour'", sagte Burke. „Bitte."

Es klang wie etwas, das er in einem Video gesehen hatte. Arschloch. Ich dachte nicht wirklich darüber nach, aber ich zögerte ein paar Sekunden, damit er glaubte, ich hätte es in Erwägung gezogen. „Ich denke, ich nehme die leichte Tour."

„Kluger Mann", sagte Mallory. „Gehen wir."

Ich folgte ihnen zur Vordertür hinaus und nahm die Blicke der paar Dutzend Leute auf, die zufällig vorbeigekommen waren, und derjenigen, die aufgetaucht waren, als sie die Nachricht vernommen hatten. Ich schätze, es dauerte neunzig Sekunden, bis sie sich im Rest des Gebäudes verbreitete.

Mallory öffnete die Hintertür ihres Hover-Cars, ein massiges, gepanzertes Ding, das zwanzig Jahre alt aussah, aber irgendwie immer noch funktional aussah. Eher klassisch als veraltet. Sie ignorierten all meine Versuche, während der Fahrt Informationen aus ihnen herauszubekommen, was bedeutete, dass sie mich nicht wissen lassen wollten, was sie hatten. Ich fragte mich, wer gestorben war. Ich hatte ein paar Minuten gebraucht, um zu dem Schluss zu kommen, dass es das sein musste. Jemand war gestorben und irgendwie hatte die Polizei eine Verbindung zu mir hergestellt. Die Liste der Leute in ihrem Zuständigkeitsbereich, die ich wirklich mochte, war ziemlich kurz. Ganos hatte ich gerade erst gesehen, also blieben Plazz, Sheila Jackson und Serata, die ich als Freunde betrachtete. Jackson arbeitete für VPC und die anderen beiden hätten große Schlagzeilen verursacht, wenn es also einer oder eine von ihnen gewesen wäre, hätte ich vermutlich davon gehört. Das beantwortete allerdings meine Frage nicht. Beinahe bat ich Mallory, mir zu sagen, wer gestorben war, aber ich entschied, mir das für einen Moment aufzusparen, in dem ich ihre Gesichter sehen und ihre Reaktionen einschätzen konnte. Hier im Fahrzeug konnte ich nur ihre Hinterköpfe anstarren und die gaben mir keine Antworten.

Auf dem Revier bugsierten sie mich durch eine Seitentür in der Nähe des Parkplatzes für Polizeifahrzeuge. Wir liefen – Mallory vor und Burke hinter mir –

durch einen Bereich voller Schreibtische und niedriger Trennwände, an denen mindestens ein Dutzend Polizistinnen und Polizisten an modernen Computern arbeiteten, während einige mit Zivilisten sprachen und Aussagen aufnahmen oder so was in der Art. Ein paar Leute sahen auf, aber niemand für länger als einen kurzen Moment, ehe sie wieder weiterarbeiteten. Warum auch immer sie mich aufs Revier gebracht hatten – es war entweder nicht so wichtig oder niemand sonst hier wusste davon.

Mallory führte mich in dasselbe Verhörzimmer, in dem ich gewesen war, als ich sie das letzte Mal aufgesucht hatte, aber mit einem kleinen Unterschied. Dieses Mal konnte ich nicht gehen, wann ich wollte, und das ließ den Raum kleiner und dunkler wirken. Die Anwesenheit des ununterbrochen wütenden Burke half der Atmosphäre nicht gerade.

„Also, wer ist tot?", fragte ich. Burkes langer Blick in Richtung seiner Partnerin bestätigte meine Vermutung. Sie schüttelte leicht den Kopf, wie um ihn verstummen zu veranlassen. Ich verstand das so, dass er mich hatte fragen wollen, woher ich wusste, dass jemand tot war, sie aber in eine andere Richtung wollte.

„Sie müssen uns sagen, wo Sie die letzten zwölf Stunden gewesen sind", sagte sie.

„Ich bin vor Einbruch der Dunkelheit nach Hause gekommen. Ich war in meiner Wohnung, bis ich vor Kurzem zur Arbeit aufgebrochen bin."

„Um wieviel Uhr sind Sie zur Arbeit aufgebrochen?"

„Weiß ich nicht", sagte ich. „Vielleicht vor einer Stunde. Ich habe eine Menge Sirenen gehört, als ich

VPC betrat. Das gibt Ihnen vielleicht eine ungefähre Zeit.“

Dieses Mal war es Mallory, die ihren Partner ansah. Ich war mir nicht sicher, aber ich glaubte, die Sirenen zu erwähnen, hatte etwas in ihr ausgelöst. „Hat jemand Sie in der Nähe Ihrer Wohnung gesehen?“

„Nicht dass ich wüsste“, sagte ich.

„Sie wissen, dass wir Kameraüberwachung aus der Gegend–“

Erhobene Stimmen aus dem Flur unterbrachen Mallory. „Sir! Sir! Sie können da nicht reingehen!“

Die Tür öffnete sich und ein großer, dunkelhäutiger Mann in einem feinen, anthrazitfarbenen Anzug trat ein. Er trug sein Haar kurz, makellos getrimmt, und er lächelte die Officers auf die Art an, wie ein Raubtier seine nächste Mahlzeit ansieht. „Entschuldigen Sie, Officers. Ich würde mich gerne mit meinem Klienten besprechen, ehe Sie ihn weiter befragen.“

Mallory sah mich an. „*Das* ist Ihr Anwalt?“

„Mein Klient wird keine Fragen beantworten, bis wir uns unterhalten haben. Ich bin Mark Gaspard. Ich wurde zur Vertretung von Colonel Butler engagiert.“

Mark Gaspard. Ich erkannte ihn nicht, aber ich kannte den Namen. Jeder kannte den Namen. Er war der prominenteste Strafverteidiger in der Stadt, wenn nicht sogar auf dem Planeten. Jemand wie ich konnte keinen Termin mit ihm bekommen. Und jemand wie ich konnte ihn sich definitiv nicht leisten.

„Colonel Butler?“, fragte Mallory. „Ungeachtet dessen, was dieser hochpreisige Gentleman behauptet, haben Sie nur das Recht, sich mit ihm zu beraten, wenn er Ihr

Anwalt *ist*. Also fürchte ich, dass Sie antworten *müssen*.“

„Sie brauchen nur einen Anwalt, wenn Sie was zu verbergen haben“, sagte Burke.

„Lassen Sie den Scheiß, Officer“, sagte Gaspard. „Das ist ungebührlich.“ Einen Moment lang sah Burke beinahe peinlich berührt aus. Allein dafür hätte ich mich von Gaspard vertreten lassen.

„Ja. Mr. Gaspard vertritt mich.“

„Wir überlassen Ihnen das Zimmer.“ Mallory klappte ihr Device etwas härter zu als nötig.

„Das wird nicht nötig sein“, sagte Gaspard. „Es ist nicht so, dass ich Ihnen mit Ihren Abhörgeräten nicht vertraue. Nennen Sie es eine Vorsichtsmaßnahme. Das verstehen Sie, richtig?“

„Aber er kann nicht gehen …“

Gaspard lächelte. „Ist er verhaftet? Wie lautet die Anklage? Schauen Sie, ich will kein sturer Hund sein. Geben Sie mir fünf Minuten draußen, dann kommen wir sofort wieder. Sie haben mein Wort.“

Mallory seufzte und sah Burke an, der mit den Schultern zuckte. „In Ordnung“, sagte sie.

Ich setzte zu sprechen an, während wir durch die Polizeistation liefen, um herauszufinden, wo mein anwaltlicher Retter hergekommen war, aber der unterbrach mich mit einer Handbewegung, bis wir die Straße erreicht hatten.

„Würden sie uns wirklich abhören?“, fragte ich.

„Schwer zu sagen“, sagte Gaspard. „Aber warum sollten wir sie in Versuchung führen? Hauptsächlich wollte ich Ihnen blöd kommen.“

Ich kicherte. „Ich nehme an, VPC hat sie geschickt?“

„Javier Sanchez hat mich persönlich angerufen. Entschuldigen Sie, dass ich nicht schon hier war, ehe Sie eintrafen, aber Ihr Gewahrsam war eine kleine Überraschung, wie ich hörte.“

„Eine ziemliche Überraschung. Ich weiß nicht mal, weshalb ich hier bin.“

„Ich bin mir auch nicht sicher, was vermutlich bedeutet, dass ich Sie ohne weitere Befragung rausbekomme, wenn Sie wollen.“

Ich lächelte. „So spaßig das auch klingt, wenn sie zulässige Fragen haben und ich helfen kann, macht es mir nichts aus. Und wenn möglich, hätte ich auch gern Informationen von ihnen. Irgendetwas ist passiert und sie haben zumindest den leisen Verdacht, dass es etwas mit mir zu tun hat.“

„Okay. Ich werde die Einführung machen und dann für die Befragung hierbleiben. Das wird vermutlich genug sein, um dafür zu sorgen, dass sie nicht aus der Reihe tanzen, und die beiden davon abhalten, Sie zu sehr fertigzumachen. Geben Sie mir eine kurze Zusammenfassung der Situation, dann gehen wir wieder rein.“

„Klingt gut“, sagte ich. „Nur aus Neugier, was kostet so was?“

„Das wollen Sie nicht wissen. Ich habe außerdem eine Nachricht für Sie, direkt von Mr. Sanchez.“

„Sicher, solange er die Rechnung übernimmt, bin ich ganz Ohr.“

„Er sagte, Sie sollen sämtliche Aktivitäten einstellen, die mit der Omicron Corporation in Verbindung stehen. Er sagte, Sie wüssten, was das bedeutet.“

„Weiß ich", sagte ich. Darüber würde ich später nachdenken. Zuerst musste ich mich auf die dringendere Angelegenheit mit der Polizei konzentrieren. Ich briefte Gaspard über die Ereignisse der vergangenen Woche, einschließlich Gylikas Tod und der Schießerei auf der Straße. Ich erwähnte ausdrücklich *nicht* die Hybride oder unser Eindringen in Omicrons System. Er war mein Anwalt, aber er war auch Javiers.

Mallory und Burke warteten auf uns, als wir zurückkehrten, und unterhielten sich mit gesenkten Stimmen.

„Mein Klient stimmt vorbehaltlich meiner Anwesenheit einer weiteren Befragung zu", sagte Gaspard.

„Wie großzügig von ihm", sagte Burke.

„Ja, nicht wahr?" Gaspard lächelte.

„Setzen Sie sich", sagte Mallory. Ich nahm den Stuhl, auf dem ich zuvor gesessen hatte, und Gaspard setzte sich links neben mich. Mallory setzte sich auf einen Stuhl auf der anderen Seite des Polymertisches, während Burke seinem Naturell entsprechend im Zimmer auf und ab ging.

„Ich glaube, Sie waren gerade dabei, uns von diesem Morgen zu erzählen", sagte Mallory.

„Ich will offen zu Ihnen sein", sagte ich. „Ich habe keine Ahnung, warum ich hier bin. Ich bin gerne bereit, Ihnen auf jede erdenkliche Weise zu helfen, aber Sie müssen mich erst mal ins Bild setzen, worum es geht. Alles, was ich weiß, ist: Ich habe nichts getan außer zu schlafen, an meinem Computer Zeit zu vertändeln und dann zur Arbeit zu gehen."

Mallory seufzte. „Die Sirenen, die Sie heute früh gehört haben ... sie hatten mit einer Explosion zu tun."

Das erwischte mich etwas unvorbereitet. „Was hat das mit mir zu tun?"

„Es hat etwas mit Ihnen zu tun, weil die Leute, die bei der Explosion starben, dieselben waren, von denen wir vermuten, dass sie sich vor ein paar Tagen in Ihrer Nähe ein Feuergefecht geliefert haben. Jemand schießt Sie an, dann stirbt jemand. Klingt nach einem verdammt eigenartigen Zufall, oder nicht?"

„Das klingt nach einer Anschuldigung", sagte Gaspard.

Mich durchfuhr ein Schauer, trotz der Wärme im Zimmer. „Es ist okay", sagte ich. Es war definitiv kein Zufall. Aber ich wusste auch nicht, welche Seite gestorben war. Waren es die Hybride oder die andere Gruppe gewesen? Ich wollte nicht direkt fragen, weil sie das wissen lassen würde, wie wichtig es mir war. „Sind Sie sich sicher, dass es Mord war und kein Terroranschlag oder so was?"

Sie schüttelte den Kopf. „Terroristen geben sich größte Mühe, so viel Schaden wie möglich anzurichten. Diese Explosion hat genau einen Raum betroffen und die beiden Personen darin getötet, aber dem Rest des Gebäudes keinen Schaden zugefügt."

„Wow", sagte ich.

„Wer immer das getan hat, kannte sich aus. Können Sie damit was anfangen?"

Ich schüttelte den Kopf. „Das ist wirklich nicht mein Fachgebiet. Ich kenne mich mit Explosionen aus, aber so was in einem Zimmer, das übersteigt meine Fähigkeiten. Das klingt eher nach …" Ich brach mitten im Satz ab. Das klang eher nach Spezialeinheits-Fähigkeiten.

Ich hatte eine Vermutung, wer gestorben war, und es waren nicht die Hybride.

„Beenden Sie den Gedanken." Mallory sah Gaspard an, um zu schauen, ob er dagegen Einspruch erhob, dass sie mich unter Druck setzte.

„Mein Klient würde Ihnen diese Informationen als Experte auf diesem Gebiet geben, nicht als Verdächtiger", sagte Gaspard.

„Sicher", sagte Mallory.

„Es ist eine Fähigkeit, die zu einer Spezialeinheit passt", sagte ich. „Das Ziel in einem begrenzten Raum ohne Kollateralschaden auszuschalten ... ja. Falls es jemand vom Militär war, würde ich gutes Geld daraufsetzen, dass es Leute von einer Spezialeinheit waren."

„Und was haben Soldaten einer Spezialeinheit mit einer Schießerei in einer Gasse zu tun? Angenommen, dieselben Leute sind für beide Taten verantwortlich."

„Darauf müssen Sie nicht antworten", sagte Gaspard.

Mallory setzte zu sprechen an, aber ich unterbrach sie. „Es ist in Ordnung. Ich antworte darauf. Aber Tatsache ist, dass ich es nicht weiß." Ich hatte ihnen einen Teil der Wahrheit gesagt, aber ich zog eine Grenze, wenn es darum ging, über die Hybrid-Frau zu reden. Es würde mich weiter in Polizeiangelegenheiten hineinziehen und sie hatten nichts, das für mich von Wert war. Zumindest nicht, soweit ich es sehen konnte. „Vielleicht könnte ich mehr Licht ins Dunkel bringen, wenn ich wüsste, wer die Toten sind."

Mallory dachte darüber nach. „Wir wissen es nicht. Sie hatten beide ziemlich gute falsche Ausweise. Sie sind Ex-Militärs, da sind wir uns recht sicher, aber das ist so ziemlich alles, was wir haben."

„Shit“, sagte ich.

„Was?“, fragte Mallory.

„Ich will wissen, wer diese Leute sind.“

„Sie wissen es wirklich nicht?“

„Ich weiß es wirklich nicht.“

„Butler … worin sind Sie da verstrickt?“, fragte sie.

Gaspard räusperte sich.

„Egal“, sagte Mallory.

Ich lächelte. Es spielte keine Rolle, ob ich antwortete oder nicht. Ich hatte keine Ahnung.

Kapitel achtzehn

Kaum dass ich meine Wohnung betreten hatte, spürte ich, dass etwas nicht stimmte. Ich weiß nicht, was mich warnte, aber ich sprang zu Boden und suchte Deckung.

„Guten Abend, Colonel Butler." Die Stimme einer Frau. Vertraut. „Sie können aufstehen. Wir werden Ihnen nichts tun. Wir wollen nur reden."

Mein Herz pochte. Die Frau von der Straße. Der cappanische Hybrid. Dieselben Worte, die sie gesagt hatte, ehe ich angeschossen worden war. „Wie sind Sie hier reingekommen?" Ich wollte, dass sie weiterredete. Wollte Zeit schinden. Ich hatte einen Taser neben dem Bett versteckt. Es schien unwahrscheinlich, dass ich ihn erreichen würde, aber ‚vielleicht' war besser als ‚ausgeschlossen'.

„Sie haben ein gutes Sicherheitssystem. Hochmodern."

„Offenbar nicht", sagte ich.

„Nein, das ist es. Aber wir sind gut darin, solche Dinge zu umgehen." Die Frau saß auf dem Sofa, ihr Partner stand hinter ihr, derselbe Kerl, der auch zuvor bei ihr gewesen war. Keiner von ihnen schien eine Waffe zu haben. Aber sie schienen deswegen auch nicht sonderlich besorgt zu sein. Sie strahlten Ruhe aus. „Ich muss Sie bitten, ihr Device wegzulegen", sagte die Frau. „Ich will nicht, dass Sie die Polizei rufen."

Ich holte mein Device hervor und legte es auf die Ablage. Ich hatte keinen Grund, ihr nicht zu gehorchen. Wenn sie mich hätten töten wollen, wäre ich bereits tot. Wenn sie es noch vorhatten, würde es passieren, lange bevor irgendjemand, den ich angerufen hatte, herkommen könnte. Ich schätze, ich hätte jemanden anrufen können, damit meine Leiche weggeschafft wird. Ich schüttelte diesen Gedanken ab und versuchte, mich auf etwas weniger Morbides zu konzentrieren. „Sicher. Sie sind hier, also können wir uns genauso gut unterhalten.“

„Sie wissen, wer wir sind“, sagte der Mann. Eine Aussage, keine Frage.

„Ich weiß ... was Sie sind. Wer? Nein, das weiß ich nicht.“

„Mein Name ist Sasha. Das ist Riku“, sagte die Frau.

„Carl Butler. Macht es Ihnen etwas aus, wenn ich mich setze?“ Ich hatte das Vorhaben, zu meiner Waffe zu gelangen, noch nicht aufgegeben, aber mehr noch wollte ich Antworten.

„Bitte“, sagte Sasha. „In Anbetracht der Umstände sind Sie erstaunlich ruhig.“

Dem stimmte ich nicht zu. Seit ich die Wohnung betreten hatte, hämmerte mir das Herz in der Brust, und ich hatte gerade erst angefangen, es unter Kontrolle zu kriegen. Langsam zu meinem Stuhl zu gehen, half dabei. „Ich versuche, nicht übermäßig zu reagieren. Wie sind Sie hergekommen?“ Ich erwartete nicht, dass sie antworteten, aber wenn ich den Tenor der Unterhaltung ändern und sie dazu bringen konnte, mir zu antworten, konnte das nur helfen.

„Das haben wir bereits beantwortet“, sagte Riku.

„Nein, ich meine nicht, wie Sie in meine Wohnung gekommen sind. Wie sind Sie auf den Planeten gekommen?“

„Wie wir es Ihnen schon bei unserem letzten Treffen sagten, brauchen wir Ihre Hilfe“, sagte er und ignorierte meine Frage, was mir noch mehr veranschaulichte, dass ich es mit Profis zu tun hatte.

„Ja. Ich erinnere mich daran, dass Sie das gesagt haben. Kurz bevor Leute anfingen, auf mich zu schießen.“

„Das war unerfreulich“, sagte Sasha.

Ich schnaubte. „Wem sagen Sie das?“

„Die Leute, die Sie angeschossen haben … wollten eigentlich uns treffen“, sagte sie.

„Woher wissen Sie das?“, fragte ich.

„Es ist nicht das erste Mal, dass sie es versucht haben.“

„Sie hatten freie Schussbahn. Wenn sie Sie hätten treffen wollen, hätten sie es getan.“

„Vielleicht“, sagte sie. „Bei so einer Sache spielen viele Dinge eine Rolle.“

Ich hielt inne, ehe ich den Kurs änderte. „Also haben Sie hier Feinde. Sie haben zurückgeschlagen. Diese Leute wurden heute tot aufgefunden. Ich nehme an, das war Ihr Werk.“

Sie warf ihrem Partner über die Schulter hinweg einen Blick zu. „Wir haben überall Feinde.“

„Und ich bin der Mann, der ganz allein für den Mord an einer großen Zahl von Cappanern verantwortlich ist“, sagte ich. „Ich nehme also an, dass ich ziemlich weit oben auf der Liste stehe.“

„Nicht notwendigerweise“, sagte Sasha.

„Okay. Da komme ich nicht mehr mit. Ich mache mir einen Drink. Wollen Sie etwas?“

„Nein, danke", sagte sie. Riku schüttelte den Kopf.

Ich stand auf, ging hinüber zum Tresen und schenkte mir einen Doppelten ein. „Wieso bin ich nicht Volksfeind Nummer eins?"

„Unter einigen Cappanern sind Sie das ganz sicher. Aber was die Gruppe betrifft, für die wir arbeiten, haben Sie nichts getan, was das rechtfertigen würde."

Mir fiel beinahe der Drink aus der Hand. „Ich habe nichts getan?"

Sasha dachte über ihre Worte nach, ehe sie sprach. „Genauer gesagt liegt das, was Sie getan haben, in der Vergangenheit. Eine einmalige Sache. Sie – wir – sind bereit, es hinter uns zu lassen, wenn es uns heute hilft."

„Das ist erstaunlich ... reif von Ihnen. Und den Cappanern. Ich nehme an, die stecken hinter Ihrem Besuch?" Ich nahm einen Schluck von meinem Drink, ohne mich darum zu sorgen, dass es etwa elf Uhr morgens war.

„Sie haben uns gebeten, Kontakt zu Ihnen aufzunehmen, ja", sagte Sasha. „Sie wollen mit Ihnen reden. Aber es nicht so, als könnte ein Cappaner auf Talca 4 auftauchen, ohne Aufmerksamkeit auf sich zu ziehen."

„Vergeben Sie mir, wenn es mir schwerfällt, das zu glauben", sagte ich. Ich kam nicht dahinter, was ihr Plan war, und die Verwirrung bereitete mir ein ungutes Gefühl.

„Lassen Sie mich Ihnen eine Frage stellen, Colonel Butler", sagte Sasha. „Das letzte Mal, als Sie mit jemandem wie uns zu tun hatten – hätten Sie sie als reif beschrieben?"

Augenblicklich erinnerte ich mich an Mallot, dem ich ins Gesicht geschossen hatte, weil er verrückt geworden war und mich wahrscheinlich getötet hätte, und an

Karikov, einen hochdekorierten Offizier, der dabei war, seinen Verstand zu verlieren. „Nein, das ist nicht das Wort, das ich verwendet hätte."

„Welches Wort hätten Sie verwendet?", fragte sie.

Ich dachte darüber nach; wollte sie nicht beleidigen oder in die Defensive zwingen. „Ich würde sagen ... instabil."

„Exakt", sagte sie.

„Sie wollen andeuten ..." Ich setzte mich wieder. „Sie behaupten, Sie sind anders als die?"

„Ja", sagte sie.

„Interessant? Würden Sie das weiter ausführen?"

„Die Prozedur, die cappanische und menschliche DNA gespleißt hat, hat damals nicht funktioniert. Jetzt tut sie es." Sie begegnete meinem Blick ohne zu blinzeln, ihrer war aber nicht herausfordernd. Sie glaubte an das, was sie sagte, erwartete aber nicht notwendigerweise, dass ich es tat.

„So einfach?", fragte ich.

Sie schüttelte den Kopf. „Ganz und gar nicht einfach. Die Wissenschaft dahinter, so sagte man mir, ist unfassbar kompliziert. Zuvor standen die beiden genetischen Informationen im Konflikt miteinander. Jetzt harmonieren sie."

„Ich verstehe nicht, wie das möglich ist."

„Ich verstehe es auch nicht unbedingt." Sie deutete auf sich und ihren Partner. „Aber hier sind wir nun."

„Hier sind Sie nun", wiederholte ich und versuchte mehr als alles andere, mir Zeit zu verschaffen, um nachdenken zu können. „Was hat sich verändert?"

„Als Sie den Planeten angegriffen haben, haben Sie die medizinischen Einrichtungen der Menschen zerstört.“

Ich nickte. „Ja.“

„Jene von uns mit gespleißter cappanischer DNA, die auf dem Planeten gestrandet waren, konnten ohne Behandlung nicht überleben“, fuhr sie fort. „Also gingen wir zur einzigen Quelle, die wir hatten.“

„Welche Quelle?“

„Zu den Cappanern.“

Ich nahm einen Schluck, um meine Überraschung zu verbergen. „Den Cappanern?“

„Ihr Verständnis von Genetik ist recht fortgeschritten“, sagte sie.

„Genetik. Die Cappaner.“ Ich schaffte es nicht, die Skepsis aus meiner Stimme herauszuhalten.

„Das war der eigentliche Ursprung des Projekts. Ein gemeinsames Bestreben von Cappanern und Menschen. Bis die Menschen es übernahmen und zu ihren eigenen Zwecken nutzten.“

„Vergeben Sie mir ... die Cappaner sind ein rückwärtsgewandtes Volk.“

Sie verzog ihr Gesicht. „Sagt wer? Die Menschen?“

„Alle. Sie hatten nicht die Fähigkeit, ins All zu reisen, als wir eintrafen.“

„Raumfahrt ist ein willkürliches Merkmal. Sie hatten nicht das Verlangen, ihren Planeten zu verlassen“, antwortete sie.

„Aber sie ...“ Ich hielt inne. Was wusste ich wirklich über sie? „Sie sagen also, sie hätten den Planeten verlassen können, wenn sie es gewollt hätten?“

„Die Bevölkerung hatte nicht begonnen, die Ressourcen ihrer eigenen Welt auszuschöpfen. Sie sind ein ziemlich effizientes Volk. Und zugegeben, vor dem Eintreffen der Menschen besaßen sie keine Fusionstechnologie."

„Bis sie sie gestohlen haben", sagte ich mit sanfter Stimme.

„Wie schnell haben Sie sie assimiliert?", fragte sie.

Ich starrte in die bernsteinfarbene Flüssigkeit in meinem Glas, ohne sofort zu antworten. „Sie haben alles verstanden."

„Anfangs nicht", sagte sie. „Aber Wissenschaft ist viel leichter, wenn man etwas hat, worauf man aufbauen kann."

Ich war kein Wissenschaftler, aber es fiel mir nicht schwer, diesen Teil der Geschichte zu glauben. „Also sind Sie … Sie beide … sind stabil?"

„So stabil wie Sie", sagte Riku.

„Das ist nicht unbedingt ein guter Maßstab", sagte ich, aber sie reagierten nicht auf den Witz. „Sie behaupten, die Cappaner haben das getan. Sie repariert."

„*Repariert* ist ein ziemlich hässliches Wort", sagte er. „Aber ja."

Ich nahm noch einen Schluck von meinem Drink. Ich konnte das nicht verarbeiten. „Wie hängt das mit Omicron zusammen?" Beide Gesichter verdunkelten sich, als ich den Namen sagte. „Mit Omicron stimmt etwas nicht", fügte ich nur für den Effekt hinzu.

Ihre lange Pause sagte mir, dass ich ins Schwarze getroffen hatte. Es sagte mir außerdem, dass sie über Omicron Bescheid wusste. „Omicron ist ein Problem, ja. Das ist einer der Gründe, warum die Cappaner mit Ihnen reden wollen."

„Wir reden doch gerade." Ich gab jeden Gedanken daran auf, eine Waffe in die Finger zu bekommen. Sasha wusste etwas über Omicron, und da sie in meiner Wohnung war, konnte ich mir ziemlich sicher sein, dass es etwas mit mir zu tun hatte.

„Es ist nicht an uns, Ihnen das zu sagen. Die Cappaner werden entscheiden, wie viel sie preisgeben wollen", sagte sie.

„Ich brauche mehr als das", sagte ich.

Sie dachte darüber nach. „Ich sage Ihnen Folgendes: Die Leute, die auf Sie geschossen haben – die auf uns geschossen haben –, waren bei Omicron angestellt."

„Haben Sie Beweise?", fragte ich. Wenn dem so war, könnte ich sie bei Mallory verwenden.

„Nein."

„Aber Sie sind sich sicher", sagte ich.

„Ja." Sie spuckte das Wort aus, beinahe wie ein Schimpfwort.

„Warum sollten die auf Sie schießen?"

Sie sahen einander an, und obwohl niemand sprach, bekam ich das Gefühl, als übermittle sich etwas zwischen ihnen. „Wir haben unsere Nachricht überbracht", sagte sie. „Werden Sie sich mit den Cappanern treffen oder nicht?"

„Wir treffen uns doch gerade", sagte ich, während sich Enttäuschung in mir breitmachte. Sie hatte Antworten, würde sie mir aber nicht geben.

„Wir sind nicht die Cappaner", sagte Riku. „Wir tun ihnen einen Gefallen. Sie helfen uns, wir helfen ihnen."

„Das letzte Mal, als ich mich mit den Cappanern ge-troffen habe, haben sie mich zusammengeschlagen und versucht, medizinische Experimente an mir durch-zuführen."

„Sie scheinen die Cappaner für eine homogene Gruppe zu halten", sagte Sasha. „Ich würde behaupten, dass sie in ihrem Denken so divers sind wie die Men-schen. Die Cappaner, denen Sie begegnet sind, waren wahrscheinlich Teil des Widerstands gegen die Inva-sion. Daraus ergibt sich, dass sie auf der radikalen Seite waren, so wie alle Freiheitskämpfer. Aber ich verstehe Ihre Haltung", sagte Sasha.

Ich setzte zu einer Antwort an, unterbrach mich aber. Jetzt, wo ich darüber nachdachte, wurde mir bewusst, dass ich sie tatsächlich hauptsächlich als eine Gruppe betrachtet hatte, und jetzt, da Sasha mich darauf hinge-wiesen hatte, erschien mir dieser Gedanke auf törichte Weise holzschnittartig. „Und die Gruppe, die Sie reprä-sentieren?", fragte ich schließlich.

„Hauptsächlich Wissenschaftler", sagte Sasha. „Viel progressiver. Sie vertrauen Menschen zwar nicht, aber sie sehen den Nutzen – oder die Notwendigkeit – einer friedlichen Koexistenz."

„Ihr mangelndes Vertrauen kann ich ihnen nicht ver-übeln", sagte ich, „also hoffe ich, dass Sie mir mein mangelndes Vertrauen nicht verübeln. Können Sie für meine Sicherheit garantieren, wenn ich zustimme, mich mit den Cappanern zu treffen?"

„Würden Sie uns glauben, wenn wir ja sagen wür-den?", fragte Sasha.

Guter Punkt. „Ich brauche Zeit, um darüber nachzu-denken."

„Unglücklicherweise haben wir nicht viel davon", sagte Sasha. „Die Cappaner haben einen ziemlich engen Zeitplan. Sie können nicht lange auf Talca 4 bleiben."

„Sie sind *hier*?"

„Wie sollten Sie sich sonst treffen?", fragte Riku.

„Ich weiß nicht, ich dachte an eine Videoübertragung oder so etwas." Ich nuschelte leicht, weil ich Mühe hatte, diese neue Information zu verarbeiten. „Sie sind von der Rückseite von Cappa gestartet, haben die Satellitenüberwachung umgangen und sind *hierhergekommen*?"

Sasha blickte ihren Partner bedeutungsvoll an. Ich überraschte sie wieder mit meinem Wissen. Gut zu wissen, dass sie nicht alle Antworten hatten.

Nach ein paar Sekunden wiederholte ich: „Ich brauche Zeit zum Nachdenken." Ich war mir beinahe sicher, dass ich mich mit den Cappanern treffen würde. Wie könnte ich nicht? Sasha gab mir keine Antworten obwohl sie es könnten. Aber indem ich um Zeit bat, konnte ich abschätzen, ob ich wirklich eine Wahl hatte oder ob die beiden Hybriden mich zwingen würden. Zu wissen, wo ich stand, war eine wertvolle Information.

„Wir können Ihnen zwei Tage geben", sagte sie. „Aber Sie müssen versprechen, nichts zu unternehmen, um die Anwesenheit der Cappaner auf Talca zu enthüllen. Wir werden Sie beobachten."

„Dem stimme ich zu", sagte ich ohne Pause.

„Das schließt Ms. Ganos ein, die versucht, Informationen über uns auszugraben", sagte Sasha.

Jetzt war ich an der Reihe damit, von *ihrem* Wissen überrascht zu sein. Ich erwog, zu bluffen, zu leugnen, dass ich etwas wusste, aber etwas an Sasha sagte mir, dass das Zeitverschwendung gewesen wäre. „Sie wissen von ihr?"

„Ja, wir verraten sie aber nicht."

Sie wollte andeuten, dass sie es könnten, wenn ich ihnen nicht half. Sie fragten mich freundlich, aber nicht wirklich freundlich.

„Haben Sie ihre Bemühungen, das Netz nach Informationen zu durchsuchen, vereitelt?"

„Mitarbeiter von uns", sagte Sasha. „Sie ist sehr talentiert."

Es beruhigte mich ein wenig, dass sie und nicht Omicron Ganos gefunden hatten. Das war vermutlich mein Unterbewusstsein, das mir sagte, welche Seite ich wählen sollte. Aber ich war mir immer noch nicht sicher, also entschied ich, einen anderen Ansatz zu versuchen, um sie zu testen. Ich suchte immer noch nach einem Grund, um nein zu sagen. „Was ließ Sie Partei für die Cappaner ergreifen?"

„Wir haben viel Zeit mit ihnen verbracht, als sie uns behandelt haben, und wir haben gesehen, wie die Menschen sie misshandelt haben. Das ist falsch. Wir haben das Gefühl, dass die Gruppe, mit der wir jetzt zusammenarbeiten, geeignete Maßnahmen ergreift."

„Und alle ... alle Leute, die von den Cappanern medizinisch behandelt wurden, denken wie Sie?"

„Absolut nicht", sagte Riku. „Wir haben einen freien Willen. Tatsächlich haben sich die meisten dazu entschieden, sich nicht einzumischen. Sie werden für Menschen gehalten, also integrieren sie sich wieder in die Gesellschaft. Sie sehen keinen Grund, zu kämpfen."

Darüber hatte ich nie nachgedacht. So wie ich die Cappaner über einen Kamm geschoren hatte, hatte ich die Hybride als eine zusammenhängende Gruppe betrachtet. Und wieder ergab es Sinn, dass sie das nicht waren. Wieso sollten sie auch? Ich unterlag einem schwerwiegenden Denkfehler.

„Wie viele Cappaner haben sich dieser Gruppe angeschlossen? Wie viele halten es für eine gute Idee, mit mir zusammenzuarbeiten? Wie viele wollen mich tot sehen?"

Sasha lächelte. „Jetzt stellen Sie die richtigen Fragen. Aber es ist nicht an mir, sie Ihnen zu beantworten. Sie sollten das fragen, wenn Sie sich mit ihnen treffen. Nehmen Sie sich die zwei Tage Zeit und denken Sie darüber nach. Wir haben nicht vor, Sie zum Handeln zu zwingen."

„Sie sind in meine Wohnung eingebrochen. Sie haben nicht ganz so subtil gesagt, dass Sie Ganos belasten könnten. Sie müssen verstehen, dass mich das skeptisch macht."

„Das war notwendig", sagte Riku. „Was Ganos betrifft, mussten wir Leute, die *uns* bloßstellen könnten, im Auge behalten. Und wir sind bei Ihnen eingebrochen, weil wir keine weitere Interaktion wie neulich auf der Straße riskieren konnten."

„Das sehe ich ein", sagte ich. „Aber wenn Sie nicht hier sind, um mich zu zwingen, wieso sind Sie dann hier?"

Sasha lächelte mich ausdruckslos an. „Um Sie zu bitten, das Richtige zu tun."

Shit. Wenn Sie mich entführt und zu den Cappanern geschleppt hätten, hätte ich vielleicht Widerstand geleistet, und sie hätten getan, was sie vorgehabt hatten.

Wir hätten uns einen Kampf geliefert und das wäre es dann gewesen. Aber sie appellierten an meinen Gerechtigkeitssinn.

Sie kämpften schmutzig.

„Wieso wollen sie mich?"

„Sie sind davon überzeugt, dass Sie der richtige Mensch sind, um ihnen zu helfen", sagte Sasha.

Ich schüttelte den Kopf. „Ihr Vertrauen in mich ist schmeichelhaft. Aber ich glaube, sie liegen falsch." Ich hob mein Glas. „Ich bin nur ein abgewrackter Säufer, der zu viele Schlachtfelder gesehen hat."

„Blödsinn", sagte Sasha mit einer Heftigkeit, die mich für einen Augenblick erschreckte. Andererseits glaubte ich es selbst nicht, also konnte ich ihren Gefühlsausbruch nachvollziehen.

„Sie wissen, dass ich das Falsche getan habe, richtig? Auf Cappa?"

Sasha lächelte. „Wissen wir. Aber richtig und falsch sind nichts Absolutes. Was in einem Moment richtig ist, mag in einem anderen falsch sein."

„Das ist Quatsch! Es *gibt* moralisch Absolutes. Und was ich getan habe–"

„Falls es ein moralisches Absolutum ist, warum haben Sie es dann getan?", fragte Riku. „Sind Sie ein unmoralischer Mensch?"

Ich lächelte ihn ausdruckslos an, dann schüttelte ich den Kopf. „Ich weiß nicht. Vielleicht bin ich das."

Wieder blickten sie einander an. Diesmal meldete die Frau sich zu Wort. „Unsere Verbündeten sind bereit zu glauben, dass Sie es nicht sind."

„Okay. Sie sagten, dass ich zwei Tage Zeit bekommen würde. Ich verstehe Ihre Bedingung, dass ich nichts unternehmen soll, um Ihnen irgendwie zu schaden. Was ist mit Aktionen gegen Omicron?“ Es schien nicht vernünftig, das zu präzisieren, da ich bereits eine solche Aktion durchgeführt hatte, indem ich in ihr System eingebrochen war.

„Solange sie nicht zu uns zurückführen“, sagte Sasha.

„Okay. Wie nehme ich Kontakt zu Ihnen auf?“

„Schicken Sie das Wort ‚Entscheidung‘ an diese Nummer.“ Auf der Ablage vibrierte mein Device.

„Zwei Tage“, sagte ich.

Sobald sie gegangen waren, sank ich auf mein Sofa, trank meinen Drink aus und dachte über meine lächerliche Situation nach. Ich hatte mich bereits mehr oder weniger entschieden, zu dem Treffen zu gehen. Die einzige Sache, über die ich mir klarwerden musste, war, wie ich mich in den zwei Tagen, die mir blieben, am besten darauf vorbereiten konnte.

Kapitel neunzehn

Am nächsten Tag ging ich früh zur Arbeit. Sasha hatte mir gesagt, dass die Leute, die mich angeschossen hatten, für Omicron arbeiteten. Das war bei mir hängengeblieben und mein Bauchgefühl sagte, dass Omicron etwas damit zu tun hatte, weshalb die Cappaner sich mit mir treffen wollten. Es gab zu viele Zufälle, als dass sie nicht miteinander in Verbindung standen, besonders angesichts dessen, was Ganos über das Phoenix Project herausgefunden hatte. Ich hatte den Großteil der Nacht wachgelegen und über das nachgedacht, was Sasha und Riku mir erzählt hatten. Verdammt, natürlich glaubte ich ihnen. Verdammt, ich glaubte, dass die Cappaner die Guten waren. Vielleicht hatte ich zu viel Zeit in der Nähe von Firmen wie Omicron verbracht und kannte die Missstände, die dort herrschten. Vielleicht dachte ich, dass ich den Cappanern etwas schuldete, nachdem ich so viele von ihnen getötet hatte. So oder so hatte ich in zwei Tagen ein Treffen mit den Cappanern, und ich wollte so viel wie möglich wissen.

Omicrons Lobby zu betreten und Antworten zu verlangen, würde nicht funktionieren. Ich hätte wieder über ihr Computernetzwerk auf sie losgehen können, aber ich wollte Ganos nicht tiefer mit in die Sache hineinziehen – ich hatte immer noch die Hoffnung, dass sie meinen Rat angenommen und die Stadt verlassen hatte. Und Javier hatte mir sämtliche offizielle Unterstützung entzogen, die ich gehabt hatte, um als Angestellter von VPC auf sie loszugehen. Da meine Optionen begrenzt waren, hatte ich das Gefühl, nur noch einen anderen Weg zu haben.

Sehr inoffiziell vorzugehen.

Es war an der Zeit, Javier ein wenig wegen seiner Kontaktperson unter Druck zu setzen. Er wusste Dinge, die er nicht preisgab, und ich wollte sie wissen. Alles, was mir im Weg stand, war die Tatsache, dass er mir durch einen sehr teuren Anwalt hatte mitteilen lassen, ich solle meine Ermittlung einstellen.

Aber da ich nur zwei Tage hatte, musste ich Risiken eingehen. Wenn das eine potenzielle Kündigung bedeutete; so sei es. Ich war VPC sowieso überdrüssig. Ich holte mir einen Kaffee und ging nach oben zu seinem Büro, um zu schauen, ob er mich in seinem Terminkalender unterbringen konnte.

Es stellte sich heraus, dass ich keinen Termin brauchte; Javier begrüßte mich, kaum dass ich sein Vorzimmer betrat. „Carl! Genau der Mann, mit dem ich reden wollte. Sie haben es mir erspart, jemanden zu schicken.“

Ich versuchte, meine Überraschung zu verbergen. Ich hatte verschiedene potenzielle Herangehensweisen geprobt, aber keine beinhaltete, dass Javier mich einlud. „Sicher, Boss“, sagte ich nach einer, wie ich hoffte, nicht allzu peinlichen Pause. Ich folgte ihm in sein Büro.

„Ich will mit Ihnen über Omicron reden.“ Javier ergriff das Wort, ehe er die Tür schloss. Ich war froh, dass er nicht in mein Gesicht gesehen hatte, als er es sagte, weil er vielleicht wieder Überraschung gesehen hätte.

Ich tat so, als sähe ich aus seinen riesigen Fenstern, wo rotes, frühmorgendliches Sonnenlicht die Stadt überzog und lange Schatten warf. Ich nutzte die Zeit, um mich zu sammeln. „Ich habe die Nachricht vom Anwalt bekommen, mich zurückzuziehen", sagte ich und drehte mich um, um ihn anzusehen.

Er schüttelte den Kopf. „Ich bin enttäuscht, Carl."

Meine Gedanken rasten. Was wusste er? Er konnte nichts davon wissen, dass wir ihr Netzwerk gehackt hatten. Ausgeschlossen. „Ich bin etwas ratlos."

„Dachten Sie, ich würde nichts davon erfahren, dass Sie wegen einer Stelle bei Omicron waren?", fragte er.

Oh. Erleichterung durchfuhr mich, aber nur für einen Moment. Ich steckte nicht wegen des illegalen Einbruchs ins Netzwerk einer konkurrierenden Firma in Schwierigkeiten. Gut. Aber ich musste meinem Boss von meiner vorgeschobenen Geschichte erzählen, zu der es gehört hatte, so zu tun, als kehre ich dem Unternehmen, bei dem ich angestellt war, den Rücken. Schlecht. Und ich konnte ihm nicht sagen, dass der Besuch bei Omicron nur ein Vorwand für unsere Operation gewesen war. Sehr schlecht. Ich dachte etwa drei Sekunden über meine Optionen nach, ehe ich mich für einen Kurs entschied: Unverfroren lügen. Als ich mich zu Wort meldete, tat ich mein Bestes, um entspannt zu klingen. „Ach, das. Das war nichts. Ein Ablenkungsmanöver." Die besten Lügen haben ein bisschen Wahrheit in sich.

Javier setzte zu sprechen an, unterbrach sich aber zweimal. Er hatte diese Konfrontation vermutlich geübt und ich hatte ihn aus dem Konzept gebracht. Er hatte meine Antwort nicht erwartet. „Jetzt bin ich ratlos“, sagte er.

„Ich habe versucht, eine neue Spur bei Omicron zu finden … das war, ehe Sie mir die Nachricht geschickt haben, dass ich meine Ermittlung einstellen soll. Also habe ich so getan, als sei ich auf Arbeitssuche, um eine Entschuldigung zu haben, ihr Gebäude zu betreten und zu schauen, ob ich *versehentlich* jemandem begegnen könnte, der vielleicht etwas weiß.“

Er ging um seinen Schreibtisch herum und setzte sich, dann zeigte er auf einen Stuhl und bedeutete mir, mich zu setzen. Ich nahm mir ein paar zusätzliche Sekunden, um mich zu setzen, sodass ihm meine Worte ins Bewusstsein dringen konnten, und hoffte, dass er es mir abkaufte. *Komm schon. Es ist eine gute Story. Kauf sie mir ab!*

„Das ergibt eine Menge Sinn“, sagte er schließlich. „Sie sollten wissen, dass sie Ihr Angebot ernstgenommen haben. Das könnte Probleme verursachen.“

„Kein Problem“, sagte ich und wurde warm mit der Lüge. „Ich werde ihnen sagen, dass Sie es herausgefunden, mich zur Rede gestellt und mir ein besseres Angebot gemacht haben.“

Darüber lachte er beinahe. „Das trifft sich gut für Sie.“

„Es muss nicht wirklich ein besseres Angebot *geben.* Sie werden es nicht wissen. Und wenn doch, muss es nichts mit Geld zu tun haben. Es kann vage sein. Sagen Sie so was wie, dass Sie mir neue Verantwortung gegeben haben, die ich herausfordernd finde.“

Er dachte darüber nach. „Das könnte ich unterstützen. Wir könnten eine Art interne Taskforce ins Leben rufen, mit Ihrem Namen drauf. Auf diese Weise würden Omicrons Quellen in unserem Unternehmen das Ganze bestätigen."

„Sie haben Spione hier?"

„Natürlich haben sie das", sagte er.

Ich musste noch eine Menge über konkurrierende Unternehmen lernen.

„Und wir haben Spione bei Omicron, so haben Sie auch davon erfahren, dass ich dort gewesen bin."

„Nicht in diesem Fall. Jemand von Omicron hat mir davon erzählt. Aus Höflichkeit."

Ich konnte nicht anders, als mich zu fragen, ob diese Person dieselbe war, die ihm anfangs von der Sicherheitslücke berichtet hatte. Er hatte gesagt, es wäre jemand vom Militär gewesen, aber ich war mir nicht sicher, ob ich das noch glaubte. Ehe ich ihn zur Rede stellen konnte, stand er auf und zwang mich, ebenfalls aufzustehen.

„Es tut mir leid, dass ich Sie rauswerfen muss, aber ich habe ein Meeting. Ich will hoffen, dass ich nichts mehr davon höre, dass Sie sich anderswo nach einem Job umsehen. Wenn Sie ein Problem haben, kommen Sie zuerst zu mir. Deal?"

„Deal", sagte ich. Die Tür öffnete sich und ich wurde von seinem erschöpften Assistenten hinausgeführt, dann stand ich dümmlich im Vorzimmer herum und fragte mich, was aus meinem Plan geworden war, Javier unter Druck zu setzen, damit er mir Informationen gab.

Nachdem ich in mein Büro zurückgekehrt war, um mich etwas zu sammeln, entschied ich, es noch mal zu versuchen, also machte ich mich erneut auf ins oberste

Stockwerk. Jemand war bei Javier im Büro, als ich eintraf, also wartete ich zwanzig Minuten, bis sie fertig waren, und vertrieb mir die Zeit damit, auf meinem Device die Nachrichten zu lesen. Die Titelgeschichte behandelte eine Schießerei etwa drei Blocks von meiner Wohnung entfernt. Ich fragte mich, ob ich einen der Beteiligten kannte. Die Chancen standen gut. Die Polizei hatte keine Hinweise.

Javier kam hinter zwei Führungskräften aus seinem Büro, ein Mann und eine Frau, beide in teuren Anzügen. Den Mann konnte ich nicht zuordnen, obwohl ich ihn irgendwo schon mal gesehen hatte. Die Frau erkannte ich nicht. Javier sah mich, führte die beiden anderen aber hinaus, ohne uns einander vorzustellen. Seltsam. Mich Leuten vorzustellen schien der Grund dafür zu sein, warum er mich angestellt hatte.

„Carl. Was kann ich für Sie tun? Ich habe nur zehn Minuten bis zum nächsten Meeting.“

„Ich habe ein paar Fragen über Omicron.“

„Ich dachte, ich hätte mich klar ausgedrückt. Das ist vorbei.“

„Ist es. Und ich tue nichts, um diese Anordnung zu missachten. Aber ich habe noch ein paar Gedanken, zu denen ich gerne Ihre Meinung hätte.“

Ein Ausdruck huschte über sein Gesicht, aber ich konnte ihn nicht deuten. Es hätte Enttäuschung oder Resignation sein können. So oder so, es war ein Fehler gewesen, noch mal zu ihm zu kommen. „Lassen Sie es gut sein, Carl.“

Ich zögerte für den Bruchteil einer Sekunde. „Okay. Entschuldigen Sie, dass ich Sie behelligt habe, Boss.“

„Machen Sie sich deswegen keinen Kopf", sagte er. „Wenn Sie mich jetzt entschuldigen würden."

„Sicher."

Ich verließ das Büro, ohne zu wissen, was ich als Nächstes tun sollte. Ich hatte die Identität von Javiers Kontaktperson gewollt, von der ich glaubte, dass es jemand bei Omicron war, weil ich mir für meinen Plan mit den Hybriden dort Zugang verschaffen musste. Dem aber hatte er einen Riegel vorgeschoben. Allerdings schien irgendetwas an der Sache nicht zu stimmen, und dass er gesagt hatte, ich solle es gut sein lassen, führte lediglich dazu, dass ich es weiter untersuchen wollte. Einer Eingebung folgend, ging ich zurück ins Vorzimmer. Javier war wieder in seinem Büro und hatte die Tür geschlossen, also ging ich auf seinen Assistenten zu.

„Entschuldigung", sagte ich. „Mr. Sanchez hat mich gebeten, der Frau, mit der er sich gerade getroffen hat, noch weitere Fragen zu stellen, und gerade ist mir bewusst geworden, dass ich ihre Kontaktinformationen nicht habe. Haben Sie die vielleicht?"

„Sicher, Sir", sagte der junge Mann. Er drückte ein paar Tasten und mein Device vibrierte. „Bitte sehr."

„Danke", sagte ich. „Sie sind ein Lebensretter." Ich blickte auf mein Device, sobald ich den Flur erreicht hatte. Ich strauchelte beinahe, als ich die Kontaktdaten las. Sheilla Ranier. *Omicron Industries.* Dafür hätte es eine plausible Erklärung geben können, schätze ich. Aber Javier hatte mir gesagt, dass die Sache mit Omicron vorüber war, kurz nachdem er sich mit deren Stellvertreterin getroffen hatte. Es schien unwahrscheinlich, dass sie so wenig miteinander zu tun hatten, dass er vergessen würde, es zu erwähnen. Ich versuchte, mir eine harmlose Erklärung für sein Handeln einfallen zu lassen. Ich schaffte es nicht.

Zu viele Dinge überschnitten sich, aber nichts passte zusammen. Javier hatte mich auf den Fall angesetzt, war aber nie mitteilsam gewesen. Anfangs hatte ich das akzeptiert, aber jetzt fragte ich mich, wieso er mich mit einer Aufgabe losschickte, ohne mir alle Informationen zu geben. Ich verstand es nicht. Vielleicht sollte ich das auch nicht. VPC hatte zwar gewollt, dass ich die Ermittlung einstellte, aber war das jetzt ausgeschlossen.

Als ich wieder in meiner Wohnung war, brauchte ich einen Drink. Nachdem ich mir eingeschenkt hatte, rief ich Plazz an, um mich nach dem Stand der Dinge zu erkundigen. Vielleicht hatte sie etwas über Omicron oder Gylika herausgefunden. Es war weit hergeholt, aber ich hatte auch den Hintergedanken, dass ich nach dem Treffen mit den Cappanern vielleicht ihre Hilfe brauchen würde. Es ist ein beschissener Grund, jemanden anzurufen – um ihn später auszunutzen –, aber ich wollte ihr auch etwas mitteilen, das ihr gegebenenfalls half, und sie vielleicht davon überzeugen, dass ich kein Arschloch war.

Vielleicht wollte ich mich auch selbst davon überzeugen, wenn ich schon dabei war.

„Ich habe mich schon gefragt, wann Sie mich wieder anrufen würden", sagte Plazz. Sie hatte die Privatsphäre-Einstellung an ihrem Device gewählt, sodass es kein Bild übertrug. „Was wollen Sie?"

„Kann ein Mann nicht einfach anrufen, um sich mal wieder zu melden?"

„Könnte er. Sie aber nicht", sagte sie. „Wie geht es Ihnen nach der Schießerei? Sind Sie okay?"

„Ja. So gut wie neu. Wie steht es bei Ihnen?"

„Was ist los?", fragte sie.

„Was meinen Sie?", fragte ich.

„Ich bin Reporterin. Ich spüre es, wenn Sie was verheimlichen. Sie wissen was Gutes. Raus damit."

„Geht nicht", sagte ich.

„Sie wissen, dass Sie scheiße sind."

„Das ist eine ziemlich weit verbreitete Ansicht, ja."

„Was *können* Sie mir sagen?"

„Noch nichts", sagte ich. „Aber vielleicht habe ich bald etwas."

„Geben Sie mir einen Hinweis", sagte sie.

„Okay." Ich hatte sowieso vorgehabt, ihr das zu sagen, dachte aber, dass es überzeugender wirken würde, wenn sie es aus mir herausholen musste. Vielleicht zerbrach ich mir auch unnötig den Kopf. „Javier Sanchez hat mir den Auftrag erteilt, die Sicherheitslücke bei Omicron zu untersuchen. Kürzlich hat er mir gesagt, ich solle alle Aktionen einstellen, die damit zu tun haben. Heute hat er sich, nachdem er wiederholt hat, dass ich die Arbeit einstellen soll, mit Führungskräften von Omicron getroffen. In seinem Büro."

„Interessant", sagte sie. „Was glauben Sie, was das bedeutet?"

„Keine Ahnung."

„Sie *haben* eine Ahnung", sagte sie. „Sonst hätten Sie es nicht erwähnt."

„Ich denke noch darüber nach. Ich habe es mit Ihnen geteilt, für den Fall, dass Ihnen etwas einfällt." In Wahrheit musste ich jemandem davon erzählen, und sie war die Einzige, der ich vertraute. Es war eine traurige Tatsache, dass der vertrauenswürdigste Mensch in meinem Leben eine Reporterin war.

„Ich könnte etwas über das Meeting zwischen Javier und Omicron bringen und schauen, was dabei herauskommt", bot sie an. „Ist es das, was Sie wollen?"

„Das würde zu mir führen", sagte ich. „Davon abgesehen würden Sie, wenn sie das täten, das Risiko eingehen, die größere Story zu begraben."

„Es gibt eine größere Story?"

„Gibt es", sagte ich, „aber das letzte Mal, als ich eine gute Spur hatte, hat es eine Leiche gegeben." Ich unterbrach mich. Ich hatte es als Witz gemeint, aber es war der Wahrheit unangenehm nahegekommen. Jemand hatte Gylika getötet, und sie hatten es vermutlich getan, weil er etwas hatte leaken wollen. Oder weil jemand geglaubt hatte, dass er das vorgehabt hatte. Sie würden mit mir das Gleiche machen, wenn sie glaubten, dass ich eine Bedrohung war.

„Okay. Bis auf Weiteres warte ich mit der Story, und ich stochere etwas herum und schaue, ob ich etwas finden kann, ohne mich zu verraten. Aber geben Sie mir schnell etwas. Ich muss los", sagte Plazz. „Ich habe ein Date."

„Jemand, den ich kenne?", fragte ich.

„Absolut nicht."

„Ich kenne eine Menge Leute", stichelte ich.

Sie lachte. „Warten Sie nicht zu lange mit Ihrem Rückruf. Ich will noch diese Woche von Ihnen hören. Sie schulden mir eine Story." Sie legte auf, ehe ich widersprechen konnte. Jetzt hatte ich zwei Deadlines.

Dr. Baqri stand auf und ging zum Fenster, um die Jalousie zu verstellen und das grelle Licht im Zimmer zu reduzieren.

„Glauben Sie, es ist möglich, dass Schuldgefühle einen dazu bringen können, schlechte Entscheidungen zu treffen?“, fragte ich.

„Wie meinen Sie das? So ganz allgemein?“

„Ist es möglich, dass man sich der Vergangenheit wegen so schuldig fühlt, dass man einer aktuellen Situation gegenüber blind ist?“

Sie dachte einen Moment darüber nach, allerdings vermutlich mehr für den Effekt als für alles andere. „Ich glaube, dass Schuld eine ganze Menge bewirken kann. Weswegen fühlen Sie sich schuldig?“

„Was glauben Sie?“, fragte ich.

Sie nickte. „Und was glauben Sie, zu welcher Entscheidung Sie das führt?“

Ich hatte mich auf diese Frage vorbereitet, also hatte ich eine Antwort, die nicht zu viel verriet. „Ich glaube, ich will etwas tun, das den Cappanern hilft.“

„Also eine Art Wiedergutmachung“, sagte sie.

„Ich weiß nicht, ob ich je wiedergutmachen kann, was ich getan habe. Aber ja, so was in der Art.“

„Ich denke, Sie sollten mit so was vorsichtig sein“, sagte sie. „Es ist sicher in Ordnung, etwas zu tun, um zu helfen. Aber wenn Sie es in der Hoffnung tun, dass Ihre Schuldgefühle abnehmen, werden sie vielleicht enttäuscht.“

Ich dachte darüber nach. Ich wusste nicht, worum die Cappaner mich bitten würden – sie würden mich um etwas bitten, dessen war ich mir sicher –, und ich musste in Betracht ziehen, dass mein Urteilsvermögen fragwürdig war, was sie betraf. Was auch immer ihre Interessen waren, sie würden sich vermutlich nicht mit meinen decken. Aber das setzte voraus, dass ich meine eigenen Interessen durchschaute.

„Können Sie mir folgen, Carl?", fragte sie.

„Sorry. Meine Gedanken sind etwas abgeschweift."

„Sie wirken abwesend. Haben Sie vor, sich etwas anzutun?"

„Schonungslos wie immer, was, Doc?" Ich lächelte. „Nein. Ich habe nicht vor, mir etwas anzutun. Ich bin seit über einem Jahr nicht an diesem Punkt gewesen."

„Sie wissen, dass ich fragen musste", sagte sie.

„Verstehe ich. Ich bin okay."

Ich hatte noch einen Tag, aber keine Hinweise, und ich zerbrach mir den Kopf darüber, was die Cappaner wohl von mir wollten. Ich schickte das Wort *Entscheidung* an die Nummer in meinem Device, noch ehe ich ihre Praxis ganz verlassen hatte.

Kapitel zwanzig

Sasha und Riku warteten in meiner Wohnung, als ich nach Hause kam. „Hand aufs Herz", sagte ich. „Dieses ganze Aus-dem-Nichts-auftauchen-Ding ist ziemlich unheimlich."

„Wir können nicht gerade draußen auf der Straße warten", sagte Sasha.

„Ich verstehe. Ich bin bereit für das Treffen."

„Sie sind früh dran", sagte sie.

„Als ich mich erst mal entschieden hatte, erschien es mir sinnlos, es hinauszuschieben."

„Was hat Sie zu der Entscheidung geführt?"

„Ich bin mir nicht sicher", sagte ich. „Es gehen Dinge vor sich, die ich nicht verstehe, und ich hoffe, dass die Cappaner etwas Licht ins Dunkel bringen können. Ein anderer Grund sind vermutlich meine Schuldgefühle."

Sasha lächelte mich an, obwohl es ein trauriges Lächeln war. „Ihre Schuldgefühle wollen wir nicht. Aber wir wollen Ergebnisse, und wenn wir sie auf diese Weise bekommen, akzeptieren wir das."

„Was passiert als Nächstes?"

„Wir melden uns", sagte Sasha. „Bald."

Sasha hatte nicht gelogen, als sie gesagt hatte, dass es bald sein würde. Sie fasste neben mir Tritt, als ich am nächsten Morgen aus dem Bus stieg, um ein paar Sachen aus dem Lebensmittelladen zu holen.

„Gehen Sie etwas langsamer“, sagte ich. „Schlimmer Fuß.“

„Das letzte Mal, als Sie und ich zusammen auf der Straße waren, hat jemand auf uns geschossen“, rief sie mir ins Gedächtnis.

„Warum sind Sie dann nicht wieder in meine Wohnung gekommen?“

„Jemand überwacht sie.“

Shit. „Wer?“

„Wissen wir noch nicht. Profis.“

„Mit meiner Drohne habe ich sie nicht gesehen.“

„Es ist wahrscheinlich, dass Sie auf so eine Maßnahme vorbereitet sind.“

„Sie waren es nicht“, sagte ich.

„Ich *wollte*, dass Sie mich sehen“, sagte sie.

Shit. Diese Sache war eine Nummer zu groß für mich. „Bin ich in Gefahr?“

„Omicron hat gesehen, wie Sie sich mit uns unterhalten haben. Ich denke, man kann mit Sicherheit sagen, dass Sie jetzt *immer* in Gefahr sind. Aber wir vertreiben die Beobachter, ehe Sie nach Hause zurückkehren.“

Es war gut, Verbündete zu haben. „Danke.“

„Bezüglich der Polizeiermittlung wegen des toten Mannes haben wir etwas herausgefunden. Unsere Agenten haben letzte Nacht das System der Polizei geknackt. Sie stehen nicht in der Akte, Carl. Sie standen drin, aber Ihr Teil des Falles ist vor ein paar Tagen geschlossen worden. Die Polizei hat keine anderen Spuren.“

Ich legte die Stirn in Falten. „Wieso haben die mir das nicht erzählt?“

„Das weiß ich nicht.“

„Gehen wir jetzt zum Meeting?"

Sie blieb stehen, so als würde sie lauschen. „Zuerst müssen wir unsere Verfolger loswerden." Sie hielt wieder inne und ich bekam den Eindruck, dass sie irgendeine Art unsichtbaren Kommunikator hatte, der mit ihr sprach.

„Dieselben Leute, die meine Wohnung überwachen?" Ich musste vorsichtiger sein. Ich widerstand dem Verlangen, mich umzusehen. „Was tun wir jetzt?"

„Folgen Sie meinem Beispiel." Sie beobachtete die Straße, während wir gingen und bewegten beinahe unmerklich den Kopf. Ein paar Sekunden später schnellte ein Hover-Car aus dem Verkehr und hielt vor uns an. Sie packte meinen Arm und zog mich auf den Rücksitz. Das Auto setzte sich in Bewegung, ehe sich die Tür hinter mir schloss. An der nächsten Kreuzung bogen wir von der falschen Spur aus ab und wichen gerade so einem entgegenkommenden Truck aus, dann rasten wir über drei Kreuzungen hinweg, ehe wir erneut abbogen und so abrupt zum Stehen kamen, dass ich in den Sitz vor mir geschleudert wurde.

„Wir steigen hier aus", sagte sie, und die Tür klappte auf. Ich fiel halb auf den Gehsteig, Sasha wich mir geschickt aus und ging mit schnellen Schritten voraus. Ich humpelte ihr hinterher. Wir bogen nach etwa hundert Meter noch einmal ab, vermutlich um zu schauen, ob wir immer noch Verfolger hatten. Vier Häuser weiter betraten wir ein Antiquitätengeschäft.

„Morgen", sagte Sasha.

„Morgen", sagte der Mann in dem kleinen Laden, ohne von seinem Device aufzusehen. Er stand hinter einem Tresen, der gleichzeitig als Schaukasten fungierte

und in dem Etliches an Nippes lag, alles ordentlich aufgereiht. Wir gingen am Tresen vorbei und betraten das
Hinterzimmer.

Da wir so schnell gefahren waren, hatte ich bis zu diesem Moment nicht über die emotionalen Auswirkungen nachgedacht, die das Treffen verursachen würde.
Zu meiner Verteidigung zögerte ich nur einen Moment
beim Anblick des vollblütigen Cappaners, der auf der
anderen Seite des fensterlosen Raumes auf einem Stuhl
mit harter Rückenlehne saß, der zu seiner schmalen Figur passte. Er hatte ein blau-gelb-gesprenkeltes Gesicht,
mit einem ausgeprägten gelben Kreis um ein Auge.
Eine locker sitzende, graue Robe bedeckte den Rest seines Körpers. Ich sage *er*, ohne dass ich das Geschlecht
des Cappaners gekannt hätte. Ich hatte noch nicht gelernt, das zu erkennen.

Sasha führte mich zu einem Stuhl gegenüber des Cappaners, der ähnlich konstruiert war wie seiner, aber
größer, um menschlicher Anatomie gerecht zu werden.
Sie sagte nichts, und sobald ich saß, sahen der Cappaner und ich einander schweigend an, so lange, dass es
etwas unangenehm wurde. Abgesehen von Sasha lehnten zwei andere menschlich aussehende Personen an
der Wand: Riku und eine Frau, die ich nicht kannte. Ich
hatte mehr als einen Cappaner erwartet, aber ich sah
keine anderen.

„Es tut mir leid“, sagte der Cappaner. Seine Stimme
passte nicht zu den Bewegungen seiner Lippen, da er
über einen digitalen Übersetzer kommunizierte. Der
hatte eine computergenerierte, leicht gekünstelt klingende, männliche Stimme, die meinen Eindruck verstärkte, dass es sich um einen Mann handelte, obwohl

es auch das Übersetzungsprogramm sein konnte. „Ich wusste nicht, was ich empfinden würde, wenn ich endlich hier mit Ihnen zusammensitze. Es ist ein wenig überwältigender, als ich erwartet habe."

Ich unterdrückte ein Kichern und hielt einen teilnahmslosen Gesichtsausdruck aufrecht. Ich musste glauben, dass ich mindestens so überwältigt war wie er. Aber ich verstand ihn. Für alles, was Menschen über mich denken mochten, ob richtig oder falsch, mussten Cappaner tiefergehender Gefühle empfinden. „Nehmen Sie sich so viel Zeit, wie Sie brauchen", sagte ich.

„Danke, dass Sie einverstanden waren, sich mit mir zu treffen", sagte er. Es klang in meinen Ohren sehr förmlich, konnte aber auch am Übersetzungsprogramm liegen.

„Es ist das Mindeste, was ich tun kann. Ich muss gestehen, dass ich bis vor Kurzem nicht wusste, dass Sie auf dem Planeten sind", sagte ich.

„Ja. Wir haben versucht, das geheim zu halten, aus offensichtlichen Gründen. Es ist nicht legal. Ich bin mir sicher, dass Sie das wissen."

„Ja. Das Embargo-Gesetz."

Er wand sich auf seinem Stuhl und führte mit der Hand eine kreisförmige Bewegung aus. Es sah aus wie eine Geste, aber die Übersetzungssoftware bezog Körpersignale nicht mit ein. „Ich komme gleich zum Punkt. Wir haben unsere Optionen erwogen und glauben, dass Sie die beste Person sind, um uns zu helfen."

„Das habe ich mir schon gedacht, immerhin haben Sie sich so viel Mühe gemacht, um sich mit mir zu treffen. Was ich nicht weiß, ist, wobei ich Ihnen helfen soll."

„Sie haben mit einer Firma namens Omicron zu tun gehabt. Was wissen Sie über sie?"

„Eine ganze Menge", sagte ich. „Ich habe sie untersucht."

„Wussten Sie, dass wir im Geschäft sind? Im Geheimen natürlich, da es gegen das Gesetz ist."

In diesem Moment machte es Klick. Ganos hatte entdeckt, dass Omicron an der Weiterentwicklung von Ortho-Robotik arbeitete. Ich hatte angenommen, dass sie Elliots alte Forschungsergebnisse hatten, aber die brauchten sie nicht. Sie hatten die Cappaner. „Project Phoenix", sagte ich.

Falls der Cappaner von dieser Schlussfolgerung beeindruckt war, kam das über den Übersetzer nicht rüber. „Das war ihr Name dafür, ja."

„Sie haben mit ihnen daran gearbeitet", sagte ich. „Ich nehme an, dass dem nicht mehr so ist. Wieso?"

„Unsere Ziele wurden inkompatibel." Er hielt einen Augenblick inne, als würde er nachdenken. „Wir haben eine lange Zeit zusammengearbeitet. Schon vor der Vernichtung."

Die Vernichtung. So nannten sie es also. „Sie haben schon mit Omicron zusammengearbeitet, als die menschlichen Soldaten Cappa noch besetzt hatten?"

„Anfangs haben wir mit dem Militär zusammengearbeitet, aber die Beziehung veränderte sich, als sich die Ziele des Militärs änderten."

„Aber ich habe gesehen, wie Cappaner mit Dr. Elliot zusammengearbeitet haben."

„Soldaten, ja. Wissenschaftler? Nein. Dr. Elliot hat cappanische Freiwillige für ihre Experimente bezahlt.

Wir hatten lange zuvor aufgehört, an diesem Projekt mitzuarbeiten, und das war ihre Lösung."

„Welche Rolle spielt Omicron da?"

„Sie hatten Mitarbeiter auf dem Planeten, die mit Technologie handelten und Ideen austauschten. Anfangs hatten sie nichts mit dem Genetik-Programm zu tun. Das kam später."

Ich saß da und war für einen Moment sprachlos. Omicron hatte von Anfang an mit den Cappanern zusammengearbeitet. Ich hatte angenommen, dass Elliot ihnen Zugang zur Fusionstechnologie verschafft hatte. Vermutlich hatten sie einen anderen Weg gehabt. „Ich habe vier Schiffe entdeckt, die den Planeten verlassen haben. Waren sie das?"

„Anfangs vier", sagte er. „Später mehr. Ja. Um den Schaden, den die Vernichtung angerichtet hatte, schlimmer zu machen, brach auf unserem Planeten auch noch ein Bürgerkrieg aus. Omicron half einigen von uns, dem zu entfliehen."

„Und als Gegenleistung halfen Sie ihnen bei Project Phoenix."

„Zum Teil. Aber wir hatten auch andere Ziele. Wir erkannten den ökonomischen Wert der Gentechnik und wollten sie nutzen, um über unsere Position in der Galaxis zu verhandeln. Um unsere Arbeitsbeziehungen mit den Menschen von einer neuen, gewaltfreien Position aus wiederherzustellen."

„Nach dem, was wir ... was *ich* Ihnen angetan habe? Wieso?"

„Wieso lassen sich Leute miteinander ein? Handel, Technologie, Ressourcen. Der Planet, den Sie Cappa nennen, ist in schlechtem Zustand, und wir haben viele Bedürfnisse.“

Das war zu viel, um es zu verarbeiten. Aber er hatte keinen Grund, mich anzulügen, also versuchte ich, es für bare Münze zu nehmen und von da aus weiterzumachen. Wenn er mir etwas antun wollte, hätte er es viel einfacher haben können. Nein, wir waren hier, und er brauchte etwas. Nach einigen Sekunden stellte ich die Verbindung her. „Etwas an Ihrer Beziehung mit Omicron hat sich verändert.“

„In der Tat. Ähnlich unserer früheren Zusammenarbeit mit dem Militär haben sich ihre Ziele geändert. Jemand bei Omicron hat entschieden, dass sie ohne uns Geld machen könnten und dass unsere politischen Bedürfnisse zu teuer und schwer umsetzbar wären.“

„Also haben sie die Technologie gestohlen?“, fragte ich.

„Sie haben mehr als das getan. Sie haben unsere Leute angegriffen. Sie haben gedroht, zu verraten, auf welchen Planeten wir umgesiedelt waren. Sie verlangten cappanische Versuchspersonen. Sie haben Geiseln genommen und versucht, unsere Wissenschaftler zur Arbeit zu zwingen, um den Prozess weiterzuentwickeln.“

„Wenn sie die Technologie hatten, wozu brauchten Sie dann Ihre Wissenschaftler?“, fragte ich.

„Sie haben die Technologie, aber ihre Methoden sind nicht so fortgeschritten wie unsere. In ein paar Jahren finden sie vermutlich von selbst eine Lösung. Wir haben sie jetzt. Wir haben einige Dinge zurückgehalten. Wir waren vertrauensvoll, aber nicht dumm.“

Ich nickte, merkte aber, dass das nicht übersetzt werden würde. „Ich verstehe. Was soll ich also tun? Ihnen helfen, die Technologie zurück zu stehlen?"

„Das haben wir bereits getan", sagte er.

Ich hielt einen Augenblick inne, ehe mich die Erkenntnis traf. „Heilige Scheiße. Sie haben Omicron gehackt."

Er antwortete nicht.

„Sie waren das. Moment … wenn Sie bei Omicron eingebrochen sind, bedeutet das … dass Sie Gylika getötet haben."

„Wir haben nichts dergleichen getan", sagte er.

„Dann haben Ihre Verbündeten es getan." Ich zeigte auf die Hybride, die an die Wand gelehnt dastanden.

Der Cappaner machte wieder eine Geste, die ich nicht verstand. Beunruhigung? „Weder wir noch irgendjemand, der mit uns zu tun hat, hat irgendetwas mit dem Tod des Menschen zu tun."

„Wer war es dann?", fragte ich.

„Das wissen wir nicht. Aber wenn Sie einverstanden sind, uns zu helfen, werden wir unser Bestes geben, um das herauszufinden. Die Logik gebietet, dass es Omicron selbst war."

Ich holte tief Luft und atmete aus. Ich weiß nicht wieso, aber ich glaubte ihm. „Wobei soll ich Ihnen dann helfen? Sie haben die Informationen bereits zurück gestohlen. Moment … wie haben Sie das tun können? Omicron muss Kopien gehabt haben."

„Wir sind sehr gründlich gewesen", sagte er. Vielleicht bildete ich es mir nur ein, aber ich hätte schwören können, dass die Übersetzung einen Hauch von Stolz übermittelte.

„Wenn Sie sie also wiederhaben, was ist dann das Problem? Die Geiseln?“, fragte ich.

„Wie gesagt, sie wissen, wo unser neues Zuhause ist. Sie haben damit gedroht, diese Information ans Militär weiterzugeben.“

Das traf mich wie ein Schlag in die Eingeweide. Sie würden das Militär informieren und das würde jemanden wie mich schicken, um sich darum zu kümmern. „Sie wollen von der Medizintechnologie profitieren und sind bereit, dafür die cappanische Rasse auszulöschen.“

„Ja, das nehmen wir an.“

„Was glauben Sie, kann ich tun?“

„Wir müssen eine Lösung mit Omicron aushandeln, die es uns erlaubt, unsere bisherigen Ziele zu erreichen“, sagte er.

„Moment ... Sie würden nach dieser Sache noch mit Omicron zusammenarbeiten?“

Er hielt inne. „Was haben wir sonst für eine Option? Wir können die Vergangenheit hinter uns lassen, wenn es uns hilft, unsere Ziele zu erreichen. Ihre Anwesenheit ist ein Beweis dafür.“

Da hatte er recht. „Wieso ich?“

Sein Gesicht verzog sich zu etwas, das die cappanische Version eines Lächelns sein mochte. „Sie sind in einer einzigartigen Position. Sie haben Zugang zum Unternehmen, das wir beeinflussen müssen, und Sie haben das Ansehen, um es umzusetzen. Wenn Sie über Cappaner sprechen, ist es naheliegend, dass andere Menschen Ihnen zuhören. Wir brauchen eine Lösung, die größer ist als ein Unternehmen. Etwas, das Bestand hat.“

„All das ergibt Sinn." Ich hielt inne und überlegte, wie ich den nächsten Gedanken ausdrücken sollte. Ich hatte eine Ahnung, wie die Antwort ausfallen würde, aber ich wollte sie von ihm hören. „Aber Sie sollten mich hassen."

„Hass ist ein Gefühl für jemanden, der den Luxus besserer Optionen hat."

Das schien weiser als das, was ich im Moment verarbeiten konnte. „Um klarzustellen, weshalb wir hier sind, und sicherzustellen, dass wir dieselben Erwartungen haben: Sie haben mir gesagt, dass Sie ganz allgemein wollen, dass alles wieder so wird, wie es war, aber das ist vielleicht unmöglich. Was sind Ihre genauen Ziele?"

„Selbst jetzt arbeiten sie daran, uns dazu zu zwingen, zurückzugeben, was wir gestohlen haben."

„Was tun sie?", fragte ich

„Wir glauben, dass sie eine Mission vorbereiten, deren Ziel es ist, zu unserem neuen Planeten zu fliegen und uns durch militärische Mittel ihren Willen aufzuzwingen."

„Sind Sie sich dessen sicher?", fragte ich.

„Unsere Informationen sind verlässlich, ja."

„Wie viele von Ihnen sind auf dem Planeten?" Falls Omicron eine physische Aktion plante, mussten wir uns zuerst damit befassen.

„Weniger als zwanzigtausend. Wir kennen das volle Ausmaß ihrer Mission nicht", sagte er. „Aber wir können Vermutungen anstellen."

„Auf kurze Sicht brauchen wir also eine Lösung, die sie davon abhält, bewaffnete Aktionen durchzuführen oder damit zu drohen." Ich hatte *wir* gesagt. Ich hatte bereits begonnen, von uns als Wir zu denken. Theoretisch sollte ein Unternehmen nicht in der Lage sein, eine militärische Mission umzusetzen, aber wenn es die Hälfte aller von Menschen genutzten Waffen und Raumschiffe herstellte, wäre es nicht überraschend, wenn es ein bisschen was für sich selbst behielt. Außerdem war es eine große Galaxis und es war nicht gerade so, als könnten sich die Cappaner zum Schutz an die Behörden wenden. Selbst *wenn* es jemand Offiziellem auffiel, gab es überall Piraten, und es wäre unmöglich, einer bestimmten Organisation etwas zuzuordnen. „Bekommen wir alle vom Planeten runter?“

„Ehe wir Pläne schmieden, denke ich, dass es wichtig ist, über Ihre Rolle zu sprechen. Offiziell.“

Ich sah mich im Zimmer um und warf den Hybriden einen Blick zu. Sie alle sahen gespannt zu, aber keiner von ihnen schien bereit zu sein, der Unterhaltung etwas hinzuzufügen. „Ich bin dabei.“

Der Cappaner faltete die Hände. Ich wusste nicht, ob die Geste für sie dieselbe Bedeutung hatte wie für Menschen, aber sie schien universell zu sein. „Das ist gut. Ich glaube nicht, dass es möglich ist, uns vom Planeten zu evakuieren. Erstens beobachten sie uns, und zweitens – wo sollen wir hin? Es gibt keine Menschen auf dem Planeten, und bewohnbare Planeten ohne Menschen sind rar.“

„Was glauben Sie, wie viele von Ihrer Bevölkerung Ihre Ansichten über die Zusammenarbeit mit Menschen teilen?“

„Unmöglich zu sagen“, sagte er. „Obwohl jeder, der mit uns auf den neuen Planeten gereist ist, das freiwillig getan hat. Viele wissen nichts von der Technologie, mit der wir arbeiten, aber sie unterstützen unsere allgemeine Philosophie der Zusammenarbeit mit Menschen. Unsere Gruppe wird angeführt von Wissenschaftlern. Intelligente, vernünftige Leute. Es gibt Meinungsverschiedenheiten, aber kein Übermaß an politischen Ansichten. Allerdings sind wir keine hundertprozentige Hegemonie.“

Er hatte die Frage nicht gänzlich beantwortet, und das konnte ich nicht auf sich beruhen lassen. Ich stellte mir vor, dass es einfach war, Freiwillige zu finden, wenn die Alternative lautete, auf einem vom Krieg zerrissenen Planeten zu bleiben. „Ist es möglich, dass es andere Gruppen gibt, die *mit* Omicron zusammenarbeiten? Cappaner, die ihnen helfen könnten, an die Macht zu kommen? Entweder jemand, der mit Ihnen auf dem neuen Planeten ist, oder jemand von denen, die auf Cappa zurückgeblieben sind?“

„Wir halten das für unwahrscheinlich“, sagte der Cappaner. „Ihr Angriff hat Menschen beim Großteil unserer Bevölkerung unbeliebt gemacht.“

Das konnte ich nachvollziehen. Das machte eine unmögliche Mission zumindest ein kleines bisschen leichter. Wenn sie willige Cappaner hatten, hätten wir überhaupt kein Druckmittel. Die Tatsache, dass Omicron etwas von den Cappanern wollte, ließ uns immerhin eine kleine Möglichkeit offen. „Das ist gut.“

„Haben Sie bereits einen Plan?“

„Ich habe einen Anfang. Was haben wir für Ausrüstung? Was Sie mit dem System von Omicron angestellt haben, war beeindruckend. Können wir uns auf so etwas verlassen, wenn wir es brauchen?“

„Omicron erneut zu hacken ist ein Risiko. Sie erwarten uns."

„Wie groß ist das Risiko?", fragte ich.

„Zu groß", sagte er. „Da ihr Sicherheitsteam nach uns Ausschau hält, sind unsere Erfolgschancen sehr klein. Zu klein, als dass es sich lohnen würde. Das erste Mal haben wir erreicht, was wir wollten, weil sie nicht vorbereitet waren."

„Okay", sagte ich. Mir schoss Ganos' Einbruch durch den Kopf. Wir hatten auch dieses Fenster geschlossen, aber die Vorstellung, dass Omicron zum Zeitpunkt ihres Einbruchs auf genau so etwas geachtet hatte, gab mir ein ungutes Gefühl. „Können wir ihr System angreifen, um Schaden zu verursachen?"

„Möglich", sagte der Cappaner. „Aber vermutlich nicht genug, um sie umzustimmen."

„Okay", sagte ich und ertappte mich dabei, wieder nicken zu wollen. Es wäre nett gewesen, einen Angriff auf ihr Netzwerk als Drohung zu haben. Aber ich hatte noch eine andere Idee, wie man Omicron drohen könnte. „Ich brauche ein paar Tage, um über alles nachzudenken. Wie kann ich mich mit Ihnen in Verbindung setzen, wenn ich bereit bin?"

„Ich werde den Planeten heute Abend verlassen", sagte der Cappaner. „Meine Mitarbeiter sind hier, um Ihnen bei Bedarf zu helfen." Ich kam nicht umhin, zu denken, dass er viel Vertrauen in mich setzte. Zu viel. Er hatte sicher Ausweichpläne, aber ich hatte nicht die Hoffnung, dass er sie mir anvertrauen würde. Von meinem Schützenloch aus waren es ein paar Hybride und ich gegen das mächtigste Unternehmen der Galaxis. Ein Kampf nach meinem Geschmack.

Kapitel einundzwanzig

Nachdem ich mein Meeting mit dem Cappaner verlassen hatte, landete ich in Gedanken immer wieder bei seiner vermeintlichen Überzeugung, wir könnten Omicron dazu bekommen, einen Deal einzugehen. Der zweite dominante Gedanke war, dass ich ein Idiot gewesen war, diese Sache anzunehmen, weil Risiko und Verantwortung viel zu groß waren. Aber da ich beabsichtigte, es zu tun – und Erfolg zu haben – waren wir vielleicht beide auf der richtigen Spur.

Ja, der Zirkelschluss ist mir bewusst.

Um die potenzielle Stupidität meiner Entscheidung, den Cappanern zu helfen, noch schlimmer zu machen, machte ich mich auf den Weg zur Polizei – nach etlichen Autowechseln, um sicherzustellen, dass ich nicht verfolgt wurde. Kaum, dass ich eingetroffen war, wusste ich, dass es eine schlechte Entscheidung gewesen war. Aber nachdem ich mich mit dem Cappaner unterhalten hatte, hatte sich ein Schalter umgelegt. Und das fühlte sich gut an. Ich musste Omicron dazu zwingen, auf mich zu reagieren, also war es Zeit zum Angriff. Um das zu tun, musste ich wissen, wie ich in Mallorys Gunst stand. Ich musste herausfinden, ob ich mich auf dem weiteren Weg auf sie verlassen konnte, oder ob sie gegen mich arbeiten würde. Ich hatte eine ungefähre Vorstellung davon, wie ich die Polizei nutzen konnte, um Omicron unter Druck zu setzen und sie für meine Vorschläge empfänglicher zu machen.

„Kann ich Ihnen helfen?", fragte der Officer am Empfang.

„Ich bin hier, um Lieutenant Mallory zu sehen." Ich blieb nicht stehen.

„Sir, Sie können nicht ohne Begleitung nach hinten durchgehen."

Ich war schon etliche Meter an ihm vorbei, ehe er mir hinterherkam. Ich schätze, er hatte nicht damit gerechnet, dass jemand in ein Polizeirevier hereinmarschiert, aber ich wollte Mallory nicht die Zeit geben, sich zusammen mit Burke auf ein Treffen mit mir vorzubereiten. „Lieutenant Mallory!"

Das gesamte Großraumbüro drehte sich zu mir um. Drei Officers, einer davon ein Riese, standen hinter ihren Schreibtischen auf.

„Mallory!" Ich war bereits in Schwierigkeiten, weil ich am Empfang vorbeigegangen war. So würde es sich wenigstens lohnen.

Zwei der Officers erreichten mich zeitgleich, ich erhob meine Hände und ließ mich ohne Gegenwehr von ihnen packen. Mein Verlangen, nicht aufgemischt zu werden, überstieg mein Bedürfnis, mit dem Lieutenant zu sprechen.

„Ich finde selbst hinaus", bot ich an und zwang mich zu einem Grinsen.

Sie erwiderten das Grinsen nicht, aber schleppten mich nur ein kleines Stück in Richtung Ausgang.

„Butler? Was geht hier vor?" Mallory kam zum Haupteingang herein, kurz bevor wir ihn erreichten.

„Dieser Depp ist am Empfang vorbeigerannt und hat drinnen nach Ihnen gerufen", sagte einer der Officers, die mich gepackt hatten, eine stämmige Frau.

Mallory schüttelte den Kopf. „Wenn Sie vorher angerufen hätten, hätten Sie gewusst, dass ich nicht hier war."

„Jetzt erkenne ich die Weisheit darin."

Sie versuchte, ein Lachen zu unterdrücken, scheiterte aber ziemlich. „Kommen Sie." Die beiden Officers ließen mich frei und ich gab mein Bestes, um nicht selbstgefällig auszusehen, als ich sie stehen ließ und Mallory ins Verhörzimmer folgte.

„Wollen Sie mir sagen, worum es geht?", fragte sie.

„Ich bin sauer", sagte ich. Ich wollte sie in die Defensive zwingen. „Sie schließen mich nicht aus Ihren Ermittlungen im Fall Gylika aus, obwohl Sie wissen, dass ich nichts damit zu tun habe."

„Ja? Wie kommen Sie darauf?"

Ich hatte mir das nicht sonderlich gut überlegt. „Ich kenne Leute, die Dinge wissen."

Sie dachte einen Augenblick lang darüber nach. „Habe ich Sie nicht neulich im Krankenhaus gesehen? Irgendwas wegen einer Schussverletzung?"

„Das hatte nichts mit Gylika zu tun."

Sie hob die Augenbrauen. „Sind Sie sich da sicher?"

„Sie wissen, dass es so ist."

„Tue ich das? Woher weiß ich, dass es so ist? Was wollen Sie mir sagen?"

Ich hätte mich ohrfeigen können. Ich hätte es besser wissen müssen, als einem Profi wie Mallory mit einem halbgaren Plan zu kommen. Sie hatte den Spieß umgedreht, ohne ins Schwitzen zu geraten. „Omicron steckt hinter den Ex-Militär-Typen, die mich angeschossen haben."

„Können Sie das beweisen?", fragte sie.

„Kann ich nicht. Aber es stimmt. Setzen Sie sie etwas unter Druck und Sie finden es heraus."

Sie schüttelte den Kopf. „So läuft das nicht. Ich kann nicht zu einem mächtigen Unternehmen gehen und mit haltlosen Anschuldigungen um mich werfen. Sie behaupten, Sie könnten es mir nicht erzählen, aber Sie verheimlichen mir etwas. Darauf würde ich meine Marke verwetten."

„Also behalten Sie diesen Fall gegen mich in der Hand, um mich dazu zu kriegen, Ihnen etwas zu liefern."

„Das würde ich nie tun", sagte sie. „Das wäre unethisch."

Ich schüttelte den Kopf. „Sie sind eine Nervensäge."

„Tja, Sie auch. Aber ich habe eine Leiche und einen ungeklärten Fall, also kann ich damit leben."

„Was wollen Sie von mir?", fragte ich. „Ich habe Ihnen gesagt, dass Omicron involviert ist. Was brauchen Sie?"

„Das weiß ich, wenn ich es höre", sagte sie.

„Bullshit. Was wollen Sie?"

Sie blickte mich wütend an. „Also schön. Ich sage Ihnen, was ich will. Ich will wissen, was so wichtig war bei Omicron, dass ein Mann dafür getötet wurde."

„Das weiß ich nicht", sagte ich.

„Ficken Sie sich, Butler. Sie sind ein schlechter Lügner."

Ich setzte zu sprechen an, unterbrach mich aber. Ich wollte auf ihren Kommentar antworten und mich verteidigen, aber deswegen hatte sie ihn gebracht. Die

Lady war gut. Ich *hatte* gelogen. Nicht zuletzt wusste ich genau, was bei Omicron so wichtig war. Ich brauchte ein paar Sekunden, um mich zu sammeln. „Ich kann meinen Anwalt rufen und wir machen das auf eine andere Weise."

„Sie verschwenden meine Zeit." Sie stand auf. Es war ein Bluff, aber ein guter. Ich konnte sie nicht dazu bringen, ihre Karten zu zeigen. Ich wollte, dass sie Omicron auf die Pelle rückte. Sie zu einer Reaktion zwang.

„Okay, warten Sie", sagte ich, dann wartete ich, während sie sich Zeit damit ließ, sich wieder hinzusetzen. Sie zog eine Show ab. „Sie haben recht. Da ist etwas, das ich Ihnen nicht sage. Ich kann es nicht beweisen, aber ich habe ein paar ziemlich gute Ideen, wieso Omicron in Gylikas Tod verwickelt ist. Gylika hat an einem Projekt namens Phoenix gearbeitet. Es geht um bahnbrechende Medizintechnologie, und sie ist Milliarden wert. Es gab eine Sicherheitslücke, und ich habe Grund zu der Annahme, dass sie Gylika verdächtigt haben."

„Jetzt sagen Sie die Wahrheit." Sie konnte mich gut einschätzen, das war sicher. „Wie sicher sind Sie sich?"

„Sehr sicher", sagte ich.

„Aber Sie können es nicht beweisen."

„Nein. Aber das gibt Ihnen Ansatzpunkte."

Sie dachte darüber nach. Ich versuchte, meinen Atem zu beruhigen, ruhig zu bleiben und ihr Zeit zum Nachdenken zu geben. Sie musste niemanden verhaften. Sie musste Fragen stellen, die Leute nervös machen würden. Die es wahrscheinlicher machten, dass diese Leute mit mir verhandelten. Sie konnten Gylika töten, um ihn zum Schweigen zu bringen, aber Mallory konnten sie nicht töten. „Das ist nicht genug."

Ich seufzte. „In Ordnung. Dann will ich ein öffentliches Statement, dass ich im Mordfall Gylika nicht länger verdächtigt werde."

„Das können Sie vergessen", sagte sie.

Ich stand auf und ging zur Tür, dann drehte ich mich um. „Sie haben vierundzwanzig Stunden."

„Was passiert dann?"

„Dann gehe ich zur Presse und erzähle von der skrupellosen Polizistin, die versucht, sich einen Namen zu machen, indem sie einen renommierten Veteranen schikaniert."

„Sie labern Scheiße. Sie wollen wegen dieser Sache nicht durch die Medien gezerrt werden."

„Sie haben gesagt, ich wäre ein schlechter Lügner. Sehe ich so aus, als würde ich gerade lügen?" Ich drehte mich um und ging, ehe sie antworten konnte.

Es war nicht so gelaufen, wie ich gehofft hatte, aber etwas hatte ich herausgefunden. Angesichts meiner Pläne für Omicron, musste ich wissen, wie es zwischen Mallory und mir aussah. Sie hatte gesagt, dass ich ihr nicht genug verraten hatte, aber je länger sie darüber nachdachte, desto länger würde es an ihr nagen. Hoffentlich hatte ich ihr Interesse genug geweckt, sodass sie etwas herumstochern würde. Wie sie gesagt hatte, hatte sie einen ungeklärten Todesfall, der für ihre Vorgesetzten nicht gut aussehen würde. Sie brauchte eine Antwort, und ich hatte sie immerhin mit der richtigen Frage versorgt.

Und wenn sie mich aus dem Kreis der Verdächtigen ausschloss, würde Omicron es mitbekommen und das würde sie aufhorchen lassen.

Als ich nach Hause kam, rief ich als Erstes Ganos an, um zu schauen, ob sie meinen Rat befolgt und die Stadt verlassen hatte, was sie, meiner Vermutung entsprechend, nicht getan hatte. Ich wiederholte meinen Rat und schlug vor, dass es wünschenswert wäre, wenn sie den Planeten verließe; wenn sie Urlaub machen würde. Sie bestand darauf, mir zu helfen, und ich brauchte fast zwanzig Minuten, um sie davon zu überzeugen, dass sie das nicht konnte; und weitere zehn, um sie dazu zu bringen, einzusehen, in welche Gefahr ich sie gebracht hatte, und dass sie tun sollte, was ich sagte. Sie hatte sowieso versprochen, irgendwann mal Parkers Mutter zu besuchen, die nicht auf dem Planeten lebte, also beschloss sie, diese Reise vorzuziehen. Da das geklärt war, wandte ich meine Aufmerksamkeit Plazz zu.

Ich konnte sie nicht anrufen, weil sie dann zu viel aus mir rausbekommen hätte, und dafür war ich noch nicht bereit. Aber ich brauchte ein Backup, für den Fall, dass die Sache in die Hose ging. Mein Plan machte mich angreifbar, und ich musste jederzeit damit rechnen, dass man mich vom Spielfeld entfernte. Dieser Gedanke machte mir nicht viel aus. Risiko gehörte zu jeder Mission dazu. Aber obwohl ich mich selbst in Gefahr bringen konnte, konnte ich nicht riskieren, dass die Informationen, über die ich verfügte, im Falle meines Ablebens verschwanden. Ich tippte alles, was ich wusste, in eine verschlüsselte Datei, protokollierte jedes Detail, ob bestätigt oder nur vermutet, dokumentierte Dinge und nannte Quellen, wo sie mir zur Verfügung standen, und erklärte meinen Denkprozess, wo ich es nicht konnte. Ich schrieb über den Cappaner, den ich getroffen hatte, und die cappanischen Schiffe, die ich in der Datenbank von SPACECOM gefunden hatte. Ich schrieb ausführlich von Javiers Meeting mit Omicron und meiner Vermutung bezüglich Gylikas Tod. Ich brauchte fast zwei Stunden, um fertig zu werden. Dann speicherte ich es auf einem Wechsellaufwerk, das ich in meinen Safe legte, und bereitete eine verschlüsselte E-Mail an Plazz vor. Ich stellte es so ein, dass sie in drei Tagen automatisch abgeschickt werden würde, sofern ich sie nicht stoppte.

Nachdem ich damit fertig war, rief ich Turkov bei Omicron an. Sein Assistent brauchte drei Minuten, um ihn ans Telefon zu kriegen, und ich brauchte fünf Minuten, um ihn wegen unseres Gesprächs, das bis zu Javier vorgedrungen war und mich in Schwierigkeiten gebracht hatte, zusammenzuscheißen. Nachdem das geklärt war, sagte ich ihm, dass ich den Job immer noch wollte und fragte, ob er es geheim halten könnte, wenn ich morgen käme, um darüber zu reden. Ich plante, ihn dafür zu benutzen, ein Meeting mit Ellen Haverty zu bekommen, dem CEO, aber diesen Teil des Plans behielt ich für mich.

Als ich damit fertig war, genehmigte ich mir endlich einen Drink. Ich war so angespannt, dass ich zum Einschlafen mehr als meine übliche Dosis brauchte. Das war für mich schon etwas Besonderes. Zum ersten Mal seit langer Zeit träumte ich nicht.

Das war noch ungewöhnlicher.

Kapitel
zweiundzwanzig

Turkov empfing mich, als ich Omicrons Lobby betrat, und kurz fragte ich mich, wie lange er dagestanden und auf mich gewartet hatte. „Schön, Sie wiederzusehen, Carl."

„Gleichfalls. Sie hätten nicht nach unten kommen müssen, um mich zu empfangen."

„Tatsächlich musste ich das. Wir gehen nicht in mein Büro." Er ging auf den Fahrstuhl zu, der Führungskräften vorbehalten war, und ich folgte ihm.

„Wo gehen wir hin?", fragte ich.

„Der CEO will Sie kennenlernen."

„Äh ... okay", verhaspelte ich mich. Einer der größten Fehler in jedem Plan ist, zu versäumen, Erfolg vorauszusehen. Ich war in diese Falle getappt. Ich hatte mich mit jemandem treffen wollen, der verhandeln konnte, aber ich hatte nicht erwartet, dass es an diesem Morgen passieren würde.

„Oberster Stock", sagte Turkov, obwohl der Mann, der im Fahrstuhl auf uns gewartet hatte, den Knopf bereits gedrückt hatte. Die Tür öffnete sich etwa zwanzig Sekunden später und gab den Blick auf eine kleine Lobby frei, die mit dunklem Holz und Marmor ausgestattet war. Ich sah nicht genau hin, aber ich nahm an, dass es echt war, was den Raum extrem teuer machte.

Ellen Haverty kam auf uns zu, als wir ausstiegen. Ich sollte sagen, sie kam auf mich zu, weil sie ihren Blick nicht von mir abwandte. Ich war ihr nie zuvor begegnet, aber natürlich hatte ich Fotos gesehen. Sie wurde ihnen gerecht: Sie trug einen grauen Blazer und hatte kurzgeschnittenes Haar, eine Kreuzung zwischen blond und weiß. Einem Modejournalisten hatte sie mal gesagt, dass sie ihre Haare kurz trug, weil das weniger Zeit brauche, sie zu pflegen, was ihr mehr Zeit für Geschäfte gab.

„Colonel Butler, es ist schön, dass wir uns endlich kennenlernen. Ich habe so viel von Ihnen gehört."

„Nennen Sie mich Carl. Es ist auch schön, Sie kennenzulernen, Ms. Haverty."

„Bitte. Sagen Sie Ellen. Möchten Sie etwas? Wasser? Whisky?" Sie schüttelte meine Hand und wandte den genau richtigen Druck an, drückte zwei Mal zu und ließ dann los.

„Nein, danke", sagte ich. „Ich will nicht zu viel von Ihrer Zeit stehlen."

Sie winkte ab. „Das macht ganz und gar keine Mühe." Natürlich log sie, aber sie war wirklich überragend darin. CEOs von großen Unternehmen hatten nicht zufällig freie Zeit. Sie hatte irgendetwas verschoben, um dieses Meeting möglich zu machen. Ich wusste nicht, was das bedeutete, aber es war bedeutsam. „Kommen Sie, unterhalten wir uns in meinem Büro, abseits vom Lärm."

Ich ignorierte die Tatsache, dass es abgesehen von unserem Gespräch leise war, und folgte ihr in ihr Büro. Es hatte auf zwei Seiten die erforderlichen deckenhohen

Fenster, unter uns breiteten sich Gebäude aus wie Soldaten der Königin. Der polierte Parkettboden leuchtete fast so hell wie die sechs in die hohe Decke eingelassenen Lampen.

„Mr. Turkov sagte mir, dass Sie an einem Job interessiert sind." Sie sagte es nebensächlich, aber ich erkannte es augenblicklich als ihren ersten Schachzug. Unglücklicherweise wusste ich nicht, was sie im Schilde führte, und das brachte mich etwas aus dem Konzept. Ich wollte das Thema ‚Cappaner' aufs Tapet bringen, aber es fühlte sich falsch an, das einfach so zu erwähnen. Ihr Verhalten sagte mir, dass Ellen Haverty mich aus einem bestimmten Grund in ihr Büro gebeten hatte, ich aber ziemlich sicher nicht wusste, warum. Sie hatte ihre eigenen Pläne.

„Ja. Ich lote meine Möglichkeiten aus", sagte ich. In diesem Moment konnte ich nichts tun, als es sich entwickeln zu lassen.

„Ich bin mir sicher, dass ein Mann wie Sie viele Möglichkeiten hat", sagte sie.

„Einige. Es ist kein reiner Segen, wissen Sie?"

Sie betrachtete mich für einen Moment. „Ich komme direkt zum Punkt. Sie wissen, wieso Sie hier sind; ich weiß, wieso Sie hier sind. Aber Sie wissen nicht, wieso ich hier bin."

„Stimmt", sagte ich. Ich nahm an, dass Sie *nicht* wusste, weshalb ich hier war, aber ich konnte sie deswegen nicht zur Rede stellen, ohne etwas zu verraten.

„Ich will, dass Sie einen Job für mich machen."

Ich zögerte. Das hatte ich nicht erwartet. „Ich hatte den Eindruck, dass ich genau deswegen hergekommen bin."

„Nicht diesen Job. Etwas anderes.“

„Ich glaube–“

„Lassen Sie mich ausreden. Sie müssen nur zuhören. Erst zuhören, dann reden.“ Sie sprach mit der selbstsicheren Stimme von jemandem, der daran gewöhnt war, seinen Willen durchzusetzen.

„Sicher.“

„Jemand hat mir etwas gestohlen. Ich will es wiederhaben. Und ich will, dass Sir mir dabei helfen, es wiederzubeschaffen.“

Für einen Augenblick wünschte ich, ich hätte das angebotene Wasser akzeptiert, sodass ich etwas hätte, um mein Gesicht dahinter zu verbergen, während ich um Fassung rang. Ich bin mir sicher, dass meine Überraschung zu sehen war. Die Cappaner wollten, dass ich mit Omicron einen Deal aushandelte, und es schien, als wollte Omicron, dass ich dasselbe für sie tat. Es konnte unmöglich so einfach sein. „Ich bin mir ziemlich sicher, dass wir auf einer Wellenlänge sind.“

„Sind wir das?“

„Ich denke schon. Lassen Sie mich Ihnen eine Frage stellen“, sagte ich. „Wieso ich?“

„Ich glaube, Sie sind besonders geeignet, es zu beschaffen.“

Beinahe dieselben Worte zu hören, die der Cappaner verwendet hatte, ließ mich erschaudern. „Wie das?“

„Ich denke, das wissen Sie.“

„Ich glaube nicht, dass dem so ist.“

„Bitte, Carl. Heuchelei steht Ihnen nicht. Ich weiß, wer in meine Firma eingebrochen ist, ich weiß, was sie gestohlen haben, und ich will es wiederhaben.“

„Angenommen, ich weiß, wovon Sie reden“, sagte ich.

„Ja, nehmen wir das an." Sie stand etwa einen Meter entfernt und hatte sich nicht bewegt, seit wir das Zimmer betreten hatten. Ich war ein paar Zentimeter größer, aber ihre eindrucksvolle Erscheinung machte ihre Größe irrelevant.

„Noch mal: Wieso ich?"

„Wer wäre besser geeignet, sich mit der fraglichen Gruppe zu befassen?"

„Ich will hören, wie Sie es sagen", sagte ich.

„Was sagen? Dass die Cappaner unser System infiltriert und irgendwie sämtliche Spuren des Ortho-Robotik-Projekts, das wir Phoenix nennen, ausgelöscht haben, und wir nicht dahinterkommen, wie das möglich war? Ist es das, was ich sagen soll?"

Ich hielt inne. Ich hatte nicht wirklich erwartet, dass sie es aussprechen würde. „Ja."

„Ich habe es gesagt. Können wir das nun hinter uns lassen und zu dem Punkt kommen, an dem Sie mir helfen, es zurückzubekommen?"

„Okay", sagte ich. „Ich hatte Kontakt mit Leuten, die mit den Cappanern zusammenarbeiten." Ihr Gesicht zeigte keine Regung. Vielleicht war sie eine so gute Verhandlungsführerin, dass sie jede Spur von Überraschung verbergen konnte, aber mein Bauchgefühl sagte mir, dass sie es bereits wusste. Sie wusste, dass ich mich mit den Cappanern getroffen hatte.

„Und?", hakte sie nach.

„Ich bin bereit, Bedingungen auszuhandeln", sagte ich. „Ein Mittelsmann zu sein."

„Bedingungen? Die Bedingungen sind wie folgt. Sie geben mir zurück, was sie gestohlen haben. Nachdem sie das getan haben, werde ich liebend gerne über Probleme reden, die sie vielleicht haben, und schauen, was wir tun können, um ihnen entgegenzukommen."

„Ich glaube nicht, dass sie aus gutem Willen auf Ihr Wort vertrauen werden", sagte ich.

„Weswegen ich auch nicht wirklich verhandle." Sie wandte schließlich ihren Blick von mir ab und ging ein paar Schritte Richtung Fenster. „Es gibt keine Bedingung, die sie vorschlagen können und die ich akzeptieren würde. Denn sobald ich anfange, Geschäfte mit ihnen zu machen, haben sie keinen Grund mehr, über diese Geschäfte zu schweigen."

Ich rang um einen neutralen Gesichtsausdruck. Damit zu drohen, eben das der gesamten Galaxis zu verraten, war Teil meines Plans gewesen, obwohl ich noch nicht genau wusste, wie ich das anstellen und Omicron gleichzeitig davon halten würde, sich an den Cappanern zu rächen. Tatsächlich war das mein Problem. *All* meine Pläne scheiterten daran, dieses Problem zu lösen. Ich hatte gedacht, ich hätte mehr Zeit, darüber nachzudenken. Ich hatte nicht erwartet, so schnell hier zu sein und vor dem CEO von Omicron zu stehen. Ich hatte geblufft und sie hatte nicht nur sehen wollen, sie hatte meine Karten gekannt und ihren Einsatz erhöht.

„Also befinden wir uns in einer Sackgasse", sagte ich.

„Das glaube ich nicht", sagte sie. „Ich habe einen Plan in Gang gesetzt. Er braucht vielleicht *etwas* Verhandlung, aber ich habe vor, sie mit entscheidenden Druckmitteln zu führen."

„Wozu brauchen Sie dann mich?"

„Sie können die Dinge einfacher machen. Mir die Informationen jetzt verschaffen und mir den Ärger ersparen, ihre Kolonie auszulöschen.“

„Das ist ein Bluff“, sagte ich. „Wenn Sie die Kolonie auslöschen, haben Sie Ihre Unterlagen immer noch nicht zurück.“

Sie lächelte, obwohl das Lächeln ihre Augen nicht erreichte. „Vielleicht. Aber selbst wenn es ein Bluff ist, geht es darum, wer zuerst blinzelt.“

Ich wollte ihr sagen, dass es nicht funktionieren würde, aber ich war mir nicht sicher, was die Cappaner tun würden, wenn sie mit diesem Dilemma konfrontiert waren. Sie konnten die Kolonie evakuieren, aber Omicron würde nach so etwas Ausschau halten. Sie konnten Schiffe, die die Atmosphäre verließen, leichter abschießen, als auf den Planeten selbst zu feuern. „Das ist ein großes Risiko“, sagte ich nach einer langen Pause.

„Ist es. Und ich bin nicht glücklich darüber. Deswegen will ich, dass Sie mit meinem Team zu dem Planeten fliegen.“

Ich setzte zu einer Antwort an, unterbrach mich aber. „Was?“

„Ich will, dass Sie die Verhandlung führen, aber ich will, dass Sie das an einem Ort tun, der den größtmöglichen Vorteil bietet. Ich denke, Sie vor Ort zu haben – einen Mann, der Bereitschaft gezeigt hat, ihre Bevölkerung auszulöschen – wird unsere Verhandlungsposition stärken. Sie werden nicht die Zugeständnisse bekommen, die ich haben will, wenn Sie von hier aus verhandeln.“

„Sie wollen also, dass ich mit vorgehaltener Waffe mit ihnen verhandle." Ich hatte immer noch Mühe, meinen Rückstand aufzuholen, also hielt ich sie hin.

„So hätte ich es nicht ausgedrückt", sagte sie, „aber ja."

Ich stand einen Moment lang schweigend da und tat so, als würde ich über ihre Forderung nachdenken, während ich versuchte, einen Weg zu finden, um den Spieß umzudrehen. Sie hatte mich von Anfang an in die Enge getrieben und ich hatte sie nicht mal ins Schwitzen gebracht. „Ich kann den Deal auch verhandeln, ohne Talca zu verlassen", sagte ich.

Sie täuschte einen gelangweilten Blick vor. „Ich glaube, ich habe mich deutlich ausgedrückt, als ich sagte, dass wir das so nicht tun würden. Das bringt uns keinen Vorteil."

„Doch, tut es", sagte ich. „Denn ich habe eine Akte bei VPC gelassen, und wenn ich innerhalb von zwei Tagen nicht zurückkehre, geht sie an die komplette Adressliste des Unternehmens raus."

Sie lächelte. „Wirklich? Und was ist in dieser Akte?"

„Genug Details über Ihr gentechnisches Programm mit Cappaner-Mensch-Kreuzungen, um VPC zu einem ernsten Konkurrenten zu machen. Wie viele Milliarden wird Sie das kosten, was glauben Sie?"

Sie lächelte immer noch, und das wollte ich nicht sehen. „Netter Schachzug. Um ehrlich zu sein, wenn Sie sich kampflos ergeben hätten, wäre ich enttäuscht gewesen." Sie ging zu ihrem Schreibtisch und drehte einen schwenkbaren Bildschirm zu mir herum. Javier starrte mich an. „Ich gehe davon aus, dass Sie unsere Unterhaltung mitangehört haben, Javier?"

„Habe ich", sagte er.

„Und?"

„Und wir kooperieren auf jede erdenkliche Weise mit Omicron. Das schließt Sie ein, Carl. Was diese Akte angeht, darum kümmere ich mich."

„Danke, Javier." Sie schaltete den Bildschirm aus. „Wie Sie sehen, sind wir gar nicht so gierig, Carl. Wir sind mehr als bereit, ein anderes Unternehmen am Gewinn zu beteiligen, wenn es Sinn ergibt."

Ich stand fassungslos da. Was für ein Trottel ich gewesen war. Ich hatte Javier in Verdacht gehabt und gewusst, dass er mit Omicron in Kontakt gestanden hatte, aber das Ausmaß war mir nicht bewusst gewesen. Ich fragte mich, an welchem Punkt er begonnen hatte, mit Omicron zusammenzuarbeiten, und ob es vor oder nach Gylikas Tod gewesen war. Ich musste mich konzentrieren. Aber ich konnte das nicht auf sich beruhen lassen. „Wie lange arbeiten Sie schon zusammen?"

„Lange genug", sagte sie. „Da fällt mir ein. Ich sollte Ihnen dafür danken, unsere undichte Stelle gefunden zu haben."

Es traf mich wie ein Schlag in die Magengrube. Gylika. Wenn ich mich nicht mit ihm getroffen hätte, würde er noch leben. Und das Schlimmste war, dass er nicht mal eine undichte Stelle gewesen war. Als wir uns das erste Mal getroffen hatten, hatte er nichts gewusst. Ich hatte ihn aktiv werden lassen. „Ich muss mich setzen."

Sie deutete auf einen gepolsterten Stuhl. „Wir glauben, es ist unsere beste Option, zu ihrem neuen Planeten zu fliegen, und die Informationen physisch in die Finger zu bekommen."

„Sie planen einen Kampfeinsatz", sagte ich. Meine Augen mussten weit aufgerissen sein. Mein Herz raste und ich konnte es nicht kontrollieren, was allerdings mehr mit den Andeutungen über Gylika zu tun hatte und weniger mit den Cappanern.

„*Kampf* ist ein hässliches Wort. Sie sind keine Menschen. Es gibt kein Gesetz dagegen, sie zu töten, wie Ihnen sicher bewusst ist. Es ist mehr wie ... eine Jagd. Sie werden die beste Ausrüstung und das beste Team bekommen, das man für Geld kaufen kann."

Ich schüttelte den Kopf. „Das ist krank."

„Dass gerade Sie das sagen, finde ich etwas unaufrichtig."

„Ficken Sie sich. Es ist nicht ansatzweise das Gleiche."

„Ich schätze, ich würde dasselbe sagen, wenn ich an Ihrer Stelle wäre."

Ihr Gesichtsausdruck war neutral, trotz ihrer Worte ließ sie nicht zu, dass Selbstgefälligkeit zu sehen war. Das hielt mich nicht davon ab, ihre eine schmieren zu wollen. Es gab keine sichtbare Security und ich muss gestehen, dass ich für einen Augenblick darüber nachdachte.

„Sie werden mich nicht dazu anstacheln", sagte ich.

„Das habe ich nicht vor. Sie werden fliegen, Sie werden mir die Technologie zurückbringen und das war es dann."

Ich starrte sie an, unfähig, die richtigen Worte zu finden. Die Arroganz dieser Dame machte mich fertig. Aber zuzustimmen war vielleicht die beste Chance, noch etwas auszuhandeln, und darum hatten die Cappaner mich schließlich gebeten. Vorausgesetzt, es wären noch irgendwelche Cappaner am Leben, wenn die

Söldner von Omicron erst mit ihrer Arbeit fertig waren. „Ich werde darüber nachdenken.“

„Tja, Ihre andere Option ist, dass wir Sie für den Einbruch in unser System belangen.“

Ich zuckte zusammen, sagte aber nichts.

„Was, dachten Sie, dass wir nichts davon gewusst haben? Haben sie nicht erwartet, dass wir nach einer massiven Sicherheitslücke genau aufpassen? Ich bin enttäuscht.“

„Ist mir egal. Belangen Sie mich.“

„Ich dachte mir, dass Sie das sagen würden. Ich bezweifle aber, dass Sie dasselbe über Ihre Komplizin Ms. Ganos sagen werden.“

„Wer?“

„Bitte. Wir haben Gesichtserkennung in unserem Sicherheitssystem.“

„Sie werden sie belangen?“

„Oh, nein. Obwohl meine Leute aus der Rechtsabteilung glauben, dass sie zwischen sechs und zehn Jahren kriegen würde, ist sie viel zu wertvoll, um sie in eine Zelle zu sperren. Zumindest sperren wir sie nicht in eine Gefängniszelle. Nein, wir holen sie uns und verwenden, was wir gegen sie in der Hand haben, um sie an den Meistbietenden zu verkaufen. Sie wird den Rest ihres vermutlich kurzen Lebens damit zubringen, für uns oder jemanden wie uns zu arbeiten, bis sie aufgebraucht ist. Dann liefern wir sie aus. Sie wird aber nicht viel Zeit absitzen. Man wird sie tot in ihrer Zelle finden. Vermutlich Suizid. Tragisch.“

„Arschloch." In diesem Moment fiel mir nichts anderes ein. Ich hoffte, dass Ganos es vom Planeten geschafft hatte, aber wenn sie die legale Route nahm, würde ihr das nicht sehr lange helfen.

„In der Tat. Ich verstehe das als ein Ja?"

Ich wandte den Blick von ihr ab.

„Ich muss es hören", sagte sie. „Ich brauche ein Ja."

„In Ordnung. Ja."

Kapitel dreiundzwanzig

Obwohl ich nicht genau wusste, was sie von mir erwarteten, zeigte sich eine Sache sofort: Sie vertrauten mir nicht. Sie konfiszierten meine elektronischen Geräte und schickten mich durch einen Hintereingang zu einem Privatfahrzeug. Ein Fahrer und zwei Wachen brachten mich fort, von den sich auftürmenden Wolkenkratzern in der Stadtmitte in die Außenbezirke, in ein Industriegebiet mit alten drei- und vierstöckigen Gebäuden, alles rechteckig und mit geraden Linien. Wir hielten vor einem Haus ohne irgendwelche Schilder und sie führten mich zu einer Doppeltür hinauf. Der Hightech-Identifikationsscanner stand in krassem Kontrast zur abgenutzten Fassade des Gebäudes, das mindestens fünfundsiebzig Jahre alt sein musste.

Ich trat durch die Tür und helles Licht blendete mich einen Moment, bis sich meine Augen daran gewöhnt hatten. Der Zementboden des großen Raumes, grau gestrichen wie in den meisten militärischen Einrichtungen, sah so sauber aus, dass man davon hätte essen können, und er reflektierte das Licht der Lampen, die von der hohen Decke herabhingen. Eine Reihe Bildschirme säumte die nächstgelegene Wand, alle dunkel, mit Ausnahme von einem, auf dem die Nachrichten liefen. Ich erkannte die Hardware als militärisch. Es erinnerte mich an eine Vielzahl von Räumen, in denen ich in der Vergangenheit Soldatinnen und Soldaten dabei zugesehen hatte, wie sie an Computern ausgebildet wurden.

Ein paar Männer und Frauen liefen geschäftig hin und her, konzentriert auf verschiedene Aufgaben, und obwohl sie keine Uniformen trugen, verhielten sie sich wie Soldaten. Ihre Körperhaltung, wie sie sich bewegten, alles an ihnen schrie Militär. Oder Ex-Militär, was wahrscheinlicher war, allerdings noch nicht allzu lange aus dem Dienst ausgeschieden, angesichts der Tatsache, dass sie alle noch relativ jung waren.

„Colonel Butler, willkommen auf dem Ostcampus." Ein großer Mann von etwa fünfunddreißig Jahren mit kantigem Kinn, Haar, das beinahe kurz genug war fürs Militär, und schlaksiger Statur durchquerte den Raum, um mich und die beiden Gorillas, die mich eskortiert hatten, zu begrüßen. „Ich muss schon sagen, Sir. Es ist eine Ehre, mit Ihnen zusammenzuarbeiten." Er wandte sich an eine meiner beiden Wachen. „Ich übernehme hier. Danke."

Ich musterte ihn. Wer immer er war, er hatte mich im Hintertreffen, weil er eindeutig darüber gebrieft worden war, dass ich mich dem Team anschließen würde, und ich keine Ahnung hatte, wer er war. Ex-Militär, selbstverständlich. Vermutlich Spezialeinheit, wenn ich raten müsste. Ich hielt ihn für jemanden, der den Dienst als Captain quittiert hatte, nachdem er bei ein paar Einsätzen dabei gewesen war. Das passte zumindest zum Alter. Ich machte es mir leicht und sagte nichts, was ihn dazu zwang, das Gespräch am Laufen zu halten oder verlegen da zu stehen.

„Ich bin Eric Tanaka." Er hielt mir eine Hand hin und ich schüttelte sie. „Ich bin der Teamleader für die Mission."

„Gut zu wissen." Ich verhielt mich wie ein Arschloch, aber die Scheiße, die sich mit Haverty ereignet hatte, berechtigte mich dazu. Nach dem wenigen, das ich gesehen hatte, schlussfolgerte ich, dass wir den Planeten verlassen würden.

Mir würde genug Zeit bleiben, um es wieder gut zu machen. Ich erwog, die Situation eskalieren zu lassen, indem ich ihm die Stirn bot und ihn bat, auf klassische Militär-Alphatier-Art seine Vertrauenswürdigkeit unter Beweis zu stellen, aber ich entschied, dass eine sanftere Herangehensweise mich weiterbrächte. „Was ist das für ein Laden?"

„Der Ostcampus? Auf dem Papier ist es eine Prüfeinrichtung. Hightech-Zeug, Waffen. Unser Team gibt Ex-Soldaten Omicrons Ideen in die Hände und die geben den Entwicklern Feedback. Aber er ist auch für die Ausbildung ausgestattet. Ich mache hier viel Arbeit, bereite Teams auf verschiedene Missionen vor. Wir haben hinten einen vollausgestatteten Simulator und eine Reihe Schießstände. Es ist eine großartige Umgebung für die Ausbildung. Ich führe Sie gleich ein bisschen herum."

Er sagte Missionen, was mich dazu veranlasste, zu glauben, dass er eine stehende Truppe hatte. Ich fragte mich, was die Regierung davon halten würde, dass ein Unternehmen seine eigene Armee hatte. Man wusste es wahrscheinlich und es war ihnen vermutlich auch egal. „Wie groß ist das Team?"

„Das hängt vom Bedarf ab. Für diese Mission? Etwa zweihundert."

Die Größe überraschte mich, aber ich ließ mir nichts anmerken. Ich hatte ein kleines Team erwartet, ein Infiltrationsszenario. Das hier war eher eine Angriffstruppe, wenn auch vielleicht nicht groß genug, falls wir auf ernsthaften Widerstand stoßen würden. „Die Größe erscheint mir seltsam."

„Darüber können wir später reden. Uns fehlen Informationen über die Position des Feindes, also haben wir für den Moment entschieden, es nicht mit einem zu kleinen Team zu versuchen. Falls wir irgendetwas Größeres brauchen, können wir auf unsere Kräfte im All zurückgreifen. Vielleicht können Sie ein paar Informationslücken schließen."

„Vielleicht." *Kräfte im All.* Das war ein Euphemismus für hochleistungsfähige Waffen. „Wie viele von den zweihundert kämpfen?"

„Die meisten", sagte er. „Etwa hundertsechzig gehen auf die Oberfläche. Der Rest wird das Schiff bemannen, mit dem wir fliegen, sowie das kleinere Angriffsschiff."

Ich nickte leicht, um Zustimmung zu zeigen, obwohl ich die Situation ohne weitere Informationen nicht beurteilen konnte. Es fühlte sich an, als wollte er meine Mitwirkung, also bekam er sie. Irgendwann in der vergangenen Minute hatte ich entschieden, die Arschlochrolle an den Nagel zu hängen, mich für eine Weile zu benehmen und zu schauen, wohin mich das führte. Ich hatte mich noch nicht damit abgefunden, bei der Mission mitzumachen. Sasha und Riku waren immer noch da draußen. Sie würden wissen, dass ich verschwunden war, und hatten bewiesen, dass sie ziemlich fähig

waren. Ich war im Rückstand, hatte aber noch Spiel-
züge in der Hinterhand. „Sie sind also der Teamleader.
Was ist meine Rolle bei dieser Sache?“

Er rieb die Hände aneinander und wandte den Blick
ab. „Nun, Sir … Ihr offizieller Titel ist Berater, aber ich
bin nicht arrogant genug, um Ihnen zu sagen, was das
bedeutet. Jemand denkt, dass Sie hilfreich sein könnten. Ich bin mir sicher, dass der- oder diejenige recht
hat, und ich bin froh, dass Sie hier sind. Aber wenn es
darum geht, was Sie tun? Ich dachte, das überlasse ich
Ihnen. Ich bin mir sicher, Sie wissen am besten, wo Sie
etwas ergänzen können.“

Ich unterdrückte ein Kichern. Das war Militärspra-
che für „die haben Sie mir zugeteilt und ich habe keine
verdammte Ahnung“. Ich muss zugeben, dass er mir
das freundlich mitteilte. „Sicher. Improvisieren wir. Sobald ich sehe, was wir machen, und womit wir es zu tun
haben, sehe ich, wo ich am besten reinpasse. Keine
Sorge, Tanaka. Ich werde nicht versuchen, Ihne die
Show zu stehlen.“ Ich sagte mit Absicht *wir*. Es schien
das Beste zu sein, ihn glauben zu lassen, ich wäre an
Bord. Fürs Erste.

„Roger, Sir. Wir rüsten Sie für einen Einsatz an der
Oberfläche aus, nur für den Fall. Wenn Sie sich entscheiden, im All zu bleiben, ist das auch okay, aber wir
wollen, dass Sie vorbereitet sind. Außerdem wird
Ihnen die Ausrüstung gefallen.“

Tanaka verbrachte den Rest des Nachmittags damit,
mich in der Einrichtung herumzuführen, die sich beinahe einen halben Block weit erstreckte, soweit ich das
einschätzen konnte. Es schien beinahe so, als wolle er
mich beeindrucken. Ich spielte mit – und ehrlich gesagt

war ich beeindruckt. Sie hatten viele Sachen und einige hatte ich noch nie gesehen. Zu jeder anderen Zeit hätte ich die Tour geliebt und Spaß gehabt, mit der ausgestellten Technik rumzuspielen. Aber meine Rolle als erzwungener Gast dämpfte jede Begeisterung, die ich vielleicht verspürt hätte.

Man ließ Tanaka und mich nie allein, zwei oder drei Leute wuselten stets um uns herum und versorgten uns mit irgendeiner Information über verschiedene Aspekte der Basis. Ich gab mein Bestes, um mir den Grundriss zu merken, aber ich hatte noch nie ein sonderlich gutes räumliches Vorstellungsvermögen innerhalb eines Gebäudes gehabt, besonders dann nicht, wenn es keine Fenster gab. Mir fiel auf, dass das Gebäude genau sechs Türen hatte, die nach draußen führten, drei auf der Vorderseite und zwei plus eine Laderampe auf der Rückseite. Die meisten der Türen, sowohl Zimmertüren als auch Außentüren, waren mit Scan-Bedienfeldern ausgestattet. Niemand hatte Zugangskarten, was auf ein biometrisches Sicherheitssystem hindeutete.

Irgendwann schloss sich uns ein großer Mann mit pechschwarzen Haaren und bräunlichem Teint an und blieb Teil unserer Gruppe. Seine lockere Körperhaltung und sein wachsamer Blick wiesen ihn als eine Art Sicherheitsmann aus, aber ich wusste nicht, ob er Tanakas Bodyguard oder mein Gefängniswärter war. Der Mann sagte nichts, und ich fragte nicht, weil der Unterschied keine große Rolle spielte.

In einer gut ausgestatteten Kantine aßen wir spät zu Abend. An langen, rechteckigen Tischen war Platz für etwa hundertfünfzig Leute, obwohl die Hälfte der Tische leer war und unser Tisch abgesehen von Tanaka, dem großen Corporal und mir leerblieb. Sie servierten ein Militärmenü, das sattmachend und vermutlich nahrhaft, aber nichts Besonderes war. Wenigstens ein paar Leute erkannten mich, zumindest bekam ich die Sorte Blicke, an die ich mich an der Öffentlichkeit gewöhnt hatte, aber niemand näherte sich. Wichtiger noch, ich erkannte niemanden. Es war nicht sehr realistisch, aber bei genügend Ex-Soldaten an einem Ort gab es immer die Chance, dass ich mit einem gedient hatte. Das hätte sich als nützlich erweisen können.

Nachdem wir fertig waren, brachten meine beiden Begleiter mich auf mein Zimmer, ein drei mal drei Meter Quadrat, aus dem eine kleine Ecke für ein winziges Badezimmer mit Dusche, Toilette und Waschbecken ausgeschnitten worden war. Ein kleiner Schreibtisch, ein Stuhl, ein Bett und ein Spind an der Wand waren die einzigen anderen Einrichtungsgegenstände. „Entschuldigen Sie die spärliche Unterkunft", sagte Tanaka. „Wir sind nur ein paar Tage hier."

„Ich war schon schlechter untergebracht", sagte ich. Mein Zimmer sah ein bisschen aus wie eine Zelle, andererseits sahen eine Menge militärische Zimmer so aus. Ich fragte ihn nicht nach Beschränkungen, weil ich nicht wollte, dass er mir sagte, ich solle auf dem Zimmer bleiben. Auf diese Weise könnte ich, wenn ich zu entkommen versuchte, immer noch sagen, dass ich nicht gewusst hatte, dass ich nicht gehen durfte. Er würde es natürlich als Lüge erkennen, aber wir konnten beide so tun als ob, und das Gesicht wahren. Das setzte voraus, dass ich die Tür öffnen konnte, nachdem sie gegangen waren.

„Falls Sie irgendetwas brauchen, Corporal Matua hier ist Ihr Mann." Tanaka deutete auf den Soldaten, der uns den ganzen Tag begleitet hatte, und der große Mann lächelte.

Nachdem sie gegangen waren, wartete ich vielleicht dreißig Minuten, ehe ich mich an der Tür versuchte. Ich konnte nicht länger warten, allein, mit nichts anderem als meinen Gedanken. Das ist an einem guten Tag schon kein schöner Umstand, erst recht nicht nach all den Dingen, die ich in letzter Zeit hatte verkraften müssen. Sicher erwarteten sie nicht, dass ich ohne Beschäftigung in einem leeren Zimmer sitzen würde. Zu meiner Überraschung öffnete sich die Tür zischend, als ich meine Hand auf das Bedienfeld legte.

Ich steckte meinen Kopf in den Flur und erwartete, Matua oder eine andere Wache zu sehen, aber der Flur war leer. Er war kaum breit genug, dass zwei Leute aneinander vorbeigehen konnten, ohne sich zu berühren, hatte weiße Wände, grauen Boden und auf beiden Seiten waren in regelmäßigen Abständen Türen. Ich nahm an, dass sie zu weiteren Unterkünften führten, aber ich wusste nicht, wie viele von der Truppe hier stationiert waren und wie viele pendelten. Es konnten auch Zellen sein, wenn das hier ein Arrestbereich war. Es erschien mir unwahrscheinlich. Die Wände endeten am Boden in Metallschienen, was vermutlich bedeutete, dass sie das Gebäude für andere Zwecke umgestalten konnten, abhängig von der Mission.

Ich entschied mich wahllos, nach links zu gehen, und lief den Flur hinunter. Ich hatte mir auf der Tour ein paar entscheidende Punkte gemerkt, und sobald ich sie fand, konnte ich mich hoffentlich in diesem verwirrenden Labyrinth von Gleichförmigkeit orientieren. Ich drückte meine Handfläche auf das Bedienfeld neben einer Tür, die aussah, als könnte sie in eine Abstellkammer führen, und versuchte es dann bei einer, die wie eine aussah, hinter der eine Werkstatt lag. Keine davon öffnete sich. Zwei Soldaten kamen im Flur an mir vorbei und plauderten miteinander über ein Beta-Ball-Match, das sie offenbar gerade gesehen hatten. Sie würdigten mich mit einem Nicken und gingen weiter. Das bedeutete zweierlei: Es war mir gestattet, mich frei zu bewegen, oder niemand kannte meinen Status. Beides war für mich in Ordnung. Ich kam durch einen großen, offenen Trainingsbereich, den ich von meiner Tour her kannte. Vier Soldaten spielten Fußball in Zweierteams und benutzten dabei Netze, die in vorgegebenen Bahnen im Boden verankert waren. Sie trugen alle irgendeine Art Hightech-Ausrüstung, die es ihnen erlaubte, übermenschlich schnell zu springen und zu rennen, was zu einem unmöglich akrobatischen Tor führte, das alle vier Spieler mit Jubel würdigten.

Ich folgte einem Flur, der in den großen Raum führte, durch den ich hindurchgekommen war, als ich eingetroffen war. Zwei Soldaten kamen auf mich zu, vermutlich kamen sie von draußen.

„Hey, kriegt man hier irgendwo einen Drink?", fragte ich.

Sie blieben ein paar Schritte von mir entfernt stehen. „Nein, Sir." Die große Frau lächelte, als hätte ich eine dumme Frage gestellt. „Die meisten von uns bringen was zum Trinken mit."

„Ich hatte keine Gelegenheit. Ich glaube, ich werde ausgehen und was suchen.“

„Hier in der Gegend, Sir?“, fragte der Mann, der ein paar Zentimeter kleiner war als seine Kameradin. „In diesem Teil der Stadt ist die nächste Bar etwa fünf Klicks entfernt.“

„Ich kann Bewegung gebrauchen. Und ich brauche wirklich einen Drink.“ Ich blickte so freundlich drein, wie ich konnte. *Es gibt hier nichts zu sehen. Nur einen alten Soldaten, der seinen Schnaps braucht.* Ich brauchte nicht wirklich einen Drink, aber es war eine passende Ausrede. Und natürlich würde ich einen Drink auch nicht ablehnen. „Ich bin mir sicher, dass ich ein Auto finden kann, das mich zurückbringt.“

Wenn es sie kümmerte, ließen sie sich nichts anmerken, und wir alle gingen in unsere jeweiligen Richtungen weiter. Ich hatte keine Ahnung, ob ich nach draußen kommen würde, aber Omicron hatte sich die Mühe gemacht, mich am Leben zu lassen, also würden sie mich vermutlich nicht erschießen, wenn ich meine Grenzen austestete. Ich dachte darüber nach, wie ich einen Kommunikator in die Finger bekommen, jemanden kontaktieren und die Person wissen lassen konnte, wo ich war. Ich hatte die Kontaktinformationen von Sasha und Riku verloren, als sie mein Device konfisziert hatten, aber ich hatte das Gefühl, dass die beiden nach mir suchen würden, also glaubte ich, dass sie mich finden würden, wenn ich eine Nachricht absetzen könnte. Wenn nicht, hatte ich immer noch die Nachricht an Plazz, die ich vorprogrammiert hatte und die in etwa zwei Tagen rausgehen würde. Hoffentlich wäre ich dann noch hier.

Ich erreichte die Außentür und legte meine Hand aufs Bedienfeld. Nichts. Das überraschte mich nicht. Ich rief den beiden Soldaten zu, an denen ich vorbeigekommen war, da sie den Raum noch nicht ganz verlassen hatten. „Hey, ich bin gerade erst angekommen und sie haben mich noch nicht im System. Macht es Ihnen was aus?"

Sie kamen ein Stück des Weges zurück, sodass wir uns nicht anbrüllen mussten, und flüsterten unterwegs miteinander. Zweifelsohne debattierten sie darüber, was sie tun sollten. Die Frau meldete sich zu Wort. „Sir, es ist uns nicht gestattet, jemanden durch eine Tür zu lassen, für die er keine Berechtigung hat. Man ist hier, was das betrifft, sehr streng."

„Ich bin mir sicher, dass ich eine Berechtigung haben werde, sobald sie auf dem neusten Stand sind. Ich will nur einen Drink." Ich konnte die Verzweiflung hören, die sich in meine Stimme schlich, was bedeutete, dass sie sie auch hören konnte. Ich war am Arsch.

„Sorry, Sir."

„Kein Problem", sagte ich. „Ich will nicht, dass Sie in Schwierigkeiten geraten."

Ich versuchte es bei allen anderen Außentüren, für den unwahrscheinlichen Fall, dass sich eine von ihnen öffnen würde, aber ich hatte keinen Erfolg. Ich traf eine Gruppe von drei Soldaten und versuchte es mit meiner rührseligen Geschichte, bekam aber dasselbe Ergebnis wie beim ersten Versuch. Sie wirkten, als täte es ihnen ehrlich leid, aber sie konnten mir nicht helfen. Als ich zu meinem Zimmer zurückging, machte ich mir einen Moment lang Sorgen, dass ich nicht wieder hineinkommen würde, aber ich kam um die Ecke und sah Corporal Matua, der vor der Tür auf mich wartete. Er hielt eine Flasche Whisky in einer Hand, in der anderen ein Glas und einen kleinen Eimer Eis.

Ich lachte. „Ich schätze, Sie haben mich am Ende doch beobachtet.“

Er zuckte mit den Schultern. „Ich bin für Ihre Sicherheit verantwortlich. Es ist mein Job, aufmerksam zu sein.“

„Bedeutet Sicherheit, dass sie mich beschützen oder sicherstellen, dass ich nicht abhaue?“

Er lächelte mich breit an, ein Lächeln, das sein ganzes Gesicht erhellte. „Es ist mein Job, dafür zu sorgen, dass Ihnen nichts zustößt.“

Er hatte die Frage nicht beantwortet, aber gleichzeitig hatte er es doch getan, so gut wie. Ich legte es nicht drauf an. Es war das Mindeste, das ich tun konnte, nachdem er keine große Sache aus meinem Fluchtversuch gemacht hatte. Außerdem hatte er eine Flasche bei sich. Ich nahm sie dankbar an. Es war beim besten Willen nicht Ferra 3, aber auch kein Fusel. Er ging, ich betrat mein Zimmer und goss mir drei Finger breit ein.

Kapitel
vierundzwanzig

Nach einer Nacht, in der ich beschissen geschlafen hatte, was durch Frühstück und Kaffee mit Matua etwas besser wurde, gingen wir in die Waffenkammer, um meine Ausrüstung zu holen. Tanaka hatte nicht gelogen, als er gesagt hatte, dass mir die Ausrüstung gefallen würde. Zwei Techs brauchten vier Stunden, um Körperpanzer und Helm auf mich anzupassen, aber als sie erst fertig waren, wollte ich beinahe tanzen. Der Ganzkörperanzug war wie eine robotische Hülle, die jede meiner natürlichen Bewegungen nachahmte, aber verstärkte. Sie fingen langsam an, brachten mir bei, wie ich mich bewegen und meine Augen benutzen musste, um die die verschiedenen Funktionen des Helms auszulösen, und kalibrierten alles auf meine exakten Maße. Nach etwa fünf Minuten war ich die Geschwindigkeit ihrer Lektionen leid, machte ein Vorwärtssalto und landete auf meinen Hightech-Stiefeln, die auf den Zementboden knallten. Ich stieß einen Freudenschrei aus und Matua, der an der Wand lehnte, lachte.

„Ha!" Ich rannte ein halbes Dutzend Schritte und machte einen Satz, um die Fähigkeiten der Beine zu testen. Ich kam etwa zwei Meter hoch und als ich wieder auf dem harten Boden aufkam, absorbierte der Anzug den Großteil des Aufpralls. „Wir hätten dieses Zeug bei der Infanterie gebraucht.“

„Die Army konnte sie sich nicht leisten“, sagte Tanaka, der auf der anderen Seite des Raumes gestanden hatte. „Zum Preis von vier dieser Dinger kann man ein ganzes Bataillon mit Standardausrüstung ausstatten.“

„Vier Leute in diesen Dingen könnten es vielleicht mit einem Bataillon aufnehmen“, scherzte ich. Ich musste zugeben, dass es mir ein wenig meines alten Feuers zurückgab, so ausgerüstet zu werden. Das gefiel mir. Ich fragte mich, ob Kerle wie Tanaka es deswegen taten: Das Militär verließen und denselben Job in der zivilen Welt annahmen. Etwas daran gab mir das Gefühl, mehr am Leben zu sein als in den zwei Jahren zuvor. Ich bin mir sicher, dass nicht nur ich der Grund war. „Sind die meisten in Ihrem Team Ex-Militärs?“

„Beinahe ausschließlich“, sagte Tanaka. „Wir rekrutieren sehr intensiv aus Elite-Einheiten. Wir haben ein gutes Team.“

Ich blickte zu dem großen Corporal hinüber. „Wie haben die Sie überzeugt?“

„Einfach. Sie zahlen besser. Viel besser.“

Tanaka mischte sich ein. „Sicher, man setzt sein Leben immer noch aufs Spiel, aber hier wird es wertgeschätzt. Außerdem geht es beim Großteil des Jobs darum, Ausrüstung zu testen, und wir haben alles Mögliche an cooler Ausrüstung.“ Er deutete auf die Ausrüstung, die den Großteil der Werkhalle einnahm.

„Das haben Sie“, sagte ich. „Was ist mit Waffen?“

„Lassen Sie den Anzug hier und wir zeigen sie Ihnen."
Er lächelte das breite, ehrliche Lächeln eines stolzen El-
ternteils.

„Sind Sie sich sicher, dass ich ihn nicht anbehalten
kann?", fragte ich. „Das Ding könnte sich als nützlich
erwiesen."

„Er wird für Sie auf dem Schiff sein."

Ein paar Minuten später liefen wir durch eine
schwere Tresortür in eine Waffenkammer. Tanaka
nahm ein Hightech-Pulsgewehr von einem Ständer
und reichte es mir. „Das ist das Beste auf dem Markt,
Sir. Die PR-21."

„Ja?" Ich nahm ihm das Gewehr ab.

„Es ist wasserfester, der Akku hält länger und es hat
einen klarer definierten Strahl als alles, was Sie je abgefeuert haben", sagte Tanaka. „Es ist die tödlichste per-
sönliche Waffe in der Galaxis."

Ich ging an beiden vorbei und gab die Waffe zurück,
ehe ich ein Projektilgewehr von einem Ständer nahm.
Es sah dem Bikovsky, das ich zu meiner Dienstzeit be-
vorzugt hatte, sehr ähnlich, hatte aber schlankere Linien. „Ich nehme das hier."

„Ich habe Ihnen doch gesagt, dass er die Bitch will",
sagte Matua, der den Soldaten-Spitznamen der Bikovsky verwendet hatte. „Sie schulden mir einen Fün-
fer."

Tanaka schnaubte. „Ja, ja. Ich weiß, dass Sie mit der
Bitch vertraut sind, Sir. Dieses Modell funktioniert
identisch, bietet aber mehr Optionen, was die Projek-
tile betrifft. Sie haben Funk- und Infrarot-Suchge-

schosse, und die Lenkgeschosse lassen sich um zusätzliche sieben Grad beugen. Alles natürlich mit Ihrem Helm verbunden.“

„Sie hat Infrarot-Geschosse? Hitzesuchend?“

„Ja, Sir. Nicht super effektiv, wegen der begrenzten Reichweite, aber hin und wieder sind sie ganz nützlich.“

Ich nickte und ging weiter zu den Handfeuerwaffen. Ich wählte eine Pulspistole in Standardausführung. „Die hier auch.“

„Na klar.“

„Was ist Ihre Vorgeschichte, Tanaka?“, fragte ich. Es war eine ungefährliche Frage, jetzt, da wir Gelegenheit gehabt hatten, über Waffen und Ausrüstung eine Beziehung aufzubauen. Es würde nicht wie eine Kampfansage rüberkommen.

„Ach, Sie wissen schon, Sir. Captain bei der Army. Hauptsächlich Spezialeinheit. Davor ein Einsatz bei der Infanterie.“

„Wo haben Sie gedient?“ Wir verglichen Einsätze, stellten fest, dass wir ein paarmal an denselben Orten gewesen waren, aber nie zur selben Zeit. Wenn wir weitergesucht hätten, hätten wir sicher gemeinsame Bekannte gefunden, aber nicht viele, da wir unterschiedlich alt waren und verschiedene Ränge hatten.

„Also, wie wird das laufen?“, fragte ich schließlich. „Ich bin mir sicher, dass Matua Ihnen erzählt hat, dass ich gestern Abend versucht habe, das Gebäude zu verlassen.“

„Für einen Drink“, sagte Tanaka und bestätigte meinen Verdacht.

„Genau. Für einen Drink.“

Matua schnaubte.

„Sie sind kein Gefangener, Sir“, sagte Tanaka.

„Nein? Also kann ich gehen?“, fragte ich.

Er wandte den Blick für den Bruchteil einer Sekunde ab.

„Das habe ich mir gedacht. Nicht Ihre Schuld. Ich nehme es Ihnen nicht übel.“ Ich sah die Erleichterung in seinem Gesicht. Beinahe durchschaute ich ihn. Er hatte nicht um mich gebeten, das wusste ich. Jemand hatte mich ihm aufgenötigt, also hatten wir einander am Hals.

Nein, ich hatte gelogen. Ich *nahm* es ihm übel, ein wenig, aber ihn das wissen zu lassen, hätte nichts gebracht. Bis ich einen Ausweg gefunden hatte, musste ich mit ihm und seinem Team koexistieren. Falls ich es nicht rausschaffte, würden wir uns in eine Situation begeben, die vielleicht feindlich wäre, und alle hatten Waffen. Ich musste mich nützlich machen. Oder mindestens zu jemandem werden, den sie nicht umbringen und auf einem entfernten Planeten loswerden wollten.

Nach einem Vormittag mit dem coolen Zeug verbrachten wir den Nachmittag mit dem dumpfen, aber notwendigen Teil der Mission: Den Hintergrundinformationen. Tanaka saß neben mir, an der Mitte eines langen, rechteckigen Tischs, während Matua hinter mir an der Wand Stellung bezog. Drei Einweiser standen am entgegengesetzten Ende, auf militärische Weise vor der Wand aufgereiht und in graue Kampfanzüge gekleidet. Theoretisch brieften sie Tanaka, aber sicher war er mit den Grundlagen der Mission längst vertraut, also hatten sie das alles in Wirklichkeit für mich vorbereitet. Eine große, schlanke Frau mit kurzen, schwarzen Haaren sah Tanaka an und er nickte. Sie gab jemandem hinten im Raum ein Zeichen und ein Hologramm leuchtete vor uns auf, das einen Planeten zeigte.

„Sir, das ist Zeta 4. Der Planet kreist um einen Stern der Intensität 1,14, der Orbitalradius beträgt etwa hundertfünfundsiebzig Millionen Kilometer, was eine gemäßigte Klimazone bedeutet. Der Planet ist weit genug von seinem Stern entfernt, dass er nicht gebunden rotiert, also ihm nicht immer dieselbe Seite zuwendet. Das macht ihn ideal." Sie sah Tanaka an, während sie sprach, warf mir aber einen Blick zu, um sicherzugehen, dass ich verstanden hatte. „Der Planet hat sowohl Eis als auch Wasser, was Leben ermöglicht. Mit weiterem Terraforming könnte man die suboptimale Atmosphäre dicker machen. Der Sauerstofflevel liegt momentan bei achtundsechzig Prozent des Standards."

Ich lehnte mich zu Tanaka hinüber. „Zeta 4. Das ist ein verlassener Bergbauplanet, oder nicht?"

Er nickte und zeigte auf die Einweiserin, womit er andeutete, dass sie darauf noch eingehen würde.

„Angesichts der dünnen Atmosphäre variieren die Temperaturen zwischen den Regionen und zwischen Tag und Nacht stark. Die Durchschnittstemperatur liegt zwar innerhalb der Norm für menschliches Leben, die intensiven Schwankungen machen es aber ziemlich ungemütlich."

„Man könnte also dort leben, es würde aber keinen Spaß machen", sagte ich zur Einweiserin.

„Exakt, Sir. Der Planet hat eine 0,9 Standardgröße und 0,9 Standarddichte. Die Gravitation liegt bei etwa 0,8. Die Rotation dauert vierundzwanzig Stunden und die zwei Monde haben im Vergleich zum Planeten eine relativ hohe Masse, was zu einigermaßen extremen Fluteffekten führt."

„Wie schlimm?", fragte ich.

„Die Küsten sind beinahe unbewohnbar, Sir." Sie ging ein Dutzend weitere Holo-Bilder durch und etwa fünfzehn Minuten grundlegende Fakten über die Kontinente, den Boden und andere Umweltfaktoren, ehe sie fertig war. „Wenn es keine weiteren Fragen gibt, gebe ich weiter an Mr. Sherzinski."

Tanaka warf mir einen Blick zu und ich schüttelte den Kopf. „Keine Fragen", sagte er.

Sherzinski begann ohne zu zögern. „Wie Sie sagten Sir, befand sich auf Zeta 4 ursprünglich eine Bergbau-Operation. Hauptsächlich Erkundungsmissionen."

„Okay", sagte ich. „Aber sie haben sie aufgegeben. Wieso?"

„Aus demselben Grund, aus dem alle Bergbaubetriebe irgendetwas aufgeben, Sir. Geld. Es gibt dort Eisen und einen Haufen Fels, aber beinahe keine Edelmetalle, die eine große Operation rentabel machen würden."

„Und angesichts des Wetters, der Gravitation und der Fluten ist es kein Ort für Siedlungen", sagte ich.

„Korrekt, Sir. Im Grunde genommen ist er nur für Wasser zu gebrauchen, und für diesen Zweck ist er nicht nah genug an anderen Systemen, damit sich der Export lohnt. Der Planet könnte für Sportlerinnen und Sportler interessant sein, angesichts der Brandung für Surfer und wegen der großartigen unterirdischen Höhlen, von denen es eine ganze Menge gibt. Ein paar Unternehmen besitzen kleine finanzielle Beteiligungen, aber niemand hat bisher etwas entwickelt."

Ich machte mir keine Notizen, merkte mir aber alles. Jetzt bedeutete es noch nichts, aber ich hatte keine Ahnung, was die Zukunft bereithielt, und ich wollte vorbereitet sein.

„Okay. Wir haben also einen toten Planeten mitten im Nirgendwo. Ich nehme an, der dritte Einweiser wird uns bezüglich der Cappaner aufklären?"

„Ja, Sir." Der dritte Einweiser übernahm. „Obwohl auf Zeta 4 keine Menschen leben, seit die letzten Forscher der Bergbaubetriebe vor sechzig Jahren weggegangen sind, ist der Planet jetzt bewohnt. Vor schätzungsweise zwei Jahren hat eine Gruppe Cappaner den Planeten besiedelt."

„Hätte das damals nicht jemandem auffallen müssen?", fragte ich.

Er schüttelte den Kopf. „Nicht wirklich, Sir. Es gibt keinen Grund. Obwohl der Planet nach galaktischen Maßstäben nicht weit entfernt ist, ist er eine Sackgasse. Der Sprung, der ins Zeta-System führt, führt nicht weiter."

„Wie ... wie haben wir dann herausgefunden, dass sie dort sind?"

„Ich weiß es nicht, Sir."

Ich warf Tanaka einen Blick zu, aber der hielt den Blick nach vorne gerichtet. Ich kannte die Antwort auf die Frage – Omicron hatte ihnen überhaupt erst geholfen, von Cappa zu entkommen –, aber ich wollte herausfinden, was die anderen wussten. Ich konnte Tanaka nicht lesen. Ich nickte dem Einweiser zu, damit er fortfahren konnte.

„Unsere Schätzung ist, dass die Bevölkerung zwischen zehn und fünfzehntausend–"

„Moment. Tut mir leid, dass ich Sie schon wieder unterbreche, aber Sie haben fünfzehntausend gesagt.“ Ich kannte die Bevölkerungszahl bereits von meinem Gespräch mit ihrem Anführer, aber es gab mir eine weitere Möglichkeit, nachzubohren.

„Ja, Sir.“

„Ich weiß nur von vier Schiffen, die von Cappa geflohen sind. Ausgeschlossen, dass sie so viele Leute an Bord hatten. Nicht bei dieser Entfernung. Sie hätten Cryo gebraucht.“ Ein großer Truppentransport konnte Hunderttausende transportieren, aber die Schiffe, die Cappa verlassen hatten, waren nicht so groß gewesen. „Gab es mehr Schiffe?“

Jeder im Raum starrte mich an, Tanaka drehte sich dafür sogar auf seinem Stuhl um.

„Was? Glauben Sie, ich wüsste nicht auch ein paar Dinge über das, was auf Cappa passiert ist?“ Ich hatte ein paar Informationen preisgegeben, aber wenn es half, sie aus dem Konzept zu bringen und dazu, sich zu fragen, was ich wusste, war es das allemal wert.

„Ich weiß nicht, wie sie dort hingekommen sind, Sir, aber wir sind uns ziemlich sicher, was die Zahl angeht“, fuhr der Einweiser fort. „Wir haben Satellitenaufnahmen, die zeigen, dass sie hauptsächlich in einer Siedlung leben. Wir haben minimale Bewegungen gesehen, die von diesem Bereich wegführen. Hier ist eine Ansicht.“ Das Bild änderte sich und zeigte ein Dorf, das aus Fertigbauhäusern bestand, in einer flachen Gegend, die von einer Art Erhebung aus Erde umgeben war, beinahe wie eine Schüssel.

„Und wenn wir rauszoomen“, fuhr er fort, „sehen wir, dass sie auf dieser großen Insel sind. Die ist etwa fünfzehntausend Quadratkilometer groß.“

„Insel ... Ich dachte, die Küste käme nicht infrage“, sagte ich.

„Kommt sie auch nicht, Sir“, sagte die Einweiserin von ihrem Platz an der Wand. „Aber diese Insel erhebt sich recht schnell zu etwa tausend Metern Höhe. Eine Reihe Klippen und Steilufer beschützen die Insel vor den Effekten der Flut.“

„Wie läuft die Lebensmittelversorgung? Bringen sie Lebensmittel auf den Planeten oder bauen sie die vor Ort an?“

„Hauptsächlich vor Ort, Sir“, sagte der aktuelle Einweiser. „Es gibt Hinweise darauf, dass sie in den Höhlensystemen anbauen. Die scheinen recht dienlich zu sein, um verschiedene Arten von Pilzen und Flechten zu ziehen, die zum Nahrungsbedarf der Cappaner passen. Wir haben nicht beobachtet, dass Waren von außerhalb des Planeten geliefert wurden.“

„Okay. Ich habe einen guten Überblick über die Beschaffenheit des Geländes. Wie lautet die Mission?“ Ich sah Tanaka an.

„Das wäre alles“, sagte er zu den Einweisern. Sie gingen geordnet durch eine dünne Tür hinaus und schwiegen dabei peinlich berührt.

„Keine weiteren Einweiser?“, fragte ich.

„Sir ... was das betrifft. Es tut mir wirklich leid. Aber wir werden Sie über die Mission briefen, sobald wir an Bord sind.“

Ich starrte ihn einige Sekunden lang an. „Wirklich?“

„Sorry, Sir.“

Seinem Gesichtsausdruck nach zu urteilen war es ihm wirklich unangenehm. Es war nicht seine Idee gewesen, mich im Dunkeln zu lassen. Mir es war egal. Das gab mir Munition, um mich mit ihm anzulegen. Ich hatte kaum ein Druckmittel, also musste ich nutzen, was immer ich hatte. „Nur, um das klarzustellen. Sie sperren mich ein, ich habe keine Möglichkeit der Kommunikation und doch kann man mir immer noch nicht mit der Information vertrauen, was wir zu erreichen versuchen?"

Er wandte den Blick ab. „Das ist korrekt, Sir."

„Was bedeutet, dass es so abgefuckt ist, dass Sie Angst haben ... nein, streichen Sie das. Es bedeutet, dass *jemand* Angst hat, dass ich einen Rückzieher mache."

„Davon weiß ich ehrlich gesagt nichts, Sir. Die Sache scheint mir ziemlich geradeheraus zu sein."

„Sie kennen die Mission also?"

„Ja, Sir." Ich hätte es genau in diesem Moment auf sich beruhen lassen und ihn beim Wort nehmen können, aber ich wollte ein bisschen Druck ausüben und schauen, was passierte.

„Dann erzählen Sie mir davon."

„Sir, ich bin nicht befugt–"

„Sie sagten, die Mission sei geradeheraus."

„Sir, ich kann nicht–"

„Gut, dann komme ich nicht mit", sagte ich. Ich traf die Entscheidung spontan, aber nachdem ich es erst mal ausgesprochen hatte, gefiel mir die Idee. Ich sah keinen Weg aus dem Gebäude, also musste ich für etwas Chaos sorgen und schauen, ob sich irgendwelche Möglichkeiten ergaben.

„Wie bitte, Sir?"

„Sie haben den Befehl, mir nicht zu erzählen, worum es bei der Mission geht. Wie lauten Ihre Befehle, wenn ich mich weigere, das Schiff zu betreten?“

„Sir–“

„Werden Sie mich betäuben? Mich gegen meinen Willen in Kälteschlaf versetzen, mich zu einem Sackgassenplaneten schleifen und hoffen, dass ich tue, was Sie von mir verlangen, wenn wir dort sind? Kommen Sie, Tanaka, ist es das?“

Er wand sich auf seinem Stuhl. Mein Ausbruch war ihm unangenehm, denn obwohl er für die Mission verantwortlich war, war er dazu ausgebildet worden, ranghöheren Offizieren nicht ans Bein zu pissen. „Ich habe keine derartigen Befehle, nein, Sir.“

„Also müssen Sie jemanden anrufen.“

„Ja, Sir.“

„Dann rufen Sie sie an.“

Er zögerte. „Sir, Sie wollen wirklich, dass ich–“

„Was ich wirklich will ist wissen, wieso jemand glaubt, dass eine Gruppe von ausgebildeten Profis einen abgewrackten alten Colonel dabeihaben muss. Und bis mir jemand erzählt, worum es bei der Mission geht, habe ich keine Antwort darauf. Da Sie nicht in der Lage sind, sie mir zu geben, will ich mit jemandem reden, der das kann. Liege ich falsch? Sie brauchen mich nicht für eine einfache Infiltration. Es muss etwas anderes sein.“

Nach einem Moment nickte er. „Ich mache einen Anruf, Sir.“

Ich hatte nicht erwartet, dass mein Ausbruch irgendetwas bewirken würde, und obwohl er spontan gewesen war, hatte ich ihn so getimt, dass nur Tanaka und

Matua zugegen gewesen waren. Matua würde den Mund halten, andernfalls wäre er mir nicht zugeteilt worden. Bei Tanaka konnte ich mich später dafür entschuldigen, mich wie ein Arschloch verhalten zu haben, da niemand anderes es mitangesehen hatte. Wenn ich ihn vor seinen Leuten in Verlegenheit gebracht hätte, wäre das ein ganz anderes Problem gewesen. So oder so war das vermutlich mein letzter Schachzug, ehe die E-Mail an Plazz rausging. Ich war nicht scharf auf diese Option, also griff ich auf das zurück, was ich immer tat: Ich versuchte, dafür zu sorgen, dass etwas passierte. Entweder gab mir das die Gelegenheit, meine Position zu verbessern, oder nicht, aber es schien unwahrscheinlich, dass es sie verschlechtern würde.

Ellen Haverty betrat den Konferenzraum des Ostcampus mit dem Gesichtsausdruck von jemandem, der in einen Haufen Scheiße getreten war. Ich wusste nicht, ob ihre Abneigung mit der dürftigen Einrichtung oder mit mir zu tun hatte, aber ich hatte eine Vermutung. Zumindest setzte sie ein falsches Lächeln auf, als sich unsere Blicke trafen. „Colonel Butler. Und ich dachte, wir hätten unseren Teil der Angelegenheit abgeschlossen.“

„Ms. Haverty. Ich wäre nur zu gern zu Ihnen gekommen oder hätte das hier via Video erledigt. Es tut mir wirklich leid, Ihnen so zur Last zu fallen.“ Ich erwiderte ihr „Ficken Sie sich“-Lächeln.

„Ich finde es dieser Tage am besten, nicht auf Technologie zu vertrauen. Man kann nicht vorsichtig genug sein, wissen Sie?“

„Haben Sie das von Gylika gelernt?“

Ihr Blick versteinerte sich. „Ich bin aus Respekt hier. Das Mindeste, das Sie tun könnten, wäre, sich zivilisiert zu verhalten.“

„Vergeben Sie mir, wenn ich Sie wie eine Erpresserin behandle. Keine Ahnung, wie ich auf die Idee gekommen bin.“ Offenbar verspürte ich nicht das Bedürfnis, mich zivilisiert zu verhalten.

„Passen Sie auf. Sie wollten mit mir reden. Ich hätte nicht herkommen müssen. Ich schlage vor, Sie kommen zum Punkt, ehe ich meine Meinung ändere.“

„Meinetwegen. Ich will wissen, worum es bei der Mission geht.“

Sie setzte sich mir gegenüber auf einen der niedrigpreisigen Bürostühle. „Warum müssen Sie das wissen? Mir wurde gesagt, dass Sie die Details einer Mission nicht wissen wollen, ehe Sie fliegen, da sich Dinge ändern können, während Sie im Kälteschlaf sind, und Sie im Anschluss sowieso Zeit haben, alles zu klären.“

Ich konnte nicht anders, als sie anzulächeln, ungeachtet der Tatsache, dass sie ein übler Troll war. Sie hatte ihre Hausaufgaben gemacht und sie hatte recht. Sie hatte durchschaut, wie ich normalerweise vorging. „Das hier ist anders. Wenn ich zu militärischen Missionen aufbrach, hatte ich immerhin eine Vorstellung davon, was zu erwarten war. Worauf ich gewartet habe, waren die Details. Ich hatte erwartet, Mr. Tanaka würde mir Änderungen mitteilen, wenn wir in zwei oder drei Monaten aus dem Kälteschlaf aufwachen.“

„In einem Monat“, sagte sie. „Sie sind nicht mit einem militärischen Transport unterwegs. Unsere Schiffe sind schneller.“

Ich nickte leicht. „Das weiß ich zu schätzen. Dann hat man es schneller hinter sich."

„In der Tat."

„Hier ist mein Problem. So wie ich es jetzt verstehe, ergibt diese Mission keinen Sinn. Es gibt Tausende Cappaner und wir gehen mit zweihundert Leuten rein. Das sind nicht genug Truppen, um die Cappaner dazu zu kriegen, etwas rauszugeben, wenn sie das nicht wollen. Es sind zu wenige für einen Kampf, zu viele für eine Infiltration."

„Deswegen schicken wir Sie. Um zu verhandeln."

Ich hatte darüber nachgedacht, wie ich das anstellen würde. Wir würden damit drohen, den Planeten aus dem All in die Luft zu jagen und das als Druckmittel verwenden. Dann würde es davon abhängen, wie gut und glaubhaft ich den Cappanern das vermitteln könnte. Das Ganze berücksichtigte nicht, dass ich auch mit den Cappanern zusammenarbeitete, was die bereits lächerlich vertrackte Situation noch komplizierter machte. „Sie brauchen mich bei dieser Mission nicht", sagte ich. „Tanaka wird Ihnen das bestätigen. Tatsächlich wäre er verdammt glücklich, wenn ich ihm nicht über die Schulter schauen würde."

„Ich pflege meine Angestellten nicht nach Ihrer Meinung zu meinen Entscheidungen zu fragen. Wir bezahlen Mr. Tanaka sehr gut. Es ist mir egal, ob er glücklich ist, solange er den Job erledigt."

„Bei einer militärischen Mission sollten Sie vielleicht ... Sie wissen schon ... auf die Jungs vom Militär hören."

Sie lächelte mich an wie eine Mutter, die ihrem Kind seinen Willen lässt. „Ich werde darüber nachdenken."

„Das war's also? Sie sind den ganzen Weg hierhergekommen, um mir zu sagen, dass Sie mir nichts über die Mission sagen? Das hätten Sie auch von Ihrem Büro aus tun können."

Sie beobachtete mich ein paar Sekunden lang. „Ich hielt es für nötig, mir das selbst anzusehen. Manchmal muss man das als Führungskraft tun. Ich bin mir sicher, dass Sie das verstehen."

„Ich brauche mehr als das."

„Ach, Carl. Sie sind ein kluger Mann. Wir wissen beide, dass Sie kein Druckmittel haben." Sie stand auf.

Ich stand ebenfalls auf, stemmte die Hände auf den Tisch und lehnte mich vor. „In Ordnung. Ohne weitere Informationen komme ich nicht mit."

„Das meinen Sie nicht ernst. Ich habe Ms. Ganos von einem Team lokalisieren lassen. Ich bluffe nicht."

Shit. „Dann sagen Sie mir wenigstens eins", sagte ich. „Wann hat Javier sich mit Ihnen zusammengetan? War das von Anfang an der Plan?"

Es sah aus, als würde sie darüber nachdenken, ob sie es mir sagen sollte oder nicht. „Kurz nachdem Mr. Gylika gestorben war, hat er mich kontaktiert. Sie sollten ihm danken, falls Sie ihn je wiedersehen. Ich wollte Sie eliminieren lassen. Javier hat mich davon überzeugt, dass Sie nützlich sein könnten."

„Klar werde ich mich bei ihm bedanken, wenn ich ihn sehe."

„Seien Sie nicht so traurig. Das ist eine großartige Gelegenheit." Etwas an ihrem herablassenden Tonfall ließ mich durchdrehen.

„Ich tue es nicht." Ich hatte bis zu diesem Moment nicht vorgehabt, sie herauszufordern, aber je mehr ich darüber nachdachte, desto mehr glaubte ich, dass sie ihre Ganos-Karte nicht spielen würde. Wenn sie das tat, hatte sie kein weiteres Druckmittel mehr gegen mich in der Hand. Sie wusste das.

„Also gut, machen wir es auf Ihre Tour." Sie drückte einen Knopf an ihrem Device und vier Wachen in grauen Uniformen eilten zur Tür herein. Sie trugen Helme. Verfickte Helme. Als wäre ich eine Bedrohung. Zwei von ihnen kamen um den Tisch herum, einer von links, einer von rechts, und ich nahm die Hände über den Kopf.

Ich sah Matua in die Augen, der sich von der Wand abgestoßen hatte und nun einsatzbereit dastand, sich aber nicht bewegt hatte, um die anstürmenden Wachen aufzuhalten. Er zuckte mit den Schultern, als wolle er „Sorry" sagen.

„Locker, Jungs", sagte ich und beäugte den Betäubungsstab, den ein kleiner, gedrungener Mann in der Hand hielt. „Schlagen Sie mich nicht mit dem Betäubungsstab. Keiner von uns wird das Ergebnis mögen."

„Ich bin auch aus einem anderen Grund hergekommen", sagte Haverty.

„Weswegen?", fragte ich.

„Ich wollte Ihr Gesicht sehen, wenn ich Ihnen erzähle, dass wir Ihre E-Mail gehackt haben. Wir haben die Verschlüsselung noch nicht geknackt, um zu sehen, was Sie geschrieben haben, aber wir haben gesehen, dass sie in weniger als zwei Tagen automatisch an eine Reporterin rausgehen sollte. Ich hoffe, das war nicht wichtig."

Ich setzte zu einer Antwort an, aber eine große weibliche Wache kam mir zuvor und drückte etwas gegen

meinen Arm. Ich spürte einen stechenden Schmerz,
dann nichts mehr. Autoinjektor.

„Was war das verf–"

Die Welt um mich herum wurde schwarz.

Kapitel fünfundzwanzig

Ich erwachte mit einem Kater, Schwindel und einem trockenen Hals, das Resultat der Stasis während einer Reise durchs All. Diese Bastarde hatten mich betäubt, bis wir für den Trip in Stasis versetzt wurden. Ich nahm mir einen Moment Zeit, um meine Umgebung zu sondieren. Leute, die aus der Stasis erwachten, neigten dazu, ein paar Stunden unbeweglich zu sein und nichts mitzubekommen, also würde niemand vermuten, dass ich schon komplett wieder da war.

Fünf oder sechs Leute bewegten sich durch eine teuer aussehende Reisesuite. Gemütlich aussehende, schwarze Ruhesessel säumten eine Wand und kleine, funktionale Stehtische die andere. Mindestens eine Person war noch nicht aus ihrer Stasis erwacht und saß wie ich in ihrer Röhre. Drei Leute standen um einen kleinen Kombüsenbereich herum und der Geruch frischen Kaffees schwebte durch die Kabine.

„Sind Sie wieder da, Colonel?", fragte Tanakas Stimme.

„Das kommt darauf an", sagte ich mit kratziger Stimme. „Gibt es noch Kaffee."

„Ja."

„Sie Arschlöcher haben mich unter Drogen gesetzt", sagte ich.

„Zu meiner Verteidigung muss ich sagen, dass ich dagegen gestimmt habe. Ms. Haverty hört nicht immer zu.“

„Das glaube ich gern.“ Er hätte es nicht befohlen, da er wusste, dass er mit mir würde zusammenarbeiten müssen. Ich musste auch mit ihm arbeiten, also ließ ich es auf sich beruhen. Das All ist ein kalter Ort, und kein guter, um sich Feinde zu machen. „Wie lange waren wir weg?“

„Etwas länger als einen Monat“, sagte Tanaka. „Wir verlangsamen gerade auf unter etwas weniger als ein G, weswegen wir aufstehen und rumlaufen können.“

„Großartig“, sagte ich.

„Die Dusche ist am Ende des Abteils, und wenn Sie fertig sind, gibt es Kekse und Bratensoße.“

Mein Magen freute sich. Endlich jemand, der Reisen durchs All verstand. Es machte mich so glücklich, dass es mir egal war, dass sie vermutlich Leute kontaktiert hatten, die mich kannten, um herauszufinden, ob ich das Essen mochte. Ich nahm an, dass sie alles wussten, was ich je getan hatte. Das machte es einfacher. Ich musste mir nicht den Dienstplan der Soldaten ansehen, die an Bord waren. Omicron hatte das bereits getan und dafür gesorgt, dass keiner von ihnen je mit mir gedient hatte. Es klingt seltsam, aber das gab mir ein angenehmes Gefühl. Es ist immer schön zu wissen, dass man mit Profis arbeitet, auch wenn es einem im Moment keinen Vorteil bringt.

Die Dusche hatte den besten Wasserdruck, den ich je auf einem Schiff erlebt hatte, und ich genehmigte mir dreißig extra Sekunden. Ich hätte mich daran gewöhnen können, kommerziell zu reisen. Ich zog mir die Arbeitsuniform an, die jemand bereitgelegt hatte – sie passte perfekt – und ging wieder hinaus in den Hauptbereich. Ich zählte acht Leute, mich ausgeschlossen. Das war also die Führungsriege. Die Fußsoldaten reisten vermutlich auf einem anderen Schiff, das weniger fürstlich und komfortabel war als unseres. Ich wettete, dass es dennoch besser war als ein Standardschiff des Militärs.

Während ich mich durch den Raum zu meinen geliebten Keksen bewegte, machte ich es mir zur Aufgabe, mit jedem, an dem ich vorbeikam, Augenkontakt aufzunehmen und ihn oder sie anzulächeln. Ich brauchte Verbündete und wenn das nicht klappte, brauchte ich angesichts der Möglichkeit eines bevorstehenden Kampfes Leute, die mir nicht in den Rücken schossen. Ein kleiner Mann mit dunkler Haut nickte und erwiderte das Lächeln, also blieb ich stehen.

„Ich bin mir nicht sicher, was die Rangabzeichen bedeuten", sagte ich, obwohl ich es ziemlich gut durchschaute. „Zwei Kreise, das bedeutet …"

„Lieutenant, Sir. Lieutenant Darce Jackson."

„Schön, Sie kennenzulernen, Jackson. Ich bin–"

Er lachte. „Ich weiß, wer Sie sind, Sir. Jeder in der Galaxis weiß das."

Ich tat so, als würde ich zusammenzucken, und sog Luft ein. „Ja. Das ist nicht so toll, wie alle denken."

Er lachte wieder. „Hat aber vermutlich auch seine Vorteile."

„Ich weiß nicht. Es hat mich aufs selbe Schiff gebracht wie Sie."

„Stimmt“, sagte er. „Lassen Sie sich von mir nicht aufhalten, Sir. Das Essen ist heiß.“

Ich lächelte erneut und berührte ihn am Oberarm. „Danke.“

Ich schnappte mir einen Plastikteller, bedeckte ihn mit Keksen und verteilte dann lebensspendende Bratensoße darauf. Ich stopfte mir etliche Kekse in den Mund, ehe ich es zu einem Tisch schaffte, und der elende Kälteschlaf-Kater begann nachzulassen. Der Effekt mag nur in meinem Kopf stattgefunden haben, aber das war mir egal. Ich stellte meine Beute auf dem Tisch ab, an dem Tanaka mit einem seiner Lieutenants stand. Ich wollte die anderen kennenlernen, aber den Kommandanten zu ignorieren, wäre unangebracht gewesen. Es wäre den Leuten aufgefallen und es hätte gewirkt, als behandelte ich ihn geringschätzig. Das würde Leute dazu zwingen, sich für eine Seite zu entscheiden, und ich zahlte ihren Sold nicht. Eine Konfrontation konnte ich mir noch nicht leisten.

Tanaka erwartete vermutlich, dass ich nach Informationen über die Mission fragen oder mich noch etwas mehr darüber beklagen würde, wie sie mich schanghait hatten, also wählte ich einen anderen Kurs. „Holen Sie alle so früh aus der Stasis oder nur die Offiziere?“

„Fürs Erste nur uns, Sir. Wir holen die Truppen etwa acht Stunden bevor wir den Orbit erreichen aus dem Kälteschlaf, sodass sie Zeit haben, sich zu erholen.“

„Ist Matua dabei?“ Ich mochte den großen Corporal, trotz der Tatsache, dass er sozusagen mein Gefängniswärter war.

„Ist er“, sagte Tanaka. „Er wird während der Mission für Ihre Sicherheit verantwortlich sein.“

„Gut." Ich deutete auf die uns umgebende Opulenz und sprach dann mit einem Mund voll Keksen. „Nette Bude."

„Ja, Sir. Besser als mit dem Militär zu reisen, oder nicht?"

„Wenn wir so gereist wären, wäre ich vielleicht dabeigeblieben. Schneller ist es auch. Obwohl ich nicht weiß, an welchem Tag wir gestartet sind."

Tanaka lächelte und hielt es für den beabsichtigten Witz. „Es war schnell, Sir. Und als wir gestartet sind, waren Sie weniger als einen Tag bewusstlos."

Ich nickte, während ich einen Schluck des wundervollen Kaffees nahm.

„Das ist meine zweite Offizierin, Chelsea Larsson."

„Sir." Die Frau, die mit uns aß, war einen Kopf kleiner als ich, und ich bin nicht groß. Sie starrte mich mit einem Blick an, der härter war als der Rumpf eines Raumschiffs.

„Bleiben Sie auf dem Schiff und befehligen hier, wenn wir runtergehen, oder sind Sie ein kämpfender XO?", fragte ich. Es war keine Beleidigung. Die Stellvertreterin hatte zwei Optionen, was es zu einer legitimen Frage machte.

Ihr Gesichtsausdruck wurde für einen Moment sanfter und strahlte Stolz aus. „Ich kämpfe, Sir. Der Stabsoffizier bemannt das Schiff."

„Gut zu hören. Ich bevorzuge es so." Ich hätte dasselbe gesagt, egal wie sie geantwortet hätte. Ich wandte mich an Tanaka. „Wie sind Sie für den Kampf organisiert?"

„Wir haben vier Platoons, Sir. Jeweils vierzig Soldaten, angeführt von einem Lieutenant. Der XO geht auf den Planeten, wie sie schon sagte, und ich natürlich auch. Der Stabsoffizier bleibt auf dem Schiff und die Nachrichtenoffizierin kann beides machen. Ich tendiere dazu, sie für diese Sache mitzunehmen."

„Ich glaube, das ergibt Sinn. Wir werden von hier oben nicht viel mitbekommen, also schafft man sie runter auf den Planeten, wo die Informationen sind. Man verliert zwar etwas an analytischer Leistung, aber sie kann ihrem Team auf dem Schiff Informationen zukommen lassen und sie via Reachback abrufen."

„Ja, Sir. Genau so habe ich mir das gedacht."

Ich kicherte. „Schauen Sie mich nur an, wie ich versuche, Ihre Mission zu übernehmen. Sie haben alles im Griff."

Er lächelte wieder und es sah echt aus. Gut. Meine Zustimmung bedeutete ihm immer noch etwas. Das würde ich brauchen. „Ich bin für alles offen, was Sie anzubieten haben, Sir."

„Macht es Ihnen was aus, wenn ich ein bisschen rumlaufe und das Team kennenlerne? Das Schlimmste daran, aus dem Dienst auszuscheiden, ist, dass man sich nicht mehr mit Soldatinnen und Soldaten unterhalten kann."

„Nur zu. Sobald sich alle erholt haben und wir Gelegenheit hatten, durchzugehen, was sich im letzten Monat ereignet hat, setzen wir uns für ein Missionsbriefing zusammen."

„Keine Eile", sagte ich. Ich deutete ihm mit einem Kopfnicken an, sich von seiner Stellvertreterin zu entfernen, damit ich vertraulich mit ihm sprechen konnte. Er tat es. „Wie ist meine Kommunikationssituation?

Senden und erhalten? Ich will vor den Junior-Offizieren keine große Sache daraus machen, aber ich muss es wissen."

„Ich weiß das zu schätzen, Sir", sagte Tanaka. „Erhalten ist kein Problem. Alle Übertragungen, die wir kriegen, bekommen Sie auch. Senden geht nicht."

Ich nickte. „Okay. Die Leute werden sich aber fragen, wo ich bin."

„Sorry, Sir. Ich muss darauf vertrauen, dass jemand zu Hause einen Plan hat, um damit fertigzuwerden."

„Meinetwegen." Ich hatte die Antwort gekannt, ehe ich gefragt hatte, aber ich wollte, dass er ein Nein aussprach, sodass es auf ihm lastete, wenn ich ihn das nächste Mal um etwas bat. Außerdem wollte ich mich absichern, wenn ich die Nachrichten checkte. Ich musste sehen, ob über mein Verschwinden berichtet worden war, oder wenigstens die Geschichte finden, die sie sich ausgedacht hatten. Wenn es bekannt geworden war, würde ich wahrscheinlich so oder so davon erfahren. Vermutlich dann, wenn sie mich durch eine Luftschleuse ins All pusteten. Tanaka hatte noch keinen derartigen Befehl erhalten. Wenn er mich tot sehen wollte, hätte er das erledigen können, während ich im Kälteschlaf gewesen war.

„Ich weiß Ihre Kooperation zu schätzen, Sir. Sie hätten es mir viel schwerer machen können."

„Das hat jetzt keinen Zweck mehr", sagte ich. „Welche Geschichte haben Sie Ihren Leuten erzählt, weshalb ich so früh im Kälteschlaf war? Das muss seltsam gewesen sein."

„Ich habe ihnen gesagt, dass Sie abergläubisch und gerne der erste im Kälteschlaf sind. Ich machte eine vage Andeutung auf etwas, das bei einer früheren Mission passiert ist."

Ich schnaubte. „Das haben sie Ihnen abgekauft?"

„Sir, wenn ich ihnen erzählen würde, dass Sie fliegen können, würden sie mir glauben. Sie sind für die meisten von der Truppe überlebensgroß."

„Hauptsache, sie werfen mich nicht von einem Gebäude runter, um das zu testen", sagte ich.

Er lachte. „Richtig. Sir, wenn es Ihnen nichts ausmacht, ich muss die letzten geheimdienstlichen Informationen durchgehen, ehe wir den Rest des Teams briefen. Wenn Sie mich entschuldigen würden?"

„Aber sicher. Es ist Ihre Show. Ich werde die Nachrichten checken. Es passiert eine Menge, wenn man einen Monat lang schläft."

Ich überflog die Schlagzeilen der größten Seiten aus dem vergangenen Monat und hielt nach allem Ausschau, das mir einen Hinweis darauf geben könnte, wo ich stand. Ich wollte wissen, was Plazz herausgefunden hatte, und ich wollte Neuigkeiten über Gylika lesen, aber ich wollte keine Suchbegriffe eingeben. Sie erlaubten mir, das System zu benutzen, aber ich machte mir keine Illusionen. Sie überwachten mich. Ich klickte zur Tarnung auf wahllose Links, und die halfen mir, auf den neusten Stand zu kommen und den letzten Monat aufzuholen. Das Erste, was mir auffiel, war Teil der Wirtschaftsnachrichten. Omicron und VPC hatten ein gemeinschaftliches Projekt bekanntgegeben. Der Artikel war zwei Absätze lang und ihm fehlten Details, aber er deutete an, dass sie mit dem Militär zusammen an Medizintechnologie arbeiten würden.

Das war es also. Man musste kein Genie sein, um herauszufinden, an welchem Projekt sie zusammenarbeiten würden. *Ich* war das gemeinschaftliche Projekt … wir waren das … unsere Mission war es. Wir würden die Technologie zurückbringen und die beiden Unternehmen, die mich hierhergebracht hatten, würden davon profitieren. Haverty hatte gesagt, dass ich Javier danken sollte, aber ich fühlte mich nicht sonderlich nachsichtig. Ich glaubte ihr aber, was den Zeitpunkt seiner Kontaktaufnahme betraf. Jetzt, wo ich daran zurückdachte, fiel mir auf, dass er sich nach Gylikas Tod verändert hatte. Ob Haverty ihm ein Angebot gemacht und er mich gegen Unternehmensprofit getauscht oder mich verkauft hatte, um den eigenen Arsch zu retten, würde ich vermutlich nie erfahren. Und ich wusste immer noch nicht, welche Rolle sie beim weiteren Vorgehen für mich vorsahen. Soviel war sicher: Ich befand mich in einer misslichen Lage, da ich mich in potenziell feindliches Gebiet begab, wo mich beide Seiten tot sehen wollten. Aber ich hatte eigene Pläne. Bei den meisten ging es darum, ihre Pläne auf jede erdenkliche Art und Weise zu durchkreuzen, obwohl das in Wahrheit wohl eher eine Absichtserklärung als ein tatsächlicher Aktionsplan war.

Ich rief die Seite der *Galactic Times* auf, bei der Plazz arbeitete, und tat so, als würde ich lesen, während ich sie nach ihrem Namen überflog. Sie hatte einen großen Artikel über einen Regierungsvertreter, der seine Stellung offenbar genutzt hatte, um dem Unternehmen seiner Geliebten Kunden zu verschaffen, aber kein Wort über Omicron, kein Wort über mich. Ich glaubte Haverty, dass sie meine Nachricht abgefangen hatten, und ich nahm an, dass sie sie decodiert hatten, obwohl das schwer gewesen sein musste, weil ich sie Ende-zu-Ende-verschlüsselt hatte.

Ich suchte weiter. Ich weiß nicht, was ich bei meiner allgemeinen Suche zu finden erwartete. Ich vermute, dass ich die leise Hoffnung hegte, dass Plazz mich zu kontaktieren versucht, mich nicht gefunden und nachzuforschen begonnen hatte.

Schließlich entschied ich, es zu riskieren und Gylikas Namen zu suchen. Ich hatte es Haverty bei unserem letzten Treffen an den Kopf geworfen, also würde es mich schwerlich weiter belasten, wenn ich jetzt nachsah. Es brachte nichts. Das jüngste Ergebnis war von einem Datum, das vor meiner Gefangennahme durch Omicron lag. Der Fall war vollkommen aus der Öffentlichkeit verschwunden. Ich schüttelte den Kopf.

„Was ist los, Sir?“, fragte ein Lieutenant, der am Terminal neben mir saß. Sie sah zu mir herüber, obwohl ihre schlanken Finger weiter über die Tasten flogen.

„Ach, nichts“, sagte ich. „Ein Freund von mir ist ein paar Wochen, bevor wir geflogen sind, gestorben. Ich hatte gehofft, dass etwas in den Nachrichten stünde.“

„Oh, das ist traurig“, sagte sie. „Wie ist er gestorben?“

„Mord“, sagte ich. Es war besser, so nah wie möglich bei der Wahrheit zu bleiben.

„Das ist schrecklich!“

„Die Stadt kann hart sein. Was ist mit Ihnen? Irgendwelche guten Neuigkeiten von zu Hause?“ Ich wollte zu den Offizieren eine Beziehung aufbauen, aber nicht auf der Grundlage des Mordes.

„Nicht viel, Sir. Immer das Gleiche. Mein Freund besteigt nächste Woche einen Fünftausender. Ich schätze, das ist die größte Sache.“

„Nice. Klettern Sie auch?“

„Wenn ich die Gelegenheit kriege, Sir. Aber nichts so Großes. Ich bin zu viel im All. Das macht es schwer, in Form zu bleiben.“

„Sicher“, sagte ich. „Wo wir gerade davon reden: Gibt es auf dieser Kiste ein Fitnessstudio?“

„Ja, Sir. Ein kleines. Aber wir werden kaum lange genug im All sein, um es zu benutzen, wenn alles nach Plan läuft.“

„Straffer Zeitplan? Ich wurde noch nicht gebrieft.“

„Ein Tag, bis wir den Orbit erreichen, dann zwölf Stunden später ein schneller Abstecher auf die Oberfläche.“

„Hm. Schätze, wir sind in Eile.“

„Schwer zu sagen bei diesen Unternehmenseinsätzen. Aber der Sold ist unschlagbar.“

„Ist er.“ Ich fragte mich einen Moment lang, ob VPC mich immer noch bezahlte. Vermutlich taten sie es, als Tarnung. Es würde mir Spaß machen, ihr Geld auszugeben, wenn ich die Sache überlebte.

Ich überflog noch ein paar Nachrichten, langweilte mich aber und entschied, mir das Fitnessstudio anzusehen. Oder zu schauen, ob das Schiff eine Bar hatte. Das eine oder das andere, ganz sicher. Ich schlängelte mich an den Kälteschlaf-Kabinen vorbei in Richtung Rückseite des Schiffs, als Larsson vor mich trat und mir den Weg versperrte.

„Ich durchschaue, was Sie vorhaben, Sir.“ Ihre Stimme war eiskalt.

„Tut mir leid, habe ich etwas falsch gemacht?“

„Mit den Offizieren. Ich durchschaue, was Sie vorhaben. Sie sind nett zu ihnen und versuchen, sich einzuschmeicheln.“

„Hätten Sie es lieber, wenn ich ein Arschloch wäre? Ich verfüge auch über diese Fähigkeit.“ Ich lächelte und verbarg mein Unbehagen darüber, dass ich mich so offensichtlich verhalten hatte. Nicht dass es eine Rolle gespielt hätte.

„Glauben Sie ja nicht, dass Captain Tanaka der Einzige ist, der weiß, was mit Ihnen los ist. Er ist der Kommandant. Er muss nett zu Ihnen sein. Aber ich? Ich beobachte Sie, und ich würde Ihnen genauso gern ins Gesicht schießen wie Sie nach Hause zurück zu schleppen.“

„Okay. Larsson. Gutes Gespräch.“ Sie blickte mich einige Sekunden lang wütend an, ehe sie mir aus dem Weg ging. So viel dazu, mir keine Feinde zu machen.

Ich versuchte, Larsson nicht anzusehen, als sich die Offiziere fürs Briefing versammelten, um die Mission durchzusprechen, aber sie durchbohrte mich mit ihren Blicken und machte das schwierig. Wenn es irgendjemand anderem auffiel, sagten sie nichts. Ich hoffte, dass sie und ich auf verschiedenen Schiffen fliegen würden. Tanaka würde mich vermutlich an seiner Seite haben wollen, und der Kommandant und der XO flogen nie zusammen, also bekäme ich meinen Wunsch vermutlich erfüllt.

„Wir gehen in vier Schiffen runter, zu diesem Landepunkt hier“, sagte Tanaka und deutete auf eine Holo-Karte. „Von dort aus bewegen wir uns in Platoons entlang dieser vier Routen.“ Vier farblich gekennzeichnete

Wege leuchteten auf, die über etliche bewaldete Hügel führten. Jede Route war zwischen fünfzehn und zwanzig Kilometer lang. Es sah nach einem elenden Weg aus, aber die niedrige Gravitation und die energiebetriebenen Anzüge würden helfen. Ich fragte mich, wieso er eine Landezone gewählt hatte, die so weit vom Ziel entfernt lag. Unter normalen Umständen hätte ich gefragt, da es mir wie ein fehlerhafter Plan vorkam, aber ich wollte die Aufmerksamkeit nicht auf mich ziehen.

Tanaka ließ den potenziellen Feind auf der Karte in Rot aufleuchten und es wurde deutlicher. „Wir landen außerhalb der uns bekannten cappanischen Gebiete, und werden uns so nah wie möglich an den erwarteten Zielort heranwagen. Wenn wir nicht angreifen müssen, tun wir es nicht. Lassen Sie mich das ganz klar sagen. Die gestohlenen Daten zurückzuholen und dabei keinen Schuss abzugeben würde ich als vollen Erfolg betrachten.“

Einer der Gruppenführer schnaubte, ein großer fleischiger Typ, den ich noch nicht kennengelernt hatte. „Das sind Cappaner. Ausgeschlossen, dass es friedlich läuft.“

„Das wissen wir nicht“, sagte Tanaka. „Es sind Wissenschaftler. Und deswegen landen wir außerhalb ihres hauptsächlichen Siedlungsbereichs. So haben sie genug Zeit, sich damit anzufreunden, dass wir kommen. Ich will nicht aus Versehen in ein Feuergefecht geraten.“

„Es sind verdammte Cappaner, Sir.“ Der fleischige Typ warf mir einen Blick zu, aber ich hielt keinen Augenkontakt. Er war vermutlich ein treuer Anhänger dessen, was ich auf Cappa getan hatte. Er war vermutlich ein Arschloch. Aber wenn ich mich zwischen ihm und Larsson entscheiden müsste, würde ich ihn wählen. Besser ein Arschloch, das mich mochte, als jemand, der mich vielleicht erschoss. Trotzdem musste ich ihn ja nicht ermutigen.

Tanaka blaffte ihn an. „Haben Sie den Befehl verstanden, Jurcovik?"

„Ja, Sir", sagte Fleischi.

„Gut. Wenn wir uns der Hauptsiedlung nähern, hier", sagte er und ließ ein Icon grün aufleuchten, „werden drei Platoons von diesen Positionen aus Feuerschutz geben." Drei Ovale leuchteten auf. „Ich, Colonel Butler und das erste Platoon werden an die Cappaner herantreten und versuchen, eine friedliche Herausgabe der erforderten Daten auszuhandeln. Sobald wir bestätigt haben, dass wir die richtigen Informationen haben ... eine Aufgabe, die etwa fünfunddreißig Minuten dauern wird, wegen der Übertragungsverzögerung ... wird sich unsere Einheit als erste entfernen, gefolgt von den Feuerschutz-Platoons. Der Abholort ist hier."

Er deutete auf einen anderen Punkt, etwa fünf Kilometer vom Ziel entfernt. Ich vermutete, dass er erwartete, der Abflug würde reibungsloser laufen als die Landung. Wahrscheinlicher war, dass er nicht wusste, wie die Landung verlaufen würde. Wenn wir uns drauf vorbereiteten, den Planeten zu verlassen, würden wir auf die eine oder andere Weise wissen, was die Cappaner dachten. Wenn es zu einem Kampf kam, würden wir spontan umdisponieren und einen geeigneten Abholort suchen.

„Die übrigen Informationen, einschließlich alternativer Landezonen, Notfallpläne und was Sie sonst gebrauchen könnten, finden Sie in Ihren Devices. Irgendwelche Fragen?“

Ich hatte kein Tablet, also war ich den anderen gegenüber im Nachteil. Aber anders als die anderen, für die „irgendwelche Fragen“ eine rhetorische Frage war, konnte ich tatsächlich eine Frage stellen. „Was haben wir für Feuerschutz? Luftunterstützung, Feuer aus dem Orbit, so was?“

„Wir haben eine Formation aus zwei schnellen Angriffsschiffen, Sir“, sagte Tanaka. „Das Schiff, auf dem wir sind, hat Raketen, aber nichts, das wir aus der Nähe einsetzen wollen. Wir sind hauptsächlich auf uns allein gestellt. Am Boden haben wir standardisierte Box-Raketen und schultergestützte.“

Ich nickte. Das änderte meine Meinung über die Mission nicht, aber ich wusste immer gern, was wir hatten, für den Fall, dass die Sache in die Hose ging. Denn für gewöhnlich gingen Sachen in die Hose. Tanaka hatte nicht spezifiziert, was für Raketen es waren, aber dass er gesagt hatte, dass wir sie nicht aus der Nähe einsetzen würden, erregte meine Aufmerksamkeit. Ich machte mir eine gedankliche Notiz, zu checken, über welche Bewaffnung das Schiff verfügte. Da es ein Nichtregierungsschiff war, sollte es gar keine haben. Andererseits hätte es als Nichtregierungsschiff auch nicht eine aus hundertsechzig bis an die Zähne bewaffneten Soldaten bestehende Angriffstruppe an Bord haben dürfen.

Ich nahm Tanaka beiseite, nachdem das Briefing vorüber war. „Ich wollte vor den Soldaten keine weiteren

Fragen stellen, aber ich habe eine wichtige. Was passiert, wenn sie uns die Daten nicht geben? Wir können sie nicht aus ihnen rausschießen."

„Wir hoffen, dass es nicht dazu kommt, aber wir haben zwei Spezialisten für Datenrückgewinnung in der Crew. Larsson ist eine Spezialistin, der andere ist ein Fußsoldat, der noch schläft."

„Larsson macht Datenrückgewinnung?"

„Sie ist eine der besten", sagte er. „Wieso ist das überraschend?"

„Sie scheint auf mich nicht der Typ zu sein. Außerdem ist sie XO. Sie hat eine andere Mission."

„Wir sind alle übergreifend ausgebildet", sagte er. Er musste etwas in meinem Gesichtsausdruck gesehen haben, weil er die Stirn für eine Sekunde in Falten legte, ehe er sich fing. „Kommen Sie, Sir. Die Bar ist geöffnet. Ich lade Sie auf Omicrons Rechnung auf einen Drink ein."

„Ich könnte mich an dieses kommerzielle Söldnerleben gewöhnen", sagte ich.

Wenn ich nur nicht entführt worden wäre, um daran teilzuhaben.

Kapitel sechsundzwanzig

Ich wartete, bis sie die Truppen aus dem Kälteschlaf geholt hatten, ehe ich herumzuschnüffeln begann. Die zusätzlichen Leute, die sich auf dem Schiff bewegten, gaben mir immerhin ein wenig Schutz vor den neugierigen Blicken von Larsson, die mich zu ihrem persönlichen Projekt gemacht hatte. Ich ließ meinen Weg zufällig erscheinen, ging durch den Bereich der einfachen Soldaten, schüttelte Hände und machte Fotos mit Soldaten, die um mich herumschwärmten, sobald sie wussten, wer ich war. Der XO konnte starren so viel sie wollte, aber was sollte sie tun? Wenn es zu einer Entscheidung zwischen ihr und mir kam, hatte ich bei den Infanteristen bessere Chancen. Und sie konnte nicht zulassen, dass die Infanteristen es ihr verübelten, ihnen diese (scheinbar) unschuldige Begegnung mit einer echten Berühmtheit zu verwehren. Nicht zuletzt würde, es Omicron schwerfallen, meinen Tod zu vertuschen, wenn viele Fotos von mir im Umlauf waren, angenommen das war es, was sie vorhatten.

Nach einer Weile fand ich Matua, der sich über eine Mahlzeit beugte und mit erschreckender Geschwindigkeit Essen in sich hineinschaufelte. „Hungrig?"

„Hey, Sir! Ja. Aus welchem Grund auch immer verursacht die Stasis, dass ich mich anschließend vollstopfen will."

„Ist bei mir dasselbe", sagte ich.

„Ich hoffe, Sie nehmen mir nicht übel, wie die Dinge in der Einrichtung auf Talca gelaufen sind", sagte er. Ich hegte etwas Groll, aber das war eigentlich nicht fair, da er sowieso nichts dagegen hätte unternehmen können.

„Alles gut", sagte ich. „Sorgen Sie nur dafür, dass Sie das nächste Mal, wenn sich mir jemand nähert, so mit ihm umspringen wie mit dem Fleisch auf Ihrem Teller."

Er lachte und Krümel eines Kekses flogen ihm aus dem Mund. „Alles klar, Sir."

Ich fuhr fort mit meinem Rundgang durch den Bereich der Fußsoldaten und ergriff die Gelegenheit, jeden Soldaten etwas Persönliches zu fragen: wo sie lebten, ob sie verheiratet waren, welche ihre Lieblingssportmannschaft war. Ich fragte jeden und jede, was ihre Aufgabe auf der Mission war, und merkte mir die, die auf dem Schiff blieben – ich hatte Fragen über das Schiff, und niemand wusste mehr darüber, als die Soldaten, die es betrieben. Die Truppen, die auf den Planeten runtergingen, wären mir physisch näher, aber die Leute, die im All blieben, würden mehr über die kritischen Aspekte der Mission wissen.

Nachdem ich mich mit etwa fünfzehn Soldatinnen und Soldaten unterhalten hatte, fand ich endlich eine, die im Schiffsbetrieb arbeitete. Lopez trug ihr schwarzes Haar raspelkurz und hatte eine Narbe direkt unter dem linken Ohr. „Muss nett sein, mit so was Fortschrittlichem unterwegs zu sein", sagte ich.

Sie zuckte mit den Schultern. „Ist okay, Sir. Es ist beinahe zu hübsch, wissen Sie?"

„Angesichts der großartigen Duschen akzeptiere ich, dass es zu hübsch ist", sagte ich.

„Kann man wohl sagen, Sir."

„Sie haben gesagt, dass Sie am Zielsystem arbeiten."

„Ja, Sir."

„Ich kenne mich ein bisschen mit Zielführung aus." Ich lächelte und erlaubte mir beinahe ein Kichern.

Sie lachte. „Ja, Sir. Ich schätze, das stimmt."

„Was haben wir dabei?"

„XB25er, Sir. Vier Stück."

„Heilige Scheiße." Das rutschte mir so raus. XB25er waren leistungsstarke Fusionswaffen. Planetenbrecher. Die Dinger, die ich auf Cappa abgefeuert hatte. „Ich hätte nicht erwartet, dass ein ziviles Schiff so was hat."

„Es ist ein Schiff von Omicron, Sir. Wer, glauben Sie, stellt die Dinger her?"

Shit. Ich hatte nie darüber nachgedacht, aber *Omicron* stellte die XB25er her. Nicht dass es eine Rolle spielte. Was eine Rolle spielte, war, dass wir sie auf dem Schiff hatten, was bedeutete, dass jemand glaubte, sie hätten hier einen Zweck. Sie hatten sie nicht aus Versehen geladen. Mich durchfuhr ein Schaudern. Ich fragte mich, ob sie ein letzter Ausweg waren oder ihr Einsatz der eigentliche Plan. Angesichts des kleinen Bereichs der Insel, auf der die Cappaner lebten, konnten vier XB25er alles in Schutt und Asche legen, wenn man richtig zielte, und niemand würde überleben.

Lopez starrte mich an und mir wurde bewusst, dass ich zu lange nichts gesagt hatte. „Nun, hoffen wir, dass wir sie nicht einsetzen müssen."

„Ja, Sir. Hoffen wir es."

Ich entschuldigte mich, als Lieutenant Danner an uns vorbeiging. Er war acht bis zehn Zentimeter größer als alle anderen und hatte außerordentlich dunkle Haut. Für mich war er interessant, weil er der Stabsoffizier war und das Schiff befehligen würde, wenn wir auf den Planeten runtergingen. Bis Tanaka und der XO wieder auf dem Schiff waren, hatte Danner den Finger am Abzug der XB25er.

„Hey Danner, waren Sie in Ihrer Zeit bei der richtigen Army Unteroffizier?", fragte ich. Er sah ein bisschen zu alt aus für einen Lieutenant, also war es eine naheliegende Vermutung.

„Ja, Sir. Ich war Fluglotse."

„Ich mochte FLs immer", sagte ich. „Vermutlich der wichtigste Mann bei einer Mission."

Er lächelte. „Ich habe ein paar Einsätze gehabt, bei denen ich–"

„Colonel Butler?" Larsson warf sich beinahe zwischen uns, als sie uns unterbrach. „Es ist Zeit, dass Sie sich fertigmachen."

Was bedeutete, dass die Zeit, in der ich mich bei der Crew einschmeicheln konnte, vorüber war.

Ich hatte mehr als genug Zeit, um mich für den Trip auf den Planeten vorzubereiten, dank Larsson, die mich von Danner fernhalten wollte. Als wir an Bord gingen, hatte ich dreimal meine Munition gecheckt und war zweimal auf die Toilette gegangen. In meinem Alter lasse ich mir keine Gelegenheit entgehen. Ich schnallte mich an, hinter mir das vordere Schott, Tanaka neben mir. Vor uns saß das erste Platoon in vier Zehnerreihen, zwei jeweils gegenüber voneinander in ein einem der beiden Gänge. Matua saß in der Nähe und sah in meine Richtung, stellte sicher, dass ich mich korrekt angeschnallt hatte. Ich sagte nichts. Jemandem, der mir den Rücken freihielt, würde ich nie sagen, dass er seinen Job weniger ernstnehmen soll.

Die Mission war so beschissen wie eine Kaserne mit kaputter Latrine. Jedes Mal, wenn ich versucht hatte, Tanaka in die Ecke zu drängen und nach Notfallplänen auszufragen – für den Fall, dass unser eigentlicher Plan in die Hose ging –, war Larsson mit irgendeiner Angelegenheit, die seine augenblickliche Aufmerksamkeit erforderte, aus dem Nichts aufgetaucht. Ich hatte es heruntergespielt, aber es hatte einen schlechten Nachgeschmack hinterlassen. Wir landeten in einer Gegend, die voll war von Orten für mögliche Hinterhalte, verfügten aber über wenig Feuerkraft. Der Plan stand und fiel mit der Hoffnung, dass die Cappaner mit uns kooperierten, wozu sie keinen Grund hatten. Ein weiser Mann hat mir mal gesagt, dass Hoffnung keine gute Grundlage für einen Plan ist.

Jetzt, da Larsson weit weg auf einem anderen Schiff und Tanaka neben mir angeschnallt war, konnte er mir endlich nicht mehr entkommen. „Wozu sind die XB25er, Sir?", fragte ich.

„Was meinen Sie, Sir?"

„Die Planetenbrecher. Wieso haben wir die dabei?"

Er zögerte eine halbe Sekunde zu lang. „Für den Fall, Sir. Das ist alles."

Lügner. Wenn sie die Daten hatten und die Cappaner vernichteten, gäbe es niemanden mehr, der hinter ihnen her war. Es gäbe niemanden mehr, der eine andere Geschichte erzählen könnte als die offizielle Omicron-Version. Niemanden außer mir.

Shit.

Ich hatte es schon zuvor vermutet, aber so wie Tanaka es gesagt hatte, war ich mir plötzlich sicher. Ich würde auf diesem Planeten sterben. Ich wusste zu viel. Sie konnten mich nicht in der Zivilisation töten. Das würde zu viele Fragen aufwerfen. Sie hatten diese Lektion nach Gylikas Tod gelernt, und meinen Tod würde man zehn Mal genauer untersuchen als seinen. Aber wenn ich hier draußen starb, konnten sie es so drehen, wie sie wollten. Sie konnten mir sogar die Schuld für die XB25er geben. Ich persönlich hätte mich entschieden für: „Eigenwilliger Colonel konnte sich nicht vom Kampf fernhalten, und nun hat es ihn erwischt." Die Leute würden das glauben. Shit, ich würde es bei nahezu jedem Colonel glauben, den ich je kennengelernt hatte. Die Anziehungskraft war groß. Ich glaube nicht, dass ich gänzlich verstanden hatte, wie mächtig sie war, bis ich die Gelegenheit hatte, zurückzukehren. Dein ganzes Leben tust du große, wichtige Dinge. Du sprichst und Leute hören zu. Dann ist das plötzlich vorbei und du verschwendest dein Leben damit, einen blödsinnigen Job zu machen, der keinen Sinn hat, und bei dem es niemanden kümmert, was du tust, solange du bei den Feierlichkeiten des Unternehmens auftauchst.

Ja, diese Story würde ich glauben. Denn obwohl ich mir über meine Taten im Klaren war und in einem

Schiff saß, das ein potenzielles Kampfgebiet und mein eigenes Ende ansteuerte, musste ich zugeben, dass ich ein bisschen aufgeregt war.

Beinahe fragte ich Tanaka, wie es passieren würde – wie er mich umbringen würde –, aber ich hielt den Mund. Ich wusste, was er tun würde, aber es gab die Möglichkeit, dass er nicht wusste, dass ich das wusste. Nicht nötig, ihm diesen Vorsprung zu geben. Ich hatte nicht viel, aber das hatte ich. Und ich hatte meine zivile Hochgeschwindigkeitsversion einer Bitch, zusammen mit einem Dutzend Magazinen voller Munition. Das war wenigstens etwas.

„Denken Sie, ich kann die Übertragung des Piloten bekommen?" Ich zeigte auf meinen Helm. „Ich fliege ungern, ohne zu wissen, was vor sich geht. Gewohnheit."

„Sicher." Tanaka löste etwas in seinem Helm aus, was die Übertragung in meinem öffnete. „Bereit. Sir, ich will, dass Sie etwas wissen. Unter uns."

„Worum geht es?", fragte ich.

„Ich weiß, dass Sie nicht dumm sind. Ich weiß, wie diese ganze Sache aussehen muss. Aber es ist mir egal, wie die Mission lautet. Ich habe vor, Sir mit uns zurückzubringen. Lebend."

Mich durchfuhr ein Schaudern. Es war, als hätte er meine Gedanken gelesen. Ich dachte einen Moment lang über seine Worte nach, ehe ich antwortete. „Sie wissen, dass Sie dadurch mit Ihrem Arbeitgeber in Konflikt geraten könnten."

„Ich weiß. Ist mir egal."

„Sie sind ein guter Mann, Tanaka. Ich weiß das zu schätzen. Ich bin mir allerdings nicht sicher, ob Ihr XO es genauso sieht."

„Sie befolgt meine Befehle, Sir.“

Ich setzte meinen Helm auf, schloss die Augen und tat so, als würde ich bis zum Start dösen. Vielleicht hatte er gelogen, aber ich bin ein ziemlich guter Menschenkenner, und etwas sagte mir, dass dem nicht so war. Vielleicht war ich wirklich für einen Moment eingenickt – die Art Halbschlaf, bei der man nicht merkt, dass man weg ist –, weil ich zusammenzuckte, als die Pilotin sich durch meinen Ohrhörer zu Wort meldete. Sie hatte eine rauchige Stimme. „Fünfzehn Sekunden bis zum Start.“

Aus Gewohnheit zählte ich im Kopf mit. Das Schiff begann zu vibrieren und dann drückte mich die Bewegung in den Sitz. Nach etwa einer halben Minute wurde der Flug ruhiger und das Schiff glitt gemächlich durchs All.

„Sechs Minuten, bis wir die Atmosphäre erreichen, dreiundzwanzig bis zum Ziel“, sagte die Pilotin. Niemand sonst sprach via Kommunikator. Für mich war das ein gutes Zeichen. Professionelle Einheiten plaudern nicht auf dem Befehlskanal; das tun sie auf Privatkanälen. Ein paar Soldaten checkten ihre Ausrüstung. Ein paar schliefen. Veteranen. Ich nahm die Gelegenheit wahr, um einen privaten Kanal zu Matua zu öffnen.

„Ich will nicht, dass das seltsam wird“, sagte ich, „aber wenn die Sache in die Hose geht und es für mich Zeit ist zu gehen, stellen Sie sich nicht in den Weg.“

„Wovon reden Sie, Sir?“

„Passen Sie auf. Ich weiß nicht, was Sie bereits wissen, und sagen Sie das hier auf keinen Fall weiter. Es ist nicht wahrscheinlich, dass ich die Sache überlebe. Es ist im Interesse Ihres Arbeitgebers, dass ich nicht wiederkomme. Wenn Sie also sehen, wie das passiert, bringen Sie sich in Deckung."

Die Leitung war etliche Sekunden lang tot. „Scheiß drauf, Sir. Meine Mission ist, Sie zu beschützen. Wenn die Sie wollen, müssen sie an mir vorbei."

Ich lächelte in mich hinein. Soldaten blieben trotz der beschissenen Situation Soldaten, und Tanaka und Matua waren gute. Vielleicht hatte ich eine Chance.

Das Schiff ruckte, als wir auf die Atmosphäre trafen, und alles wackelte. Selbst, wenn ich tausend solcher Flüge mitmachen würde, würde ich mich nie an die zähneklappernde Vibration des Wiedereintritts gewöhnen. Oder Eintritt, in diesem Fall.

„Alle Systeme normal", sagte die Pilotin. „Das Wackeln sollte in einer Minute nachlassen."

Wir näherten uns dem Planeten etliche hundert Kilometer von unserem Ziel entfernt und trafen in einem präzisen Winkel auf die Atmosphäre, bis auf etliche Nachkommastellen genau vom Schiffscomputer berechnet. Zumindest war es das, was sie mir sagten. Da ich hinten saß, ohne Fenster, hatte ich keine Möglichkeit, es zu überprüfen. Ich war noch nie mit einem Schiff beim Eintritt explodiert, also gab ich ihnen einen Vertrauensvorschuss.

„Nähern uns der Landezone. Noch zwei Minuten. Das Wetter sieht ... Scheiße! Was war das?"

„Vorsicht!" Eine zweite Stimme. Der Co-Pilot vielleicht. Das Schiff ruckte nach rechts, dann mit einer Rolle wieder nach links. Mein Körper wurde gegen die Gurte geschleudert, als die Bewegung des Schiffs mich in Tanakas Richtung warf. Draußen ein Donnerschlag, gefolgt von einem näheren, unverwechselbaren Knall.

Wir hatten Gegenmaßnahmen gegen Raketen eingeleitet. Leute hatten schon zuvor versucht, mich abzuschießen, und das war kein Geräusch, das ich so bald vergessen würde. Unser Schiff stieß Infrarot- und Radartäuschkörper aus, um feindliche Waffen abzulenken.

„Vier ist getroffen!", sagte die Pilotin, etwas Panik schlich sich in ihre Stimme. Kein Donner. Eine Explosion.

„Was ist da los?", fragte Tanaka, als das Schiff sich stabilisierte. Keine Antwort. Er erhob die Stimme. „Was ist da los?"

Ich legte ihm eine Hand auf den Arm, um auf mich aufmerksam zu machen, und öffnete einen privaten Kanal. „Lassen Sie die Pilotinnen kämpfen. Sie können von hier hinten aus nichts tun, und wenn sie Ihnen antworten müssen, lenkt sie das nur ab."

Er zögerte einen Moment, dann nickte er. Er wusste das, aber ich hatte das Gefühl, dass er länger, als er zugeben wollte, nicht mehr im Gefecht gewesen war.

Es käme allerdings schnell zurück – das tat es immer.

Das Schiff ruckte erneut, unterstrichen vom Knall eines weiteren ausgestoßenen Täuschkörpers. Eine ohrenbetäubende Explosion ließ mich zusammenzucken, und das Schiff machte einen Satz nach links, wie es Flugobjekte nicht tun sollten. Einer der Soldaten erbrach sich zwischen seine Stiefel. Glücklicherweise waren wir aus der Schwerelosigkeit raus. Das wäre sonst übel gewesen.

Shit. Keiner der Geheimdienstberichte hatte Luftabwehrwaffen erwähnt. Ich hätte es besser wissen müssen, anstatt den Informationen über die Cappaner zu vertrauen. Selbst, wenn wir es nach unten schafften, brauchten wir einen neuen Plan. „Wir sind aus der oberen Atmosphäre raus. Schauen Sie, ob Sie das vierte Platoon auftreiben können", sagte ich zu Tanaka.

Er nickte. Die Schiffe hatten Kommunikationssysteme, aber wir hatten auch welche in unseren Helmen, und jetzt, da wir die Interferenzen der oberen Atmosphäre hinter uns gelassen hatten, würden sie funktionieren. Tanaka schaltete zwischen den Frequenzen hin und her und sagte Worte, die ich nicht hören konnte. Vor mir bewegten Soldaten ihre Köpfe vor und zurück. Sie sprachen nicht auf der Frequenz des Schiffs, also konnte ich sie nicht hören, aber jetzt unterhielten sie sich. Panik. Die Angst davor, nicht zu wissen, was verdammt noch mal passiert. Die ist universell. Sie hatten eine leichte Mission erwartet und es war erschreckend klar geworden, dass sie die nicht bekommen würden. Ich hoffte, dass meine frühere Einschätzung, es handele sich um Veteranen, weiterhin gültig war, jetzt, da wir eine Abzweigung nach In-die-Hose-Town genommen hatten.

Tanaka sah mich an und schüttelte den Kopf. Schlechte Neuigkeiten.

„Okay. Wie lautet der Plan? Rückzug?", fragte ich über unseren privaten Kanal.

Er blickte zu seinen Soldaten hinüber. „Ich muss das Team beruhigen."

„Müssen Sie. Aber zuerst müssen Sie der Pilotin sagen, wo sie hinsoll." Ich deutete mit meinem Kopf auf die Soldaten. „Die werden warten. Das nicht."

Er nickte. „Ja, Sir. Cockpit, können wir immer noch die Landezone erreichen?"

„Roger. Das Feuer scheint abgeebbt zu sein. Es war eine einzelne Salve Raketen. Es könnte aber noch mehr geben, also will ich nicht zu viel Zeit damit verbringen, im Kreis zu fliegen."

„Da bin ich Ihrer Meinung. Wissen Sie, was mit Schiff vier passiert ist?"

„Es sieht nicht gut aus. Ich sehe keine Schleudersitze", sagte die Pilotin.

Keine Schleudersitze. Keine Überlebenden. Tanaka ließ den Kopf sinken und starrte zu Boden. Ich kannte das Gefühl, und ich hatte Mitgefühl mit ihm. Seine Geheimdienstinformationen hatten ihn im Stich gelassen und Leute waren gestorben. Der Trick ist zu lernen, dass man nie alles vorhersehen kann, dass Menschen sterben und man das schnell hinter sich lassen muss, sodass nicht noch mehr Leute sterben. Man braucht lange, um das zu lernen. Ich hoffe immer noch, diesen Punkt eines Tages zu erreichen. Aber es ist leichter, es von außen zu betrachten, wenn es um jemand anderen geht und man selbst nicht betroffen ist. Ich stieß ihn an und deutete auf den Rest des Teams. Nicht jeder starrte uns an, aber genug, um einen Unterschied zu machen.

„Konzentrieren Sie sich auf die, die Sie noch haben", sagte ich über den privaten Kanal.

Tanaka erwachte wieder zum Leben und schaltete einen schiffweiten Kanal ein. „Der Feind hatte mehr Verteidigungsmaßnahmen, als wir angenommen hatten.

Wir sind durch und fliegen weiter zur Landezone. Gegenwärtig hat sich der Plan nicht geändert.“

Köpfe nickten. Er hatte es voller Zuversicht gesagt, was wichtiger war als der Inhalt der Nachricht. Er musste zuversichtlich sein, denn wenn er nicht klang, als glaubte er daran, würde es auch niemand anderes tun. Die Wahrheit war, dass wir keine Ahnung hatten, ob wir unseren Plan ändern mussten oder nicht. Vielleicht war die Luftabwehrbatterie eine einmalige Sache gewesen, vielleicht war sie die Ankündigung allgemein verstärkter Verteidigungsmaßnahmen. Das würden wir noch eine Weile nicht herausfinden. Aber er musste so tun, als wüsste er Bescheid, denn nichts zerstörte eine Einheit so wie der Gedanke, dass der Kommandant nicht Bescheid wusste. Nach einem kurzen Schluckauf war er gut damit umgegangen. Nicht alle kauften es ihm ab – sie waren nicht dumm –, aber auch die Soldatinnen und Soldaten kannten das Spiel. Sie wollten es von ihm hören, selbst, wenn sie es in einigen Minuten selbst erleben würden.

Eine Sache wussten wir. Wenn wir erwarteten, dass die Cappaner sich zurücklehnten und auf uns warteten, lagen wir falsch.

Das Schiff schlug hart auf, sodass ich in die Gurte geschleudert wurde. Der Sitz fing das meiste ab, dafür war er immerhin entworfen worden, dennoch schoss mir stechender Schmerz in den unteren Rücken.

„Behandeln Sie es wie eine feindliche Landezone“, bellte Tanaka.

Mit diesem einfachen Befehl verwandelte sich das Chaos in militärische Präzision, als müssten sie alle nur einen Schalter umlegen. Der Gruppenführer begann

augenblicklich, auf demselben Kanal zu funken.
„Trupp eins geht links raus und sichert die Umgebung,
Trupp zwei rechts raus. Drei und vier bleiben zurück,
bis wir einen ersten Lagebericht über die Situation haben."

Vier Stimmen sagten gleichzeitig: „Roger." Die vier
Gruppenführer. Mein Herzschlag beschleunigte sich
und trommelte mir in den Ohren, als die Leitung für einen Moment tot war, während die Gruppenführer auf
anderen Kanälen Befehle an ihre Untergebenen weiter-
leiteten. Ich erwartete Angst, aber die spürte ich nicht.
Es war Begeisterung. Meine Seelenklempnerin würde
eine fantastische Zeit haben, vorausgesetzt, ich schaffte
es zurück. Während der Stille erlaubte ich mir eine Minute lang den Wunsch, dass anstelle von Schiff vier
Schiff drei getroffen worden wäre. Das ist ein abgefuck-
ter Wunsch, aber Selbsterhaltung verursacht so was.
Sie hatte immerhin damit gedroht, *mich* zu töten.

All das verschwand aus meinen Gedanken, als sich
auf beiden Seiten des Schiffs zischend Türen öffneten
und die Soldaten sich in Bewegung setzten.

Kapitel
siebenundzwanzig

Die ersten Trupps stiegen zügig aus, ohne in Eile zu sein. Die Furcht war von den Soldaten abgefallen, jetzt, da sie ein Ziel hatten. In der Luft hatten wir keine Kontrolle; egal was passierte, wir waren hinten angeschnallt und mussten mitfliegen. Hier, mit den Füßen auf dem Boden, konnten wir immerhin zurückschießen. Das machte für die Infanterie einen großen Unterschied.

„Kontakt. Drei Personen an der Baumgrenze, dreihundertfünfzig Meter." Eine Stimme über Funk. Einer der Gruppenführer von draußen.

„Was tun sie?", fragte Tanaka und Frustration schlich sich in seine Stimme. Diese Information hätte Teil des ersten Lageberichts sein sollen.

„Sie sind … sie scheinen, nichts zu tun. Sie beobachten nur. Sollen wir angreifen?"

Ich konnte beinahe hören, wie Tanaka die Augen verdrehte. „Nehmen sie uns ins Visier oder ist es möglich, dass sie sich lediglich fragen, wieso drei Schiffe auf einer Lichtung gelandet sind?"

„Keine sichtbaren Anzeichen für irgendwelche Ausrüstung", sagte der Gruppenführer ein paar Sekunden später. Ich stellte mir vor, wie er die anderen Soldaten ansah, um ihre Meinung einzuholen. Ich wollte ebenfalls die Augen verdrehen.

Ich nickte mit dem Kopf in Richtung Ausgang und Tanaka ging in diese Richtung. Wir mussten aussteigen, ehe irgendjemand Dummheiten machte. Wir hatten auf dem Weg nach unten ein Schiff verloren, aber das bedeutete nicht, dass alle hier unten gegen uns waren. Die Vernichtung des vierten Platoons konnte ein einziger Cappaner mit dem entsprechenden Waffensystem gewesen sein. Aber die Soldaten würden das nicht so sehen. Ihre Freunde waren tot und vielleicht wollten sie um sich schlagen, egal, ob sie das richtige Ziel hatten. Wenn sie anfingen, alle in Sichtweite zu erschießen, konnte das die Mission verkomplizieren. Uns durch die gesamte Bevölkerung zu schießen, war für eine Truppe unserer Größe unhaltbar, besonders wenn der Erfolg davon abhing, sie davon zu überzeugen, uns Informationen zu geben. Tanaka hatte einen Notfallplan, für den Fall, dass sie nicht kooperierten, aber er wollte es dennoch erst mal auf die leichte Tour versuchen.

Nichts davon änderte etwas an der Tatsache, dass sie irgendwo schwere Waffen *hatten*, die sie nicht hätten haben sollen. Wir mussten uns damit auseinandersetzen, wenn es so weit war.

Meine Stiefel sanken in den Boden ein, als ich von der Rampe trat. Die Temperatur lag laut meinem Anzug bei einunddreißig Grad Celsius, außerdem war es feucht, aber das machte mir nichts aus, da mein Hightech-Anzug über Temperaturregulierung verfügte. Noch ein Punkt fürs Söldnerleben. In der leichten Brise wiegte sich das kniehohe Gras, das grünem Weizen ähnelte, hin und her. Auf allen Seiten umgab uns Wald mit seltsamen, hohen Bäumen in einem helleren Grün, das beinahe zu leuchten schien.

Ich stellte meinen Bildschirm auf sechsfache Vergrößerung und scannte die Baumgrenze nach unseren Beobachtern. Drei Cappaner. Sie sahen nicht uns, sondern einander an, so als unterhielten sie sich. Ich schaltete die Vergrößerung aus und warf Tanaka einen Blick zu. Er hatte sie ebenfalls gesehen.

„Ignoriert sie", verkündete er über den Befehlskanal und stellte sicher, dass alle drei Gruppenführer ihn gehört hatten. „Es ist ja nicht so, als würden wir uns reinschleichen. Wir rücken auf unseren geplanten Wegen vor. Drittes Platoon, Sie haben jetzt zusätzlich zur eigenen die vierte Unterstützungsposition. Kundschaften Sie sie aus und entscheiden Sie, ob sie sich aufteilen oder alle zusammen einen der beiden Punkte einnehmen. Ihre Entscheidung, basierend auf dem Gelände."

Ich stimmte seinem Befehl zu. Karten waren großartig für Pläne, aber nichts verlief wie geplant, wenn man erst mal Truppen am Boden hatte.

Der erste Gruppenführer funkte an sein Platoon: „Zu mir." Ich hatte den Kanal ebenfalls offen, da wir uns zusammen mit der Einheit bewegen würden. Tanaka war auch dabei, um die räumlich gesehen nächste Einheit im Auge zu behalten, während er gleichzeitig die gesamte Kompanie führte. Vielleicht versuchte er, bei all seinen Platoons zuzuhören, damit er auf dem Laufenden blieb und sie ihm nicht über den Befehlskanal Bericht erstatten mussten. Ich würde es nicht so machen, aber das war kein Dogma, sondern mehr eine Frage des

Führungsstils. Ich fand, dass es zu viel meiner Aufmerksamkeit erforderte und ich mich nicht mehr auf das konzentrieren konnte, was um mich herum passierte. Und obwohl der hiesige Gruppenführer den Kampf anführen würde, blieb ich gerne aufmerksam. Die entfernten Gruppenführer könnten sich bei mir melden und mit mir reden, wenn sie es mussten.

Die vier Fünftel normaler Gravitation glichen die schwere Rüstung aus, die ich trug, und die eingebaute mechanische Unterstützung half ebenfalls. Ich wollte beinahe schauen, wie weit ich in der niedrigen Gravitation springen konnte. Ich war mir sicher, dass die Soldaten es ausprobieren würden, sobald die Gruppenführer ihnen den Rücken gekehrt hatten. Angesichts des niedrigen Sauerstoffgehalts in der Atmosphäre ließen wir unsere Helme geschlossen. Das Display zeigte 14,4 Prozent an, was etwa das Äquivalent zu dreitausend Metern Höhe in Standardatmosphäre war. Menschen konnten damit leben, aber es würde ihnen elend gehen, besonders, wenn sie sich körperlich betätigen mussten. Unsere Anzüge konnten uns in dieser Umgebung auf unbestimmte Zeit mit Sauerstoff versorgen, da sie zusätzlichen Sauerstoff aus der Luft aufnahmen und den Gehalt dann wie benötigt regulierten. Es war dennoch gut zu wissen, dass mich ein Riss im Anzug nicht umbrachte.

Als wir uns von den anderen Platoons entfernten und in Richtung Wald bewegten, blieb ich etwas zurück und ließ mich hinter Tanaka zurückfallen. Er war beschäftigt, bekam vermutlich zwei oder dreimal so viele Informationen auf sein Display wie ich, also nahm ich an, dass es ihm nicht auffallen würde. Corporal Matua folgte mir und ließ sich ebenfalls zurückfallen, seine Größe identifizierte ihn, ohne dass ich auf meinem Display nach seinem Namen schauen musste. Unser Platoon formte einen Keil, und Tanaka ging etwa am Ende des vorderen Drittels. Ich ließ mich zurückfallen bis zum Nachhut-Drittel.

Während ich lief, nahm ich die Gelegenheit wahr, mich sichtbar zu machen. Die Namen von Soldaten tauchten automatisch auf meinem Display auf und das gab mir die Möglichkeit, mich auf ihren privaten Kanälen zu melden. Ich tat es nicht, aber sie sahen auch meinen Namen. Das wollte ich. Sie sahen, wie ich neben ihnen entlanghumpelte, dieselbe Mühsal auf mich nahm, ohne Privilegien. Das würde mir ein paar Punkte einbringen. Punkte, die ich irgendwann in der Zukunft vielleicht brauchte, wenn jemand sich entschloss, mich zu töten. Soldaten sind komisch, was das angeht. Wenn jemand ein Feind oder Außenseiter ist, können sie ihre Emotionen ausschalten und tun, was zu tun ist. Wenn es einer von ihnen ist? Nicht ganz so. Ich musste einer von ihnen sein.

Das hier waren Söldner, keine Meuchelmörder.

Die hohen Bäume formten schwere Baumkronendächer über unseren Köpfen, die das Sonnenlicht abhielten und dafür sorgten, dass der Waldboden relativ frei von Unterholz war. Die nächsten drei Kilometer liefen wir allgemein bergan, aber langsam. Mein Display zeigte mir an, dass wir einundsechzig Höhenmeter zurückgelegt hatten, seit wir die Landezone verlassen hatten, aber das lag daran, dass wir eine Reihe kleiner Hügel überqueren mussten; rauf, runter und den nächsten wieder rauf.

„Halt“, meldete der Gruppenführer. Die Soldaten ließen sich gleichzeitig auf ein Knie hinab und jeder konzentrierte sich auf den ihm zugewiesenen Sektor, wodurch wir dreihundertsechzig Grad abdecken konnten. Mit einer Augenbewegung konnte ich jeden Sektor auf meinem Display aufrufen, und wenn irgendjemand einen Feind wahrnahm, bekämen wir alle ein rotes Warnsignal angezeigt. Im Augenblick blieb der Bildschirm sauber.

„Was haben Sie?“, fragte Tanaka.

„Da ist ein erster Engpass, Sir.“ Etwa fünfhundert Meter vor uns erhoben sich felsige Klippen aus dem Wald, vielleicht sechzig Meter hoch. Sie erstreckten sich in beide Richtungen, ein schmaler Durchgang beinahe direkt vor uns.

„Dran vorbei oder durch?“, fragte Tanaka. Ich rief die Karte auf meinem Display auf, um zu sehen, wie weit wir laufen müssten, um sie zu umgehen. Der Gruppenführer hatte es auf seiner Aufklärungskarte bereits gesehen und bestimmt schon einen Plan gefasst. Ich hatte eine genaue Vorstellung davon, welchen Weg ich wählen würde, aber ich behielt sie für mich.

„Der Plan ist, durchzugehen, Sir. Es ist ein weiter Weg, den Engpass zu umgehen. Würde uns eine Stunde kosten“, antwortete der Gruppenführer.

„Roger“, sagte Tanaka. „Ich will auf beiden Seiten oben Soldaten haben. Wir gehen auf keinen Fall da durch, ohne Augen von oben.“

Nicht die Entscheidung, die ich getroffen hätte.

Etwas an der Lücke fühlte sich falsch an, obwohl ich nicht genau sagen konnte, was. Ich konnte einer Entscheidung, die Tanaka und sein Gruppenführer bereits gefällt hatten, nicht widersprechen, ohne sie schwach erscheinen zu lassen, also behielt ich meine Einschätzung für mich. Aber ich achtete definitiv genauer auf meine Umgebung.

„Roger, Sir. Ich empfange keine Wärmesignaturen."

„Ist mir egal", sagte Tanaka. „Wenn sie einen Hinterhalt vorbereiten würden, was wäre das Erste, das sie tun? Sie würden dafür sorgen, dass es keine sichtbaren Wärmesignaturen gibt."

„Ja, Sir. Verstanden, Sir."

„Setzen Sie die Leute in Bewegung", sagte Tanaka. „Ich will keine Zeit verlieren." Der Gruppenführer schaltete auf eine andere Frequenz um und zwanzig Sekunden später trennten sich sechs Soldaten von der Gruppe und rannten mechanisch unterstützt auf die Klippen zu, zwei Gruppe à drei Soldaten trennten sich, während sie vordrangen.

„Ausrücken", sagte der Gruppenführer. „Halbe Geschwindigkeit. Geben wir den Spähern Zeit, nach oben zu kommen." Ein paar Sekunden später starteten zwei andere Soldaten faustgroße Drohnen, die einen Moment lang in der Luft schwebten, ehe sie in Richtung der Klippen davonschnellten.

Ich nahm die Gelegenheit wahr, um zu Tanaka aufzuschließen. „Drohnen und Männer oben auf den Klippen. Halten Sie das für einen Hinterhalt?"

„Ich weiß es nicht", sagte er. „Irgendetwas fühlt sich komisch an."

„Sehe ich auch so. Irgendwas stimmt hier nicht", sagte ich. „Irgendwelche Nachrichten von den anderen Platoons?"

„Nichts. Das setzt mir ebenfalls zu. Es ist zu still. Wir haben nichts erwartet, aber nach dem Feuer, das wir auf dem Weg nach unten abgekriegt haben, weiß ich nicht.“

„Wenn sie uns angreifen wollen, hätten sie sich keinen besseren Ort aussuchen können“, sagte ich. „Wir sind in einiger Entfernung gelandet. Ihre Siedlung sah von oben zusammenhängend aus. Aber dann haben wir diese drei Cappaner gesehen, als wir gelandet sind, also haben es ein paar von ihnen nach hier draußen geschafft.“

Er dachte einen Moment lang darüber nach. „Sie haben den Nagel auf den Kopf getroffen. Das ist es, was mir zu schaffen macht. Sie hatten keine Zeit, hier rauszukommen, nachdem sie uns kommen gesehen haben. Sie hatten kein sichtbares Fahrzeug. Das bedeutet, dass sie vermutlich schon hier draußen waren. Wenn Cappaner hier draußen leben würden, hätten wir mehr von ihnen gesehen. Das haben wir aber nicht. Sie waren aus einem bestimmten Grund hier, selbst wenn dieser Grund nichts mit uns zu tun hat.“

„Ich glaube nicht an Zufälle“, sagte ich.

„Ich auch nicht. Was also treiben sie hier draußen?“

Ich biss mir unter meinem Helm auf die Lippe. „Denken wir mal an den schlimmsten Fall. Was wäre das?“

„Schlimmstenfalls … wussten sie, dass wir kommen.“

„Aber wie?“, fragte ich. Ich kannte die Antwort, da die Cappaner mir davon erzählt hatten, aber es würde nichts bringen, Tanaka das zu sagen. Es war besser, ihn selbst darauf kommen zu lassen.

„Ich weiß es nicht. Es kommt mir wirklich unwahrscheinlich vor. Sie könnten einen Spion auf Talca haben, der ihnen Bescheid gegeben hat, als wir aufgebrochen sind. Aber vorauszusehen, wann wir hier eintreffen würden, angesichts der Unwägbarkeiten von Reisen durchs All, und zu wissen, wo wir landen würden ... ausgeschlossen. Richtig?"

„Es ist stets am besten, anzunehmen, dass der Feind fähiger ist, als er es in Wirklichkeit ist, richtig?"

„Aber es ist unwahrscheinlich, oder nicht?" Er sah mich an, obwohl ich sein Gesicht wegen der Blende nicht sehen konnte. „Ich meine ... es ist mindestens weit hergeholt."

„Schwer zu sagen", gab ich zu. Es *war* weit hergeholt, egal wie rational man es analysierte. Aber die Cappaner wussten, dass wir kommen würden. Soviel hatten sie mir gesagt. Sie hatten vermutlich nicht wissen können, wann wir eintreffen oder was wir dabeihaben würden.

Wir erreichten den Eingang des Engpasses ein paar Minuten später, und gingen noch langsamer, weil die Späher Schwierigkeiten hatten, einen Weg auf die Klippe zu finden. Selbst mit der Unterstützung ihrer Anzüge war es ein schwerer Aufstieg. Wir hielten inne, um sie Stellung beziehen zu lassen, und der Gruppenführer erstattete Bericht. „Alles sauber, Sir. Laut der Drohnen wartet nichts auf der anderen Seite der Klippen, und die Späher sagen, oben ist auch nichts."

„Roger", sagte Tanaka. „Ausrücken."

Der Keil teilte sich wie selbstverständlich in engere Formationen kleiner Keile auf, vier Soldaten in jedem, die sich aufteilten, so gut das auf dem schmalen Terrain ging. Tanaka und ich gingen hinter der dritten Vierergruppe.

Eine Explosion drückte meine Brust durch die Panzerung hindurch zusammen und stieß mich einen Schritt zurück, gefolgt von einer zweiten, weniger als eine Sekunde später. Ich hatte Schwierigkeiten, während der Erschütterung auf den Beinen zu bleiben.

„Kartoffelminen!", rief jemand über Funk.

Shit. Kartoffelminen waren eine typisch cappanische Waffe, ihr geringer Metallgehalt machte es beinahe unmöglich, sie aufzuspüren. Wir hatten meine Antwort auf die Frage gefunden, wie die Cappaner antworten würden. Sie hatten den naheliegendsten Zugang vermint.

Tanakas Stimme meldete sich über den Befehlskanal und funkte an die entfernten Platoons. „An alle Einheiten, achten Sie auf Kartoffelminen. Das erste Platoon hat Kontakt." Seine Gelassenheit beeindruckte mich. Der natürliche Instinkt ist, auf die unmittelbare Situation zu reagieren, er aber blieb alles in allem konzentriert und dachte daran, den Rest der Kompanie zu informieren.

„Zweites Platoon hat Kontakt", kam die Antwort von einer der entfernten Einheiten.

Shit. Es ergab Sinn, dass die Cappaner ihre Stellung verteidigten, aber es brachte mich in eine missliche Lage, weil ich gehofft hatte, mich mit ihnen in Verbindung zu setzen. Einer Mine war es egal, wen sie tötete. Ich wollte eine Karte aufrufen und mir die allgemeine Situation anschauen, meine Optionen abschätzen, aber dazu hatte ich keine Zeit, da ich mitten in einem Minenfeld stand. Jetzt gerade waren wir in einem Gefecht, und obwohl es nicht meines war, machte das keinen Unterschied. Wir waren stehen geblieben, was in einem Minenfeld Standardprozedur war, aber das hieß, dass wir ortsgebunden und leichte Ziele waren. Wir hatten Drohnen und Späher auf den Klippen, sodass der Feind uns nicht direkt beschießen konnte, was den Druck etwas verringerte. Aber wenn sie keine Gewehre auf uns gerichtet hatten, bedeutete das vermutlich, dass sie Artillerie oder Raketen hatten.

Tanaka und ich sahen einander im gleichen Moment an. Wir waren beide zu demselben Schluss gekommen. Wir konnten entweder dem Minenfeld trotzen oder weglaufen, aber wir konnten nicht stillstehen. „Vor oder zurück?", fragte ich auf einem privaten Kanal.

„Vorwärts", sagte er ohne zu zögern. „Erstes Platoon, ausrücken. Laufschritt. Los!"

Ich rannte los, mein erster mechanisch unterstützter Schritt warf mich nach vorne. Corporal Matua lief Schritt für Schritt neben mir. Ich wollte ihm sagen, dass er sich lösen sollte, da wir beide von einer Mine getroffen werden würden, die der andere auslöste, aber ich hatte keine Zeit. Ich war vielleicht sechs Schritte weit gekommen, als die erste Rakete heranpfiff. Manchmal ist es echt scheiße, recht zu haben. Um mich herum wurde Erde aufgeworfen und Körper flogen durch die Luft, Schrapnelle tanzte in meinem Sichtfeld wie ein Schwarm heißer, tödlicher Glühwürmchen. Mein Helm schaltete den Lärm automatisch stumm, um mein Gehör zu schützen, was mich etwas isolierte und mir den Eindruck vermittelte, als kämen die Geräusche von hinter einer dicken Wand.

Ich machte große, mechanisch verstärkte Schritte, jeder von ihnen zehn Meter lang, und hoffte, dass ich nicht auf einer Mine landete. Mehr konnte ich nicht tun. Der Feind hatte niemanden oben auf den Klippen gebraucht. Er hatte irgendwo eine winzige Kamera installiert und Raketen auf den wahrscheinlichsten Weg voreingestellt. Die nächste Erschütterung warf mich zur Seite, ich prallte hart auf die Erde und überschlug mich, ehe ich zum Stillstand kam. Ich sprang wieder auf die Beine, ohne zu prüfen, ob ich verletzt war oder nicht. Stehen zu bleiben bedeutete den Tod.

Ich verlor den Überblick über die Explosionen. Sieben. Vielleicht acht. Ich könnte mir später die Aufnahme meines Helms ansehen und nachzählen, vorausgesetzt, dass ich es überlebte. Etwas Großes traf mich, hob mich von den Füßen und warf mich zu Boden. Den Bruchteil einer Sekunde später verwandelte sich meine Welt in eine Explosion aus Felsen und Erde. Ich versuchte, mich zu bewegen, aber etwas über mir hielt mich am Boden.

Nach ein paar Sekunden beruhigte ich mich, fand einen Hebel, stieß mich hoch und rollte zur gleichen Zeit herum. Das Gewicht bewegte sich und ich kam frei. Ich kämpfte mich auf die Knie und versuchte, auf die Beine kommen. Alles, um zu entkommen. Ich brauchte einen Moment, um zu erfassen, dass das, was mich am Boden gehalten hatte, ein gepanzerter Körper gewesen war, und eine weitere Sekunde, bis sich mein Display wiedereingestellt hatte und mir sagte, dass es Matua war. Ich atmete erleichtert aus, als er sich bewegte und versuchte, sich aufzusetzen.

Er hatte oberhalb des Ellenbogens ein Stück Schrapnell abbekommen, das seine Panzerung etwa zwanzig Zentimeter bis runter zu seinem Handgelenk zerschmettert und einen Brei aus Blut, Polymer und Knochen hinterlassen hatte. Ich kniete mich neben ihn und legte ihm eine Hand auf seine gesunde Schulter. Er drehte den Kopf zu mir herum und ich öffnete einen privaten Kanal.

„Sie kommen in Ordnung. Wir holen einen Vogel, der uns evakuiert." Die Worte blieben mir etwas im Halse stecken. Auch wenn er mein Wärter war, war es mir nicht egal, was mit ihm geschah. „Jetzt müssen wir verdammt noch mal aus der Todeszone raus. Können Sie laufen?"

„Ich ... ich weiß es nicht." Er klang so verwirrt wie jemand, den es schwer erwischt hatte. Ich war mir ziemlich sicher, dass er sich zwischen mich und die letzte Explosion geworfen hatte.

„Versuchen Sie, aufzustehen. Ich helfe Ihnen." Ich packte seinen gesunden Arm und zog, und mit seiner Hilfe bekam ich ihn auf die Füße. Er wankte und ging beinahe wieder zu Boden. „Nope", sagte ich. „Ich werde Sie tragen müssen."

„Tut mir leid, Sir."

„Gehen wir." Ich ging in die Hocke und warf ihn mir über beide Schultern, wie ein Feuerwehrmann es getan hätte, dabei achtete ich darauf, dass ich seinen gesunden Arm erwischte und sein verletzter unberührt blieb. Ohne die verstärkte Kraft meines Anzugs hätte ich den großen Kerl niemals tragen können. Selbst mit dem Anzug stellte ich mir vor, wie ich meine Gelenke ächzen hören konnte, als ich ihn mir richtig auf die Schultern legte. Ich schwankte ein wenig, dann bewegte ich mich. Ich konnte nicht rennen, aber ich setzte einen Fuß vor den anderen und fürchtete, dass ich hinfallen würde, wenn ich stehenblieb, und Matua dann nicht wieder hochbekommen würde. Eine weitere Explosion erschütterte den Bereich hinter mir, nah genug, dass ich die Druckwelle durch meine Rüstung spüren konnte. Ich lief weiter und hielt den Kopf unten.

Als ich aus dem Gefahrenbereich raus war, setzte ich Matua ab und lehnte ihn mit dem Rücken an einen großen Baum. Schweiß strömte mir vom Gesicht und den Nacken hinab, und ich rang nach Luft, trotz meines temperaturregulierten Anzugs.

Kampf war was für jüngere Männer. „Sir, es tut mir so leid."

„Wovon reden Sie, Mann? Sie haben mir das Leben gerettet."

Er schüttelte beinahe unmerklich den Kopf, schien damit zu kämpfen. „Das meine ich nicht. Das andere Zeug."

„Machen Sie sich deswegen keine Gedanken. Wir sind alle auf Missionen gewesen, die wir lieber ausgelassen hätten. Jetzt müssen wir Sie hier rausholen." Ich nahm das Erste-Hilfe-Set aus der Stecktasche seines gesunden Arms und holte den Autoinjektor heraus. Das würde seinen Stoffwechsel verlangsamen und ihm bei der Gerinnung helfen. Er wäre nutzlos, aber es würde ihm vermutlich das Leben retten, bis er bessere medizinische Versorgung erhalten konnte.

Er sprach undeutlich. „Passen Sie auf sich auf, okay?"

„Tue ich immer", sagte ich. Mit Matuas Ausscheiden aus dem Kampf war die Situation schwieriger geworden, aber ich hatte immer noch Tanaka und sein Versprechen. Ich hatte immer noch die Hoffnung, dass ich es hier rausschaffen würde, auch wenn ich im Moment keinen Ausweg sehen konnte.

Genauso wie zuvor, konnte ich nichts anderes tun, als einen Fuß vor den anderen zu setzen und zu beten, dass nichts in die Luft flog.

Kapitel achtundzwanzig

Ich kroch um einen Baum mit glatter Borke herum und sah mich nach Feinden um. Unsere Drohnen hatten den Bereich gecheckt, aber ich vertraute ihnen nicht. Ich konnte nicht glauben, dass die Cappaner uns nach dem Minen-Hinterhalt vom Haken gelassen hatten. Sie hätten Leute hierhaben sollen, die uns abknallen, während wir uns sammelten, nachdem die Raketen uns auseinandergetrieben hatten. Aber mein Display blieb leer – keine Icons von Feinden – und eine unheimliche Stille breitete sich aus, etliche Sekunden lang, wie eine dicke Decke. Ich nutzte die Zeit, um nach dem Ursprung der Raketen zu suchen. Das Radar in unseren Anzügen hatte eine Flugbahn aufgezeichnet und sie zu dem Punkt zurückverfolgt, an dem die Raketen abgefeuert worden waren. Jeder Anzug hatte diese Software und miteinander verbunden errechneten sie einen genauen Standort. Mein Display zeigte an, dass der fünfzehn Kilometer entfernt lag, was bedeutete, dass sie von jenseits unseres Ziels geschossen hatten. Jemand hatte bereits eine unserer Drohnen ausgesandt, damit sie Fotos machte. Sie flog mit einer Geschwindigkeit von hundert Metern pro Sekunde und wäre in unter drei Minuten dort.

Tanaka unterbrach die Funkstille mit einem Funkspruch ans gesamte Netzwerk. „Erstes Platoon, Status."

Etliche Sekunden lang meldete sich niemand, dann ertönte eine unbekannte Stimme. „Der Lieutenant ist ausgeschaltet. Red Seven ist jetzt Red Six. Truppführer, Bericht." Red Seven. Das bedeutete, dass der Platoon Sergeant, normalerweise der zweite Offizier, das Platoon übernommen hatte, um Red Six, den Lieutenant, zu ersetzen, der getroffen worden war. Das war Fleischi. Jeder Trupp meldete seine Verluste, Tote, Verwundete und die Schwere der Verwundungen. Es dauerte länger, als es hätte dauern sollen, weil zwei Truppführer ebenfalls getroffen worden waren und ihre Stellvertreter jetzt das Sagen hatten. Während einer Mission die Führung zu wechseln war eine Standardprozedur, aber eine, die nie zu hundert Prozent reibungslos verlief.

„Insgesamte Zählung: Sieben Tote, elf Verwundete. Sieben der Verwundeten müssen evakuiert werden. Einer sofort."

„Roger", sagte Tanaka. „Richten Sie einen Evakuierungspunkt ein. Ich rufe den Vogel."

Eine andere Stimme, über den Kanal der Kompanie, verschaffte mir einen allgemeinen Überblick. Es war einer der anderen Lieutenants. „Sir, hier ist White Six. Das zweite Platoon hat Verluste erlitten."

„Bericht", sagte Tanaka.

„Drei Tote. Vierzehn Verwundete. Minenfeld, dann Raketen."

„Roger, White. Wie viele müssen evakuiert werden?"
„Zwölf, Sir."

Tanaka schüttelte den Kopf. Ich wusste, was er dachte. Drei Tote und zwölf zu evakuierende Soldaten ließen einem Platoon gerade so mehr als fünfzig Prozent seiner eigentlichen Truppenstärke und brachten es in Gefahr, seine Mission nicht zu Ende führen zu können. All das, ohne den härtesten Punkt der Action erreicht zu haben. Zu meiner Linken hatten zwei Soldaten schultergestützte Raketen vorbereitet. Sie warteten auf die Drohnen, um zu schauen, ob es bei der feindlichen Raketenstellung noch etwas gab, das sie beschießen konnten.

Tanaka riss sich zusammen und kontaktierte das dritte Platoon. „Blue Six, irgendwelcher Feindkontakt?"

„Hier ist Blue Six. Negativ."

„Passen Sie auf Kartoffelminen auf. Besonders in Engpässen."

„Wird gemacht, Sir."

Tanaka schwieg einen Moment auf dem Kanal, obwohl sich seine Lippen unter seinem Visier bewegten. Vermutlich rief er Evakuierungsschiffe. Entweder das, oder er sprach mit jemandem auf einem privaten Kanal. Vielleicht Larsson. Das hätte ich getan. Wir hatten so viele Verluste erlitten, dass er einen Rückzug in Betracht ziehen musste.

Nachdem er zu sprechen aufgehört hatte, öffnete ich einen privaten Kanal zu ihm. „Was denken Sie?"

„Diese Raketen waren wirklich gut koordiniert. Und genau. Sie hatten das voreingestellt."

„Die Drohne hat den Startpunkt der Raketen erreicht", sagte ich. Wir hielten beide inne, um die Videoübertragung aufzurufen. Auf einer Lichtung standen leere Rampen in einem Loch von einem halben Meter

Tiefe. Eine radarabweisende Plane lag auf der Erde. Offensichtlich hatte sie die Raketen bis kurz vor dem Abfeuern bedeckt. Keine Lebenszeichen, was bedeutete, dass alles ferngesteuert gewesen war. Wir hatten keine Ziele, die wir angreifen konnten.

„Shit“, sagte Tanaka.

„Es war gut geplant, ohne Zweifel“, sagte ich. „Was jetzt?“

„Die Frage ist, wie viel sie haben“, sagte er. „Wenn sie uns hier mit den Raketen beschossen, aber dahinter nichts haben, kann es sein, dass sie damit bezwecken wollten, uns zu vertreiben. Uns dazu zu kriegen, dass wir aufgeben.“

„Möglich“, sagte ich. „Würden Sie es so machen, wenn Sie sie wären?“

„Wenn alles, was ich hätte, ein paar Minen und Raketen sind? Vermutlich. Wenn ich einen Angreifer davon überzeugen könnte, dass das erst der Anfang war, würde ich ihn vielleicht dazu kriegen, umzukehren und zu fliehen. Wenn ich keine Möglichkeit hätte, am Boden zu kämpfen ... ja, dann würde ich es vielleicht so machen.“

Das war ein gutes Argument. Es war ein Münzwurf. Entweder hatten sie weitere Überraschungen oder nicht, und wir konnten es nicht herausfinden, ohne die Mission fortzuführen, es sei denn, wir hatten Glück und fanden etwas mit Hilfe der Drohnen. „Sie haben recht. Es könnte so oder so laufen. Wie lautet die Entscheidung?“, fragte ich.

Er dachte lange genug darüber nach, sodass ich ihn beinahe noch einmal fragte, als er antwortete. „Wir gehen weiter.“

„Roger." Ich hatte Zweifel, aber ich wollte sie nicht mitteilen. Er brauchte seine Zuversicht. Wenn die verschwand, waren wir alle gefickt. Davon abgesehen hatte ich eine bessere Chance, zu fliehen, als wenn wir uns zurückzogen.

Wir waren seit fünf Minuten weitergegangen, als das dritte Platoon Feindkontakt meldete.

„Scharfschützen auf einer Erhöhung", ertönte die Meldung über den Kanal der Kompanie.

„Roger. Wie viele?", fragte Tanaka.

Niemand antwortete. Gut. Er hätte nicht fragen sollen, obwohl es zugegebenermaßen schwer war, zu widerstehen. Er war nicht dort, also konnte er nicht helfen. Sie mussten ihren eigenen Kampf kämpfen, und sie hatten einen Gruppenführer und Larsson, um ihn zu koordinieren. Aber gleichzeitig hielten wir alle den Atem an und warteten auf eine Antwort. Ein Schiff heulte über unseren Köpfen auf, unsere Luftunterstützung, die dem dritten Platoon helfen würde.

„Wir sollten ein paar Bomben auf das Wohngebiet abwerfen", sagte ein Soldat, der sich nicht identifizierte, auf dem Kanal des ersten Platoons. „Das würde sie dazu bringen, aufzuhören." Niemand antwortete über Funk, aber etliche Köpfe nickten. Ich checkte die beiden Soldaten mit den Raketenwerfern, um sicherzustellen, dass sie nicht darüber nachdachten, Dummheiten zu machen. Keiner schien feuerbereit zu sein. Gut. Nichts war härter, als beschossen zu werden und keine Möglichkeit zu haben, das Feuer zu erwidern, während die Nerven blank lagen.

Weit entfernt ertönte eine Explosion, angesichts unserer Distanz nur eine schwache Erschütterung. Das Schiff hatte Ziele gefunden.

„Black Six, hier ist Blue Six." Der Gruppenführer des dritten Platoons meldete sich.

„Sprechen Sie", sagte Tanaka.

„Drei feindliche Schützen ausgeschaltet. Drei von uns tot, einer verwundet, nicht dringend."

„Roger", sagte Tanaka und der Funk verstummte.

„Tanaka. Ich habe eine Idee für eine alternative Vorgehensweise", sagte ich über einen privaten Kanal.

„Ich bin ganz Ohr", sagte er.

„Bei dieser Mission geht es darum, aus einer Position der Stärke heraus zu verhandeln, aber wir werden von Minute zu Minute schwächer. Wenn wir von hier eine Funkverbindung zu den Cappanern aufbauen könnten, könnten wir–"

„Kann ich nicht tun, Sir", unterbrach er mich. „Das liegt außerhalb der Parameter der Mission."

Ich hielt einen Moment lang entmutigt inne. Ich hatte gehofft, dass, wenn ich mich mit ihnen in Verbindung setzen könnte, ich die Cappaner warnen und es dabei irgendwie schaffen könnte, nicht erwischt zu werden. „Dann ändern Sie die Parameter. Sie sind der Kommandant."

„So einfach ist das nicht", sagte er mit Enttäuschung in der Stimme.

„Was sind die Kriterien für einen Abbruch?", fragte ich.

Er brauchte einen Moment für die Antwort. „Es gibt keine."

Shit.

Tanaka hatte es nicht wörtlich gemeint, als er gesagt hatte, dass er keine Abbruchkriterien hatte, weil er ab einem gewissen Punkt nicht mehr genug Kampfkraft hatte, um weiterzumachen, und wir aufgeben müssten. Aber es ließ mich dennoch erschaudern. Er hatte die Absicht, vorzurücken, bis er nicht mehr konnte. Ich hatte ihm vor ein paar Minuten zugestimmt, als wir uns Minen und Raketen gegenübergesehen hatten, aber feindliche Scharfschützen fügten ein weiteres Element hinzu. Es bedeutete, dass Cappaner sich dem Kampf physisch angeschlossen hatten, und das änderte alles. Sie waren fünfzehn- oder zwanzigtausend, und wir wussten nicht, wie viele bewaffnet waren. Trotz unserer technologischen Vorteile hatten wir nicht ansatzweise genug Feuerkraft, um dagegen anzukommen. Aber ich konnte mich nicht mit Tanaka streiten, dem Kerl, der vielleicht versuchen würde, mir das Leben zu retten. Es passte außerdem zu meinem Verlangen, den Cappanern näherzukommen. Falls es überhaupt irgendjemand von uns so weit schaffte.

Dennoch, die tiefere Bedeutung seines Handelns beunruhigte mich. Jemand hatte genug Einfluss auf ihn, um ihn dazu zu kriegen, in einer Situation weiter zu marschieren, in der er es nicht hätte tun sollen, und seine Leute schienen ihm ohne Murren zu folgen. Es musste einen großen Bonus geben, damit sie weitermarschierten und ihre Leben riskierten. Vielleicht war es mehr als nur Geld. Ich kannte die internen Abläufe der Einheit nicht, also konnte ich es nicht wissen. Soldaten taten Dinge für ihre Vorgesetzten, aus Gründen, die über das Verständnis von Außenseitern hinausgingen. So viele nicht greifbare Faktoren spielten eine

Rolle bei Loyalität, dass der Versuch, sie zu verstehen … ich konnte es nicht. Ich kannte die Beziehungen nicht. Als Tanaka sagte, dass wir weiter vorrücken sollten, meldete ich mich über Funk und sagte: „Roger."

Wir ließen eine kleine Einheit von Verwundeten, die gehen konnten, zurück, um die die medizinische Evakuierung zu überwachen, und rückten aus. Die Soldaten bewegten sich jetzt mit noch mehr Vorsicht vorwärts, obwohl es für untrainierte Beobachter unverändert ausgesehen hätte. Wir bewegten uns in derselben Keilformation mit etwa der gleichen Geschwindigkeit, aber mit einem anderen Level an Aufmerksamkeit. Einer der Soldaten mit den schultergestützten Raketen hielt seine Waffe im Anschlag. Das nächste Ziel, das sich bot, würde er erst beschießen und dann Fragen stellen. Die Drohnen waren zurückgekehrt, bewegten sich etwa einen Kilometer vor uns über unserer Route und übermitteln uns die Aufnahmen ihrer Sensoren. Ich stellte meinen Bildschirm so ein, dass er alles herausfilterte, was nicht tatsächlicher Feindkontakt war, da ich der Meinung bin, dass zu viele Daten bei einer solchen Operation überwältigend sein konnten.

Datenflut konnte ein echtes Problem für einen Anführer sein. Lieutenants konnten sich so sehr auf all die Dinge konzentrieren, die in ihre Helme gespeist wurden, dass sie grundlegende Dinge übersahen, die sich um sie herum ereigneten. Jeder zog seine Grenze an einem anderen Punkt, abhängig von den eigenen Fähigkeiten und Erfahrungen. Ich hoffte, dass Tanaka und seine Offiziere es draufhatten. Es war ein seltsames Gefühl, den Leuten die Daumen zu drücken, die mich in diese schwierige Situation hineingezwungen hatten, aber hier war ich nun einmal. Die Cappaner waren nicht wirklich meine Feinde und die Omicron-Soldaten waren nicht wirklich meine Freunde, aber diese Dinge wurden weniger wichtig, sobald Schüsse fielen. Die Soldaten um mich herum taten, was sie tun mussten, um zu überleben, und ich konnte es ihnen nicht verübeln. Alle Spitzfindigkeiten und Politik spielten keine Rolle mehr, wenn man im Einsatz war und ein Gewehr im Anschlag hatte. Bis ich einen Punkt erreichte, von dem aus ich mit den Cappanern kommunizieren konnte, würde sich das nicht ändern.

Selbst in diesem Augenblick, mit der unklaren Situation, die über mir schwebte, wollte ein Teil von mir hier sein. Ein großer Teil. Als wäre es besser, mein Leben für eine dubiose Sache zu riskieren, als dafür bezahlt zu werden, gemütlich in einem Unternehmensgebäude mit Air-Condition zu sitzen. Ich glaube, mir war vage bewusst, wie falsch dieser Gedankengang war, aber diese Art der Selbstanalyse spart man sich besser für außerhalb des Kriegsgebiets auf.

Das Gelände öffnete sich und wurde flacher und die Bäume wurden weniger, was das Vorrücken erleichterte. Wir verteilten uns, was uns zu schwereren Zielen machte, und fast eine Stunde lang bewegten wir uns, ohne auf Gegenwehr zu stoßen. Auch keine der anderen Einheiten meldete Feindkontakt und ich begann, Tanakas Theorie Glauben zu schenken, dass die Cappaner uns mittels einer ersten Verteidigung hatten vertreiben wollen.

Ich hätte auf mein Bauchgefühl vertrauen sollen.

Das dritte Platoon meldete Feindkontakt und kaum, dass sie mit der Übertragung fertig waren, funkte der

zweite Gruppenführer und meldete ebenfalls Feindkontakt.

Tanaka stellte diesmal keine Fragen, sondern wartete
auf weitere Berichte. Die Luftunterstützung kreiste
über unseren Köpfen, aber ohne zu wissen, welches
Platoon es am schwersten hatte, gab Tanaka keine An-
weisungen. Er würde sich die Übertragungen der einzelnen Platoons anschauen und versuchen, herauszufinden, womit wir es an den verschiedenen Standorten
zu tun hatten und wer am meisten Hilfe benötigte.

Der Kopf des Soldaten vor mir explodierte.

„Kontakt, dreißig Grad. Scharfschütze!“ Ich konnte
nicht sagen, wer das gefunkt hatte. Es war mir egal. Ich
warf mich auf den Boden, als zwei weitere Schüsse er-
tönten und bevor die Soldaten um mich herum das
Feuer erwiderten und sie übertönten. Rote Punkte erschienen auf meinem Display. Feinde. In der Nähe
schnitt das Rauschen startender Raketen durch die
Schüsse. Unser Mann mit dem Raketenwerfer hielt
sich nicht zurück.

„Drei Feinde ausgeschaltet.“ Eine weitere unbekannte
Stimme. Die Lächerlichkeit der gesamten Situation
wurde mir bewusst. Körperlose Stimmen teilten mir
Sachen mit, die ich auf meinem Display bereits gesehen
hatte. Berichteten von Toden, die sich bereits ereignet
hatten. Dankenswerterweise hatte ich keine Zeit, darüber nachzudenken oder es zu verarbeiten. Ich blickte
durchs Zielfernrohr meiner Waffe, erhöhte die Vergrößerung und suchte nach einem Ziel. Ich visierte einen
Cappaner mit Gewehr an. Ich betätigte den Abzug, aber
der Alien machte einen Ruck, kurz bevor ich feuerte, er
war bereits getroffen worden.

Zu unserer Linken leuchtete weiteres Mündungsfeuer auf, zu viel für mich, um es händisch zu zählen, aber mein Helm zählte dreiundzwanzig. Der Feind hatte uns im Kreuzfeuer, beschoss uns aus einer L-Formation heraus. Hinterhalt wie aus dem Lehrbuch.

Irgendwie hatten sie die Drohnen und unsere Sensoren gemieden, um uns überraschen zu können. Ich gab diesen Gedanken auf, als die ersten Raketen unsere Position trafen, Erde und Holzsplitter aufwarfen und einen gepanzerten Körper durch die Luft schleuderten. Ich scannte die Umgebung nach Tanaka, während ich mich auf den Boden presste. Wir brauchten Befehle, aber die Kanäle der Kompanie und des Platoons schwiegen. Ich fand ihn, vierzig Meter entfernt, wo er sich auf ein Knie herabgelassen hatte und die neuen Ziele beschoss. Ich begann, in seine Richtung zu kriechen, während ich einen privaten Kanal öffnete.

Eine Explosion erschütterte die Erde vor Tanaka und warf ihn fünf oder sechs Meter rückwärts. Sein Rücken prallte gegen einen großen Baumstamm, wo er absurderweise einen Moment wie ans Holz geheftet hing, ehe er zu Boden fiel. Ohne zu überlegen sprang ich auf und rannte mit einigen mechanisch verstärkten Schritten zu ihm. Etwas schlug laut gegen meinen gepanzerten Rücken, als ich ihn erreichte, aber ich spürte es kaum. Mein System zeigte keine Warnungen, also dankte ich der guten Technologie im Stillen und untersuchte Tanaka. Einer seiner Arme war auf eine Weise unter ihm verbogen, wie menschliche Arme sich nicht verbiegen sollten, aber sein ramponierter Anzug schickte meinem ein Signal, dass er lebte.

Ich versuchte, mich zwischen ihn und den Großteil des feindlichen Feuers zu stellen, basierend auf dem, was mein Computer mir über ihren Standort sagte. Fünf rote Punkte waren auf meinem Display zurückgeblieben. Sie hatten das Überraschungsmoment, aber sobald wir sie gefunden hatten, forderten unsere überlegenen Waffen ihren Tribut, obwohl auch etliche blaue Symbole erloschen waren. Abgesehen vom Lebensnotwendigsten schaltete ich alles in den Hintergrund, um mich auf Tanaka zu konzentrieren. Ich schnappte mir das Erste-Hilfe-Set aus der Stecktasche der Schulterpanzerung seines gesunden Arms und aktivierte es. Die zwölf Sekunden, die es für einen Diagnose-Scan brauchte, krochen dahin, als würde ich auf eine Sonnenuhr starren. Als der Bildschirm endlich aufleuchtete, zuckte ich ob des Ergebnisses zusammen. Gebrochene Rippen, der verletzte Arm, den ich sehen konnte, und mindestens ein gebrochener Rückenwirbel.

Ich wollte ihn nicht bewegen, aber wir konnten auch nicht hierbleiben. Es gab genug rote Punkte, die immer noch auf uns schossen, sodass es gefährlich war, und weitere schlossen sich ihnen an. Vielleicht zwanzig Meter entfernt lag ein übel zugerichteter Soldat, aber mein Blick ging an ihm vorbei, zugunsten des Raketenwerfers, der ein paar Zentimeter außerhalb der Reichweite seiner toten Arme lag. Er sah intakt aus. Ich sprintete hin, drückte den Knopf fürs Synchronisieren und wartete die drei Sekunden, die es dauerte, bis er sich mit meinem Helm verbunden hatte. Kugeln prallten in der Nähe meiner Füße vom Boden ab und ich sprang instinktiv zur Seite, was auch immer das bringen würde.

Ich prüfte die Waffe und stellte fest, dass sie nicht geladen war.

Shit.

Ich rollte den toten Soldaten herum, durchsuchte seine Ausrüstung und fand die letzte Rakete. Ich schäme mich nicht, zuzugeben, dass ich mich hinter seiner Leiche verbarg, während ich auf dem Rücken lag und die große Patrone in den Werfer lud. Ich erhob mich auf die Knie und zielte in einem Winkel von sechzig Grad in die grobe Richtung der größten Gruppe roter Punkte und feuerte. Die Rakete rauschte mit sehr wenig Rückstoß davon und ich konnte nicht anders, als ihrer kurzen, leuchtenden Flugbahn zu folgen. Als sie ihren höchsten Punkt erreichte, explodierte sie in einer kleinen Rauchwolke, sechs Tochtergeschosse flogen nach unten in Richtung der Feinde und steuerten sie basierend auf der Übertragung meines Helms an. Die Sprengköpfe hatte nicht viel Sprengstoff geladen – vielleicht jeder ein halbes Kilo –, aber mit der präzisen Zielführung brauchten sie auch nicht viel. Etliche weitere rote Punkte erloschen und das gegnerische Feuer wurde langsam immer weniger.

Ich sprintete zu Tanaka zurück, kniete mich neben ihn und drückte sein Erste-Hilfe-Set an ihn, dort, wo sich seine Rüstung abgeschält hatte. Es vibrierte in meiner Hand, als es ihm Stabilisatoren injizierte, die ihm hoffentlich das Leben retteten. Für den Kampf fiel er aus, aber wenn ich ihn zurück aufs Schiff bekam, konnten sie ihn wieder zusammenflicken. Ich positionierte sein Gewicht auf meinen Schultern, etwa wie ich es mit Matua gemacht hatte, und kämpfte mich auf die Beine.

Ihn zu erschüttern, während er einen gebrochenen Rückenwirbel hatte, würde ihn vielleicht lähmen, aber das war besser als zu sterben.

Etwas krachte gegen meinen Rücken, wirbelte mich herum und warf mich nach vorne auf die Knie. Tanakas regloser Körper stürzte von mir, beinahe wie in Zeitlupe. Es spielte keine Rolle. Er hatte die Hauptlast der Puls-Detonation abbekommen, die ich gespürt hatte, und sie hatte seine Rüstung verschmort und ein rauchendes Loch zurückgelassen. Ich kniete einige Sekunden lang da, vielleicht länger. Als ich mich endlich gesammelt hatte, hatten die Schüsse aufgehört.

„Captain Tanaka wurde ausgeschaltet", sagte ich, erst über den Kanal des Platoons, dann über den der Kompanie.

„Erstes Platoon, wie ist Ihr Status?" Die Antwort kam nach ein paar Sekunden. Eine weibliche Stimme. Larsson. Jetzt, wo Tanaka ausgeschaltet war, hatte sie das Sagen. Mein Leben hatte sich gerade verschlechtert. Allerdings nicht so sehr wie Tanakas.

Niemand antwortete. Nach ein paar Sekunden dachte ich darüber nach, selbst Bericht zu erstatten, aber mein Bauchgefühl sagte mir, dass ich es nicht tun sollte. Nach einer Weile fragte sie erneut, diesmal auf dem Kanal des Platoons. Klug. Alle Vorgesetzten auf dem Kanal der Kompanie waren vermutlich ausgeschaltet, also hatte niemand sie gehört, als sie dort gefunkt hatte.

„Ma'am ... hier ist Sergeant Kapoor. Ich weiß nicht, wer das Sagen hat. Red Six ist ausgeschaltet, Red Seven auch. Wir haben ... ich weiß nicht. Vielleicht sind sechs von uns übrig. Sie waren überall. Schätzungsweise hundertfünfzig Feinde. Vielleicht mehr. Wir haben nicht aufgehört, auf sie zu schießen, aber es kamen immer mehr."

Die Verbindung war für ein paar Sekunden tot, ehe sie antwortete. „Ist Colonel Butler noch bei Ihnen?"

„Ich bin hier", sagte ich.

„Sichern Sie ihn und gehen Sie auf dem ursprünglichen Kurs weiter", sagte sie.

„Was verdammt noch mal reden Sie da?" Ich konnte nicht länger schweigen. „Wir müssen diese Mission abbrech–"

Mein Transmitter fiel aus. Nach ein paar Sekunden Stille wurde mir bewusst, dass sie auch meinen Empfänger ausgeschaltet hatte. Ich konnte weder etwas sagen, noch etwas hören. Die plötzliche Isolation verwirrte mich für einen Moment, auf eine Weise, wie es der Kampf nicht getan hatte. Ich kam schnell zur Besinnung und ging zu Kapoor hinüber, die anscheinend das befehligte, was von unserer Einheit übrig war. Leichen lagen zwischen den Bäumen verstreut. Jemand bewegte sich am Boden zu meiner Linken, und ich wandte mich stattdessen in diese Richtung. Ich musste nachdenken, bevor ich handelte. Ich hatte vielleicht nur eine Chance mit Kapoor und ich musste sie nutzen.

Blut sickerte an den gepanzerten Beinen der Soldatin hinunter, es kam aus einem Riss an ihrer Taille. Ich zog ihr Erste-Hilfe-Set heraus und machte einen Scan. Sie hatte keine Chance. Ich nahm ihr den Helm ab, presste ihr das Erste-Hilfe-Set an den Hals und wartete aufs Geräusch der Injektion. Ich konnte sie nicht retten, aber wenigstens würde sie sich in ihren letzten Minuten wohlfühlen.

Ich weiß nicht, wie ich in einer sitzenden Haltung landete oder wie lange ich so dasaß ... es war zu viel. Der Tod. Ich erinnerte mich daran, an Gefechte in der Vergangenheit, ich hatte Träume, aber hier ... ich saß benommen da, unfähig mich zu bewegen.

Ich schrie in mein totes Mikrofon und das Geräusch erschütterte das Innere meines Helms. Ich schrie und schrie, bis meine Kehle schmerzte, dann weinte ich.

Ich wusste nicht, wie lang ich dort saß, ehe ich aufhörte. Vermutlich nicht lange. Ein Soldat bewegte sich in mein Sichtfeld und meine Instinkte meldeten sich. Ich riss mich zusammen. Wir waren immer noch im Gefecht, und wir hatten keine Zeit, also verdrängte ich den ganzen Mist.

Ich musste wissen, wie es den anderen Einheiten ergangen war, ob es sie so hart getroffen hatte wie uns. Wenn ja, würde jemand Larsson zur Vernunft bringen. Wir hatten keine zehn Soldaten in unserem Platoon übrig, die gehen konnten. Wir hatten Verletzte, die wir evakuieren mussten. Wenn Larsson weiter vorrücken wollte, würden die Soldaten ihre Befehle nicht befolgen. Nicht jetzt. Nicht nach dem, was wir durchgemacht hatten.

Ein Schatten fiel erneut auf meine Blende, ich sah auf und erblickte eine Soldatin – mein Anzug identifizierte sie als Kapoor –, die mir mit ihrem Gewehr bedeutete, aufzustehen. Dann schloss sich ihr eine zweite Soldatin an und erleichterte mich um meine Waffe. Was verdammt noch mal dachten sie sich dabei? Wir brauchten jeden Schützen, den wir hatten, wenn wir es lebend von diesem Planeten herunterschaffen wollten. Wenn sie das verstanden, wenn es sie kümmerte, ließen sie sich das nicht anmerken. Zumindest konnte ich sie nicht hören. Ich wusste nicht, was Larsson befohlen oder ob sie ihr überhaupt widersprochen hatten. Was sie ihnen versprochen hatte. Ich war ein Gefangener, schlicht und ergreifend, schlimmer aber war die Isolation. Nicht Bescheid zu wissen.

Ich hatte keinen Zweifel, dass Larsson vorhatte, mich zu töten. Aber wenn das der Fall war, hätte einer der Soldaten mich einfach erschießen können. Vielleicht hatten sie sich geweigert. Vielleicht gab sie ihnen den Befehl nicht, weil sie ihre Loyalität nicht auf die Probe stellen wollte. Sie konnte ihnen befohlen haben, mich zu ihr zu bringen, um es selbst tun. Ich erwog, einen der Soldaten anzugreifen, um eine Waffe in die Finger zu kriegen, aber das würde sie provozieren. Ungeachtet ihrer Befehle hatten sie mich *nicht* erschossen und das wollte ich nicht ändern. Das hier war für mich nicht länger ein Gefechtseinsatz, sondern wieder eine Geiselnahme.

Natürlich hatte das niemand den Cappanern erzählt. Ich begann, die Grundlage eines Plans zu schmieden. Wenn sie wieder angriffen, wäre das meine Gelegenheit. Ich wusste nicht, wo ich hingehen würde, gestrandet auf einem hauptsächlich verlassenen Planeten, aber ich würde die Verwirrung ausnutzen und verschwinden. Vielleicht konnte ich mich verstecken und darauf warten, dass die Menschen den Planeten verließen. Ich konnte mein Glück bei den Cappanern versuchen.

Kapitel
neunundzwanzig

Wir begutachteten das Massaker, das einst unser Platoon gewesen war. Ich trug meinen Teil dazu bei und half, mich um die Verwundeten zu kümmern. Ich mochte vielleicht ein besserer Gefangener sein, aber ich war immer noch Soldat, und das waren sie auch, egal ob sie auf der falschen Seite dienten. Ich hatte kein Recht, sie zu verurteilen. Denn trotz allem, was sie getan hatten, seit sie sich für diese Mission gemeldet hatten, hatte ich in der Vergangenheit viel Schlimmeres getan. Ich bin ein Heuchler, aber kein *solcher*Heuchler.

Wir trennten die Toten von den Verwundeten, markierten eine Landezone und ließen die gehfähigen Verwundeten zurück, um die Evakuierung zu überwachen. Sie würden in Sicherheit sein, sobald die Schiffe unseren Standort erreichten. Ich konnte die Kommunikation nicht hören, aber ich nahm an, dass auch die anderen Einheiten schwere Verluste erlitten hatten. Fünf von unserem Platoon waren weitestgehend unverletzt.

Jemand musste entschieden haben, dass es unpraktisch war, nicht in der Lage zu sein, mit mir zu reden, denn es öffnete sich ein Kanal und Sergeant Kapoor meldete sich. Der Klang der Stimme eines anderen Menschen ermutigte mich, obwohl meine Lage immer noch beschissen war. „Sie haben keinen Zugang zu den

Kompaniekanälen, aber Sie können auf privaten Kanälen antworten, wenn jemand anderes ihn öffnet.“

„Danke.“ Ich hatte ein Dutzend andere Antworten vorbereitet, von Fluchen bis Betteln, aber das war alles, was ich herausbrachte. Vermutlich klug.

„Wir rücken bald aus. Ich hoffe, Sie machen uns keine Schwierigkeiten, Sir.“

„Wie lautet der Plan?“

„Weiß ich nicht“, sagte sie. „Der XO hat eine Idee, aber sie sagt uns nicht viel. Wir gehen weiter zum ursprünglichen Ziel.“

„Um was zu tun? Wir sind zu fünft und müssen drei Klicks weit gehen. Wer weiß, was dazwischen liegt?“

„Die Scans zeigen nichts, was auch immer das heißen mag.“ Ihr Tonfall ließ durchblicken, dass sie wusste, dass die Cappaner schon den ganzen Tag unsere Scans getäuscht hatten, also ging ich nicht weiter darauf ein. Aber ich konnte diesen Wahnsinn nicht auf sich beruhen lassen.

„Wieso weitergehen? Wieso treffen Sie nicht die Entscheidung, abzubrechen?“ Ich achtete darauf, dass meine Stimme neutral klang, nicht verurteilend. Ich war eher neugierig als alles andere, und wollte herausfinden, was eine Soldatin dazu brachte, in einer solch lächerlichen Situation weiterzumarschieren.

„Weil keine Exfiltration kommt, wenn wir nicht weitergehen. Nicht für uns, nicht für die Verwundeten.“

„Was?“ Ich konnte es nicht glauben.

„Sie haben mich verstanden, Sir. Wenn wir weitergehen, evakuieren sie die Verwundeten. Falls nicht, sitzen wir alle hier bis … tja, bis wer weiß wann.“

„Heilige Scheiße“, sagte ich. „Schwere Entscheidung.“

„Nicht wirklich. Sehen Sie sich um." Sie deutete auf die toten Soldaten auf der anderen Seite der Lichtung. „Denken Sie, wir wären nicht entbehrlich?"

„Das ist abgefuckt."

Sie nickte. „Jepp. Ich schätze aber, dass wir es verdient haben. Wir haben in der Vergangenheit eine Menge Gehaltschecks für leichte Missionen eingesammelt. Die Rechnung wird aber immer irgendwann fällig, richtig?"

„Kann ich dann wenigstens mein Gewehr wiederhaben?", fragte ich. „Wenn wir wieder in ein Gefecht geraten, kann ich helfen. Ich verspreche, ich werde niemanden von Ihnen erschießen."

„Ich kann nicht."

„Wenn Sie sterben, sterbe ich auch. Sie sind mein einziges Ticket von diesem Planeten. Lassen Sie mich Ihnen helfen, mein eigenes Leben zu retten."

Sie dachte einen Moment lang darüber nach. Ich versuchte zu erkennen, ob sich ihre Lippen bewegten, also ob sie über Funk jemand anderen nach seiner Meinung fragte, aber das Licht funkelte auf ihrer Blende, sodass ich nichts sehen konnte. „Versprechen Sie mir, dass Sie nicht abhauen."

Ich dachte für den Bruchteil einer Sekunde darüber nach. „Ich verspreche, dass ich nicht versuchen werde, *Ihnen* zu entkommen oder irgendetwas zu tun, dass der Mission schadet. Oder dieser Gruppe hier. Aber wenn Sie fliehen, fliehe ich mit Ihnen. Und wenn Sie alle tot sind, tue ich, was ich will."

„Deal." Sie ging und holte mein Gewehr. „Holen Sie sich außerdem so viel Munition, wie Sie tragen können."

„Danke." Ich ging zu dem Haufen, auf dem wir die Munition des Platoons gesammelt hatten. Ich hatte noch das meiste meiner Ladung, aber ich schnappte mir ein paar zusätzliche Magazine. Hauptsächlich Explosivgeschosse. Da wir nur so wenige waren, wollte ich alle Feuerkraft, die ich aufbringen konnte, so wenig es auch war. Ich hatte ernst gemeint, was ich Kapoor gesagt hatte. Sie steckte genauso tief in dieser Sache wie ich, wenn auch aus anderen Gründen, und es schien, als läge unser Ausweg für den Moment in derselben Richtung. Wenn dieser Weg sich irgendwann in der Zukunft teilte, würde ich noch mal darüber nachdenken.

Wir legten ein hohes Tempo vor, obwohl die Anzüge es beinahe mühelos machten. Irgendwo unterwegs verloren wir eine unserer Drohnen, aber wir ließen die andere tief zwischen den Bäumen vor uns hin und her fliegen, trotz der Tatsache, dass sie uns bisher nichts genutzt hatte. Über uns hallten die Triebwerke unserer Luftunterstützung, zu weit entfernt, um sagen zu können, wo genau sie war. Aber sie war nah genug, um zu reagieren.

Der Wald endete am Kamm eines steilen Abhangs, der etwa dreißig oder vierzig Meter in eine Senke führte, die sich rund zehn oder zwölf Kilometer weit erstreckte. Hunderte von grauweißen Fertigbauhäusern standen nicht sondern ordentlich gruppiert zusammen, sodass sie beinahe wie kleine Dörfer wirkten, die durch schmale Grasstreifen voneinander getrennt wurden. Wir waren unbehelligt eingetroffen. Die Cappaner mussten wissen, dass wir in der Nähe waren, wenn sie auch nicht unseren genauen Standort kannten. Aber es bewegte sich nichts, abgesehen von dem wadenhohen Gras, das in der Brise leicht hin und her wogte.

Ich drehte die Vergrößerung meines Helms herauf, scannte die Umgebung und gab Kapoor mit einer peinlichen Handbewegung ein Signal, die Drohne vorzuschicken, damit wir eine Videoübertragung hatten. Hier und dort lehnten Werkzeuge und andere Geräte an den Häusern, die Überbleibsel von Leben. Jemand hatte hier gelebt und war bis vor Kurzem vor Ort gewesen, aber nichts legte nahe, dass die Cappaner in den letzten paar Stunden hier gewesen waren. Vielleicht hatten sie evakuiert, als wir gelandet waren. Es würde Sinn ergeben, immerhin hätten wir mühelos Raketen und Schiffe benutzen können, um ihre verwundbare Niederlassung anzugreifen.

„Kontakt", sagte Kapoor. Eine Sekunde später erschienen feindliche Icons auf meinem Display. Ich orientierte mich an ihnen und lokalisierte so ein halbes Dutzend Cappaner in einer beinahe verborgenen Stellung auf der von unserer Position aus rechten Seite des Lagers.

„Hab sie", sagte ich. „Ich kann nicht sagen, ob sie bewaffnet sind oder nicht."

„Gehen Sie davon aus, dass sie Waffen haben", sagte sie unnötigerweise.

„Haben wir Befehle?", fragte ich. Die Cappaner waren außerhalb der Reichweite von Gewehren, also hatten wir begrenzte Möglichkeiten.

„Stillhalten und abwarten", sagte sie. „Beobachten."

Ich seufzte und scannte weiter. Ich identifizierte einen zweiten Außenposten von Cappanern, dieser noch besser versteckt – beinahe unter der Erde, so gut hatten sie gegraben. Ich ließ mein System die roten Punkte an die Gruppe übertragen, sodass die anderen sie sehen konnten. Ich hatte keine Zeit für weitere Einschätzungen, da eine Gruppe blauer Icons auftauchte und dann beinahe augenblicklich noch eine kleinere Gruppe. Die Überbleibsel der anderen beiden Platoons waren in Reichweite gekommen. Ihrer Anzahl nach zu urteilen, waren sie beinahe so schwer getroffen worden wie wir. Sieben in einer Gruppe, zehn in der anderen. Mit unseren fünf lag die Gesamtzahl bei zweiundzwanzig von ursprünglich einhundertsechzig. Das bedeutete eine Verlustrate von etwa fünfundachtzig Prozent, was weit über das hinausging, was eine Einheit verlieren konnte, ohne ihre Funktion einzubüßen. Aber hier waren wir und machten weiter. Wenn wir die Guten gewesen wären, hätte man es heldenhaft genannt.

Aber wir waren nicht die Guten.

Wie um das zu unterstreichen, wurde das Dröhnen von Schiffen lauter, als sich unsere beiden Luftunterstützungsvögel schnell näherten. Ich hoffte, es wäre nur eine Machtdemonstration. Mir drehte sich der Magen um, als sie beide je zwei Objekte abwarfen. Die Bomben schienen beinahe zu schweben, als wären sie Blätter im Wind und nicht zweihundert Kilogramm Metall, Sprengstoff und Tod. Aber sie schienen nur wegen der Geschwindigkeit der Schiffe zu schweben, die sie abgeworfen hatten, und wegen des Schreckens, etwas Entsetzliches, aber Unvermeidliches mitanzusehen. Sie schlugen alle innerhalb von Sekunden ein, blitzen auf und warfen Erde und Polymertrümmer von Gebäuden am Rand des Lagers empor. Die Wand eines Gebäudes, scheinbar intakt, flog etwa fünfzig Meter in die Luft und überschlug sich etliche Male, ehe sie wieder zu Boden fiel. Der Knall erreichte uns ein paar Sekunden später, viermal charakteristisches Knirschen, gefolgt vom leiseren Aufprallen des fallenden Schutts.

Das Schiff gewann an Höhe, wendete und flog auf anderem Kurs in unsere Richtung zurück. Ich schaltete meinen Helm auf maximale Vergrößerung und scannte die Trümmer, aber ich sah keine Leichen.

„Was zur Hölle macht sie?", fragte ich und vergaß, dass mein Mikrofon tot war. Die Siedlung zu zerstören, würde uns nicht das verschaffen, was wir brauchten, es sei denn, die Mission hatte sich geändert und lautete jetzt „Rache". Ich glaubte nicht, dass sie sich geändert hatte. In der Theorie hielt jemand in einem dieser Gebäude den Schlüssel zu einer Multimilliarden schweren Industrie in der Hand. Vernünftige Leute warfen so was nicht weg. Unternehmen taten es definitiv nicht, und ich hatte keinen Zweifel, dass Omicron bei der Mission immer noch die Strippen zog, auf die eine oder andere Weise.

Das Schiff steuerte wieder nach unten, ehe es im letzten Moment abdrehte, hart wendete und dann begann, im Kreis zu fliegen, ohne je außer Sicht zu geraten. Einen Moment später verstand ich, wieso, als am Rand des Talkessels ein Lautsprecher ertönte, vielleicht neunzig Grad zu unserer Linken, am nächsten an der Stelle, wo die Bomben eingeschlagen waren.

„Achtung! Wir wollen uns mit Ihren Anführern treffen. Sie haben fünf Minuten, um uns zuzustimmen, oder wir werden weitere Bomben abwerfen." Ich brauchte ein paar Sekunden, um zu begreifen, dass die Ansage auf Cappanisch war und ich eine Übersetzung hörte. Offenbar hatte Larsson diese Funktion meines Helms nicht ausgeschaltet.

Mindestens zwei Minuten bewegte sich in der Siedlung unter uns nichts. Ich fragte mich, ob irgendjemand in den Gebäuden war. Wenn die Anführer, die Larsson zu treffen verlangte, evakuiert worden waren, würde es ein harter Tag für die cappanische Siedlung werden. Das warf allerdings die Frage auf, wo sie waren, wenn nicht hier? Und würde es eine Rolle spielen, ihre Häuser zu zerstören? Jemand in meiner Gruppe zeigte auf etwas und ich wandte meinen Blick zur Tür eines Gebäudes, die sich geöffnet hatte. Es war mir wegen der identischen Farbe und Fertigbauweise vorher nicht aufgefallen, aber das Gebäude war vielleicht viermal größer als die anderen Bauten. Ich ertappte mich dabei, wie ich den Atem anhielt, obwohl ich nicht wusste, was ich erwartete.

Drei Cappaner traten heraus, entfernten sich vom Gebäude und winkten. Ich weiß nicht, ob sie es als Signal zur Identifikation meinten oder um den nächsten Angriff zu verhindern. Da wir nur einen Lautsprecher zur Kommunikation hatten, konnten wir es nicht wissen.

„Wir sehen Sie", sagte der Lautsprecher. „Warten Sie dort und bewegen Sie sich nicht. Wir kommen zu Ihnen. Wenn jemand auf uns feuert, werden wir Sie und Ihre gesamte Siedlung vernichten."

Ich kam nicht mehr mit. Larsson musste irgendeine Art Spiel spielen, um an die Informationen zu kommen, aber es schien eine beiderseitige Bereitschaft zur Vernichtung zu sein, vorausgesetzt sie hatte vor, selbst in den Talkessel zu gehen, wovon ich ausging. Anzunehmen, dass die Cappaner ihre Siedlung genug wertschätzten, um nicht zu feuern, war ein ziemlich hohes Risiko. Nichts, auf das ich mein Leben gesetzt hätte, was Larsson aber tat.

„Gehen wir", sagte Sergeant Kapoor und riss mich aus meinen Gedanken.

„Ich?", fragte ich.

„Sie und ich", sagte sie. „Die anderen bleiben hier und geben uns Deckung."

„Okay. Was ist meine Funktion?" Larsson wollte vielleicht immer noch, dass ich einen Deal aushandelte, aber sie hatte bereits auf Drohungen zurückgegriffen, also hatte ich nicht viel Spielraum übrig, mit dem ich arbeiten konnte.

„Kommen Sie mit mir mit und machen Sie keine Dummheiten", sagte Kapoor.

Ich wollte fragen: *Sie meinen, wie ohne Plan ins Freie zu laufen?*, sagte aber nur: „Roger." Entweder wusste sie es nicht oder sie sagte es mir nicht. So oder so, es half nicht, mich mit ihr zu streiten.

Den sechzig Grad steilen Abhang runterzukommen, wäre ohne die Unterstützung unserer Rüstungen schwierig gewesen, aber unsere Fersen gruben sich in weiche Stellen und machten es leicht, wenn auch unbeholfen. Wir erreichten den Grund des Kessels und die ersten Gebäude, die größtenteils drei Mal vier Meter maßen, obwohl einige von Nahem betrachtet etwas größer waren als die anderen. Ich spähte durch ein paar der transparenten Polymerfenster. Aus etwa einem Dutzend Gebäuden blickte mich Augenpaare an. Sie hatten evakuiert, aber nicht komplett, was die Frage aufwarf, ob die Zurückgebliebenen Teil eines Plans waren oder sich zu gehen geweigert hatten. Ich verbannte diesen Gedanken aus meinem Kopf. Die Cappaner hatten ihre Gründe und ich konnte sie nicht beeinflussen.

Wir erreichten das, was ich jetzt für die Kommandozentrale des cappanischen Lagers hielt, zur selben Zeit wie Larsson, der zwei Soldaten folgten. Die drei Cappaner hatten sich nicht bewegt. Ich bin sehr schlecht darin, cappanische Körpersprache zu lesen, aber sie machten auf mich einen ruhigen Eindruck, was ich als gutes Zeichen verstand. Vorschnelle Entscheidungen, egal auf welcher Seite, würden zu diesem Zeitpunkt nur auf eine Weise enden, und es wäre keine gute.

„Haben Sie das Sagen?", fragte Larsson. Wir alle standen ein paar Meter voneinander entfernt, etwa in Form eines Dreiecks. Kapoor und ich, die Cappaner und Larsson mit ihren Gorillas. Ich hätte mich um Einiges besser gefühlt, wenn Tanaka überlebt hätte.

„Hier entlang", sagte der Cappaner, der ein kleines Stück vor den anderen beiden stand, und ging auf das Gebäude zu. Larsson folgte ohne zu zögern. Ich blickte Kapoor an, die mit den Schultern zuckte und ihnen dann folgte. Larssons Wachen blieben draußen stehen, auf ihren Befehl hin, wie ich vermutete. Kapoor bedeutete mir, hineinzugehen, dann drehte sie ab und wartete mit den anderen beiden, nicht aber, ohne mir vorher mein Gewehr abzunehmen. Larsson musste eine

Menge Vertrauen in ihren Plan haben, wenn sie nur mit mir zusammen reinging und ich unbewaffnet war. Ich fragte mich, was sie wusste und ich nicht.

Meine Blende brauchte einen Moment, um sich in dem schummrigeren Innenbereich aufzuhellen. Ein einzelner Cappaner wartete am Ende eines langen, rechteckigen Raumes auf uns. Computerterminals säumten die Wände, acht oder neun auf jeder Seite, aber niemand saß auf den Stühlen davor. Als wir den Cappaner erreichten, sah ich, dass er einen gelben Kreis um ein Auge hatte, der aussah wie eine Augenklappe, und obwohl er anders gekleidet war, erkannte ich ihn von unserem Treffen auf Talca. Ich behielt einen neutralen Gesichtsausdruck, lächelte aber in mich hinein. Was immer Larsson wusste, ich hatte wenigstens eine Sache, um es auszugleichen.

„Grüße", sagte sie.

„Gleichfalls", sagte der Cappaner. „Ich wünschte, wir hätten uns unter anderen Umständen treffen können."

„In der Tat. Aber noch ist Zeit, um die Situation zu retten."

Der Cappaner neigte den Kopf leicht. „Das wäre gut. Wir haben beide genug Soldaten verloren."

„Wir haben Ihnen ein Geschenk mitgebracht", sagte Larsson. „Das ist Colonel Butler. Der Zerstörer Ihrer Welt."

Mein Herz klopfte in meiner Brust, nicht weil ich beleidigt war, in dieser Verhandlung ein Druckmittel zu sein. Das war ich von Anfang an gewesen. Stattdessen sorgte ich mich darum, dass der cappanische Anführer verraten würde, dass wir uns bereits kennengelernt hatten und damit den einen Vorteil zunichtemachte den ich hatte.

„Sie haben meinem Volk großes Leid zugefügt“, sagte er.

„Das tut mir sehr leid“, sagte ich.

„Wenn Sie uns die Informationen geben, die wir haben wollen, lassen wir ihn hier, und Sie können mit ihm machen, was Sie wollen“, sagte Larsson.

„Das ist ein großzügiges Angebot“, sagte der Cappaner. „Aber er ist bereits hier. Sie verhandeln über etwas, das wir bereits haben.“

„Meine Leute sind immer noch da draußen“, sagte Larsson. „Wichtiger noch, sie sind ebenfalls im Orbit. Wenn ich nicht mit den Daten herauskomme, die ich benötige, haben sie den Befehl, diese komplette Insel dem Erdboden gleichzumachen.“

Also das war der Schachzug. Sie hatten nie gewollt, dass ich verhandle. Sie wollten mich als Tauschware. Was den Cappaner betraf, so änderte sich sein Ausdruck nicht, beinahe so, als hätte er ihre Antwort erwartet. Er musste gewusst haben, dass sie nicht ohne Notfallplan hier war. Er hatte mir sozusagen gesagt, dass er diese Drohung erwartete. Seit meinem Treffen mit dem Cappaner auf Talca verstand ich, was ich in den vergangenen Jahren nicht verstanden hatte. Die Cappaner wussten stets mehr, als wir ihnen zutrauten.

„Colonel Butler, was ist Ihre Meinung dazu?“

„Seine Meinung spielt keine Rolle“, sagte Larsson.

„Tut sie“, sagte der Cappaner. „Er kennt Ihre Leute und weiß, wie sehr ich Ihnen vertrauen kann.“

„Sie können Ihnen überhaupt nicht vertrauen“, sagte ich.

Larsson wandte sich zu mir um und blickte mich durch ihre transparente Blende hindurch wütend an, aber sie war in einer Sackgasse. Sie hatte mich den Cappanern als Preis versprochen, also konnte sie nichts tun, ohne ihr Angebot zu gefährden. Ich wusste die Gelegenheit zu schätzen, die ihr Fehler mir eröffnet hatte.

„Sie wissen nicht, wovon Sie reden", sagte sie.

„Sicher weiß ich das", sagte ich. „Sobald Sie haben, was Sie wollten, und vom Planeten runter sind, werden Sie ihn so oder so in Schutt und Asche legen."

„Warum sollten wir das tun? Wir hätten die Technologie, die wir haben wollen. Das ist der Auftrag."

Ich wandte mich an den Cappaner. „Um ihre Spuren zu verwischen. Wenn sie ihr Angebot ernst meinen würden, würden sie Ihnen anbieten, gemeinsam an dem Projekt zu arbeiten. Die Cappaner haben in zwei Jahren mehr erreicht als Menschen in zwanzig. Aber das können sie aus politischen Gründen nicht tun."

„Er lügt", sagte Larsson.

Ich ignorierte Larsson weiterhin und hielt stattdessen mit dem Cappaner Augenkontakt. Er war der Schlüssel zu allem. Sie spielte keine Rolle. Ich hatte auf Talca eine leichte Verbindung zu ihm gespürt und hoffte, dass es ihm auch so gegangen war – hoffte, dass er danach handeln würde.

„Er lügt, um seine eigene Haut zu retten", wiederholte Larsson und ein leichtes Zittern schlich sich in ihre Stimme.

Ich schüttelte den Kopf. „Das habe ich in dem Moment aufgegeben, als ich Havertys Büro verließ. Diese Sache endet für mich nur auf eine Weise. Ich will lediglich etwas Gutes tun, ehe ich gehe."

„Er ist–“ Larsson verkniff sich ihre Antwort. Ich konnte beinahe sehen, wie ihr Verstand arbeitete. „Wenn ich nicht kriege, weshalb ich gekommen bin, ist das das Ende für diese Siedlung und Ihr Volk auf diesem Planeten.“

„Und wenn sie bekommt, weshalb sie gekommen ist, ist es immer noch das Ende. Warum sollten Sie Ihr einziges Druckmittel aus der Hand geben?“

Larsson zielte mit ihrem Gewehr auf mich. Ich wich einen Schritt zurück, auch wenn das nichts brachte. Ich hätte diese Reaktion kommen sehen müssen, so wie ich sie provoziert hatte. Andererseits hätte sie mich vor einer Stunde erschießen sollen, anstatt mich für ein falsches Geschäft zu benutzen. Larssons Gesichtsausdruck war eine Mischung aus Entschlossenheit und Hass … und dann explodierte ihr Kopf mit zwei leisen Explosionen, Schüssen, die durch die Bauweise des Raums abgedämpft wurden. Ich stolperte zurück, meine Blende war mit Blut, Knochensplittern und Gehirnmasse bespritzt. Einer der Cappaner stand hinter Larsson, sein Gewehr folgte ihrer Leiche, die wie ein Sack Erde zu Boden fiel.

„Die Soldaten draußen–“

Der Cappaner mit der Augenklappe ließ mich mit einer Handbewegung verstummen. „Wir haben uns um sie gekümmert.“ Ich wusste nicht, ob das hieß, dass sie tot waren oder lebten. Ich hatte keine Schüsse gehört, aber angesichts des Schallschutzes in den Wänden bedeutete das nichts. „Um die auf dem Kamm ebenfalls.“

„Da ist immer noch das Schiff im Orbit“, sagte ich. „Es hat XB25er geladen.“

„Es ist, wie Sie gesagt haben. Das war immer unser Schicksal. Wir haben die meisten unserer Leute evakuiert, unter die Erde. Wir hoffen, dass sich der Schaden begrenzen lässt.“

Ich dachte darüber nach. Unter der Erde zu sein würde helfen, aber es spielte keine Rolle. Wenn sie überlebten, würde Omicron wiederkommen. Es war zu viel Geld für sie im Spiel. Sie waren verloren, egal, was passierte.

Vielleicht aber auch nicht.

„Was, wenn es einen anderen Weg gäbe?“, fragte ich.

„Ich bin ganz Ohr.“

Kapitel dreißig

Die nächsten paar Minuten vergingen wie im Flug. Ich wusste nicht, wie lange wir hatten, bis das Schiff das Feuer eröffnete, wenn die Crew nichts von Larsson hörte. Trotz allem, was auf dem Planeten passiert war, spielten jetzt die Dinge im All eine Rolle. Ich hoffte, dass sie zögern würden, den Abzug zu betätigen, weil ihre eigenen Leute hier unten waren, aber angesichts dessen, was ich bisher von der Söldnertruppe gesehen hatte, hätte ich nicht viel darauf gewettet. Ein cappanischer Techniker brauchte fast acht Minuten, um meinen Helm zu hacken und die Kommunikation wiederherzustellen, und ich nutzte die Zeit, um dem cappanischen Anführer meinen Plan zu unterbreiten.

„Sie wollen also, dass wir einfach die Informationen aus der Hand geben", sagte er, als ich fertig war.

„Ich glaube, es ist unsere einzige Option. Ich hatte diesen Gedanken bereits, als wir uns auf Talca unterhielten, und ich bin jetzt nur noch überzeugter davon. Sobald die Information einmal da draußen ist und alle sie haben, gibt es keinen Grund, Sie weiter zu verfolgen."

„Und Sie sind sich sicher, dass Sie sie auf diese Weise nach draußen kriegen?"

„Ich werde Ihre Hilfe brauchen", sagte ich. „Sie haben Leute, die eine Nachricht an jemanden außerhalb des Planeten übermitteln können, richtig?"

„Ja, das bekommen wir hin. Es ist schwierig, ohne dass sie abgefangen wird, aber auch wenn sie es wahrscheinlich mitbekommen, können sie sie nicht aufhalten.“

„Dann helfen Sie mir, eine Nachricht an Karen Plazz zu schicken. Ich schreibe etwas und Sie fügen hinzu, was immer Sie sie wissen lassen wollen. Sie wird es in der Galaxis verbreiten.“

Er dachte einen Moment lang darüber nach. „Schreiben Sie Ihre Nachricht. Ich werde mich anschließend entscheiden. Und beeilen Sie sich. Ich glaube nicht, dass wir viel Zeit haben.“

Ich hatte mir vor diesem Moment etliche Male durch den Kopf gehen lassen, was ich sagen würde, also dauerte es nicht lange.

Karen, sorry, dass ich mich nicht gemeldet habe, aber ich wurde von Omicron gekidnappt, mit der bereitwilligen Teilnahme von VPC – Sie haben vermutlich von deren „Gemeinschaftsprojekt“ gehört –, um auf eine Mission zu gehen, bei der ich einer cappanischen Kolonie Technologie abpressen sollte. Ich werde den Standort nicht nennen, um die Cappaner nicht zu gefährden, obwohl sie selbst ihn vielleicht preisgeben, außerdem kennen die Unternehmen ihn bereits. Omicron hat von den Cappanern Technologie gestohlen und an ihnen Experimente durchgeführt, um im Rahmen des sogenannten Phoenix Project medizinische Forschung zu ermöglichen. Die Cappaner haben die Technik perfektioniert, an der Colonel Elliot auf Cappa gearbeitet hat – die Prozedur, die Menschen hilft, Ortho-Robotik anzunehmen. Alles, was folgt, ist eine Nachricht von den

Cappanern selbst. Sie können darauf vertrauen, dass sie die Wahrheit sagen. Bitte verbreiten Sie sie so umfassend wie möglich. Wenn dieser Gruppe Cappanern etwas zustößt, war es Omicron. Sie haben XB25er an Bord ihres Schiffs und sie beabsichtigen, sie einzusetzen. Bitte halten Sie diese Nachricht sechsundneunzig Stunden nach Erhalt unter Verschluss, ehe Sie sie veröffentlichen.

Eine letzte Bitte – und das ist das Wichtigste, was ich sagen werde: Es gibt eine ehemalige Angestellte von VPC namens Ganos. Sie hat mir geholfen, diesen Punkt der Operation zu erreichen, und ich habe Grund zur Annahme, dass Omicron und/oder VPC sie ins Visier genommen haben. Vielleicht haben sie sie bereits. Finden Sie sie und sorgen Sie für Ihre Sicherheit, koste es, was es wolle. Betrachten Sie es als meine Bezahlung für diese Information. Falls ein Mensch mit cappanischer DNA namens Sasha Sie kontaktiert, vertrauen Sie ihr. Carl.

Ich zeigte es Augenklappe. Er nickte. „Wir werden unsere Leute ebenfalls einsetzen, um Ganos zu beschützen. Aber ich verstehe die sechsundneunzig Stunden nicht."

„Wenn alles nach Plan läuft, wird die Crew des Schiffs im Orbit ihre Mission abgeschlossen haben und auf dem Heimweg sein. Sie werden in Stasis, also nicht in der Lage sein, Nachrichten zu empfangen, wenn die Information an die Öffentlichkeit gelangt."

„Aber das wird keine Rolle spielen, wenn sie bereits ihre Raketen abgefeuert haben."

„Überlassen Sie das mir", sagte ich. „Ich habe einen Plan. Aber ich muss wissen, wo Ihre Standorte unter der Erde sind."

Augenklappe sah mich mit einem Ausdruck an, den ich, wäre er ein Mensch gewesen, für Skepsis gehalten hätte. „Sie verlangen viel Vertrauen."

„Das tue ich. Aber Sie haben mich ausgewählt, auf Talca. Etwas hat Sie dazu bewogen."

Der Cappaner starrte mich an und ich musste annehmen, dass er nachdachte. Schließlich fragte er: „Sind Sie sich sicher, dass Sie uns beschützen können?"

„Bin ich nicht", sagte ich. „Aber wenn ich es zurück auf das Schiff schaffe, bin ich Ihre beste Chance."

Er entfernte sich von mir und rief einem seiner Landsmänner etwas zu. Sie unterhielten sich leise, erhoben ihre Stimmen einmal, der Neuankömmling hob wütend die Hände. Nach etlichen Minuten der Diskussion kam er zurück. „Wir werden Ihnen zeigen, was Sie wollen. Aber nur Sie können gehen. Die anderen bleiben hier."

„Ich muss Sie mitnehmen. So viele wie möglich."

Er schüttelte den Kopf. „Sie verlangen zu viel. Wir vertrauen Ihnen, aber die Soldaten aufzugeben ist unbesonnen."

„Was wird mit ihnen passieren?"

„Sie werden bei uns bleiben. Wenn wir überleben, überleben sie."

Ich nickte. „Und danach?"

„Sie werden hierbleiben müssen. Wir werden ihnen nichts tun und sie werden frei leben dürfen. Hoffentlich kommt in der Zukunft der Punkt, an dem wir sie freilassen können."

Ich seufzte. Ich verdammte die Soldaten zu einem Leben in Gefangenschaft, wenn ich den Cappanern erlaubte, sie hierzubehalten. Entscheidender für meinen Plan war, dass Omicron und unmittelbarer das Schiff im Orbit einen Grund hatten, wiederzukommen, solange lebende Soldaten auf dem Planeten waren. Diese Soldaten hatten Freunde dort oben und wenn man Gefühle ins Spiel brachte, änderte es das Ergebnis. „Wenn sie glauben, dass ihre eigenen Leute noch leben, werden sie wiederkommen, um sie zu retten. Es ist wichtig für unseren Plan, dass sie das nicht tun."

„Wir könnten sie töten", sagte Augenklappe.

Ich versuchte, nicht zusammenzuzucken. Trotz unserer Abmachung gab es immer noch ernste Unterschiede zwischen meiner Vorstellung von Moral und der der Cappaner. Ich musste mich daran erinnern, dass das hier Leute waren, die ihre eigenen Toten zur Warnung an Pfähle gebunden hatten. „Oder Sie könnten den Eindruck erwecken, als *wären* sie tot. Die Sensoren in ihren Anzügen. Sie müssen die Ortungsfunktion so oder so deaktivieren. Es wäre nicht viel aufwändiger, die anderen Sensoren ebenfalls zu modifizieren."

Wieder dachte er darüber nach. „Das könnten wir tun."

Ich nickte, wandte mich ab und versuchte, meine Erleichterung zu verbergen. Ich durfte mich nicht so sehr in der Zusammenarbeit verlieren, dass ich vergaß, dass wir nicht auf derselben Seite standen. Ich wollte ihnen helfen, und ich glaube, das erkannten sie, aber das ging nur bis zu einem gewissen Punkt. „Dann fehlt nur noch, dass Sie mir zeigen, wohin sie evakuieren."

„Was werden Sie anschließend tun?"

„Ich werde mit den Daten fliehen und versuchen, die Leute auf dem Schiff dazu zu bringen, mir zu glauben.“

Ich eilte den Hang hinauf, meine Füße rutschten auf der Erde aus, kleine Steine rollten hinter mir nach unten, bis ich die Kante erreichte und in den Wald lief. Ich joggte anderthalb Kilometer weit, ehe ich Kontakt zum Schiff aufnahm. Ich wollte, dass es so aussah, als wäre ich so weit wie möglich vor den Cappanern geflohen, um mir einen Puffer zu verschaffen, ehe ich einen Funkspruch riskierte: als befürchtete ich, dass sie mein Signal verfolgten. Die Cappaner würden mir nachjagen, sobald ich Kontakt herstellte, um die Illusion abzurunden.

„*Basilisk*, hier ist Butler.“ Ich gab mein Bestes, um meine Stimme verzweifelt klingen zu lassen. Niemand antwortete. Ich überprüfte den Kanal und versuchte es erneut. „*Basilisk*, hier spricht Colonel Butler. Bitte melden.“

„Sprechen Sie, Sir.“

„Ich habe die Daten.“

Es war eine Weile still, länger als die gute Sekunde, die es brauchte, bis die Nachricht in den Orbit gelangt war und eine Antwort mich erreichen würde. „Sagen Sie das noch mal.“

„Die Daten. Die Mission. Das, weswegen wir hergekommen sind. Ich habe sie!“

„Wie?“

„Larsson hatte sie, ehe sie sie getötet haben. Sie vermutete, dass sie sie verraten würden, und gab sie mir. Als unsere Truppen reinkamen, habe ich die Verwirrung genutzt, um zu entkommen. Ich weiß nicht, ob sie mich verfolgen oder nicht. Es wäre wirklich fantastisch, wenn mich jemand abholen würde."

Eine weitere Pause. „Ist sonst noch jemand am Leben?"

„Ich weiß es nicht. Meine Sensoren zeigen nichts an, aber ich habe mich vom letzten bekannten Standort entfernt und bewege mich jede Minute weiter weg." Das war eine glatte Lüge, aber es würde sie dazu zwingen, ihre eigenen Systeme zu checken und eigene Schlüsse zu ziehen. So würden sie es eher glauben. Sie würden mir nicht vertrauen, aber sie vertrauten ihren Maschinen mehr als sie sollten. Eine Menge Sachen mussten gutgehen, damit meine Täuschung klappte, und wenn eine davon schiefging, würde mein Plan scheitern, also half alles, was ich zu meinen Gunsten hinzufügen konnte.

„Wir nehmen keine Lebenszeichen wahr. Aber da sind Cappaner, die sich in Ihre Richtung bewegen."

„Shit. Wo?", fragte ich.

„Etwa anderthalb Klicks hinter Ihnen. Sie empfangen vermutlich das Signal Ihrer Übertragung. Schalten Sie Ihren Kommunikator auf Nur-Empfangen um. Das können sie nicht so leicht verfolgen."

„Roger", sagte ich.

„Wir schicken Ihnen Koordinaten auf Ihr Display. Bewegen Sie sich sofort zu diesem Standort. Sie werden in vierzehn Minuten abgeholt. Keine Antwort erforderlich. Gehen Sie einfach da hin."

Mein Computer berechnete den Standort im Bruchteil einer Sekunde und schickte ihn auf mein Display. Bei meiner gegenwärtigen Geschwindigkeit würde ich ihn mit zwei Minuten Puffer erreichen. Ich änderte die

Richtung um neunzehn Grad nach links und rannte weiter. Die niedrige Gravitation und mein Anzug, der mich mit Sauerstoff versorgte und meine Beine unterstützte, machten das Laufen beinahe unbekümmert – es half außerdem, zu wissen, dass ich nicht wirklich verfolgt wurde. Diese gedankenlosen Minuten erlaubten mir, jedes Szenario durchzugehen, das ich mir vorstellen konnte, wissend, dass ich unmöglich an alle denken konnte. Es würde sich etwas ereignen, das ich nicht vorausgesehen hatte. Im Grunde genommen würde ich von dem Moment an, in dem ich einen anderen Menschen sah, eine Rolle spielen, bis es eine finale Entscheidung gab. Oder bis sie mich durch eine Luftschleuse ins All pusteten. Das war eine reale Möglichkeit, ungeachtet dessen, ob mein Plan funktionierte, aber ich ertappte mich dabei, festzustellen, dass es mir nichts ausmachte. Zu erwarten, dass man stirbt, hat etwas Befreiendes. Wenn ich die Cappaner retten konnte, wäre das ein Erfolg, egal, was sonst passierte.

Das klingt nach Bullshit. Das weiß ich. Eine Menge Leute sagen, dass sie bereit sind, dem Tod gegenüberzutreten, sperren sich aber, wenn sie diesen Punkt wirklich erreichen. Aber mein Leben spielte nicht länger eine Rolle. Ich wollte nicht sterben. Ich suchte den Tod nicht aktiv. Aber ich wollte auch nicht länger leben. Wenn ich irgendwie überlebte, musste ich dieses Gefühl zusammen mit Dr. Baqri analysieren. Noch eine Sache mehr auf meiner Liste.

Ich erreichte die Koordinaten, ging am Rand der Lichtung auf ein Knie und scannte die Richtung, aus der ich gekommen war, nach meinen cappanischen „Verfolgern". Sie würden mich nicht einholen, da sie es nicht wirklich versuchten, aber ich musste mich daran gewöhnen, alles genau richtig aussehen zu lassen. Es war beinahe ausgeschlossen, dass irgendein Mensch mich in diesem Moment sehen konnte, zumindest nicht genau genug, um zu sehen, in welche Richtung mein Gewehr zeigte. Aber beinahe ausgeschlossen ist nicht dasselbe wie ausgeschlossen. Ich musste jede noch so kleine Gelegenheit ergreifen, um potenzielle Enttarnung zu vermeiden. Sie summierten sich.

Das Schiff kam schnell herangeflogen, der Pilot erinnerte sich vermutlich an das Luftabwehrfeuer, das wir abbekommen hatten, als wir auf den Planeten runtergeflogen waren. Ich wünschte, ich hätte daran gedacht, den Cappanern zu sagen, dass sie das Schiff beschießen sollen, um es besser aussehen zu lassen. Vermutlich war es eine gute Sache, dass ich es vergessen hatte, denn bei meinem Glück hätten sie es aus Versehen getroffen und alles ruiniert.

Ich sprintete in Richtung des Schiffs, ehe es landete. Gerade als sie sich öffnete, erreichte ich die Tür, eilte hindurch, stolperte und landete auf dem Boden, als das Schiff abhob, ehe ich mich irgendwo festhalten konnte. Zwei Soldaten halfen mir auf einen Sitz und schnallten mich an, während eine weitere Soldatin eine Pulskanone bemannte und die Gegend scannte, die wir gerade verlassen hatten. Ich beobachtete sie aus dem Augenwinkel, um zu sehen, ob sie feuerte, um zu sehen, ob sie die cappanischen Verfolger gesehen hatte. Hatte sie nicht.

Ich setzte den Helm ab, da ich jetzt auf dem Schiff war, das seine eigene Sauerstoffversorgung hatte, fuhr mir mit der Hand über die Glatze und wischte mir den

Schweiß weg. Jemand warf mir ein Handtuch zu, ich benutzte es gründlich auf meinem Kopf und Nacken und nahm mir Zeit, mich auf meinen Text vorzubereiten.

„Was ist da unten passiert, Sir?", fragte einer der Soldaten, die mir geholfen hatten. Er war klein und sein Haar war so hell, dass es beinahe weiß wirkte. Er sah jung aus, hatte keine Falten um die Augen, andererseits sah jeder auf der Mission im Vergleich zu mir jung aus.

„Ich habe keine verdammte Ahnung." Je einfacher die Antwort, desto einfacher ist es zu lügen.

„Wie haben–"

„Leute sind gestorben", sagte ich und unterbrach ihn, ehe er seine Frage stellen konnte. Ich sagte es langsam, in einem Tonfall, den Kriegsveteranen erkennen würden. Der Tonfall, der begleitet wurde vom Blick ins Nichts, dem Blick eines Mannes, der zu viel gesehen hat. „Einfach ... alle. Verdammte Raketen, Scharfschützen und Kartoffelminen. Wir hätten uns zurückziehen sollen."

Er beobachtete mich eine Minute lang, aber nicht so, wie es ein argwöhnischer Vernehmender tun würde. Mehr wie ein Soldat – und vermutlich einer, der mir zustimmte. Das musste ich erreichen. Dass sie mich als Soldat sahen. Gut, dass ich einige Übung in der Rolle hatte. Aus welchem Grund auch immer sagte er nichts mehr, und niemand sonst auf dem Schiff näherte sich mir. Ich verstand das so, dass ich den ersten Test bestanden hatte, was sicherlich der Leichteste, aber notwendig gewesen war. Als Nächstes käme ein Meeting mit dem Stabsoffizier. Da mein Treffen mit Lieutenant Danner von Larsson unterbrochen worden war, hatte ich keine Gelegenheit gehabt, ihn kennenzulernen, und jetzt brauchte ich ihn für den nächsten Teil meines Plans. Er hatte das Team befehligt, das auf dem Schiff geblieben war. Jetzt war er der Kommandant für die gesamte Mission. Wichtiger noch, er wäre derjenige, der wegen weiterer Befehle mit Omicron kommunizieren würde.

Und er wäre vermutlich derjenige, der die Luftschleuse bedienen würde, wenn sie sich dafür entschieden, mich ins All zu befördern.

Wir landeten auf der *Basilisk* und warteten darauf, dass sich die Landebucht mit Luft füllte. Ich blieb etwas länger als nötig auf meinem Sitz, bis sich alle anderen abgeschnallt hatten. Ich kannte meinen Status nicht und wollte nicht fragen. Ihr Handeln würde mir verraten, ob ich für sie ein Gefangener war oder nicht. Ich nahm an, dass ja, hoffte aber auf ein Nein. Als nach ein paar Sekunden niemand kam, um mir zu helfen, schnallte ich mich ab und stand auf. Ich gesellte mich zu den anderen, ging die Rampe hinunter und suchte nach Danner. Niemand erwartete uns, abgesehen vom Luftunterstützungsteam, das die Hülle des Schiffs checkte, volltankte und die hundert anderen Dinge tat, die zu tun waren, wenn ein Schiff landete. Die Crew kümmerte sich um ihre Angelegenheiten, was mich etwas aus dem Konzept brachte. Selbst wenn ich kein Gefangener war, hatte ich die Daten, die der Dreh- und Angelpunkt unserer gesamten Mission gewesen waren. Das allein hätte Aufmerksamkeit wert sein sollen.

Ich war zwar verwirrt, musste mich aber bewegen, also folgte ich der Gruppe in den Raum, in dem wir unsere Ausrüstung ablegten, und ich zog meine Rüstung mit ein wenig Hilfe des Mannes aus, mit dem ich mich auf dem Schiff unterhalten hatte. Von dort aus ging es zur Dekontamination in eine kleine Kammer, die mit einem ganzen Platoon schrecklich voll gewesen wäre, für meinen einsamen Helfer und mich aber funktionierte. Ich war am Boden gewesen und er hatte mich berührt. Die Dekontamination hatte ich ganz vergessen. Auch wenn ich entscheidende Informationen dabeihatte, gab es Sicherheitsvorschriften beim Umgang mit außerirdischen Planeten. Das erklärte, wieso sich mir niemand genähert hatte. Ich benutzte die sieben Minuten lange Prozedur als Atempause.

Danner wartete auf mich, als ich herauskam. Er lächelte nicht, aber sah so aus, als würde er sich freuen, mich zu sehen, wie es Soldaten eben tun. „Brauchen Sie was zu essen, Sir, oder können wir gleich zum Debriefing?" Professionell. Kein Bullshit. Noch konnte ich nicht sagen, ob das gut oder schlecht war.

„Ich könnte eine Tasse Kaffee vertragen", sagte ich. „Aber es gibt keinen Grund, weshalb wir uns zur selben Zeit nicht unterhalten könnten."

Er nickte und ein Soldat hinter ihm eilte davon, vermutlich, um mir mein Getränk zu besorgen. Was ich wirklich wollte, war ein Drink, aber ich musste einen klaren Kopf bewahren. Ich würde trinken, wenn ich mein Schicksal kannte. Sobald sie ihre Entscheidung getroffen hatten, würde ich mich betrinken. Wenn sie mich durch eine Luftschleuse ins All warfen, hätte ich einen im Tee.

Ich setzte mich mit Danner an einen runden Tisch, nicht ihm gegenüber, sondern eher neben ihm. Er suchte die Plätze aus und sagte dann: „Das ist kein Verhör. Wir reden nur." Genau, was ich gesagt hätte, wenn ich jemanden verhört hätte.

„Das Wichtigste zuerst, Sir. Sie haben gesagt, Sie hätten die Daten?"

„Sie sind in meinem Anzug", sagte ich, wohl wissend, dass sie ihn vermutlich bereits durchsucht und den Chip gefunden hatten. Ich hatte ihn Larssons Leiche abgenommen und die Cappaner hatten ihn bespielt, was zu meiner Geschichte passte. „Ich wollte ihn nicht mit in die Dekontamination nehmen. Ich weiß nicht, wie diese Dinge funktionieren, aber kein Grund, ein Risiko einzugehen, richtig?"

„Natürlich, Sir. Wir werden die Sachen hochladen und nach Talca schicken, um sicherzugehen, dass es das ist, was sie brauchen."

„Großartig", sagte ich. Ich nahm an, dass drauf war, was sie haben wollten, aber in diesem Moment kam mir aus welchem Grund auch immer der Gedanke, dass ich keine Ahnung hatte. Die Cappaner hätten irgendetwas aufspielen können. Scheiße, der Chip könnte leer sein und ich würde es nicht wissen.

„Sind Sie okay, Sir?"

„Ja. Ich hoffe, wir haben die Daten. All die Toten ... Ich weiß nicht, ob sie es wert sind, aber immerhin wären sie nicht bedeutungslos gestorben."

Er nickte. „Ja. Was zur Hölle ist passiert?"

„Wir wurden den ganzen Weg über aufgerieben. Ich bin mir sicher, dass Sie die Berichte gesehen haben." Ich hielt inne. „Es war schlimm. Kartoffelminen ... ich hasse diese verdammten Dinger."

Er saß da, sein Gesichtsausdruck unverändert, und wartete darauf, dass ich fortfuhr.

„Als wir ihre Siedlung erreichten, haben unsere Vögel Bomben auf ein paar ihrer Gebäude abgeworfen. Einen Augenblick lang schien es so, als hätte ihnen das den Kampfgeist genommen. Sie hörten auf, zurückzuschießen, und dann hat Larsson die Entscheidung getroffen, weiterzugehen und die Informationen zu holen." Ich gab mein Bestes, alles zu erzählen, was sie verifizieren konnten. Ich wollte die Lüge so klein wie möglich halten.

„Das haben wir gesehen", sagte er.

„Kapoor ist mit mir runter und wir haben eine Verbindung zu Larsson hergestellt. Die Cappaner haben uns in ein Gebäude geführt und waren einverstanden, uns die Daten zu geben. Dann ... ich weiß nicht. Leute fingen an, in einem geschlossenen Raum zu feuern. Larsson ... sie wurde getroffen, aber sie hat auch ein paar von ihnen erwischt. Wir sind hinter einem umgefallenen Tisch in Deckung gegangen und sie hat mir die Daten gegeben. Ihr Bein war zertrümmert. Sie dachte vermutlich, dass ich bessere Chancen hätte, zu entkommen. Das Letzte, das ich von ihr gesehen habe, war, dass sie mir Feuerschutz gab und ... ich weiß nicht. Ich nahm an, dass sie mich verfolgen würden, aber das taten sie nicht. Sie ist eine verdammte Heldin." Den letzten Satz fügte ich spontan hinzu.

Danners Gesicht entspannte sich ein wenig, was mich annehmen ließ, dass er es mir abgekauft hatte. Der zweifelhafte Teil war der, bei dem es um die Übergabe der Daten ging, aber Larsson-die-Heldin überstrahlte das ein wenig. Sie wollten das glauben. Menschen wollen immer an Helden glauben, obwohl die Wahrheit solcher Geschichten selten dem Mythos gerecht wird. Irgendjemand würde wissen, dass sie und ich uns nicht verstanden hatten, also würde mein positiver Bericht über sie nur noch glaubhafter wirken.

Natürlich war es nicht Danner, den ich reinlegen musste. Er war das zweite Tor. Den echten Test musste ich vor Omicron bestehen, und ich hatte abgesehen von Danner beinahe keine Möglichkeit, den zu beeinflussen. „Wir werden in ein paar Minuten wissen, ob die Daten was taugen. Lassen Sie mich der Heimatbasis ein Update von Ihrem Debriefing geben." Er fügte nicht hinzu, dass er einen Rat erbeten würde, was mit mir zu tun wäre, andererseits musste er das auch nicht. Ich nippte an meinem Kaffee und sah mich beiläufig im Zimmer um. Ich wollte wissen, wer sonst interessiert war, denn das waren die Leute, die ich später beobachten musste. Danner war die wichtigste Verbindung, aber die Art, wie sich die Soldatinnen und Soldaten auf dem Planeten verhalten hatten, verriet mir, dass Omicron Leute hatte, die auch ihn beobachteten. Niemand fiel mir auf.

Ich stand auf und lief herum, meine Ausrede war, mir weiteren Kaffee zu holen. Niemand schenkte mir Aufmerksamkeit, also machte ich mir das zunutze und ging in die Einsatzzentrale. Danner saß auf der einen Seite des Raumes und starrte auf ein Terminal, aber ich ging ihm aus dem Weg und suchte nach Lopez. Ich erkannte sie an ihren raspelkurzen Haaren, sie saß an der Zielstation. Genau, was ich zu sehen gehofft hatte.

„Haben Sie die Ziele schon ausgewählt?", fragte ich.

Sie schloss ein Fenster, in dem sie ein Puzzle gelöst hatte und blickte auf. „Oh, hi, Sir! Ziele wofür?"

„Die XB25er. Um die cappanische Siedlung zu vernichten."

Ihre Augen weiteten sich und ihr stockte der Atem. Niemand hatte ihr davon erzählt. Fairerweise muss ich sagen, dass ich geraten hatte, was den Befehl betraf, also überraschte es mich nicht, dass sie nicht Bescheid wusste. „Haben wir das vor?"

„Oh … ähm … vergessen Sie's. Ich dachte, sie hätten Ihnen den Befehl gegeben." Es war scheiße von mir, eine junge Soldatin so auszunutzen. Es käme ihr nie in den Sinn, dass ich sie angelogen hatte, sie würde stattdessen annehmen, dass ich mehr wusste als sie. Angesichts meiner anderen Sünden schien diese im Vergleich klein.

„Sollte ich daran arbeiten?"

„Noch nicht. Warteten wir auf den Stabsoffizier. Vielleicht gibt es einen anderen Weg. Wenn wir es tun müssen, ist das eine schwierige Aufgabe. All die Leben dort unten. Vielleicht auch ein paar von uns. Die Sensoren zeigen nichts an, aber ich muss annehmen, dass es ein paar von ihnen geschafft haben." Ich ging weg, ehe sie die Gelegenheit hatte, zu antworten. Ich hatte getan, was ich hatte tun müssen. Ich hatte sie dazu gebracht, darüber nachzudenken.

Lieutenant Danner rief mir zu, ehe ich den Raum verlassen hatte. „Sir, haben Sie einen Moment?"

„Sicher. Hier oder in dem anderen Zimmer?"

„Im anderen Zimmer", sagte er.

Ich nickte, ging voraus und wartete dann, bis er die Tür hinter uns geschlossen hatte, dann meldete ich mich zu Wort, ehe er etwas sagen konnte. „Ehe Sie irgendetwas sagen: Ich will es nicht wissen. Falls sie Ihnen befohlen haben, mich zu töten ... oder falls sie es Ihnen in der Zukunft befehlen ... sagen Sie es mir nicht. Versetzen Sie mich einfach in Stasis, so als würden wir nach Hause fliegen, und machen Sie es dann.“

Er setzte zu sprechen an, unterbrach sich aber und dachte für ein paar Sekunden über seine Worte nach. „Danke, Sir. Ich kann Ihnen jetzt sagen, dass ich diesen Befehl nicht habe, aber ich verstehe, wieso es zur Diskussion stehen könnte. Ich verstehe, was Sie sagen.“

Es spielte wirklich keine Rolle für mich. Tot war tot. Aber ich hatte es ihm leichter gemacht. Bei all den beschissenen Dingen, die ich getan hatte und weiter tun würde, würde ich gerne glauben, dass diese Tat die Waage etwas ausgleichen könnte. „Also, was haben sie gesagt?“

„Die Informationen, die Sie beschafft haben, Sir. Es sind die richtigen. Es ist genau das, was sie wollten.“

Ich lächelte. „Gut. Aber dieser Ausdruck auf Ihrem Gesicht ... Sie sehen nicht aus wie ein Mann, der gute Neuigkeiten bekommen hat.“

„Sie wollen, dass wir die cappanische Siedlung zerstören.“

Ich nickte. Das war der Moment, den ich geplant hatte. Alles hing von der nächsten Minute der Unterhaltung ab. „Wie fühlen Sie sich dabei?“

Er seufzte. „Es gefällt mir nicht. Aber so lautet die Mission. Und wenn ich es nicht tue, werden sie jemand anderen abstellen, der es tut.“

„Sie sind der letzte Offizier an Bord.“

„Wir sind hier nicht beim Militär, Sir. Sie können befördern, wen sie wollen.“

„Guter Punkt. Sie sollten mit Lopez sprechen, der Ziel-Technikerin. Ich schätze, sie wird das schwer verkraften. Besonders, falls sie Freunde auf dem Planeten hat.“

„Shit“, sagte er. „Darüber habe ich nicht nachgedacht.“

Ich nippte an meinem Kaffee und ließ es ein paar Sekunden nachwirken, ehe ich weitersprach. „Ich könnte es tun.“

„Es Lopez sagen? Darum könnte ich Sie nicht bitten, Sir. Sie ist meine Untergebene.“

„Nein. Ich meine, ich könnte die Zieleinstellung übernehmen. Ich habe einige Erfahrung mit der Maschine.“

„Daran besteht kein Zweifel, Sir.“

„Wichtiger noch, ich habe einige Erfahrung wie es ist, mit so etwas zu leben. Glauben Sie mir, es ist viel schwieriger als nur der reine Akt. Es ist nichts, das ich irgendjemandem wünsche. Lopez nicht und Ihnen auch nicht.“

„Ich bin immer noch zuständig, Sir.“

„Sicher“, sagte ich. „Aber das muss niemand wissen. Besonders nicht zu Hause. Wenn das rauskommt – und es *wird* rauskommen, es kommt alles raus, immer –, werden die Medien nach jemandem suchen, dem sie die Schuld geben können. Ich bin ein geeignetes Ziel, da sie mich bereits kennen. Scheiße – wenn sie die Passagierliste sehen und meinen Namen lesen, werden sie davon *ausgehen*, dass ich es war.“

Er dachte darüber nach. „Wie Sie sagten, Sir. Die Dinge kommen immer ans Licht. Sie werden die Wahrheit herausfinden.“

„Vielleicht nicht. Erzählen Sie ihnen die Story, die sie hören wollen ..." Ich zuckte mit den Schultern. „Nun, erzählen Sie ihnen das und sie neigen dazu, nicht weiter nachzuforschen. Davon abgesehen wissen die Soldaten an Bord, wer ich bin, aber sie wissen nicht, wieso ich hier bin. Wenn ich übernehme, denken Sie wahrscheinlich, dass das Teil des Plans ist. Warum sonst nimmt man einen Massenmörder mit?"

Er dachte ein paar Sekunden darüber nach. „Es könnte funktionieren."

„Wenn nicht, haben wir nicht viel verloren. Es ist nicht so, als würde ein Vertuschungsversuch die Sache schlimmer machen." Ich beobachtete ihn genau. Bisher hatte er nicht mal eine Spur Argwohn gezeigt, aber bald würde er so weit sein. Ich durfte ihn nicht überholen. Er musste selbst auf das Problem stoßen, ehe ich ihm die Lösung präsentieren konnte. Aber ich konnte es ihm soufflieren. Ich wartete, bis wir in die Einsatzzentrale zurückgingen. „Zum Feuern brauche ich die Autorisierungscodes."

Für den Bruchteil einer Sekunde stockte er. Da war es. Er blieb stehen und zögerte, ehe er etwas sagte. „Ich bin mir nicht sicher, ob das eine gute Idee ist."

Ich tat so, als dächte ich darüber nach. „Ach, richtig. Daran hätte ich denken sollen. Sie vertrauen mir nicht."

„Das ist es nicht, Sir–"

„Es ist vollkommen okay. Ich kann verstehen, warum Sie sich Sorgen machen. Ich sage Ihnen was. Ich stelle die Ziele ein und bereite alles vor, abgesehen von den Ausführungscodes. Sie können überprüfen, was ich ins System eingegeben habe, ehe Sie autorisieren." Er biss sich auf die Unterlippe. Ich hatte ihn fast so weit. „Und natürlich werden Sie den Zielbereich über die Sensoren einsehen. Sie werden die Ergebnisse deutlich genug sehen können.“

Er stand etliche weitere Sekunden da. Ich wusste nicht, was in ihm vorging. Dann nickte er. „Tun wir es.“

„Okay. Sagen Sie Lopez Bescheid.“

„Richtig.“ Er ging zu der Soldatin hinüber und sprach leise mit ihr. Sie nickte und stand von ihrem Platz auf. Ich bin mir nicht sicher, wie viel er ihr gesagt hatte, aber sie sah nicht verärgert aus, und das war alles, was zählte. Ich setzte mich ans Terminal, rief die nötigen Seiten auf und nahm mir einen Moment Zeit, um mich mit dem Interface vertraut zu machen. Es war beinahe dasselbe wie das System des Militärs, was mich nicht überraschte, da Omicron beide herstellte. Ich gab die Parameter der Mission ein und wählte den Waffentyp aus und auf einem anderen Bildschirm rief ich eine dreidimensionale Karte der Insel auf.

Ich wählte alle vier Raketen aus, die wir an Bord hatten, was für den Bereich Overkill war. Ich hätte den Job auch mit zwei oder drei erledigen können, wenn sie korrekt gezielt waren. Weil ich vier ausgewählt hatte, spuckte der Computer über zwanzig mögliche Szenarien aus, von denen alle die Anforderungen der Mission erfüllten. Ich hatte es absichtlich so eingestellt, so viele Möglichkeiten zu bekommen, weil ich eine auswählen wollte, die dem am nächsten kam, was ich wollte. Ich hatte Informationen, die der Computer nicht hatte. Ich wollte außerdem sämtliche Munition einsetzen, damit sie nicht noch eine Rakete abfeuern konnten, nur für den Fall.

Ich studierte die Zahlen einige Minuten lang. Ich konnte spüren, wie Danner nervös wurde und hinter mir auf und ab ging, also beschwichtigte ich ihn. „Der Computer hat dreiundzwanzig effektive Szenarien zum Beschuss ausgespuckt. Ich überprüfe sie händisch, um das Beste zu finden.“

Ich wählte das aus, das meine Parameter am besten erfüllte und begann, die vier Zielpunkte zu verarbeiten. Leute denken, mit leistungsstarken Waffen zu zielen sei einfach, und dass Fusionswaffen eine so große Explosion erzeugen, dass man nur nah genug dran sein muss. Es ist subtiler als das. So groß die Waffen auch sind, der Planet ist größer, und den Punkt des Aufpralls um ein paar hundert Meter zu bewegen, kann einen entscheidenden Unterschied machen. Ein Hügel oder ein Kamm können eine Schockwelle ableiten und die Wirkung auf einen bestimmten Bereich verringern und auf einen anderen vergrößern. Die Energie muss irgendwo hin. Das ist ein Gesetz der Physik. Wo sie hingeht? Das ist Kunst. Und ich bin ein meisterhafter Künstler. Die Effekte einer kleinen Veränderung des Zielpunkts werden wichtiger, wenn das Ziel unter der Erde ist. Die Szenarien des Computers rechneten unterirdische Ziele nicht mit ein. Meins schon.

Nicht jeder, der Zieleinstellungen vornahm, konnte tun, was ich versuchte. Leute neigen dazu, sich auf Maschinen zu verlassen, ohne die zugrundeliegende Wissenschaft zu kennen. Sie akzeptierten, was der Computer ausspuckte, und es funktionierte. Ich gehörte zur alten Schule. Ich hatte gelernt, wie man es händisch macht, ehe ich es auf einem Computer gelernt hatte. Ich glaube nicht, dass Lopez das getan hatte. Ich wusste, dass Danner es nicht getan hatte. Ich bewegte den Zielpunkt von zwei der Raketen und ließ den Computer eine Simulation durchführen. Grüne Kreise leuchteten auf, was bedeutete, dass mein Szenario die Erfordernisse der Mission erfüllte. Laut Computer würde es alles an der Oberfläche zerstören. Daran führte kein Weg vorbei. Aber wenn ich es richtig machte, würden Leute überleben, die an bestimmten Orten unter der Erde waren. Vielleicht. Wie gesagt, es ist eine Kunstform. Es ist nicht vollkommen. Es war die beste Chance, die ich ihnen geben konnte, und ich glaubte, dass es funktionieren würde.

„Fertig." Ich stand auf und ließ Danner ans Terminal. Ich ließ die grünen Kreise in einer Ecke des Bildschirms offen, sodass er sehen konnte, dass das Szenario die Parameter erfüllte. „Ich habe das Autorisierungsfeld hervorgehoben. Sie müssen nur Ihre biometrischen Daten eingeben."

Er blieb hinter dem Stuhl stehen, statt sich hinzusetzen. „Lassen Sie mich den Bildschirm mit den detaillierten Parametern sehen."

Ich zögerte, aber nur, weil ich es nicht erwartete hatte. „Sicher, natürlich." Es war klug von ihm, das zu checken. Wenn ich die Parameter geändert hatte, würde der Computer grünes Licht für eine andere Mission geben. Es war einfach, aber ich hatte nicht daran gedacht, das zu versuchen. Theoretisch hätte ich auch grünes Licht bekommen, wenn ich die Parameter umprogrammiert, die Siedlung unbeschadet gelassen und die XB25er aufs Meer abgefeuert hätte, wo sie zwar massiven Schaden angerichtet hätten, aber harmlos für die Cappaner im Wasser gelandet wären. Ich lehnte mich vor, rief den Bildschirm mit den Parametern auf und ließ Danner ihn ohne zu kommentieren überprüfen. Ich hatte nichts von dem, was Lopez eingestellt hatte, verändert. Er zeigte immer noch die Siedlung und alles Leben auf der Oberfläche als primäres Ziel.

„Das wird alle töten?", fragte er.

„Vermutlich nicht", sagte ich. „Selbst mit den größten Waffen gibt es immer Überlebende. Jemand, der außerhalb des Bereichs ist oder zufällig gerade hinter einem großen Fels oder in einer Mulde steht. Aber es werden nicht viele sein."

„Shit", sagte er.

„Was ist?"

„Ich musste an unsere eigenen Leute denken, falls noch welche von ihnen am Leben sind. Es ist schwer zu glauben, dass wir eine komplette Kompanie verloren haben."

„Ja. Das ist übel", sagte ich und ließ meinen Gesichtsausdruck so teilnahmslos wie möglich aussehen. „Andererseits würde man nicht wollen, dass irgendjemand von uns den Cappanern in die Hände fällt. Sie wissen, wie sie sind."

„Ja." Er seufzte schwer. Er wusste nicht wie ich aus erster Hand, wie einige Cappaner ihre Gefangenen behandelten, aber er hatte sicherlich Geschichten gehört. „Okay. Es hat keinen Sinn zu warten. Die Angriffsflugzeuge sind aus der Atmosphäre raus."

Ich rief den Autorisierungsbildschirm wieder auf und trat beiseite, als Danner ihn mit seinem Daumenabdruck, dann mit einem Retina-Scan autorisierte. „Das wird genügen."

Ich drückte auf den Feuerknopf, ehe er die Sache noch mal überdenken konnte.

Das Schiff vibrierte kaum, als die vier Raketen ihre Abschussrampen verließen. Ihre Antriebe wurden erst gezündet, nachdem sie das Schiff verlassen hatten. Von dort aus würde der Computer in jeder Rakete diese bis zu den Zielen führen, die ich programmiert hatte. Theoretisch konnten sie zurückgerufen werden, obwohl es riskant war, das zu versuchen, sobald sie einmal in die Atmosphäre eingetreten waren. Ab diesem Moment wäre die beste Option, sie zu neutralisieren. Das würden wir nicht tun.

„Wie lange bis zum Einschlag?", fragte Danner.

Ich checkte den Computer. „Etwas über neun Minuten." Raketen mussten sich nicht an G-Kräfte halten, die für Menschen überlebenswichtig waren, also beschleunigten sie schneller als Schiffe.

„Flugsicherung, ich will einen bemannten Überflug des Zielgebiets in fünfzehn Minuten", sagte Danner. Er sah mich an, so als wolle er fragen, ob das sicher wäre. Ich nickte.

„Roger, Sir. Flugsicherung hat den Auftrag", antwortete ein älter aussehender Sergeant.

„Intel, ich will auch, dass unbemannte Drohnen Überflüge machen. Scans von jedem Spektrum, über das wir verfügen."

„Roger, Sir." Diesmal eine weibliche Stimme. Ich drehte mich nicht um. Ich war mir sicher, dass jeder die Nervosität in meinem Gesicht sehen würde, also konzentrierte ich mich auf den Bildschirm vor mir. Der Ausgang der Sache lag nicht mehr in meinen Händen. Die Cappaner hatten unsere Drohnen und Sensoren ausgetrickst, als wir unten auf dem Planeten gewesen waren. Ich musste darauf vertrauen, dass sie es jetzt wieder tun konnten. Wenn nicht ... nun, dann hatte ich ihnen einen Monat verschafft, bis Omicron mehr Leute herschaffen würde.

Es war still im Raum, oder zumindest so still, wie es in einer Einsatzzentrale sein kann. Niemand sagte etwas. Es war, als schwiege sogar die Luft selbst und erwiese denen Respekt, die unten auf dem Planeten waren. Die Bürde der ganzen Sache würde auf jedem im Raum lasten. Sie hatten es nicht getan, aber sie waren dabei gewesen. Sie hatten es gesehen. Manche würde es stärker beeinflussen als andere ... es war unmöglich zu sagen. Einige würden an sich und ihrer Rolle in dieser Sache zweifeln. Manche würden nie wieder daran denken. Und andere ... andere würden nichts fühlen, sich aber fragen, warum dem so war.

Ich hätte sie alle davon befreien können. Ich hätte ihnen sagen können, dass, wenn ich es richtig gemacht hatte, diese sehr teuren Raketen eine riesige Sauerei anrichten, die Leute aber in Sicherheit sein würden. *In Sicherheit.* Ich lachte beinahe. Das war ein dummer Gedanke. Wenn ich es ihnen erzählte, würde Omicron ein weiteres Schiff schicken. Mehr Raketen–

„Einschlag", sagte jemand.

Ein paar Bildschirme wurden weiß, ehe sie dunkel wurden; ihre internen Systeme schalteten die Sensoren aus, um Schaden zu vermeiden. Sie würden ein paar Sekunden brauchen, um wieder hochzufahren. Es war vollkommen still im Raum, während wir darauf warteten, dass sie wieder angingen. Der visuelle Spektralsensor war zuerst wieder da und schenkte uns ein Bild dessen, was die cappanische Siedlung gewesen war. Die Fertigbauhäuser waren jetzt nur noch ein Haufen Schutt, verstreut und zu unerkennbarer Schlacke geschmolzen. Eine Person klatschte, als das Bild auftauchte, hörte aber sofort auf, als sie feststellte, dass sich ihr niemand angeschlossen hatte.

Junge Gesichter starrten das Display an und dann ein anderes, als es sichtbar wurde, sprachlos, aber unfähig, den Blick abzuwenden. Ich sah nicht hin. Ich beobachtete stattdessen die Leute. Das hatte ich das letzte Mal nicht getan, bei Cappa. Ich hatte keine Zeit gehabt. Jetzt hatte ich *nichts als Zeit.* Ich fragte mich, ob ich so aussah wie sie, ob ich die letzten Jahre so ausgesehen hatte, weil ich die Last tausender Tode mit mir herumgetragen hatte. Mehr als Tausende, in meinem Fall. Irgendwann schickte die Flugsicherung Schiffe, um sich die Sache aus der Nähe anzusehen. Auch Drohnen flogen los. Entweder fanden sie die Cappaner oder nicht. Ich hatte getan, was ich konnte. Ich verließ den Raum, ohne mit jemandem zu reden. Soldaten gingen mir aus dem Weg, stolperten beinahe in ihrer Hast, als würde ich sie anstecken können, wenn sie mich berührten.

Ich erreichte die Krankenstation ohne wirklich zu wissen, dass das mein Ziel gewesen war. In beinahe jedem Bett in dem langen, schmalen Raum lag ein Soldat oder eine Soldatin. Ich fand Matua etwa in der Mitte einer Reihe von beinahe zwanzig Betten, die an einer Wand aufgereiht standen. Er sah auf, als ich über ihm stand.

„Sie haben es geschafft, Sir." Seine Stimme war ein Krächzen.

Ich lächelte ihn an. „Habe ich. Zum Teil dank Ihnen."

„Ausgeschlossen, Sir. Sie wissen, dass das nicht stimmt.“

„Sie haben Ihren Job gemacht, Matua. Mehr kann keiner von uns tun. Vertrauen Sie mir.“

„Es tut mir so leid, Sir.“

Ich lächelte wieder, diesmal aber dünner, und schüttelte den Kopf. Ich traute mir nicht zu, etwas zu sagen, ohne die Beherrschung zu verlieren.

Ich machte mich auf in die Bar.

Ich hatte drei Drinks intus, als Danner mich fand. „Sie machen vielleicht lieber langsamer, Sir. Wir haben die Nachricht bekommen, aufzubrechen.“

Ich hob mein Glas und prostete ihm zu. Es heißt, es sei nicht gesund, in Stasis zu gehen, während man Alkohol im Blut hat. Andererseits heißt es auch, dass viele Dinge nicht gesund sind, und das hatte mich nie davon abgehalten. „Also waren die Scans sauber?“

„Waren sie. Keine Lebenszeichen. Wir lassen die Satelliten im Orbit, um die Dinge im Auge zu behalten, aber die Leute zu Hause wirken ziemlich zufrieden.“

Ich nickte und schenkte mir noch einen Drink ein. Er wollte, dass ich nach meiner eigenen Situation fragte, sodass er mir davon erzählen und sich erleichtern konnte. Ich wollte nicht. „Wann geht es in die Stasis?“

„Innerhalb der nächsten Stunde.“

Ich sah ihn an, nickte erneut und wandte mich wieder meinem Drink zu. Nach ein paar Sekunden peinlicher Stille ließ Danner mich allein.

Die Cappaner waren nicht außer Gefahr. Sie mussten vermeiden, von den Satelliten entdeckt zu werden, und einen Weg finden, den Planeten zu verlassen, ehe jemand anderes kam, um nachzuschauen. Sie hatten

Leute wie Sasha und Riku auf Talca, und vermutlich andere in anderen Systemen. Nach den Fähigkeiten zu urteilen, die ich gesehen hatte, gefielen mir ihre Chancen. Ich schenkte mir einen letzten Drink ein. Meine größte Angst galt Ganos. Sie hatte keinen Wert mehr für Omicron, jetzt da die Mission vorüber war, aber sobald alles in den Nachrichten war, würde ich es ihnen zutrauen, so kleinkariert zu sein, sich an ihr zu rächen. Aber sie war klug, und Plazz und die Cappaner würden auf sie aufpassen. Darauf musste ich vertrauen.

Was mich betraf, würde ich mich in Stasis begeben und entweder aufwachen oder nicht. Ich schätzte, ich hätte gute Chancen, abhängig davon, wie sie mit dem, was gerade geschehen war, umgehen wollten. Sie konnten versuchen, es zu vertuschen, aber ihnen musste bewusst sein, dass das nicht funktionieren würde. Jemand aus der Crew würde reden, und wenn sie das nicht taten, würde Plazz es so oder so herausfinden, mit der Hilfe, die ich ihr gegeben hatte. Vielleicht wollten sie mich als Sündenbock behalten. Andererseits vielleicht auch nicht.

Ich wollte nur schlafen, tief und friedlich, ohne die Träume. Ich wusste nicht, ob das passieren würde oder nicht, aber ich hoffte es.

„Sir?" Jemand stand in respektvollem Abstand zu mir da. „Es ist Zeit."

Ich stand auf und lächelte. „Ich bin so weit."

Danksagung

Während meiner andauernden Reise als Schriftsteller haben mir so viele Menschen geholfen, dass ich sie unmöglich alle aufzählen kann, aber ich will einige würdigen, die für dieses Projekt besonders entscheidend gewesen sind.

Ich danke meiner Agentin Lisa Rodgers, die mir exzellenten Rat gibt, was meine Schriftstellerkarriere allgemein betrifft, und die einen klaren Verstand hat, der dieses spezielle Buch in vielerlei Hinsicht besser gemacht hat. Ich könnte keine bessere Partnerin für meine Schreibprojekte haben.

Ich danke David Pomerico und dem gesamten Team von Harper Voyager für ihren kontinuierlichen Glauben an meine Arbeit und ihren Einsatz dafür, sie zu dem Produkt zu machen, das Sie hier auf diesen Seiten sehen. Ohne das herausragende Lektorat wäre dieses Buch viel weniger, als es ist. Zusätzlicher Dank geht an die Leute vom Layout für das Cover und an alle, die hinter den Kulissen daran arbeiten, das Buch auf den Markt zu bringen. Ich danke besonders Andrew Gibeley dafür, dass er *Planetside* promotet und es mehr Leserinnen und Lesern zugänglich gemacht hat, als ich es selbst gekonnt hätte. Bücher zu promoten ist hart, und ich hätte mir keine bessere Unterstützung wünschen können.

Dieses Buch hatte weniger Erstleser als meine vorherige Arbeit, also war jede Person *per definitionem* wichtiger. Red Levine hat mir essenzielles Feedback gegeben, besonders was Figuren und ihr Verhalten betrifft, was ihnen Tiefe hinzugefügt hat, die sonst fehlen würde. Rebecca Enzor hat früh Anmerkungen gemacht und dem Projekt etliche Male das Leben gerettet. Jason Nelson hat mir entscheidende Einblicke in Computernetzwerke verschafft, sowie spezielle Gedanken für Butler und Ganos. Ohne sie hätte ich es nicht hinbekommen.

Besonderer Dank gilt Dan Koboldt, der sich den Titel ausgedacht und hervorragende Anmerkungen zum Projekt gemacht hat. Mehr noch, er gibt mir immer wieder Ratschläge und Einblicke bezüglich meiner Karriere. Viele Jahre nachdem er mir bei Pitch Wars als Mentor zur Seite stand, lerne ich immer noch von ihm. Danke an Pancho, der mich dazu inspiriert hat, mir Cisco einfallen zu lassen, Ganos' Hund.

Ich danke allen, die *Planetside* gelesen haben, und besonders jedem, der es gelesen und jemand anderem davon erzählt hat. Das überwältigt mich immer wieder – und bedeutet mir sehr viel. Eure Zeit ist wertvoll, und die Tatsache, dass ihr sie mit meinem Buch verbringt, ist großartig. Danke. Wirklich.

Schließlich, und das ist das Wichtigste, möchte ich meiner Frau Melody danken. Ihre Unterstützung, ihr Rat und Verständnis sind entscheidender für meinen Erfolg als alles andere zusammen. Ohne sie hätte ich nichts hiervon tun können.